THE COMPANIES ACT 1989

A Practitioners' Guide

Nigel Furey LLM, Solicitor
Lecturer in Law,
University of Bristol

David Parkes FCA,
KPMG Peat Marwick McLintock
(Consulting Editor)

Jordans
1990

Published by
Jordan & Sons Limited
21 St Thomas Street
Bristol BS1 6JS

© Jordan & Sons Limited 1990

Reprinted March 1990

British Library Cataloguing in Publication Data

Furey, Nigel E.
  The Companies Act 1989: a practitioners' guide.
  1. Great Britain. Companies. Law
  I. Title
  344.106'66

ISBN 0 85308 152 2

Typeset by Afal, Cardiff
Printed by Billing & Sons Ltd, Worcester

PREFACE

It was never anticipated that the consolidation of the companies legislation in 1985 would herald the same sort of breathing space in company law reform that followed earlier consolidations in 1862, 1908, 1929 and 1948. If nothing else, the necessity to implement European Community directives on the harmonisation of company law was bound to ensure a continued flow of legislative changes. The need to implement the Seventh Directive on group accounts and the Eighth Directive on qualifications of auditors was the original reason for the Companies Act 1989. But the opportunity has been taken not only to make changes to other areas of company law but also to reform areas of law that are not part of company law at all. This commentary concentrates, however, on those areas which do principally affect company law: accounts, auditors, ultra vires, the registration of charges, the de-regulation of private companies and the many miscellaneous changes to company law. The changes to the DTI's powers of investigation, the strengthening of the provisions relating to the control of mergers, and the amendments to the regime for regulating the conduct of investment business under the Financial Services Act are given less detailed treatment. Finally, the Act also introduces an entirely new legislative structure to govern the settlement of a defaulter's debts on financial markets. These provisions are of highly specialised application and are only briefly summarised in the commentary.

Writing this commentary has been made a great deal easier than it would otherwise have been thanks to the willingness and unfailing courtesy with which officials of the Department of Trade and Industry have supplied information and dealt with questions about the Bill. They are, of course, not responsible for any of the views expressed but their assistance with information has been greatly appreciated. I should also like to thank David Parkes for many helpful suggestions in relation to the chapters on accounts and auditors. In a work like this, time is of the essence and Jackie Williams assisted me tremendously by the speed with which she typed the manuscript. Finally, my thanks also go to the staff at Jordans who have been enormously helpful and efficient.

NIGEL FUREY
30 November 1989

CONTENTS

TABLE OF CASES

TABLE OF PARLIAMENTARY DEBATES

House of Lords

First Reading:
HL Deb Vol 502   21 December 1988, cols 1363–1364

Second Reading:
HL Deb Vol 503   16 January 1989, cols 6–82

Committee Stage:
(Considered by a committee of the whole house.)
HL Deb Vol 503   30 January 1989, cols 876–977
HL Deb Vol 503   31 January 1989, cols 995–1001, 1016–1067
HL Deb Vol 504   14 February 1989, cols 73–140, 151–168
HL Deb Vol 504   21 February 1989, cols 508–584, 600–636
HL Deb Vol 504   2 March 1989, cols 1145–1204, 1214–1249
HL Deb Vol 504   6 March 1989, cols 1260–1318

Report Stage:
HL Deb Vol 505   20 March 1989, cols 461–530, 541–566
HL Deb Vol 505   6 April 1989, cols 1195–1197, 1209–1231

Recommitment on Part V:
HL Deb Vol 505   6 April 1989, cols 1231–1290
HL Deb Vol 506   11 April 1989, cols 131–236

Report Stage resumed:
HL Deb Vol 506   11 April 1989, cols 236–238
HL Deb Vol 506   20 April 1989, cols 902–926, 945–976
HL Deb Vol 506   21 April 1989, cols 988–1009

Third Reading:
HL Deb Vol 506   27 April 1989, cols 1377–1402

House of Commons

First Reading:
HC Deb Vol 151   27 April 1989, col 1092

Second Reading:
HC Deb Vol 152   4 May 1989, cols 291–332

Committee Stage:
(Considered by Standing Committee D.)
The committee held fifteen sittings between 16 May 1989 and 29 June 1989
which are reported in cols 1–724 of the Official Report.

Report Stage:
HC Deb Vol 158   25 October 1989, cols 879–992
HC Deb Vol 158   26 October 1989, cols 1126–1249

Third Reading:
HC Deb Vol 158   26 October 1989, cols 1249–1250

House of Lords

Consideration of Commons Amendments:
HL Deb Vol 512   7 November 1989, cols 548–573, 673–697
HL Deb Vol 512   9 November 1989, cols 948–962, 1046–1074
HL Deb Vol 512   13 November 1989, cols 1088–1193

CHAPTER 1

INTRODUCTION

Drafting Techniques in the Companies Act 1989

1.1   The scope of the Companies Act 1989 (CA 1989) has been outlined in the Preface. There are, however, several notable features of the drafting of the Act which also require special attention. First, in relation to accounts, the appointment etc of auditors and the registration of charges, the practice has been adopted of both reforming the law and at the same time consolidating the changes within the existing law. This procedure is very much to be welcomed since it enables users to find all the relevant provisions in one place. What is less welcome is that this reform and consolidation consists of inserting provisions back into the Companies Act 1985 (CA 1985). It is not obvious why this was done. Although it gives a superficial appearance of neatness, it carries with it the danger of confusion because in large areas of the CA 1985 there will be two sections bearing the same number but with completely different content. Although both will not be in force at the same time, during the transitional period (which in relation to dealing with accounts and the impact of registration of charges could, in reality, last several years) practioners will need to refer to both old and new legislation. Because in these areas each section of the CA 1989 inserts several sections into the CA 1985, it is not possible to refer to the CA 1989 instead.[1] Reference must be made, therefore, to the section number a provision will have in the CA 1985. Fortunately, this can easily be located in the CA 1989 because the provisions appear in the numerical order they will have in the CA 1985. But to avoid confusion with a section bearing the same number in the original CA 1985, the practice is followed of using the term 'new section' or the abbreviation 'ns' when referring to a provision inserted into the CA 1985 by the CA 1989.

1.2   The second drafting point is that the Act includes provision for what seems to be an even greater amount of delegated legislation than usual, including powers to amend the primary legislation itself. Thirdly, the drafting is in a more informal, on occasions almost coloquial, style. Whether this will be an aid to interpretation in the long run remains to be seen. New section 416(2) inserted into the CA 1985 by the CA 1989, s 103 is an example of such drafting which may present difficulties of interpretation in future[2]. Students of different styles of

---

[1]   Thus, although there are 216 sections of the CA 1989 there are approximately 284 sections *in* the CA 1989.
[2]   Discussed in paragraph 5.18 below.

1

statutory drafting may like to compare the style of drafting of ns 416(2) with that of s 75C(2) inserted into the Fair Trading Act 1973 by s 146 of the CA 1989.

Parliamentary Debates

1.3 One of the consequences of debate on the Companies Bill being foreshortened by a timetable motion was that the meaning of provisions like ns 416(2), referred to in the previous paragraph, was never discussed. It is a pity because for the most part the debates on the Bill were marked by the informed nature of the contributions and the high degree of preparation for debates, particularly by front bench spokesmen on both sides of both houses. Reference is frequently made to these debates in the commentary. Details of full reports of the debates are given in the Table of Parliamentary Debates on page xv.

Commencement

1.4   The Act received the Royal Assent on 16 November 1989 and a number of provisions came into force then[1]; in particular, many of the changes relating to mergers. Most of the Act, however, will come into force at different times to be appointed during the following eighteen months. Where expected dates of commencement are available, these are referred to in the commentary. Different commencement dates make for difficulty in referring to the existing law or the future law. The practice has therefore, been adopted throughout of referring to the 'old law' as in the past and the 'new law' as in the future. It is hoped this causes no confusion while the old law still applies or after the new law has come into force.

---

[1]   CA 1989, s 215.

CHAPTER 2

THE ACCOUNTING PROVISIONS

Introduction

Reform and consolidation

2.1 It is essential in understanding the accounting provisions to notice that the legislation includes not only reforming measures, but also consolidation of that reform together with the existing accounting provisions. Consolidation has the obvious advantage that the reader need only refer to one place for all the accounting provisions. The means by which this reform and consolidation is achieved is that Part VII of the CA 1985 is entirely replaced by provisions contained in Part I of the CA 1989.[1] The replacement provisions, however, take the form of new sections inserted into a new Part VII of the CA 1985. It will be necessary to refer to a new section by reference to its number in the CA1985 because each section of the CA 1989 inserts *several* new sections into the CA 1985.[2] As the new sections inserted into the CA 1985 are contained in the CA 1989 in numerical order it is, fortunately, just as easy to find a section by reference to its number in the CA 1985 as by reference to its number in the CA 1989. However, the reader must be aware of the danger that a reference to, say, CA 1985, s 230 could be a reference to the old s 230 or the new s 230. To avoid confusion in this commentary we shall refer to new sections of the CA 1985 inserted by the CA 1989 as 'new sections' and use the abbreviation 'ns'.

2.2 As far as the accounting schedules to the CA 1985 (ie Schedules 4 to 11) are concerned, the position is that some of these are merely amended by the CA 1989 while others are replaced entirely. As all the provisions will, however, continue to form part of the CA 1985, reference will frequently be made to the schedule number as it will be to the amended CA 1985. To avoid confusion with the old schedule numbers we shall again refer to 'new schedule' or 'nSch' to indicate a

---

[1] Consequential amendments are set out in the CA 1989, Sch 10, including nss 700–703 containing revised provisions for delivery of accounts by oversea companies in place of the existing CA 1985, ss 700–703: Sch 10, para 13. The new provisions are expected to apply to accounts in respect of financial years commencing on or after 1 January 1990.

[2] Thus ss 2 to 22 of the CA 1989 are used to insert fifty-two new sections into Part VII of the CA 1985. Why they were not simply enacted as ss 2 to 53 of the CA 1989 is not immediately obvious. A destination table showing where accounting provisions contained in the original CA 1985 are now located is included at the end of this chapter.

reference to a revised schedule, a replaced schedule or, in the case, for example, of the new Schedule 4A, to an entirely new schedule.

Use of delegated legislation

2.3   The second key feature of the accounting provisions, and one they have in common with other parts of the Act, is the amount of delegated legislation for which provision is made. In four areas there is a specific provision for regulations to be issued which will be necessary before sections can be made fully effective. These are:

(i)   consequential provisions in relation to revised annual accounts – ns 245;
(ii) summary financial statements for listed companies – ns 251;
(iii) banking partnerships – ns 255D;
(iv) prescribing bodies making accounting standards – ns 256.

More significantly, however, the Secretary of State's general power to amend the provisions of Part VII of the CA 1985 is increased. In the past the legislation specified which areas could be amended. Effectively this limited the Secretary of State's power to alter the content of accounts. New section 257 now gives the Secretary of State power to amend *any* of the provisions of the new Part VII of the CA 1985.

The Influence of the EEC on Accounting Provisions

2.4   One of the major reasons for the Companies Act 1989 was the need to implement the EEC Seventh Directive[1] on the harmonisation of group accounts. In the end implementation of the Seventh Directive has proved a relatively minor part of the accounting provisions, let alone of the Act as a whole. However, the influence of the EEC generally on company accounting is very considerable and likely to increase. It may help in understanding not only the Seventh Directive but also other accounting provisions to place them in the context of other EEC accounting measures taken or proposed.[2]

The Fourth Directive[3] adopted in 1978 and implemented in the UK in the CA 1981 provided for the harmonisation of the annual accounts of limited liability companies. It has yet to be implemented in Italy, Portugal and Spain. The definition of small- and medium-sized companies in the Fourth Directive was revised in 1984[4] and certain further amendments were made by the Seventh Directive. There are, however, two proposals being discussed by the Commission which, if adopted, would have a considerable impact on the scope of the Fourth and Seventh Directives. In 1986 the Commission issued a draft proposal[5] to extend the Fourth and Seventh Directives to cover partnerships, limited

[1]   83/349/EEC; OJ 1983 L 193/1. See Wooldridge (1988) 37 ICLQ 714.
[2]   There is a very useful two part article by Karel van Hulle published in *Accountancy*. Part I is in the September 1989 issue, p 76. Part 2 is in the October 1989 issue, p 96.
[3]   78/660/EEC; OJ 1978 L 222/11.
[4]   84/569/EEC; OJ 1984 L 314/28.
[5]   OJ 1986 C 144/10.

partnerships and unlimited companies where all the partners or members have limited liability themselves. The proposal was apparently aimed at including within the scope of the directives a category of German partnership called 'GmbH & Co KG' which had been excluded by Germany from its national legislation implementing the directives.[1] Since the 'GmbH & Co KG' category includes a number of partnerships larger than the GmbHs which are covered by the directives, the Commission felt that such an exemption was liable to distort competition. The German Government, however, has been anxious to resist this extension because it would affect a large number of smaller enterprises. Instead, they suggested excluding all small- and medium-sized enterprises from the Fourth and Seventh Directives altogether. The Commission took up this idea and have issued a proposal[2] aimed at easing the accounting requirements of small- and medium-sized enterprises. One of the proposals would exempt small companies from the requirement to have their accounts audited by a qualified person. Since, in order to avoid distorting competition between small companies in different member states, these proposed exemptions would be mandatory on member states, this is highly controversial.[3] The question of exempting small companies from accounting and particularly auditing requirements is, therefore, still very much on the agenda.

2.5 The Commission has also issued a directive on the annual and consolidated accounts of banks and other financial institutions.[4] Corresponding to that there is also a draft directive on the annual and consolidated accounts of insurance companies.[5] Some account has been taken of these directives in the accounting requirements for banking and insurance companies in CA 1985, ns 255–255D and nSchs 9 and 10. There is also in draft an Eleventh Directive[6] on the harmonisation of disclosure requirements imposed by member states when branches are set up of companies established elsewhere. Since these requirements extend to company accounts separate provision will be made for banking and insurance companies and the directive relating to the publication of accounts by branches of banks has already been published.[7]

2.6 Whether harmonisation of the legal requirements relating to company accounts alone can be effective is a moot point.[8] It raises the question whether there should not also be harmonisation of accounting standards as well. That in

---

[1]   Nieuwdorp (1989 17 Int Bus Lawyer 35, 37.
[2]   OJ 1988 C 287/ 6.
[3]   For earlier discussion see the DTI consultative document 'Accounting and Audit Requirements of Small Firms' (1985), particularly section 3. See also the DTI consultative document on 'The Delivery of Annual Accounts and Returns to the Registrar of Companies' (1986), pp 28–29.
[4]   86/ 635/ EEC; OJ 1985 L 372/ 1.
[5]   OJ 1987 C 131/ 1.
[6]   OJ 1988 C 105/ 6.
[7]   89/ 117/ EEC; OJ 1989 L 44/ 40.
[8]   See the results of a survey by Touche Ross reported by Richard Waters in the *Financial Times*, 5 July 1989.

turn raises the question whether these would need to be enforced by law. It also involves the complicated issue of relations with the International Accounting Standards Committee and the question whether it would be better to develop global rather than European accounting standards.[1] Some developments in these areas can be expected to emerge from a conference on harmonisation of accounting standards to be hosted by the Commission in Brussels in January 1990. The Commission has also asked member states to consider what subjects not covered by the Fourth Directive ought to be the subject of harmonisation and whether there is scope for a reduction in the number of options that were included in the Fourth Directive.

The Dearing Committee on the Making of Accounting Standards

2.7 The Committee, under the chairmanship of Sir Ronald Dearing, was appointed by the Consultative Committee of Accountancy Bodies to review and make recommendations on the standard setting process. Among other things it was particularly asked to look at the relationship of standards to company law and at procedures for the monitoring of compliance with standards and the enforcement of standards. These are issues which other countries have also considered in recent years. In the UK, however, there was increasing concern about the extent to which standards were being ignored, exemplified particularly by the experience of SSAP 16 on inflation accounting which was finally withdrawn after being increasingly disregarded.

2.8 The Committee's report,[2] published in November 1988, contained many recommendations which would require legislation. The Department of Trade and Industry (DTI) issued a consultation paper in January 1989 and some of the Committee's recommendations for changes regarding compliance with and enforcement of standards are included in the CA 1989. However, it has not proved possible to reach agreement on implementation of the Committee's recommendations regarding the new institutional framework, in particular how it should be financed, and it is possible that further measures will be introduced by delegated legislation. Whenever it is relevant during the commentary reference is made to the Dearing Committee's proposals. It is intended here to give an overview of their proposals so that the reader can see how they interrelate and the extent to which further subordinate legislation can be expected.

[1]   See the article by David Waller in the *Financial Times*, 16 October 1989. Part 2 of Karel van Hulle's article (see footnote 4, above) puts the pro-European harmonisation argument.
[2]   'The Making of Accounting Standards' (The Dearing Report) available from the ICAEW. For discussion of the report see articles in *Accountancy* in January 1989, p 38; June 1989, p 92; and August 1989, p 77.

2.9 At present, accounting standards are prepared by the Accounting Standards Committee. This is a body of part-timers, mainly professional accountants, and is entirely funded by the accountancy profession. Before standards are issued by the six professional accountancy bodies they must be unanimously agreed upon. This has led to delay in agreeing appropriate standards and a tendency to compromise in order to obtain unanimous agreement. The Committee's recommendation was to replace this body by a smaller Accounting Standards Board with a full-time chairman and technical director which would itself have authority to issue accounting standards.[1] These, moreover, could be agreed to by a two-thirds majority of its members. The broad policy objectives of the Accounting Standards Board would be set, under the Dearing Committee proposals, by a Financial Reporting Council.[2] This body would have around twenty members, half being practising accountants with the remainder representing other relevant areas of interest such as the Stock Exchange, institutional investors and other users of accounts, industry, commerce and employees. The third body recommended by the Committee was the establishment of a Review Panel.[3] The rôle of the Review Panel would be to examine alleged material departures from accounting standards by public or large private companies which the Panel felt involved an issue of principle or might in its opinion result in the accounts not giving a true and fair view. The Review Panel might then draw matters to the attention of the Stock Exchange or any relevant professional accountancy body and would have power ultimately, as would the DTI and the Stock Exchange, to take legal proceedings to compel a company to produce acceptable accounts.

2.10 None of this institutional framework is established in the Companies Act, although it came close to being so at one stage. The possibility that such bodies will be established is recognised, however, in various places in the legislation[4] and ns 256 expressly authorises the Government to make grants to, or for the purposes of, bodies concerned with issuing accounting standards (by which it is understood to refer to the Accounting Standards Board), overseeing and directing the issue of such standards (the Financial Reporting Council), or investigating departures from such standards or from statutory accounting requirements and taking steps to secure compliance with them (the Review Board). The main areas of controversy are whether such bodies should be established by statute, how they should be funded and who should be responsible for appointing the members.[5] The accountancy bodies take the view that this is an issue of public concern and that it is therefore the Government's duty to establish and fund the necessary institutional framework. The Government's view is that the Financial Reporting Council is designed to create a bridge between the practitioners (auditors), the

[1] The Dearing Report, Chapter 12.
[2] Ibid, Chapter 11.
[3] Ibid, Chapter 15.
[4] For example, ns 245C.
[5] The issues were well aired in the House of Commons Committee stage of the Companies Bill. See HC Committee, cols 106–136.

preparers of accounts (companies) and the users of accounts; the responsibility for devising and promoting the adoption of SSAPs should therefore rest with these groups and the government's role should be one of facilitation. In the Government's view the commitment of major interest groups, which is vital, is most likely to be achieved if they play a full rôle in managing and financing the relevant bodies. The Dearing Committee estimated that the new structure would cost £1.5m per annum compared with the Accounting Standards Committee's budget of £440,000 for 1989. It now seems to be agreed that a figure of at least £3m is more realistic and the cost is likely to be met entirely from three private sector sources – a levy on all companies filing an annual return collected by the DTI, a levy on all listed companies collected by the Stock Exchange and a contribution from the accountancy profession.

Apart from a new institutional framework the Dearing Committee also made recommendations to secure greater compliance with accounting standards.[1] The recommendation that public and large private companies reveal any material departures from applicable accounting standards has been implemented.[2] On the other hand the proposal to include a statutory presumption that accounts which involved such a material departure did not give a true and fair view has not been enacted. The Committee's proposal to restrict the criminal offence of producing defective accounts to cases involving a deliberate attempt to mislead has been enacted[3] as has their related proposal that a civil action should be available to compel companies to produce proper accounts.[4] All these matters are discussed more fully in the appropriate context.

New Definitions of Parent and Subsidiary Undertakings

2.11   Although the question whether one undertaking is a subsidiary of another is principally important in relation to the preparation of group accounts, the terminology is also relevant in relation to individual company accounts. Under the old law[5] there were three ways in which one company (S) became the subsidiary of another (P). First, if P was a member of S and controlled the composition of its board of directors. Secondly, if P held more than half in nominal value of S's equity share capital. Thirdly, any subsidiary of S was also a subsidiary of P. The major problem with this definition, in practice, was that it might exclude situations where one company controlled another which factually, though not legally, would be described as its subsidiary. This led to disagreement as to whether, in order to give a true and fair view, group accounts should reflect the substance of the relationship between companies rather than the formal legal

---

[1]   The Dearing Report, Chapter 15.
[2]   NSch 4, para 36A (CA 1989, Sch 1, para 7).
[3]   Ns 233(5) (CA 1989, s 7).
[4]   Ns 245B (CA 1989, s 12).
[5]   CA 1985, s 736.

relationship. In 1980 a successful prosecution was mounted against a company for including in its consolidated accounts the results of a company which it factually controlled but which did not legally become its subsidiary until after the end of the financial year.[1] The DTI then reminded auditors that emphasis on substance should never be at the expense of formal legal requirements.[2] Relying on this, companies justified making deliberate use of controlled non-subsidiaries as a means of keeping assets or liabilities off the consolidated balance sheet.[3]

2.12 The Seventh Directive provides for mandatory implementation by member states of tests based on legal control[4] while tests based on factual control are optional.[5] However, to help deal with the problem of off-balance sheet financing described above, the UK has implemented the tests based on factual control as well as those based on legal control. The new definition is drafted in terms of undertakings rather than companies. This makes it clear that subsidiaries for accounting purposes now encompasses not only bodies corporate but also partnerships and other unincorporated associations carrying on a trade or business with or without a view of profit.[6]

2.13 There are now six ways in which an undertaking may be a parent undertaking (P) in relation to a subsidiary undertaking (S).
These are where:

    (i) P holds a majority of the voting rights in S.[7] This may be contrasted with the previous test of holding a majority of the equity share capital which might or might not have voting rights attached.

    (ii) P is a member of S and controls alone a majority of the voting rights pursuant to an agreement with other shareholders or members.[8]

In both the above definitions the reference to voting rights in an undertaking basically means the rights conferred on shareholders or members (if the undertaking has no share capital) to vote at general meetings on all, or substantially all, matters.[9] If the undertaking has no general meetings at which votes are taken then holding a 'majority of voting rights' means the right to direct overall policy or alter the constitution.[10]

    (iii) P is a member of S and has the right to appoint or remove directors who have a majority of the voting rights at board meetings.[11]

---

[1] See (1981) 2 Co Law 275.
[2] See *Tolley's Company Law* (2nd edn, 1988) Appendix 3.
[3] See Bird [1986] JBL 132.
[4] Seventh Directive, art 1(1) (*a*), (*b*), (*d*).
[5] Ibid, art 1(1)(*c*), (2).
[6] Ns 259(1) (CA 1989, s 22).
[7] Ns 258(2)(*a*) (CA 1989, s 21).
[8] Ns 258(2)(*d*).
[9] NSch 10A, para 2(1) (CA 1989, Sch 9).
[10] Ibid, para 2(2).
[11] Ns 258(2)(*b*). As to the circumstances in which P is regarded as having the right to appoint to a directorship, see nSch 10A, paras 3(2) and (3).

(iv) P has the right to exercise a dominant influence over S by virtue of a provision in S's memorandum or articles or by virtue of a control contract.[1] P is not regarded as having the right to exercise a dominant influence over S unless it has a right to direct the operating and financial policies of S and the directors of S are obliged to comply with such directions whether or not they are for the benefit of S.[2] A 'control contract' is a contract in writing which confers on P the right to exercise a dominant influence over S and which is both expressly authorised by the memorandum or articles of S and permitted by the law under which S is established.[3] Such provisions for control of one undertaking by another are almost completely unknown in the UK and so this test is not likely to be of great significance where the putative subsidiary is incorporated in the UK. This test for establishing the relationship of parent and subsidiary is in fact optional so far as member states are concerned under the Seventh Directive. It has been implemented in the UK, however, because it might be useful if the putative subsidiary is established in, say, West Germany, where provisions for control are recognised by law. There is also, under discussion in Brussels, a proposed Ninth Directive to harmonise the treatment of groups in areas of company law besides that of consolidated accounts. The Ninth Directive, if it is ever issued, is likely to provide for control contracts to be recognised by member states and including this provision in the accounting legislation could prove helpful in preparing the ground for the Ninth Directive.

(v) P holds a participating interest in S and either actually exercises a dominant influence over S, or P and S are managed on a unified basis.[4] A 'participating interest' means an interest in the shares of S held [5] on a long-term basis for the purpose of securing a contribution to the activities of any undertaking in the group or of the group as a whole.[6] Neither the term 'dominant influence' nor the term 'managed on a unified basis' is defined in the Act. In particular the definition of 'right to exercise a dominant influence' referred to in the previous section does not apply here.[7] The terms are taken straight from the Seventh Directive and are deliberately left undefined. This test for establishing a parent subsidiary relationship is also an option for member states in the Seventh Directive. It has been implemented in the UK in the hope that it will curb the use of off-balance sheet financing whereby assets or liabilities are acquired by controlled non-subsidiaries with the intention

---

[1]   Ns 258(2)(c) (CA 1989, s 21).
[2]   NSch 10A, para 4(1) (CA 1989, Sch 9).
[3]   Ibid, para 4(2).
[4]   Ns 258(4).
[5]   By or on behalf of P or any of its subsidiary undertakings: ns 260(4), (5)(a) (CA 1989, s 22).
[6]   Ns 260(1).
[7]   NSch 10A, para 4(3).

of keeping them off the consolidated balance sheet. Any statutory definition of the relevant terms would merely encourage attempts at evasion. It also leaves it open for the accountancy profession to give guidance as to its practical meaning, and in this respect attention is particularly drawn to Exposure Draft 42.

(vi) Where P is a parent undertaking of S, it is treated as a parent undertaking in relation to all S's subsidiary undertakings.[1]

Individual Company Accounts and Reports: Changes in Content and Preparation

Financial year and accounting reference dates

2.14   Under the old law a company's financial year, although defined as the period in respect of which a profit and loss account had to be made up, coincided with the company's accounting reference period because a profit and loss account had to be prepared for each such period. Under the new law this link is maintained but made explicit, without the cross reference to preparing a profit and loss account. The end of a company's financial year must fall within seven days of the end of an accounting reference period.[2] The ending of an accounting reference period is still fixed by reference to the company's accounting reference date.[3] However, for a company incorporated after the commencement of Part I of the CA 1989, unless it gives due notice of a different date, its accounting reference date will be the last day of the month in which the anniversary of its incorporation falls.[4] In the past, the accounting reference date for such a company would have always been 31 March.

Amendments to the Companies Act 1985, Schedule 4

2.15   The changes to the CA 1985, Sch 4 are contained in Sch 1 to the CA 1989. Many of these are consequential upon the new terminology of 'undertakings' in place of 'companies' and 'participating interests' replacing 'shares in related companies'.[5] Others are relatively minor amendments. Thus, under Sch 4, para 11, it becomes a statutory requirement that accounting policies must now be applied consistently within the same accounts as well as from year to year.[6] This will be of particular significance in the preparation of consolidated accounts. Schedule 4, para 34(3) is revised to make clearer the implementation of the Fourth Directive, art 33(2).[7] It is made explicit that, apart from being used to pay

---

[1]   Ns 258(5) (CA 1989, s 21).
[2]   Ns 223 (CA 1989, s 3).
[3]   Ns 224(1) (CA 1989, s 3).
[4]   Ns 224(3).
[5]   CA 1989, Sch 1, paras 2–4.
[6]   Ibid, para 5.
[7]   Ibid, para 6.

up bonus shares or being transferred to the profit and loss account in appropriate cases, the revaluation reserve shall only be reduced to the extent that the amounts transferred to it are no longer necessary for the purposes of the valuation method used. It is now clear therefore that it is not permissible to write off goodwill to the revaluation reserve. Some companies had been doing this on the basis of interpreting the former wording, 'for the purpose of the accounting policies adopted by the company', to refer to *any* of their accounting policies rather than the relevant valuation method. This change is likely also to have more impact on consolidated accounts since it is in connection with acquisition of other companies that goodwill is most likely to arise. Finally, Sch 4, para 47 is amended to require provision for deferred taxation to be stated as well as (but separately from) provision for other taxation.[1]

Disclosure about related undertakings

2.16 The changes to disclosure requirements about related undertakings are also relatively minor. The term 'related undertakings' is now used to refer to subsidiary undertakings, associated undertakings, joint ventures and significant holdings in non-subsidiary undertakings. A revised set of disclosure requirements is contained in Sch 3 to the CA 1989 which becomes a new Sch 5 to the CA 1985. Part I of the Schedule deals with disclosure by companies not required to prepare group accounts and Part II with companies which are required to prepare group accounts. In Part I the main changes arise from the inclusion of unincorporated undertakings for the first time. The more significant changes in Part II are referred to below in relation to group accounts.

Disclosure about directors' emoluments and other benefits

2.17 There are some important extensions to the disclosure requirements regarding directors' emoluments and other benefits. Emoluments in respect of a person's accepting office as a director ('golden hellos') must now be included in a director's overall emoluments.[2] These were not caught previously, provided the payment was made before the director joined the company and without any obligation being imposed on the prospective director to take up the appointment. Sums paid to or receivable by persons connected with the director or by a body corporate controlled by the director will in future be treated as received by the director and thus require disclosure.[3] This will cover, for example, sums paid to the firm of a solicitor or accountant director. Sums paid to third parties in respect of the director's services will also have to be disclosed.[4] This will cover so-called compensation payments or transfer fees as well as any damages arising from possible inducement of breach of contract. This provision also requires disclosure of benefits in kind.

---

[1]   Ibid, para 8.
[2]   NSch 6, para 1(4) (CA 1989, Sch 4, para 3).
[3]   Ibid, paras 10(4) and 13(4).
[4]   Ibid, para 9.

2.18   There are important extensions requiring the disclosure of benefits in kind where they form part of compensation for loss of office[1] or pension provision.[2] The nature of the benefit or compensation must be disclosed and its estimated money value included in the relevant total figure. In contrast, the provisions requiring disclosure of the emoluments of higher paid employees[3] have been repealed. The importance of disclosure regarding directors is because of the obvious potential for conflict between duty and interest in relation to a director's dealings with the company. The same applies in relation to shadow directors and accordingly the disclosure requirements relating to loans, quasi-loans and other dealings now cover transactions with shadow directors as well as with directors.[4]

There is one significant change also to the directors' report. This extends disclosure of the directors' interests in the company's shares or in those of other companies in the group so it covers the grant or exercise of rights or obligations to subscribe for shares.[5] This effectively extends disclosure to share options granted or exercised by directors or their immediate families, unless the relevant family member is also a director.

Compliance with Statements of Standard Accounting Practice (SSAPs)

2.19   There is one change to CA 1985, Sch 4 which deserves separate treatment. A new para 36A inserted into CA 1985, Sch 4 requires public companies and large private companies to disclose in notes to the accounts whether the accounts have been prepared in accordance with applicable accounting standards.[6] They must also give particulars of, and the reasons for, any material departures from such standards. 'Applicable accounting standards' are defined as statements of standard accounting practice which are, in accordance with their terms, relevant to the company's circumstances and to the accounts.[7]

This provision implements one of the principal recommendations of the Dearing Committee on the Making of Accounting Standards.[8] It applies in addition to the professional but non-statutory requirement upon auditors to note any departures from accounting standards that do not have their support. It represents the latest stage in a long running debate over incorporating accounting standards into law. In many ways this raises similar issues to the debate over whether accounts should reflect the legal form or the economic substance of a transaction. The danger with statutory legal requirements is that companies and

---

[1]   Ibid, para 8(3).
[2]   Ibid, para 7(4).
[3]   CA 1985, Sch 5, Part VI. See HC Committee cols 165–177.
[4]   NSch 6, para 27 (CA 1989, Sch 4, para 5).
[5]   NSch 7, para 28 (CA 1989, Sch 5, para 3). In addition the report must state if the company effected any liability insurance for its officers or auditors: nSch 7, para 5A (CA 1989, s 137(2)).
[6]   CA 1989, Sch 1, para 7.
[7]   Ns 256(2) (CA 1989, s 19).
[8]   Dearing Report, para 10.3(*a*).

their advisers seek ways round the precise letter of the requirement, while ignoring the spirit of the legal provision which may be much broader in application. This is the problem at the heart of the controversy over off-balance sheet financing. The Dearing Committee were conscious of the danger of a legalistic approach and also of the fact that it is generally easier to adapt non-statutory requirements to new developments quickly. They therefore rejected the approach, which has been followed in both Australia and Canada, of a general move towards incorporating accounting standards into law.[1]

2.20   The Dearing Committee foresaw three advantages in requiring public and large private companies to reveal non-compliance with accounting standards.[2] First, to bring to the attention of the whole board of directors any proposed material departure from accounting standards; secondly, to help the user to understand the accounts; and thirdly, to facilitate the task of monitoring compliance with accounting standards. The new provision requires only that particulars of any departure from SSAPs plus the reasons for it be given. The government resisted an amendment which would have added the requirement that the financial effects of departures be set out, on the grounds that this came too close to giving SSAPs legal effect.[3] The proposal as it has been enacted more closely reflects the Dearing Committee recommendation.

2.21   The Dearing Committee also made an associated recommendation for a rebuttable presumption to be incorporated into statute to the effect that compliance with accounting standards is necessary to give a true and fair view.[4] Thus, if there were a material departure from accounting standards the onus would be on those arguing that the accounts nevertheless gave a true and fair view to show that they did. The Government, however, did not accept this recommendation on the basis that it was also getting too close to giving legal force to SSAPs with all the disadvantages of excessive legalism that that might entail. No such presumption therefore appears in the Act. It may be questioned whether a statutory presumption would, in any case, make all that much difference. In an opinion given to the Accounting Standards Committee in 1983[5] leading counsel stated that 'the courts will treat compliance with accepted accounting principles as prima facie evidence that the accounts are true and fair. Equally, deviation from accepted principles will be prima facie evidence that they are not.' Similarly, in a case involving alleged negligence by auditors, Woolf J, referring to the duty to comply with SSAPs, said 'while they are not conclusive so that a departure from their terms necessarily involves a breach of the duty of care, . . . they are very

---

[1]   Ibid, para 10.2

[2]   Dearing Report, para 10.4.

[3]   See HC Committee cols 105–136. It remains a requirement of the professional bodies, that when SSAPs are not followed the financial effects of departures be stated or the reasons for such non-disclosure given. See Explanatory Foreword to the SSAPs in *Accounting Standards* published by the ICAEW.

[4]   Dearing Report, paras 15.14–15.17.

[5]   See *Accounting Standards* published by the ICAEW.

strong evidence as to what is the proper standard which should be adopted and unless there is some justification, a departure from this will be regarded as constituting a breach of duty.'[1]

Group Accounts

Introduction

2.22 As has been explained above, one of the main reasons for the CA 1989 is to implement the Seventh Directive on the harmonisation of rules relating to the preparation of group accounts. A vital aspect of the Directive is the definition of parent and subsidiary undertaking and before reading these pages the reader should first consult the pages dealing with the new definitions.[2] In summary, their effect so far as a test based on legal control is concerned is to replace a test based on holding a majority of the equity by one based on holding a majority of the votes. They also introduce new tests reflecting factual control based on the ability of the parent to exercise a dominant influence over the subsidiary. Altogether there are now six ways in which an undertaking may become a subsidiary of another undertaking.

When must group accounts be prepared?

2.23 Any company which is a parent company, ie it has one or more subsidiary undertakings, must prepare group accounts[3] unless it falls within one of three exceptions: (i) the group qualifies as a small or medium-sized group; (ii) the parent is itself a subsidiary and is included in the accounts of a larger group; or (iii) *all* the subsidiary undertakings in the group are excluded for one reason or another.

Small or medium-sized group exemption

2.24 Under the old law the parent company of a small or medium-sized group was entitled to deliver to the registrar modified group accounts comparable to those for small or medium-sized companies.[4] The UK has now taken advantage of an option in the Seventh Directive[5] to exempt the parent company of small or medium-sized groups from the obligation *even to prepare* group accounts at all.[6] The conditions for qualifying as a small or medium-sized group remain the same as before except that there are now alternative 'net' or 'gross' figures for

---

1   *Lloyd Cheyham & Co Ltd v Littlejohn & Co* [1987] BCLC 303, 313.
2   See paras 2.11–2.13 above.
3   Ns 227(1) (CA 1989, s 5).
4   CA 1985, s 250(6).
5   Seventh Directive, art 6(1).
6   Ns 248(1) (CA 1989, s 13).

aggregate turnover and aggregate balance sheet total.[1] The net figures, which are the same as the figures in the old legislation, are calculated by taking into account the set-offs and other adjustments required in the case of group accounts; the gross figures are without such set-offs and adjustments. Companies may qualify on the basis of either the net or the gross figure.[2] In addition, as before, no company in the group must be engaged in an ineligible activity and the old list of such activities has been augmented by the addition of 'an authorised person under the Financial Services Act'.[3] Finally, the auditors' report stating that the company is entitled to the exemption must be attached to the individual accounts of the company.[4]

Intermediate parent company

2.25   Under the old law a holding company was exempt from preparing group accounts if it was the wholly owned subsidiary of a company incorporated in Great Britain.[5] This exemption is continued under the new law with the modification that the immediate parent undertaking may now be established anywhere in the EEC.[6] The exemption is also extended to cases where the company's immediate parent does not own all the shares but owns more than 50 per cent. In such a case, however, shareholders holding in aggregate more than half of the remaining shares or 5 per cent of the total shares in the company may none the less demand that the company does prepare group accounts.[7]

Whether the intermediate parent is wholly or partly owned there are a number of other new conditions, all of which must be satisfied before the company is entitled to the exemption from preparing group accounts. First, no securities in the company may be listed on a stock exchange within the EEC.[8] Secondly, the company must be included in the group accounts of a larger group headed by a parent undertaking established within the EEC, and the accounts must have been drawn up and audited and the directors' report drawn up in accordance with the Seventh Directive.[9] Thirdly, the company's individual accounts must disclose the exemption, state the name and origin of the EEC parent in whose group accounts the company is included, and the company must deliver to the registrar a copy of the group accounts, directors' and auditors' report, together with a certified English translation of any document not in English.[10]

---

[1]   Ns 249(3) (CA 1989, s 13).
[2]   Ns 249(4).
[3]   Ns 248(2) (CA 1989, s 13).
[4]   Ns 248(4).
[5]   CA 1985, s 229(2).
[6]   Ns 228(1)(*a*) (CA 1989, s 5).
[7]   Ns 228(1)(*b*).
[8]   Ns 228(3). The word 'listed' indicates that so far as the London Stock Exchange is concerned the restriction only applies to companies listed on the Official List.
[9]   Ns 228(2)(*a*), (*b*).
[10]   Ns 228(2)(*c*)–(*f*).

All subsidiaries excluded from group accounts

2.26 For the avoidance of doubt it is expressly stated that if all a parent's subsidiaries are excluded from the group accounts, no group accounts need be prepared.[1] When a subsidiary may be excluded from the group accounts is dealt with next.

Exclusion of undertakings from group accounts

2.27 The rule is that all subsidiary undertakings must be included in the group accounts unless they are covered by one of the exceptions.[2] A number of exceptions existing under the old law continue. Thus, a subsidiary *must* be excluded if its activity is so different that its inclusion would be incompatible with a true and fair view[3] and *may* be excluded if it is not material for the purpose of giving a true and fair view,[4] or if the necessary information cannot be obtained without disproportionate expense or undue delay.[5] The former exclusions on the grounds that inclusion would be misleading, or, with the approval of the Secretary of State, on the grounds that it would be harmful to the company, have not been re-enacted. There are two new optional grounds for exclusion, however. First, if the exercise of the parent's rights over the assets or management of the subsidiary undertaking is substantially hindered by severe long-term restrictions.[6] Secondly, if the interest of the parent in the subsidiary is held with the sole intention of resale. In order to prevent parent companies taking advantage of this exception to include or exclude subsidiaries at will it is provided that once a subsidiary has been included it is not possible subsequently to decide that the shares in it were held exclusively for resale.[7]

General requirements regarding preparation of group accounts

2.28 Group accounts must in future consist of a consolidated profit and loss account and balance sheet.[8] The option which parent companies had in the past of preparing group accounts in something other than consolidated form has not been re-enacted. The wording of the requirement that the accounts give a true and fair view[9] follows very closely the wording of the old legislation rather than the wording of the Seventh Directive.[10] It is very unlikely, however, that there is any difference in law between the different wordings. It is also now made clear

---

[1]   Ns 229(5) (CA 1989, s 5).
[2]   Ns 229(1).
[3]   Ns 229(4). See also nSch 4A, para 17 (CA 1989, Sch 2). If the accounts of such a subsidiary undertaking are not otherwise required to be delivered to the registrar then they must be appended to the parent company's own accounts: ns 243 (CA 1989, s 11).
[4]   Ns 229(2).
[5]   Ns 229(3)(*b*).
[6]   Ns 229(3)(*a*).
[7]   Ns 229(3)(*c*).
[8]   Ns 227(2) (CA 1989, s 5).
[9]   Ns 227(3).
[10]   Seventh Directive, art 16(3).

that the requirement to depart from detailed statutory provisions, if in special circumstances this is necessary to give a true and fair view,[1] is independent of the requirement to give any additional information necessary to give a true and fair view.[2]

2.29   An issue which provoked considerable debate prior to the Act concerned the extent to which parent companies should be permitted or required to include controlled non-subsidiaries within the group accounts.[3] To a great extent the new test of parent/ subsidiary relationship based on the parent holding a participating interest and actually exercising a dominant influence or managing itself and the subsidiary on a unified basis[4] should help to solve the problems of off-balance sheet financing. However, there may continue to be cases of undertakiings which are in fact controlled by the parent but do not fall within the new definition of subsidiary. It may be necessary to give more information about such undertakings than will be shown using the equity method of accounting in order to give a true and fair view of the state of affairs of these undertakings which are included in the group accounts. In such circumstances, in order to comply with the true and fair view requirement, the parent company effectively has two options. It may either give any necessary additional information by way of notes to the accounts;[5] or, in such special circumstances, it may override the statutory provisions and include the controlled non-subsidiary in the group accounts.[6]

2.30   Many of the detailed rules contained in the Seventh Directive regarding group accounts were foreshadowed by provisions included, in 1981, in what became Sch 4 to the CA 1985. So the extent of the changes now is less than would otherwise have been the case. The starting point for the detailed rules regarding group accounts is now Sch 2 to the CA 1989 which becomes a new Sch 4A to the CA 1985. As a general rule, group accounts must comply so far as practicable with the rules contained in Sch 4 for individual company accounts.[7] Thus, rules as to format and general rules as to presentation are still those contained in Sch 4.

   The group accounts must be drawn up as at the same date as the individual accounts of the parent company.[8] Unless there are good reasons against this, the financial year of each subsidiary undertaking must coincide with that of the parent company.[9] If this is not the case then the group accounts are made up using the accounts of the subsidiary undertaking for its financial year last ending before the end of the parent company's financial year, provided that year ended

1   Ns 227(6) (CA 1989, s 5).
2   Ns 227(5).
3   See above, para 2.11.
4   Ns 258(4) (CA 1989, s 21). This test is described in para 2.13 above.
5   Ns 227(5).
6   Ns 227(6).
7   NSch 4A, para 1(1) (CA 1980, Sch 2).
8   Ns 227(1)(3).
9   Ns 223(5) (CA 1989, s 3).

no more than three months before that of the parent company.[1] If the parent company's financial year does end more than three months after that of a subsidiary undertaking, then interim accounts must be prepared by the subsidiary as at the end of the parent company's financial year and these will be the accounts incorporated into the group accounts.[2]

2.31 Under the Seventh Directive, assets and liabilities are to be valued by a uniform method; normally that used by the parent company in its individual accounts. If this is not so it must be recorded in a note to the group accounts and the reasons given.[3] If assets and liabilities have been valued under different rules, unless these are not material for the purpose of giving a true and fair view,[4] they must be adjusted to accord with the method used for the group accounts.[5] If the directors of the parent company have some special reason not to make the adjustments they need not do so, but particulars must be disclosed in notes to the accounts together with the reason and its effects.[6]

Accounting for acquisitions and mergers

2.32 Apart from the problem of off-balance sheet financing, the most controversial issue in accounting practice in the past few years has been the methods by which acquiring companies incorporate their acquisitions into their consolidated accounts. The economic justification of takeovers is that they should lead to assets being redeployed to more efficient uses or being managed by more efficient managers. If the takeover market is itself working efficiently, assets should thus be put to more productive use as a result of a takeover, with the consequence that the overall wealth of society is increased. Over the last few years fears have been expressed that some acquiring companies have artificially inflated their earnings through the way in which they have accounted for their acquisitions.[7] The methods used have strictly speaking been within the rules laid down in company law and accounting practice, but within those rules some companies have managed to present their accounts so as to create a particular impression or to make it difficult to judge the true effects of an acquisition. If investors cannot judge the true effects of an acquisition then they cannot judge whether the takeover really has resulted in more productive use of the assets involved. In this way assets may end up not being managed by the most efficient managers but by those managers with the most creative accountants, so the market for corporate control is itself distorted and assets are not put to their most productive use.

---

[1] NSch 4A, para 2(2)(*a*) (CA 1989, Sch 2).
[2] Ibid, para 2(2)(*b*).
[3] Ibid, para 4.
[4] Ibid, para 3(3).
[5] Ibid, para 3(1).
[6] Ibid, para 3(2).
[7] See, for example, the CBI report 'Merger and Acquisition Accounting' (1987). See also the research of Chris Higson of the London Business School reported in the *Financial Times*, (1989) 12 October.

2.33   The two methods by which an acquisition may be incorporated into consolidated accounts are known as acquisition accounting and merger accounting. The difference between these methods may be illustrated by an example in which company A is acquiring or merging with company B. In year 1 A makes £100 profit and B makes £60. In year 2 A makes £120 and B makes £80, but halfway through year 2 A acquires or merges with B. Under acquisition accounting B is incorporated into the consolidated accounts as from the date of acquisition. As this is halfway through the year, one half of B's profits for that year will be included in the consolidation. Compared with A's profit of £100 in the year before acquisition its profit at the end of the year of acquisition will be £160 (£120 + £40).

Merger accounting, on the other hand, is based on a pooling of the interests of the two companies that have merged. Thus, the whole of the profit of B in the year of acquisition is combined with that of A to give a total of £200 (£120 + £80). This will be compared in the consolidated accounts with the combined total from the previous year of £160 (£100 + £60). As is explained in more detail below the two methods of accounting also require differing treatments for consolidating the balance sheets. Under acquisition accounting the assets of the acquired company are only brought in to the group accounts from the date of acquisition and at cost to the acquiring company. Under merger accounting the balance sheets are amalgamated as if the two companies had always been together.

2.34   The Seventh Directive contains provisions to harmonise the manner in which acquisitions are incorporated into consolidated accounts and these are duly enacted in paras 7–15 of the new Sch 4A to the CA 1985. Until now accounting for acquisitions and mergers has only been regulated by an accounting standard.[1] The normal method of accounting for acquisitions throughout the member states of the EEC is by the acquisition method. However, at the insistence of the UK, member states were given the option of allowing merger accounting as an alternative in certain defined circumstances.[2] The UK has exercised this option so that while acquisition accounting is the norm, merger accounting may be used where the conditions for merger accounting are met.[3] Accordingly, consolidated accounts must in future not only state the names of any undertakings acquired (or the name of the parent undertaking where a group of undertakings has been acquired), but also whether they are accounted for in the consolidation by the acquisition method or the merger method.[4] As we shall see it can be important to know whether the acquisition was paid for in cash or by the issue of shares or in some other form of consideration, and so there is a requirement that the composition and the fair value of the consideration given by the parent company and any of its subsidiary undertakings must also be stated.[5]

---

[1]   SSAP 23.
[2]   Seventh Directive, art 20.
[3]   NSch 4A, para 8 (CA 1989, Sch 2).
[4]   Ibid, para 12(1)(2).
[5]   Ibid, para 12(3).

2.35 It will be apparent from the examples given above[1] that acquisition accounting gives the impression of faster growing profits after the acquisition. The apparent boost to the profits of A in the example can be particularly misleading if the business of B is highly seasonal and the bulk of B's profits were generated before the acquisition took place. To avoid this the profit or loss of the acquired undertaking or group must be stated for the period from the start of the financial year to the date of the acquisition. In order that proper comparisons with past performance can be made, the profit or loss for the previous financial year must also be given.[2] Where an acquisition takes place in stages, there is further scope for presenting the figures in a way which makes the most favourable impact on the post acquisition profits. To an extent this will be controlled under the new rules which provide that the income and expenditure of the undertaking acquired are to be brought into the group accounts only as from the date of acquisition,[3] which is the date at which the undertaking becomes a subsidiary undertaking of the parent company.[4]

2.36 Any apparent boost to profits represented by using acquisition accounting should not be misleading at all if a proportionate increase in turnover and an accurate figure for the value of assets acquired are also recorded in the consolidated accounts. It is likely that the acquiring company will have paid a premium for the assets acquired and that the value at which they are recorded in the consolidated balance sheet will be lower than the consideration paid for them. There is, however, an advantage in putting as low a value as possible on the assets acquired in that less provision for depreciation need be made in future. Furthermore, if the low valued asset is subsequently sold by its new owners, the amount of any profit will appear to be greater. So the new rules for acquisition accounting lay down that identifiable assets and liabilities of the undertaking acquired (ie assets and liabilities which are capable of being disposed of or discharged separately, without disposing of a business of the undertaking)[5] shall be included in the consolidated balance sheet at their fair values as at the date when the undertaking acquired became a subsidiary.[6]

Sometimes the value of assets to the original owner and to the new owner have appeared to be so disproportionately different as to raise questions as to the basis of the valuation and even the point of the takeover itself. In order to help investors assess the figures in future, the value at which each class of assets and liabilities of the undertaking or group acquired were entered in the books of such undertaking or group immediately before the acquisition must be given together with the fair value at the date of the acquisition.[7] There is no definition of class of assets, but

---

[1] In para 2.33.
[2] NSch 4A, para 12(4) (CA 1989, Sch 2).
[3] Ibid, para 9(3).
[4] Ibid, para 7.
[5] Ibid, para 9(2).
[6] Ibid, para 9(1). Fair value rules already apply under SSAP 14 and SSAP 23.
[7] Ibid, para 12(5).

this is likely to be covered by professional guidance as is the extent to which goodwill arising in relation to one class of assets can be netted off against a negative consolidation difference in relation to another class. Likewise, there is no statutory definition of fair value, but accounting standards define it as the amount for which an asset or liability could be exchanged in an arm's length transaction. That will require estimating what the acquiring company would have to pay if it were purchasing the relevant asset direct instead of as part of a package. An SSAP is due to be published dealing specifically with the meaning of 'fair value'. This will need to be taken into consideration because the incorporation of individual accounts into the consolidated balance sheet is to take account of any appropriate adjustments required in accordance with generally accepted accounting principles and practice.[1]

2.37   The difference between what the acquiring company paid and the value of the assets it received represents goodwill. That is itself an asset of the acquiring company and should be written off in future years as its value depreciates. The effect of such writing off will be to reduce the profit in subsequent years and so companies using acquisition accounting have found ways to reduce the goodwill element. In the past one method used has been to subtract from the consideration paid by the acquiring company a figure for the cost of 'reorganising' the company taken over. By apparently reducing the price paid for the assets this reduces the goodwill element and therefore reduces the impact on the future profits of the acquiring company. This is the case even though had such reorganisation costs been incurred by the acquired company instead they would have had to be set off against its profits unless they justified being treated as extraordinary items. In future, this practice will no longer be possible because under the new rules the only permitted set off against the acquisition costs of the shares in the acquired undertaking will be the acquiring company's interest in the capital and reserves of the acquired undertaking.[2] The resulting difference, if positive, is to be treated as goodwill and, if negative, as a negative consolidation difference.[3] In addition, the amount of any goodwill or negative consolidation difference arising on the acquisition of each class of assets and liabilities must be stated.[4]

2.38   In order to avoid goodwill having an adverse effect on profits some companies have in the past written off goodwill against a revaluation reserve. As explained above,[5] the Government's view was that this was contrary to art 33(2)(*c*) of the Fourth Directive which is applied to consolidated accounts by art 29(1) of the Seventh Directive. As a result the relevant provision of the Companies Act 1985, Sch 4, para 34, has now been amended[6] to make it clear

1   Ibid, para 2(1).
2   Ibid, para 9(4).
3   Ibid, para 9(5).
4   Ibid, para 12(5).
5   Para 2.15.
6   CA 1989, Sch 1, para 6.

that goodwill cannot be written off against a revaluation reserve and this applies to consolidated accounts as well as to individual company accounts.[1] In addition, consolidated accounts will have to state the net cumulative goodwill arising from acquisitions less disposals which has been written off in that and earlier financial years.[2]

2.39   Another method of disposing of goodwill without it having an impact on subsequent profits is to write it off via a reduction in the share premium account. If the acquiring company has paid for the acquisition by issuing its own shares the difference between the nominal value of shares issued and the value of the acquisition is share premium and must be credited to the share premium account.[3] However, with the sanction of the court, the share premium account can be reduced,[4] the effect being to reduce the apparent consideration paid by the acquiring company thus reducing the goodwill element.[5] In some cases companies have even managed to eliminate any goodwill by avoiding having to credit the share premium account in the first place. This is done by structuring the deal so as to qualify for merger relief under the CA 1985, s 131. When this section was introduced in 1981 it was intended to facilitate merger accounting and there is no doubt that using it in conjunction with acquisition accounting smacks of having the best of both worlds. Nevertheless, it is not the Government's intention to prohibit such a practice at present pending the outcome of a review of the relevant accounting standards. When that is complete the Government may restrict or prohibit the practice using delegated legislation.

2.40   An alternative way to prevent goodwill arising is to use merger accounting. In future, however, the circumstances in which merger accounting may be used will be regulated by statute.[6] The essence of a merger as opposed to an acquisition is that in a merger not only are the assets of the two separate businesses merged but the owners of the two separate businesses all remain and become owners of the merged business. The value of the merged business is basically the sum of the two original businesses. No value has been paid out because no owner has left. In contrast, in an acquisition the increase in the value of the acquiring company will be the value of the business acquired less any consideration paid for its acquisition.

2.41   As we have seen merger accounting is based on a pooling of interests and is appropriate where businesses are merged under the combined ownership of the owners of the previously separate businesses. The conditions for merger

---

1   NSch 4A, para 1(1) (CA 1989, Sch 2).
2   Ibid, para 13.
3   CA 1985, s 130.
4   Ibid, s 135.
5   Alternatively, the share premium account can be reduced to create or increase the accumulated profit reserve and goodwill can then be written off against this without affecting current profits: *Re Thorn EMI plc* [1989] BCLC 612.
6   NSch 4A, paras 10 and 11.

accounting, although reflecting this situation in principle, do not require that 100 per cent of previous owners remain as owners of the merged business. Instead the minimum conditions to be satisfied in order to allow merger accounting to be used are:[1]

(i)   that after the merger at least 90 per cent of the nominal value of shares in the undertaking acquired having unrestricted rights to participate in distributions and on liquidation are held by or on behalf of the parent company or its subsidiary undertakings;

(ii) that that 90 per cent figure was attained pursuant to an arrangement providing for the issue of equity shares by the parent company or its subsidiary undertakings; (There is no requirement that the whole 90 per cent was attained as a result of the arrangement. The 90 per cent figure thus includes shares already held. However, accounting practice restricts the prior holding to 20 per cent.)[2]

(iii) that the fair value of any consideration, other than the issue of equity shares, given pursuant to the arrangement by the parent company and its subsidiary undertakings did not exceed 10 per cent of the nominal value of the equity shares issued;

(iv) the adoption of merger accounting accords with generally accepted accounting principles and practice.

Satisfying conditions (ii) and (iii) will ensure that the bulk of the owners of the acquired undertaking become owners of the new parent company or one of its subsidiary undertakings. Conditions (i), (ii) and (iii) represent the minimum conditions laid down in the Seventh Directive, but it is open to member states to impose stricter conditions and the UK has provided for this possibility by requiring in condition (iv) that any relevant accounting standard must also be complied with.

2.42 Where merger accounting is used, the assets and liabilities of the undertaking acquired are brought into the group accounts at the figures at which they stood in the undertaking's accounts, subject to any adjustments, for example, to bring the valuation methods into line.[3] Any significant adjustments must be explained.[4] As already mentioned, in merger accounting the income and expenditure of the undertaking acquired for the whole year are included in the group accounts, including therefore the period before acquisition.[5] Likewise, the figures for the previous year must be based on the assumption that the undertakings had been merged throughout that period.[6] It is usual for the acquiring company in merger accounting to take advantage of merger relief

---

[1]   NSch 4A, para 10 (CA 1989, Sch 2).
[2]   SSAP 23.
[3]   NSch 4A, para 11(2).
[4]   Ibid, para 3.
[5]   Ibid, para 11(3).
[6]   Ibid, para 11(4).

under the CA 1985, s 131 to avoid creating a share premium. Only the *nominal* value of the issued capital of the undertaking acquired which is held by the parent company and its subsidiary undertakings is set off therefore against the consideration given. And in calculating the consideration only the *nominal* value of shares issued by the parent company or its subsidiary undertakings is aggregated to the fair value of any other consideration, determined as at the date of acquisition.[1] The resulting figure is simply a balancing item which is shown as an adjustment to the consolidated reserves.[2]

Accounting for subsidiary undertakings not included in the consolidation

2.43 Where a subsidiary undertaking is excluded from consolidation under ns 229(4) (ie on the grounds that its activities are so different that inclusion would be incompatible with giving a true and fair view), the interest of the group in the excluded subsidiary undertaking, and the amount of any profit or loss attributable to that interest, must be shown by the equity method of accounting[3] (including dealing with any goodwill arising in accordance with Sch 4, paras 17–19 and 21).[4]

Accounting for associated undertakings

2.44 An associated undertaking is one in which an undertaking included in the consolidation has a participating interest and over whose operating and financial policy it exercises a significant influence.[5] It specifically excludes, however, any undertaking which is either a subsidiary undertaking of the parent company or dealt with as a joint venture under para 19 of Sch 4A. The logic of such exclusions is that those undertakings will already have been dealt with in the consolidated accounts. The interest in an associated undertaking is to be shown by the equity method of accounting in a similar manner to that in a subsidiary undertaking excluded from the consolidation.[6]

Accounting for unincorporated joint ventures

2.45 Where an undertaking included in the consolidation manages, jointly with an undertaking not included in the consolidation, an unincorporated undertaking ('the joint venture'), it may be dealt with in the group accounts by proportional consolidation.[7] Under this method a proportionate share of the assets and

---

[1]   Ibid, para 11(5).
[2]   Ibid, para 11(6).
[3]   This is where the investing company reflects in its consolidated profit and loss account its share of the investee company's profits and losses and, in its consolidated balance sheet, its share of the investee company's retained profits or accumulated deficits.
[4]   NSch 4A, para 18 (CA 1989, Sch 2).
[5]   Ibid, para 19.
[6]   Ibid, para 21.
[7]   Ibid, para 18.

liabilities are brought into the consolidated balance sheet line by line. It is particularly appropriate for accounting for a stake in an unincorporated joint venture because the undertaking's interest in the joint venture can be seen as akin to a direct interest in the assets and liabilities. As regards assets there is no difficulty with ascertaining a proportionate share, likewise with liabilities if they are several. Where liabilities are joint it is likely that attention will be drawn to this in a note to the accounts. Particulars of unincorporated joint ventures dealt with in this way must also be included in a note to the accounts including the factors on which the joint management is based and the proportion of capital in the joint venture held by undertakings included in the consolidation.

Minority interests

2.46   Minority interests arise where subsidiary undertakings included in the balance sheet are not wholly owned. Part of what has been included in the consolidated accounts is therefore attributable not to the shareholders in the parent company but to the minority shareholders in the subsidiary undertakings. The appropriate adaptations to the accounts formats laid down in Sch 4 are dealt with in nSch 4A, para 17.

Information about related companies

2.47   The provisions requiring disclosure of details about related undertakings are revised and consolidated in Sch 3, Part II to the CA 1989 which in turn becomes a new Sch 5, Part II to the CA 1985. The main changes are as follows. In future the notes to the accounts will have to give not only the name and place of incorporation of each subsidiary undertaking, but also by virtue of which of the conditions specified in ns 258(2) or (4) it is a subsidiary undertaking of its immediate parent undertaking.[1] Likewise, in relation to unincorporated joint ventures which are dealt with in the accounts by proportional consolidation, the factors on which the joint management is based must be stated.[2]

Finally, where a parent company is also a subsidiary undertaking so that it is included within a larger set of group accounts, it must give details of the parent company which heads the largest group of undertakings for which group accounts are drawn up and in which it is included. This may perhaps conveniently come to be referred to as the 'ultimate group parent'. It must also give similar details of the parent company which heads the smallest group of undertakings for which group accounts are drawn up and in which it is included. This in turn may perhaps conveniently come to be referred to as the 'immediate group parent'.[3]

---

[1]   NSch 5, para 15(5) (CA 1989, Sch 3).
[2]   Ibid, para 21.
[3]   Ibid, para 30.

Parent company's individual profit and loss account

2.48 There are significant changes to the exemptions available to a parent company which prepares group accounts, in respect of the publication of its own individual profit and loss account.[1] These reflect the fact that a new version of art 58 in the Fourth Directive is substituted by art 44 of the Seventh Directive. The new provisions also cure certain important drafting defects in the previous legislation. A parent company which prepares group accounts is entitled to the exemptions, provided its profit or loss, determined in accordance with the CA requirements, is shown in the notes to the company's individual balance sheet[2] and, provided the fact that advantage is being taken of the exemptions is disclosed in the group accounts.[3]

The exemptions now permitted consist of omitting the supplementary information specified in paras 52 to 57 of Sch 4 regarding matters such as taxation, turnover and staff costs.[4] In addition, although the company's individual profit and loss account must be approved by the board of directors, it does not need to be audited, circulated to members, laid before the general meeting or delivered to the registrar.[5] It will also count as non-statutory accounts for the purposes of ns 240.

Special Provisions for Banking and Insurance Companies and Groups

2.49 The provisions in the CA 1989, s 18[6] plus Schs 7 and 8[7] replace the provisions that dealt with 'special category' companies under the old legislation. Shipping companies which used to qualify as special category will no longer do so. Their accounts must therefore be prepared under the normal rules. Banking and insurance companies and groups, however, will continue to be given the option to prepare their accounts under special provisions. In the case of individual company accounts the option is to prepare accounts in accordance with the CA 1985, Sch 9, Part I rather than Sch 4. Schedule 9, Part I contains what was formerly in Sch 9, Parts I–IV as further amended by the provisions of the CA 1989, Sch 7, Part I. The accounts of banking or insurance groups may in turn be prepared under the new CA 1985, Sch 9, Part II which is inserted by the CA 1989, Sch 7, Part II. The modifications to disclosure requirements about related undertakings and the emoluments and other benefits of directors and others now only apply to banking companies and groups. The normal provisions in the revised CA 1985, Schs 5 and

---

[1]   Ns 230 (CA 1989, s 5).
[2]   Ns 230(1)(*b*).
[3]   Ns 230(4).
[4]   Ns 230(2).
[5]   Ns 230(3).
[6]   This inserts nss 255–255D into the CA 1985.
[7]   These become Schs 9 and 10 to the CA 1985.

6 must be read, in the case of banking companies and groups, subject to the modifications contained in the CA 1989, Sch 7, Parts III and IV which become, in the CA 1985, Sch 9, Parts III and IV. The modifications to the directors' report which apply to both banking and insurance companies or groups are contained in the CA 1985, ns 255C and Sch 10, a revised version of which is substituted by the CA 1989, Sch 8.

2.50   The accounts of banking and insurance companies are also the subject of two separate EC harmonisation directives. The directive affecting insurance companies is still a draft under discussion.[1] The directive on annual accounts and consolidated accounts of banks and other financial institutions, however, was adopted by the Council of Ministers on 8 December 1986.[2] It must be implemented into national law by 31 December 1990 and apply no later than in respect of accounting periods beginning on or after 1 January 1993. It will be implemented at the same time as a directive harmonising the documents, including accounting documents, which must be filed at the relevant local registry by branches of credit and other financial institutions established in one member state but whose head office is outside that member state.[3] The method of implementation will be via regulations under ns 257. The scope of the directive is wider than just banks incorporated under the companies legislation and would also apply to banking partnerships. The Government's belief is that although there are no such partnerships in the UK at present, while the possibility of their authorisation exists it is necessary to have powers to bring them within the scope of the implementation of the directive. New section 255D therefore gives the Secretary of State power to make regulations applying the accounting provisions of the CA 1985 to banking partnerships with such modifications as may be appropriate.

Signing, Presentation and Registration of Accounts and Reports

Signing of accounts and reports

2.51   There are a number of changes to the requirements regarding the signing of accounts and reports. The copy of the accounts approved by the board of directors and the copy delivered to the Registrar of Companies will in future need only to be signed by one director instead of two.[4] For the first time the directors'

---

[1]   OJ 1987 C 131/ 1.
[2]   86/ 635/ EEC; OJ 1986 L 372/ 1.
[3]   89/ 117/ EEC; OJ 1989 L 44/ 40.
[4]   Ns 233(1)(4)(CA 1989, s 7). One reason for this is that Companies House often found accounts were submitted with only one signature when there should have been two: HL Committee col 953. For other common defects in filing accounts see *Accountancy*, August 1989, p 125.

report approved by the board and the copy delivered to the Registrar must also be signed, either by a director or the secretary of the company.[1] Likewise the auditors' report to the company and the copy delivered to the Registrar must state the names of the auditors and be signed by them.[2] Signing by the auditors refers, where the office is held by a body corporate or partnership, to signature in the name of the body corporate or partnership by someone authorised to sign on its behalf.[3] In many cases these represent a common practice becoming a statutory requirement. This will also be true of the new statutory requirements to include the name of the signatory to the accounts and directors' report and the names of the auditors on copies laid before the general meeting or otherwise circulated, published or issued.[4]

Circulation of accounts to shareholders: summary financial statements for listed companies

2.52 The basic provisions regarding circulation of the accounts, directors' report and auditors' report to shareholders and the requirements regarding publication of accounts are unchanged except that the terms 'full accounts' and 'abridged accounts' are replaced by the terms 'statutory accounts' and 'non-statutory accounts'.[5] There is, however, a potentially very significant new provision enabling the Secretary of State to make regulations[6] allowing listed companies to send their members a summary financial statement in place of the accounts and directors' and auditors' reports.[7] The main pressure for this facility to be made available seems to have come from companies, particularly recently privatised ones, which have a very large number of small shareholders and for whom it may represent a cost saving. However, it is also believed that the use and understanding of company reports and accounts by individual shareholders is typically not very great and summary financial statements may give an opportunity to present the information in a more readily understood and meaningful way.[8]

The companies that will be able to offer summary financial statements are those any of whose shares are admitted to the Official List of the International Stock Exchange. The restriction to listed companies is because the inequality of information that arises if some shareholders receive full accounts and others receive a summary matters far less where there is an active market in the shares. The information contained in a company's report and accounts is normally assimilated by the market and reflected in the share price very quickly indeed so

---

1. Ns 234A(1)(3) (CA 1989, s 8).
2. Ns 236(1)(3) (CA 1989, s 9). As to the requirement to use the term 'registered auditor', see below, p 43.
3. Ns 236(5).
4. Nss 233(3), 234A(2) and 236(2).
5. See nss 238–240 (CA 1989, s 10).
6. The DTI published a consultative document on the issues involved in August 1989.
7. Ns 251 (CA 1989, s 15).
8. Mumford, *Accountancy*, June 1989, p 111.

that shareholders are unlikely to be prejudiced if they choose to receive only the summary financial statement. The legislation allows for further conditions to be laid down in the regulations, but there are unlikely to be any. In particular, it is not expected that there will be any requirement for amending a company's articles or for requiring the general meeting to decide whether summary financial statements should be available. It will probably be for the directors to decide whether to issue summary financial statements and for each shareholder to choose instead to receive the full report and accounts.

2.53 The full report and accounts must be sent to any member who wishes to receive them. The Government has indicated that this must be completely free of charge to the member, so companies are likely to have to send out reply-paid cards which members can return to the company if they wish to receive the full accounts. One possibility would be to send the summary financial statement to every member in advance of publication of the full accounts together with the reply-paid card. It is more likely, however, that the card will be sent first, perhaps with the interim accounts, allowing members to choose which set of accounts they wish to receive. Both sets of accounts could then be published simultaneously.

The form and content of a summary financial statement will be laid down in the regulations. These will set the minimum contents and companies will be free to include more information, but there is an overriding requirement that all the information is derived from the company's annual accounts and reports.[1] There are also certain statements that must be included by statute.[2] It must state that it is only a summary of information in the annual accounts and directors' report. It must contain a statement by the auditors as to whether it is consistent with the accounts and report and complies with the legislative requirements. It must also state whether the auditors' report on the accounts was qualified or unqualified, and if qualified it must set out the report and any further information needed to understand the qualification. Finally, it must state whether the auditors' report contains a statement under ns 237(2) or (3), and if so (ie that proper accounting records, information and explanations were not available), set out the statement in full. It does not need to contain the other warnings which non-statutory accounts must contain under ns 240(3).[3] Companies will be free to issue summary financial statements within a more wide ranging document which could therefore include information not derived from the annual accounts and reports. But it would have to be clear what was the statutory summary financial statement and what was not. Separate regulations will be made for banks and insurance companies to reflect the CA 1985, Sch 9 rather than Sch 4 and because they will need to be amended when first the bank accounts directive and then the insurance companies accounts directive come into force.

---

[1]   Ns 251(3) (CA 1989, s 15).
[2]   Ns 251(4).
[3]   Ns 251(7).

Laying accounts before the general meeting: power for private companies to dispense with this altogether

2.54   There are no changes to the basic provisions under which directors are obliged to lay accounts and reports before the general meeting of shareholders.[1] The Government has, however, indicated its intention at some time in the future progressively to reduce the ten-month and seven-month periods allowed for filing accounts which also represent the periods in which accounts must be laid before the general meeting.[2] As part of the programme of de-regulation of business the legislation now also permits private companies to elect to dispense with laying their accounts and reports before the general meeting altogether.[3] The election is only open to private companies and must be made by an 'elective resolution'[4] which means that members must be given at least twenty-one days' notice of the proposed resolution and it must receive the unanimous consent of those entitled to attend and vote at the meeting.

2.55   Once the election is made it has effect as regards the accounts and reports in respect of the current financial year and subsequent years.[5] It cannot therefore be made in respect of any financial year which has already finished, even if the period in which the accounts should be laid before the general meeting has not yet elapsed. Even where an election is in force there is provision for any member or auditor of the company to require that the accounts be laid before a general meeting. The accounts and reports must be sent out to those entitled to receive them under ns 238 at least twenty-eight days before what would otherwise be the expiry of the period for laying the accounts before the general meeting and the members must also be informed of their right to require the accounts to be laid before a general meeting.[6] If during the twenty-eight days after the accounts were sent out any member or auditor requires, in writing, that the accounts and reports be presented to a general meeting, the directors must, within twenty-one days, call a meeting to take place within the next twenty-eight days.[7] If the directors fail to convene such a meeting, any member or auditor can do so at the expense of the company which can recoup itself from any fees or remuneration payable to the defaulting directors.[8]

Delivery of accounts to the registrar

2.56   Apart from the possibility that in future the time limits for delivery of

1   Nss 241 and 244 (CA 1989, s 11).
2   HC Committee, col 219.
3   Ns 252 (CA 1989, s 16).
4   Ns 252(1). As to elective resolutions see ns 379A (CA 1989, s 16) discussed in Chapter 6, below.
5   Ns 252(2).
6   Ns 253(1) (CA 1989, s 16).
7   Ns 253(2), (3), (6).
8   Ns 253(3)–(5).

accounts to the Registrar may be reduced[1] there is another shock in store for the company that fails to file its accounts in time. The penalties on the company for late filing of accounts, which thus far have lain dormant on the statute book, are increased in the new legislation[2] and are to be brought into force. The only other change is one which requires a parent company to append the accounts of subsidiary undertakings which have been excluded from the consolidation under ns 229(4) on the grounds of difference of activity and whose accounts will not otherwise have been registered in the UK. This may occur either because the subsidiary undertaking is incorporated outside Great Britain and has no established place of business here, or because it is an unincorporated undertaking.[3]

Remedies for Failure to Comply with Accounting Requirements

2.57 Following recommendations made by the Dearing Committee,[4] a completely new set of procedures for dealing with failure to comply with accounting requirements is introduced. The Committee recognised that the overriding objective should be to ensure that good accounting information is ultimately produced, rather than the punishment of transgressors. Accordingly, the criminal offence of laying before the general meeting or delivering to the registrar accounts which do not comply with the Companies Act is repealed and not re-enacted. It is, however, appropriate for the criminal law to be involved where there has been a deliberate attempt to mislead and a new offence is introduced where directors approve annual accounts which they know do not comply with the requirements of the Act or they are reckless as to whether the accounts comply or not.[5] The new civil procedures are based on three stages: first, an opportunity for directors voluntarily to prepare revised annual accounts or directors' reports; secondly, provision for the Secretary of State to require companies to explain possible defects in their annual accounts or prepare revised accounts; and thirdly, power for the courts to order companies to prepare revised accounts where the existing accounts do not comply with the Companies Act.

2.58 The reason a statutory power[6] is needed to enable directors voluntarily to prepare revised annual accounts or directors' report is that otherwise the registrar, having received one set of accounts or report from the company, would have no basis on which to register the revised versions. Where the annual

---

[1]   See footnote 174, above.
[2]   Ns 242A(2) (CA 1989, s 11).
[3]   Ns 243 (CA 1989, s 11).
[4]   *The Making of Accounting Standards*, Chapter 15.
[5]   Ns 233(5) (CA 1989, s 7).
[6]   Ns 245 (CA 1989, s 12).

accounts or directors' report have been laid before the general meeting or delivered to the Registrar it cannot simply be open to the directors to change their minds about something and prepare revised accounts. So, in such a case, the revisions must be confined to correction of those aspects in which the previous accounts and report did not comply with the Act, plus any necessary consequential amendments.[1] Regulations will need to be made[2] dealing with such matters as the audit of the revised accounts and whether the same auditors can be used, the manner in which changes in the revised accounts are indicated and explained, and the circumstances in which revised accounts need to be circulated to all shareholders. It is expected that the regulations will make it clear that revised accounts can be used as the basis for paying dividends.[3]

2.59 It may seem strange that once directors have realised the accounts or directors' report do not comply with the Act it is not compulsory for them to prepare revised versions. The Government's hope is that by leaving it as a voluntary matter more directors will be encouraged to act in an openly responsible manner. However, the Secretary of State is given power,[4] where there appears to him to be a question whether a company's annual accounts (but not, it seems, the directors' report) comply with the Act, to require the directors to give an explanation of the accounts or prepare revised accounts. If neither a satisfactory explanation nor revised accounts is forthcoming then the Secretary of State may apply for a court order to the directors to prepare revised accounts.[5] In making such an order the court may also give directions regarding auditing, the revision of any directors' report or summary financial statement, and publicity for the revised accounts.[6]

2.60 There is also provision for the Secretary of State to authorise other suitable persons to make court applications in respect of defective accounts.[7] The Dearing Committee proposals for a new institutional framework to secure compliance with accounting standards and legislation were discussed above.[8] The Committee recommended the establishment of a Review Body and suggested that it would be appropriate for the Stock Exchange and for the new Review Body to be given power to initiate civil proceedings in respect of defective accounts. Fears have been expressed, however, that if these bodies and the Secretary of State each have power they will merely pass the buck to one another and no action will be taken. It has been suggested that the responsibility should lie on the

---

1   Ns 245(2) (CA 1989, s 12).
2   Ns 245(3), (4).
3   HC Committee, col 196.
4   Ns 245A (CA 1989, s 12).
5   Ns 245B (CA 1989, s 12).
6   Ns 245B(3).
7   Ns 245C (CA 1989, s 12).
8   Paras 2.7–2.10.

Secretary of State with the Review Panel and the Stock Exchange having a purely advisory role.[1]

Destination Table of Accounting Provisions

The following table shows in relation to section numbers in the old CA 1985, Part VII where the *equivalent* section number is in the new CA 1985, Part VII. It must be remembered this is not pure consolidation and so although the contents of the new section may be very similar or even identical to the old, in many cases they may be totally different. This table is therefore intended only as a guide to where to find the *equivalent* material.

OLD	NEW	OLD	NEW	OLD	NEW
221(1)	221(1)	226(3)	–	231(1)	231(1), 232(1)
(2)	221(1)	227(1)	226(1)	(2)	231(2), 232(2)
(3)	221(2)	(2)	223(2), (3)	(3)	–
(4)	221(3)	(3)	226(1)	(4)	232(3), (4)
222(1)	222(1)	(4)	223(5)	232(1)	232(1), (2)
(2)	222(2)	228(1)	226(3)	(2)	232(1), (2)
(3)	222(3)	(2)	226(2)	(3)	232(1)
(4)	222(5)	(3)	226(4)	(4)	–
223(1)	221(5), 222(4)	(4)	226(4)	(5)	Sch 9, Part IV,
(2)	222(6)	(5)	226(5)		para 2
(3)	221(6), 222(4), (6)	(6)	226(5)	233(1)	232(1), (2)
224(1)	224(1)	(7)	230	(2)	232(1), (2)
(2)	224(2)	229(1)	227(1)	(3)	Sch 9, Part IV,
(3)	224(2), (3)	(2)	228		para 3
(4)	224(4), (5)	(3)	229	(4)	232(1)
(5)	224(6)	(4)	–	(5)	–
225(1)	225(1)	(5)	227(2)	234(1)	–
(2)	225(2)	(6)	–	(2)	–
(3)	225(2), (5)	(7)	–	(3)	–
(4)	225(3)	230(1)	227(4)	235(1)	234(1)
(5)	225(6)	(2)	227(3)	(2)	234(2)
(6)	225(4)	(3)	–	(3)	234(3), (4)
(7)	225(4)	(4)	227(5)	(4)	234(3), (4)
(8)	225(2), (4), (6)	(5)	227(6)	(5)	234(3), (4)
226(1)	–	(6)	227(6)	(6)	255C(5)
(2)	–	(7)	Sch 4A, para 2 (2)	(7)	234(5), (6)
		(8)	–	236(1)	235(1)

---

[1]   HC Committee, cols 115–136.

OLD	NEW	OLD	NEW	OLD	NEW
236(2)	235(2)	247(5)	–	256(5)	257(2)
237(1)	237(1)	248(1)	247(3)	(6)	257(3)
(2)	237(2)	(2)	247(3)	257(1)	–
(3)	389A(1)	(3)	247(5)	(2)	–
(4)	237(3)	(4)	247(6)	(3)	255(1), (2), 255A (1), (2)
(5)	237(4)	(5)	247(4)	(4)	255(3), 255A(5)
(6)	235(3)	249(1)	–	258(1)	–
238(1)	233(1), (2), (4)	(2)	247(1)	(2)	255(1)
(2)	233(6)	(3)	–	(3)	–
(3)	–	(4)	247(1)	(4)	255(4)
(4)	233(1)	(5)	247(2)	(5)	–
239	–	(6)	247(2)	259(1)	–
240(1)	238(1)	250(1)	248(1)	(2)	–
(2)	238(3)	(2)	246(5)	(3)	255A(1)
(3)	238(2)	(3)	249(4)	(4)	255A(6)
(4)	238(4)	(4)	249(4)	260(1)	255B(1)
(5)	238(5)	(5)	249(5)	(2)	Sch 9, Part I, para 18C
241(1)	241(1)	(6)	–		
(2)	–	251(1)	257(1)	(3)	–
(3)	242(1)	(2)	257(2)	261(1)	255C(1)
(4)	254(1), (2), (3)	(3)	257(3)	(2)	255C(3)
242(1)	244(6)	252(1)	250(1), 388A(1)	(3)	255C(2)
(2)	244(1)	(2)	250(1)	(4)	–
(3)	244(3)	(3)	250(1)	(5)	255C(4), (5)
(4)	244(2)	(4)	250(2)	(6)	255C(5)
(5)	244(4)	(5)	250(3)	(7)	–
(6)	244(5)	(6)	250(5)	262(1)	Sch 9, para 28A
243(1)	241(2), 242(2)	(7)	388A(2)–(5)	(2)	Sch 9, para 28A
(2)	241(3), 242(4)	253(1)	250(4)		
(3)	242A(1)	(2)	250(4)		
(4)	242A(2)	(3)	250(4), Sch 8, para 9		
(5)	241(4), 242(5), 242A(4)	254(1)	240(5)		
(6)	–	(2)	240(1)		
244(1)	242(3)	(3)	240(2)		
(2)	242(3)	(4)	240(1)		
(3)	–	(5)	240(1)		
245(1)		(6)	240(6)		
(2)	233(5), 245–245C	255(1)	240(5)		
		(2)	240(5)		
(3)		(3)	240(3), 254(4)		
246(1)	239(1)	(4)	240(3)		
(2)	239(3), (4)	(5)	240(6)		
247(1)	246(1)	256(1)	257(1)		
(2)	246(3)	(2)	–		
(3)	246(4), 248(2)	(3)	–		
(4)	250(4)	(4)	257(4)		

What happens to existing Accounting Schedules to CA 1985

Schedule 4 is amended by Sch 1 to CA 1989 (s 4(2)).

Schedule 4, Part IV is now largely dealt with by Schs 4A and 5.

Schedule 4, Part VI is now dealt with by Sch 5, para 10.

(Sch 4A is inserted by Sch 2 to CA 1989 (s 5(2)).)

Schedule 5, Parts I–IV: an amended version is substituted by Sch 3 to CA 1989 (s 6(2)).

Schedule 5, Part V becomes Sch 6, Part I and an amended version is substituted by Sch 4, para 3 to CA 1989 (s 6(4)).

Schedule 5, Part VI is repealed and not re-enacted.

Schedule 6, Parts I and II become Sch 6, Parts II and III and are amended by Sch 4, paras 4–6 to CA 1989 (s 6(4)).

Schedule 7 is amended by Sch 5 to CA 1989 (s 8(2)).

Schedule 8, Part I: an amended version is substituted by Sch 6 to CA 1989 (s 13(2)).

Schedule 8, Parts II and III are repealed and not re-enacted.

Schedule 9 is amended by Sch 7 to CA 1989 (s 18(3)).

Schedule 10: an amended version is substituted by Sch 8 to CA 1989 (s 18(5)).

(Schedule 10A is inserted by Sch 9 to CA 1989 (s 21(2)).)

CHAPTER 3

AUDITORS

Qualification of Auditors

Introduction

3.1 Part II of the CA 1989 (ie ss 24–54) together with Schs 11–14 introduce an entirely new regime for the regulation of auditors. The main reason for the new provisions is the need to implement the EEC Eighth Directive[1] on the harmonisation of approval of persons responsible for carrying out statutory audits. The broad effect of the directive, which must be in force by 1 January 1990,[2] is to set minimum criteria for approval of auditors covering educational qualifications and practical training and to require member states to prescribe and enforce standards of professional integrity and independence. Complying with these requirements is unlikely to make significant changes to the ways in which individuals qualify as accountants. However, the directive permits member states to allow companies or multi-disciplinary partnerships to act as auditors provided certain conditions are fulfilled. The UK has taken up these options and this is likely to have profound long-term significance for the structure of the accountancy and auditing profession in the UK.

3.2 The Eighth Directive is not the only EEC measure likely to have an impact on auditors. In December 1988 the Council adopted a directive[3] on a general system for the mutual recognition of professional qualifications. Although this directive does not have to be implemented by member states until 4 January 1991,[4] some account has been taken of its provisions in drafting Part II of the CA 1989. The broad effect of this directive in terms of the UK is that the UK must allow auditors qualified in other member states ('EEC auditors')

---

[1] 84/ 253/ EEC; OJ 1984 L 126/ 20.
[2] Eighth Directive, art 30(2). In fact, provisions enabling bodies to apply for recognition are likely to be in force in early 1990, the remaining provisions in early 1991, with recognition being granted in March 1991. The significance of 1 January 1990 is explained in para 3.5 below.
[3] 89/ 48/ EEC; OJ 1989 L19/ 16. The term used in the directive to signify professional qualifications is 'higher education diplomas'.
[4] Recognition of Higher Education Diplomas Directive, art 12. There are useful articles on the directive in *Accountancy*, by Currie in May 1989, p 92, and Plender in September 1989, p 125. The directive also has implications, of course, for a UK-qualified auditor wishing to practise in another member state.

to practise here on the same terms as its own nationals.[1] Such auditors can be required to complete an adaptation period or take an aptitude test where the education and training they have received differs substantially from that covered by UK requirements.[2] As auditing and accounting require precise knowledge of national law it will be open to the UK authorities rather than the EEC auditor to specify whether an adaptation period or an aptitude test is appropriate.[3] EEC auditors will be entitled to use the new professional designation 'registered auditor',[4] but will not be entitled to use additional designations like 'chartered accountant' unless they actually belong to an appropriate institute.[5] The institutes must however apply the same criteria for membership to EEC auditors as they apply to UK nationals.[6]

Eligibility for appointment as company auditor

3.3   In order to be eligible for appointment as a company auditor, persons must fulfil two basic conditions. First, they must be members of a recognised supervisory body,[7] although it should be noted here that 'members' includes persons supervised by the body, although they are not full members of it.[8] Secondly, they must be eligible under the rules of their supervisory body to be appointed as company auditor.[9] There will, in other words, be no direct authorisation at all by the DTI in future. To be eligible all persons must be members of a recognised supervisory body. As before individuals or firms may be appointed company auditors,[10] but 'firms' now includes bodies corporate as well as partnerships.[11] The former prohibition on a company acting as auditor is repealed.

3.4   Being eligible under the rules of a recognised supervisory body itself involves two elements. First, persons must be independent of the company concerned. Certain relationships with the company concerned which are fundamentally likely to be incompatible with independence are prohibited outright,[12] as they were under the previous legislation. The Secretary of State is, however, given a new power to make regulations specifying other connections between auditors and clients that would make a person ineligible.[13]

---

[1]   Recognition of Higher Education Diplomas Directive, art 3(1).
[2]   Ibid, art 4(1).
[3]   Ibid, art 4(1), final paragraph.
[4]   Ibid, art 7(1). See footnote 9 of p 43 below.
[5]   Ibid, art 7(2), 1.
[6]   Ibid, art 7(2), para 2.
[7]   S 25(1)(*a*). As to recognised supervisory bodies, see paras 3.9–3.12, below.
[8]   S 30(2).
[9]   S 25 (*a*), (*b*).
[10]   S 25(2).
[11]   S 53(1). See below, para 3.7.
[12]   S 27(1).
[13]   S 27.

The Government envisages that one thing the regulations will prohibit is a corporate auditor being appointed to audit a company which is one of its shareholders.[1] Independence will also be secured by the requirement that recognised supervisory bodies have rules designed to prevent persons from being appointed auditors in circumstances in which they have any interest likely to conflict with the proper conduct of the audit.[2] This will allow a more flexible approach to securing independence in cases where the circumstances are not covered by statutory provisions. An example given by the minister of a possible circumstance in which independence might be jeopardised, but which is better covered by flexible professional guidance, is if the income a practice received from a particular client was disproportionately large in relation to its total income.[3]

3.5 The second condition for eligibility under the rules of a recognised supervisory body is holding appropriate qualifications.[4] There are five ways of doing this:[5]

(i) The first two cover persons holding existing qualifications for
and appointment as auditor under the old CA 1985, s 389 as at 1 January 1990
(ii) and who are still so qualified when the new regime comes into operation, which is likely to be in early 1991.[6] If such persons are qualified by virtue of their membership of a body recognised for the purposes of the old CA 1985, s 389 (1)(*a*), that itself suffices as holding appropriate qualifications.[7] If they are not members of any such recognised body they will none the less automatically be regarded as holding appropriate qualifications for twelve months after the new regime commences. Thereafter they may continue to be so regarded if they notify the Secretary of State in writing that they wish to retain the benefit of this qualification.[8]

(iii) The third route to holding appropriate qualifications covers persons who start training for a professional accountancy qualification before 1 January 1990 but only complete it after that date. Provided such persons obtain their qualifications before 1 January 1996 they are treated as holding an appropriate qualification.[9]

---

[1]   HC Committee, col 337.
[2]   Sch 11, para 7.
[3]   A suggestion that companies should be obliged to appoint different auditors every five years is not included in the Act. Nor is there any restriction on non-audit work being undertaken by auditors although provision is made for regulations requiring disclosure of fees for non-audit work: ns 390B (CA 1989, s 121).
[4]   Sch 11, paras 4 and 5.
[5]   These are the only ways: s 31(6).
[6]   The reason for the reference to 1 January 1990 is that art 12 of the Eighth Directive permits member states to confirm the rights of those with existing rights to practise only as at the date when the directive comes into force which is 1 January 1990: HC Committee, col 357.
[7]   S 31(1)(*a*).
[8]   S 31(2), (3).
[9]   S 31(4), (5).

(iv) For persons who only start their training on or after 1 January 1990 holding an appropriate qualification means[1] holding a recognised professional qualification[2] obtained in the UK.[3]

(v) The final way covers persons holding approved overseas qualifications[4] and who satisfy any additional educational requirements that might be imposed for ensuring that they have an adequate knowledge of the law and practice in the UK relevant to the audit of accounts.[5]

Consequences of ineligible person holding office

3.6 The consequences for the person concerned are broadly the same as under the old law. In other words there is a duty not to act as company auditor if ineligible and a duty to resign if a person becomes ineligible while in office and both these duties are enforced by the threat of criminal sanctions for breach.[6] However, a significant new power is introduced whereby, if an ineligible person held office during any part of the period in which the audit was conducted, the Secretary of State may direct the company, within twenty-one days, to retain an eligible auditor either to do the audit again or to review the first audit and report whether a second is needed.[7] An ineligible auditor who acts while knowing of the ineligibility is liable to reimburse the company's costs in complying with the Secretary of State's direction.[8]

Appointment of companies or partnerships as company auditor

3.7 One of the most significant changes the new regime on auditors will introduce is to allow corporate bodies to act as auditor.[9] Where a firm (which in the Act covers a partnership[10] or a corporate body)[11] is appointed

---

[1] S 31(1)(*b*).
[2] As to the meaning of 'recognised professional qualification', see s 32. This is discussed in paras 3.13 and 3.14, below.
[3] 'Obtained in the UK' is defined in s 53(2) by reference to a body established in the UK. This will therefore cover recognition of the Institute of Chartered Accountants of Ireland which is established under Royal Charter granted in the UK.
[4] S 31(1)(*c*). As to what qualifications may be approved, see s 33(1)–(3).
[5] S 33(4). A person holding an approved overseas qualification would still need to become a member of a recognised supervisory body in the UK. As to the possible impact of the Directive on Recognition of Higher Education Diplomas (89/ 48/ EEC; OJ 1989 L 19/ 16) as regards persons from other EC countries, see the articles in *Accountancy* by Currie, May 1989, p 92 and Plender, September 1989, p 125. See also para 3.2 above.
[6] S 28.
[7] S 29(1).
[8] S 29(6).
[9] Ss 25(2), 53(1).
[10] Where a partnership which is not a legal person is appointed as company auditor, the appointment is (unless a contrary intention appears) of the partnership as such and not of the partners: s 26(1), (2). There are rules dealing with succession where such a partnership ceases: s 26(3)–(5).
[11] S 53(1).

company auditor it is the firm which must be a member of a recognised supervisory body and be eligible for appointment as company auditor under the rules of the relevant body. In terms of holding appropriate qualifications this means that the individuals within the firm responsible for audit work must hold appropriate qualifications *and* the firm must be controlled by qualified persons.[1] The controllers themselves may, of course, be individuals or firms and 'qualified' in this context means for an individual, holding appropriate qualifications, and for a firm, being eligible for appointment as company auditor.[2] A firm is then 'controlled by qualified persons', if, but only if, a majority of its members and members of its management body are qualified persons.[3] These are minimum requirements and there is nothing to stop a recognised supervisory body imposing more stringent conditions if it wishes.[4] Firms must also have arrangements to prevent individuals who do not hold appropriate qualifications and persons who are not members of the firm being able to exert influence over the conduct of the audit in a way which might affect the independence or integrity of the audit.[5] Finally, regulations will be made requiring recognised supervisory bodies to keep and make available to the public certain information about firms eligible under their rules for appointment as company auditor.[6]

3.8 If partnerships are to take full advantage of these rules enabling them to include as partners persons who are not eligible to act as company auditor a change will need to be made in the exemption from the twenty partner limit in the CA 1985, ss 716 and 717. The existing exemption only applies to firms all of whose partners are individually qualified to undertake audits.[7] It is expected that the Secretary of State will make regulations[8] amending the exemption to apply to any firm eligible to undertake audits.

Recognised supervisory bodies

3.9 Under the new regime any person seeking eligibility to be appointed as company auditor must belong to a recognised supervisory body.[9] These are

[1]   Sch 11, para 4(1)(*b*).
[2]   Sch 11, para 5(2).
[3]   Sch 11, para 5(3)–(6). If a firm consists of only two members, therefore, both of them must be qualified. However, in the case of the management body, if that consists of only two persons, it is sufficient if one of them is qualified: para 5(3)(*b*).
[4]   These minimum provisions have important implications for the possible development of multidisciplinary practices, requiring as they do that an auditing firm consists of at least a majority of members holding appropriate qualifications or eligible for appointment as company auditor. The present proposals of the ICAEW are to restrict outside shareholders in incorporated accountancy firms to a maximum holding of 25 per cent of voting shares.
[5]   Sch 11, para 7(2).
[6]   S 36.
[7]   See CA 1985, ss 716(2)(*b*) and 717(1)(*b*).
[8]   Under s 50.
[9]   S 25(1)(*a*).

defined as bodies established in the UK, whether corporate or unincorporated, which maintain and enforce rules as to the eligibility of persons to be company auditors and the conduct of company audit work.[1] The rules must be binding on persons seeking appointment or acting as company auditors either because they are members or because they are otherwise subject to its control.[2] Unlike the previous law which specified the recognised bodies to which auditors could belong, the CA 1989 does not specify which supervisory bodies are recognised. Instead it provides a procedure whereby supervisory bodies may apply to the Secretary of State for recognition.[3]

3.10   The crucial condition to be fulfilled in obtaining recognition is that the rules and guidance issued by the supervisory body must meet the requirements laid down in Sch 11, Part II.[4] These include requirements designed to ensure that persons eligible under their rules to conduct company audits hold appropriate qualifications,[5] are fit and proper persons to undertake such work,[6] and are free from any possible conflict of interest with the proper conduct of audit work.[7] The body must also have rules and practices as to the technical standards to be applied in company audit work,[8] procedures designed to ensure that its members maintain an appropriate level of competence[9] and arrangements and resources for monitoring and enforcing compliance with its rules.[10] It must have arrangements for the investigation of complaints both against itself and against its members[11] and an appeals procedure with regard to the principal aspects of the relationship between itself and its members.[12]

3.11   In carrying out their functions recognised supervisory bodies, their officers, employees and members of their governing bodies are granted the now familiar[13] immunity from liability in damages[14] unless the relevant act or omission

[1]   S 30(1).
[2]   In the Act all such persons are referred to as members of the supervisory body: s 30(2).
[3]   Sch 11 Part II.
[4]   The rules and guidance must also be considered by the Director General of Fair Trading who must report to the Secretary of State as to whether they are intended or likely to have, to any significant extent, the effect of distorting or preventing competition. If this is the case, the Secretary of State must not make a recognition order unless it appears to him that the effect is reasonably justified having regard to the purposes of CA 1989, Part II: s 47(1) and Sch 14, para 1.
[5]   Sch 11, paras 4, 5.
[6]   Ibid, para 6.
[7]   Ibid, para 7.
[8]   Ibid, para 8.
[9]   Ibid, para 9.
[10]   Ibid, para 10.
[11]   Ibid, para 12.
[12]   Ibid, para 11.
[13]   It is also granted to the SIB, the SROS and the Stock Exchange under the Financial Services Act 1986, s 187.
[14]   The actions of supervisory bodies may still be subject to judicial review: Beatson (1987) 8 Co Law 34.

is shown to be in bad faith.[1] This immunity will cover actions by members of the public affected, for example, by the negligent authorisation of a person to act as company auditor.[2] It will also cover actions by members, ex-members or would-be members of the supervisory body adversely affected by some negligent administration of the rules.[3] No such immunity has been granted to auditors themselves in the conduct of their audit work although there are certain straws in the wind that may lead to limitations on liability being introduced in future.[4] In the meantime, in contrast to the supervisory bodies' immunity, their rule books must contain provision designed to ensure that auditors are able to meet claims against them arising out of company audit work, whether by professional indemnity insurance or otherwise.[5] In framing this and all their rules supervisory bodies must have arrangements for taking account of the costs of compliance with the rules.[6]

3.12 Finally, regulations will be made requiring each supervisory body to maintain a public register of firms or individuals eligible for appointment as company auditor showing, in the case of firms, the individuals holding appropriate qualifications who are responsible for the company audit work on behalf of such firms.[7] Regulations will also require supervisory bodies to maintain a public register giving information about directors, shareholders or partners in firms eligible to be appointed as company auditors.[8] The

---

[1] S 48(1)(2).
[2] There may be immunity at common law anyhow: *Yuen Kun Yeu v AG of Hong Kong* [1988] AC 175, PC.
[3] See further on this Feldman 'Liability of regulatory and disciplinary bodies' (1987) 3 Professional Negligence 23.
[4] As regards liability to the client the Likierman Report (see *Professional Liability: report of the study teams*) contained a proposal that the CA 1985, s 310 should be amended to allow companies and their auditors to agree a limit on the auditors' potential liability. This would be subject to the reasonableness test in the Unfair Contract Terms Act 1977. Any such limitation would also be included in the resolution appointing the auditors and disclosed in the accounts. The DTI published a discussion paper on this topic in June 1989. However, the only relevant provision included in the CA 1989 is one confirming that it is not contrary to s 310 for companies to effect insurance in respect of their auditors' liability. It would be a remarkably altruistic company that would effect such insurance, however! As regards liability to other parties the Court of Appeal in *Caparo Industries plc v Dickman* [1989] 1 All ER 798 held that while a duty of care may be owed to existing shareholders in certain circumstances, no duty is owed to non-shareholders. See also *Al Saudi Banque v Clark Pixley* [1989] 3 All ER 361. Both decisions are subject to appeal to the House of Lords.
[5] Sch 11, para 13.
[6] Ibid, para 15.
[7] S 35. The rule books of supervisory bodies must require persons eligible for appointment as company auditor to comply with obligations in regulations under ss 35 or 36: Sch 11, para 14. These are likely to include a requirement to use the term 'registered auditor' when signing audit reports under CA 1985, ns 236. Chartered and certified accountants may still additionally use that description. It is an offence to use the term 'registered auditor' when not entitled to be so described: s 41(2).
[8] S 36.

Government's intention had been for the professional bodies jointly to maintain a single register. It now seems that there will be separate registers because the professional bodies thought they would not be able to agree on setting up a single register.[1] The bodies will, however, be obliged to exchange information in a manner that will enable them to comply with the Eighth Directive.

Recognition of professional qualifications

3.13   For persons who start training towards becoming eligible for appointment as a company auditor on or after 1 January 1990 holding an 'appropriate qualification'[2] will mean holding a recognised professional qualification.[3] Bodies offering professional qualifications in accountancy can seek recognition for their qualifications from the Secretary of State provided the body   itself satisfies certain pre-conditions so that it counts as a qualifying body.[4] One condition is that the body, which may be incorporated or unincorporated, must be established in the UK.[5] It must also have power to enforce rules, whether or not laid down by the body itself, relating to, amongst other things: (i) admission to or expulsion from a course of study leading to a professional accountancy qualification; (ii) the award or deprivation of such qualification; and (iii) the approval of persons for the purpose of giving practical training or the withdrawal of such approval.[6]

3.14   Only a qualifying body can apply for recognition of a professional accountancy qualification.[7] If recognition is granted the body is then referred to in the legislation as a recognised qualifying body.[8] The procedure for obtaining recognition of a qualification is set out in Sch 12, Part I.[9] The requirements which a qualification must fulfil in order to be recognised are set out in Sch 12, Part II. These represent the minimum requirements for compliance with the Eighth Directive so as to allow recognised qualifying bodies the maximum flexibility to develop new courses and make other adjustments. They include such matters as entry requirements,[10] provision for examinations to test theoretical knowledge

---

1   HC Committee, cols 351–352.
2   As required by Sch 11, para 4(1). See para 3.5 above.
3   S 31(1)(*b*).
4   Sch 12, para 1(1).
5   S 32(1).
6   S 32(2).
7   Sch 12, para 1(1).
8   Ibid, para 2(1). It is known that the ICAEW and CACA intend to apply to be recognised qualifying bodies.
9   The rules and guidance must also be considered by the Director General of Fair Trading who must report to the Secretary of State as to whether they are intended or likely to have, to any significant extent, the effect of distorting or preventing competition. If this is the case the Secretary of State must not make a recognition order unless it appears to him that the effect is reasonably justified having regard to the purposes of CA 1989, Part II: s 47(1) and Sch 14, para 1.
10   Ibid, para 4.

and the ability to apply such knowledge in practice[1] and provision for at least three years' practical training.[2] The Act requires that a substantial part of the practical training must be in company audit work or other audit work designated in regulations as similar to company audit work.[3]

Powers of the Secretary of State

3.15 The Secretary of State is authorised to require recognised supervisory or qualifying bodies to give him certain specified information on a regular basis and also to give him any other information as he may reasonably require.[4] He also has power to request a court to issue a compliance order as an alternative to revoking recognition of a supervisory or qualifying body or a professional qualification.[5] Finally, he can direct such bodies to behave in a way which would not be incompatible with EEC obligations or other international obligations of the UK.[6]

The statute also includes provision for the delegation by the Secretary of State of most of his functions under the CA 1989, Part II.[7] At present the Government has no intention of exercising the delegation power,[8] but it is there in case there are moves among the professional bodies to create something along the lines of a General Auditing Council.

Other Provisions Relating to Auditors

Introduction

3.16 There are a considerable number of changes to the provisions relating to the appointment, rights, remuneration, removal and resignation of auditors and in the light of these the whole of Part XI, Chap V of the CA 1985 (ie ss 384–394) is repealed. In its place CA 1989, ss 118–123 insert eighteen new sections as a new CA 1985, Part XI, Chap V. As before, since each section of the CA 1989 inserts several sections into the CA 1985, we shall again use the term 'new section' or the abbreviation 'ns' to avoid any possible confusion with a repealed provision[9]. The

---

[1]   Ibid, para 7.
[2]   Ibid, para 8.
[3]   Ibid, para 8(1)(*b*). This is designed to cover persons most of whose training is in doing non-company audit, such as local authorities. Some part of everyone's training must, however, be in company audit work: para 8(1)(*a*).
[4]   Ss 37, 38.
[5]   S 39.
[6]   S 40.
[7]   S 46. The status, constitution and proceedings of any body established by a delegation order must be in accordance with Sch 13. It will have the benefit of limited immunity from liability in damages: s 48(3).
[8]   HC Committee, cols 367–371.
[9]   A destination table showing where provisions from the existing CA 1985, Part XI, Chap V are now located is included at the end of this Chapter. The provisions are expected to come into force in March 1990.

changes to the rights of auditors are in relation to the obligation on parent companies to help in getting information from overseas subsidiary undertakings[1] and in relation to proposed written resolutions.[2] The changes in relation to remuneration relate to the possibility of regulations being made requiring disclosure in the auditors' report or companies' accounts of fees received by auditors and their associates for non-audit work.[3]

Appointment of auditors

3.17   The introduction of provisions allowing private companies to dispense with laying accounts before the general meeting and to dispense with the annual appointment of auditors has necessitated a complete recasting of the material previously contained in the CA 1985, s 384. There are now four possibilities to consider in relation to the appointment of auditors:

(i)   The most common method of appointment, and the one used under the old law, is likely to be annual appointment at the general meeting at which the accounts are considered.[4]   This is the only method open to a public company.

(ii)   A private company which has elected under ns 252 to dispense with laying accounts before a general meeting must make an annual appointment at a general meeting held within twenty-eight days of sending out the accounts or, if a general meeting to consider the accounts is validly demanded under ns 253(2), at that meeting.[5]

(iii) A private company may instead of adopting either (i) or (ii) elect under ns 386(1) to dispense with annual appointment of auditors altogether, in which case the auditors are automatically deemed to be re-appointed.[6] This possibility is open to a private company whether or not it has elected to dispense with laying accounts before a general meeting. Obviously, however, it is a particular advantage to a company which has made such an election since it obviates the need to call a meeting at all in connection with the accounts and auditors. The election to dispense with annual reappointment of auditors must be made by an 'elective resolution'[7] and will therefore require the unanimous consent of all the members entitled to attend and vote at meetings.[8] Any such election lasts until a resolution is

---

1   Ns 389A(4) (CA 1989, s 120).
2   Ns 390(2).
3   Ns 390B (CA 1989, s 121).
4   Ns 385(2) (CA 1989, s 119).
5   Ns 385A(2).
6   Ns 386(2).
7   Ns 386(1).
8   Ns 379A(2) (CA 1989, s 116).

ns 393[1] terminating the auditors' appointment.[2] Any member may propose such a resolution although only one proposal may be made per member per year.[3] Notice of such a proposal must be deposited with the directors who must convene a general meeting to take place within twenty-eight days of the notice being deposited.[4] If the decision is to terminate the appointment the auditors are not deemed to be re-appointed when next they would be.[5]

(iv) Finally, a private company which has declared itself dormant[6] is, as under the old law, exempt altogether from the requirement to appoint auditors.[7]

Removal and resignation of auditors

3.18 The main change in this area extends the requirement for a statement by persons ceasing to hold office as auditor from cases where auditors resign to those where, for whatever reason, they cease to be the company's auditors.[8] The statement sets out whether there are any circumstances connected with the auditors ceasing to hold office which they consider should be brought to the attention of the members or creditors of the company. If there are none the statement must say so. In the past, although an auditor's resignation was not effective unless accompanied by such a statement, auditors would avoid the requirement in awkward cases by the simple device of not seeking re-election rather than resigning.

Destination Table of Auditing Provisions

The following table shows in relation to section numbers in the old CA 1985, Part XI, Chap V where the *equivalent* section number is in the new CA 1985, Part XI, Chap V. It must be remembered that this is not pure consolidation and so, although the contents of the new section may be very similar or even identical to the old, in many cases they may be totally different. This table is therefore intended only as a guide to where to find the *equivalent* material.

---

1 CA 1989, s 122.
2 Or until a resolution is passed declaring the company dormant: ns 386(2)(*a*).
3 Ns 393(1) (CA 1989, s 122).
4 Ns 393(2).
5 Ns 393(3).
6 Under Ns 250 (CA 1989, s 14).
7 Ns 388A(1) (CA 1989, s 119).
8 Ns 394(1) (CA 1989, s 123).

OLD	NEW	OLD	NEW	OLD	NEW
384(1)	385(2)	388(2)	388(4), 391A(2)	391(1)	392A(1), (2)
(2)	385(3)	(3)	391A(3), (4)	(2)	391A(3)
(3)	385(4)	(4)	391A(5)	(3)	391A(4)
(4)	388(1), (2)	(5)	391A(6)	(4)	391A(5)
(5)	387	389(1)		(5)	391A(6)
385(1)	390A(1)	– (10)	CA 1989, Part II	(6)	391A(7)
(2)	390A(2)	390(1)	392(1), (2)	(7)	391A(8)
(3)	390A(4)	(2)	394(1)	392(1)	389A(3)
386(1)	391(1)	(3)	392(3),	(2)	389A(3)
(2)	391(2)		394(3)(*a*)	393	389A(2)
(3)	391(3)	(4)	394(3)(*b*)	394(1)	
387(1)	390(1)	(5)	394(6)	– (3)	Trade Union and
(2)	391(4)	(6)	394(6)(*a*) (7)		Labour Relations
388(1)	388(3), 391A(1)	(7)	392(3), 394A(4)		Act 1974 s 11 (9)

CHAPTER 4

ULTRA VIRES AND THE AUTHORITY OF CORPORATE AGENTS

Introduction

4.1 Sections 108–112 of the CA 1989 contain important provisions dealing with the drafting of companies' objects clauses, their amendment and the consequences if companies go outside their stated objects.[1] Section 108 replaces the existing CA 1985, s 35 with three new sections and, as before, the practice of referring to these as ns 35, ns 35A and ns 35B will be followed. As with the old s 35 which they replace they deal also with the consequences of the board of directors going beyond limitations on its authority. Section 109 inserts ns 322A into the CA 1985 dealing with the particular problem where the other party to a transaction with the company is one of its directors or an associate of a director. Section 110 introduces a new form of objects clause for a 'general commercial company' (by inserting ns 3A into the CA 1985) and allows companies the general right to change their objects by special resolution (by substituting ns 4 for the existing s 4 of the CA 1985). Finally, ss 111 and 112 make special provision for charitable companies. Before examining the new sections in detail it is proposed to highlight the issues raised in reform of the ultra vires doctrine, first by briefly examining the way in which the doctrine operates today and then discussing the methods by which reform may be effected.

Present Operation of the Ultra Vires Doctrine

4.2 In understanding the issues involved in reform of the ultra vires doctrine it is important to appreciate the reality of its present operation in order to see what problems needed to be solved and what, if any, useful purposes are served by the doctrine. In doing this it is helpful to divide up the consideration of the doctrine into its internal aspect (ie operation as between the company and its members) and its external aspect (ie operation as between the company and outsiders dealing with the company).

---

[1]   The new provisions reflect in part suggestions contained in a report by Dr D D Prentice entitled 'Reform of the Ultra Vires Rule' published by the DTI in 1986 (the Prentice Report). These provisions are expected to come into force in March 1990.

Internal dimension

4.3 The traditional justification for the ultra vires doctrine is that shareholders know the type of activity they have invested in and can ensure, by obtaining an injunction, that the company does not go beyond that activity. The legal basis for such an injunction is that it is part of the membership contract between the company and its members under the CA 1985, s 14 that the company will observe the terms of the objects clause in the memorandum. It is because creditors are not party to this contract that they are not entitled to injunctions to restrain the company from carrying on an ultra vires activity, even though they, just as much as shareholders, may have given credit to a company because it was only able to carry out certain activities. If creditors do wish to restrict the company to activities stated in the objects clause they must do so by inserting terms to that effect in their separate contracts with the company.

4.4 Traditionally therefore the doctrine protects the shareholders as a body vis à vis the directors by giving shareholders power to control the type of activities the directors cause the company to engage in. In practice this protection has been rendered largely illusory by the adoption of long all-embracing objects clauses together with clauses stating that the objects are to be construed as independent of each other,[1] or by giving the company power to carry on any business which, in the directors' opinion, could be combined with that of the company.[2] Nevertheless, the theoretical position, that it is for the shareholders and not the directors to decide what nature of business the company carries on, is maintained in the requirement that the consent of the shareholders is still needed for a change to the objects of the company.[3] Without the benefit of empirical research it is not possible to say whether the ultra vires doctrine ever does serve to protect the interests of the shareholders as a group vis à vis the directors but the absence of reported cases on this issue suggests that it is not a burning issue. As Dr Prentice pointed out, it is far more likely that shareholders are concerned with the financial and economic significance of a transaction than they are with its constitutional correctness.[4]

4.5 On the other hand, the ultra vires doctrine does occasionally form the basis on which a minority shareholder seeks protection against the combined wishes of the majority shareholders and the directors. In particular the doctrine has been invoked where the majority shareholders and the directors wished to give away the company's property to a cause for which the minority shareholder did not have the same philanthropic feelings.[5] Whether a minority shareholder can

[1]   *Cotman v Brougham* [1918] AC 514.
[2]   *Bell Houses Ltd v City Wall Properties Ltd* [1966] 2 QB 656.
[3]   CA 1985, s 4.
[4]   Prentice Report, p 40.
[5]   For example *Evans v Brunner Mond & Co* [1921] 1 Ch 359 and *Parke v Daily News Ltd* [1962] Ch 927.

successfully resist such a donation on the grounds of ultra vires depends entirely on the drafting of the objects clause. In any case, today minority shareholders would be far more likely to object to a donation they disapproved of on the grounds of unfair prejudice under the CA 1985, s 459, particularly since it is no longer a bar to complaint under s 459 that the conduct was equally prejudicial to all members of the company.[1]

External dimension

4.6 Turning to the operation of the ultra vires doctrine as between the company and outsiders, the stark reality here is that the doctrine is relied on almost exclusively only when the company is in liquidation. Quite apart from the limited protection for outsiders introduced in 1973 in what became the CA 1985, s 35, companies which are still in business and trading successfully do not about turn and refuse to perform contracts they have entered into on the grounds that the contract is ultra vires. If they did they would soon find themselves the outcasts of the commercial world and no longer in business. Furthermore, the agents who entered into the ultra vires contract for the company might find they were personally liable for breach of warranty of authority.[2] Finally, the other party, although unable to enforce the contract, might have a tracing claim against the company which would probably provide very effective protection against a solvent company still carrying on business.[3]

4.7 The external dimension can also have an impact on minority shareholder protection in relation to donations which the directors and the majority shareholders have agreed the company should make. Once a donation has been made by a company it is no longer possible for a shareholder who objects to the payment to seek an injunction. The remedy for the minority shareholder then becomes one of seeking to enforce the company's right of action to recover the money from the third party to whom it was given.[4] Again whether the payment is ultra vires or not is often a fortuitous matter of the drafting of the objects clause and again a petition under the CA 1985, s 459 should now be possible in these circumstances[5] and might provide a better basis on which to resolve the problem of balancing the interests of the minority against those of the majority.

4.8 It is when the company is in liquidation that the ultra vires doctrine has had most impact. Liquidators have used the doctrine in two ways. First, as a basis to seek to exclude creditors' proofs from the liquidation.[6] Where the liquidator has

---

[1] The difference of interpretation between *Re A Company (No 00370 of 1987)* [1988] BCLC 570 and *Re Sam Weller & Sons Ltd* (1989) 5 BCC 810 is now resolved in favour of the latter by CA 1989, Sch 19, para 11. See further, para 7.21 below.
[2] *Firbanks Executors v Humphreys* (1889) 18 QBD 54.
[3] *Sinclair v Brougham* [1914] AC 398.
[4] *Simmonds v Heffer* [1983] BCLC 298.
[5] See footnote 1, above.
[6] For example in *Cotman v Brougham* [1918] AC 514.

been successful the result has been to exclude the ultra vires creditor entirely, the effect presumably being in most cases that the intra vires creditors received a larger dividend than they otherwise would have done. But it seems highly probable that in cases like *Re Beauforte (Jon) Ltd*[1] and *Re Introductions Ltd*[2] there was not the slightest distinction on the merits between the intra vires and the ultra vires creditors.[3] And if the consequence of excluding the ultra vires creditors is that there is now enough to pay the intra vires creditors in full and leave a surplus, what happens to the surplus? It would be monstrously unfair if it went to the members, especially in cases like *Re Beauforte (Jon) Ltd* and *Re Introductions Ltd* where it was the members' failure to change the objects that led to an ultra vires problem arising at all. Fortunately the members do not benefit. What happens is that if there are funds remaining after the intra vires creditors have been paid, the ultra vires creditors are entitled to claim it by the fiction of having proprietary claims which enable them to trace into whatever remains undistributed.[4]

4.9   Secondly, liquidators use the ultra vires doctrine as a basis for seeking to recover assets which the company disposed of before the liquidation. Cases like *Re Horsley & Weight Ltd*[5] and *Rolled Steel Products Ltd v British Steel Corporation*[6] are examples of this technique. As those cases show, however, whether the liquidator is successful in pleading ultra vires depends on the drafting of the objects clause, which is something over which the creditors whose interest the liquidator is protecting have no say or influence whatsoever. It may be entirely fortuitous, therefore, whether the ultra vires doctrine can be used as a measure of creditor protection in these circumstances. It may be entirely inappropriate, also, because the real question is whether the transaction prejudiced the creditors or not. This depends essentially on whether or not the company was solvent at the time. That issue never arises in relation to the question whether or not the transaction was ultra vires. Furthermore, since 1986 liquidators have had a far more appropriate means by which to recover property disposed of by an insolvent company.[7]

---

[1]   [1953] 1 Ch 131.

[2]   [1970] Ch 199.

[3]   The old CA 1985, s 35 was designed to deal with these problems but its drafting was such that it merely added to the complexities, uncertainties and inconsistencies.

[4]   *Sinclair v Brougham* [1914] AC 398. The normal consequence of a proprietary claim is to give the claimant priority, as regards those particular assets, over unsecured creditors. This is an indefensible conclusion in relation to ultra vires contracts where the claimant was taking the same risk as the unsecured creditors. Moreover, it did not happen in *Sinclair v Brougham* because the intra vires creditors had been paid in full before the proprietary claim was even considered. Therefore, *Sinclair v Brougham* only recognises the ultra vires creditors' right to trace vis à vis the members. In effect they are in the position of deferred creditors.

[5]   [1982] Ch 442.

[6]   [1986] Ch 246.

[7]   Insolvency Act 1986, s 238.

Reform of the Doctrine

4.10   The earliest modification to the ultra vires doctrine came in 1890 when companies were first allowed to change their objects on certain limited grounds provided the court consented. This has gradually been relaxed and, as we shall see, the latest stage in this relaxation process is included in the CA 1989.[1] In relation to transactions which none the less fall outside the objects of a company there are two approaches to solving the problems that arise. The first is to extend the capacity of companies so that they are not constrained by their objects clause at all. This is the approach taken, for example, by the Canada Business Corporations Act which provides: 'A corporation has the capacity and, subject to this Act, the rights, powers and privileges of a natural person.'[2] It has been followed in Australia[3] and New Zealand[4] where, however, it was felt necessary to add that the company can also do a range of acts, like issue shares or debentures, which individuals cannot do. This approach was suggested by Dr Prentice in his proposal that '[a] company shall possess the capacity to do any act whatsoever', which neatly sidestepped the necessity for stating additional powers as in Australia and New Zealand.[5]

4.11   The alternative approach to reform is to continue to restrict the company's capacity but to protect outsiders dealing with the company against the consequences of the company's lack of capacity. This was the approach followed in art 9 of the EC First Directive[6] harmonising the protection of persons dealing with companies. This was implemented in the UK in the European Communities Act 1972, s 9(1) which subsequently was re-enacted as the CA 1985, s 35. In many ways it was dissatisfaction with the drafting of this provision which prompted the present review of the law. Both approaches to reform deal primarily with the external aspect of ultra vires and leave open the possibility of a company having objects and of members being able to restrain the company from carrying on activities beyond its objects.

Effect of the 1989 Legislation

Provision for general commercial company

4.12   Under the CA 1985, ns 3A inserted by the CA 1989, s 110(1), it will in future be possible to register a company where the memorandum simply states

---

[1]   Ns 4 (CA 1989, s 110). See below, para 4.14.
[2]   Canada Business Corporations Act 1975, s 7.
[3]   Australian Companies Act 1983, s 67(1).
[4]   New Zealand Companies Act 1955, s 15A(1).
[5]   Prentice Report, p 5.
[6]   68/ 151/ EEC; OJ 1968 L 65/ 8.

that the object of the company is 'to carry on business as a general commercial company'.[1] Where this is done then, under ns 3A:

'(a) the object of the company is to carry on any trade or business whatsoever, and
(b) the company has power to do all such things as are incidental or conducive to the carrying on of any trade or business by it.'

The clear intention behind this provision is to allow companies wishing to have the maximum flexibility in their commercial activity the freedom to do so. It is likely that the management of such a company will welcome this freedom and, where the management and shareholders are basically the same people, it may prove very useful.[2] Where the management and shareholders are different it may be less easy to persuade shareholders of the advantage of this arrangement even though it probably gives shareholders no less protection than they have under many existing objects clauses. Advisers might well consider, however, adopting a suggestion made by Dr Prentice[3] that shareholders' interests could be protected by requiring their consent to transactions involving either a quantitative economic relationship to the company's assets or a stipulated value.[4]

4.13   The hope obviously is that adopting the new provision will enable the draftsman to dispense with objects clauses that set out every type of activity the company may wish to enter into. Whether the draftsman will be prepared to dispense with the practice of setting out a long list of ancillary powers and then for good measure declaring them to be independent objects remains to be seen. It is arguable that neither para (a) nor (b) would enable a company to dispose of an entire business or its entire undertaking and that a specific power to do this should be included. Draftsmen may also wish to include express power to make gifts, grant pensions, or guarantee and grant security for debts of other persons, firms or companies. These issues have all arisen in recent reported cases and the context has usually involved the power being exercised for purposes unconnected, or only loosely connected, with the carrying on of any trade or business by the company. It would be advisable, therefore, that any such additional express powers should either be *deemed* to be incidental or conducive, or should be

---

[1]   This will meet the requirement in the Second Directive (77/ 91/ EEC; OJ 1977 L 26/ 10, art 2(*b*)) that a public company must state the objects of the company in the memorandum or articles of association.

[2]   cf 'It has always been the ambition apparently of the commercial community to stretch the objects clause of a memorandum of association, thus obtaining the advantage of limited liability with as little fetter on the activities of the company as possible. But still you cannot have an object to do every mortal thing you want, because that is to have no object at all' per Harman LJ in *Re Introductions Ltd* [1970] Ch 199, 209.

[3]   Prentice Report, p 40.

[4]   Such an approach is taken by the Stock Exchange with respect to Major Class 1 transactions: *Admission of Securities to Listing*, Section 6, Ch 1, para 3.4.

expressed to be capable of being carried out whether or not they were incidental or conducive to any business of the company.[1]

Alteration of the objects

4.14 Companies will in future be able to alter their objects by special resolution for any reason whatever.[2] The seven grounds for the alteration of objects that were previously stated in the old CA 1985, s 4 are no longer relevant. In the past, if the alteration was not within one of the seven grounds any member could object to the alteration and, provided the objection was made within twenty-one days, it was bound to succeed.[3] In future, any objection to the alteration of the objects[4] will need the support of holders of 15 per cent in nominal value of the issued share capital or any class thereof, or, if the company is not limited by shares, 15 per cent of the members.[5] It will, of course, still be open to shareholders to argue that an understanding existed between the members that the power to alter the objects would not be exercised without their consent, and breach of such understanding might warrant a just and equitable winding-up order.[6] There must also be the possibility that an alteration to the objects could constitute unfair prejudice under CA 1985, s 459, particularly since it is now clear that conduct can be prejudicial even though it affects the interests of a company's members generally.[7]

Validating acts outside the objects of the company

External dimension

4.15 Despite the possibility of registering as a general commercial company and the power of companies to change their objects for any reason, it is likely that some companies will still end up acting outside the scope of their objects clause. New sections 35, 35A and 35B, inserted into the CA 1985 by CA 1989, s 108 in place of the former s 35, are intended to deal with the consequences of this situation. The first issue that arises in relation to any such act or transaction is its validity vis à vis the other parties. New section 35(1) provides that:

---

[1] Ns 3A(*a*) does not appear to allow for the addition of further objects as such.
[2] Ns 4(1) (CA 1989, s 110(2)). A private company may also change its objects under the written resolution procedure in future: ns 381A(6) (CA 1989, s 113).
[3] This is because under the CA 1985, s2(7) 'A company may not alter the conditions contained in its memorandum except in the cases, in the mode and to the extent, for which express provision is made by this Act'. The only alterations to the objects authorised by the Act were on the seven grounds in s 4. If the alteration was not within those grounds, the company had no authority to make it.
[4] Ns 4(2).
[5] CA 1985, s 5(2). Previously objectors only needed the support of 15 per cent if the alteration was within the seven grounds listed in the old s 4. Any objection must still be made within twenty-one days: s 5(3).
[6] Under the Insolvency Act 1986, s 122(1)(*g*) as applied in *Re Westbourne Galleries Ltd* [1973] AC 360.
[7] See CA 1989, Sch 19, para 11.

'The validity of an act done by a company shall not be called into question on the ground of lack of capacity by reason of anything in the company's memorandum.'

There are a number of comparisons that can be made with the former CA 1985, s 35. First, the new section refers to 'acts' rather than 'transactions' and will therefore cover donations such as gifts to charity or political parties[1] as well as commercial transactions.[2] Secondly, there is no reference to 'decided on by the directors' which had appeared to restrict the effectiveness of the former s 35 in protecting outside parties. Thirdly, the operation of ns 35 is not restricted to being in favour of a person dealing with the company. The position is now therefore quite clear that neither companies nor outside parties may plead the company's lack of capacity.[3] Fourthly, there is no requirement that outsiders be in good faith. So, even if outsiders, or the company, know full well that the transaction they are entering into is outside the company's objects, the company's lack of capacity still cannot be relied on. Finally, it was pointed out during the passage of the Bill through Parliament that the capacity of a company may be restricted by provisions in the memorandum other than the objects clause. So, a reference to 'the objects of the company' became 'anything in the company's memorandum'. The full effect of this has yet to be worked out, but one consequence will be that in future where a company issues shares over and above the authorised capital stated in its memorandum it will not be possible to argue that the issue of shares is thereby invalid.[4]

4.16   Lack of capacity, however, is not the only ground on which an act, which is beyond the objects of a company, may be questioned. If a company is confined to pursuing activities stated in its objects then it must follow that the authority of the board of directors as agents of the company is likewise circumscribed. The possibility of the directors' lack of authority being pleaded in relation to acts and transactions between the company and outsiders is dealt with in ns 35A. Subsection (1) is as follows:

'In favour of a person dealing with a company in good faith, the power of the board of directors to bind the company, or authorise others to do so, shall be deemed to be free of any limitation under the company's constitution.'

---

[1]   See, for example, *Simmonds v Heffer* [1983] BCLC 298: donation to the Labour Party by League Against Cruel Sports Ltd.

[2]   Consider the effect on *Ashbury Railway Carriage & Iron Co v Riche* (1875) LR 7 HL 653: agreement to finance the construction of a railway by a company authorised to make railway rolling stock.

[3]   Under the old law there was some confusion as to whether outsiders could plead lack of capacity: *Anglo-Overseas Agencies Ltd v Green* [1961] 1 QB 1 and *Bell Houses Ltd v City Wall Properties Ltd* [1966] 2 QB 656.

[4]   Under the old law an issue of shares in such circumstances was void. See Pennington, *Company Law* 5th edn (1985) p 34 citing *Bank of Hindustan, China and Japan Ltd v Alison* (1871) LR 6 CP 222.

It will be noted that ns 35A(1) only applies in favour of the outsider. It also refers to a person 'dealing' with the company, but in ns 35A(2)(a) it is made clear that 'dealing' includes being party to any transaction or other act to which the company is party. In other words, it includes the receipt of donations or gifts as much as being a party to a commercial transaction.[1] New section 35A(1) only operates if the person dealing with the company is in good faith. As under the old law, the onus is on the company to prove that the outsider lacked good faith. Likewise, no constructive notice of the contents of the memorandum or articles can be relevant to the issue of good faith. This is made clearer than it was under the old law. New section 711A[2] abolishes constructive notice of documents registered at the Companies Registry[3] and this is reinforced by ns 35B[4] which, while intended no doubt to repeat the old CA 1985, s 35(2) seems to have removed any duty of inquiry on the outside. There remains the possibility that the outsider actually knows that the transaction is outside the objects and thus outside the directors' powers. Under ns 35A(2)(b) possessing even this knowledge does not in itself mean that the outsider is acting in bad faith.[5] One purpose of this provision is to deal with the problem of an organisation 'knowing' something because an ex-employee knew it or two employees each knew pieces of information which when combined mean the organisation 'knows' something which no individual knows.[6] It seems that to be in bad faith outsiders must know that the directors are engaged in some act or transaction which is, at the very least, not in what the directors honestly regard as the best interests of the company.

4.17 As noted above, ns 35A(1) only protects the outsider dealing with the company. If instead the outsider pleads the lack of authority of the company's agent against the company, the solution for the company is to ratify the act of its agent and then enforce any resulting contract. In the past, if the lack of authority stemmed from going beyond the objects the act could not be ratified. In future, it will be capable of ratification but only by special resolution.[9] This ties in with the company's new power to alter its objects for any purpose by special resolution.[10] If the board of directors has committed the company to an act which is beyond the

---

[1] Consider ns 35A(1) in relation to *Simmonds v Heffer* and *Ashbury Railway Carriage & Iron Co v Riche*. See above, para 4.15.

[2] Inserted by CA 1989, s 142.

[3] This does not affect constructive notice of the registration of charges: ns 711A(4).

[4] Ns 35B refers to 'a party to a transaction with a company'. It can hardly have been intended that the recipient of a gift should be under a duty to inquire and it might have been clearer to refer to 'a party dealing with a company' as in ns 35A(1).

[5] This would certainly acquit the bank in *Re Introductions Ltd* [1970] Ch 199 who, at the time, reasonably misunderstood that the contents of the memorandum meant the directors could not borrow money for pig-breeding. Even if the facts occurred today the bank's knowledge that the directors could not borrow money for pig-breeding would not of itself put the bank in bad faith. In *Barclay's Bank Ltd v TSOG Trust Fund Ltd* [1984] BCLC 1, 17–18, Nourse J accepted that good faith in this context required a genuine and honest, but not necessarily reasonable, belief.

[6] Prentice Report p 34. See also *Wedderburn* (1984) 47 MLR 345.

[7] Ns 35(3) (CA 1989, s 110).

[8] Ns 4(1).

objects of the company the general meeting may ratify that by special resolution.[1]

Internal dimensions

4.18   The provisions we have looked at so far deal only with the issue of the validity of any act or transaction vis à vis the outside party. There remains the question of the consequences of acts outside the objects as between the company and its members. New section 35(2) provides:

> 'A member of a company may bring proceedings to restrain the doing of an act which but for subsection (1) would be beyond the company's capacity; but no such proceedings shall lie in respect of an act to be done in fulfilment of a legal obligation arising from a previous act of the company.'

This makes clear that if members bring proceedings before the company enters into a legal obligation and the proposed action is found to be outside the objects of the company, they will be entitled to an injunction to prevent the act being carried out. If, however, members do not bring proceedings until after the company is legally bound to act then it is too late.[2] It was pointed out in the debates on the Bill that members are often unlikely to find out about proposed action until after the company is legally committed and therefore this right of objection may not be very effective.

4.19   The right to object before the company is legally committed must also now be seen in the light of the members' new general power to change a company's objects by special resolution.[3] If such a resolution is passed then the minority can only object if they have the necessary 15 per cent support.[4] An interesting question arises as to whether the power of ratification under ns 35(3) allows the members to pass a special resolution authorising the directors in advance to do something which would otherwise be outside the company's objects. It is submitted that this is not permitted. If it were, the right of members holding 15 per cent of shares to object to an alteration of the objects could easily be circumvented. It is suggested instead that the power of ratification under ns 35(3) relates only to action already taken by the directors which it now turns out is outside the objects of the company. Finally, it should be noted in relation to ns 35(2) that the power to bring proceedings is only open to members and not to

---

[1]   In a case like *Simmonds v Heffer* [1983] BCLC 298, therefore, if the members of League Against Cruel Sports Ltd passed a special resolution they could alter the objects to permit the donation to the Labour Party; or they could ratify a donation which was outside the objects.

[2]   The legislation has not, in other words, followed the pattern set by the United States Model Business Corporations Act of allowing members to restrain performance of executory ultra vires acts but also permitting the outsider to sue for breach of contract. In such actions, however, the outsider is restricted to restitutionary damages and cannot claim lost anticipated profits from the contract. This provision was followed by the Ontario Business Corporations Act 1970, s 16(2) and the New Zealand Companies Act 1955, s 18A(3), (4).

[3]   Ns 4(1) (CA 1989, s 110(2)).

[4]   CA 1985, s 5(2). The objection must also be made within twenty-one days: s 5(3).

creditors. This is consistent with the proposition that the members' right of action is based on enforcing the contract constituted by the memorandum and articles of association.[1] Creditors are not party to that contract, and if they wish to restrict the company's activities in some way they must do so by a specific term in their contract with the company.

4.20   The other internal aspect of a company acting beyond its capacity is that it may involve a breach of the directors' duty to the company to ensure that the company's assets are not used for ultra vires purposes. That this duty continues is clear from ns 35(3):

'It remains the duty of the directors to observe any limitations on their powers flowing from the company's memorandum; and action by the directors which but for subsection (1) would be beyond the company's capacity may only be ratified by the company by special resolution. A resolution ratifying such action shall not affect any liability incurred by the directors or any other person; relief from any such liability must be agreed to separately by special resolution.'

Thus, even if the members have passed a special resolution ratifying an action by the directors which was outside the company's objects, that does not relieve the directors from any liability for breach of duty. Relief from any such liability must be agreed to separately by special resolution. Nor does the ratification resolution relieve any other person who may be liable to the company in consequence of the directors acting outside the company's objects. It must be remembered so far as outsiders dealing with the company are concerned that this can only refer to persons not in good faith; those in good faith will be protected by ns 35A(1). It may also refer to persons who knowingly assist the directors in a breach of duty. In these cases, as with the directors' own breach of duty, relief from liability to the company must be agreed to by a special resolution separate from that ratifying the action itself.

Acts beyond other constitutional limitations on the authority of agents

4.21   As we have seen[2] ns 35A has an impact where the lack of authority of the board of directors arises because the act would be, but for ns 35(1), beyond the capacity of the company. But ns 35A can also apply in relation to any other limitation on the power of the board of directors to bind the company, or authorise others to do so, arising under the company's constitution. It is also made clear that the company's constitution for this purpose includes not only the memorandum and articles, but also resolutions passed or agreements made by members of the company.[3] The kinds of limitation breach which might well be

[1]   Ibid, s 14.
[2]   See para 4.16, above.
[3]   Ns 35A(3).

covered by ns 35A include: a requirement that the directors obtain the consent of the general meeting before exercising a particular power;[1] a requirement that directors exercise a power only as may seem expedient;[2] or a prohibition on directors interested in a matter from being counted towards the quorum at a meeting with the result that the meeting becomes inquorate.[3] Before considering the impact of ns 35A on these examples it is important to remember that in future there will be no constructive notice of limitations on the powers of the board of directors arising from the contents of any documents lodged at Companies House.[4] The only problem, therefore, will be with situations in which the outside party has actual notice of the limitation, although not necessarily notice that the limitation has been breached.

4.22   It has already been pointed out[5] how ns 35A(1) protects a person dealing with a company in good faith by deeming the power of the board of directors to be free of any limitation under the company's constitution. It follows therefore that even if outsiders have actual notice of the limitation on the directors' powers they will still be protected provided they are dealing with the company in good faith. It is now clear from ns 35B that just because the limitation consists of something that could be checked by outsiders (for example, a requirement for a special resolution to authorise the exercise of a power by the directors),[6] this does not make outsiders in bad faith if they fail to check. In fact, ns 35A(2)(*b*) goes further and says that even if outsiders know that the directors are acting beyond their powers, that alone does not make outsiders in bad faith. To be in bad faith seems to require that outsiders at least realise that directors are not acting in what they honestly regard as the best interests of the company.[7]

4.23   If it is an outsider who pleads the directors' lack of authority against the company then the company's solution is to ratify the transaction. There is no question here of the transaction being outside the company's capacity so there is no requirement of a special resolution. Apart from the impact on transactions with outsiders there is also an internal aspect to directors going beyond their authority. This is recognised in ns 35A(4) which, like ns 35(3), allows members to

---

[1]   See, for example, *Royal British Bank v Turquand* (1856) 6 E & B 327.

[2]   As in *Rolled Steel Products Ltd v British Steel Corporation* [1986] Ch 246, where the Court of Appeal interpreted such a requirement as limiting not the capacity of the company but the authority of the directors.

[3]   See, for example, Table A, reg 95. Regulation 92 might appear to protect an outsider but the effect of a regulation like reg 92 may depend on the outsider actually having read it. See *South London Greyhound Racecourses Ltd v Wake* [1931] 1 Ch 496. An inquorate board meeting was the problem of the 'no due authorisation' point in *Rolled Steel Products Ltd v British Steel Corporation* [1986] 2 Ch 246.

[4]   Ns 711A (CA 1989, s 142) and ns 35B.

[5]   See para, 4.16 above.

[6]   Because special resolutions have to be registered: CA 1985, s 380(4)(*a*).

[7]   On the effect of ns 35A(2)(*b*) see also para 4.16 above.

bring proceedings to restrain the doing of an act[1] beyond the powers of the directors, except where the act is to be done in fulfilment of a legal obligation arising from a previous act of the company. Likewise, any liability of the directors, or any other person, by reason of the directors exceeding their powers is not affected by protection afforded the outsider by ns 35A.

Transactions between a company and directors or their associates

4.24   New section 322A, inserted by CA 1989, s 109, is intended to prevent ns 35 or ns 35A being used by directors or their associates as a means of validating dubious transactions between themselves and the company. Although ns 35A(1) only protects persons dealing with the company in good faith, this was not felt to be sufficient. So, ns 322A(1) and (2) provide that:

'where a company enters into a transaction[2] to which the parties include:

(a)   a director of the company or its holding company,

or

(b)   a person connected with such a director or a company with whom such a director is associated,[3]

and the board of directors, in connection with the transaction, exceed any limitation on their powers under the company's constitution, the transaction is voidable at the instance of the company.'

The Government had originally intended such transactions to be void, unless ratified, in order to force directors to disclose them to shareholders and seek their approval.[4] It was felt that this put the interests of other innocent parties too much at risk[5] and so the transaction is voidable instead.

4.25   Whether or not the transaction is avoided, the section also provides that any such party as mentioned in subsection (1)(*a*) or (*b*) and any director who authorised the transaction is liable to account to the company for any profits and to indemnify the company for any loss or damage.[6] In line with the existing provision in the CA 1985, s 322(2), the transaction ceases to be voidable if restitution is no longer possible, the company has been indemnified, third party rights have intervened or the transaction is ratified by ordinary or special

---

[1]   'Act' is the term used in ns 35A(4). In this context it is intended to encompass both transactions where there are other parties, and acts like donations where it is not realistic to talk of another party.

[2]   'Transaction' includes 'act': ns 322A(8). It might have been neater to say 'where the company deals with', which per ns 35A(2)(a) covers being party to any transaction or other act to which the company is a party.

[3]   These relationships are defined in CA 1985, s 346.

[4]   HC Committee, cols 419–420.

[5]   In particular, the Land Registry and Registrars in Scotland which indemnify the purchaser of land for any defect in title.

[6]   Ns 322A(3). Persons other than directors are not liable if they show that at the time of the transaction they did not know that the directors were exceeding their powers: ns 322A(6).

resolution depending presumably on whether the limitation on their powers which the directors exceeded arose from a limitation on the company's capacity or not.[1] Finally, it may happen that a transaction is voidable in relation to one party under ns 322A(1) and (2) and yet valid in relation to another by virtue of ns 35A(1). In such cases either the person in whose favour the transaction is valid, or the company, may ask the court to affirm, sever or set aside the transaction on such terms as appear to the court to be just.[2]

Changes Affecting Charitable Companies

4.26 Sections 111 and 112 of the CA 1989 make a number of changes to the law regarding charitable companies.[3] First, s 111(2) extends to Scotland a provision which already applies to charities in England or Wales which are corporate bodies.[4] This is the provision which ensures that property donated to the charity continues to be held for charitable purposes even after the charity has changed its constitution so as to cease to be a charity. Secondly, for charities subject to the Companies Act whether incorporated in England, Wales or Scotland, nss 35 and 35A do not apply to acts of the company except in two cases: (i) in favour of a purchaser who gives full consideration without notice that the act is not permitted by the company's memorandum or is beyond the powers of the directors; or (ii) in favour of a person who does not know at the time the act is done that the company is a charity.[5] Even where nss 35 and 35A do not apply to protect a purported transfer or grant of an interest in property by the company, the title of a subsequent transferee of the property is unaffected, provided the subsequent transferee gave full consideration and was without notice of the circumstances affecting the validity of the company's act.[6] Thirdly, for charitable companies incorporated in England and Wales the ratification of any act under ns 35(3) or any act to which ns 322A applies,[7] or the alteration of the company's objects,[8] is ineffective without the prior written consent of the Charity Commissioners. Finally, a charity which is a company whether incorporated in England, Wales or Scotland whose name does not include the word 'charity' or 'charitable' must state that it is a charity in correspondence and on certain documents.[9]

---

[1]   Ns 322A(5).

[2]   Ns 322A(7).

[3]   More far-reaching changes concerning charitable companies are contemplated in *Charities: A Framework for the Future* (1989) Cm 694, paras 5.21 and 5.22.

[4]   In England and Wales the provision is the Charities Act 1960, s 30(2). Under CA 1989, s 111(1) this is renumbered as the Charities Act 1960, s 30A(1).

[5]   For charities incorporated in England or Wales see ns 30B(1),(3) inserted into the Charities Act 1960 by CA 1989, s 111(1). For charities incorporated in Scotland see CA 1989, s 112(3)(5).

[6]   See Charities Act 1960, ns 30B(2) and CA 1989, s 112(2).

[7]   Charities Act 1960, s 30B(4) (CA 1989, s 111(1)).

[8]   Charities Act 1960, s 30A(2) (CA 1989, s 111(1)).

[9]   For charities incorporated in England and Wales see Charities Act 1960, ns 30C (inserted by CA 1989, s 111(1). For charities incorporated in Scotland see CA 1989, s 112(6). Conveyances were added to the list because the land registries in England and Scotland are going to require charitable companies to warrant that transactions are ultra vires. They therefore need to be able to identify charitable companies.

CHAPTER 5

REGISTRATION OF COMPANY CHARGES

Introduction

5.1   There has been disquiet about the system for the registration of company charges for some considerable time. Part of this disquiet stems from dissatisfaction with the general state of the law regarding security over moveable property, but it has been exacerbated by a feeling of uncertainty about the whole rationale behind having a separate register of company charges.[1] The question of security over moveable property was the subject of recommendations made by the Crowther Committee in 1971.[2] These were never acted upon and in 1986 the DTI asked Professor Diamond to look again at the need for alteration of the law relating to security over property other than land. He was specifically asked to consider the case for a single scheme of registration and to consider the position of the registration of charges created by companies in the context of such a scheme. Professor Diamond produced a consultative paper in 1986[3] and his final report was published in 1989.[4] His proposals for a radical reform to the system of security over property other than land are still the subject of consultation. But it is chiefly his recommendations for reform of the registration of company charges[5] that led to the changes implemented in the CA 1989. It is hoped that they will prove to be only temporary; not because of any particular defects in the new system, but because Professor Diamond's main proposals deserve to be the subject of legislation before too long.

5.2   The implementation of the changes takes the now familiar pattern of a complete substitution of the existing CA 1985, Part XII by provisions inserted by the CA 1989, ss 93–107.[6] Since they insert twenty-six sections into the CA 1985, the practice will again be followed of referring to the section by the number it will have in the CA 1985 and doing so by using the abbreviation ns. One particularly welcome change is that the opportunity has been taken to rationalise the statute book by producing a single set of provisions applicable to England, Wales and

[1]   See Goode *Commercial Law* (1982) pp 761–762.
[2]   Report of the Committee on Consumer Credit (1971) Cmnd 4596 Chap 5.
[3]   'Security Interests in Property other than Land'.
[4]   'A Review of Security Interests in Property'. ('The Diamond Report').
[5]   See Part III of the Report.
[6]   The provisions are not expected to come into force until at least December 1990. A destination table of the provisions in the old CA 1985, Part XII is included at the end of this chapter.

Scotland. It should also be noted that the provisions for the registration of charges by oversea companies are revised and set out in greater detail as part of the CA 1985, Part XXIII.

Which Charges are Registrable

5.3   The new legislation adopts the same approach as the old law of only requiring charges to be registered if they fall within the list of registrable charges set out in the Act.[1] As before, charges arising by operation of law are excluded[2] so that, for example, repairers' liens or unpaid vendors' liens continue to be exempt from registration.[3] There is no change either in the requirement that a charge included in the list falls to be registered in the companies' charges register, even though it may also be registered elsewhere. There are, however, a number of changes to the list of registrable charges.

Charges on goods or any interest in goods

5.4   As far as England and Wales are concerned, this provision[4] replaces the category that was founded on the analogy of a bill of sale created by an individual. The effect is to extend this category to a wider range of goods and to cover charges whether or not they are created or evidenced by an instrument in writing.[5] For Scotland it makes non-possessory security in goods registrable for the first time.[6] The legislation specifically excludes charges under which the chargee is entitled to possession either of the goods or a document of title to them, the effect being to exclude pledges and liens from registration. There is no provision in the legislation specifically requiring registration of retention of title clauses, hire-purchase contracts or other forms of conditional sale agreement, nor of finance leases. If Part II of the Diamond Report were to be implemented and more comprehensive changes introduced for the registration of security interests in moveable property, it is likely that all those categories of contract would become registrable.[7]

Charges over debts

5.5   The legislation continues to require registration of a charge over the book debts of a company, whether the debt was created by the company or assigned to

---

[1]   Ns 396(1),(2) (CA 1989, s 93). This approach was supported by the Diamond Report, para 23.1.6. The Secretary of State may amend the list by regulation: ns 396(4).
[2]   Ns 395(2) (CA 1989, s 93).
[3]   See *Capital Finance Co Ltd v Stokes* [1969] 1 Ch 261 and *London and Cheshire Insurance Co Ltd v Laplagrene Property Co Ltd* [1971] Ch 499; cf *Re Wallis & Simmonds (Builders) Ltd* [1974] 1 All ER 561.
[4]   Ns 396(1) (*b*).
[5]   See Diamond Report, paras 23.9.14–23.9.19.
[6]   Ibid, paras 23.3.1–23.3.6.
[7]   Ibid, paras 23.6 and 23.7.

it.[1] Professor Diamond suggested that book debts could be defined as 'debts due or to become due to the company in respect of goods supplied or to be supplied or services rendered or to be rendered by the company in the course of the company's business.'[2] No definition is included in the Act, but the Government has announced[3] that one will be included in regulations to be made under the Act.[4]

Charges over bank accounts

5.6   The most common of debts due to a company, but which is not earned in the course of its business activities, and arguably therefore is not a book debt, is a credit balance in the company's bank account. Indeed, in *Re Brightlife Ltd*,[5] Hoffmann J decided that a bank account was not even included in the phrase 'book debts or other debts' as it was not natural to talk of a bank account as a debt at all. However, the practice of the Registrar has been to accept charges over bank accounts for registration. In future it will still be possible to register a charge over a bank account because the Registrar will not be concerned with whether a charge is registrable or not. The Registrar will merely file the particulars delivered and will not even see, let alone inspect, the charge itself.[6] It will therefore depend on whether the definition of book debts adopted by the Government includes bank accounts as to whether it becomes obligatory to register any charge over a bank balance. Professor Diamond's view was clearly that it should not, at least until Part II of his report is implemented.[7] Because bank accounts are usually secret, other creditors are unlikely to be misled by the existence of an undisclosed charge. The same reasoning applies to rights of set off in relation to bank accounts and to contractual restrictions on the right to withdraw money from the account (the 'flawed asset' technique).

Liens on sub-freights

5.7   The entitlement of a charterer of a ship to sub-freight is a book debt of the charterer and since a lien is a form of charge it was held in *Re Welsh & Irish Ferries Ltd*[8] that a lien on sub-freights is a registrable charge. In practice, registration for the purposes of giving publicity is not important because the existence of liens on sub-freights is a well-known feature of the standard forms of charter party. At

---

1   Ns 396(1)(*c*)(iii) (CA 1989, s 93).
2   Diamond Report, para 23.9.22.
3   HC Committee, Cols 404–406.
4   Under ns 396(4). See also ns 413 (CA 1989, s 102).
5   [1987] Ch 200.
6   Ns 398(4) (CA 1989, s 95).
7   Diamond Report, paras 23.4.7–23.4.12. This only deals with whether a charge over a bank balance can constitute a charge over a book debt. Of course, if a bank balance is covered by another charge, for example a floating charge, it may be the subject of registration. Neither the Diamond Report nor the legislation deals with the question of whether a charge back, ie a charge over a bank account in favour of the bank, is conceptually possible.
8   [1986] Ch 471. See also *Annagel Glory v Golodetz* [1988] PCC 37.

the same time, requiring registration would prove particularly burdensome because it would involve registration of each charter party. So Professor Diamond recommended[1] that they should no longer be registrable and this exemption is implemented in ns 396(2)(*g*).

Deposits of negotiable instruments to secure book debts

5.8   The argument about the registration of liens over sub-freights harks back to a recommendation of the Davey Committee[2] in 1895 which noted that 'there are liens, mortgages and charges of daily occurrence in the usual transactions of business which it would be inconvenient to register, and the validity of which should not be dependent on their registration'.[3] This reasoning also applies to a common device whereby a company sells goods on credit to A, thereby creating a book debt of the company. To pay the debt, A ,ives the company a post-dated cheque, which the company deposits with a bank in return for an advance. That deposit creates a charge over the book debt, but according to a Government spokesman: 'In view of the commercial frequency of such transactions, it is important that the facility to create security by depositing negotiable instruments in this way should be flexible and informal.'[4] Accordingly, such a deposit continues to be exempt from registration under ns 396(2)(*f*).

Insurance policies

5.9   In *Paul & Frank Ltd v Discount Bank (Overseas) Ltd*,[5] it was held that a charge on an insurance policy before a claim arises is not a charge on a book debt, because the debt under the policy is contingent and it is not the practice to enter it into the books of the company as a debt. There are also dicta in the case suggesting that the same conclusion applies even when a debt is due under the policy, because again it would not be the practice to enter such debt in a book. Professor Diamond recommended that charges on insurance policies should be registrable.[6] No change to implement this is included in the Act, but it may be included in regulations, perhaps in relation to the definition of book debts.

Charges securing an issue of debentures

5.10   Professor Diamond pointed out that under the old law read literally the requirement to register a charge securing an issue of debentures could cover any debt evidenced in writing.[7] It was always intended to refer to the issue of a series of debentures and this is now made clear in ns 419(1) (CA 1989, s 104).

[1]   Diamond Report, para 23.4.16.
[2]   Committee on Company Law Amendment (C 7779).
[3]   Ibid, para 48.
[4]   HL Committee, Col 124.
[5]   [1967] Ch 348.
[6]   Diamond Report, para 23.5.
[7]   Ibid, paras 23.9.3–23.9.13.

Charges over shares

5.11 If a company is seriously intent on creating unregistrable security, one way to do it is to vest the relevant asset in a subsidiary company and then create a charge over the shares in the subsidiary company. Whereas a charge over the asset would be registrable, a charge over the shares is not. In 1962, the Jenkins Committee recommended that a charge over the shares in a subsidiary should be registrable, but this was never implemented. Professor Diamond foresaw various difficulties in treating shares in subsidiaries differently from other shares and serious practical problems in requiring registration of charges on all shares.[1] He therefore recommended no change. The Government accepted this and it remains the case that charges over shares are not *per se* registrable.

Method and Effect of Registration

Time limit and priority point

5.12 As under the old law the method of registration is by delivering prescribed particulars to the Registrar within twenty-one days of creation of the charge.[2] Unlike under the old law, however, it will no longer be necessary to produce the charge itself. In consequence the former rule that, in the case of a charge created abroad of property situated abroad, the twenty-one days ran from the date when the instrument creating the charge or a copy of it could, in due course of posts, have been received in the UK is not re-enacted. Now in the case of a charge over property situated abroad, wherever it was created, the twenty-one days runs from creation of the charge.[3]

5.13 No change is made to the rule that priority as between successive charges on the same property is determined by reference to the date of creation and not the date of registration. This, coupled with the fact that chargees have twenty-one days in which to deliver paticulars, can create a problem for holders of subsequent charges on the same property. Suppose that charge A is created on 1 February and registered on 20 February, and charge B is created over the same property on 10 February and registered on 12 February. Charge A will rank ahead of charge B, even though charge B was registered first and even though, if the second chargee searched the register on 9 February, it would have found nothing to indicate the existence of charge A. To solve this problem, Professor Diamond recommended a system of priorities related to the date of registration, rather than the date of creation, but this was not accepted by the Government.[4]

---

[1] Diamond Report, para 23.8.
[2] Ns 398(1) (CA 1989, s 95). As to the date of creation of the charge, see ns 414 (CA 1989, s 103).
[3] Ns 414(4).
[4] Diamond Report, para 24.2.8.

5.14 One reason it was not accepted is that on its own it would not solve the problems. The second chargee might search the register on 19 February, find nothing, and so create charge B. But, by the time it seeks to register on, say, 21 February, charge A will have been registered and will take priority. Professor Diamond's solution to this was for a system of provisional registration to be introduced.[1] This was also rejected by the Government because provisional registration on its own, without a system of priority based on time of registration, offered no better protection.[2] And, as the Government had rejected changing the priority rules, there was no point in introducing provisional registration. If the present priority rules were retained, Professor Diamond recommended an official search system under which the Registrar would give a certificate in effect guaranteeing the holder priority if a charge was registered within a certain period of time.[3] This, however, was also rejected by the Government, presumably because of the administrative burden it would place on the Registrar.

Prescribed particulars[4]

5.15 It is provided that the prescribed particulars which must be delivered to the Registrar in order to register a charge will be laid down by regulations.[5] These are certain to include a requirement that a negative pledge, ie a clause in a floating charge restricting the right of the company to create other charges ranking in priority to, or *pari passu* with, the floating charge, must be registered.[6] This is already the position in Scotland,[7] but will represent a change in the law of England and Wales.

Ranking provisions in Scottish Law [8]

5.16 In Scotland the prescribed particulars under the old law also included provisions in a floating charge 'which vary or otherwise regulate the order of ranking of the floating charge in relation to subsisting securities'.[9] Such ranking provisions are more usual in Scottish floating charges, because they are specifically permitted under the CA 1985, s 464(1)(*b*) as a means of contracting out of the statutory order of priority that would otherwise apply. Section 464(1)(*b*) is amended by the CA 1989, s 140(3) to make it clear that a floating charge can only contain ranking provisions which adversely affect the holder of any subsisting floating charge or fixed security with the consent of such holder. It is also made explicit that where, as permitted by the CA 1985, s 464(1)(*a*), a floating charge contains a negative pledge, the effect is to give the floating charge

1   Diamond Report, para 26.6.
2   HL Committee, Col 134–136.
3   Diamond Report, para 26.7.
4   Diamond Report, paras 22.4.1–22.4.7.
5   Ns 415(1) (CA 1989, s 103).
6   Ns 415(2)(*a*). HC Committee, Col 408.
7   CA 1985, s 417(3)(*e*).
8   Diamond Report, paras 22.4.8–22.4.11.
9   CA 1985, s 417(3)(*e*).

priority over any subsequent fixed security or floating charge.[1] The provisions are subject to Part XII of the CA 1985, so that the rules will presumably depend on any registration requirements being fulfilled.[2] It is not, however, expected that ranking provisions, as opposed to negative pledges, will be included in the prescribed particulars, since by definition all those affected by such provisions will have consented to them. For the avoidance of doubt, the CA 1985, s 464(3) is reworded to make it clear that the ranking provisions in s 464(4) and (5) apply only where the ranking is not controlled by provisions made under s 464(1).[3]

Effect of registration

5.17 In future the Registrar will merely file the statement of prescribed particulars delivered by the parties.[4] The charge itself will not even be produced to the Registrar, so there will be no question of checking the accuracy of the particulars.[5] As under the old law, registration of a charge at Companies House will continue to give rise to constructive notice. Although constructive notice generally is abolished by ns 711A(1),[6] this is subject to ns 416,[7] subs (1) of which provides that:

'A person taking a charge over a company's property shall be taken to have notice of any matter requiring registration and disclosed on the register at the time the charge is created.'

Thus, subsequent chargees, but not anyone else dealing with the company, will be taken to know of the existence of registrable charges which are registered. They will also be presumed to know of any matters relating to the charges, such as the existence of negative pledges, which come within the prescribed particulars and which have been duly registered.

5.18 Subsequent chargees will not, however, be presumed to know any additional information voluntarily included on the register which does not fall within the prescribed particulars. This appears to follow from ns 416(2), but as it is worded rather obscurely it is worth setting out in full:

'Otherwise, a person shall not be taken to have notice of any matter (i) by reason of its being disclosed on the register or (ii) by reason of his having failed to search the register in the course of making such inquiries as ought reasonably to be made.'[8]

---

[1]   CA 1985, s 464(1A) inserted by CA 1989, s 140(4).
[2]   CA 1985, s 464(6) as amended by CA 1989, s 140(7).
[3]   CA 1985, s 464(3) as amended by CA 1989, s 140(5).
[4]   Ns 398(4) (CA 1989, s 95).
[5]   Diamond Report, para 22.2. The Registrar will send a copy of the filed particulars together with a note as to the date on which they were filed to interested parties: ns 398(5).
[6]   See CA 1989, s 142.
[7]   See CA 1989, s 103.
[8]   The figures (i) and (ii) have been added for ease of reference.

It is not clear what situations (ii) refers to which are not already covered by (i). It might conceivably be that (i) is intended to abolish actual notice and (ii) deemed notice, but that is unlikely to have been intended and the phrase 'not be taken to have notice' surely refers only to deemed notice. If (i) therefore prevents deemed notice arising as regards additional material voluntarily included in the registered particulars, what situations are left to be covered by (ii)?

A further problem arises in ns 416(2) over the meaning of 'person'. It is presumed that the 'person' referred to is the 'person taking a charge over a company's property' mentioned in ns 416(1). If that is the case, it would have been clearer to refer to '*such* a person' and clearer still to say 'shall not be taken to have notice of any *other* matter'. But it seems possible to read the opening phrase 'Otherwise, a person' as referring to anyone who is not taking a charge, such as a purchaser. It would mean that purchasers would not be taken to have notice of any matter on the register: (i) by reason of its being on the register; or (ii) by reason of having failed to search the register in the course of making such inquiries as ought reasonably to be made. The only redeeming feature of this obscurity is that it does not seem to make any difference. Purchasers are not deemed to have notice of anything on the companies register by virtue of ns 711A.[1] The only exception is that ns 711A does not affect the operation of the rule whereby the registration of certain land charges at Companies House is deemed to constitute actual notice for all purposes connected with the land affected.[2]

Effect of Non-registration

Penalty on company and officers

5.19   The duty to deliver particulars of the charge continues to fall on the company that creates the charge.[3] Anyone else may deliver the particulars, but if no one does, the company and its officers are liable to a fine.[4] The real consequence of non-delivery, however, is that the charge becomes void on the happening of certain relevant events.[5] The usual practice is likely to be, therefore, as under the old law, for lenders and their solicitors to undertake the delivery of the particulars.[6]

---

[1]   CA 1989, s 142. This accords with the Diamond Report, para 24.3.5. See further the discussion at paragraphs 7.5–7.7 below.

[2]   Ns 711A(4)(*b*).

[3]   Ns 398(1) (CA 1989, s 95).

[4]   Ns 398(3).

[5]   Ns 399. (CA 1989, s 95).

[6]   In certain circumstances, however, the company's solicitors could be liable in negligence for failing to register a charge: *Trustee of PAF Foster v Crusts* [1986] BCLC 307.

Charge may become void against creditors

5.20 If the particulars are not delivered within twenty-one days, the charge does not immediately become void. Instead, it becomes void on the happening of a so-called relevant event.[1] There are two relevant events referred to in the new legislation. One is the beginning of insolvency proceedings,[2] by which is meant the presentation of a petition on which an administration order or compulsory winding-up order is made, or the passing of a resolution for voluntary winding up.[3] Thus, if particulars of a registrable charge are not delivered within twenty-one days, it will become void against an administrator or liquidator of the company.[4] The charge will be void even if the beginning of insolvency proceedings occurs during the twenty-one days in which the particulars may be delivered.[5] If this does occur, but particulars are then delivered within twenty-one days of creation of the charge, the charge is not void for non-registration. It may, however, be vulnerable under the Insolvency Act 1986 as a preference,[6] or as a transaction at an undervalue,[7] or if it is a floating charge, under s 245.

5.21 The other relevant event is the acquisition of an interest in or right over property subject to the charge.[8] Thus, an unregistered charge becomes void against any person who for value acquires such an interest or right.[9] This means that, as under the old law, creditors, who subsequently take security over the same property and which, if registrable, is duly perfected by delivery of particulars to the Registrar,[10] will be unaffected by the prior unregistered charge. This is so even if the subsequent chargee had actual notice of the prior unregistered charge, unless the subsequent charge was expressly subject to the prior charge.[11] 'Acquisition of an interest in or right over property' also covers a judgment creditor levying execution on company property. This means that judgment creditors can ignore the existence of unregistered charges, even if they know about them, except in the unlikely event of a judgment creditor having agreed expressly to be subject to the charge. As in relation to the beginning of insolvency proceedings, it does not matter whether the subsequent security interest or

---

1   Ns 399(1) and (2) (CA 1989, s 95).
2   Ns 399(2)(*a*).
3   Ns 419(5) (CA 1989, s 104).
4   Ns 399(1).
5   Ns 399(1). Where the beginning of the insolvency proceedings occurs on the same day as the charge is created, the charge is presumed to be created first, unless the contrary is proved: ns 399(3).
6   Insolvency Act 1986, s 239.
7   Ibid, s 238.
8   Ns 399(2)(*b*).
9   Ns 399(1)(*b*).
10 Ns 404(1) (CA 1989, s 99). As to what happens if the particulars of the second charge are incomplete or inaccurate, see ns 404(2). See para 5.37 below.
11 Ns 405(1). This represents a change in the law. In some cases it may be easy to tell whether a subsequent charge is expressly subject to an earlier one: *Watson v Duff Morgan and Vermont (Holdings) Ltd* [1974] 1 All ER 794. In others it may not be so easy: *Re Monolithic Building Co* [1915] 1 Ch 643.

judgment creditors' rights were acquired during the twenty-one days after creation of the first charge,[1] provided particulars of the first charge were not, in fact, delivered within twenty-one days of its creation.

Charge may become void against purchasers

5.22   Under the old law, the non-registration of a charge did not render it void against a purchaser from the company of the property subject to the unregistered charge. Professor Diamond recommended that 'a purchaser of an asset subject to an unregistered (but registrable) charge should take free of it unless he actually knew of the charge'.[2] Under the new legislation, a purchaser from the company of property subject to an unregistered charge is a 'person who for value acquires an interest in or right over property subject to the charge'. Such purchasers, therefore, will in future take free of the unregistered charge,[3] unless they acquired their interest in or right over property expressly subject to the charge.[4]

Repayment of money secured by unregistered charge

5.23   Under the old law, the money secured by an unregistered charge became automatically repayable at the expiry of the twenty-one day period. Under the new law, such money becomes repayable, together with any interest, only when the charge becomes void to any extent, ie on the happening of one of the relevant events outlined above, and then only if repayment is demanded.[5]

Late Delivery of Particulars

5.24   Under the new system, although there will still be a duty to deliver prescribed particulars of a registrable charge within twenty-one days of its creation,[6] failure to do so will not render the charge void until the happening of a relevant event.[7] In the meantime, it will be possible to perfect the charge by delivering the prescribed particulars after the twenty-one day period has expired.[8] The difference compared with the old system of late registration is that the procedure will no longer involve obtaining a court order, and will be available regardless of the reasons for failure to deliver within twenty-one days.

---

[1]   Ns 399(1) (CA 1989, s 95).
[2]   Diamond Report, para 24.3.5.
[3]   Ns 399(1).
[4]   Ns 405(1) (CA 1989, s 99). Where a chargee exercises a power of sale, as opposed to the company selling the property, the purchaser is not concerned with whether particulars of the charge have been delivered to the registrar: ns 406(1). As to the chargee's duty with regard to the proceeds of sale, see ns 406(2) (CA 1989, s 99).
[5]   Ns 407 (CA 1989, s 99).
[6]   Ns 398(1) (CA 1989, s 95).
[7]   Ns 399(1).
[8]   Ns 400(1) (CA 1989, s 95).

5.25   Late delivery of particulars will not act retrospectively to defeat the rights of creditors which have been acquired by the happening of relevant events. Thus, if insolvency proceedings have begun,[1] the rights of unsecured creditors will be unaffected by any late delivery of particulars.[2] If another charge over the same property has been granted and perfected by any necessary delivery of particulars, or if a charge granted before the unregistered charge has in the meantime been perfected by registration, they will have priority over the late registered charge.[3] As we have seen, this will be so even if the relevant event giving rise to the protected rights occurred during the twenty-one days after the creation of the charge in respect of which late delivery is taking place.[4] An example, assuming two registrable charges over the same property and assuming that the second charge is not expressly subject to the first,[5] may illustrate this. If charge A is created on 1 February and particulars are delivered on 1 October, but particulars of charge B are delivered before 1 October, then charge B will have priority *whenever charge B was created* — whether before 1 February, during the first twenty-one days of February,[6] or thereafter.

5.26   Protection against subsequent relevant events will provide some incentive to deliver particulars promptly, but there is a further incentive to deliver particulars within twenty-one days of creation of the charge. This is because the charge becomes void against an administrator or liquidator if insolvency proceedings begin within a certain period of time after late delivery of the particulars.[7] The period of time depends on the nature of the charge. It is two years in the case of a floating charge granted to a connected person, one year for other floating charges, and six months for any other charges.[8] In each case, the charge will not be void unless, at the time of the late delivery of particulars, the company was unable to pay its debts or subsequently became unable to pay its debts as a result of the transaction under which the charge was created.[9]

---

[1]   Ns 399(2)(*a*) (CA 1989, s 95) and ns 419(5) (CA 1989, s 104).
[2]   cf *Victoria Housing Estates Ltd v Ashpurton Estates Ltd* [1983] Ch 110. See also *Re Resinoid and Mica Products Ltd* (1967) [1983] Ch 132n.
[3]   Ns 399(2)(*b*).
[4]   Ns 399(1). See paras 5.20 and 5.21 above.
[5]   Ns 405(1) (CA 1989, s 99).
[6]   Thus, but for the fact that the second charge was expressly subject to the first, the decision in a case like *Watson v Duff Morgan and Vermont (Holdings) Ltd* [1974] 1 All ER 794, would in future be different. Likewise, the decision in *Ram Narain v Radha Kishen* (1929) LR 57 Ind App 76.
[7]   Ns 400(2) (CA 1989, s 95).
[8]   Ns 400(2)(*b*).
[9]   Ns 400(2)(*a*). Consider the application of these new rules to facts like those in *Re Braemar Investments Ltd* [1989] Ch 54, where the charge was created on 17 June 1986, but not registered until 10 November 1986 and the resolution for voluntary winding up was passed on 2 December 1986. Whether the charge was void against the liquidator would depend on whether the company was unable to pay its debts at the date of the late delivery of particulars, ie 10 November 1986.

Supplementing or Varying Registered Particulars

5.27   Under the old law, if a mistake was made in the registered particulars, it was necessary to apply for a court order allowing rectification of the omission or misstatement. If part of the property charged was released, or if the amount secured was reduced, then a memorandum of satisfaction had to be registered. If the charged property was changed by substitution, or if the charged sum was increased, then a completely new charge had to be registered. Under the new law, all of these alterations can be achieved by filing further particulars supplementing or varying the registered particulars.[1] This may be done at any time and without a court order. The further particulars must be signed by or on behalf of both the company and the chargee.[2] The further particulars are filed[3] and a copy sent to the company and the chargee.[4]

5.28   Whether extending the scope of an existing charge is varying it or creating a new charge will be a matter for decision by the company, the chargee and their advisers. It will usually be preferable to treat the extension as the creation of a new charge, because that will give twenty-one days in which to deliver the prescribed particulars. If they are delivered within twenty-one days, the charge is valid from the date of the extension. It will therefore gain priority over charges created after that date. It will also be protected against relevant events occurring after that date, but before delivery of the particulars.

Errors and Omissions in Registered Particulars

Effect of Registrar's certificate

5.29   Under the old law, despite the fact that the charge itself was sent to the Registrar together with the prescribed particulars, errors and omissions appeared in the register of charges. The problems this caused were exacerbated by the fact that the certificate of registration of the charge was deemed to be conclusive evidence that the requirements as to registration had been satisfied.[5] Under the new law, the charge itself will not be sent when the prescribed particulars are delivered and the Registrar will merely file the particulars as they are submitted.[6]

---

1   Ns 401(1) (CA 1989, s 96).
2   Ns 401(2). As to the power of the court to dispense with signatures of the chargee or the company, see ns 417 (CA 1989, s 103).
3   Ns 401(3).
4   Ns 401(4).
5   *National Provincial Union Bank of England v Charnley* [1924] 1 KB 431; *Re Mechanizations (Eaglescliffe) Ltd* [1966] Ch 20; *Re C L Nye Ltd* [1971] 1 Ch 442. For an attempt to go behind the conclusive nature of the certificate via judicial review, see *R v Registrar of Companies* [1986] QB 1114.
6   Ns 397(2) (CA 1989, s 94).

The only certificate the Registrar will issue in future will be one stating the date on which the particulars were delivered.[1] This certificate will give rise to an irrebuttable presumption that the particulars were delivered not later than the date shown, and a rebuttable presumption that they were delivered not earlier than the date shown.[2] The certificate will not therefore carry any sort of representation or warranty that the registered particulars accurately represent either the property charged or the debt secured.

Effect of errors and omissions in registered particulars

5.30   In these circumstances, it is important to understand what incentive there will be for parties to deliver accurate particulars to the Registrar. The incentive will be that where the particulars delivered are not complete and accurate the charge will be void, to the extent that it confers rights which would have been disclosed by complete and accurate particulars, if a relevant event[3] occurs and the court does not order otherwise.[4] If the charge does become void to any extent under these provisions, then the whole of the money secured by it, together with interest, becomes repayable on demand.[5]

5.31   One relevant event is the beginning of insolvency proceedings. Thus, the charge will be void against an administrator or liquidator in respect of inaccurate particulars at the date insolvency proceedings begin,[6] unless the chargee satisfies the court that either: (i) the omission or error is not likely to have misled any unsecured creditor in a way materially to prejudice the creditor; or (ii) that no person became an unsecured creditor at a time when the registered particulars were incomplete or inaccurate.[7] If the insolvency proceedings begin on the same day as particulars, or further particulars, are delivered to the Registrar, the insolvency proceedings are presumed to have begun first, unless the contrary is proved.[8]

5.32   The other relevant event is the acquisition of an interest in or right over the charged property. Thus, the charge will be void against any person who for value acquires an interest in or right over the charged property[9] unless either: (i) the chargee satisfies the court that the person acquiring the interest or right did not rely, in connection with the acquisition, on particulars which were incomplete

---

[1]   Ns 397(3) (CA 1989, s 94).
[2]   Ns 397(5). It is left open for the chargee to show that particulars were delivered earlier, as this might be important in the context of escaping invalidity where the time limit is important.
[3]   Ns 399(2) (CA 1989, s 95).
[4]   Ns 402(1) (CA 1989, s 97).
[5]   Ns 407 (CA 1989, s 99).
[6]   Ns 402(2)(*a*).
[7]   Ns 402(4).
[8]   Ns 402(3).
[9]   Ns 402(2)(*b*).

or inaccurate;[1] or (ii) the person acquiring the right or interest did so expressly subject to the charge.[2]

5.33   The facts in the case of *National Provincial Union Bank of England v Charnley*[3] can be slightly adapted to illustrate the operation of these new provisions. A company granted to the bank a floating charge covering its leasehold factory and moveable plant. The charge was registered, however, as a 'mortgage on leasehold premises' without any mention of the plant. Subsequently, an execution creditor seized some of the plant and shortly afterwards a liquidator was appointed. The case involved a dispute between the bank and the execution creditor and one issue was as to whether the plant was covered by the charge in view of the inaccurate registered particulars. If these facts arose under the new law and particulars were delivered and filed which omitted any reference to plant, the charge would be void as regards the plant unless the bank as chargee could show that the execution creditor did not rely, in connection with the execution, on the incomplete or inaccurate particulars.[4] Since, in the case, the execution creditor had not searched the register, it seems likely the chargee could satisfy this test. However, the issue would also arise of the charge on the plant being void against the liquidator. Here the chargee would have to show that the incomplete or inaccurate particulars were not likely to have misled any unsecured creditor in a materially prejudicial way or (which seems unlikely) that no person became an unsecured creditor while the registered particulars were incomplete or inaccurate.[5]

5.34   The natural consequence of these provisions may be for chargees to err on the side of caution and deliver particulars which cover as much property as might possibly fall within their charge. In this context, it is important to remember that when particulars are delivered and filed, the Registrar will send a copy of the particulars and a note as to their delivery to the company and the chargee.[6] If the particulars have been delivered by the chargee, it will be in the company's interest to check that the particulars do not overstate the extent of the charge.

Priority as between Successive Charges over the same Property

5.35   The power to deliver particulars or further particulars at any time, and the effect of failure to correct errors or omissions in registered particulars necessitate

1   Ns 402(5) (CA 1989, s 97).
2   Ns 405(1) (CA 1989, s 99). See cases cited at para 5.21.
3   [1924] 1 KB 431.
4   Ns 402(2)(*b*), (5).
5   Ns 402(2)(*a*), (4).
6   Ns 398(5) (CA 1989, s 95).

a further refinement in the rules relating to priority between successive charges on the same property. In the following example it must again be assumed that both charges are registrable and that neither is expressly subject to the other.

5.36 Where relevant particulars of charge A (ie particulars relating to rights inconsistent with those under another charge, charge B), are not delivered within twenty-one days of its creation and remain undelivered when particulars of charge B are delivered, then charge A is void as against charge B which will therefore have priority. This is so whenever charge B was created: whether before charge A was created; during the twenty-one days after charge A was created; or more than twenty-one days after charge A was created. The authority for this proposition if no particulars at all of charge A have been delivered is ns 399(1)(*b*) and (2)(*b*).[1] If particulars of charge A have been delivered, but they are inaccurate or incomplete as regards a right which is inconsistent with those under charge B, then the authority is ns 402(1), (2)(*b*), (3) and (5).[2]

5.37 The particular problem that arises is where the relevant particulars of charge B which are delivered are themselves incomplete or inaccurate. Then charge A is only void to the extent that rights under charge B were disclosed by the registered particulars of charge B, delivered before the particulars of the corresponding rights in charge A were delivered.[3]

Registration of Discharge

5.38 The new legislation continues to treat as optional the delivery to the Registrar of a memorandum that a registered charge no longer affects certain property.[4] Professor Diamond had recommended that it should be obligatory,[5] but the Government felt that the absence of any effective sanction made this unrealistic. In any case, there ought to be sufficient incentive on the company in making sure that its assets do not appear more encumbered than they are. Any memorandum which is delivered must be signed by or on behalf of both company and chargee[6] and the Registrar will send interested parties a copy of the memorandum and a note as to the date of delivery.[7] If a memorandum is wrongly delivered, the charge becomes void to the same extent as if the charge

---

[1] See para 5.21 above.
[2] See para 5.32 above.
[3] Ns 404(2) (CA 1989, s 99).
[4] Ns 403(1) (CA 1989, s 98).
[5] Diamond Report, para 28.2.
[6] Ns 403(2). As to the power of the court to dispense with signatures: ns 417 (CA 1989, s 103).
[7] Ns 403(4).

had been unregistered.[1] Similarly, the money secured by the charge becomes repayable on demand.[2]

Notice of Crystallisation of Floating Charge

5.39 A growing problem in relation to floating charges has been the increasingly prevalent use of clauses providing for the charge to crystallise either automatically[3] or on service of a notice on the company.[4] The use of such clauses to defeat statutory restrictions on floating charges has been prevented by the Insolvency Act 1986, s 251 which defines a floating charge as a charge which, as created, was a floating charge. However, there still remains the problem that such crystallising occurs in secret without other creditors of the company necessarily being aware of it. To deal with this, ns 410[5] allows the Secretary of State to make regulations requiring notice to be given to the Registrar of: (i) the occurrence of crystallising events or action taken to crystallise a charge;[6] and (ii) the consequences of failure to give such notice which may include treating the crystallisation as ineffective.[7]

5.40 In a consultation document circulated in July 1988, the DTI suggested that registration should be required within seven days of the occurrence of a crystallising event which occurred at any time before a resolution for voluntary winding up was passed or a winding-up order made. Where the crystallising event was already notified under a different provision of the Act,[8] such notification would be treated as notification of crystallisation if given within seven days. Under these proposals, the effect of notification within seven days seems to be that crystallisation is effective from the moment it occurred. If notification was not made within seven days, the crystallisation would be void unless and until it had been notified at which time it would be effective except against: (i) persons acquiring an interest in or security over the relevant property in the period between crystallisation and notification; and (ii) the liquidator where a winding up had commenced and the administrator where an administration order had been made, prior to notification of the crystallisation.

---

1   Ns 403(5) (CA 1989, s 98). See paras 5.20–5.22 above. If the relevant event occurs on the same day as the memorandum is delivered, it is rebuttably presumed to have occurred before delivery of the memorandum so not making the charge void: ns 403(6).
2   Ns 407 (CA 1989, s 99).
3   For earlier discussion see *Davey & Co v Williamson & Son Ltd* [1898] 2 QB 194 and *Evans v Rival Granite Quarries Ltd* [1910] 2 KB 979. See also *Re Brightlife Ltd* [1987] Ch 200.
4   *Re Woodroffe's (Musical Instruments) Ltd* [1986] Ch 366; *Re Brightlife Ltd* above.
5   CA 1989, s 100.
6   Ns 410(1).
7   Ns 410(2),(3).
8   For example, the appointment of a receiver under ns 409 (CA 1989, s 100).

Charges on Property of Oversea Companies

5.41 A new set of provisions, nss 703A-703N inserted into the CA 1985 by the CA 1989, Sch 15, governs the registration of charges by oversea companies. The most important change is that the obligation on oversea companies to register charges applies only if they have registered a place of business in Great Britain under the CA 1985, s 691.[1] In other words, the so called Slavenburg[2] register, on which were kept particulars of charges created by companies which had not registered under s 691, is abolished. The Government accepted that this is not a perfect solution to the problem in that companies which do not register under s 691, or trade in Great Britain but do not establish a place of business, are excluded. It was felt, however, that a practicable solution was better than aiming at theoretical perfection. The main consideration was that the register should not mislead. In so far as some companies will be left out of the system, persons dealing with them would be on notice of that fact and able to take decisions accordingly.

5.42 A company which registers under s 691, and has at that time property in Great Britain subject to a registrable charge, must deliver particulars relating to the charge at that time.[3] A company which is already registered under s 691 and which creates a registrable charge on property in Great Britain or acquires such property subject to an existing registrable charge, must deliver particulars relating to the charge within twenty-one days of the charge's creation or the acquisition unless the property is no longer in Great Britain at the end of twenty-one days.[4] If neither of the above applies, but a company already registered under s 691 brings property subject to a registrable charge to Great Britain and keeps it here continuously for four months, particulars relating to the charge must be delivered before the end of the four-month period.[5] As regards the location of property, a ship, aircraft or hovercraft is treated as being in Great Britain if it is registered in Great Britain; other vehicles are treated as in Great Britain if they are managed from a place of business in Great Britain.[6]

---

[1]   Ns 703A(1),(3).
[2]   See *Slavenburg's Bank NV v Intercontinental Natural Resources Ltd* [1980] 1 All ER 955.
[3]   Ns 703D(1). The particulars are to be delivered to the Registrar to whom the documents are delivered under s 691: ns 703E(1).
[4]   Ns 703D(2). As to which Registrar documents should be delivered if the company is registered in both parts of Great Britain, see ns 703E(2).
[5]   Ns 703D(3).
[6]   Ns 703L(1).

Destination Table of Company Charges Provisions

The following table shows in relation to section numbers in the old CA 1985, Part XII where the *equivalent* section number is in the new CA 1985, Part XII. It must be remembered that this is not pure consolidation and so, although the contents of the new section may be very similar or even identical to the old, in many cases they may be totally different. This table is therefore intended only as a guide to where to find the *equivalent* material.

OLD	NEW	OLD	NEW	OLD	NEW
395(1)	399(1)	404(2)	–	415(1)	398(1)
(2)	407	405(1)	409(1)	(2)	398(2)
396(1)	396(1), (2)	(2)	409(2)	(3)	398(3)
(2)	396(2)(f)	(3)	409(3)	416(1)	398(1)
(3)	396(2)(a)	(4)	409(4)	(2)	–
(4)	395(2)	406(1)	411(1)	(3)	398(3)
397(1)	408	(2)	411(1)	417(1)	397(1), (2)
(2)	–	407(1)	411(2)	(2)	397(1), (2)
(3)	–	(2)	411(2)	(3)	397(2), 415
398(1)	–	(3)	411(4)	(4)	–
(2)	–	408(1)	412(1)	418(1)	397(3)
(3)	414(4)	(2)	412(1)	(2)	397(4), (5)
(4)	–	(3)	412(4)(a)	419(1)	401(1), 403 (1)
399(1)	398(1)	(4)	412(4)(b)	(2)	403(4)
(2)	398(2)	409(1)	703A–703N	(3)	417
(3)	398(3)	(2)		(4)	–
400(1)	–	410(1)	395(1)	(5)	–
(2)	398(1)	(2)	399(1)	420	400, 401
(3)	–	(3)	407	421(1)	411(1)
(4)	398(3)	(4)	396(1), (2)	(2)	411(1)
401(1)	397(1), (2)	(5)	395(4)(b), 414 (3)	422(1)	411(2)
(2)	397(3), (4), (5)	411(1)	–	(2)	411(2)
(3)	–	(2)	414(4)	(3)	411(4)
402(1)	–	412	396(2)(f)	423(1)	412(1)
(2)	–	413(1)	396(2)(a)	(2)	412(1)
(3)	–	(2)	408	(3)	412(4)(a)
403(1)	401(1), 403 (1)	(3)	–	(4)	412(4)(b)
(2)	403(4)	414(1)	–	424(1)	703A–703N
404(1)	400, 401	(2)	–	(2)	

CHAPTER 6

DE-REGULATION OF PRIVATE COMPANIES

Introduction

6.1 Sections 113–117 of the CA 1989 introduce a set of provisions designed to ease the burden of running a small private company.[1] They have their origin in a report produced in November 1986 by the Institute of Directors entitled 'De-regulation for Small Private Companies'. The thesis of the report was that small private companies would benefit from a much simplified legal regime which distinguished more clearly between company law requirements designed to protect creditors and customers and those designed to protect shareholders.[2] The former would remain unchanged, but as regards the latter, shareholders would be able to dispense with certain formalities and requirements where this would not weaken the protection of outside parties. Some of these requirements are of a purely formal nature like having to decide something by a particular type of resolution, or at a general or class meeting. Others are substantive in the sense that they require a company to do something, or more commonly prevent it from doing something.

6.2 It is these proposals which ss 113–117 are designed to implement. The key principle governing shareholders' decisions to opt for a more de-regulated regime is that unanimous consent is required. Therefore, although the new regime is available to all private companies, in practice it is closely-held private companies and wholly-owned subsidiaries which will benefit from it most. The Institute of Directors envisaged the new regime becoming available by stages.[3] First, there would be clarification of the law relating to the status of written resolutions. Secondly, the Secretary of State would be given powers to designate by statutory instrument which Companies Act provisions a company could elect to disapply. Both these stages are included in the CA 1989 and the Act also designates the first five provisions which companies can disapply. Thirdly, the Institute of Directors foresaw the possibility of a company, by a single resolution, adopting the entire de-regulation package or 'elective regime' as they suggested it should be known.[4]

---

[1] These provisions are expected to come into force in March 1990.
[2] 'Deregulation for Small Private Companies', p 2.
[3] 'Deregulation for Small Private Companies', p 4.
[4] This would probably be something similar to the United States close corporation model code.

Written Resolutions

Procedure

6.3   Section 113 of the CA 1989 introduces statutory written resolutions by inserting nss 381A–381C and ns 382A into the CA 1985. Under ns 381A(1), anything which a private company may do by a resolution of a general or class meeting may in future be done by written resolution. The procedure is that a written resolution has to be signed by or on behalf of all members who, at the date of the resolution, would be entitled to attend and vote at such a meeting.[1] The signatures may be on separate documents, provided each sets out the terms of the resolution.[2] Once agreed to in this manner a written resolution is as effective as if it had been passed at the appropriate meeting, although no meeting at all need be held and no previous notice of the resolution need be given.[3] It is specifically provided that a written resolution passed in accordance with ns 381A can be used to pass any sort of resolution, whether ordinary, special, extraordinary or elective.[4]

Scope for using written resolutions

6.4   Of course, any company, public or private, may already include in its articles a power for members to agree to resolutions in writing, rather than at a meeting.[5] It is important therefore to see what can be done under these new rules which could not be achieved by a provision in a company's articles. In some cases, this will depend how widely the clause in the articles is drafted. Table A, art 53, for example, does not extend to resolutions of class meetings, whereas the new legislation does. More importantly, however, the new legislation allows written resolutions to be used in situations where previously the Companies Act itself would have prevented this. For example, the CA 1985, s 2(7) prohibits a company from altering the conditions in its memorandum 'except in the cases, in the mode and to the extent, for which express provision is made by this Act'. When, therefore, the CA 1985, s 4 provides that 'a company may by special resolution alter its memorandum with respect to the objects of the company',[6] that is the *only* way in which the objects may be changed. Even a unanimous agreement, like that in *Cane v Jones*,[7] which was effective to change the articles,[8]

---

[1]   Ns 381A(1) (CA 1989, s 113(2)).
[2]   Ns 381A(2).
[3]   Ns 381A(1) and (4).
[4]   Ns 381A(6). As to 'elective resolutions', see below, paras 6.8–6.11.
[5]   See, for example, Table A, art 53.
[6]   Ns 4 (CA 1989, s 110) is to the same effect.
[7]   [1981] 1 All ER 533.
[8]   *Cane v Jones* above, held that it was always possible for a company to alter its articles by unanimous agreement. When, therefore, CA 1985, s 9 provides that 'a company may by special resolution alter its articles' that is merely providing an alternative route, one by which a particular majority may bind a minority. The word 'may' in s 9 merely facilitates an easier method of altering the articles. The word 'may' in s 4 constitutes the only way of altering the objects.

would not be effective to change the objects. In future, however, a statutory written resolution will be as good as a special resolution and can therefore be used to change the objects clause of a private company. Likewise, the power to reduce share capital is entirely statute based and requires a special resolution.[1] Even a unanimous agreement not in the form of a special resolution has therefore been unacceptable.[2] But in future a statutory written resolution will be effective.

Exceptions and consequential amendments

6.5 Section 114 of the CA 1989 inserts new Sch 15A into the CA 1985. Part I of the new Schedule lists the two cases where it will still not be possible to use written resolutions. These are in relation to the removal of directors[3] or auditors[4] from office before the expiry of their term of office. The reason for these exceptions is that the director or auditor in such a case has the right to make representations at a general meeting of the company.[5] Part II of the new Schedule sets out certain consequential amendments that are needed as to formalities for valid resolutions in certain cases. Where information has to be given with the notice of a meeting[6] or documents made available for inspection[7] or information supplied[8] at the meeting, it will suffice if such information is given or documents made available at or before the time when the resolution is supplied for signature. In cases where resolutions are ineffective if passed only as a result of the votes of interested parties,[9] the consent of the members concerned is not needed for a unanimous resolution.

Rights of auditors in relation to written resolutions

6.6 One procedure the legislation requires, which was not envisaged by the Institute of Directors, concerns the rights of auditors. A copy of any proposed written resolution must be sent to the auditors.[10] If it concerns the auditors as auditors, they have seven days in which to say that in their opinion the resolution should be considered by a general or class meeting, as appropriate.[11] A written resolution cannot take effect unless either the auditors do not reply within seven days, or they notify the company that the resolution does not concern them as auditors, or if it does concern them as auditors, that nevertheless no meeting is needed.[12] This procedure seems likely to present a serious impediment to the speedy or easy use of written resolutions, unless the auditors are prepared to give

[1] CA 1985, s 135.
[2] *Re Barry Artists Ltd* [1985] BCLC 283.
[3] Under CA 1985, s 303.
[4] Under CA 1985, s 386 (replaced by ns 391) (CA 1989, s 122).
[5] See CA 1985, ss 304 and 387(2) (replaced by ns 391(4)).
[6] CA 1985, s 95(5).
[7] CA 1985, ss 157(4)(*a*), 164(6), 173(2) and 319(5).
[8] CA 1985, s 337.
[9] CA 1985, ss 164(5) and 173(2).
[10] Ns 381B(1) (CA 1989, s 113(2)).
[11] Ns 381B(2).
[12] Ns 381B(3).

some clearance in advance or otherwise indicate the type of resolutions to which they will automatically consent.

Written resolutions under the articles and doctrine of acquiescence

6.7   The rights of auditors do not apply to written resolutions under the articles and this raises the question whether it will still be possible to agree to written resolutions under the articles. It seems that for a private company the answer is no, because ns 381A and ns 381B are stated to 'have effect notwithstanding any provision of the company's memorandum or articles'.[1] However, the common law doctrine of unanimous acquiescence is unaffected by the new sections.[2] Maybe it will still be possible to sign a document setting out a resolution that makes it clear that it is not a written resolution under ns 381A, but that each member signing will be regarded as acquiescing in the resolution being treated as passed and precluded from alleging that a resolution in that form has not been duly passed.

Elective Resolutions

Scope for using elective resolutions

6.8   An elective resolution is a procedure by which a private company may disapply certain Companies Act requirements. As we have seen, the Institute of Directors envisages that in the long run a large number of such requirements will be capable of being disapplied[3] and the Secretary of State is given power to extend elective resolutions to cover other areas of internal administration or procedure.[4] The idea is that the requirements disapplied are ones which do not affect creditors or other outsiders dealing with the company.

6.9   Thus far, the CA 1989 provides for elective resolutions disapplying Companies Act requirements in five cases:[5]

Authority to issue shares

Under the CA 1985, s 80 before the directors of a company, public or private, issue shares, they must have authority from the shareholders. Such authority under s 80 can last up to a maximum of five years. Under ns 80A, inserted into

---

[1]   Ns 381C(1) (CA 1989, s 113(2)). It is possible that ns 381C(1) merely invalidates any more restrictive provision in a company's articles, but that interpretation would allow companies to ignore the auditor's rights by using written resolutions under their articles.

[2]   Ns 381C(2). The best known example of this doctrine is in the case of *Re Duomatic Ltd* [1969] 2 Ch 365.

[3]   'Deregulation for Small Private Companies', p 4.

[4]   CA 1989, s 117.

[5]   Ns 379A(1) (CA 1989, s 116(2)).

the CA 1985 by the CA 1989, s 115(1), private companies may by elective resolution adopt an alternative whereby authority to issue shares may last indefinitely or for a fixed period, but which can be longer than five years.

Laying accounts before a general meeting

Under the CA 1985, ns 252 inserted by the CA 1989, s 16, a private company may dispense with laying accounts before the general meeting unless required by a member or the auditors to do so.

Annual general meeting

Under CA 1985, ns 366A inserted by the CA 1989, s 115(2), a private company may dispense with holding an annual general meeting unless required to so by a member.

Consent to short notice

Companies Act 1989, s 115(3) allows a private company to reduce the 95 per cent majority needed for consent to short notice under the CA 1985, ss 369(4) or 378(3), but not to less than 90 per cent.[1]

Appointment of auditors

Under the CA 1985, ns 386 inserted by the CA 1989, s 119, a private company may dispense with annual appointment of auditors in which case the auditors in office are automatically deemed to be reappointed.

Procedure

6.10 In order to pass an elective resolution, all the members entitled to attend and vote at meetings of the company must agree.[2] In other respects, the procedure is similar to that for a special resolution. At least twenty-one days' notice in writing must be given of the meeting, stating that an elective resolution is to be proposed and stating the terms of the resolution.[3] The new procedure for written resolutions can, however, be used to pass an elective resolution.[4] When it is passed, an elective resolution must be registered within fifteen days.[5] An elective resolution may be revoked by an ordinary resolution,[6] but that too must be registered.[7] Any private company will be able to pass an elective resolution as

---

[1]   If this is de-regulation one is tempted to wonder what bureaucracy would look like!
[2]   Ns 379A(2) (*b*) (CA 1989, s 116(2)).
[3]   Ns 379A(2) (*a*).
[4]   Ns 381A(6) (CA 1989, s 113(2)).
[5]   Ns 380(4) (*bb*) (CA 1989, s 115(3)).
[6]   Ns 379A(3).
[7]   Ns 380(4) (*bb*).

soon as the legislation is in force. There will be no need for companies to change their articles of association before they can pass elective resolutions.

6.11   At present, a separate elective resolution must be passed in relation to each of the five options outlined above. How long it will be before a fully fledged 'elective regime' is introduced, capable of being adopted by a single elective resolution, is a matter for speculation. What is apparent, but was only to be expected, is that the process which began in 1980 of the Companies Act increasingly differentiating public and private companies is taken a stage further by this legislation. How long it will be before we have a Public Companies Act and a Private Companies Act is an even more interesting matter for speculation.

CHAPTER 7

MISCELLANEOUS CHANGES TO COMPANY LAW

Definition of Subsidiary and Holding Company for Non-accounting Purposes

7.1 The new definitions of parent and subsidiary undertakings which were examined in Chapter 2[1] apply only in relation to accounts, chiefly the preparation of consolidated accounts. The CA 1989, however, also introduces new definitions of 'subsidiary' and 'holding company' which will apply for all non-accounting purposes.[2] Compared with the accounting definitions it will be noticed that these definitions refer only to companies, which in this context includes any body corporate,[3] but does not include unincorporated associations. It will also be noticed that the term holding company is used rather than parent, which should provide a helpful means of avoiding confusion between the two sets of definitions.

7.2. In other respects the new non-accounting definitions mirror ways in which a body could be a subsidiary undertaking of a parent company. Thus, S will be H's subsidiary in four situations. These are where:

(i) H holds a majority of the voting rights in S.[4] This may be contrasted with the previous test of holding a majority of the equity share capital which might or might not have had voting rights attached.

(ii) H is a member of S and controls alone a majority of the voting rights pursuant to an agreement with other shareholders or members.[5]

In both the above definitions the reference to voting rights means the rights conferred on shareholders or members to vote at general meetings of the company on all, or substantially all, matters.[6]

---

[1] See para 2.13, above.
[2] CA 1989, s 144(1). Inevitably this is done by substituting for the old CA 1985, s 736, a new s 736 plus new ss 736A and 736B. There is more justification for a substitution where the provision has the same section number. Even so there is the possibility of confusion – see para 7.4 below.
[3] Ns 736(3) (CA 1989, s 144(1)).
[4] Ns 736(1)(*a*).
[5] Ns 736(1)(*c*).
[6] Ns 736A(2) (CA 1989, s 144(1)).

(iii) H is a member of S and has the right to appoint or remove directors who have a majority of the voting rights at board meetings.[1]

(iv) S is a subsidiary of a company which itself is a subsidiary of H.[2] This is the company law equivalent of the grandchild/grandparent relationship.

7.3   Each of these tests is capable of relatively precise application. The two methods by which a body could be a subsidiary undertaking for accounting purposes which are not included in this definition involve either the exercise of a dominant influence, or the management of parent and subsidiary on a unified basis.[3] These are not included in the definition for non-accounting purposes because they depend too much on an element of judgment about the relationship between the two companies. The tests were incorporated into the accounting definitions because they were important to help control off-balance sheet financing for which definitions that enabled the true substance of a relationship to be identified were necessary. In non-accounting contexts the need is far more for precision and certainty. Nevertheless, in case the new definitions are shown to need amendment the Secretary of State is given power to amend them by regulations.[4]

7.4   One important issue in relation to the new definitions is whether they apply to existing references to 'subsidiary' or 'holding company' within the meaning of the CA 1985, s 736. The position as regards statutes (including subordinate legislation) is that such references are deemed to refer to the new definitions except in so far as an express amendment or saving is made by the CA 1989, Sch 18.[5] As far as existing private deeds or other instruments or documents are concerned there is no presumption that the new definition applies.[6] It will therefore depend on the construction of the particular deed, instrument or document, whether the old or the new definition applies. Although this may seem a rather uncertain state of affairs, the arguments are convincing that this is better than having a presumption that the new definition should apply.[7]

Abolition of Deemed Notice

7.5   Section 142(1) of the CA 1989 inserts ns 711A into the CA 1985, subs (1) of which is as follows:

---

[1]   Nss 736(1)(*b*) and 736A(3) (CA 1989, s 144(1)).
[2]   Ns 736(1).
[3]   Ns 258(2)(*c*), (4) (CA 1989, s 21(1)).
[4]   Ns 736B(1) (CA 1989, s 144(3)).
[5]   CA 1989, s 144(2).
[6]   Ibid, s 144(6).
[7]   See the article by Steven Sugar (1989) 139 NLJ 377.

'A person shall not be taken to have notice of any matter merely because of its being disclosed in any document[1] kept by the registrar of companies (and thus available for inspection) or made available by the company for inspection.'

This, at last, removes[2] a presumption introduced into company law by the House of Lords in *Ernest v Nicholls*.[3] The reasoning behind the presumption given by Lord Wensleydale in the case shows that he was concerned with protecting the large number of shareholders who invested in joint stock companies and who had relatively little control over what the management of the company did. The shareholders could, therefore, put restrictions on the power of the directors in the articles and persons dealing with the company had to take notice of them. As Lord Wensleydale explained: 'If they [the persons dealing with the company] do not choose to acquaint themselves with the powers of the directors, it is their own fault, and if they give credit to any unauthorised person they must be content to look to them only, and not to the company at large.'[4] *Ernest v Nicholls* was decided at a time when unlimited liability was still the norm for shareholders.[5] With the increased use of limited liability, the risk borne by shareholders from unauthorised transactions diminished, but the doctrine of deemed notice lived on, albeit subjected to increasingly severe criticism.[6]

7.6 The abolition of deemed notice arising from documents being kept available for inspection by the Registrar or by the company does not affect the general question of notice arising from failure to make reasonable inquiries.[7] In this context, reasonable inquiries presumably means other than by searching the companies register. In this connection it is worth remembering that ns 35B[8] says that a party to a transaction with a company need make no inquiries as to the memorandum of a company or limitations on the authority of the board of directors. As to what would constitute reasonable inquiries in other situations, the type of transaction and the general antipathy of commercial law towards any doctrine of constructive notice should be borne in mind. The words of Lindley LJ in *Manchester Trust v Furness*[9] are a useful reminder of the principles involved:

---

[1] 'Document' includes any material which contains information: ns 711A(3).
[2] It does not affect the question of notice arising from the registration of charges. See para 7.7, below.
[3] (1857) 6 HL Cas 410.
[4] Ibid, at p 418.
[5] Limited liability had been made generally available in the Limited Liability Act only two years earlier in 1855.
[6] See Goode *Commercial Law* (1982), pp 775–6; Sealy *Company Law and Commercial Reality* (1984) pp 29–31. See also Dr Prentice's Report 'Reform of the Ultra Vires Rule' (1986), pp 21–24 and Professor Diamond's Report 'A Review of Security Interests in Property' (1989), para 24.4.
[7] Ns 711A(2) (CA 1989, s 142(1)).
[8] CA 1989, s 108.
[9] [1895] 2 QB 539, 545. See also Lord Blackburn in *Jones v Gordon* (1877) 2 App Cas 616, 628–9 on the difference between not making reasonable inquiries and turning a blind eye to suspicious circumstances.

'As regards the extension of the equitable doctrines of constructive notice to commercial transactions, the Courts have always set their faces resolutely against it. The equitable doctrines of constructive notice are common enough in dealing with land and estates, with which the Court is familiar; but there have been repeated protests against the introduction into commercial transactions of anything like an extension of those doctrines, and the protest is founded on perfect good sense. In dealing with estates in land title is everything, and it can be leisurely investigated; in commercial transactions possession is everything, and there is no time to investigate title; and if we were to extend the doctrine of constructive notice to commercial transactions we should be doing infinite mischief and paralysing the trade of the country.'

7.7   The abolition of deemed notice by ns 711A(1) is subject to two further exceptions. The first[1] is ns 416[2] under which a person taking a charge over a company's property is presumed to have notice of any matter requiring registration in the charges register and which is disclosed in the register at the time the charge is created. The second[3] is the rule under which registration of certain land charges at Companies House is deemed to constitute actual notice.

Changes Affecting Company Administration

Abolition of the mandatory seal

7.8   The CA 1989, s 130 makes a number of changes to provisions relating to the making of contracts and the execution of documents by companies, the most important of which stem from the fact that in England, Wales and Scotland a company will no longer need to have a common seal.[4] The CA 1989, s 130 substitutes for the existing CA 1985, s 36:

> (i)   ns 36 dealing with company contracts in England and Wales;
> (ii) ns 36A dealing with the execution of documents by companies in England and Wales;
> (iii) ns 36B dealing with the execution of documents by companies in Scotland[5]; and
> (iv) ns 36C which repeats the old s 36(4)[6] provision as to the liability of agents on pre-incorporation contracts and makes clear that it extends to

---

[1]   Ns 711(4)(*a*) (CA 1989, s 141(1)).
[2]   CA 1989, s 102. See paras 5.17–5.18, above.
[3]   Ns 711(4)(*b*).
[4]   CA 1989, Sch 17 makes various amendments consequential on the abolition of mandatory seals.
[5]   The background is explained in 'Report on Requirements of Writing' Scot Law Com No 112, paras 6.41–6.56.
[6]   The wording is substantially identical including the proviso at the end which appears to suggest, in accordance with the First Directive, art 7 on which it is based, that it only makes the agent liable on the contract and does not enable the agent to enforce the contract. The CA 1989 does not contain any provision allowing companies to ratify pre–incorporation contracts. Cf the Companies Bill 1973, cl 6.

the making of deeds in England and Wales and the undertaking of an obligation in Scotland.

7.9   As a formality, under the law of England and Wales, documents are still to be executed by a company by the affixing of its common seal.[1] However, since a company need no longer have a common seal,[2] it is provided that documents executed in the manner set out in ns 36A(4) have effect as if they were sealed. Furthermore, this provision applies even if a company has a common seal but has not used it. New section 36A(4) provides that:

> 'A document signed by a director and the secretary of a company or by two directors of the company, and expressed (in whatever form of words) to be executed by the company has the same effect as if executed under the common seal of the company.'

If a document executed by a company makes clear on its face that it is intended by those making it to be a deed,[3] it has effect upon delivery as a deed.[4] Furthermore, there is a rebuttable presumption that such a document is delivered upon being so executed.[5]

Company's registered office

7.10   The CA 1989, s 136 substitutes ns 287 in the CA 1985. The main effect is to clarify uncertainty regarding when a change in the address of the registered office takes effect. There were three possibilities: (i) the day the company resolved on the change; (ii) the day notification was received at Companies House; or (iii) the day notification was registered by the Registrar. The decision was to opt for the third solution, so the change takes effect on the notice being registered by the Registrar.[6] However, for fourteen days beginning on that date documents may validly be served at the old registered office. It should also be remembered that the company may not be able to rely on a change in the address of its registered office against other parties for fifteen days after the change has been officially notified in the appropriate Gazette.[7] It would therefore be sensible for the Registrar to register the change on the same day that it is officially notified so that the two periods of uncertainty coincide. As regards the duty to keep registers, etc at the registered office or mention the address in correspondence, the company

---

1   Ns 36A(2) (CA 1989, s 130).
2   Ns 36A(3).
3   The Law Commission suggested a form of words such as 'executed as a deed', Law Com No 163, para 2.16.
4   Ns 36A(5).
5   The importance of delivery of a deed is that it fixes the moment at which the deed takes effect. Rebutting the presumption will therefore involve showing that this was not the intention.
6   Ns 287(4) (CA 1989, s 136).
7   CA 1985, ss 42, 711(2).

may decide at what date the change is to take effect provided it is within fourteen days after notice of the change was given to the Registrar.[1]

Company's obligations as to the inspection of registers

7.11   A quite remarkable number of problems have arisen in recent years over the right of members of the company and the general public to search registers kept by the company.[2] The following are some of the questions which have arisen. Should it suffice to allow inspection on a visual display unit or must hard copy be made available? Is it permissible to take notes during a search? Should searchers be entitled to demand copies of parts of the register on a selective basis? Should it be permissible to supply copies in non-legible form? Should the purpose for which an inspection or copy is requested be relevant? Should charges be based on economic cost? Can a single inspection extend over several visits? Does the extent of the exemption under the Data Protection Act 1986, s 34(1) need to be clarified?

7.12   To deal with the problems, the CA 1989, s 143 inserts ns 723A into the CA 1985 enabling the Secretary of State to answer all these questions by regulations. It is expected there will be some consultation before answers are forthcoming. The regulations will also allow for a whole series of anomalies and inconsistencies in the present legislation to be resolved regarding charging for inspection, hours for inspection, right to copies and time within which copies are to be sent. Finally, the use of regulations will enable a whole series of repetitions in the statute book to be removed.

Company annual returns

7.13   The CA 1989, s 139(1) substitutes a new Chapter III into Part XI of the CA 1985[3] dealing with the duty to file and the contents of annual returns. The annual return continues to be a separate document, the filing of which is not linked to delivery of the accounts to the Registrar, and every company, whether public or private, limited or unlimited continues to be liable to make an annual return. There is a change in the method of fixing the date to which the return must be made up. Instead of being made up to a date linked to the date of the annual general meeting, the annual return will in future have to be made up to a date not later than the date which is from time to time the company's 'return

---

[1]   Ns 287(5) (CA 1989, s 136).

[2]   See two Memoranda of the Company Law Committee of the Law Society on 'Inspection and Availability of Information on Company Share and Similar Registers' (1985) and 'The Improper Use of the Right to Inspect Company Share Registers' (1987).

[3]   Thus, the CA 1985, ss 363–365 are replaced by nss 363, 364, 364A and 365. Apart from these changes it is also likely that the annual return will in future be updated on a shuttle basis under which a copy of the previous annual return is sent to the company which indicates any changes that have taken place. See 'A New Approach to the Annual Return' published by the Companies House Executive Agency (June 1989).

date'.[1] A company's return date is the anniversary of: (i) the company's incorporation; or (ii) the date to which the company's previous annual return was made up, provided that return was in accordance with the Act.[2] In future, the annual return will only need to be signed by a director or secretary, instead of by both.[3] It must then be delivered to the Registrar within twenty-eight days of the date to which it is made up.[4]

7.14 There are a considerable number of changes to the contents of the annual return and the Secretary of State is given power to make further changes by regulation.[5] The layout of the legislation is changed so that ns 364 deals with the requirements which are common to all types of company, with or without a share capital and ns 364A deals with additional requirements for companies with a share capital.[6] The new requirements include a statement of the type of company, given by reference to a classification scheme which will be prescribed for this purpose.[7] They also include a statement of the company's principal business activities given by reference to one or more categories used in systems of classifying business activities which will be prescribed for this purpose.[8] In addition, a private company will be required to give the date of birth of its directors[9] and state whether it has elected to dispense with laying accounts and reports before the general meeting or with holding an annual general meeting.[10]

7.15 Among the new requirements for a company with a share capital, it will have to state the total number of issued shares as at the date to which the return is made up and the aggregate nominal value of such shares.[11] Where shares are divided into classes, the nature of each class must be stated with the number and aggregate nominal value of the issued shares in each class.[12]

Other changes to company administration

7.16 The attention of those involved in company administration is also drawn to the various revisions made to the obligation to state the names of directors and the secretary of the company.[13] The CA 1989 also makes a number of changes to

---

1   Ns 363(1) (CA 1989, s 139(1)).
2   Ns 363(1) (*a*), (*b*).
3   Ns 363(2) (*c*).
4   Ns 363(4).
5   Ns 365 (CA 1989, s 139(1)).
6   Previously s 363 and Sch 15 applied to companies with a share capital and s 364 to companies without a share capital. Schedule 15 is repealed and the relevant material incorporated in nss 364 and 364A.
7   Ns 364(1)(*b*), (2) (CA 1989, s 139(1)).
8   Ns 364(1)(*b*), (3).
9   Ns 364(1)(*e*),(*i*).
10   Ns 364(1)(*i*).
11   Ns 364A(2) (CA 1989, s 139(1)).
12   Ns 364A(3).
13   CA 1989, Sch 19, paras 2–7.

the powers of the Registrar of Companies. Sections 125–127 substitute new sections dealing with delivery of documents to the Registrar and the keeping and inspection of company records held by the Registrar. In addition, Sch 19, para 14 substitutes ns 705 in the CA 1985 which gives the Registrar power to change companies' registered numbers. A potential change of great significance is foreshadowed by s 207 of the CA 1989. This authorises the Secretary of State to make regulations enabling the title to securities to be evidenced and transferred without a written instrument. This will enable computerised share transfer schemes to become fully effective and will permit the so-called dematerialisation of shares.[1]

Disclosure of Substantial Shareholdings in Public Companies

7.17   There is another important change which affects the administration of a public company, although it also has wider implications for the company and the public interest in knowing who may be seeking to build a position of influence in a public company. The change is the reduction from 5 per cent to 3 per cent in the figure for the size of shareholding in a public company at which it becomes necessary to notify the company.[2] The time within which such notification must be given is also reduced from five days to two days.[3] Companies must already keep a register of such holdings.[4] They also have the right to require shareholders to state whether they are the beneficial owners of shares registered in their names or to identify who is the beneficial owner[5] and may impose restrictions on shares if their questions are not answered.[6]

7.18   The background to the changes is outlined in a consultative document entitled 'Disclosure of Interests in Shares', published by the DTI in 1988. This highlighted some other problems arising from the Stock Exchange's Admission of Securities to Listing which inhibited companies from applying effective sanctions against shareholders who refused to identify the beneficial owner of shares. Since then changes have been made by the Stock Exchange.[7] These allow listed companies to include in their articles power for disenfranchisement to take place, in the case of larger shareholdings, fourteen days (instead of twenty-eight days)

---

1   For further information about how such a scheme might work, see the helpful consultative paper 'The Dematerialisation of Share Certificates and Share Transfers' published by the DTI in November 1988.

2   CA 1989, s 134(2), amending CA 1985, s 199(2). Transitional arrangements regarding obligations of persons whose interests become notifiable when this provision comes into force are likely to be included in the order bringing the amendment into force.

3   CA 1989, s 134(3), amending CA 1985, ss 202(1) and (4) and 206(8).

4   CA 1985, s 211.

5   Ibid, s 212.

6   Ibid, s 216. Under CA 1989, s 135, the Secretary of State may make regulations relating to orders imposing restrictions on shares regarding: protection of third parties, the circumstances in which restrictions may be relaxed or removed, and interim court orders.

7   See (1989) *Financial Times*, 21 February.

after the failure to identify the beneficial owner. In all cases, listed companies can now include in their articles power to withhold payment of dividends. Companies may also impose some restrictions on the transfer of shares.

7.19   Apart from the changes outlined above, the CA 1989, s 134(5) inserts a ns 210A into the CA 1985 which enables the Secretary of State to amend certain provisions of the CA 1985, Part VI by regulations. The provisions the Secretary of State will be able to amend are the minimum level for disclosure, the time limit for disclosure, the definitions of 'interest' and 'relevant share capital', the exemptions from disclosure and companies' powers of investigation into the ownership of shares. One use that is likely to be made of these powers is to effect any changes needed to implement an EEC Directive on disclosure when a major holding in a listed company is acquired or disposed of.[1] The Directive must be implemented by member states by 1 January 1991, but since the UK requirements are already far stricter than the Directive, the changes are expected to be relatively minor.

Redeemable Shares

7.20   The CA 1989, s 133 inserts a ns 159A into the CA 1985 dealing with the terms and the manner of redemption of redeemable shares. The problem under the old law was that under the CA 1985, s 160(3), the terms and manner of redemption of redeemable shares had to be fixed by the articles of association. It was arguable, therefore, that whenever a company wished to create redeemable shares, a general meeting had to be convened to amend the articles. As well as involving considerable inconvenience and expense, it also inhibited companies from taking advantage of favourable market conditions by preventing them from issuing redeemable shares quickly. Since 1981 it has also appeared highly restrictive when compared with the relative freedom public companies have under the CA 1985, s 166 for making a market purchase of their shares. Under ns 159A, which replaces s 160(3), the time for redemption must either be specified by the articles or, if the articles allow, may be fixed by the directors.[2] In the latter case, however, the time must be fixed before the shares are issued. Any other circumstances in which the shares are to be or may be redeemed must still be specified in the articles.[3] The amount payable on redemption must also either be specified in the articles or determined in accordance with a basis or formula contained in the articles, but the formula must not involve the amount being determined by reference to anyone's discretion.[4] Any other terms and conditions of redemption must be specified in the articles.[5]

[1]   88/627/EEC; OJ 1988 L348/62.
[2]   Ns 159A(2) (CA 1989, s 133).
[3]   Ns 159A(3).
[4]   Ns 159A(4).
[5]   Ns 159A(5).

Shareholder Protection

Conduct affecting members generally may be unfairly prejudicial

7.21 Section 459(1) of the CA 1985 is amended[1] so that it covers conduct which is unfairly prejudicial to the interests 'of its members generally'[2] as well as to the interests of some part of its members. There has been judicial disagreement[3] as well as academic uncertainty[4] about whether the phrase 'some part of the members' prevented cases where all the members were equally prejudiced from coming within the section. Such uncertainty is now removed, but the consequences of this expansion in the jurisdiction remain to be worked out. It seems clear that the alteration will enable shareholders to allege unfair prejudice in respect of matters like excessive 'golden handshakes' or excessive remuneration for directors,[5] consistently restrained dividend policy,[6] or failure to take action in respect of alleged negligence by directors.[7] Many of these involve the courts getting perilously close to sitting in judgment on business decisions which is a role they have traditionally disavowed. It will not be surprising if the courts develop an interpretation of unfair prejudice, which in the end excludes many of the cases where the conduct affects all members equally.

Rule in Houldsworth v City of Glasgow Bank reversed

7.22 Section 131 of the CA 1989 inserts into the CA 1985, ns 111A the effect of which is to reverse a rule laid down by the House of Lords in *Houldsworth v City of Glasgow Bank.*[8] The rule was to the effect that shareholders cannot claim financial compensation from a company in respect of anything to do with holding shares in the company,[9] while remaining as shareholders. In that particular case, the plaintiff had subscribed for shares in the company on the basis of a fraudulent prospectus which concealed the fact that the company was insolvent. As the company had gone into liquidation it was too late for the plaintiff to rescind.[10]

---

[1] CA 1989, Sch 19, para 11. CA 1985, s 460(1)(*b*) is also amended.

[2] The wording resembles that used in the Insolvency Act 1986, s 27 except that, of course, creditors cannot petition under CA 1985, s 459.

[3] See *Re Carrington Viyella plc* (1983) 1 BCC 98, 951 per Vinelott J at 98, 959 and *Re A Company (No 00370 of 1987) ex parte Glossop* [1988] BCLC 570 per Harman J at 574–575; but cf *Re Sam Weller & Sons Ltd* (1989) 5 BCC 810 per Peter Gibson J.

[4] See *Gower's Principles of Modern Company Law* (4th edn) 1979, p 670 and cf 1980 Supplement.

[5] See *Re Carrington Viyella plc* above.

[6] See *Re A Company (No 00370 of 1987) ex parte Glossop* above and *Re Sam Weller & Sons Ltd* above.

[7] See *Pavlides v Jensen* [1956] Ch 565. See also the Jenkins Committee Report (1962) Cmnd 1749 para 207.

[8] (1880) 5 App Cas 317. The initiative for the change came from the Law Society's Company Law Committee.

[9] Shareholders who were creditors of the company could always sue in their capacity as creditors.

[10] *Oakes v Turquand and Harding* (1867) LR 2 HL 325.

The House of Lords held that unless he could and did rescind he was unable to claim damages.

7.23 The precise reason for the rule has never been clear.[1] The City of Glasgow Bank was an unlimited liability company and there is an obvious practical difficulty in allowing shareholders to claim damages from the company in such circumstances. Allowing their claims would add to the liabilities of the company to which they, as shareholders, have to contribute. That increases their loss and thus their claim against the company, which adds to the liabilities of the company, and so on, ad infinitum. But the rule was held to apply in *Re Addlestone Linoleum Co Ltd*,[2] to a shareholder in a limited liability company as well. The justification here may have been a fear that allowing shareholders to claim money from their company involved the risk of payment being made to the shareholders out of capital. The issue of capital maintenance is likely still to be a concern of the courts in any case in which the question of the company paying compensation to a shareholder arises. It is noticeable that when the Financial Services Act 1986, ss 152(1)(*a*) and 168(1)(*a*) gave shareholders the right to financial compensation from the company while remaining shareholders, it was provided that any such compensation was to be disregarded in determining the amount paid up on the shares.[3]

7.24 Despite the uncertain basis of the rule in *Houldsworth v City of Glasgow Bank*, it remains the case that shareholders seeking to enforce the contract in the memorandum and articles have invariably sought injunctions and declarations as their only remedies. Whether shareholders deprived of a vote[4] or a dividend in cash[5] will in future seek financial compensation remains to be seen. It must be remembered that they cannot claim compensation for a decline in the value of their shares arising from a wrong done to the company.[6] The other area where this change may have an impact is in relation to unfair prejudice petitions under the CA 1985, s 459. The court has power under s 461(1) to make such order as it thinks fit and it will be interesting to see how the first petitioners fare who ask for damages under s 459.

Time limit for holding requisitioned extraordinary general meetings

7.25 One of the ways in which shareholders can air their grievances is by requisitioning the directors to call an extraordinary general meeting under the CA

---

[1]   See the discussion between Hornby and Gower (1956) 19 MLR 54, 61 and 185.
[2]   (1887) 37 ChD 191.
[3]   Financial Services Act 1986, ss 152(9) and 168(8).
[4]   *Pender v Lushington* (1877) 6 ChD 70.
[5]   *Wood v Odessa Waterworks Co* (1889) 42 ChD 636.
[6]   *Prudential Assurance Co Ltd v Newman Industries Ltd (No 2)* [1982] Ch 204.

1985, s 368. In *Re Windward Islands Enterprises (UK) Ltd*,[1] the section was held to be defective in that it did not specify a time within which a meeting called by the directors was to take place. This confirmed the view of the Jenkins Committee who, as long ago as 1962,[2] recommended that the directors should be deemed to have failed to convene a meeting if they convened one for more than twenty-eight days ahead. This was included in the Companies Bill 1973, cl 77(2) which never reached the statute book. Now, finally, it has been enacted.[3]

Directors' Contracts

7.26   Apart from the CA 1985, ns 322A, which is discussed in Chapter 4, other changes are made by the CA 1989 affecting directors. These include increasing the financial limits in the provisions governing loans and quasi-loans to directors by the CA 1989, s 138. An exemption from the CA 1985, s 320 (which requires shareholders' approval for substantial property transactions) is also introduced for transactions made on a recognised investment exchange by an independent broker which turn out to be between a company and one of its directors.[4] The CA 1985, s 310(3) is amended[5] to make clear that the section, which otherwise renders void any contract for indemnifying an officer of the company against liability for breach of duty, does not prevent a company from purchasing and maintaining, for any officer or auditor, insurance against any such liability.[6] Finally, although this by no means solely concerns directors, it may be worth pointing out that Company Securities (Insider Dealing) Act 1985, s 8(2) is amended[7] to allow the Secretary of State to consent, on a case by case basis, to other persons bringing prosecutions for insider dealing. It is likely that consent will be given for the Stock Exchange to bring prosecutions as that body is particularly concerned that the number of prima facie cases of insider dealing it discovers is not matched by the number of prosecutions.

Employee Share Ownership Plans

7.27   There are two provisions in the CA 1989 whose common purpose is the promotion of employee share ownership plans. Section 128 empowers the

---

[1]   [1983] BCLC 293.

[2]   Cmnd 1749, para 458.

[3]   CA 1989, Sch 19, para 9. In one case the courts found a way of protecting the minority by treating the directors' failure to call a meeting as unfair prejudice: *McGuinness v Bremner plc* [1988] BCLC 673. This will no longer be necessary.

[4]   CA 1989, Sch 19, para 8.

[5]   CA 1989, s 137(1).

[6]   Any such policy which is effected must be disclosed in the directors' report: CA 1985, Sch 7, para 5A (inserted by CA 1989, s 137(2)).

[7]   CA 1989, s 209.

Secretary of State to make regulations prescribing a model set of articles of association for a partnership company, that is, a company limited by shares whose shares are intended to be held to a substantial extent by or on behalf of its employees. Such companies will be free to adopt the model articles, which will be known as Table G, in whole, or in part as usual.

7.28 Section 132 substitutes a new provision for the CA 1985, s 153(4)(*b*) which exempts the provision of money in accordance with an employees' share scheme from the prohibition on a company giving financial assistance for the purchase of its own shares. The substituted version refers to the provision of 'financial assistance' in place of 'money'. This is because in employee share ownership schemes the assistance the company gives may often take the form of security given to a bank which is lending money to the trustees of the scheme. The other change is a reference to 'for the purposes of an employees' share scheme' instead of 'for the acquisition of fully paid shares in the company or its holding company'. The assistance must be given 'in good faith in the interests of the company'. This is intended to stop an illegitimate use of the power, as for example, buying up shares in the company at inflated prices to help defeat a takeover bid.

Restoring a Company to the Register After Winding Up

7.29 Under the Third Party (Rights Against Insurers) Act 1930, if a company which has insured against liability to third parties becomes insolvent, the company's rights against the insurer are transferred to and vest in the third party to whom the company was liable. The vital importance of this is that it prevents the insurance proceeds from being added to the pool of the debtor company's assets which are distributed *pari passu* among its creditors.[1] Instead, the insurance proceeds bypass the pool and go directly to the third party to provide full compensation or at least as full as the insurance policy provided for.

7.30 The operation of the 1930 Act is subject to a number of requirements being fulfilled. One of these arises from the fact that the Act only transfers to the third party such rights against the insurer as an insured company would have had. As an insured company is only entitled to be indemnified under an insurance policy when the company's liability has been established either by a court judgment, an arbitration award or an agreement between itself and the insurer, it follows that such liability must be established before any rights arise which can be transferred to the third party. In *Bradley v Eagle Star Insurance Co*[2] the plaintiff

---

[1] See *Re Law Guarantee Trust & Accident Society Ltd* [1914] 2 Ch 617 and *Re Harrington Motor Co* [1928] Ch 105, both decided before the 1930 Act was passed.

[2] [1989] 1 All ER 961.

was suffering from a disease which she claimed had been caused by the negligence of her employer. Unfortunately, her employer, who maintained an employer's liability insurance policy with the defendant, had been voluntarily wound up and then dissolved some years before any claim was brought. No liability had therefore been established against her employer and no rights arose therefore against the insurance company which could be transferred to her. Furthermore, since under the CA 1985, s 651 a company which had been dissolved after being wound up can only be restored to the register within two years, it was too late for the plaintiff to take proceedings to restore her employer to the register.

7.31   To deal with this situation the CA 1989, s 141 amends the CA 1985, s 651 by extending the period for declaring void a dissolution of a company after winding up. The extension only applies for the purposes of bringing proceedings against the company in respect of death or personal injuries.[1] The provision came into force on 16 November 1989 (on the CA 1989 receiving royal assent) and is retrospective to the extent that it applies to companies dissolved in the twenty years before that date.[2]

1   CA 1985, ns 651(5).
2   CA 1989, s 140(4).

CHAPTER 8

INVESTIGATIONS AND POWERS TO OBTAIN INFORMATION

Introduction

8.1 Part III of the CA 1989 (ie ss 55–91) makes a number of changes to the powers of investigation of the DTI[1] under the CA 1985, the Financial Services Act 1986 and the Insurance Companies Act 1982.[2] Some of the changes represent new substantive powers of investigation, while others relate to the conduct of investigations and are more procedural in character. There are also a considerable number of drafting amendments, some of which are consequential on changes introduced elsewhere. In this chapter it is intended to concentrate on the more important substantive and procedural changes.

Power to Assist Overseas Regulatory Authorities

8.2 The increasing freedom to trade across frontiers in the European Community and the globalisation of securities markets mean that co-operation between regulatory authorities in different countries becomes ever more important. Probably the most important of the new powers is a power under the CA 1989, s 82 for the Secretary of State to assist an overseas regulatory authority which has asked for help in connection with inquiries it is carrying out. The Secretary of State may exercise, or appoint others to exercise, the powers set out in s 83. Broadly, these give inspectors or competent authorities powers similar to those they would have in a domestic investigation. Under s 82(3), the Secretary of State must be satisfied that the assistance requested by the overseas regulatory authority is for the purposes of its regulatory functions. Then, in deciding whether to exercise the powers there are various factors, listed in s 82(4), which the Secretary of State may take into account, including whether corresponding assistance would be given by the requesting authority and whether it relates to a breach of a law that has no close parallel in the UK, or asserts a jurisdiction not recognised by the UK.

---

[1] The changes followed an internal review of the DTI's investigation powers and procedures, the results of which were announced on 11 May 1988. The DTI publishes a useful booklet entitled *Investigations – How They Work.*
[2] CA 1989, Part III is expected to come into force in March 1990.

New Substantive Powers Relating to Domestic Investigations

8.3   The CA 1989, s 55 introduces a new power for inspectors to be appointed under the CA 1985, s 432(2) on the basis that any report by the inspectors would not be available for publication. Broadly, s 432(2) gives the Secretary of State discretion to appoint inspectors if it appears to him there has been any dishonesty, misfeasance or misconduct. This new power will be used when the prime purpose of the appointment is to consider the case for prosecution or regulatory action and it would be inappropriate to publish the report.

8.4   New powers[1] are introduced enabling the Secretary of State to halt investigations where evidence of criminal behaviour has been found and the matter can be more appropriately handled by, for example, the Serious Fraud Office or, in Scotland, through the Lord Advocate. There is also a new power to terminate insider dealing investigations when no further purpose would be served, or to limit or extend the duration of such investigations,[2] or to confine the investigation to particular matters (but not to extend it).[3] When the Secretary of State is required by members of a company under the CA 1985, s 442(3) to investigate the ownership of a company, he will in future be able to do so using the powers conferred on him under s 444, instead of appointing inspectors.[4] The power of the Secretary of State to bring civil proceedings on the company's behalf is extended to cover reports made or information obtained under any provision of the CA 1985, Part XIV.[5]

Powers to Enter and Search Premises

8.5   The CA 1989, s 64 substitutes a ns 448 into the CA 1985, governing entry and search of premises.[6] The main changes are as follows. First, the power to obtain a warrant is extended to cover any section in Part XIV of the CA 1985, not just
s 447.[7] Secondly, there is a new power to obtain a warrant in relation to documents which have not been requested, but which the inspectors fear may be

---

[1]   CA 1985, s 437, as amended by CA 1989, s 57 and Financial Services Act 1986, s 94, as amended by CA 1989, s 72(3).

[2]   Financial Services Act 1986, s 177, as amended by CA 1989, s 74(2).

[3]   Financial Services Act 1986, s 177, as amended by CA 1989, s 74(3).

[4]   CA 1985, s 442, as amended by CA 1989, s 62. Applicants for investigation under CA 1985, s 442(3) can now be made liable to contribute to the cost of the investigation in the same way as applicants for investigations under other sections: CA 1985, s 439, as amended by CA 1989, s 59(5).

[5]   CA 1985, s 438, as amended by CA 1989, s 58.

[6]   See similar amendments to the Financial Services Act 1986, s 199, by CA 1989, s 76 and to the Insurance Companies Act 1986, s 44A, by CA 1989, s 77(3).

[7]   Ns 448(1).

removed, hidden, tampered with or destroyed.[1] Thirdly, the warrant will in future authorise the taking of copies of documents and requiring persons named in the warrant to explain the document, or to state where documents may be found.[2] Wherever appropriate in the legislation the term 'document' is now used[3] and is defined in an all-embracing way so as to include information held in a non-legible form.

Bankers' Privilege from Disclosure

8.6 The rules relating to a bankers' privilege from disclosure are revised.[4] Under the new rules a banker is not obliged to disclose information or produce documents in respect of which he owes an obligation of confidence by virtue of carrying on the business of banking unless: (i) in the case of an investigation under the CA 1985 the person to whom the obligation of confidence is owed is the company under investigation; (ii) the person to whom the obligation of confidence is owed consents; or (iii) the Secretary of State authorises the disclosure.

---

[1]   Ns 448(2) (CA 1989, s 64).
[2]   Ns 448(3)(*c*),(*d*).
[3]   See CA 1989, ss 56(2),(5), 63(3),(7),(8), 64(1), 66(3), 77(2) and 77(6).
[4]   CA 1985, s 452, amended by CA 1989, s 69(2), (3), Financial Services Act 1986, ss 94, 105(7), 106(2A) and 177(8), as amended by CA 1989, ss 72(2), 73(2),(5) and 74(4) respectively.

CHAPTER 9

MERGERS

Introduction

9.1 The CA 1989, Part VI (ie ss 146–153) and Sch 20[1] contain provisions making a number of amendments to the mergers legislation in the Fair Trading Act 1973 (FTA 1973). Many of the changes were foreshadowed in a Blue Paper (Mergers Policy) published by the DTI in March 1988. The major concern of the Government, as indicated in Mergers Policy, was that the system for consideration of mergers should operate with more flexibility and speed.[2] The introduction of a pre-notification clearance procedure and provision for the acceptance of undertakings in place of a reference to the Monopolies and Mergers Commission (MMC) reflect this concern. In addition, the minimum time limit of three months for MMC reports to be produced is removed.[3]

9.2 Other changes, outlined in Mergers Policy[4] have recently been introduced by delegated legislation. The minimum size of an MMC panel considering a merger reference has been reduced from five to three[5] and the maximum number of regular members of the entire MMC has been increased from thirty-two to fifty.[6] One other change foreshadowed in Mergers Policy[7] and implemented by the CA 1989, s 152, is that the Secretary of State is enabled to make regulations prescribing fees to be charged in connection with the exercise by the Secretary of State, the Director General of Fair Trading (DGFT) and the MMC of their functions under the FTA 1973, Part V. It is likely that these will be charged in relation to any merger qualifying to be referred to the MMC, whether or not it is referred,[8] and will be calculated by reference to the value of assets involved.[9]

9.3 The changes made by the CA 1989 do not affect any general questions of merger policy.[10] The discretion of the Secretary of State to refer mergers and the

---

[1] Ss 147-150 and parts of Sch 20 came into force on royal assent: CA 1989, s 215(1). The remainder are expected to be brought into force in January 1990.
[2] 'Mergers Policy', paras 3.1 and 4.1.
[3] CA 1989, Sch 20, para 2(1) amending the FTA 1973, s 60.
[4] 'Mergers Policy', paras 5.10–5.11.
[5] Monopolies and Mergers Commission (Performance of Functions) Order, SI 1989, No 122.
[6] Monopolies and Mergers Commission (Increase in Membership) Order, SI 1989, No 1240.
[7] 'Mergers Policy', para 5.14.
[8] CA 1989, s 152(3).
[9] Ibid, s 152(4)(*c*). A different measure is suggested as regards newspaper mergers.
[10] See Mergers Policy, Chaps I and II.

criteria considered by the DGFT and the MMC remain unaltered, although the DGFT is formally placed under the same statutory duty of consultation[1] as the MMC.[2] The burden of proof likewise remains on those who wish to stop a merger to show that it is contrary to the public interest. The alternative approach of requiring all mergers above a certain size to be shown to be in the public interest has not been adopted. Government policy towards mergers also remains unchanged, so that mergers will continue to be referred to the MMC, principally because of their effects on competition.[3] As expected, the provisions in the CA 1989 take no account of the draft EEC Mergers Regulation[4] currently still under discussion in Brussels. Further changes in the law may be necessary when the Regulation is issued, besides which there are likely to be changes in other areas of competition law resulting from the White Paper on 'Opening Markets: New Policy on Restrictive Practices'[5] published in July 1989.

Pre-notification of Mergers[6]

9.4   The CA 1989, s 146 inserts into the FTA 1973, ss 75A–75F. These sections introduce a system for voluntary pre-notification of mergers to the Office of Fair Trading (OFT), the incentive for which is that if the merger is not referred to the MMC within a certain period of time, it will be exempt from being subsequently referred. Until now UK law has contained no express provision for prior notification of mergers to the OFT. Parties to a merger in practice often do inform the OFT, frequently in order to obtain clearance for the merger before it is completed. However, because the vast majority of mergers raise no competition issues justifying reference to the MMC, the Government felt it unnecessary to introduce a compulsory requirement that mergers be notified in advance.

Procedure

9.5   For parties who wish to take advantage of pre-notification, the procedure will be for them to give notice (a 'merger notice') to the OFT.[7] The notice will have to be in the prescribed form and give various pieces of information about the parties and their businesses.[8] The precise information required will be laid down by regulations,[9] but it will include a statement that the proposal has been made

[1]   FTA 1973, s 76(2), inserted by CA 1989, Sch 20, para 11.
[2]   FTA 1973, s 81.
[3]   See 'Mergers Policy', Chap II and Appendices B and C.
[4]   OJ 1989, c 22/ 14.
[5]   Cm 727.
[6]   See 'Mergers Policy', Chap III.
[7]   FTA 1973, s 75A(1) (CA 1989, s 146).
[8]   Ibid, s 75A(2). See 'Mergers Policy', para 3.13.
[9]   Ibid, s 75D (CA 1989, s 146).

public so that third parties have an opportunity to register objections. The DGFT must take steps to notify parties likely to be affected by the proposed merger of the pre-notification merger notice and its meaning.[1] The DGFT can request further information from the parties and can reject the merger notice altogether if he suspects any information is false or misleading, that it is not proposed to carry out the merger, or if any required information is not supplied.[2]

9.6 After the merger notice is served and any fee paid, the DGFT and the Secretary of State then have four weeks[3] in which to consider the proposal and for the Secretary of State to decide whether to refer the matter to the MMC. The four weeks can be extended by the DGFT (and must be if so requested by the Secretary of State), but only twice. The first extension will be for two weeks and the second, if needed, will be for a further three,[4] but there can be no further extensions after that. If the matter has not been referred before the period has expired then, subject to certain exceptions, no reference can subsequently be made of that merger.[5] The first exception covers the situation where the Secretary of State is seeking undertakings in place of referring a merger to the MMC.[6] Once the DGFT has informed the person who gave the merger notice of this, time ceases to run until the DGFT gives notice that undertakings are no longer being sought and two further weeks have elapsed. The other exceptions, listed in s 75C, cover situations such as inadequate or false information having been supplied or a change of circumstances, including giving effect to the proposed merger during the pre-notification period, or, conversely, failing to carry it out within the following six months.

9.7 If the Secretary of State wishes to refer a pre-notified merger he must therefore decide to do so within a maximum of nine weeks from the service of the merger notice and payment of fee. To cover the possibility that the advice of the DGFT may not have been received by then, the Secretary of State is authorised, during the ninth week of such period, to make a reference to the MMC without considering the advice of the DGFT.[7] This provision is necessary because, although the Secretary of State has no legal obligation to follow the advice of the DGFT, if a reference to the MMC were made without such advice even being received or considered, it would be open to challenge.[8]

1   Ibid, s 75B(1) (CA 1989, s 146).
2   Ibid, s 75B(7).
3   Ibid, s 75B(2),(9). More precisely the period is twenty working days.
4   Ibid, s 75B(3).
5   Ibid, s 75A(3).
6   Ibid, s 75B(5).
7   Ibid, s 75B(8).
8   HC Committee, cols 566–568.

Undertakings as an Alternative to Merger Reference[1]

9.8 The CA 1989, s 147 inserts ss 75G–75K into the FTA 1973. These sections introduce a statutory power for the Secretary of State to accept undertakings from the parties to divest part of a merged business as an alternative to his referring the merger to the MMC. Although on occasions in the past the Secretary of State has accepted such undertakings, it is doubtful whether they were enforceable other than by threatening to refer the merger to the MMC if they were broken. Until now the Secretary of State has only had power to accept legally binding obligations after the MMC has reported against a merger.

Procedure

9.9 Under the new legislation the procedure is that the parties discuss the matter with the OFT,[2] but it is the Secretary of State who finally decides whether or not to accept the undertakings.[3] He can do so if he could refer the merger to the MMC, the DGFT has recommended such a reference specifying the effects adverse to the public interest the merger may cause, the undertakings comply with s 75G(2) and (3), and the undertakings are to take specific action which the Secretary of State considers appropriate to remedy or prevent the adverse effects.[3] The specific action must include, under s 75G(2), provision to divest part of a merged business[4] and may include, under s 75G(3), various ancillary provisions.

Publicity

9.10 In order to promote equality of access to information in securities markets and discourage insider dealing[5] there is provision for the undertakings, and the advice of the DGFT specifying the adverse effects, to be published.[6] This will also apply in future to undertakings given after an MMC report.[7] The provisions

---

[1] See 'Mergers Policy', Chap IV.
[2] It will be possible to seek confidential guidance both about whether a possible merger is likely to be referred and whether an appropriate undertaking might avoid a reference: 'Mergers Policy', para 4.9.
[3] FTA 1973, s 75G(1) (CA 1989, s 147).
[4] So far as possible the divestment must take place before clearance can be given and normally all divestment must have been carried out before the merger takes place: 'Mergers Policy', paras 4.5–4.6.
[5] See 'Mergers Policy', para 4.8.
[6] FTA 1973, s 75H(1). Before then the fact that the Secretary of State was seeking undertakings would have been published with enough information to enable third parties to know what area any undertakings cover and to express a view on them: HC Committee, col 570.
[7] FTA 1973, s 88(2A), inserted by CA 1989, Sch 20, para 14(2).

for prejudicial material[1] to be excluded from reports of the MMC[2] is extended to apply to advice by the DGFT[3] and there is an exemption from publishing such material in either MMC reports[4] or the DGFT's advice.[5] In order to cut the time between an MMC report being delivered to the Secretary of State and its publication, the MMC will in future pass on to the DTI the parties' own requests for excisions from the published report.[6]

Enforcement of undertakings

9.11 The DGFT is placed under a duty to keep under review the parties' observance of their undertakings and to advise the Secretary of State of any matters relating to them.[7] If the undertakings are broken, the Secretary of State may exercise various powers[8] including direct enforcement of the undertakings. In addition, the CA 1989, s 148 inserts a new s 93A into the FTA 1973 which allows any person to bring civil proceedings in respect of a failure to fulfil undertakings given under the FTA 1973, s 75G (in lieu of a reference to the MMC), s 88 (following a report of the MMC) or under ss 4 or 9 of the Competition Act 1980. The effect of s 93A is to treat such undertakings as if they were covered by the FTA 1973, s 90. That would bring such undertakings within the scope of the existing FTA 1973, s 93. There are, however, doubts about the scope of s 93(2). It is worded so as not to take away any rights rather than confer them. It may also be confined to actions for injunctions, although it seems possible that only the Crown is confined to bringing proceedings for an injunction.[9] In contrast, s 93A confers the right to bring civil proceedings, thus creating a cause of action which presumably can include a claim for damages. Section 93A confers this right on 'any person', the interpretation of which may give rise to problems. It will no doubt cover a competitor injured by a failure to abide by undertakings, but will it allow a minority shareholder to enforce an undertaking given by another shareholder to reduce their holding in the company, and in the meantime not to cast more than a certain number of votes?[10]

---

1   FTA 1973, s 75H(4) (CA 1989, s 147).
2   Ibid, s 82(1).
3   Ibid, s 75H(2).
4   Ibid, s 83(3A), inserted by CA 1989, Sch 20, para 12.
5   Ibid, s 75H(3).
6   'Mergers Policy', para 5.12.
7   FTA 1973, s 75J (CA 1989, s 147).
8   Ibid, s 75K(2) (CA 1989, s 147).
9   See Whish *Competition Law*, 2nd edn (1989), p 90.
10 The problem that was left unresolved in *Re Carrington Viyella plc* (1983) 1 BCC 98, 951, see especially 98, 956–98, 958.

Temporary Restrictions on Share Dealing

9.12   Where a reference is made to the MMC before a merger, any further share buying by parties involved in the transaction in companies covered by the reference is liable to prejudice the outcome of the MMC's inquiry. In the past, further share buying was prevented by an order made after the reference had been announced. Following a case in which the gap between the announcement of the reference and the making of the order banning share purchases was used by a bidder to increase its holding in the target, the law has been strengthened. The CA 1989, s 149 amends the FTA 1973, s 75 by inserting new sub-sections (4A)–(4M) so as to impose an automatic ban on share dealing once a reference to the MMC is made.[1] The prohibition is subject to exceptions with the consent of the Secretary of State.[2] It is possible that such consent will be given up to a level which will not prejudice the outcome of the MMC inquiry,[3] but any consent must be published in order to prevent the creation of a false market.[4] The persons who are prohibited from dealing are identified in the FTA 1973, s 75(4A) and the extent of extra-territorial application is covered by s 75(4M).[5] The period of the prohibition is from the making of the reference until the occurrence of one of the events listed in s 75(4B).

Obtaining Control by Stages

9.13   The Secretary of State normally has six months from the date of a merger in which to refer it to the MMC.[6] Where a merger comes about in stages it can be difficult to judge when the crucial step occurred that led to two enterprises ceasing to be distinct. To avoid the risk that a merger might be referred only to discover that the crucial step had occurred more than six months before, the FTA 1973, s 66 allows the Secretary of State[7] to treat a series of events taking place within a two-year period as if they all occurred on the date of the latest of them. Section 66, however, is limited to an acquisition in stages from one person, and where each stage creates a distinct addition to the degree of control. So the CA 1989, s 150(1) inserts a new s 66A[8] into the FTA 1973. Under this section, a gradual acquisition of control, such as through a series of share acquisitions, can

---

[1]   FTA 1973, s 75(4A) (CA 1989, s 149).
[2]   A general consent issued on 24 November 1989 allows acquisition by one company of shares in companies with which it is interconnected under the FTA 1973, s 137(5).
[3]   HL Committee, col 1204 (2 March 1989).
[4]   FTA 1973, s 75(4C).
[5]   Cf FTA 1973, s 90(3).
[6]   FTA 1973, s 64(4).
[7]   FTA 1973, s 66 is amended by CA 1989, Sch 20, para 4 to apply to the MMC as well as the Secretary of State. This is because the MMC also has to decide whether a merger qualifying for investigation has occurred or is proposed.
[8]   FTA 1973, s 66A is made to apply to s 75 as well so that it applies to prospective mergers as well as those which have occurred: CA 1989, Sch 20, para 9.

be treated by the Secretary of State or MMC as having occurred simultaneously, on the date on which the latest of them occurred, regardless of the number of stages or the number of sources of the acquisitions.[1]

Consequences of Supplying False or Misleading Information

9.14 The CA 1989, s 151 inserts a new s 93B into the FTA 1973 as part of a strengthening and rationalisation of certain criminal offences under the FTA 1973. Two previous offences of supplying false or misleading information to the MMC are replaced[2] by a new offence of knowingly or recklessly supplying information to the Secretary of State, the DGFT or the MMC which is false or misleading in a material particular.[3] It is also made an offence knowingly or recklessly to give false or misleading information to a person who is known to be going to supply that information to the Secretary of State, the DGFT or the MMC.[4]

---

[1]   FTA 1973, s 75C(2) and (3) (CA 1989, s 146) are designed to deal with the problem where one of the stages was part of a series of events which, taken together, led to a merger situation being pre-notified but not referred to the MMC and a further stage has now occurred.

[2]   FTA 1973, s 46(3) is repealed by CA 1989, Sch 20, para 1 and FTA 1973, s 85(6)(*b*) is repealed by CA 1989, Sch 20, para 13(2).

[3]   FTA 1973, s 93B(1) (CA 1989, s 151). For circumstances in which allegations were made of behaviour which might in future fall within this section, see *Lonrho plc v Secretary of State for Trade and Industry* [1989] 2 All ER 609. See also *Lonrho plc v Fayed* [1989] 2 All ER 65.

[4]   FTA 1973, s 93B(2).

CHAPTER 10

AMENDMENTS TO THE FINANCIAL SERVICES ACT

Introduction

10.1 The CA 1989, Part VIII (ie ss 192–206) and Sch 23[1] make a number of changes to the operation of the regime set up under the Financial Services Act 1986 (FSA 1986). The background to the changes was outlined in a DTI consultative document entitled 'Possible Changes to the Financial Services Act 1986'. There are also useful publications from the Securities and Investments Board (SIB) entitled 'A Wider Role for SIB's Principles of Conduct' and 'Regulation of the Conduct of Investment Business'. The main changes consist of reducing the scope of civil liability for breach of the rules and regulations, introducing new forms of regulation and changes to the criteria for recognition by the SIB.

Restriction on Civil Liability for Breach of Rules

10.2 The CA 1989, s 193(1) inserts a new s 62A into the FSA 1986, the effect of which is to restrict actions under s 62 to private investors.[2] Under the FSA 1986, s 62, in addition to any common law liability in tort or for breach of contract, any breach of rules relating to the conduct of investment business (other than financial resources) of the SIB, SROs or RPBs may be actionable as if it constituted a breach of statutory duty. At least as far as SROs and RPBs are concerned, this constituted a novel action in that their rules are not statutory at all, but a matter of private contract between the organisation and its members. So it is not an action for breach of statutory duty, but an action 'subject to the defences and other incidents applying to actions for breach of statutory duty'. The liability also extends to contravention of: (i) advertising rules made under the FSA 1986, s 58(3); (ii) employment of disqualified persons in investment business contrary to the FSA 1986, s 59; (iii) prohibitions or requirements imposed under

---

[1]   These provisions are expected to come into force in early to mid 1990.
[2]   CA 1989, s 193(3) inserts into the FSA 1986, Sch 11 a new para 22A making equivalent provision to s 62A for friendly societies.

enforcement measures in the FSA 1986, ss 65–68;[1] and (iv) requirements to supply information.[2]

10.3   The potential for making claims under s 62 was felt to tilt the balance too far in favour of the complainant. To remedy this, s 62A restricts actions under s 62 to private investors, except in circumstances specified in regulations made by the Secretary of State. The term 'private investor' will also be defined in regulations.[3] It may not be an easy distinction to draw. As was pointed out in the debates on the Bill,[4] an investor in a unit trust is a private investor; the fund managers of a unit trust are professionals. But what of individuals whose affairs are handled by professional brokers and whose brokers invest in the unit trust on their behalf? Presumably the test will depend on whether the principal is a private investor.

Changes to the Forms of Regulation

10.4   Although there is obvious necessity for SROs and RPBs to have different rules to cover the different circumstances in which they operate, the changes in the CA 1989 are based on the assumption that there is scope for a greater alignment of the rules of the various organisations. The aim is to achieve this in such a way that preserves the flexibility of the system of regulation, while reducing as far as possible the risk that diversity may create uncertainty and add to the burdens of business. The changes introduce three new forms of regulation: (i) statements of principle promulgated by SIB; (ii) designated rules and; (iii) codes of practice.

Statements of principle

10.5   Under the FSA 1986, s 47A[5] the SIB may issue statements of principle with respect to conduct and financial standing expected of persons engaged in investment business which will apply directly to all authorised persons, including members of SROs and persons certified by RPBs. At first, the power will be used to issue broadly expressed statements which briefly and clearly establish certain fundamental requirements that everyone engaged in investment business must satisfy. Breach of a statement of principle will not give rise to civil action, but can result in disciplinary proceedings.[6] Under the FSA 1986, s 47B, the body responsible for regulating an authorised person may waive or modify statements

---

[1]   FSA 1986, s 71.
[2]   Ibid, s 104(4).
[3]   FSA 1986, s 62A(2) (CA 1989, s 193).
[4]   HL Committee, cols 1307–1309 (6 March 1989).
[5]   CA 1989, s 192.
[6]   FSA 1986, s 47A(3).

of principle as they apply to that person. This is similar to the power that the SIB, SROs and RPBs already have to alter the requirements of rules.[1]

Designated rules

10.6   The FSA 1986, s 63A[2] allows the SIB to designate certain rules made under Part I, Chapter V of the FSA 1986, the effect being that those rules will then apply directly to members of SROs as if they were rules of the SRO concerned.[3] There will thus be a common core of rules which will help to prevent difficulties that arose in the past where persons were members of more than one SRO and had to comply with different rules, sometimes depending on which client they were dealing with. The designated rules will not apply to RPBs and their members. RPBs have many general rules which also cover investment business and to apply designated rules to them would result in unnecessary duplication at best, and confusion at worst. However, RPBs will continue to be required to achieve investor protection of the same standard as that achieved by SROs. This is because the recognition criteria applied by the SIB will be identical for SROs and RPBs.[4] Furthermore, if consistency of rules was important for adequate investor protection, the SIB could no doubt persuade an RPB to comply, if necessary by applying for a compliance order under the FSA 1986, s 12.

Codes of practice

10.7   Under the FSA 1986, s 63C,[5] the SIB is authorised to issue codes of practice relating to any matter which is covered by a statement of principle, or by rules or regulations made under Part I, Chapter V of the FSA 1986. The SIB needs an explicit power to do this, because its rules, etc are made under statutory power and without explicit authority it could not issue a code of this sort. SROs make rules under their own constitutions and it is open to them to incorporate codes of practice which are not rules, but give guidance as to the interpretation of rules. Codes of practice are not legally binding, but will have evidential value in determining whether an authorised person has complied with any applicable principle or rule.[6] Codes of practice which amplify statements of principle and designated rules will apply directly to members of SROs. In cases where designated rules have been modified by the SRO's own rules,[7] the SIB may restrict the application of its codes of practice.[8]

---

[1]   FSA 1986, s 50.
[2]   CA 1989, s 194.
[3]   The SIB will have power to modify the application of designated rules in relation to an SRO (FSA 1986, s 63A(1)) and the SRO likewise in particular cases (FSA 1986, s 63B).
[4]   CA 1989, s 203. See para 10.8 below.
[5]   Ibid, s 195.
[6]   FSA 1986, s 63C(3).
[7]   Ibid, s 63A(2).
[8]   Ibid, s 63C(4).

Changes to Criteria for Recognition of SROs and RPBs

Adequacy of investor protection

10.8   The CA 1989, ss 203 and 204 amend the requirements for recognition of SROs[1] and RPBs.[2] The old test had required that the rules of SROs or RPBs afford protection to investors at least equivalent to that afforded for the same kinds of investment business by rules and regulations made by the SIB under the FSA 1986, Part I, Chap V. This had been intended as a flexible test, but had been interpreted to a greater or lesser degree as requiring slavish adherence to the SIB rules. The new rules make two main changes. First,[3] the statements of principle, the designated rules and any codes of practice to which members are subject are considered, along with the organisation's own rules, in assessing the level of protection afforded by the organisation's arrangements. Secondly,[4] it is made clear that it is the effect of the rules, etc that is to be taken into account rather than the mere form. This is achieved by changing from 'equivalence', linked to the SIB rules, to 'adequacy', having regard to the nature of the investment business of members of the organisation, the kinds of investors and the effectiveness of the organisation's arrangements for securing compliance. In other words, 'adequacy' takes account of the fact that the appropriate level of investor protection may vary according to the kind of business and investors involved and also takes account, not just of the form of rules, but the vigour with which they are enforced. For a time, SROs and RPBs will be able to use either the old equivalence basis or the new adequacy model on which to base their rules, but eventually it is envisaged that 'adequacy' will become the basis for assessing the rules of all SROs and RPBs.[5]

Costs of compliance

10.9   The rule books of SROs have also been criticised on the ground that they imposed rules without considering the cost of compliance with the rules and comparing this with the benefits to be achieved. To meet this criticism, SROs, RPBs and the SIB must in future have satisfactory arrangements for taking account, in framing their rules, etc of the cost of compliance with those rules.[6] It is also provided that the SIB, in determining whether the requirements for recognition of an SRO or RPB are met, shall take into account the effect of any other controls to which members of the organisation or body are subject.[7]

---

[1]   See FSA 1986, Sch 2.
[2]   Ibid, Sch 3.
[3]   Ibid, Sch 2(1) and Sch 3(1). (CA 1989, s 203).
[4]   Ibid, Sch 2(2) and Sch 3(2).
[5]   CA 1989, s 203(3).
[6]   CA 1989, s 204.
[7]   FSA 1986, s 128A (CA 1989, s 196).

Recognised investment exchanges

10.10 Finally, a new para 6 is added to the FSA 1986, Sch 4 clarifying the criteria for recognition of an investment exchange.[1] The purpose of para $6(1)^2$ is to make clear that the Sch 4 requirement, that an exchange should restrict dealing to investments in which there is a proper market, does not prevent an exchange allowing dealings in things that are not within the definition of investment. Paragraph 6(2) is intended[3] to make clear that 'ensuring the performance of transactions' does not mean that the exchange is required to guarantee completion of the transaction in the event of default. For satisfactory investor protection, the exchange's default procedures must deal effectively with a member's contracts with his investor clients, as well as his contracts with other members of the exchange. The latter will be on the exchange, the former may not. The wording is restricted to transactions which are on the exchange. The main concern in the case of transactions which might not be on the exchange are 'back to back' transactions, but these are dealt with in the CA 1989, Part VII.

Relations between Regulatory Authorities

10.11 Improved co-operation between regulators at both a domestic and international level is a feature of several provisions in the CA 1989.[4] Markets are becoming increasingly international and multidisciplinary. Regulators need to co-operate to do their jobs effectively. At the same time there is a danger that firms operating in more than one business, market or country may be subject to excessive regulation. The FSA 1986, s 128B allows the SIB to rely on action taken by other regulatory authorities, and s $128C^5$ authorises the Secretary of State to exercise disciplinary or intervention powers at the request of or for the purpose of assisting, an overseas regulatory authority. Also in this connection, the CA 1989, s 201 substitutes a new FSA 1986, s 192 giving the Secretary of State revised powers to direct authorities to take or desist from action in order to secure compliance with international obligations.[6]

Changes affecting Offers of Shares and Debentures

10.12 A number of relatively minor changes are made to the FSA provisions

---

[1] CA 1989, s 205. NB: the additional requirements for recognition of investment exchanges and clearing houses in the CA 1989, s 156 and Sch 21.
[2] HC Committee, cols 591–592.
[3] HL Committee, col 1312 (6 March 1989).
[4] See para 8.
[5] These provisions are set out in CA 1989, s 196.
[6] The substantive change is that recognised investment exchanges and recognised clearing houses are now included because of their new functions under the CA 1989, Part VII.

governing offers of shares or debentures. The CA 1989, s 202[1] amends the FSA 1986, s 195, which exempts certain offers of debentures from being offers to the public and thus means they can be offered without issuing a prospectus. The old exemption applied to sterling commercial paper repayable within one year. The 1989 Budget included proposals to unify the sterling commercial paper market with that for short term corporate bonds, which are repayable within five years of issue. Accordingly, five years is substituted for one year.

10.13   The CA 1989, s 198 inserts a new FSA 1986, s 160A. This rewrites the exemption-making power previously in the FSA 1986, s 160(6)–(9) (and which applies only to s 160), so that it applies to both ss 159 and 160. One of the main purposes of this change is to ensure that draft prospectuses shown to underwriters can continue to be exempt from registration. The CA 1989, s 199 substitutes new provisions for the FSA 1986, s 170(2)–(4A). This rewrites the exemption-making power under s 170 expanding it slightly so that it corresponds to that in s 160A. According to a Government spokesman this allows for an exemption for companies limited by guarantee that they had possessed under the CA 1985, s 81.[2] Finally, the CA 1989, s 197 amends the FSA 1986, ss 150(6) and 154(5) to make clear that not incurring liability includes not being liable to any civil remedy or to rescission or repudiation of any agreement.

[1]   This provision came into force on the Act receiving royal assent: CA 1989, s 215(1)(*c*).
[2]   HC Committee, cols 690–691.

CHAPTER 11

INSOLVENCY AND FINANCIAL MARKETS

11.1 It is a common feature of the rules of investment exchanges that they include provision for the in-house clearance of debts and liabilities and for dealing with the rights and liabilities of members *inter se* when a member defaults. The validity of such rules in relation to the general insolvency law has been in doubt since the House of Lords' decision in *British Eagle International Airlines Ltd v Cie Nationale Air France.*[1] One of the fundamental principles of insolvency law is that creditors of the same rank share the debtor's assets *pari passu* so that, if there is insufficient to pay them all in full, their claims all abate proportionately. The principle came to be expressed in a rule (known as 'the rule in *ex parte Mackay'*[2] after the bankruptcy case in which it was laid down) that declared void any contractual arrangement designed to operate on insolvency and take property of the debtor out of the insolvency and give it to one or more creditors ahead of the rest.

11.2 It was apparently not sufficient just to have the effect of preferring a creditor[3] – an intention to prefer was also necessary. However, in *British Eagle International Airlines Ltd v Cie Nationale Air France*,[4] it was held that the rule in *ex parte Mackay*[5] did not depend on intention, but invalidated any provision that had the effect of preferring one creditor or a group of creditors ahead of the rest. The case concerned the clearing house operated by members of the International Air Transport Association, and the decision that the clearing house scheme was unenforceable in a member's insolvency caused widespread concern among organisations operating clearing houses.

11.3 The provisions contained in Part VII of the CA 1989 (ie ss 154–191)[6] are designed not only to counteract the effects of the *British Eagle* decision, but to isolate the clearance schemes and default procedures covered by the legislation from general insolvency law altogether. The provisions do three basic things: (i) allow for the separate settlement of debts arising from default on market

---

[1]   [1975] 2 All ER 390.
[2]   *Re Jeavons, ex parte Mackay* (1873) 8 Ch App 643.
[3]   *Re Wilkinson, ex parte Fowler* [1905] 2 KB 713; *Re Tout and Finch Ltd* [1954] 1 All ER 127.
[4]   [1975] 2 All ER 390.
[5]   *Re Jeavons, ex parte Mackay* (1873) 8 Ch App 643.
[6]   The provisions are expected to come into force in March 1990. There are important transitional provisions in CA 1989, s 182(4) and Sch 22.

contracts;[1] (ii) protect property provided as cover for margin[2] to persons operating clearing house facilities; and (iii) facilitate charges being given to recognised investment exchanges (RIEs) or recognised clearing houses (RCHs), in return for such bodies undertaking settlement or ensuring performance of market contracts, or to the Stock Exchange, in return for it making payments in relation to the transfer of securities. Such charges may be fixed or floating and are referred to in the legislation as 'market charges'.[3] The provisions are specialised and complex and it is not proposed to describe them in detail.

11.4   The default procedure must be contained in the rules of an RIE or RCH.[4] In the case of an RIE, the procedure involves: (i) the discharge of rights and liabilities on unsettled market contracts; and (ii) the setting-off of debts arising between members. In the case of an RCH, or where an RIE provides its own clearing arrangements, the rights and liabilities of defaulters will be towards the RCH or RIE. The procedure is for the rights and liabilities of the defaulter to be discharged, and for there to be a set-off of the net sum, taking into account the cover for margin provided by the defaulter.

11.5   To ensure that the separate settlement of debts operates effectively, it is isolated from normal insolvency rules. Only on completion of the default procedure is a debt or liability arising out of a market contract which is the subject of default proceedings provable or capable of set-off.[5] If the default procedure has operated effectively, the only sum provable should be the net figure owing by the defaulter to the clearing house.[6] In addition most, if not all, of the provisions in insolvency law which can invalidate transactions or dispositions are excluded to a greater or lesser extent. Likewise, market charges are given priority over certain competing claims to the same property, are protected from being set aside under certain provisions, and can be enforced notwithstanding that procedures have begun which would normally prevent the enforcement of security.[7]

---

[1]   CA 1989, s 155.
[2]   The terms 'margin' and 'cover for margin' are used interchangeably throughout the legislation: CA 1989, s 190(3).
[3]   Ibid, s 173.
[4]   The Financial Services Act 1986, Sch 4 has effect as if it included additional requirements among those required to be fulfilled for recognition by the SIB: CA 1989, s 156 and Sch 21, paras 2 and 9.
[5]   CA 1989, s 159(4),(5).
[6]   Ibid, s 163(2),(4),(5).
[7]   Ibid, ss 175, 178–180.

APPENDIX

DERIVATION TABLE OF NEW SECTIONS INSERTED INTO THE COMPANIES ACT 1985

The following table shows in relation to the new sections inserted into the CA 1985 where *equivalent* material was contained in the former provisions of the CA 1985. It must be remembered that this is not pure consolidation and so, although the contents of the new section may be very similar or even identical to the old, in many cases they may be totally different. This table is therefore intended only as a guide to where to find the *equivalent* material.

Accounting Provisions: CA 1985 Part VII

NEW	OLD	NEW	OLD
221	221, 223(1), (3)	245	–
222	222, 223	245A	–
223	227(2), (4), 742(1)(d)(ii)	245B	–
224	224	245C	–
225	225	246	247(1)–(3), 250(2)
226	227(1), (3), 228(1), (2), (4)–(6)	247	248, 249
227	229(1), (5), 230(1), (2), (4)–(6)	248	250(6)
228	229(2)	249	250(3)–(5)
229	229(3), (4)	250	252, 253
230	228(7)	251	–
231	231(1)	252	–
232	232(2), (4)	253	–
233	238(1), (2), (4)	254	241(4), 255(3)(b)
234	235(1)–(5), (7)	255	257(3), (4), 258(1), (2), (4)
234A	–	255A	257(3), (4), 259(1), (3), (4)
235	236(1), (2), 237(6)	255B	260(1)
236	–	255C	261(1)–(3), (6)
237	237(1)–(5)	255D	–
238	240	256	–
239	246	257	251, 256
240	254, 255(3)–(5)	258	–
241	241(1), 243(1), (2), (5)	259	–
242	241(3), 243(1), (2), (5), 244(1), (2)	260	–
242A	243(3), (4)	261	–
243	–	262	742
244	242	262A	–

Auditing Provisions: CA 1985 Part XI Chapter V

NEW	OLD	NEW	OLD
384	–	390A	385
385	384(1)–(3)	390B	–
385A	–	391	386, 387(2)
386	–	391A	388
387	384(5)	392	390(1), (3), (7)
388	384(4), 388(1), (2)	392A	391
388A	252(1), (7)	393	–
389A	237(3), 392, 393	394	390(2)–(6)
390	387(1)	394A	390(7)

Company Charges Provisions: CA 1985 Part XII

NEW	OLD	NEW	OLD
395	396(4), 410(1), (5)	408	397(1), 413(2)
396	396(1)–(3), 410(4), 412, 413(1)	409	405
397	401, 417, 418	410	–
398	399, 400(2), (4), 410(2), 415, 416(1), (3)	411	406, 407, 422
		412	408, 423
399	395(1)	413	–
400	404(1), 420	414	398(3), 410(5), 414(4)
401	403(1), 404(1), 419(1), 420	415	417(3)
402	–	416	–
403	403, 404(1), 419(1), (2)	417	419(3)
404	–	418	–
405	–	419	–
406	–	420	–
407	395(2), 410(3)		

COMPANIES ACT 1989

(1989 c 40)

ARRANGEMENT OF SECTIONS

PART I
COMPANY ACCOUNTS

Introduction

Consequential amendments

PART II
ELIGIBILITY FOR APPOINTMENT AS COMPANY AUDITOR

Introduction

Eligibility for appointment

Recognition of supervisory bodies and professional qualifications

Duties of recognised bodies

Offences

Supplementary provisions

PART III
INVESTIGATIONS AND POWERS TO OBTAIN INFORMATION

Amendments of the Companies Act 1985

Amendments of the Financial Services Act 1986

Amendments of other enactments

Powers exercisable to assist overseas regulatory authorities

PART IV
REGISTRATION OF COMPANY CHARGES

Introduction

Registration in the companies charges register

Copies of instruments and register to be kept by company

Supplementary provisions

PART V
OTHER AMENDMENTS OF COMPANY LAW

A company's capacity and related matters

De-regulation of private companies

Appointment and removal of auditors and related matters

Company records and related matters

Miscellaneous

PART VI
MERGERS AND RELATED MATTERS

PART VII
FINANCIAL MARKETS AND INSOLVENCY

Introduction

Recognised investment exchanges and clearing houses

Section

Other exchanges and clearing houses

Market charges

Market property

Supplementary provisions

PART VIII
AMENDMENTS OF THE FINANCIAL SERVICES ACT 1986

Section

PART IX
TRANSFER OF SECURITIES

PART X
MISCELLANEOUS AND GENERAL PROVISIONS

Miscellaneous

General

SCHEDULES:

An Act to amend the law relating to company accounts; to make new provision with respect to the persons eligible for appointment as company auditors; to amend the Companies Act 1985 and certain other enactments with respect to investigations and powers to obtain information and to confer new powers exercisable to assist overseas regulatory authorities; to make new provision with respect to the registration of company charges and otherwise to amend the law relating to companies; to amend the Fair Trading Act 1973; to enable provision to be made for the payment of fees in connection with the exercise by the Secretary of State, the Director General of Fair Trading and the Monopolies and Mergers Commission of their functions under Part V of that Act; to make provision for safeguarding the operation of certain financial markets; to amend the Financial Services Act 1986; to enable provision to be made for the recording and transfer of title to securities without a written instrument; to amend the Company Directors Disqualification Act 1986, the Company Securities (Insider Dealing) Act 1985, the Policyholders Protection Act 1975 and the law relating to building societies; and for connected purposes.   [16 November 1989]

Be it enacted by the Queen's most Excellent Majesty, by and with the advice and consent of the Lords Spiritual and Temporal, and Commons, in this present Parliament assembled, and by the authority of the same, as follows:–

PART I
COMPANY ACCOUNTS

Introduction

1   Introduction

The provisions of this Part amend Part VII of the Companies Act 1985 (accounts and audit) by –

> (a)   inserting new provisions in place of sections 221 to 262 of that Act, and
> (b)   amending or replacing Schedules 4 to 10 to that Act and inserting new Schedules.

Provisions applying to companies generally

2   Accounting records

The following sections are inserted in Part VII of the Companies Act 1985 at the beginning of Chapter I (provisions applying to companies generally) –

"Accounting records

221   Duty to keep accounting records

(1) Every company shall keep accounting records which are sufficient to show and explain the company's transactions and are such as to –

> (a)   disclose with reasonable accuracy, at any time, the financial position of the company at that time, and
> (b)   enable the directors to ensure that any balance sheet and profit and loss account prepared under this Part complies with the requirements of this Act.

(2) The accounting records shall in particular contain –

    (*a*) entries from day to day of all sums of money received and expended by the company, and the matters in respect of which the receipt and expenditure takes place, and

    (*b*) a record of the assets and liabilities of the company.

(3) If the company's business involves dealing in goods, the accounting records shall contain –

    (*a*) statements of stock held by the company at the end of each financial year of the company,

    (*b*) all statements of stocktakings from which any such statement of stock as is mentioned in paragraph (*a*) has been or is to be prepared, and

    (*c*) except in the case of goods sold by way of ordinary retail trade, statements of all goods sold and purchased, showing the goods and the buyers and sellers in sufficient detail to enable all these to be identified.

(4) A parent company which has a subsidiary undertaking in relation to which the above requirements do not apply shall take reasonable steps to secure that the undertaking keeps such accounting records as to enable the directors of the parent company to ensure that any balance sheet and profit and loss account prepared under this Part complies with the requirements of this Act.

(5) If a company fails to comply with any provision of this section, every officer of the company who is in default is guilty of an offence unless he shows that he acted honestly and that in the circumstances in which the company's business was carried on the default was excusable.

(6) A person guilty of an offence under this section is liable to imprisonment or a fine, or both.

222 Where and for how long records to be kept

(1) A company's accounting records shall be kept at its registered office or such other place as the directors think fit, and shall at all times be open to inspection by the company's officers.

(2) If accounting records are kept at a place outside Great Britain, accounts and returns with respect to the business dealt with in the accounting records so kept shall be sent to, and kept at, a place in Great Britain, and shall at all times be open to such inspection.

(3) The accounts and returns to be sent to Great Britain shall be such as to –

    (*a*) disclose with reasonable accuracy the financial position of the business in question at intervals of not more than six months, and

    (*b*) enable the directors to ensure that the company's balance sheet and profit and loss account comply with the requirements of this Act.

(4) If a company fails to comply with any provision of subsections (1) to (3), every officer of the company who is in default is guilty of an offence, and liable to imprisonment or a fine or both, unless he shows that he acted honestly and that in the circumstances in which the company's business was carried on the default was excusable.

(5) Accounting records which a company is required by section 221 to keep shall be preserved by it –

(*a*) in the case of a private company, for three years from the date on which they are made, and

(*b*) in the case of a public company, for six years from the date on which they are made.

This is subject to any provision contained in rules made under section 411 of the Insolvency Act 1986 (company insolvency rules).

(6) An officer of a company is guilty of an offence, and liable to imprisonment or a fine or both, if he fails to take all reasonable steps for securing compliance by the company with subsection (5) or intentionally causes any default by the company under that subsection.".

3　A company's financial year and accounting reference periods

The following sections are inserted in Part VII of the Companies Act 1985 –

"A company's financial year and accounting reference periods

223　A company's financial year

(1) A company's "financial year" is determined as follows.

(2) Its first financial year begins with the first day of its first accounting reference period and ends with the last day of that period or such other date, not more than seven days before or after the end of that period, as the directors may determine.

(3) Subsequent financial years begin with the day immediately following the end of the company's previous financial year and end with the last day of its next accounting reference period or such other date, not more than seven days before or after the end of that period, as the directors may determine.

(4) In relation to an undertaking which is not a company, references in this Act to its financial year are to any period in respect of which a profit and loss account of the undertaking is required to be made up (by its constitution or by the law under which it is established), whether that period is a year or not.

(5) The directors of a parent company shall secure that, except where in their opinion there are good reasons against it, the financial year of each of its subsidiary undertakings coincides with the company's own financial year.

224　Accounting reference periods and accounting reference date

(1) A company's accounting reference periods are determined according to its accounting reference date.

(2) A company may, at any time before the end of the period of nine months beginning with the date of its incorporation, by notice in the prescribed form given to the registrar specify its accounting reference date, that is, the date on which its accounting reference period ends in each calendar year.

(3) Failing such notice, a company's accounting reference date is –

(*a*) in the case of a company incorporated before the commencement of section 3 of the Companies Act 1989, 31st March;

(*b*) in the case of a company incorporated after the commencement of that section, the last day of the month in which the anniversary of its incorporation falls.

(4) A company's first accounting reference period is the period of more than six months, but not more than 18 months, beginning with the date of its incorporation and ending with its accounting reference date.

(5) Its subsequent accounting reference periods are successive periods of twelve months beginning immediately after the end of the previous accounting reference period and ending with its accounting reference date.

(6) This section has effect subject to the provisions of section 225 relating to the alteration of accounting reference dates and the consequences of such alteration.

225 Alteration of accounting reference date

(1) A company may by notice in the prescribed form given to the registrar specify a new accounting reference date having effect in relation to the company's current accounting reference period and subsequent periods.

(2) A company may by notice in the prescribed form given to the registrar specify a new accounting reference date having effect in relation to the company's previous accounting reference period and subsequent periods if –
> (*a*) the company is a subsidiary undertaking or parent undertaking of another company and the new accounting reference date coincides with the accounting reference date of that other company, or
> (*b*) an administration order under Part II of the Insolvency Act 1986 is in force.

A company's "previous accounting reference period" means that immediately preceding its current accounting reference period.

(3) The notice shall state whether the current or previous accounting reference period –
> (*a*) is to be shortened, so as to come to an end on the first occasion on which the new accounting reference date falls or fell after the beginning of the period, or
> (*b*) is to be extended, so as to come to an end on the second occasion on which that date falls or fell after the beginning of the period.

(4) A notice under subsection (1) stating that the current accounting reference period is to be extended is ineffective, except as mentioned below, if given less than five years after the end of an earlier accounting reference period of the company which was extended by virtue of this section.

This subsection does not apply –
> (*a*) to a notice given by a company which is a subsidiary undertaking or parent undertaking of another company and the new accounting reference date coincides with that of the other company, or
> (*b*) where an administration order is in force under Part II of the Insolvency Act 1986,

or where the Secretary of State directs that it should not apply, which he may do with respect to a notice which has been given or which may be given.

(5) A notice under subsection (2)(*a*) may not be given if the period allowed for laying and delivering accounts and reports in relation to the previous accounting reference period has already expired.

(6) An accounting reference period may not in any case, unless an administration order is in force under Part II of the Insolvency Act 1986, be extended so as to exceed 18 months and a notice under this section is ineffective if the current or previous accounting reference period as extended in accordance with the notice would exceed that limit.".

4 Individual company accounts

(1) The following section is inserted in Part VII of the Companies Act 1985 –

"Annual accounts

226 Duty to prepare individual company accounts

(1) The directors of every company shall prepare for each financial year of the company –
    (*a*) a balance sheet as at the last day of the year, and
    (*b*) a profit and loss account.

Those accounts we referred to in this Part as the company's 'individual accounts'.

(2) The balance sheet shall give a true and fair view of the state of affairs of the company as at the end of the financial year; and the profit and loss account shall give a true and fair view of the profit or loss of the company for the financial year.

(3) A company's individual accounts shall comply with the provisions of Schedule 4 as to the form and content of the balance sheet and profit and loss account and additional information to be provided by way of notes to the accounts.

(4) Where compliance with the provisions of that Schedule, and the other provisions of this Act as to the matters to be included in a company's individual accounts or in notes to those accounts, would not be sufficient to give a true and fair view, the necessary additional information shall be given in the accounts or in a note to them.

(5) If in special circumstances compliance with any of those provisions is inconsistent with the requirement to give a true and fair view, the directors shall depart from that provision to the extent necessary to give a true and fair view.
Particulars of any such departure, the reasons for it and its effect shall be given in a note to the accounts.".

(2) Schedule 4 to the Companies Act 1985 (form and content of company accounts) is amended in accordance with Schedule 1 to this Act.

5 Group accounts

(1) The following section is inserted in Part VII of the Companies Act 1985 –

"227 Duty to prepare group accounts

(1) If at the end of a financial year a company is a parent company the directors

shall, as well as preparing individual accounts for the year, prepare group accounts.

(2) Group accounts shall be consolidated accounts comprising –
    (a) a consolidated balance sheet dealing with the state of affairs of the parent company and its subsidiary undertakings, and
    (b) a consolidated profit and loss account dealing with the profit or loss of the parent company and its subsidiary undertakings.

(3) The accounts shall give a true and fair view of the state of affairs as at the end of the financial year, and the profit or loss for the financial year, of the undertakings included in the consolidation as a whole, so far as concerns members of the company.

(4) A company's group accounts shall comply with the provisions of Schedule 4A as to the form and content of the consolidated balance sheet and consolidated profit and loss account and additional information to be provided by way of notes to the accounts.

(5) Where compliance with the provisions of that Schedule, and the other provisions of this Act, as to the matters to be included in a company's group accounts or in notes to those accounts, would not be sufficient to give a true and fair view, the necessary additional information shall be given in the accounts or in a note to them.

(6) If in special circumstances compliance with any of those provisions is inconsistent with the requirement to give a true and fair view, the directors shall depart from that provision to the extent necessary to give a true and fair view.

Particulars of any such departure, the reasons for it and its effect shall be given in a note to the accounts.".

(2) Schedule 2 to this Act (form and content of group accounts) is inserted after Schedule 4 to the Companies Act 1985, as Schedule 4A.

(3) The following sections are inserted in Part VII of the Companies Act 1985 –

"228 Exemption for parent companies included in accounts of larger group

(1) A company is exempt from the requirement to prepare group accounts if it is itself a subsidiary undertaking and its immediate parent undertaking is established under the law of a member State of the European Economic Community, in the following cases –
    (a) where the company is a wholly-owned subsidiary of that parent undertaking;
    (b) where that parent undertaking holds more than 50 per cent. of the shares in the company and notice requesting the preparation of group accounts has not been served on the company by shareholders holding in aggregate –
        (i) more than half of the remaining shares in the company, or
        (ii) 5 per cent. of the total shares in the company.
Such notice must be served not later than six months after the end of the financial year before that to which it relates.

(2) Exemption is conditional upon compliance with all of the following conditions –

(a) that the company is included in consolidated accounts for a larger group drawn up to the same date, or to an earlier date in the same financial year, by a parent undertaking established under the law of a member State of the European Economic Community;

(b) that those accounts are drawn up and audited, and that parent undertaking's annual report is drawn up, according to that law, in accordance with the provisions of the Seventh Directive (83/349/EEC);

(c) that the company discloses in its individual accounts that it is exempt from the obligation to prepare and deliver group accounts;

(d) that the company states in its individual accounts the name of the parent undertaking which draws up the group accounts referred to above and –

(i) if it is incorporated outside Great Britain, the country in which it is incorporated,

(ii) if it is incorporated in Great Britain, whether it is registered in England and Wales or in Scotland, and

(iii) if it is unincorporated, the address of its principal place of business;

(e) that the company delivers to the registrar, within the period allowed for delivering its individual accounts, copies of those group accounts and of the parent undertaking's annual report, together with the auditors' report on them; and

(f) that if any document comprised in accounts and reports delivered in accordance with paragraph (e) is in a language other than English, there is annexed to the copy of that document delivered a translation of it into English, certified in the prescribed manner to be a correct translation.

(3) The exemption does not apply to a company any of whose securities are listed on a stock exchange in any member State of the European Economic Community.

(4) Shares held by directors of a company for the purpose of complying with any share qualification requirement shall be disregarded in determining for the purposes of subsection (1)(a) whether the company is a wholly-owned subsidiary.

(5) For the purposes of subsection (1)(b) shares held by a wholly-owned subsidiary of the parent undertaking, or held on behalf of the parent undertaking or a wholly-owned subsidiary, shall be attributed to the parent undertaking.

(6) In subsection (3) "securities" includes –

(a) shares and stock,

(b) debentures, including debenture stock, loan stock, bonds, certificates of deposit and other instruments creating or acknowledging indebtedness,

(c) warrants or other instruments entitling the holder to subscribe for securities falling within paragraph (a) or (b), and

(d) certificates or other instruments which confer –

(i) property rights in respect of a security falling within paragraph (a), (b) or (c),

(ii) any right to acquire, dispose of, underwrite or convert a security, being a right to which the holder would be entitled if he held any such security to which the certificate or other instrument relates, or

(iii) a contractual right (other than an option) to acquire any such security otherwise than by subscription.

229 Subsidiary undertakings included in the consolidation

(1) Subject to the exceptions authorised or required by this section, all the subsidiary undertakings of the parent company shall be included in the consolidation.

(2) A subsidiary undertaking may be excluded from consolidation if its inclusion is not material for the purpose of giving a true and fair view; but two or more undertakings may be excluded only if they are not material taken together.

(3) In addition, a subsidiary undertaking may be excluded from consolidation where –

(a) severe long-term restrictions substantially hinder the exercise of the rights of the parent company over the assets or management of that undertaking, or

(b) the information necessary for the preparation of group accounts cannot be obtained without disproportionate expense or undue delay, or

(c) the interest of the parent company is held exclusively with a view to subsequent resale and the undertaking has not previously been included in consolidated group accounts prepared by the parent company.

The reference in paragraph (a) to the rights of the parent company and the reference in paragraph (c) to the interest of the parent company are, respectively, to rights and interests held by or attributed to the company for the purposes of section 258 (definition of "parent undertaking") in the absence of which it would not be the parent company.

(4) Where the activities of one or more subsidiary undertakings are so different from those of other undertakings to be included in the consolidation that their inclusion would be incompatible with the obligation to give a true and fair view, those undertakings shall be excluded from consolidation.

This subsection does not apply merely because some of the undertakings are industrial, some commercial and some provide services, or because they carry on industrial or commercial activities involving different products or provide different services.

(5) Where all the subsidiary undertakings of a parent company fall within the above exclusions, no group accounts are required.".

(4) The following section is inserted in Part VII of the Companies Act 1985 –

"230 Treatment of individual profit and loss account where group accounts prepared

(1) The following provisions apply with respect to the individual profit and loss account of a parent company where –

(a) the company is required to prepare and does prepare group accounts in accordance with this Act, and (*b*) the notes to the company's individual balance sheet show the company's profit or loss for the financial year determined in accordance with this Act.

(2) The profit and loss account need not contain the information specified in paragraphs 52 to 57 of Schedule 4 (information supplementing the profit and loss account).

(3) The profit and loss account must be approved in accordance with section 233(1) (approval by board of directors) but may be omitted from the company's annual accounts for the purposes of the other provisions below in this Chapter.

(4) The exemption conferred by this section is conditional upon its being disclosed in the company's annual accounts that the exemption applies.".

6 Additional disclosure required in notes to accounts

(1) The following section is inserted in Part VII of the Companies Act 1985 –

"231 Disclosure required in notes to accounts: related undertakings

(1) The information specified in Schedule 5 shall be given in notes to a company's annual accounts.

(2) Where the company is not required to prepare group accounts, the information specified in Part I of that Schedule shall be given; and where the company is required to prepare group accounts, the information specified in Part II of that Schedule shall be given.

(3) The information required by Schedule 5 need not be disclosed with respect to an undertaking which –

  (*a*) is established under the law of a country outside the United Kingdom, or

  (*b*) carries on business outside the United Kingdom,

if in the opinion of the directors of the company the disclosure would be seriously prejudicial to the business of that undertaking, or to the business of the company or any of its subsidiary undertakings, and the Secretary of State agrees that the information need not be disclosed.

This subsection does not apply in relation to the information required under paragraph 5(2), 6 or 20 of that Schedule.

(4) Where advantage is taken of subsection (3), that fact shall be stated in a note to the company's annual accounts.

(5) If the directors of the company are of the opinion that the number of undertakings in respect of which the company is required to disclose information under any provision of Schedule 5 to this Act is such that compliance with that provision would result in information of excessive length being given, the information need only be given in respect of –

  (*a*) the undertakings whose results or financial position, in the opinion of the directors, principally affected the figures shown in the company's annual accounts, and

  (*b*) undertakings excluded from consolidation under section 229(3) or (4).

This subsection does not apply in relation to the information required under paragraph 10 or 29 of that Schedule.

(6) If advantage is taken of subsection (5) –

(*a*) there shall be included in the notes to the company's annual accounts a statement that the information is given only with respect to such undertakings as are mentioned in that subsection, and

(*b*) the full information (both that which is disclosed in the notes to the accounts and that which is not) shall be annexed to the company's next annual return.

For this purpose the "next annual return" means that next delivered to the registrar after the accounts in question have been approved under section 233.

(7) If a company fails to comply with subsection (6)(*b*), the company and every officer of it who is in default is liable to a fine and, for continued contravention, to a daily default fine.".

(2) Schedule 3 to this Act (disclosure of information: related undertakings) is substituted for Schedule 5 to the Companies Act 1985.

(3) The following section is inserted in Part VII of the Companies Act 1985 –

"232 Disclosure required in notes to accounts: emoluments and other benefits of directors and others

(1) The information specified in Schedule 6 shall be given in notes to a company's annual accounts.

(2) In that Schedule –

Part I   relates to the emoluments of directors (including emoluments waived), pensions of directors and past directors, compensation for loss of office to directors and past directors and sums paid to third parties in respect of directors' services,

Part II   relates to loans, quasi-loans and other dealings in favour of directors and connected persons, and

Part III   relates to transactions, arrangements and agreements made by the company or a subsidiary undertaking for officers of the company other than directors.

(3) It is the duty of any director of a company, and any person who is or has at any time in the preceding five years been an officer of the company, to give notice to the company of such matters relating to himself as may be necessary for the purposes of Part I of Schedule 6.

(4) A person who makes default in complying with subsection (3) commits an offence and is liable to a fine.".

(4) Schedule 6 to the Companies Act 1985 is amended in accordance with Schedule 4 to this Act.

7 Approval and signing of accounts

The following section is inserted in Part VII of the Companies Act 1985 –

"Approval and signing of accounts

233 Approval and signing of accounts

(1) A company's annual accounts shall be approved by the board of directors and signed on behalf of the board by a director of the company.

(2) The signature shall be on the company's balance sheet.

(3) Every copy of the balance sheet which is laid before the company in general meeting, or which is otherwise circulated, published or issued, shall state the name of the person who signed the balance sheet on behalf of the board.

(4) The copy of the company's balance sheet which is delivered to the registrar shall be signed on behalf of the board by a director of the company.

(5) If annual accounts are approved which do not comply with the requirements of this Act, every director of the company who is party to their approval and who knows that they do not comply or is reckless as to whether they comply is guilty of an offence and liable to a fine.

For this purpose every director of the company at the time the accounts are approved shall be taken to be a party to their approval unless he shows that he took all reasonable steps to prevent their being approved.

(6) If a copy of the balance sheet –
   (*a*) is laid before the company, or otherwise circulated, published or issued, without the balance sheet having been signed as required by this section or without the required statement of the signatory's name being included, or
   (*b*) is delivered to the registrar without being signed as required by this section,
the company and every officer of it who is in default is guilty of an offence and liable to a fine.".

8   Directors' report

(1) The following sections are inserted in Part VII of the Companies Act 1985 –

"Directors' report

234   Duty to prepare directors' report

(1) The directors of a company shall for each financial year prepare a report –
   (*a*) containing a fair review of the development of the business of the company and its subsidiary undertakings during the financial year and of their position at the end of it, and
   (*b*) stating the amount (if any) which they recommend should be paid as dividend and the amount (if any) which they propose to carry to reserves.

(2) The report shall state the names of the persons who, at any time during the financial year, were directors of the company, and the principal activities of the company and its subsidiary undertakings in the course of the year and any significant change in those activities in the year.

(3) The report shall also comply with Schedule 7 as regards the disclosure of the matters mentioned there.

(4) In Schedule 7 –
   Part I   relates to matters of a general nature, including changes in asset values, directors' shareholdings and other interests and contributions for political and charitable purposes,

Part II   relates to the acquisition by a company of its own shares or a charge on them,

Part III relates to the employment, training and advancement of disabled persons,

Part IV relates to the health, safety and welfare at work of the company's employees, and

Part V   relates to the involvement of employees in the affairs, policy and performance of the company.

(5) In the case of any failure to comply with the provisions of this Part as to the preparation of a directors' report and the contents of the report, every person who was a director of the company immediately before the end of the period for laying and delivering accounts and reports for the financial year in question is guilty of an offence and liable to a fine.

(6) In proceedings against a person for an offence under this section it is a defence for him to prove that he took all reasonable steps for securing compliance with the requirements in question.

234A Approval and signing of directors' report

(1) The directors' report shall be approved by the board of directors and signed on behalf of the board by a director or the secretary of the company.

(2) Every copy of the directors' report which is laid before the company in general meeting, or which is otherwise circulated, published or issued, shall state the name of the person who signed it on behalf of the board.

(3) The copy of the directors' report which is delivered to the registrar shall be signed on behalf of the board by a director or the secretary of the company.

(4) If a copy of the directors' report –

(*a*) is laid before the company, or otherwise circulated, published or issued, without the report having been signed as required by this section or without the required statement of the signatory's name being included, or

(*b*) is delivered to the registrar without being signed as required by this section,

the company and every officer of it who is in default is guilty of an offence and liable to a fine.".

(2) Schedule 7 to the Companies Act 1985 (matters to be included in directors' report) is amended in accordance with Schedule 5 to this Act.

9 Auditors' report

The following sections are inserted in Part VII of the Companies Act 1985 –

"Auditors' report

235 Auditors' report

(1) A company's auditors shall make a report to the company's members on all annual accounts of the company of which copies are to be laid before the company in general meeting during their tenure of office.

(2) The auditors' report shall state whether in the auditors' opinion the annual accounts have been properly prepared in accordance with this Act, and in particular whether a true and fair view is given –

    (*a*) in the case of an individual balance sheet, of the state of affairs of the company as at the end of the financial year,

    (*b*) in the case of an individual profit and loss account, of the profit or loss of the company for the financial year,

    (*c*) in the case of group accounts, of the state of affairs as at the end of the financial year, and the profit or loss for the financial year, of the undertakings included in the consolidation as a whole, so far as concerns members of the company.

(3) The auditors shall consider whether the information given in the directors' report for the financial year for which the annual accounts are prepared is consistent with those accounts; and if they are of opinion that it is not they shall state that fact in their report.

236 Signature of auditors' report

(1)The auditors' report shall state the names of the auditors and be signed by them.

(2) Every copy of the auditors' report which is laid before the company in general meeting, or which is otherwise circulated, published or issued, shall state the names of the auditors.

(3) The copy of the auditors' report which is delivered to the registrar shall state the names of the auditors and be signed by them.

(4) If a copy of the auditors' report –

    (*a*) is laid before the company, or otherwise circulated, published or issued, without the required statement of the auditors' names, or

    (*b*) is delivered to the registrar without the required statement of the auditors' names or without being signed as required by this section,

the company and every officer of it who is in default is guilty of an offence and liable to a fine.

(5) References in this section to signature by the auditors are, where the office of auditor is held by a body corporate or partnership, to signature in the name of the body corporate or partnership by a person authorised to sign on its behalf.

237 Duties of auditors

(1) A company's auditors shall, in preparing their report, carry out such investigations as will enable them to form an opinion as to –

    (*a*) whether proper accounting records have been kept by the company and proper returns adequate for their audit have been received from branches not visited by them, and

    (*b*) whether the company's individual accounts are in agreement with the accounting records and returns.

(2) If the auditors are of opinion that proper accounting records have not been kept, or that proper returns adequate for their audit have not been received from branches not visited by them, or if the company's individual accounts are not in agreement with the accounting records and returns, the auditors shall state that fact in their report.

(3) If the auditors fail to obtain all the information and explanations which, to the best of their knowledge and belief, are necessary for the purposes of their audit, they shall state that fact in their report.

(4) If the requirements of Schedule 6 (disclosure of information: emoluments and other benefits of directors and others) are not complied with in the annual accounts, the auditors shall include in their report, so far as they are reasonably able to do so, a statement giving the required particulars.".

10 Publication of accounts and reports

The following sections are inserted in Part VII of the Companies Act 1985 –

"Publication of accounts and reports

238 Persons entitled to receive copies of accounts and reports

(1) A copy of the company's annual accounts, together with a copy of the directors' report for that financial year and of the auditors' report on those accounts, shall be sent to –
  (*a*) every member of the company,
  (*b*) every holder of the company's debentures, and
  (*c*) every person who is entitled to receive notice of general meetings,
not less than 21 days before the date of the meeting at which copies of those documents are to be laid in accordance with section 241.

(2) Copies need not be sent –
  (*a*) to a person who is not entitled to receive notices of general meetings and of whose address the company is unaware, or
  (*b*) to more than one of the joint holders of shares or debentures none of whom is entitled to receive such notices, or
  (*c*) in the case of joint holders of shares or debentures some of whom are, and some not, entitled to receive such notices, to those who are not so entitled.

(3) In the case of a company not having a share capital, copies need not be sent to anyone who is not entitled to receive notices of general meetings of the company.

(4) If copies are sent less than 21 days before the date of the meeting, they shall, notwithstanding that fact, be deemed to have been duly sent if it is so agreed by all the members entitled to attend and vote at the meeting.

(5) If default is made in complying with this section, the company and every officer of it who is in default is guilty of an offence and liable to a fine.

(6) Where copies are sent out under this section over a period of days, references elsewhere in this Act to the day on which copies are sent out shall be construed as references to the last day of that period.

239 Right to demand copies of accounts and reports

(1) Any member of a company and any holder of a company's debentures is entitled to be furnished, on demand and without charge, with a copy of the company's last annual accounts and directors' report and a copy of the auditors' report on those accounts.

(2) The entitlement under this section is to a single copy of those documents, but that is in addition to any copy to which a person may be entitled under section 238.

(3) If a demand under this section is not complied with within seven days, the company and every officer of it who is in default is guilty of an offence and liable to a fine and, for continued contravention, to a daily default fine.

(4) If in proceedings for such an offence the issue arises whether a person had already been furnished with a copy of the relevant document under this section, it is for the defendant to prove that he had.

240 Requirements in connection with publication of accounts

(1) If a company publishes any of its statutory accounts, they must be accompanied by the relevant auditors' report under section 235.

(2) A company which is required to prepare group accounts for a financial year shall not publish its statutory individual accounts for that year without also publishing with them its statutory group accounts.

(3) If a company publishes non-statutory accounts, it shall publish with them a statement indicating –

- (*a*) that they are not the company's statutory accounts,
- (*b*) whether statutory accounts dealing with any financial year with which the non-statutory accounts purport to deal have been delivered to the registrar,
- (*c*) whether the company's auditors have made a report under section 235 on the statutory accounts for any such financial year, and
- (*d*) whether any report so made was qualified or contained a statement under section 237(2) or (3) (accounting records or returns inadequate, accounts not agreeing with records and returns or failure to obtain necessary information and explanations);

and it shall not publish with the non-statutory accounts any auditors' report under section 235.

(4) For the purposes of this section a company shall be regarded as publishing a document if it publishes, issues or circulates it or otherwise makes it available for public inspection in a manner calculated to invite members of the public generally, or any class of members of the public, to read it.

(5) References in this section to a company's statutory accounts are to its individual or group accounts for a financial year as required to be delivered to the registrar under section 242; and references to the publication by a company of "non-statutory accounts" are to the publication of –

- (*a*) any balance sheet or profit and loss account relating to, or purporting to deal with, a financial year of the company, or
- (*b*) an account in any form purporting to be a balance sheet or profit and loss account for the group consisting of the company and its subsidiary undertakings relating to, or purporting to deal with, a financial year of the company,

otherwise than as part of the company's statutory accounts.

(6) A company which contravenes any provision of this section, and any officer of it who is in default, is guilty of an offence and liable to a fine.".

11 Laying and delivering of accounts and reports

The following sections are inserted in Part VII of the Companies Act 1985 –

"Laying and delivering of accounts and reports

241 Accounts and reports to be laid before company in general meeting

(1) The directors of a company shall in respect of each financial year lay before the company in general meeting copies of the company's annual accounts, the directors' report and the auditors' report on those accounts.

(2) If the requirements of subsection (1) are not complied with before the end of the period allowed for laying and delivering accounts and reports, every person who immediately before the end of that period was a director of the company is guilty of an offence and liable to a fine and, for continued contravention, to a daily default fine.

(3) It is a defence for a person charged with such an offence to prove that he took all reasonable steps for securing that those requirements would be complied with before the end of that period.

(4) It is not a defence to prove that the documents in question were not in fact prepared as required by this Part.

242 Accounts and reports to be delivered to the registrar

(1) The directors of a company shall in respect of each financial year deliver to the registrar a copy of the company's annual accounts together with a copy of the directors' report for that year and a copy of the auditors' report on those accounts.

If any document comprised in those accounts or reports is in a language other than English, the directors shall annex to the copy of that document delivered a translation of it into English, certified in the prescribed manner to be a correct translation.

(2) If the requirements of subsection (1) are not complied with before the end of the period allowed for laying and delivering accounts and reports, every person who immediately before the end of that period was a director of the company is guilty of an offence and liable to a fine and, for continued contravention, to a daily default fine.

(3) Further, if the directors of the company fail to make good the default within 14 days after the service of a notice on them requiring compliance, the court may on the application of any member or creditor of the company or of the registrar, make an order directing the directors (or any of them) to make good the default within such time as may be specified in the order.

The court's order may provide that all costs of and incidental to the application shall be borne by the directors.

(4) It is a defence for a person charged with an offence under this section to prove that he took all reasonable steps for securing that the requirements of subsection (1) would be complied with before the end of the period allowed for laying and delivering accounts and reports.

(5) It is not a defence in any proceedings under this section to prove that the documents in question were not in fact prepared as required by this Part.

242A   Civil penalty for failure to deliver accounts

(1) Where the requirements of section 242(1) are not complied with before the end of the period allowed for laying and delivering accounts and reports, the company is liable to a civil penalty.

This is in addition to any liability of the directors under section 242.

(2) The amount of the penalty is determined by reference to the length of the period between the end of the period allowed for laying and delivering accounts and reports and the day on which the requirements are complied with, and whether the company is a public or private company, as follows: –

Length of period	Public company	Private company
Not more than 3 months.	£500	£100
More than 3 months but not more than 6 months.	£1,000	£250
More than 6 months but not more than 12 months.	£2,000	£500
More than 12 months.	£5,000	£1,000

(3) The penalty may be recovered by the registrar and shall be paid by him into the Consolidated Fund.

(4) It is not a defence in proceedings under this section to prove that the documents in question were not in fact prepared as required by this Part.

243   Accounts of subsidiary undertakings to be appended in certain cases

(1) The following provisions apply where at the end of the financial year a parent company has as a subsidiary undertaking –
> (*a*) a body corporate incorporated outside Great Britain which does not have an established place of business in Great Britain, or
> (*b*) an unincorporated undertaking,

which is excluded from consolidation in accordance with section 229(4) (undertaking with activities different from the undertakings included in the consolidation).

(2) There shall be appended to the copy of the company's annual accounts delivered to the registrar in accordance with section 242 a copy of the undertaking's latest individual accounts and, if it is a parent undertaking, its latest group accounts.

If the accounts appended are required by law to be audited, a copy of the auditors' report shall also be appended.

(3) The accounts must be for a period ending not more than twelve months before the end of the financial year for which the parent company's accounts are made up.

(4) If any document required to be appended is in a language other than English, the directors shall annex to the copy of that document delivered a

translation of it into English, certified in the prescribed manner to be a correct translation.

(5) The above requirements are subject to the following qualifications –

(*a*) an undertaking is not required to prepare for the purposes of this section accounts which would not otherwise be prepared, and if no accounts satisfying the above requirements are prepared none need be appended;

(*b*) a document need not be appended if it would not otherwise be required to be published, or made available for public inspection, anywhere in the world, but in that case the reason for not appending it shall be stated in a note to the company's accounts;

(*c*) where an undertaking and all its subsidiary undertakings are excluded from consolidation in accordance with section 229(4), the accounts of such of the subsidiary undertakings of that undertaking as are included in its consolidated group accounts need not be appended.

(6) Subsections (2) to (4) of section 242 (penalties, &c. in case of default) apply in relation to the requirements of this section as they apply in relation to the requirements of subsection (1) of that section.

244   Period allowed for laying and delivering accounts and reports

(1) The period allowed for laying and delivering accounts and reports is –

(*a*) for a private company, 10 months after the end of the relevant accounting reference period, and

(*b*) for a public company, 7 months after the end of that period.

This is subject to the following provisions of this section.

(2) If the relevant accounting reference period is the company's first and is a period of more than 12 months, the period allowed is –

(*a*) 10 months or 7 months, as the case may be, from the first anniversary of the incorporation of the company, or

(*b*) 3 months from the end of the accounting reference period,

whichever last expires.

(3) Where a company carries on business, or has interests, outside the United Kingdom, the Channel Islands and the Isle of Man, the directors may, in respect of any financial year, give to the registrar before the end of the period allowed by subsection (1) or (2) a notice in the prescribed form –

(*a*) stating that the company so carries on business or has such interests, and

(*b*) claiming a 3 month extension of the period allowed for laying and delivering accounts and reports;

and upon such a notice being given the period is extended accordingly.

(4) If the relevant accounting period is treated as shortened by virtue of a notice given by the company under section 225 (alteration of accounting reference date), the period allowed for laying and delivering accounts is that applicable in accordance with the above provisions or 3 months from the date of the notice under that section, whichever last expires.

(5) If for any special reason the Secretary of State thinks fit he may, on an application made before the expiry of the period otherwise allowed, by notice in

writing to a company extend that period by such further period as may be specified in the notice.

(6) In this section "the relevant accounting reference period" means the accounting reference period by reference to which the financial year for the accounts in question was determined.".

12   Remedies for failure to comply with accounting requirements

The following sections are inserted in Part VII of the Companies Act 1985 –

"Revision of defective accounts and reports

245   Voluntary revision of annual accounts or directors' report

(1) If it appears to the directors of a company that any annual accounts of the company, or any directors' report, did not comply with the requirements of this Act, they may prepare revised accounts or a revised report.

(2) Where copies of the previous accounts or report have been laid before the company in general meeting or delivered to the registrar, the revisions shall be confined to –

   (*a*)   the correction of those respects in which the previous accounts or report did not comply with the requirements of this Act, and

   (*b*)   the making of any necessary consequential alterations.

(3) The Secretary of State may make provision by regulations as to the application of the provisions of this Act in relation to revised annual accounts or a revised directors' report.

(4) The regulations may, in particular –

   (*a*)   make different provision according to whether the previous accounts or report are replaced or are supplemented by a document indicating the corrections to be made;

   (*b*)   make provision with respect to the functions of the company's auditors in relation to the revised accounts or report;

   (*c*)   require the directors to take such steps as may be specified in the regulations where the previous accounts or report have been –
      (i)   sent out to members and others under section 238(1),
      (ii)   laid before the company in general meeting, or
      (iii)   delivered to the registrar,
      or where a summary financial statement based on the previous accounts or report has been sent to members under section 151;

   (*d*)   apply the provisions of this Act (including those creating criminal offences) subject to such additions, exceptions and modifications as are specified in the regulations.

(5) Regulations under this section shall be made by statutory instrument which shall be subject to annulment in pursuance of a resolution of either House of Parliament.

245A   Secretary of State's notice in respect of annual accounts

(1) Where copies of a company's annual accounts have been sent out under section 238, or a copy of a company's annual accounts has been laid before the

company in general meeting or delivered to the registrar, and it appears to the Secretary of State that there is, or may be, a question whether the accounts comply with the requirements of this Act, he may give notice to the directors of the company indicating the respects in which it appears to him that such a question arises, or may arise.

(2) The notice shall specify a period of no less than one month for the directors to give him an explanation of the accounts or prepare revised accounts.

(3) If at the end of the specified period, or such longer period as he may allow, it appears to the Secretary of State that no satisfactory explanation of the accounts has been given and that the accounts have not been revised so as to comply with the requirements of this Act, he may if he thinks fit apply to the court.

(4) The provisions of this section apply equally to revised annual accounts, in which case the references to revised accounts shall be read as references to further revised accounts.

245B Application to court in respect of defective accounts

(1) An application may be made to the court –
    (*a*) by the Secretary of State, after having complied with section 245A, or
    (*b*) by a person authorised by the Secretary of State for the purposes of this section,
for a declaration or declarator that the annual accounts of a company do not comply with the requirements of this Act and for an order requiring the directors of the company to prepare revised accounts.

(2) Notice of the application, together with a general statement of the matters at issue in the proceedings, shall be given by the applicant to the registrar for registration.

(3) If the court orders the preparation of revised accounts, it may give directions with respect to –
    (*a*) the auditing of the accounts,
    (*b*) the revision of any directors' report or summary financial statement, and
    (*c*) the taking of steps by the directors to bring the making of the order to the notice of persons likely to rely on the previous accounts,
and such other matters as the court thinks fit.

(4) If the court finds that the accounts did not comply with the requirements of this Act it may order that all or part of –
    (*a*) the costs (or in Scotland expenses) of and incidental to the application, and
    (*b*) any reasonable expenses incurred by the company in connection with or in consequence of the preparation of revised accounts,
shall be borne by such of the directors as were party to the approval of the defective accounts.

For this purpose every director of the company at the time the accounts were approved shall be taken to have been party to their approval unless he shows that he took all reasonable steps to prevent their being approved.

(5) Where the court makes an order under subsection (4) it shall have regard to whether the directors party to the approval of the defective accounts knew or ought to have known that the accounts did not comply with the requirements of this Act, and it may exclude one or more directors from the order or order the payment of different amounts by different directors.

(6) On the conclusion of proceedings on an application under this section, the applicant shall give to the registrar for registration an office copy of the court order or, as the case may be, notice that the application has failed or been withdrawn.

(7) The provisions of this section apply equally to revised annual accounts, in which case the references to revised accounts shall be read as references to further revised accounts.

245C Other persons authorised to apply to court

(1) The Secretary of State may authorise for the purposes of section 245B any person appearing to him –

    (*a*) to have an interest in, and to have satisfactory procedures directed to securing, compliance by companies with the accounting requirements of this Act,

    (*b*) to have satisfactory procedures for receiving and investigating complaints about the annual accounts of companies, and

    (*c*) otherwise to be a fit and proper person to be authorised.

(2) A person may be authorised generally or in respect of particular classes of case, and different persons may be authorised in respect of different classes of case.

(3) The Secretary of State may refuse to authorise a person if he considers that his authorisation is unnecessary having regard to the fact that there are one or more other persons who have been or are likely to be authorised.

(4) Authorisation shall be by order made by statutory instrument which shall be subject to annulment in pursuance of a resolution of either House of Parliament.

(5) Where authorisation is revoked, the revoking order may make such provision as the Secretary of State thinks fit with respect to pending proceedings.

(6) Neither a person authorised under this section, nor any officer, servant or member of the governing body of such a person, shall be liable in damages for anything done or purporting to be done for the purposes of or in connection with –

    (*a*) the taking of steps to discover whether there are grounds for an application to the court,

    (*b*) the determination whether or not to make such an application, or

    (*c*) the publication of its reasons for any such decision,

unless the act or omission is shown to have been in bad faith.".

Exemptions and special provisions

13 Small and medium-sized companies and groups

(1) The following sections are inserted in Part VII of the Companies Act 1985, as the beginning of a Chapter II –

"CHAPTER II
EXEMPTIONS, EXCEPTIONS AND SPECIAL PROVISIONS

Small and medium-sized companies and groups

246 Exemptions for small and medium-sized companies

(1) A company which qualifies as a small or medium-sized company in relation to a financial year –

    (*a*) is exempt from the requirements of paragraph 36A of Schedule 4 (disclosure with respect to compliance with accounting standards), and

    (*b*) is entitled to the exemptions provided by Schedule 8 with respect to the delivery to the registrar under section 242 of individual accounts and other documents for that financial year.

(2) In that Schedule –

Part I relates to small companies,

Part II relates to medium-sized companies, and

Part III contains supplementary provisions.

(3) A company is not entitled to the exemptions mentioned in subsection (1) if it is, or was at any time within the financial year to which the accounts relate –

    (*a*) a public company,

    (*b*) a banking or insurance company, or

    (*c*) an authorised person under the Financial Services Act 1986,

or if it is or was at any time during that year a member of an ineligible group.

(4) A group is ineligible if any of its members is –

    (*a*) a public company or a body corporate which (not being a company) has power under its constitution to offer its shares or debentures to the public and may lawfully exercise that power,

    (*b*) an authorised institution under the Banking Act 1987,

    (*c*) an insurance company to which Part II of the Insurance Companies Act 1982 applies, or

    (*d*) an authorised person under the Financial Services Act 1986.

(5) A parent company shall not be treated as qualifying as a small company in relation to a financial year unless the group headed by it qualifies as a small group, and shall not be treated as qualifying as a medium-sized company in relation to a financial year unless that group qualifies as a medium-sized group (see section 249).

247 Qualification of company as small or medium-sized

(1) A company qualifies as small or medium-sized in relation to a financial year if the qualifying conditions are met –

    (*a*) in the case of the company's first financial year, in that year, and

    (*b*) in the case of any subsequent financial year, in that year and the preceding year.

(2) A company shall be treated as qualifying as small or medium-sized in relation to a financial year –

(*a*) if it so qualified in relation to the previous financial year under subsection (1); or

(*b*) if it was treated as so qualifying in relation to the previous year by virtue of paragraph (*a*) and the qualifying conditions are met in the year in question.

(3) The qualifying conditions are met by a company in a year in which it satisfies two or more of the following requirements –

Small company

1. Turnover	Not more than £2 million
2. Balance sheet total	Not more than £975,000
3. Number of employees	Not more than 50

Medium-sized company

1. Turnover	Not more than £8 million
2. Balance sheet total	Not more than £3.9 million
3. Number of employees	Not more than 250.

(4) For a period which is a company's financial year but not in fact a year the maximum figures for turnover shall be proportionately adjusted.

(5) The balance sheet total means –

(*a*) where in the company's accounts Format 1 of the balance sheet formats set out in Part I of Schedule 4 is adopted, the aggregate of the amounts shown in the balance sheet under the headings corresponding to items A to D in that Format, and

(*b*) where Format 2 is adopted, the aggregate of the amounts shown under the general heading "Assets".

(6) The number of employees means the average number of persons employed by the company in the year (determined on a weekly basis).

That number shall be determined by applying the method of calculation prescribed by paragraph 56(2) and (3) of Schedule 4 for determining the corresponding number required to be stated in a note to the company's accounts.".

(2) Schedule 6 to this Act is substituted for Schedule 8 to the Companies Act 1985.

(3) The following sections are inserted in Part VII of the Companies Act 1985 –

"248 Exemption for small and medium-sized groups

(1) A parent company need not prepare group accounts for a financial year in relation to which the group headed by that company qualifies as a small or medium-sized group and is not an ineligible group.

(2) A group is ineligible if any of its members is –

(*a*) a public company or a body corporate which (not being a company) has power under its constitution to offer its shares or debentures to the public and may lawfully exercise that power,

(*b*) an authorised institution under the Banking Act 1987,

(c) an insurance company to which Part II of the Insurance Companies Act 1982 applies, or

(d) an authorised person under the Financial Services Act 1986.

(3) If the directors of a company propose to take advantage of the exemption conferred by this section, it is the auditors' duty to provide them with a report stating whether in their opinion the company is entitled to the exemption.

(4) The exemption does not apply unless –

(a) the auditors' report states that in their opinion the company is so entitled, and

(b) that report is attached to the individual accounts of the company.

249 Qualification of group as small or medium-sized

(1) A group qualifies as small or medium-sized in relation to a financial year if the qualifying conditions are met –

(a) in the case of the parent company's first financial year, in that year, and

(b) in the case of any subsequent financial year, in that year and the preceding year.

(2) A group shall be treated as qualifying as small or medium-sized in relation to a financial year –

(a) if it so qualified in relation to the previous financial year under subsection (1); or

(b) if it was treated as so qualifying in relation to the previous year by virtue of paragraph (a) and the qualifying conditions are met in the year in question.

(3) The qualifying conditions are met by a group in a year in which it satisfies two or more of the following requirements –

Small group

1. Aggregate turnover	Not more than £2 million net (or £2.4 million gross)
2. Aggregate balance sheet total	Not more than £1 million net (or £1.2 million gross)
3. Aggregate number of employees	Not more than 50

Medium-sized group

1. Aggregate turnover	Not more than £8 million net (or £9.6 million gross)
2. Aggregate balance sheet total	Not more than £3.9 million net or (£4.7 million gross)
3. Aggregate number of employees	Not more than 250.

(4) The aggregate figures shall be ascertained by aggregating the relevant figures determined in accordance with section 247 for each member of the group.

In relation to the aggregate figures for turnover and balance sheet total, "net" means with the set-offs and other adjustments required by Schedule 4A in the case of group accounts and "gross" means without those set-offs and other adjustments; and a company may satisfy the relevant requirement on the basis of either the net or the gross figure.

(5) The figures for each subsidiary undertaking shall be those included in its accounts for the relevant financial year, that is –

    (*a*) if its financial year ends with that of the parent company, that financial year, and

    (*b*) if not, its financial year ending last before the end of the financial year of the parent company.

(6) If those figures cannot be obtained without disproportionate expense or undue delay, the latest available figures shall be taken.".

14 Dormant companies

The following section is inserted in Part VII of the Companies Act 1985 –

"Dormant companies

250 Resolution not to appoint auditors

(1) A company may by special resolution make itself exempt from the provisions of this Part relating to the audit of accounts in the following cases –

    (*a*) if the company has been dormant from the time of its formation, by a special resolution passed before the first general meeting of the company at which annual accounts are laid;

    (*b*) if the company has been dormant since the end of the previous financial year and –

        (i) is entitled in respect of its individual accounts for that year to the exemptions conferred by section 246 on a small company, or would be so entitled but for being a member of an ineligible group, and

        (ii) is not required to prepare group accounts for that year,

    by a special resolution passed at a general meeting of the company at which the annual accounts for that year are laid.

(2) A company may not pass such a resolution if it is –

    (*a*) a public company,

    (*b*) a banking or insurance company, or

    (*c*) an authorised person under the Financial Services Act 1986.

(3) A company is "dormant" during a period in which no significant accounting transaction occurs, that is, no transaction which is required by section 221 to be entered in the company's accounting records; and a company ceases to be dormant on the occurrence of such a transaction.

For this purpose there shall be disregarded any transaction arising from the taking of shares in the company by a subscriber to the memorandum in pursuance of an undertaking of his in the memorandum.

(4) Where a company is, at the end of a financial year, exempt by virtue of this section from the provisions of this Part relating to the audit of accounts –

    (*a*) sections 238 and 239 (right to receive or demand copies of accounts and reports) have effect with the omission of references to the auditors' report;

(*b*) no copies of an auditors' report need be laid before the company in general meeting;

(*c*) no copy of an auditors' report need be delivered to the registrar, and if none is delivered, the copy of the balance sheet so delivered shall contain a statement by the directors, in a position immediately above the signature required by section 233(4), that the company was dormant throughout the financial year; and

(*d*) the company shall be treated as entitled in respect of its individual accounts for that year to the exemptions conferred by section 246 on a small company, notwithstanding that it is a member of an ineligible group.

(5) Where a company which is exempt by virtue of this section from the provisions of this Part relating to the audit of accounts –

(*a*) ceases to be dormant, or

(*b*) would no longer qualify (for any other reason) to make itself exempt by passing a resolution under this section,

it shall thereupon cease to be so exempt.".

15 Public listed companies: provision of summary financial statement

The following section is inserted in Part VII of the Companies Act 1985 –

"Listed public companies

251 Provision of summary financial statement to shareholders

(1) A public company whose shares, or any class of whose shares, are listed need not, in such cases as may be specified by regulations made by the Secretary of State, and provided any conditions so specified are complied with, send copies of the documents referred to in section 238(1) to members of the company, but may instead send them a summary financial statement.

In this subsection "listed" means admitted to the Official List of The International Stock Exchange of the United Kingdom and the Republic of Ireland Limited.

(2) Copies of the documents referred to in section 238(1) shall, however, be sent to any member of the company who wishes to receive them; and the Secretary of State may by regulations make provision as to the manner in which it is to be ascertained whether a member of the company wishes to receive them.

(3) The summary financial statement shall be derived from the company's annual accounts and the directors' report and shall be in such form and contain such information as may be specified by regulations made by the Secretary of State.

(4) Every summary financial statement shall –

(*a*) state that it is only a summary of information in the company's annual accounts and the directors' report;

(*b*) contain a statement by the company's auditors of their opinion as to whether the summary financial statement is consistent with those accounts and that report and complies with the requirements of this section and regulations made under it;

(c) state whether the auditors' report on the annual accounts was unqualified or qualified, and if it was qualified set out the report in full together with any further material needed to understand the qualification;

(d) state whether the auditors' report on the annual accounts contained a statement under –

    (i) section 237(2) (accounting records or returns inadequate or accounts not agreeing with records and returns), or

    (ii) section 237(3) (failure to obtain necessary information and explanations),

and if so, set out the statement in full.

(5) Regulations under this section shall be made by statutory instrument which shall be subject to annulment in pursuance of a resolution of either House of Parliament.

(6) If default is made in complying with this section or regulations made under it, the company and every officer of it who is in default is guilty of an offence and liable to a fine.

(7) Section 240 (requirements in connection with publication of accounts) does not apply in relation to the provision to members of a company of a summary financial statement in accordance with this section.".

16   Private companies: election to dispense with laying of accounts and reports before general meeting

The following sections are inserted in Part VII of the Companies Act 1985 –

"Private companies

252   Election to dispense with laying of accounts and reports before general meeting

(1) A private company may elect (by elective resolution in accordance with section 379A) to dispense with the laying of accounts and reports before the company in general meeting.

(2) An election has effect in relation to the accounts and reports in respect of the financial year in which the election is made and subsequent financial years.

(3) Whilst an election is in force, the references in the following provisions of this Act to the laying of accounts before the company in general meeting shall be read as references to the sending of copies of the accounts to members and others under section 238(1) –

(a) section 235(1) (accounts on which auditors are to report),

(b) section 270(3) and (4) (accounts by reference to which distributions are justified), and

(c) section 320(2) (accounts relevant for determining company's net assets for purposes of ascertaining whether approval required for certain transactions);

and the requirement in section 271(4) that the auditors' statement under that provision be laid before the company in general meeting shall be read as a requirement that it be sent to members and others along with copies of the accounts sent to them under section 238(1).

(4) If an election under this section ceases to have effect, section 241 applies in relation to the accounts and reports in respect of the financial year in which the election ceases to have effect and subsequent financial years.

253 Right of shareholder to require laying of accounts

(1) Where an election under section 252 is in force, the copies of the accounts and reports sent out in accordance with section 238(1) –

> (a) shall be sent not less than 28 days before the end of the period allowed for laying and delivering accounts and reports, and
>
> (b) shall be accompanied, in the case of a member of the company, by a notice informing him of his right to require the laying of the accounts and reports before a general meeting;

and section 238(5) (penalty for default) applies in relation to the above requirements as to the requirements contained in that section.

(2) Before the end of the period of 28 days beginning with the day on which the accounts and reports are sent out in accordance with section 238(1), any member or auditor of the company may by notice in writing deposited at the registered office of the company require that a general meeting be held for the purpose of laying the accounts and reports before the company.

(3) If the directors do not within 21 days from the date of the deposit of such a notice proceed duly to convene a meeting, the person who deposited the notice may do so himself.

(4) A meeting so convened shall not be held more than three months from that date and shall be convened in the same manner, as nearly as possible, as that in which meetings are to be convened by directors.

(5) Where the directors do not duly convene a meeting, any reasonable expenses incurred by reason of that failure by the person who deposited the notice shall be made good to him by the company, and shall be recouped by the company out of any fees, or other remuneration in respect of their services, due or to become due to such of the directors as were in default.

(6) The directors shall be deemed not to have duly convened a meeting if they convene a meeting for a date more than 28 days after the date of the notice convening it.".

17 Unlimited companies: exemption from requirement to deliver accounts and reports

The following section is inserted in Part VII of the Companies Act 1985 –

"Unlimited companies

254 Exemption from requirement to deliver accounts and reports

(1) The directors of an unlimited company are not required to deliver accounts and reports to the registrar in respect of a financial year if the following conditions are met.

(2) The conditions are that at no time during the relevant accounting reference period –

(*a*) has the company been, to its knowledge, a subsidiary undertaking of an undertaking which was then limited, or

(*b*) have there been, to its knowledge, exercisable by or on behalf of two or more undertakings which were then limited, rights which if exercisable by one of them would have made the company a subsidiary undertaking of it, or

(*c*) has the company been a parent company of an undertaking which was then limited.

The references above to an undertaking being limited at a particular time are to an undertaking (under whatever law established) the liability of whose members is at that time limited.

(3) The exemption conferred by this section does not apply if at any time during the relevant accounting period the company carried on business as the promoter of a trading stamp scheme within the Trading Stamps Act 1964.

(4) Where a company is exempt by virtue of this section from the obligation to deliver accounts, section 240 (requirements in connection with publication of accounts) has effect with the following modifications –

(*a*) in subsection (3)(*b*) for the words from 'whether statutory accounts' to 'have been delivered to the registrar' substitute 'that the company is e mpt from the requirement to deliver statutory accounts', and

(*b*) in subsection (5) for 'as required to be delivered to the registrar under section 242' substitute 'as prepared in accordance with this Part and approved by the board of directors'.".

18 Banking and insurance companies and groups: special provisions

(1) The following sections are inserted in Part VII of the Companies Act 1985 –

"Banking and insurance companies and groups

255 Special provisions for banking and insurance companies

(1) A banking or insurance company may prepare its individual accounts in accordance with Part I of Schedule 9 rather than Schedule 4.

(2) Accounts so prepared shall contain a statement that they are prepared in accordance with the special provisions of this Part relating to banking companies or insurance companies, as the case may be.

(3) In relation to the preparation of individual accounts in accordance with the special provisions of this Part relating to banking or insurance companies, the references to the provisions of Schedule 4 in section 226(4) and (5) (relationship between specific requirements and duty to give true and fair view) shall be read as references to the provisions of Part I of Schedule 9.

(4) The Secretary of State may, on the application or with the consent of the directors of a company which prepares individual accounts in accordance with the special provisions of this Part relating to banking or insurance companies, modify in relation to the company any of the requirements of this Part for the purpose of adapting them to the circumstances of the company.

This does not affect the duty to give a true and fair view.

255A   Special provisions for banking and insurance groups

(1) The parent company of a banking or insurance group may prepare group accounts in accordance with the provisions of this Part as modified by Part II of Schedule 9.

(2) Accounts so prepared shall contain a statement that they are prepared in accordance with the special provisions of this Part relating to banking groups or insurance groups, as the case may be.

(3) References in this Part to a banking group are to a group where –
   (*a*)   the parent company is a banking company, or
   (*b*)   at least one of the undertakings in the group is an authorised institution under the Banking Act 1987 and the predominant activities of the group are such as to make it inappropriate to prepare group accounts in accordance with the formats in Part I of Schedule 4.

(4) References in this Part to an insurance group are to a group where –
   (*a*)   the parent company is an insurance company, or
   (*b*)   the predominant activity of the group is insurance business and activities which are a direct extension of or ancillary to insurance business.

(5) In relation to the preparation of group accounts in accordance with the special provisions of this Part relating to banking or insurance groups, the references to the provisions of Schedule 4A in section 227(5) and (6) (relationship between specific requirements and duty to give true and fair view) shall be read as references to those provisions as modified by Part II of Schedule 9.

(6) The Secretary of State may, on the application or with the consent of the directors of a company which prepares group accounts in accordance with the special provisions of this Part relating to banking or insurance groups, modify in relation to the company any of the requirements of this Part for the purpose of adapting them to the circumstances of the company.

255B   Modification of disclosure requirements in relation to banking company or group

(1) In relation to a company which prepares accounts in accordance with the special provisions of this Part relating to banking companies or groups, the provisions of Schedule 5 (additional disclosure: related undertakings) have effect subject to Part III of Schedule 9.

(2) In relation to a banking company, or the parent company of a banking company, the provisions of Schedule 6 (disclosure: emoluments and other benefits of directors and others) have effect subject to Part IV of Schedule 9.

255C   Directors' report where accounts prepared in accordance with special provisions

(1) The following provisions apply in relation to the directors' report of a company for a financial year in respect of which it prepares accounts in accordance with the special provisions of this Part relating to banking or insurance companies or groups.

(2) The information required to be given by paragraph 6, 8 or 13 of Part I of Schedule 9 (which is allowed to be given in a statement or report annexed to the

accounts), may be given in the directors' report instead.

Information so given shall be treated for the purposes of audit as forming part of the accounts.

(3) The reference in section 234(1)(*b*) to the amount proposed to be carried to reserves shall be construed as a reference to the amount proposed to be carried to reserves within the meaning of Part I of Schedule 9.

(4) If the company takes advantage, in relation to its individual or group accounts, of the exemptions conferred by paragraph 27 or 28 of Part I of Schedule 9, paragraph 1 of Schedule 7 (disclosure of asset values) does not apply.

(5) The directors' report shall, in addition to complying with Schedule 7, also comply with Schedule 10 (which specifies additional matters to be disclosed).".

(2) The following section is inserted in Part VII of the Companies Act 1985 –

255D   Power to apply provisions to banking partnerships

(1) The Secretary of State may by regulations apply to banking partnerships, subject to such exceptions, adaptations and modifications as he considers appropriate, the provisions of this Part applying to banking companies.

(2) A "banking partnership" means a partnership which is an authorised institution under the Banking Act 1987.

(3) Regulations under this section shall be made by statutory instrument.

(4) No regulations under this section shall be made unless a draft of the instrument containing the regulations has been laid before Parliament and approved by a resolution of each House.".

(3) Schedule 9 to the Companies Act 1985 (form and content of special category accounts) is amended in accordance with Schedule 7 to this Act.

(4) In that Schedule –

Part I   contains amendments relating to the form and content of accounts of banking and insurance companies and groups,

Part II   contains provisions with respect to the group accounts of banking and insurance groups,

Part III contains provisions adapting the requirements of Schedule 5 to the Companies Act 1985 (additional disclosure: related undertakings), and

Part IV   contains provisions relating to the requirements of Schedule 6 to that Act (additional disclosure: emoluments and other benefits of directors and others).

(5) Schedule 8 to this Act (directors' report where accounts prepared in accordance with special provisions for banking and insurance companies and groups) is substituted for Schedule 10 to the Companies Act 1985.

Supplementary provisions

19   Accounting standards

The following section is inserted in Part VII of the Companies Act 1985, as the beginning of a Chapter III –

"CHAPTER III
SUPPLEMENTARY PROVISIONS

Accounting standards

256 Accounting standards

(1) In this Part "accounting standards" means statements of standard accounting practice issued by such body or bodies as may be prescribed by regulations.

(2) References in this Part to accounting standards applicable to a company's annual accounts are to such standards as are, in accordance with their terms, relevant to the company's circumstances and to the accounts.

(3) The Secretary of State may make grants to or for the purposes of bodies concerned with –
    (*a*) issuing accounting standards,
    (*b*) overseeing and directing the issuing of such standards, or
    (*c*) investigating departures from such standards or from the accounting requirements of this Act and taking steps to secure compliance with them.

(4) Regulations under this section may contain such transitional and other supplementary and incidental provisions as appear to the Secretary of State to be appropriate.".

20 Power to alter accounting requirements

The following section is inserted in Part VII of the Companies Act 1985 –

"Power to alter accounting requirements

257 Power of Secretary of State to alter accounting requirements

(1) The Secretary of State may by regulations made by statutory instrument modify the provisions of this Part.

(2) Regulations which –
    (*a*) add to the classes of documents required to be prepared, laid before the company in general meeting or delivered to the registrar,
    (*b*) restrict the classes of company which have the benefit of any exemption, exception or special provision,
    (*c*) require additional matter to be included in a document of any class, or
    (*d*) otherwise render the requirements of this Part more onerous,
shall not be made unless a draft of the instrument containing the regulations has been laid before Parliament and approved by a resolution of each House.

(3) Otherwise, a statutory instrument containing regulations under this section shall be subject to annulment in pursuance of a resolution of either House of Parliament.

(4) Regulations under this section may –
    (*a*) make different provision for different cases or classes of case,
    (*b*) repeal and re-enact provisions with modifications of form or arrangement, whether or not they are modified in substance,

> (*c*) make consequential amendments or repeals in other provisions of this Act, or in other enactments, and
>
> (*d*) contain such transitional and other incidental and supplementary provisions as the Secretary of State thinks fit.

(5) Any modification by regulations under this section of section 258 or Schedule 10A (parent and subsidiary undertakings) does not apply for the purposes of enactments outside the Companies Acts unless the regulations so provide.".

21 Parent and subsidiary undertakings

(1) The following section is inserted in Part VII of the Companies Act 1985 –

"Parent and subsidiary undertakings

258 Parent and subsidiary undertakings

(1) The expressions "parent undertaking" and "subsidiary undertaking" in this Part shall be construed as follows; and a "parent company" means a parent undertaking which is a company.

(2) An undertaking is a parent undertaking in relation to another undertaking, a subsidiary undertaking, if –

> (*a*) it holds a majority of the voting rights in the undertaking, or
>
> (*b*) it is a member of the undertaking and has the right to appoint or remove a majority of its board of directors, or
>
> (*c*) it has the right to exercise a dominant influence over the undertaking –
>> (i) by virtue of provisions contained in the undertaking's memorandum or articles, or
>>
>> (ii) by virtue of a control contract, or
>
> (*d*) it is a member of the undertaking and controls alone, pursuant to an agreement with other shareholders or members, a majority of the voting rights in the undertaking.

(3) For the purposes of subsection (2) an undertaking shall be treated as a member of another undertaking –

> (*a*) if any of its subsidiary undertakings is a member of that undertaking, or
>
> (*b*) if any shares in that other undertaking are held by a person acting on behalf of the undertaking or any of its subsidiary undertakings.

(4) An undertaking is also a parent undertaking in relation to another undertaking, a subsidiary undertaking, if it has a participating interest in the undertaking and –

> (*a*) it actually exercises a dominant influence over it, or
>
> (*b*) it and the subsidiary undertaking are managed on a unified basis.

(5) A parent undertaking shall be treated as the parent undertaking of undertakings in relation to which any of its subsidiary undertakings are, or are to be treated as, parent undertakings; and references to its subsidiary undertakings shall be construed accordingly.

(6) Schedule 10A contains provisions explaining expressions used in this section and otherwise supplementing this section.".

(2) Schedule 9 to this Act (parent and subsidiary undertakings: supplementary provisions) is inserted after Schedule 10 to the Companies Act 1985, as Schedule 10A.

22 Other interpretation provisions

The following sections are inserted in Part VII of the Companies Act 1985 –

"Other interpretation provisions

259 Meaning of "undertaking" and related expressions

(1) In this Part "undertaking" means –

    (*a*) a body corporate or partnership, or

    (*b*) an unincorporated association carrying on a trade or business, with or without a view to profit.

(2) In this Part references to shares –

    (*a*) in relation to an undertaking with a share capital, are to allotted shares;

    (*b*) in relation to an undertaking with capital but no share capital, are to rights to share in the capital of the undertaking; and

    (*c*) in relation to an undertaking without capital, are to interests –

        (i) conferring any right to share in the profits or liability to contribute to the losses of the undertaking, or

        (ii) giving rise to an obligation to contribute to the debts or expenses of the undertaking in the event of a winding up.

(3) Other expressions appropriate to companies shall be construed, in relation to an undertaking which is not a company, as references to the corresponding persons, officers, documents or organs, as the case may be, appropriate to undertakings of that description.

This is subject to provision in any specific context providing for the translation of such expressions.

(4) References in this Part to "fellow subsidiary undertakings" are to undertakings which are subsidiary undertakings of the same parent undertaking but are not parent undertakings or subsidiary undertakings of each other.

(5) In this Part "group undertaking", in relation to an undertaking, means an undertaking which is –

    (*a*) a parent undertaking or subsidiary undertaking of that undertaking, or

    (*b*) a subsidiary undertaking of any parent undertaking of that undertaking.

260 Participating interests

(1) In this Part a "participating interest" means an interest held by an undertaking in the shares of another undertaking which it holds on a long-term basis for the purpose of securing a contribution to its activities by the exercise of control or influence arising from or related to that interest.

(2) A holding of 20 per cent. or more of the shares of an undertaking shall be presumed to be a participating interest unless the contrary is shown.

(3) The reference in subsection (1) to an interest in shares includes –
 (*a*) an interest which is convertible into an interest in shares, and
 (*b*) an option to acquire shares or any such interest;
and an interest or option falls within paragraph (*a*) or (*b*) notwithstanding that the shares to which it relates are, until the conversion or the exercise of the option, unissued.

(4) For the purposes of this section an interest held on behalf of an undertaking shall be treated as held by it.

(5) For the purposes of this section as it applies in relation to the expression "participating interest" in section 258(4) (definition of "subsidiary undertaking") –
 (*a*) there shall be attributed to an undertaking any interests held by any of its subsidiary undertakings, and
 (*b*) the references in subsection (1) to the purpose and activities of an undertaking include the purposes and activities of any of its subsidiary undertakings and of the group as a whole.

(6) In the balance sheet and profit and loss formats set out in Part I of Schedule 4, "participating interest" does not include an interest in a group undertaking.

(7) For the purposes of this section as it applies in relation to the expression "participating interest" –
 (*a*) in those formats as they apply in relation to group accounts, and
 (*b*) in paragraph 20 of Schedule 4A (group accounts: undertakings to be accounted for as associated undertakings),
the references in subsections (1) to (4) to the interest held by, and the purposes and activities of, the undertaking concerned shall be construed as references to the interest held by, and the purposes and activities of, the group (within the meaning of paragraph 1 of that Schedule).

261　Notes to the accounts

(1) Information required by this Part to be given in notes to a company's annual accounts may be contained in the accounts or in a separate document annexed to the accounts.

(2) References in this Part to a company's annual accounts, or to a balance sheet or profit and loss account, include notes to the accounts giving information which is required by any provision of this Act, and required or allowed by any such provision to be given in a note to company accounts.

262　Minor definitions

(1) In this Part –
"annual accounts" means –
 (*a*) the individual accounts required by section 226, and
 (*b*) any group accounts required by section 227, (but see also section 230 (treatment of individual profit and loss account where group accounts prepared));

"annual report", in relation to a company, means the directors' report required by section 234;

"balance sheet date" means the date as at which the balance sheet was made up;

"capitalisation", in relation to work or costs, means treating that work or those costs as a fixed asset;

"credit institution" means an undertaking carrying on a deposit-taking business within the meaning of the Banking Act 1987;

"fixed assets" means assets of a company which are intended for use on a continuing basis in the company's activities, and "current assets" means assets not intended for such use;

"group" means a parent undertaking and its subsidiary undertakings;

"included in the consolidation", in relation to group accounts, or "included in consolidated group accounts", means that the undertaking is included in the accounts by method of full (and not proportional) consolidation, and references to an undertaking excluded from consolidation shall be construed accordingly;

"purchase price", in relation to an asset of a company or any raw materials or consumables used in the production of such an asset, includes any consideration (whether in cash or otherwise) given by the company in respect of that asset or those materials or consumables, as the case may be;

"qualified", in relation to an auditors' report, means that the report does not state the auditors' unqualified opinion that the accounts have been properly prepared in accordance with this Act or, in the case of an undertaking not required to prepare accounts in accordance with this Act, under any corresponding legislation under which it is required to prepare accounts;

"true and fair view" refers –
    (*a*) in the case of individual accounts, to the requirement of section 226(2), and
    (*b*) in the case of group accounts, to the requirement of section 227(3);

"turnover", in relation to a company, means the amounts derived from the provision of goods and services falling within the company's ordinary activities, after deduction of –
    (i)   trade discounts,
    (ii) value added tax, and
    (iii) any other taxes based on the amounts so derived.

(2) In the case of an undertaking not trading for profit, any reference in this Part to a profit and loss account is to an income and expenditure account; and references to profit and loss and, in relation to group accounts, to a consolidated profit and loss account shall be construed accordingly.

(3) References in this Part to "realised profits" and "realised losses", in relation to a company's accounts, are to such profits or losses of the company as fall to be treated as realised in accordance with principles generally accepted, at the time when the accounts are prepared, with respect to the determination for accounting purposes of realised profits or losses.
This is without prejudice to –
    (*a*) the construction of any other expression (where appropriate) by reference to accepted accounting principles or practice, or
    (*b*) any specific provision for the treatment of profits or losses of any description as realised.

262A   Index of defined expressions

The following Table shows the provisions of this Part defining or otherwise explaining expressions used in this Part (other than expressions used only in the same section or paragraph) –

accounting reference date and accounting reference period	section 224
accounting standards and applicable accounting standards	section 256
annual accounts	
(generally)	section 262(1)
(includes notes to the accounts)	section 261(2)
annual report	section 262 (1)
associated undertaking (in Schedule 4A)	paragraph 20 of that Schedule
balance sheet (includes notes)	section 261(2)
balance sheet date	section 262(1)
banking group	section 255A(3)
capitalisation (in relation to work or costs)	section 262(1)
credit institution	section 262(1)
current assets	section 262(1)
fellow subsidiary undertaking	section 259(4)
financial year	section 223
fixed assets	section 262(1)
group	section 262(1)
group undertaking	section 259(5)
historical cost accounting rules (in Schedule 4)	paragraph 29 of that Schedule
included in the consolidation and related expressions	section 262(1)
individual accounts	section 262(1)
insurance group	section 255A(4)
land of freehold tenure and land of leasehold tenure (in relation to Scotland)	
– in Schedule 4	paragraph 93 of that Schedule
– in Schedule 9	paragraph 36 of that Schedule
lease, long lease and short lease	
– in Schedule 4	paragraph 83 of that Schedule
– in Schedule 9	paragraph 34 of that Schedule
listed investment	
– in Schedule 4	paragraph 84 of that Schedule
– in Schedule 9	paragraph 33 of that Schedule
notes to the accounts	section 261(1)
parent undertaking (and parent company)	section 258 and Schedule 10A
participating interest	section 260
pension costs (in Schedule 4)	paragraph 94(2) and (3) of that Schedule

period allowed for laying and delivering accounts and reports	section 244
profit and loss account (includes notes)	section 261(2)
(in relation to a company not trading for profit)	section 262(2)
provision – in Schedule 4	paragraphs 88 and 89 of that Schedule
– in Schedule 9	paragraph 32 of that Schedule
purchase price	section 262(1)
qualified	section 262(1)
realised losses and realised profits	section 262(3)
reserve (in Schedule 9)	paragraph 32 of that Schedule
shares	section 259(2)
social security costs (in Schedule 4)	paragraph 94(1) and (3) of that Schedule
special provisions for banking and insurance companies and groups	sections 255 and 255A
subsidiary undertaking	section 258 and Schedule 10A
true and fair view	section 262(1)
turnover	section 262(1)
undertaking and related expressions	section 259(1) to (3)”.

Consequential amendments

23 Consequential amendments

The enactments specified in Schedule 10 have effect with the amendments specified there, which are consequential on the amendments made by the preceding provisions of this Part.

PART II
ELIGIBILITY FOR APPOINTMENT AS COMPANY AUDITOR

Introduction

24 Introduction

(1) The main purposes of this Part are to secure that only persons who are properly supervised and appropriately qualified are appointed company auditors, and that audits by persons so appointed are carried out properly and with integrity and with a proper degree of independence.

(2) A "company auditor" means a person appointed as auditor under Chapter V of Part XI of the Companies Act 1985; and the expressions "company audit" and "company audit work" shall be construed accordingly.

Eligibility for appointment

25 Eligibility for appointment

(1) A person is eligible for appointment as a company auditor only if he –
  (*a*) is a member of a recognised supervisory body, and
  (*b*) is eligible for the appointment under the rules of that body.

(2) An individual or a firm may be appointed a company auditor.

(3) In the cases to which section 34 applies (individuals retaining only 1967 Act authorisation) a person's eligibility for appointment as a company auditor is restricted as mentioned in that section.

26 Effect of appointment of partnership

(1) The following provisions apply to the appointment as company auditor of a partnership constituted under the law of England and Wales or Northern Ireland, or under the law of any other country or territory in which a partnership is not a legal person.

(2) The appointment is (unless a contrary intention appears) an appointment of the partnership as such and not of the partners.

(3) Where the partnership ceases, the appointment shall be treated as extending to –
  (*a*) any partnership which succeeds to the practice of that partnership and is eligible for the appointment, and
  (*b*) any person who succeeds to that practice having previously carried it on in partnership and is eligible for the appointment.

(4) For this purpose a partnership shall be regarded as succeeding to the practice of another partnership only if the members of the successor partnership are substantially the same as those of the former partnership; and a partnership or other person shall be regarded as succeeding to the practice of a partnership only if it or he succeeds to the whole or substantially the whole of the business of the former partnership.

(5) Where the partnership ceases and no person succeeds to the appointment under subsection (3), the appointment may with the consent of the company be treated as extending to a partnership or other person eligible for the appointment who succeeds to the business of the former partnership or to such part of it as is agreed by the company shall be treated as comprising the appointment.

27 Ineligibility on ground of lack of independence

(1) A person is ineligible for appointment as company auditor of a company if he is –
  (*a*) an officer or employee of the company, or
  (*b*) a partner or employee of such a person, or a partnership of which such a person is a partner,
or if he is ineligible by virtue of paragraph (*a*) or (*b*) for appointment as company auditor of any associated undertaking of the company.
  For this purpose an auditor of a company shall not be regarded as an officer or employee of the company.

(2) A person is also ineligible for appointment as company auditor of a company if there exists between him or any associate of his and the company or any associated undertaking a connection of any such description as may be specified by regulations made by the Secretary of State.
  The regulations may make different provisions for different cases.

(3) In this section "associated undertaking", in relation to a company, means –
(a) a parent undertaking or subsidiary undertaking of the company, or
(b) a subsidiary undertaking of any parent undertaking of the company.

(4) Regulations under this section shall be made by statutory instrument which shall be subject to annulment in pursuance of a resolution of either House of Parliament.

28 Effect of ineligibility

(1) No person shall act as a company auditor if he is ineligible for appointment to the office.

(2) If during his term of office a company auditor becomes ineligible for appointment to the office, he shall thereupon vacate office and shall forthwith give notice in writing to the company concerned that he has vacated it by reason of ineligibility.

(3) A person who acts as company auditor in contravention of subsection (1), or fails to give notice of vacating his office as required by subsection (2), is guilty of an offence and liable –
(a) on conviction on indictment, to a fine, and
(b) on summary conviction, to a fine not exceeding the statutory maximum.

(4) In the case of continued contravention he is liable on a second or subsequent summary conviction (instead of the fine mentioned in subsection (3)(b)) to a fine not exceeding one-tenth of the statutory maximum in respect of each day on which the contravention is continued.

(5) In proceedings against a person for an offence under this section it is a defence for him to show that he did not know and had no reason to believe that he was, or had become, ineligible for appointment.

29 Power of Secretary of State to require second audit

(1) Where a person appointed company auditor was, for any part of the period during which the audit was conducted, ineligible for appointment to that office, the Secretary of State may direct the company concerned to retain a person eligible for appointment as auditor of the company –
(a) to audit the relevant accounts again, or
(b) to review the first audit and to report (giving his reasons) whether a second audit is needed;
and the company shall comply with such a direction within 21 days of its being given.

(2) If a second audit is recommended the company shall forthwith take such steps as are necessary to comply with the recommendation.

(3) Where a direction is given under this section, the Secretary of State shall send a copy of the direction to the registrar of companies; and the company shall within 21 days of receiving any report under subsection (1)(b) send a copy of it to the registrar of companies.
The provisions of the Companies Act 1985 relating to the delivery of documents to the registrar apply for the purposes of this subsection.

(4) Any statutory or other provisions applying in relation to the first audit shall apply, so far as practicable, in relation to a second audit under this section.

(5) If a company fails to comply with the requirements of this section, it is guilty of an offence and liable on summary conviction to a fine not exceeding the statutory maximum; and in the case of continued contravention it is liable on a second or subsequent summary

conviction (instead of the fine mentioned above) to a fine not exceeding one-tenth of the statutory maximum in respect of each day on which the contravention is continued.

(6) A direction under this section is, on the application of the Secretary of State, enforceable by injunction or, in Scotland, by an order under section 45 of the Court of Session Act 1988.

(7) If a person accepts an appointment, or continues to act, as company auditor at a time when he knows he is ineligible, the company concerned may recover from him any costs incurred by it in complying with the requirements of this section.

Recognition of supervisory bodies and professional qualifications

30 Supervisory bodies

(1) In this Part a "supervisory body" means a body established in the United Kingdom (whether a body corporate or an unincorporated association) which maintains and enforces rules as to –
> (*a*) the eligibility of persons to seek appointment as company auditors, and
> (*b*) the conduct of company audit work,

which are binding on persons seeking appointment or acting as company auditors either because they are members of that body or because they are otherwise subject to its control.

(2) In this Part references to the members of a supervisory body are to the persons who, whether or not members of the body, are subject to its rules in seeking appointment or acting as company auditors.

(3) In this Part references to the rules of a supervisory body are to the rules (whether or not laid down by the body itself) which the body has power to enforce and which are relevant for the purposes of this Part.
This includes rules relating to the admission and expulsion of members of the body, so far as relevant for the purposes of this Part.

(4) In this Part references to guidance issued by a supervisory body are to guidance issued or any recommendation made by it to all or any class of its members or persons seeking to become members which would, if it were a rule, fall within subsection (3).

(5) The provisions of Parts I and II of Schedule 11 have effect with respect to the recognition of supervisory bodies for the purposes of this Part.

31 Meaning of "appropriate qualification"

(1) A person holds an appropriate qualification for the purposes of this Part if –
> (*a*) he was by virtue of membership of a body recognised for the purposes of section 389(1)(*a*) of the Companies Act 1985 qualified for appointment as auditor of a company under that section immediately before 1st January 1990, and immediately before the commencement of section 25 above,
> (*b*) he holds a recognised professional qualification obtained in the United Kingdom, or
> (*c*) he holds an approved overseas qualification and satisfies any additional educational requirements applicable in accordance with section 33(4).

(2) A person who, immediately before 1st January 1990, and immediately before the commencement of section 25 above, was qualified for appointment as auditor of a company under section 389 of the Companies Act 1985 otherwise than by virtue of membership of a body recognised for the purposes of section 389(1)(*a*) –

(*a*) shall be treated as holding an appropriate qualification for twelve months from the day on which section 25 comes into force, and

(*b*) shall continue to be so treated if within that period he notifies the Secretary of State that he wishes to retain the benefit of his qualification.

The notice shall be in writing and shall contain such information as the Secretary of State may require.

(3) If a person fails to give such notice within the time allowed he may apply to the Secretary of State, giving such information as would have been required in connection with a notice, and the Secretary of State may, if he is satisfied –

(*a*) that there was good reason why the applicant did not give notice in time, and

(*b*) that the applicant genuinely intends to practise as an auditor in Great Britain, direct that he shall be treated as holding an appropriate qualification for the purposes of this Part.

(4) A person who –

(*a*) began before 1st January 1990 a course of study or practical training leading to a professional qualification in accountancy offered by a body established in the United Kingdom, and

(*b*) obtained that qualification on or after that date and before 1st January 1996, shall be treated as holding an appropriate qualification if the qualification is approved by the Secretary of State for the purposes of this subsection.

(5) Approval shall not be given unless the Secretary of State is satisfied that the body concerned has or, as the case may be, had at the relevant time adequate arrangements to ensure that the qualification is, or was, awarded only to persons educated and trained to a standard equivalent to that required in the case of a recognised professional qualification.

(6) A person shall not be regarded as holding an appropriate qualification for the purposes of this Part except in the above cases.

32 Qualifying bodies and recognised professional qualifications

(1) In this Part a "qualifying body" means a body established in the United Kingdom (whether a body corporate or an unincorporated association) which offers a professional qualification in accountancy.

(2) In this Part references to the rules of a qualifying body are to the rules (whether or not laid down by the body itself) which the body has power to enforce and which are relevant for the purposes of this Part.

This includes rules relating to –

(*a*) admission to or expulsion from a course of study leading to a qualification,

(*b*) the award or deprivation of a qualification, or

(*c*) the approval of a person for the purposes of giving practical training or the withdrawal of such approval,

so far as relevant for the purposes of this Part.

(3) In this Part references to guidance issued by any such body are to any guidance which the body issues, or any recommendation it makes to all or any class of persons holding or seeking to hold a qualification, or approved or seeking to be approved by the body for the purpose of giving practical training, which would, if it were a rule, fall within subsection (2).

(4) The provisions of Parts I and II of Schedule 12 have effect with respect to the recognition for the purposes of this Part of a professional qualification offered by a qualifying body.

33   Approval of overseas qualifications

(1) The Secretary of State may declare that persons who –
  (a) are qualified to audit accounts under the law of a specified country or territory outside the United Kingdom, or
  (b) hold a specified professional qualification in accountancy recognised under the law of a country or territory outside the United Kingdom,
shall be regarded for the purposes of this Part as holding an approved overseas qualification.

(2) A qualification shall not be so approved by the Secretary of State unless he is satisfied that it affords an assurance of professional competence equivalent to that afforded by a recognised professional qualification.

(3) In exercising the power conferred by subsection (1) the Secretary of State may have regard to the extent to which persons –
  (a) eligible under this Part for appointment as a company auditor, or
  (b) holding a professional qualification recognised under this Part,
are recognised by the law of the country or territory in question as qualified to audit accounts there.

(4) The Secretary of State may direct that a person holding an approved overseas qualification shall not be treated as holding an appropriate qualification for the purposes of this Part unless he holds such additional educational qualifications as the Secretary of State may specify for the purpose of ensuring that such persons have an adequate knowledge of the law and practice in the United Kingdom relevant to the audit of accounts.

(5) Different directions may be given in relation to different qualifications.

(6) The Secretary of State may if he thinks fit, having regard to the considerations mentioned in subsections (2) and (3), withdraw his approval of an overseas qualification in relation to persons becoming qualified as mentioned in subsection (1)(a), or obtaining such a qualification as is mentioned in subsection (1)(b), after such date as he may specify.

34   Eligibility of individuals retaining only 1967 Act authorisation

(1) A person whose only appropriate qualification is that he retains an authorisation granted by the Board of Trade or the Secretary of State under section 13(1) of the Companies Act 1967 is eligible only for appointment as auditor of an unquoted company.

(2) A company is "unquoted" if, at the time of the person's appointment, no shares or debentures of the company, or of a parent undertaking of which it is a subsidiary undertaking, have been quoted on a stock exchange (in Great Britain or elsewhere) or offered (whether in Great Britain or elsewhere) to the public for subscription or purchase.

(3) This section does not authorise the appointment of such a person as auditor of a company that carries on business as the promoter of a trading stamp scheme within the meaning of the Trading Stamps Act 1964.

(4) References to a person eligible for appointment as company auditor under section 25 in enactments relating to eligibility for appointment as auditor of a body other than a company do not include a person to whom this section applies.

Duties of recognised bodies

35 The register of auditors

(1) The Secretary of State shall make regulations requiring the keeping of a register of –
- (*a*) the individuals and firms eligible for appointment as company auditor, and
- (*b*) the individuals holding an appropriate qualification who are responsible for company audit work on behalf of such firms.

(2) The regulations shall provide that each person's entry in the register shall give –
- (*a*) his name and address, and
- (*b*) in the case of a person eligible as mentioned in subsection (1)(*a*), the name of the relevant supervisory body,

together with such other information as may be specified by the regulations.

(3) The regulations may impose such obligations as the Secretary of State thinks fit –
- (*a*) on recognised supervisory bodies,
- (*b*) on persons eligible for appointment as company auditor, and
- (*c*) on any person with whom arrangements are made by one or more recognised supervisory bodies with respect to the keeping of the register.

(4) The regulations may include provision –
- (*a*) requiring the register to be open to inspection at such times and places as may be specified in the regulations or determined in accordance with them,
- (*b*) enabling a person to require a certified copy of an entry in the register, and
- (*c*) authorising the charging of fees for inspection, or the provision of copies, of such reasonable amount as may be specified in the regulations or determined in accordance with them;

and may contain such other supplementary and incidental provisions as the Secretary of State thinks fit.

(5) Regulations under this section shall be made by statutory instrument which shall be subject to annulment in pursuance of a resolution of either House of Parliament.

(6) The obligations imposed by regulations under this section on such persons as are mentioned in subsection (3)(*a*) or (*c*) are enforceable on the application of the Secretary of State by injunction or, in Scotland, by an order under section 45 of the Court of Session Act 1988.

36 Information about firms to be available to public

(1) The Secretary of State shall make regulations requiring recognised supervisory bodies to keep and make available to the public the following information with respect to the firms eligible under their rules for appointment as a company auditor –
- (*a*) in relation to a body corporate, the name and address of each person who is a director of the body or holds any shares in it,
- (*b*) in relation to a partnership, the name and address of each partner,

and such other information as may be specified in the regulations.

(2) The regulations may impose such obligations as the Secretary of State thinks fit –
- (*a*) on recognised supervisory bodies,
- (*b*) on persons eligible for appointment as company auditor, and
- (*c*) on any person with whom arrangements are made by one or more recognised supervisory bodies with respect to the keeping of the information.

(3) The regulations may include provision –

(*a*) requiring that the information be open to inspection at such times and places as may be specified in the regulations or determined in accordance with them,

(*b*) enabling a person to require a certified copy of the information or any part of it, and

(*c*) authorising the charging of fees for inspection, or the provision of copies, of such reasonable amount as may be specified in the regulations or determined in accordance with them;

and may contain such other supplementary and incidental provisions as the Secretary of State thinks fit.

(4) The regulations may make different provision in relation to different descriptions of information and may contain such other supplementary and incidental provisions as the Secretary of State thinks fit.

(5) Regulations under this section shall be made by statutory instrument which shall be subject to annulment in pursuance of a resolution of either House of Parliament.

(6) The obligations imposed by regulations under this section on such persons as are mentioned in subsection (2)(*a*) or (*c*) are enforceable on the application of the Secretary of State by injunction or, in Scotland, by an order under section 45 of the Court of Session Act 1988.

37 Matters to be notified to the Secretary of State

(1) The Secretary of State may require a recognised supervisory or qualifying body –

(*a*) to notify him forthwith of the occurrence of such events as he may specify in writing and to give him such information in respect of those events as is so specified;

(*b*) to give him, at such times or in respect of such periods as he may specify in writing, such information as is so specified.

(2) The notices and information required to be given shall be such as the Secretary of State may reasonably require for the exercise of his functions under this Part.

(3) The Secretary of State may require information given under this section to be given in a specified form or verified in a specified manner.

(4) Any notice or information required to be given under this section shall be given in writing unless the Secretary of State specifies or approves some other manner.

38 Power to call for information

(1) The Secretary of State may by notice in writing require a recognised supervisory or qualifying body to give him such information as he may reasonably require for the exercise of his functions under this Part.

(2) The Secretary of State may require that any information which he requires under this section shall be given within such reasonable time and verified in such manner as he may specify.

39 Compliance orders

(1) If at any time it appears to the Secretary of State –

(*a*) in the case of a recognised supervisory body, that any requirement of Schedule 11 is not satisfied,

(*b*) in the case of a recognised professional qualification, that any requirement of Schedule 12 is not satisfied, or

(c) that a recognised supervisory or qualifying body has failed to comply with an obligation to which it is subject by virtue of this Part,

he may, instead of revoking the relevant recognition order make an application to the court under this section.

(2) If on such application the court decides that the subsection or requirement in question is not satisfied or, as the case may be, that the body has failed to comply with the obligation in question it may order the supervisory or qualifying body in question to take such steps as the court directs for securing that the subsection or requirement is satisfied or that the obligation is complied with.

(3) The jurisdiction conferred by this section is exercisable by the High Court and the Court of Session.

40 Directions to comply with international obligations

(1) If it appears to the Secretary of State –
- (a) that any action proposed to be taken by a recognised supervisory or qualifying body, or a body established by order under section 46 would be incompatible with Community obligations or any other international obligations of the United Kingdom, or
- (b) that any action which that body has power to take is required for the purpose of implementing any such obligations,

he may direct the body not to take or, as the case may be, to take the action in question.

(2) A direction may include such supplementary or incidental requirements as the Secretary of State thinks necessary or expedient.

(3) A direction under this section is enforceable on the application of the Secretary of State by injunction or, in Scotland, by an order under section 45 of the Court of Session Act 1988.

Offences

41 False and misleading statements

(1) A person commits an offence if –
- (a) for the purposes of or in connection with any application under this Part, or
- (b) in purported compliance with any requirement imposed on him by or under this Part,

he furnishes information which he knows to be false or misleading in a material particular or recklessly furnishes information which is false or misleading in a material particular.

(2) It is an offence for a person whose name does not appear on the register of auditors kept under regulations under section 35 to describe himself as a registered auditor or so to hold himself out as to indicate, or be reasonably understood to indicate, that he is a registered auditor.

(3) It is an offence for a body which is not a recognised supervisory or qualifying body to describe itself as so recognised or so to describe itself or hold itself out as to indicate, or be reasonably understood to indicate, that it is so recognised.

(4) A person guilty of an offence under subsection (1) is liable –
- (a) on conviction on indictment, to imprisonment for a term not exceeding two years or to a fine or both;

(*b*) on summary conviction, to imprisonment for a term not exceeding six months or to a fine not exceeding the statutory maximum or both.

(5) A person guilty of an offence under subsection (2) or (3) is liable on summary conviction to imprisonment for a term not exceeding six months or to a fine not exceeding level 5 on the standard scale or both.

Where a contravention of subsection (2) or (3) involves a public display of the offending description, the maximum fine that may be imposed is (in place of that mentioned above) an amount equal to level 5 on the standard scale multiplied by the number of days for which the display has continued.

(6) It is a defence for a person charged with an offence under subsection (2) or (3) to show that he took all reasonable precautions and exercised all due diligence to avoid the commission of the offence.

42 Offences by bodies corporate, partnerships and unincorporated associations

(1) Where an offence under this Part committed by a body corporate is proved to have been committed with the consent or connivance of, or to be attributable to any neglect on the part of, a director, manager, secretary or other similar officer of the body, or a person purporting to act in any such capacity, he as well as the body corporate is guilty of the offence and liable to be proceeded against and punished accordingly.

(2) Where the affairs of a body corporate are managed by its members, subsection (1) applies in relation to the acts and defaults of a member in connection with his functions of management as to a director of a body corporate.

(3) Where an offence under this Part committed by a partnership is proved to have been committed with the consent or connivance of, or to be attributable to any neglect on the part of, a partner, he as well as the partnership is guilty of the offence and liable to be proceeded against and punished accordingly.

(4) Where an offence under this Part committed by an unincorporated association (other than a partnership) is proved to have been committed with the consent or connivance of, or to be attributable to any neglect on the part of, any officer of the association or any member of its governing body, he as well as the association is guilty of the offence and liable to be proceeded against and punished accordingly.

43 Time limits for prosecution of offences

(1) Any information relating to an offence under this Part which is triable by a magistrates' court in England and Wales may be so tried on an information laid at any time within twelve months after the date on which evidence sufficient in the opinion of the Director of Public Prosecutions or the Secretary of State to justify the proceedings comes to his knowledge.

(2) Proceedings in Scotland for an offence under this Part may be commenced at any time within twelve months after the date on which evidence sufficient in the Lord Advocate's opinion to justify the proceedings came to his knowledge or, where such evidence was reported to him by the Secretary of State, within twelve months after the date on which it came to the knowledge of the latter.

For the purposes of this subsection proceedings shall be deemed to be commenced on the date on which a warrant to apprehend or to cite the accused is granted, if the warrant is executed without undue delay.

(3) Subsection (1) does not authorise the trial on an information laid, and subsection (2) does not authorise the commencement of proceedings, more than three years after the commission of the offence.

(4) For the purposes of this section a certificate of the Director of Public Prosecutions, the Lord Advocate or the Secretary of State as to the date on which such evidence as is referred to above came to his knowledge is conclusive evidence.

(5) Nothing in this section affects proceedings within the time limits prescribed by section 127(1) of the Magistrates' Courts Act 1980 or section 331 of the Criminal Procedure (Scotland) Act 1975 (the usual time limits for criminal proceedings).

44 Jurisdiction and procedure in respect of offences

(1) Summary proceedings for an offence under this Part may, without prejudice to any jurisdiction exercisable apart from this section, be taken against a body corporate or unincorporated association at any place at which it has a place of business and against an individual at any place where he is for the time being.

(2) Proceedings for an offence alleged to have been committed under this Part by an unincorporated association shall be brought in the name of the association (and not in that of any of its members), and for the purposes of any such proceedings any rules of court relating to the service of documents apply as in relation to a body corporate.

(3) Section 33 of the Criminal Justice Act 1925 and Schedule 3 to the Magistrates' Courts Act 1980 (procedure on charge of offence against a corporation) apply in a case in which an unincorporated association is charged in England and Wales with an offence under this Part as they apply in the case of a corporation.

(4) In relation to proceedings on indictment in Scotland for an offence alleged to have been committed under this Part by an unincorporated association, section 74 of the Criminal Procedure (Scotland) Act 1975 (proceedings on indictment against bodies corporate) applies as if the association were a body corporate.

(5) A fine imposed on an unincorporated association on its conviction of such an offence shall be paid out of the funds of the association.

Supplementary provisions

45 Fees

(1) An applicant for a recognition order under this Part shall pay such fee in respect of his application as may be prescribed; and no application shall be regarded as duly made unless this subsection is complied with.

(2) Every recognised supervisory or qualifying body shall pay such periodical fees to the Secretary of State as may be prescribed.

(3) In this section "prescribed" means prescribed by regulations made by the Secretary of State, which may make different provision for different cases or classes of case.

(4) Regulations under this section shall be made by statutory instrument which shall be subject to annulment in pursuance of a resolution of either House of Parliament.

(5) Fees received by the Secretary of State by virtue of this Part shall be paid into the Consolidated Fund.

46   Delegation of functions of Secretary of State

(1) The Secretary of State may by order (a "delegation order") establish a body corporate to exercise his functions under this Part.

(2) A delegation order has the effect of transferring to the body established by it, subject to such exceptions and reservations as may be specified in the order, all the functions of the Secretary of State under this Part except –

(*a*) such functions under Part I of Schedule 14 (prevention of restrictive practices) as are excepted by regulations under section 47, and

(*b*) his functions in relation to the body itself;

and the order may also confer on the body such other functions supplementary or incidental to those transferred as appear to the Secretary of State to be appropriate.

(3) Any transfer of the functions under the following provisions shall be subject to the reservation that they remain exercisable concurrently by the Secretary of State –

(*a*) section 38 (power to call for information), and

(*b*) section 40 (directions to comply with international obligations);

and any transfer of the function of refusing to approve an overseas qualification, or withdrawing such approval, on the grounds referred to in section 33(3) (lack of reciprocity) shall be subject to the reservation that the function is exercisable only with the consent of the Secretary of State.

(4) A delegation order may be amended or, if it appears to the Secretary of State that it is no longer in the public interest that the order should remain in force, revoked by a further order under this section.

(5) Where functions are transferred or resumed, the Secretary of State may by order confer or, as the case may be, take away such other functions supplementary or incidental to those transferred or resumed as appear to him to be appropriate.

(6) The provisions of Schedule 13 have effect with respect to the status, constitution and proceedings of a body established by a delegation order, the exercise by it of certain functions transferred to it and other supplementary matters.

(7) An order under this section shall be made by statutory instrument.

(8) An order which has the effect of transferring or resuming any functions shall not be made unless a draft of it has been laid before and approved by resolution of each House of Parliament; and any other description of order shall be subject to annulment in pursuance of a resolution of either House of Parliament.

47   Restrictive practices

(1) The provisions of Schedule 14 have effect with respect to certain matters relating to restrictive practices and competition law.

(2) The Secretary of State may make provision by regulations as to the discharge of the functions under paragraphs 1 to 7 of that Schedule when a delegation order is in force.

(3) The regulations may –

(*a*) except any function from the effect of the delegation order,

(*b*) modify any of the provisions mentioned in subsection (2), and

(*c*) impose such duties on the body established by the delegation order, the Secretary of State and Director General of Fair Trading as appear to the Secretary of State to be appropriate.

(4) The regulations shall contain such provision as appears to the Secretary of State to be necessary or expedient for reserving to him the decision –

    (*a*) to refuse recognition on the ground mentioned in paragraph 1(3) of that Schedule, or

    (*b*) to exercise the powers conferred by paragraph 6 of that Schedule.

(5) For that purpose the regulations may –

    (*a*) prohibit the body from granting a recognition order without the leave of the Secretary of State, and

    (*b*) empower the Secretary of State to direct the body to exercise its powers in such manner as may be specified in the direction.

(6) Regulations under this section shall be made by statutory instrument which shall be subject to annulment in pursuance of a resolution of either House of Parliament.

48 Exemption from liability for damages

(1) Neither a recognised supervisory body, nor any of its officers or employees or members of its governing body, shall be liable in damages for anything done or omitted in the discharge or purported discharge of functions to which this subsection applies, unless the act or omission is shown to have been in bad faith.

(2) Subsection (1) applies to the functions of the body so far as relating to, or to matters arising out of –

    (*a*) such rules, practices, powers and arrangements of the body to which the requirements of Part II of Schedule 11 apply, or

    (*b*) the obligations with which paragraph 16 of that Schedule requires the body to comply,

    (*c*) any guidance issued by the body, or

    (*d*) the obligations to which the body is subject by virtue of this Part.

(3) Neither a body established by a delegation order, nor any of its members, officers or employees, shall be liable in damages for anything done or omitted in the discharge or purported discharge of the functions exercisable by virtue of an order under section 46, unless the act or omission is shown to have been in bad faith.

49 Service of notices

(1) This section has effect in relation to any notice, direction or other document required or authorised by or under this Part to be given to or served on any person other than the Secretary of State.

(2) Any such document may be given to or served on the person in question –

    (*a*) by delivering it to him,

    (*b*) by leaving it at his proper address, or

    (*c*) by sending it by post to him at that address.

(3) Any such document may –

    (*a*) in the case of a body corporate, be given to or served on the secretary or clerk of that body;

    (*b*) in the case of a partnership, be given to or served on any partner;

    (*c*) in the case of an unincorporated association other than a partnership, be given to or served on any member of the governing body of the association.

(4) For the purposes of this section and section 7 of the Interpretation Act 1978 (service of documents by post) in its application to this section, the proper address of any person is

his last known address (whether of his residence or of a place where he carries on business or is employed) and also –

    (*a*) in the case of a person who is eligible under the rules of a recognised supervisory body for appointment as company auditor and who does not have a place of business in the United Kingdom, the address of that body;

    (*b*) in the case of a body corporate, its secretary or its clerk, the address of its registered or principal office in the United Kingdom;

    (*c*) in the case of an unincorporated association (other than a partnership) or a member of its governing body, its principal office in the United Kingdom.

50 Power to make consequential amendments

(1) The Secretary of State may by regulations make such amendments of enactments as appear to him to be necessary or expedient in consequence of the provisions of this Part having effect in place of section 389 of the Companies Act 1985.

(2) That power extends to making such amendments as appear to the Secretary of State necessary or expedient of –

    (*a*) enactments referring by name to the bodies of accountants recognised for the purposes of section 389(1)(*a*) of the Companies Act 1985, and

    (*b*) enactments making with respect to other statutory auditors provision as to the matters dealt with in relation to company auditors by section 389 of the Companies Act 1985.

(3) The provision which may be made with respect to other statutory auditors includes provision as to –

    (*a*) eligibility for the appointment,

    (*b*) the effect of appointing a partnership which is not a legal person and the manner of exercise of the auditor's rights in such a case, and

    (*c*) ineligibility on the ground of lack of independence or any other ground.

(4) The regulations may contain such supplementary, incidental and transitional provision as appears to the Secretary of State to be necessary or expedient.

(5) The Secretary of State shall not make regulations under this section with respect to any statutory auditors without the consent of –

    (*a*) the Minister responsible for their appointment or responsible for the body or person by, or in relation to whom, they are appointed, or

    (*b*) if there is no such Minister, the person by whom they are appointed.

(6) In this section a "statutory auditor" means a person appointed auditor in pursuance of any enactment authorising or requiring the appointment of an auditor or auditors.

(7) Regulations under this section shall be made by statutory instrument which shall be subject to annulment in pursuance of a resolution of either House of Parliament.

51 Power to make provision in consequence of changes affecting accountancy bodies

(1) The Secretary of State may by regulations make such amendments of enactments as appear to him to be necessary or expedient in consequence of any change of name, merger or transfer of engagements affecting –

    (*a*) a recognised supervisory or qualifying body under this Part, or

    (*b*) a body of accountants referred to in, or approved, authorised or otherwise recognised for the purposes of, any other enactment.

(2) Regulations under this section shall be made by statutory instrument which shall be subject to annulment in pursuance of a resolution of either House of Parliament.

52 Meaning of "associate"

(1) In this Part "associate", in relation to a person, shall be construed as follows.

(2) In relation to an individual "associate" means –
  (*a*) that individual's spouse or minor child or step-child,
  (*b*) any body corporate of which that individual is a director, and
  (*c*) any employee or partner of that individual.
(3) In relation to a body corporate "associate" means –
  (*a*) any body corporate of which that body is a director,
  (*b*) any body corporate in the same group as that body, and
  (*c*) any employee or partner of that body or of any body corporate in the same group.

(4) In relation to a Scottish firm, or a partnership constituted under the law of any other country or territory in which a partnership is a legal person, "associate" means –
  (*a*) any body corporate of which the firm is a director,
  (*b*) any employee of or partner in the firm, and
  (*c*) any person who is an associate of a partner in the firm.

(5) In relation to a partnership constituted under the law of England and Wales or Northern Ireland, or the law of any other country or territory in which a partnership is not a legal person, "associate" means any person who is an associate of any of the partners.

53 Minor definitions

(1) In this Part –
  "address" means –
  (*a*) in relation to an individual, his usual residential or business address, and
  (*b*) in relation to a firm, its registered or principal office in Great Britain;

  "company" means any company or other body to which section 384 of the Companies Act 1985 (duty to appoint auditors) applies;

  "director", in relation to a body corporate, includes any person occupying in relation to it the position of a director (by whatever name called) and any person in accordance with whose directions or instructions (not being advice given in a professional capacity) the directors of the body are accustomed to act;

  "enactment" includes an enactment contained in subordinate legislation within the meaning of the Interpretation Act 1978.

  "firm" means a body corporate or a partnership;

  "group", in relation to a body corporate, means the body corporate, any other body corporate which is its holding company or subsidiary and any other body corporate which is a subsidiary of that holding company; and

  "holding company" and "subsidiary" have the meaning given by section 736 of the Companies Act 1985;

  "parent undertaking" and "subsidiary undertaking" have the same meaning as in Part VII of the Companies Act 1985.

(2) For the purposes of this Part a body shall be regarded as "established in the United Kingdom" if and only if –

   (*a*) it is incorporated or formed under the law of the United Kingdom or a part of the United Kingdom, or

   (*b*) its central management and control is exercised in the United Kingdom;

and any reference to a qualification "obtained in the United Kingdom" is to a qualification obtained from such a body.

54   Index of defined expressions

The following Table shows provisions defining or otherwise explaining expressions used in this Part (other than provisions defining or explaining an expression used only in the same section) –

address	section 53(1)
appropriate qualification	section 31
associate	section 52
company	section 53(1)
company auditor, company audit and company audit work	section 24(2)
delegation order	section 46
director (of a body corporate)	section 53(1)
Director (in Schedule 14)	paragraph 1(1) of that Schedule
enactment	section 53(1)
established in the United Kingdom	section 53(2)
firm	section 53(1)
group (in relation to a body corporate)	section 53(1)
guidance	
– of a qualifying body	section 32(3)
– of a supervisory body	section 30(4)
holding company	section 53(1)
member (of a supervisory body)	section 30(2)
obtained in the United Kingdom	section 53(2)
parent undertaking	section 53(1)
purposes of this Part	section 24(1)
qualifying body	section 32(1)
recognised	
– in relation to a professional qualification	section 32(4) and Schedule 12
– in relation to a qualifying body	paragraph 2(1) of Schedule 12
– in relation to a supervisory body	section 30(5) and Schedule 11
rules	
– of a qualifying body	section 32(2)
– of a supervisory body	section 30(3)
subsidiary and subsidiary undertaking	section 53(1)
supervisory body	section 30(1)

PART III
INVESTIGATIONS AND POWERS TO OBTAIN INFORMATION

Amendments of the Companies Act 1985

55 Investigations by inspectors not leading to published report

In section 432 of the Companies Act 1985 (appointment of inspectors by Secretary of State), after subsection (2) (investigation of circumstances suggesting misconduct) insert –

> "(2A) Inspectors may be appointed under subsection (2) on terms that any report they may make is not for publication; and in such a case, the provisions of section 437(3) (availability and publication of inspectors' reports) do not apply.".

56 Production of documents and evidence to inspectors

(1) Section 434 of the Companies Act 1985 (production of documents and evidence to inspectors) is amended as follows.

(2) In subsection (1) (duty of officers to assist inspectors), for "books and documents" substitute "documents".

(3) For subsection (2) (power to require production of documents, attendance or other assistance) substitute –

> "(2) If the inspectors consider that an officer or agent of the company or other body corporate, or any other person, is or may be in possession of information relating to a matter which they believe to be relevant to the investigation, they may require him –
>> (*a*) to produce to them any documents in his custody or power relating to that matter,
>> (*b*) to attend before them, and
>> (*c*) otherwise to give them all assistance in connection with the investigation which he is reasonably able to give;
> and it is that person's duty to comply with the requirement.".

(4) For subsection (3) (power to examine on oath) substitute –

> "(3) An inspector may for the purposes of the investigation examine any person on oath, and may administer an oath accordingly.".

(5) After subsection (5) insert –

> "(6) In this section "documents" includes information recorded in any form; and, in relation to information recorded otherwise than in legible form, the power to require its production includes power to require the production of a copy of the information in legible form.".

(6) In section 436 of the Companies Act 1985 (obstruction of inspectors treated as contempt of court), for subsections (1) and (2) substitute –

> "(1) If any person –
>> (*a*) fails to comply with section 434(1)(*a*) or (*c*),
>> (*b*) refuses to comply with a requirement under section 434(1)(*b*) or (2), or
>> (*c*) refuses to answer any question put to him by the inspectors for the purposes of the investigation,

the inspectors may certify that fact in writing to the court."

57 Duty of inspectors to report

In section 437 of the Companies Act 1985 (inspectors' reports), after subsection (1A) insert –

"(1B) If it appears to the Secretary of State that matters have come to light in the course of the inspectors' investigation which suggest that a criminal offence has been committed, and those matters have been referred to the appropriate prosecuting authority, he may direct the inspectors to take no further steps in the investigation or to take only such further steps as are specified in the direction.

(1C) Where an investigation is the subject of a direction under subsection (1B), the inspectors shall make a final report to the Secretary of State only where –
   (*a*) they were appointed under section 432(1) (appointment in pursuance of an order of the court), or
   (*b*) the Secretary of State directs them to do so.".

58 Power to bring civil proceedings on the company's behalf

In section 438 of the Companies Act 1985 (power to bring civil proceedings on the company's behalf), for the opening words of subsection (1) down to "it appears to the Secretary of State" substitute "If from any report made or information obtained under this Part it appears to the Secretary of State".

59 Expenses of investigating a company's affairs

(1) Section 439 of the Companies Act 1985 (expenses of investigating a company's affairs) is amended as follows.

(2) For subsection (1) substitute –

"(1) The expenses of an investigation under any of the powers conferred by this Part shall be defrayed in the first instance by the Secretary of State, but he may recover those expenses from the persons liable in accordance with this section.
   There shall be treated as expenses of the investigation, in particular, such reasonable sums as the Secretary of State may determine in respect of general staff costs and overheads.".

(3) In subsection (4) for "the inspectors' report" substitute "an inspectors' report".

(4) For subsection (5) substitute –
   "(5) Where inspectors were appointed –
      (*a*) under section 431, or
      (*b*) on an application under section 442(3),
   the applicant or applicants for the investigation is or are liable to such extent (if any) as the Secretary of State may direct.".

60 Power of Secretary of State to present winding-up petition

(1) Section 440 of the Companies Act 1985 (power of Secretary of State to present winding-up petition) is repealed; but the following amendments have the effect of re-enacting that provision, with modifications.

(2) In section 124(4) of the Insolvency Act 1986 (application by Secretary of State for company to be wound up by the court), for paragraph (*b*) substitute –
   "(*b*) in a case falling within section 124A below.".

(3) After that section insert –

"124A Petition for winding up on grounds of public interest

(1) Where it appears to the Secretary of State from –
- (*a*) any report made or information obtained under Part XIV of the Companies Act 1985 (company investigations, &c.),
- (*b*) any report made under section 94 or 177 of the Financial Services Act 1986 or any information obtained under section 105 of that Act,
- (*c*) any information obtained under section 2 of the Criminal Justice Act 1987 or section 52 of the Criminal Justice (Scotland) Act 1987 (fraud investigations), or
- (*d*) any information obtained under section 83 of the Companies Act 1989 (powers exercisable for purpose of assisting overseas regulatory authorities),

that it is expedient in the public interest that a company should be wound up, he may present a petition for it to be wound up if the court thinks it just and equitable for it to be so.

(2) This section does not apply if the company is already being wound up by the court.".

61 Inspectors' reports as evidence

In section 441 of the Companies Act 1985 (inspectors' reports to be evidence), in subsection (1) for "sections 431 or 432" substitute "this Part".

62 Investigation of company ownership

In section 442 of the Companies Act 1985 (power to investigate company ownership), for subsection (3) (investigation on application by members of company) substitute –

"(3) If an application for investigation under this section with respect to particular shares or debentures of a company is made to the Secretary of State by members of the company, and the number of applicants or the amount of shares held by them is not less than that required for an application for the appointment of inspectors under section 431(2)(*a*) or (*b*), then, subject to the following provisions, the Secretary of State shall appoint inspectors to conduct the investigation applied for.

(3A) The Secretary of State shall not appoint inspectors if he is satisfied that the application is vexatious; and where inspectors are appointed their terms of appointment shall exclude any matter in so far as the Secretary of State is satisfied that it is unreasonable for it to be investigated.

(3B) The Secretary of State may, before appointing inspectors require the applicant or applicants to give security, to an amount not exceeding £5,000, or such other sum as he may by order specify, for payment of the costs of the investigation.
An order under this subsection shall be made by statutory instrument which shall be subject to annulment in pursuance of a resolution of either House of Parliament.

(3C) If on an application under subsection (3) it appears to the Secretary of State that the powers conferred by section 444 are sufficient for the purposes of investigating the matters which inspectors would be appointed to investigate, he may instead conduct the investigation under that section.".

63   Secretary of State's power to require production of documents

(1) Section 447 of the Companies Act 1985 (power of Secretary of State to require production of documents) is amended as follows.

(2) Omit subsection (1) (bodies in relation to which powers exercisable), and –
  (*a*) in subsections (2) and (3) for "any such body" substitute "a company",
  (*b*) in subsections (4) and (5) for "any body" and "a body" substitute "a company", and
  (*c*) in subsections (5) and (6) for "the body" substitute "the company".

(3) For "books or papers", wherever occurring, substitute "documents".

(4) In subsection (3) (power to authorise officer to require production of documents) after "an officer of his" insert "or any other competent person", after "the officer" in the first place where it occurs insert "or other person" and for "the officer" in the second place where it occurs substitute "he (the officer or other person)".

(5) In subsection (4) (power to require production of documents in possession of third party) after "an officer of his" and after "the officer" (twice) insert "or other person".

(6) In subsection (6), for the second sentence substitute –
    "Sections 732 (restriction on prosecutions), 733 (liability of individuals for corporate default) and 734 (criminal proceedings against unincorporated bodies) apply to this offence.".

(7) After subsection (8) insert –

    "(9) In this section "documents" includes information recorded in any form; and, in relation to information recorded otherwise than in legible form, the power to require its production includes power to require the production of a copy of it in legible form.".

(8) In Schedule 24 to the Companies Act 1985 (punishment of offences), in the entry relating to section 447(6), for "books and papers" substitute "documents".

64   Entry and search of premises

(1) For section 448 of the Companies Act 1985 (entry and search of premises) substitute –

"448   Entry and search of premises

(1) A justice of the peace may issue a warrant under this section if satisfied on information on oath given by or on behalf of the Secretary of State, or by a person appointed or authorised to exercise powers under this Part, that there are reasonable grounds for believing that there are on any premises documents whose production has been required under this Part and which have not been produced in compliance with the requirement.

(2) A justice of the peace may also issue a warrant under this section if satisfied on information on oath given by or on behalf of the Secretary of State, or by a person appointed or authorised to exercise powers under this Part –

(*a*) that there are reasonable grounds for believing that an offence has been committed for which the penalty on conviction on indictment is imprisonment for a term of not less than two years and that there are on any premises documents relating to whether the offence has been committed,

(*b*) that the Secretary of State, or the person so appointed or authorised, has power to require the production of the documents under this Part, and

(*c*) that there are reasonable grounds for believing that if production was so required the documents would not be produced but would be removed from the premises, hidden, tampered with or destroyed.

(3) A warrant under this section shall authorise a constable, together with any other person named in it and any other constables –

(*a*) to enter the premises specified in the information, using such force as is reasonably necessary for the purpose;

(*b*) to search the premises and take possession of any documents appearing to be such documents as are mentioned in subsection (1) or (2), as the case may be, or to take, in relation to any such documents, any other steps which may appear to be necessary for preserving them or preventing interference with them;

(*c*) to take copies of any such documents; and

(*d*) to require any person named in the warrant to provide an explanation of them or to state where they may be found.

(4) If in the case of a warrant under subsection (2) the justice of the peace is satisfied on information on oath that there are reasonable grounds for believing that there are also on the premises other documents relevant to the investigation, the warrant shall also authorise the actions mentioned in subsection (3) to be taken in relation to such documents.

(5) A warrant under this section shall continue in force until the end of the period of one month beginning with the day on which it is issued.

(6) Any documents of which possession is taken under this section may be retained –

(*a*) for a period of three months, or

(*b*) if within that period proceedings to which the documents are relevant are commenced against any person for any criminal offence, until the conclusion of those proceedings.

(7) Any person who intentionally obstructs the exercise of any rights conferred by a warrant issued under this section or fails without reasonable excuse to comply with any requirement imposed in accordance with subsection (3)(*d*) is guilty of an offence and liable to a fine.

Sections 732 (restriction on prosecutions), 733 (liability of individuals for corporate default) and 734 (criminal proceedings against unincorporated bodies) apply to this offence.

(8) For the purposes of sections 449 and 451A (provision for security of information) documents obtained under this section shall be treated as if they had been obtained under the provision of this Part under which their production was or, as the case may be, could have been required.

(9) In the application of this section to Scotland for the references to a justice

of the peace substitute references to a justice of the peace or a sheriff, and for the references to information on oath substitute references to evidence on oath.

(10) In this section "document" includes information recorded in any form.".

(2) In Schedule 24 to the Companies Act 1985 (punishment of offences), in the entry relating to section 448(5) –
(*a*) in the first column for "448(5)" substitute "448(7)", and
(*b*) for the entry in the second column substitute –

"Obstructing the exercise of any rights conferred by a warrant or failing to comply with a requirement imposed under subsection (3)(*d*).".

65 Provision for security of information obtained

(1) Section 449 of the Companies Act 1985 (provision for security of information obtained) is amended as follows.

(2) In subsection (1) (purposes for which disclosure permitted) –
(*a*) in the opening words for "body" (twice) substitute "company".
(*b*) for paragraph (*c*) substitute –
"(*c*) for the purposes of enabling or assisting any inspector appointed under this Part, or under section 94 or 177 of the Financial Services Act 1986, to discharge his functions;";
(*c*) after that paragraph insert –
"(*cc*) for the purpose of enabling or assisting any person authorised to exercise powers under section 44 of the Insurance Companies Act 1982, section 447 of this Act, section 106 of the Financial Services Act 1986 or section 84 of the Companies Act 1989 to discharge his functions;";
(*d*) in paragraph (*d*) for "or the Financial Services Act 1986" substitute ", the Financial Services Act 1986 or Part II, III or VII of the Companies Act 1989,";
(*e*) omit paragraph (*e*);
(*f*) in paragraph (*h*) for "(*n*) or (*p*)" substitute "or (*n*)";
(*g*) after that paragraph insert –
"(*hh*) for the purpose of enabling or assisting a body established by order under section 46 of the Companies Act 1989 to discharge its functions under Part II of that Act, or of enabling or assisting a recognised supervisory or qualifying body within the meaning of that Part to discharge its functions as such;";
(*h*) after paragraph (*l*) insert –
"(*ll*) with a view to the institution of, or otherwise for the purposes of, any disciplinary proceedings relating to the discharge by a public servant of his duties;";
(*i*) for paragraph (*m*) substitute –
"(*m*) for the purpose of enabling or assisting an overseas regulatory authority to exercise its regulatory functions.".

(3) For subsection (1A) substitute –

"(1A) In subsection (1) –

    (*a*) in paragraph (*ll*) "public servant" means an officer or servant of the Crown or of any public or other authority for the time being designated for the purposes of that paragraph by the Secretary of State by order made by statutory instrument; and

    (*b*) in paragraph (*m*) "overseas regulatory authority" and "regulatory functions" have the same meaning as in section 82 of the Companies Act 1989.".

(4) In subsection (1B) (disclosure to designated public authorities) for "designated for the purposes of this section" substitute "designated for the purposes of this subsection".

(5) In subsection (2), for the second sentence substitute –

    "Sections 732 (restriction on prosecutions), 733 (liability of individuals for corporate default) and 734 (criminal proceedings against unincorporated bodies) apply to this offence.".

(6) For subsection (3) substitute –

    "(3) For the purposes of this section each of the following is a competent authority –

    (*a*) the Secretary of State,

    (*b*) an inspector appointed under this Part or under section 94 or 177 of the Financial Services Act 1986,

    (*c*) any person authorised to exercise powers under section 44 of the Insurance Companies Act 1982, section 447 of this Act, section 106 of the Financial Services Act 1986 or section 84 of the Companies Act 1989,

    (*d*) the Department of Economic Development in Northern Ireland,

    (*e*) the Treasury,

    (*f*) the Bank of England,

    (*g*) the Lord Advocate,

    (*h*) the Director of Public Prosecutions, and the Director of Public Prosecutions for Northern Ireland,

    (*i*) any designated agency or transferee body within the meaning of the Financial Services Act 1986, and any body administering a scheme under section 54 of or paragraph 18 of Schedule 11 to that Act (schemes for compensation of investors),

    (*j*) the Chief Registrar of friendly societies and the Registrar of Friendly Societies for Northern Ireland,

    (*k*) the Industrial Assurance Commissioner and the Industrial Assurance Commissioner for Northern Ireland,

    (*l*) any constable,

    (*m*) any procurator fiscal.

    (3A) Any information which may by virtue of this section be disclosed to a competent authority may be disclosed to any officer or servant of the authority.".

(7) In subsection (4) (orders) for "subsection (1B)" substitute "subsection (1A)(*a*) or (1B)".

66 Punishment for destroying, mutilating, &c. company documents

(1) Section 450 of the Companies Act 1985 (punishment for destroying, mutilating, &c. company documents) is amended as follows.

(2) In subsection (1) for the opening words down to "insurance company" substitute "An officer of a company, or of an insurance company", for "body's" substitute "company's" and for "the body" substitute "the company".

(3) For subsection (4) substitute –

"(4) Sections 732 (restriction on prosecutions), 733 (liability of individuals for corporate default) and 734 (criminal proceedings against unincorporated bodies) apply to an offence under this section.".

(4) After that subsection insert –

"(5) In this section "document" includes information recorded in any form."

67 Punishment for furnishing false information

In section 451 of the Companies Act 1985 (punishment for furnishing false information), for the second sentence substitute –

"Sections 732 (restriction on prosecutions), 733 (liability of individuals for corporate default) and 734 (criminal proceedings against unincorporated bodies) apply to this offence."

68 Disclosure of information by Secretary of State or inspector

For section 451A of the Companies Act 1985 (disclosure of information by the Secretary of State) substitute –

"451A Disclosure of information by Secretary of State or inspector

(1) This section applies to information obtained under sections 434 to 446.

(2) The Secretary of State may, if he thinks fit –

(*a*) disclose any information to which this section applies to any person to whom, or for any purpose for which, disclosure is permitted under section 449, or

(*b*) authorise or require an inspector appointed under this Part to disclose such information to any such person or for any such purpose.

(3) Information to which this section applies may also be disclosed by an inspector appointed under this Part to –

(*a*) another inspector appointed under this Part or an inspector appointed under section 94 or 177 of the Financial Services Act 1986, or

(*b*) a person authorised to exercise powers under section 44 of the Insurance Companies Act 1982, section 447 of this Act, section 106 of the Financial Services Act 1986 or section 84 of the Companies Act 1989.

(4) Any information which may by virtue of subsection (3) be disclosed to any person may be disclosed to any officer or servant of that person.

(5) The Secretary of State may, if he thinks fit, disclose any information obtained under section 444 to –

(*a*) the company whose ownership was the subject of the investigation,

(*b*) any member of the company,

(*c*) any person whose conduct was investigated in the course of the investigation, (*d*) the auditors of the company, or

(*e*) any person whose financial interests appear to the Secretary of State to be affected by matters covered by the investigation.".

69 Protection of banking information

(1) Section 452 of the Companies Act 1985 (privileged information) is amended as follows.

(2) In subsection (1), omit paragraph (*b*) (disclosure by bankers of information relating to their customers).

(3) After that subsection insert –

"(1A) Nothing in section 434, 443 or 446 requires a person (except as mentioned in subsection (1B) below) to disclose information or produce documents in respect of which he owes an obligation of confidence by virtue of carrying on the business of banking unless –

(*a*) the person to whom the obligation of confidence is owed is the company or other body corporate under investigation,

(*b*) the person to whom the obligation of confidence is owed consents to the disclosure or production, or

(*c*) the making of the requirement is authorised by the Secretary of State.

(1B) Subsection (1A) does not apply where the person owing the obligation of confidence is the company or other body corporate under investigation under section 431, 432 or 433.".

(4) In subsection (3) after "officer of his" insert "or other person".

70 Investigation of oversea companies

In section 453 of the Companies Act 1985 (investigation of oversea companies), for subsection (1) substitute –

"(1) The provisions of this Part apply to bodies corporate incorporated outside Great Britain which are carrying on business in Great Britain, or have at any time carried on business there, as they apply to companies under this Act; but subject to the following exceptions, adaptations and modifications.

(1A) The following provisions do not apply to such bodies –

(*a*) section 431 (investigation on application of company or its members),

(*b*) section 438 (power to bring civil proceedings on the company's behalf),

(*c*) sections 442 to 445 (investigation of company ownership and power to obtain information as to those interested in shares, &c.), and

(*d*) section 446 (investigation of share dealings).

(1B) The other provisions of this Part apply to such bodies subject to such adaptations and modifications as may be specified by regulations made by the Secretary of State.".

71 Investigation of unregistered companies

In Schedule 22 to the Companies Act 1985 (provisions applying to unregistered companies), for the entry relating to Part XIV substitute –

"Part XIV (except   Investigation of companies and their affairs; —".
section 446)   requisition of documents.

Amendments of the Financial Services Act 1986

72 Investigations into collective investment schemes

(1) Section 94 of the Financial Services Act 1986 (investigations into collective investment schemes) is amended as follows.

(2) For subsection (7) (privilege on grounds of banker's duty of confidentiality) substitute –

> "(7) Nothing in this section requires a person (except as mentioned in subsection (7A) below) to disclose any information or produce any document in respect of which he owes an obligation of confidence by virtue of carrying on the business of banking unless –
>> (*a*) the person to whom the obligation of confidence is owed consents to the disclosure or production, or
>> (*b*) the making of the requirement was authorised by the Secretary of State.
>
> (7A) Subsection (7) does not apply where the person owing the obligation of confidence or the person to whom it is owed is –
>> (*a*) the manager, operator or trustee of the scheme under investigation, or
>> (*b*) a manager, operator or trustee whose own affairs are under investigation.".

(3) After subsection (8) (duty of inspectors to report) insert –

> "(8A) If it appears to the Secretary of State that matters have come to light in the course of the inspectors' investigation which suggest that a criminal offence has been committed, and those matters have been referred to the appropriate prosecuting authority, he may direct the inspectors to take no further steps in the investigation or to take only such further steps as are specified in the direction.
>
> (8B) Where an investigation is the subject of a direction under subsection (8A), the inspectors shall make a final report to the Secretary of State only where the Secretary of State directs them to do so.".

(4) After subsection (9) add –

> "(10) A person who is convicted on a prosecution instituted as a result of an investigation under this section may in the same proceedings be ordered to pay the expenses of the investigation to such extent as may be specified in the order.
>
> There shall be treated as expenses of the investigation, in particular, such reasonable sums as the Secretary of State may determine in respect of general staff costs and overheads.".

73 Investigations into affairs of persons carrying on investment business

(1) Section 105 of the Financial Services Act 1986 (investigation into affairs of person carrying on investment business) is amended as follows.

(2) Omit subsection (7) (privilege on grounds of banker's duty of confidentiality).

(3) In subsection (9) (interpretation), in the definition of "documents", for "references to its production include references to producing" substitute "the power to require its production includes power to require the production of".

(4) After subsection (10) add –

"(11) A person who is convicted on a prosecution instituted as a result of an investigation under this section may in the same proceedings be ordered to pay the expenses of the investigation to such extent as may be specified in the order.

There shall be treated as expenses of the investigation, in particular, such reasonable sums as the Secretary of State may determine in respect of general staff costs and overheads.".

(5) In section 106 of the Financial Services Act 1986 (exercise of investigation powers by officer, &c.), after subsection (2) insert –

"(2A) A person shall not by virtue of an authority under this section be required to disclose any information or produce any documents in respect of which he owes an obligation of confidence by virtue of carrying on the business of banking unless –
 (a) he is the person under investigation or a related company,
 (b) the person to whom the obligation of confidence is owed is the person under investigation or a related company,
 (c) the person to whom the obligation of confidence is owed consents to the disclosure or production, or
 (d) the imposing on him of a requirement with respect to such information or documents has been specifically authorised by the Secretary of State.

In this subsection "documents", "person under investigation" and "related company" have the same meaning as in section 105.".

74 Investigations into insider dealing

(1) Section 177 of the Financial Services Act 1986 (investigations into insider dealing) is amended as follows.

(2) After subsection (2) (power to limit period or scope of investigation) insert –

"(2A) At any time during the investigation the Secretary of State may vary the appointment by limiting or extending the period during which the inspector is to continue his investigation or by confining the investigation to particular matters.".

(3) After subsection (5) (duty of inspectors to report) insert –

"(5A) If the Secretary of State thinks fit, he may direct the inspector to take no further steps in the investigation or to take only such further steps as are specified in the direction; and where an investigation is the subject of such a direction, the inspectors shall make a final report to the Secretary of State only where the Secretary of State directs them to do so.".

(4) For subsection (8) (privilege on grounds of banker's duty of confidentiality) substitute –

"(8) A person shall not under this section be required to disclose any information or produce any document in respect of which he owes an obligation of confidence by virtue of carrying on the business of banking unless –

(*a*) the person to whom the obligation of confidence is owed consents to the disclosure or production, or

(*b*) the making of the requirement was authorised by the Secretary of State.".

(5) In subsection (10) (definition of "documents") for "references to its production include references to producing" substitute "the power to require its production includes power to require the production of".

(6) After subsection (10) add –

"(11) A person who is convicted on a prosecution instituted as a result of an investigation under this section may in the same proceedings be ordered to pay the expenses of the investigation to such extent as may be specified in the order.

There shall be treated as expenses of the investigation, in particular, such reasonable sums as the Secretary of State may determine in respect of general staff costs and overheads.".

75 Restrictions on disclosure of information

(1) In section 179(3) of the Financial Services Act 1986 (persons who are "primary recipients" for purposes of provisions restricting disclosure of information) –

(*a*) omit the word "and" preceding paragraph (*i*);

(*b*) in that paragraph, after "any such person" insert "as is mentioned in paragraphs (*a*) to (*h*) above;

(*c*) after that paragraph insert –
    "(*j*) any constable or other person named in a warrant issued under this Act.".

(2) Section 180 of the Financial Services Act 1986 (exceptions from restrictions on disclosure) is amended as follows.

(3) In subsection (1) (purposes for which disclosure permitted) –

(*a*) in paragraph (*c*), after "insolvency" insert "or by Part II, III or VII of the Companies Act 1989";

(*b*) for paragraph (*e*) substitute –
    "(*e*)   for the purpose –
        (i) of enabling or assisting a designated agency to discharge its functions under this Act or Part VII of the Companies Act 1989,
        (ii) of enabling or assisting a transferee body or the competent authority to discharge its functions under this Act, or
        (iii) of enabling or assisting the body administrating a scheme under section 54 above to discharge its functions under the scheme;";

(*c*) after paragraph (*h*) insert –
    "(*hh*) for the purpose of enabling or assisting a body established by order under section 46 of the Companies Act 1989 to discharge its functions under Part II of that Act, or of enabling or assisting a recognised supervisory or qualifying body within the meaning of that Part to discharge its functions as such;";

(*d*) after paragraph (*o*) insert –
    "(*oo*) with a view to the institution of, or otherwise for the purposes of, any disciplinary proceedings relating to the discharge by a public servant of his duties;";

(*e*) in paragraph (*p*), after "under" insert "section 44 of the Insurance Companies Act 1982, section 447 of the Companies Act 1985," and after "above" insert "or section 84 of the Companies Act 1989";

(*f*) after paragraph (*q*) insert –

"(*qq*) for the purpose of enabling or assisting an overseas regulatory authority to exercise its regulatory functions;".

(4) After that subsection insert –

"(1A) In subsection (1) –

(*a*) in paragraph (*oo*) "public servant" means an officer or servant of the Crown or of any public or other authority for the time being designated for the purposes of that paragraph by order of the Secretary of State; and

(*b*) in paragraph (*qq*) "overseas regulatory authority" and "regulatory functions" have the same meaning as in section 82 of the Companies Act 1989.".

(5) In subsection (3) (disclosure to designated public authorities) for "designated for the purposes of this section" substitute "designated for the purposes of this subsection".

(6) Omit subsection (6) (disclosure to certain overseas authorities).

(7) In subsection (9) (orders) for "subsection (3) or (8)" substitute "subsection (1A)(*a*), (3) or (8)".

76 Entry and search of premises

(1) Section 199 of the Financial Services Act 1986 (powers of entry) is amended as follows.

(2) For subsections (1) and (2) substitute –

"(1) A justice of the peace may issue a warrant under this section if satisfied on information on oath given by or on behalf of the Secretary of State that there are reasonable grounds for believing that an offence has been committed –

(*a*) under section 4, 47, 57, 130, 133 or 171(2) or (3) above, or

(*b*) section 1, 2, 4 or 5 of the Company Securities (Insider Dealing) Act 1985,

and that there are on any premises documents relevant to the question whether that offence has been committed.

(2) A justice of the peace may also issue a warrant under this section if satisfied on information on oath given by or on behalf of the Secretary of State, or by a person appointed or authorised to exercise powers under section 94, 106 or 177 above, that there are reasonable grounds for believing that there are on any premises documents whose production has been required under section 94, 105 or 177 above and which have not been produced in compliance with the requirement.".

(3) In subsection (3)(*b*) for "subsection (1)(*a*) or (*b*)" substitute "subsection (1)".

(4) In subsection (5) (period for which documents may be retained), for paragraph (*b*) substitute –

"(*b*) if within that period proceedings to which the documents are relevant are commenced against any person for any criminal offence, until the conclusion of those proceedings.".

(5) In subsection (6) (offences) after "Any person who" insert "intentionally".

(6) In subsection (7) for "subsection (1)(*a*) above" substitute "subsection (1) above".

(7) For subsection (8) substitute –

"(8) In the application of this section to Scotland for the references to a justice of the peace substitute references to a justice of the peace or a sheriff, and for the references to information on oath substitute references to evidence on oath.".

(8) In subsection (9) (definition of "documents"), omit the words from "and, in relation" to the end.

Amendments of other enactments

77 Amendments of the Insurance Companies Act 1982

(1) Part II of the Insurance Companies Act 1982 is amended as follows.

(2) In section 44 (power to obtain information and require production of documents), for "books or papers" (wherever occurring) substitute "documents", and for subsection (6) substitute –

"(6) In this section "document" includes information recorded in any form; and, in relation to information recorded otherwise than in legible form, the power to require its production includes power to require the production of a copy of the information in legible form.".

(3) After that section insert –

"44A Entry and search of premises

(1) A justice of the peace may issue a warrant under this section if satisfied on information on oath given by or on behalf of the Secretary of State, or by a person authorised to exercise powers under section 44 above, that there are reasonable grounds for believing that there are on any premises documents whose production has been required under section 44(2) to (4) above and which have not been produced in compliance with the requirement.

(2) A justice of the peace may also issue a warrant under this section if satisfied on information on oath given by or on behalf of the Secretary of State, or by a person authorised to exercise powers under section 44 above –

 (*a*) that there are reasonable grounds for believing that an offence has been committed for which the penalty on conviction on indictment is imprisonment for a term of not less than two years and that there are on any premises documents relating to whether the offence has been committed,

 (*b*) that the Secretary of State or, as the case may be, the authorised person has power to require the production of the documents under section 44(2) to (4) above, and

 (*c*) that there are reasonable grounds for believing that if production was so required the documents would not be produced but would be removed from the premises, hidden, tampered with or destroyed.

(3) A warrant under this section shall authorise a constable, together with any other person named in it and any other constables –

 (*a*) to enter the premises specified in the information, using such force as is reasonably necessary for the purpose;

(*b*) to search the premises and take possession of any documents appearing to be such documents as are mentioned in subsection (1) or (2), as the case may be, or to take, in relation to any such documents, any other steps which may appear to be necessary for preserving them or preventing interference with them;

(*c*) to take copies of any such documents; and

(*d*) to require any person named in the warrant to provide an explanation of them or to state where they may be found.

(4) If in the case of a warrant under subsection (2) the justice of the peace is satisfied on information on oath that there are reasonable grounds for believing that there are also on the premises other documents relevant to the investigation, the warrant shall also authorise the actions mentioned in subsection (3) to be taken in relation to such documents.

(5) A warrant under this section shall continue in force until the end of the period of one month beginning with the day on which it is issued.

(6) Any documents of which possession is taken under this section may be retained –

(*a*) for a period of three months; or

(*b*) if within that period proceedings to which the documents are relevant are commenced against any person for any criminal offence, until the conclusion of those proceedings.

(7) In the application of this section to Scotland for the references to a justice of the peace substitute references to a justice of the peace or a sheriff, and for the references to information on oath substitute references to evidence on oath.

(8) In this section "document" includes information recorded in any form.".

(4) In section 47A(1) (restriction on disclosure of information), after "section 44(2) to (4)" insert "or 44A".

(5) In section 71 (offences and penalties), after subsection (2) insert –

"(2A) A person who intentionally obstructs the exercise of any rights conferred by a warrant issued under section 44A above or fails without reasonable excuse to comply with any requirement imposed in accordance with subsection (3)(*d*) of that section is guilty of an offence and liable –

(*a*) on conviction on indictment, to a fine, and

(*b*) on summary conviction, to a fine not exceeding the statutory maximum.".

(6) In section 71(6) (defence to failure to comply with requirement to produce books or papers) for "books or papers" substitute "documents".

78 Amendment of the Insolvency Act 1986

In section 218(5) of the Insolvency Act 1986 (investigation by Secretary of State on report by liquidator), for paragraph (*a*) substitute –

"(*a*) shall thereupon investigate the matter reported to him and such other matters relating to the affairs of the company as appear to him to require investigation, and".

79   Amendment of the Company Directors Disqualification Act 1986

In section 8 of the Company Directors Disqualification Act 1986 (disqualification after investigation of company), after "section 52 of the Criminal Justice (Scotland) Act 1987" insert "or section 83 of the Companies Act 1989".

80   Amendment of the Building Societies Act 1986

In section 53 of the Building Societies Act 1986 (confidentiality of information obtained by the Building Societies Commission), in subsection (7)(*b*) (functions of Secretary of State for purposes of which disclosure may be made) after sub-paragraph (ii) insert –

> ", or
>> (iii) Part II, III or VII of the Companies Act 1989;".

81   Amendments of the Banking Act 1987

(1) In section 84(1) of the Banking Act 1987 (disclosure of information obtained under that Act), the Table showing the authorities to which, and functions for the purposes of which, disclosure may be made is amended as follows.

(2) In the entry relating to the Secretary of State, in column 2, for "or the Financial Services Act 1986" substitute ", the Financial Services Act 1986 or Part II, III or VII of the Companies Act 1989".

(3) For the entry relating to inspectors appointed by the Secretary of State substitute –

"An inspector appointed under Part XIV of the Companies Act 1985 or section 94 or 177 of the Financial Services Act 1986.	Functions under that Part or that section.".

(4) For the entry beginning "A person authorised by the Secretary of State" substitute –

"A person authorised to exercise powers under section 44 of the Insurance Companies Act 1982, section 447 of the Companies Act 1985, section 106 of the Financial Services Act 1986 or section 84 of the Companies Act 1989.	Functions under that section.".

(5) For the entry relating to a designated agency or transferee body or the competent authority (within the meaning of the Financial Services Act 1986) substitute –

"A designated agency (within the meaning of the Financial Services Act 1986).	Functions under the Financial Services Act 1986 or Part VII of the Companies Act 1989.
A transferee body or the competent authority (within the meaning of the Financial Services Act 1986).	Functions under the Financial Services Act 1986.".

Powers exercisable to assist overseas regulatory authorities

82   Request for assistance by overseas regulatory authority

(1) The powers conferred by section 83 are exercisable by the Secretary of State for the

purpose of assisting an overseas regulatory authority which has requested his assistance in connection with inquiries being carried out by it or on its behalf.

(2) An "overseas regulatory authority" means an authority which in a country or territory outside the United Kingdom exercises –

(a) any function corresponding to –
  (i) a function under the Financial Services Act 1986 of a designated agency, transferee body or competent authority (within the meaning of that Act),
  (ii) a function of the Secretary of State under the Insurance Companies Act 1982, the Companies Act 1985 or the Financial Services Act 1986, or
  (iii) a function of the Bank of England under the Banking Act 1987, or

(b) any function in connection with the investigation of, or the enforcement of rules (whether or not having the force of law) relating to, conduct of the kind prohibited by the Company Securities (Insider Dealing) Act 1985, or

(c) any function prescribed for the purposes of this subsection by order of the Secretary of State, being a function which in the opinion of the Secretary of State relates to companies or financial services.

An order under paragraph (c) shall be made by statutory instrument which shall be subject to annulment in pursuance of a resolution of either House of Parliament.

(3) The Secretary of State shall not exercise the powers conferred by section 83 unless he is satisfied that the assistance requested by the overseas regulatory authority is for the purposes of its regulatory functions.

An authority's "regulatory functions" means any functions falling within subsection (2) and any other functions relating to companies or financial services.

(4) In deciding whether to exercise those powers the Secretary of State may take into account, in particular –

(a) whether corresponding assistance would be given in that country or territory to an authority exercising regulatory functions in the United Kingdom;

(b) whether the inquiries relate to the possible breach of a law, or other requirement, which has no close parallel in the United Kingdom or involves the assertion of a jurisdiction not recognised by the United Kingdom;

(c) the seriousness of the matter to which the inquiries relate, the importance to the inquiries of the information sought in the United Kingdom and whether the assistance could be obtained by other means;

(d) whether it is otherwise appropriate in the public interest to give the assistance sought.

(5) Before deciding whether to exercise those powers in a case where the overseas regulatory authority is a banking supervisor, the Secretary of State shall consult the Bank of England.

A "banking supervisor" means an overseas regulatory authority with respect to which the Bank of England has notified the Secretary of State, for the purposes of this subsection, that it exercises functions corresponding to those of the Bank under the Banking Act 1987.

(6) The Secretary of State may decline to exercise those powers unless the overseas regulatory authority undertakes to make such contribution towards the costs of their exercise as the Secretary of State considers appropriate.

(7) References in this section to financial services include, in particular, investment business, insurance and banking.

83 Power to require information, documents or other assistance

(1) The following powers may be exercised in accordance with section 82, if the Secretary of State considers there is good reason for their exercise.

(2) The Secretary of State may require any person –

(*a*) to attend before him at a specified time and place and answer questions or otherwise furnish information with respect to any matter relevant to the inquiries,

(*b*) to produce at a specified time and place any specified documents which appear to the Secretary of State to relate to any matter relevant to the inquiries, and

(*c*) otherwise to give him such assistance in connection with the inquiries as he is reasonably able to give.

(3) The Secretary of State may examine a person on oath and may administer an oath accordingly.

(4) Where documents are produced the Secretary of State may take copies or extracts from them.

(5) A person shall not under this section be required to disclose information or produce a document which he would be entitled to refuse to disclose or produce on grounds of legal professional privilege in proceedings in the High Court or on grounds of confidentiality as between client and professional legal adviser in proceedings in the Court of Session, except that a lawyer may be required to furnish the name and address of his client.

(6) A statement by a person in compliance with a requirement imposed under this section may be used in evidence against him.

(7) Where a person claims a lien on a document, its production under this section is without prejudice to his lien.

(8) In this section "documents" includes information recorded in any form; and, in relation to information recorded otherwise than in legible form, the power to require its production includes power to require the production of a copy of it in legible form.

84 Exercise of powers by officer, &c

(1) The Secretary of State may authorise an officer of his or any other competent person to exercise on his behalf all or any of the powers conferred by section 83.

(2) No such authority shall be granted except for the purpose of investigating –

(*a*) the affairs, or any aspects of the affairs, of a person specified in the authority, or

(*b*) a subject-matter so specified,

being a person who, or subject-matter which, is the subject of the inquiries being carried out by or on behalf of the overseas regulatory authority.

(3) No person shall be bound to comply with a requirement imposed by a person exercising powers by virtue of an authority granted under this section unless he has, if required, produced evidence of his authority.

(4) A person shall not by virtue of an authority under this section be required to disclose any information or produce any documents in respect of which he owes an obligation of confidence by virtue of carrying on the business of banking unless –

(*a*) the imposing on him of a requirement with respect to such information or documents has been specifically authorised by the Secretary of State, or

(*b*) the person to whom the obligation of confidence is owed consents to the disclosure or production.

In this subsection "documents" has the same meaning as in section 83.

(5) Where the Secretary of State authorises a person other than one of his officers to exercise any powers by virtue of this section, that person shall make a report to the Secretary of State in such manner as he may require on the exercise of those powers and the results of exercising them.

85 Penalty for failure to comply with requirement, &c

(1) A person who without reasonable excuse fails to comply with a requirement imposed on him under section 83 commits an offence and is liable on summary conviction to imprisonment for a term not exceeding six months or to a fine not exceeding level 5 on the standard scale, or both.

(2) A person who in purported compliance with any such requirement furnishes information which he knows to be false or misleading in a material particular, or recklessly furnishes information which is false or misleading in a material particular, commits an offence and is liable –
- (*a*) on conviction on indictment, to imprisonment for a term not exceeding two years or to a fine, or both;
- (*b*) on summary conviction, to imprisonment for a term not exceeding six months or to a fine not exceeding the statutory maximum, or both.

86 Restrictions on disclosure of information

(1) This section applies to information relating to the business or other affairs of a person which –
- (*a*) is supplied by an overseas regulatory authority in connection with a request for assistance, or
- (*b*) is obtained by virtue of the powers conferred by section 83, whether or not any requirement to supply it is made under that section.

(2) Except as permitted by section 87 below, such information shall not be disclosed for any purpose –
- (*a*) by the primary recipient, or
- (*b*) by any person obtaining the information directly or indirectly from him,
without the consent of the person from whom the primary recipient obtained the information and, if different, the person to whom it relates.

(3) The "primary recipient" means, as the case may be –
- (*a*) the Secretary of State,
- (*b*) any person authorised under section 84 to exercise powers on his behalf, and
- (*c*) any officer or servant of any such person.

(4) Information shall not be treated as information to which this section applies if it has been made available to the public by virtue of being disclosed in any circumstances in which, or for any purpose for which, disclosure is not precluded by this section.

(5) A person who contravenes this section commits an offence and is liable –
- (*a*) on conviction on indictment, to imprisonment for a term not exceeding two years or to a fine, or both;
- (*b*) on summary conviction, to imprisonment for a term not exceeding three months or to a fine not exceeding the statutory maximum, or both.

87   Exceptions from restrictions on disclosure

(1) Information to which section 86 applies may be disclosed –

(*a*) to any person with a view to the institution of, or otherwise for the purposes of, relevant proceedings,

(*b*) for the purpose of enabling or assisting a relevant authority to discharge any relevant function (including functions in relation to proceedings),

(*c*) to the Treasury, if the disclosure is made in the interests of investors or in the public interest,

(*d*) if the information is or has been available to the public from other sources,

(*e*) in a summary or collection of information framed in such a way as not to enable the identity of any person to whom the information relates to be ascertained, or

(*f*) in pursuance of any Community obligation.

(2) The relevant proceedings referred to in subsection (1)(*a*) are –

(*a*) any criminal proceedings,

(*b*) civil proceedings arising under or by virtue of the Financial Services Act 1986 and proceedings before the Financial Services Tribunal, and

(*c*) disciplinary proceedings relating to –

(i) the exercise by a solicitor, auditor, accountant, valuer or actuary of his professional duties, or

(ii) the discharge by a public servant of his duties.

(3) In subsection (2)(*c*)(ii) "public servant" means an officer or servant of the Crown or of any public or other authority for the time being designated for the purposes of that provision by order of the Secretary of State.

(4) The relevant authorities referred to in subsection (1)(*b*), and the relevant functions in relation to each such authority, are as follows –

Authority	*Functions*
The Secretary of State.	Functions under the enactments relating to companies, insurance companies or insolvency, or under the Financial Services Act 1986 or Part II, this Part or Part VII of this Act.
An inspector appointed under Part XIV of the Companies Act 1985 or section 94 or 177 of the Financial Services Act 1986.	Functions under that Part or that section.
A person authorised to exercise powers under section 44 of the Insurance Companies Act 1982, section 447 of the Companies Act 1985, section 106 of the Financial Services Act 1986 or section 84 of this Act.	Functions under that section.
An overseas regulatory authority.	Its regulatory functions (within the meaning of section 82 of this Act).

Authority	*Functions*
The Department of Economic Development in Northern Ireland or a person appointed or authorised by that Department.	Functions conferred on it or him by the enactments relating to companies or insolvency.
A designated agency within the meaning of the Financial Services Act 1986.	Functions under that Act or Part VII of this Act.
A transferee body or the competent authority within the meaning of the Financial Services Act 1986.	Functions under that Act.
The body administering a scheme under section 54 of the Financial Services Act 1986.	Functions under the scheme.
A recognised self-regulating organisation, recognised professional body, recognised investment exchange, recognised clearing house or recognised self-regulating organisation for friendly societies (within the meaning of the Financial Services Act 1986).	Functions in its capacity as an organisation, body, exchange or clearing house recognised under that Act.
The Chief Registrar of friendly societies, the Registrar of Friendly Societies for Northern Ireland and the Assistant Registrar of Friendly Societies for Scotland.	Functions under the Financial Services Act 1986 or the enactments relating to friendly societies or building societies.
The Bank of England.	Functions under the Banking Act 1987 and any other functions.
The Deposit Protection Board.	Functions under the Banking Act 1987.
A body established by order under section 46 of this Act.	Functions under Part II of this Act.
A recognised supervisory or qualifying body within the meaning of Part II of this Act.	Functions as such a body.
The Industrial Assurance Commissioner and the Industrial Assurance Commissioner for Northern Ireland.	Functions under the enactments relating to industrial assurance.
The Insurance Brokers Registration Council.	Functions under the Insurance Brokers (Registration) Act 1977.
The Official Receiver or, in Northern Ireland, the Official Assignee for company liquidations or for bankruptcy.	Functions under the enactments relating to insolvency.
A recognised professional body (within the meaning of section 391 of the Insolvency Act 1986).	Functions in its capacity as such a body under the Insolvency Act 1986.

Authority	Functions
The Building Societies Commission.	Functions under the Building Societies Act 1986.
The Director General of Fair Trading.	Functions under the Financial Services Act 1986.

(5) The Secretary of State may by order amend the Table in subsection (4) so as to –
- (*a*) add any public or other authority to the Table and specify the relevant functions of that authority,
- (*b*) remove any authority from the Table, or
- (*c*) add functions to, or remove functions from, those which are relevant functions in relation to an authority specified in the Table;

and the order may impose conditions subject to which, or otherwise restrict the circumstances in which, disclosure is permitted.

(6) An order under this section shall be made by statutory instrument which shall be subject to annulment in pursuance of a resolution of either House of Parliament.

88   Exercise of powers in relation to Northern Ireland

(1) The following provisions apply where it appears to the Secretary of State that a request for assistance by an overseas regulatory authority may involve the powers conferred by section 83 being exercised in Northern Ireland in relation to matters which are transferred matters within the meaning of the Northern Ireland Constitution Act 1973.

(2) The Secretary of State shall before deciding whether to accede to the request consult the Department of Economic Development in Northern Ireland, and if he decides to accede to the request and it appears to him –
- (*a*) that the powers should be exercised in Northern Ireland, and
- (*b*) that the purposes for which they should be so exercised relate wholly or primarily to transferred matters,

he shall by instrument in writing authorise the Department to exercise in Northern Ireland his powers under section 83.

(3) The following provisions have effect in relation to the exercise of powers by virtue of such an authority with the substitution for references to the Secretary of State of references to the Department of Economic Development in Northern Ireland –
- (*a*) section 84 (exercise of powers by officer, &c.),
- (*b*) section 449 of the Companies Act 1985, section 53 or 54 of the Building Societies Act 1986, sections 179 and 180 of the Financial Services Act 1986, section 84 of the Banking Act 1987 and sections 86 and 87 above (restrictions on disclosure of information), and
- (*c*) section 89 (authority for institution of criminal proceedings);

and references to the Secretary of State in other enactments which proceed by reference to those provisions shall be construed accordingly as being or including references to the Department.

(4) The Secretary of State may after consultation with the Department of Economic Development in Northern Ireland revoke an authority given to the Department under this section.

(5) In that case nothing in the provisions referred to in subsection (3)(*b*) shall apply so as to prevent the Department from giving the Secretary of State any information obtained by virtue of the authority; and (without prejudice to their application in relation to disclosure

by the Department) those provisions shall apply to the disclosure of such information by the Secretary of State as if it had been obtained by him in the first place.

(6) Nothing in this section affects the exercise by the Secretary of State of any powers in Northern Ireland –
  (a) in a case where at the time of acceding to the request it did not appear to him that the circumstances were such as to require him to authorise the Department of Economic Development in Northern Ireland to exercise those powers, or
  (b) after the revocation by him of any such authority;
and no objection shall be taken to anything done by or in relation to the Secretary of State or the Department on the ground that it should have been done by or in relation to the other.

89   Prosecutions

Proceedings for an offence under section 85 or 86 shall not be instituted –
  (a) in England and Wales, except by or with the consent of the Secretary of State or the Director of Public Prosecutions;
  (b) in Northern Ireland, except by or with the consent of the Secretary of State or the Director of Public Prosecutions for Northern Ireland.

90   Offences by bodies corporate, partnerships and unincorporated associations

(1) Where an offence under section 85 or 86 committed by a body corporate is proved to have been committed with the consent or connivance of, or to be attributable to any neglect on the part of, a director, manager, secretary or other similar officer of the body, or a person purporting to act in any such capacity, he as well as the body corporate is guilty of the offence and liable to be proceeded against and punished accordingly.

(2) Where the affairs of a body corporate are managed by its members, subsection (1) applies in relation to the acts and defaults of a member in connection with his functions of management as to a director of a body corporate.

(3) Where an offence under section 85 or 86 committed by a partnership is proved to have been committed with the consent or connivance of, or to be attributable to any neglect on the part of, a partner, he as well as the partnership is guilty of the offence and liable to be proceeded against and punished accordingly.

(4) Where an offence under section 85 or 86 committed by an unincorporated association (other than a partnership) is proved to have been committed with the consent or connivance of, or to be attributable to any neglect on the part of, any officer of the association or any member of its governing body, he as well as the association is guilty of the offence and liable to be proceeded against and punished accordingly.

91   Jurisdiction and procedure in respect of offences

(1) Summary proceedings for an offence under section 85 may, without prejudice to any jurisdiction exercisable apart from this section, be taken against a body corporate or unincorporated association at any place at which it has a place of business and against an individual at any place where he is for the time being.

(2) Proceedings for an offence alleged to have been committed under section 85 or 86 by an unincorporated association shall be brought in the name of the association (and not in that of any of its members), and for the purposes of any such proceedings any rules of court relating to the service of documents apply as in relation to a body corporate.

(3) Section 33 of the Criminal Justice Act 1925 and Schedule 3 to the Magistrates' Courts Act 1980 (procedure on charge of offence against a corporation) apply in a case in which an unincorporated association is charged in England and Wales with an offence under section 85 or 86 as they apply in the case of a corporation.

(4) In relation to proceedings on indictment in Scotland for an offence alleged to have been committed under section 85 or 86 by an unincorporated association, section 74 of the Criminal Procedure (Scotland) Act 1975 (proceedings on indictment against bodies corporate) applies as if the association were a body corporate.

(5) Section 18 of the Criminal Justice Act (Northern Ireland) 1945 and Schedule 4 to the Magistrates' Courts (Northern Ireland) Order 1981 (procedure on charge of offence against a corporation) apply in a case in which an unincorporated association is charged in Northern Ireland with an offence under section 85 or 86 as they apply in the case of a corporation.

(6) A fine imposed on an unincorporated association on its conviction of such an offence shall be paid out of the funds of the association.

PART IV
REGISTRATION OF COMPANY CHARGES

Introduction

92　Introduction

The provisions of this Part amend the provisions of the Companies Act 1985 relating to the registration of company charges –

(*a*)　by inserting in Part XII of that Act (in place of sections 395 to 408 and 410 to 423) new provisions with respect to companies registered in Great Britain, and

(*b*)　by inserting as Chapter III of Part XXIII of that Act (in place of sections 409 and 424) new provisions with respect to oversea companies.

Registration in the companies charges register

93　Charges requiring registration

The following sections are inserted in Part XII of the Companies Act 1985 –

"Registration in the company charges register

395　Introductory provisions

(1) The purpose of this Part is to secure the registration of charges on a company's property.

(2) In this Part –

"charge" means any form of security interest (fixed or floating) over property, other than an interest arising by operation of law; and

"property", in the context of what is the subject of a charge, includes future property.

(3) It is immaterial for the purposes of this Part where the property subject to charge is situated.

(4) References in this Part to "the registrar" are –

    (*a*) in relation to a company registered in England and Wales, to the registrar of companies for England and Wales, and

    (*b*) in relation to a company registered in Scotland, to the registrar of companies for Scotland;

and references to registration, in relation to a charge, are to registration in the register kept by him under this Part.

396 Charges requiring registration

(1) The charges requiring registration under this Part are –

    (*a*) a charge on land or any interest in land, other than –

        (i) in England and Wales, a charge for rent or any other periodical sum issuing out of the land,

        (ii) in Scotland, a charge for any rent, ground annual or other periodical sum payable in respect of the land;

    (*b*) a charge on goods or any interest in goods, other than a charge under which the chargee is entitled to possession either of the goods or of a document of title to them,

    (*c*) a charge on intangible movable property (in Scotland, incorporeal moveable property) of any of the following descriptions –

        (i) goodwill,

        (ii) intellectual property,

        (iii) book debts (whether book debts of the company or assigned to the company),

        (iv) uncalled share capital of the company or calls made but not paid;

    (*d*) a charge for securing an issue of debentures, or

    (*e*) a floating charge on the whole or part of the company's property.

(2) The descriptions of charge mentioned in subsection (1) shall be construed as follows –

    (*a*) a charge on a debenture forming part of an issue or series shall not be treated as falling within paragraph (*a*) or (*b*) by reason of the fact that the debenture is secured by a charge on land or goods (or on an interest in land or goods);

    (*b*) in paragraph (*b*) "goods" means any tangible movable property (in Scotland, corporeal moveable property) other than money;

    (*c*) a charge is not excluded from paragraph (*b*) because the chargee is entitled to take possession in case of default or on the occurrence of some other event;

    (*d*) in paragraph (*c*)(ii) "intellectual property" means –

        (i) any patent, trade mark, service mark, registered design, copyright or design right, or

        (ii) any licence under or in respect of any such right;

    (*e*) a debenture which is part of an issue or series shall not be treated as a book debt for the purposes of paragraph (*c*)(iii);

    (*f*) the deposit by way of security of a negotiable instrument given to secure the payment of book debts shall not be treated for the purposes of paragraph (*c*)(iii) as a charge on book debts;

    (*g*) a shipowner's lien on subfreights shall not be treated as a charge on book debts for the purposes of paragraph (*c*)(iii) or as a floating charge for the purposes of paragraph (*e*).

(3)   Whether a charge is one requiring registration under this Part shall be determined –

> (a) in the case of a charge created by a company, as at the date the charge is created, and
> (b) in the case of a charge over property acquired by a company, as at the date of the acquisition.

(4) The Secretary of State may by regulations amend subsections (1) and (2) so as to add any description of charge to, or remove any description of charge from, the charges requiring registration under this Part.

(5) Regulations under this section shall be made by statutory instrument which shall be subject to annulment in pursuance of a resolution of either House of Parliament.

(6) In the following provisions of this Part references to a charge are, unless the context otherwise requires, to a charge requiring registration under this Part.

Where a charge not otherwise requiring registration relates to property by virtue of which it requires to be registered and to other property, the references are to the charge so far as it relates to property of the former description.".

94   The companies charges register

The following section is inserted in Part XII of the Companies Act 1985 –

"397   The companies charges register

(1) The registrar shall keep for each company a register, in such form as he thinks fit, of charges on property of the company.

(2) The register shall consist of a file containing with respect to each charge the particulars and other information delivered to the registrar under the provisions of this Part.

(3) Any person may require the registrar to provide a certificate stating the date on which any specified particulars of, or other information relating to, a charge were delivered to him.

(4) The certificate shall be signed by the registrar or authenticated by his official seal.

(5) The certificate shall be conclusive evidence that the specified particulars or other information were delivered to the registrar no later than the date stated in the certificate; and it shall be presumed unless the contrary is proved that they were not delivered earlier than that date.".

95   Delivery of particulars for registration

The following sections are inserted in Part XII of the Companies Act 1985 –

"398   Company's duty to deliver particulars of charge for registration

(1) It is the duty of a company which creates a charge, or acquires property subject to a charge –

> (a) to deliver the prescribed particulars of the charge, in the prescribed form, to the registrar for registration, and

(*b*) to do so within 21 days after the date of the charge's creation or, as the case may be, the date of the acquisition;

but particulars of a charge may be delivered for registration by any person interested in the charge.

(2) Where the particulars are delivered for registration by a person other than the company concerned, that person is entitled to recover from the company the amount of any fees paid by him to the registrar in connection with the registration.

(3) If a company fails to comply with subsection (1), then, unless particulars of the charge have been delivered for registration by another person, the company and every officer of it who is in default is liable to a fine.

(4) Where prescribed particulars in the prescribed form are delivered to the registrar for registration, he shall file the particulars in the register and shall note, in such form as he thinks fit, the date on which they were delivered to him.

(5) The registrar shall send to the company and any person appearing from the particulars to be the chargee, and if the particulars were delivered by another person interested in the charge to that person, a copy of the particulars filed by him and of the note made by him as to the date on which they were delivered.

399   Effect of failure to deliver particulars for registration

(1) Where a charge is created by a company and no prescribed particulars in the prescribed form are delivered for registration within the period of 21 days after the date of the charge's creation, the charge is void against –
(*a*) an administrator or liquidator of the company, and
(*b*) any person who for value acquires an interest in or right over property subject to the charge,
where the relevant event occurs after the creation of the charge, whether before or after the end of the 21 day period.

This is subject to section 400 (late delivery of particulars).

(2) In this Part "the relevant event" means –
(*a*) in relation to the voidness of a charge as against an administrator or liquidator, the beginning of the insolvency proceedings, and
(*b*) in relation to the voidness of a charge as against a person acquiring an interest in or right over property subject to a charge, the acquisition of that interest or right;
and references to "a relevant event" shall be construed accordingly.

(3) Where a relevant event occurs on the same day as the charge is created, it shall be presumed to have occurred after the charge is created unless the contrary is proved.

400   Late delivery of particulars

(1) Where prescribed particulars of a charge created by a company, in the prescribed form, are delivered for registration more than 21 days after the date of the charge's creation, section 399(1) does not apply in relation to relevant events occurring after the particulars are delivered.

(2) However, where in such a case –

(*a*) the company is at the date of delivery of the particulars unable to pay its debts, or subsequently becomes unable to pay its debts in consequence of the transaction under which the charge is created, and

(*b*) insolvency proceedings begin before the end of the relevant period beginning with the date of delivery of the particulars,

the charge is void as against the administrator or liquidator.

(3) For this purpose –

(*a*) the company is "unable to pay its debts" in the circumstances specified in section 123 of the Insolvency Act 1986; and

(*b*) the "relevant period" is –

(i)   two years in the case of a floating charge created in favour of a person connected with the company (within the meaning of section 249 of that Act),

(ii) one year in the case of a floating charge created in favour of a person not so connected, and

(iii) six months in any other case.

(4) Where a relevant event occurs on the same day as the particulars are delivered, it shall be presumed to have occurred before the particulars are delivered unless the contrary is proved.".

96   Delivery of further particulars

The following section is inserted in Part XII of the Companies Act 1985 –

"401   Delivery of further particulars

(1) Further particulars of a charge, supplementing or varying the registered particulars, may be delivered to the registrar for registration at any time.

(2) Further particulars must be in prescribed form signed by or on behalf of both the company and the chargee.

(3) Where further particulars are delivered to the registrar for registration and appear to him to be duly signed, he shall file the particulars in the register and shall note, in such form, as he thinks fit, the date on which they were delivered to him.

(4) The registrar shall send to the company and any person appearing from the particulars to be the chargee, and if the particulars were delivered by another person interested in the charge to that other person, a copy of the further particulars filed by him and of the note made by him as to the date on which they were delivered.".

97   Effect of omissions and errors in registered particulars

The following section is inserted in Part XII of the Companies Act 1985 –

"402   Effect of omissions and errors in registered particulars

(1) Where the registered particulars of a charge created by a company are not complete and accurate, the charge is void, as mentioned below, to the extent that rights are not disclosed by the registered particulars which would be disclosed if they were complete and accurate.

(2) The charge is void to that extent, unless the court on the application of the chargee orders otherwise, as against –

(*a*) an administrator or liquidator of the company, and

(*b*) any person who for value acquires an interest in or right over property subject to the charge,

where the relevant event occurs at a time when the particulars are incomplete or inaccurate in a relevant respect.

(3) Where a relevant event occurs on the same day as particulars or further particulars are delivered, it shall be presumed to have occurred before those particulars are delivered unless the contrary is proved.

(4) The court may order that the charge is effecive as against an administrator or liquidator of the company if it is satisfied –

(*a*) that the omission or error is not likely to have misled materially to his prejudice any unsecured creditor of the company, or

(*b*) that no person became an unsecured creditor of the company at a time when the registered particulars of the charge were incomplete or inaccurate in a relevant respect.

(5) The court may order that the charge is effective as against a person acquiring an interest in or right over property subject to the charge if it is satisfied that he did not rely, in connection with the acquisition, on registered particulars which were incomplete or inaccurate in a relevant respect.

(6) For the purposes of this section an omission or inaccuracy with respect to the name of the chargee shall not be regarded as a failure to disclose the rights of the chargee.".

98 Memorandum of charge ceasing to affect company's property

The following section is inserted in Part XII of the Companies Act 1985 –

"403 Memorandum of charge ceasing to affect company's property

(1) Where a charge of which particulars have been delivered ceases to affect the company's property, a memorandum to that effect may be delivered to the registrar for registration.

(2) The memorandum must be in the prescribed form signed by or on behalf of both the company and the chargee.

(3) Where a memorandum is delivered to the registrar for registration and appears to him to be duly signed, he shall file it in the register, and shall note, in such form as he thinks fit, the date on which it was delivered to him.

(4) The registrar shall send to the company and any person appearing from the memorandum to be the chargee, and if the memorandum was delivered by another person interested in the charge to that person, a copy of the memorandum filed by him and of the note made by him as to the date on which it was delivered.

(5) If a duly signed memorandum is delivered in a case where the charge in fact continues to affect the company's property, the charge is void as against –

(*a*) an administrator or liquidator of the company, and

(*b*) any person who for value acquires an interest in or right over property subject to the charge, where the relevant event occurs after the delivery of the memorandum.

(6) Where a relevant event occurs on the same day as the memorandum is delivered, it shall be presumed to have occurred before the memorandum is delivered unless the contrary is proved.".

99   Further provisions with respect to voidness of charges

The following sections are inserted in Part XII of the Companies Act 1985 –

"Further provisions with respect to voidness of charges

404   Exclusion of voidness as against unregistered charges

(1) A charge is not void by virtue of this Part as against a subsequent charge unless some or all of the relevant particulars of that charge are duly delivered for registration –

(*a*) within 21 days after the date of its creation, or

(*b*) before complete and accurate relevant particulars of the earlier charge are duly delivered for registration.

(2) Where relevant particulars of the subsequent charge so delivered are incomplete or inaccurate, the earlier charge is void as against that charge only to the extent that rights are disclosed by registered particulars of the subsequent charge duly delivered for registration before the corresponding relevant particulars of the earlier charge.

(3) The relevant particulars of a charge for the purposes of this section are those prescribed particulars relating to rights inconsistent with those conferred by or in relation to the other charge.

405   Restrictions on voidness by virtue of this Part

(1) A charge is not void by virtue of this Part as against a person acquiring an interest in or right over property where the acquisition is expressly subject to the charge.

(2) Nor is a charge void by virtue of this Part in relation to any property by reason of a relevant event occurring after the company which created the charge has disposed of the whole of its interest in that property.

406   Effect of exercise of power of sale

(1) A chargee exercising a power of sale may dispose of property to a purchaser freed from any interest or right arising from the charge having become void to any extent by virtue of this Part –

(*a*) against an administrator or liquidator of the company, or

(*b*) against a person acquiring a security interest over property subject to the charge;

and a purchaser is not concerned to see or inquire whether the charge has become so void.

(2) The proceeds of the sale shall be held by the charge in trust to be applied –
First, in discharge of any sum effectively secured by prior incumbrances to which the sale is not made subject;

Second, in payment of all costs, charges and expenses properly incurred by him in connection with the sale, or any previous attempted sale, of the property;

Third, in discharge of any sum effectively secured by the charge and incumbrances ranking *pari passu* with the charge;

Fourth, in discharge of any sum effectively secured by incumbrances ranking after the charge;

and any residue is payable to the company or to a person authorised to give a receipt for the proceeds of the sale of the property.

(3) for the purposes of subsection (2) –

    (*a*) prior incumbrances include any incumbrance to the extent that the charge is void as against it by virtue of this Part; and

    (*b*) no sum is effectively secured by a charge to the extent that it is void as against an administrator or liquidator of the company.

(4) In this section –

    (*a*) references to things done by a chargee include things done by a receiver appointed by him, whether or not the receiver acts as his agent;

    (*b*) "power of sale" includes any power to dispose of, or grant an interest out of, property for the purpose of enforcing a charge (but in relation to Scotland does not include the power to grant a lease), and references to "sale" shall be construed accordingly; and

    (*c*) "purchaser" means a person who in good faith and for valuable consideration acquires an interest in property.

(5) The provisions of this section as to the order of application of the proceeds of sale have effect subject to any other statutory provision (in Scotland, any other statutory provision or rule of law) applicable in any case.

(6) Where a chargee exercising a power of sale purports to dispose of property freed from any such interest or right as is mentioned in subsection (1) to a person other than a purchaser, the above provisions apply, with any necessary modifications, in relation to a disposition to a purchaser by that person or any successor in title of his.

(7) In Scotland, subsections (2) and (7) of section 27 of the Conveyancing and Feudal Reform (Scotland) Act 1970 apply to a chargee unable to obtain a discharge for any payment which he is required to make under subsection (2) above as they apply to a creditor in the circumstances mentioned in those subsections.

407 Effect of voidness on obligation secured

(1) Where a charge becomes void to any extent by virtue of this Part, the whole of the sum secured by the charge is payable forthwith on demand; and this applies notwithstanding that the sum secured by the charge is also the subject of other security.

(2) Where the charge is to secure the repayment of money, the references in subsection (1) to the sum secured include any interest payable.".

100 Additional information to be registered

The following sections are inserted in Part XII of the Companies Act 1985 –

"Additional information to be registered

408   Particulars of taking up of issue of debentures

(1) Where particulars of a charge for securing an issue of debentures have been delivered for registration, it is the duty of the company –
    (*a*) to deliver to the registrar for registration particulars in the prescribed form of the date on which any debentures of the issue are taken up, and of the amount taken up, and
    (*b*) to do so before the end of the period of 21 days after the date on which they are taken up.

(2) Where particulars in the prescribed form are delivered to the registrar for registration under this section, he shall file them in the register.

(3) If a company fails to comply with subsection (1), the company and every officer of it who is in default is liable to a fine.

409   Notice of appointment of receiver or manager, &c

(1) If a person obtains an order for the appointment of a receiver or manager of a company's property, or appoints such a receiver or manager under powers contained in an instrument, he shall within seven days of the order or of the appointment under those powers, give notice of that fact in the prescribed form to the registrar for registration.

(2) Where a person appointed receiver or manager of a company's property under powers contained in an instrument ceases to act as such receiver or manager, he shall, on so ceasing, give notice of that fact in the prescribed form to the registrar for registration.

(3) Where a notice under this section in the prescribed form is delivered to the registrar for registration, he shall file it in the register.

(4) If a person makes default in complying with the requirements of subsection (1) or (2), he is liable to a fine.

(5) This section does not apply in relation to companies registered in Scotland (for which corresponding provision is made by sections 53, 54 and 62 of the Insolvency Act 1986).

410   Notice of crystallisation of floating charge, &c

(1) The Secretary of State may by regulations require notice in the prescribed form to be given to the registrar of –
    (*a*) the occurrence of such events as may be prescribed affecting the nature of the security under a floating charge of which particulars have been delivered for registration, and
    (*b*) the taking of such action in exercise of powers conferred by a fixed or floating charge of which particulars have been delivered for registration, or conferred in relation to such a charge by an order of the court, as may be prescribed.

(2) The regulations may make provision as to –
    (*a*) the persons by whom notice is required to be, or may be, given, and the period within which notice is required to be given;

(*b*) the filing in the register of the particulars contained in the notice and the noting of the date on which the notice was given; and

(*c*) the consequences of failure to give notice.

(3) As regards the consequences of failure to give notice of an event causing a floating charge to crystallise, the regulations may include provision to the effect that the crystallisation –

(*a*) shall be treated as ineffective until the prescribed particulars are delivered, and

(*b*) if the prescribed particulars are delivered after the expiry of the prescribed period, shall contine to be ineffective against such persons as may be prescribed,

subject to the exercise of such powers as may be conferred by the regulations on the court.

(4) The regulations may provide that if there is a failure to comply with such of the requirements of the regulations as may be prescribed, such persons as may be prescribed are liable to a fine.

(5) Regulations under this section shall be made by statutory instrument which shall be subject to annulment in pursuance of a resolution of either House of Parliament.

(6) Regulations under this section shall not apply in relation to a floating charge created under the law of Scotland by a company registered in Scotland.".

Copies of instruments and register to be kept by company

101 Copies of instruments and register to be kept by company

The following sections are inserted in Part XII of the Companies Act 1985 –

"Copies of instruments and register to be kept by company

411 Duty to keep copies of instruments and register

(1) Every company shall keep at its registered office a copy of every instrument creating or evidencing a charge over the company's property.

In the case of a series of uniform debentures, a copy of one debenture of the series is sufficient.

(2) Every company shall also keep at its registered office a register of all such charges, containing entries for each charge giving a short description of the property charged, the amount of the charge and (except in the case of securities to bearer) the names of the persons entitled to it.

(3) This section applies to any charge, whether or not particulars are required to be delivered to the registrar for registration.

(4) If a company fails to comply with any requirement of this section, the company and every officer of it who is in default is liable to a fine.

412 Inspection of copies and register

(1) The copies and the register referred to in section 411 shall be open to the

inspection of any creditor or member of the company without fee; and to the inspection of any other person on payment of such fee as may be prescribed.

(2) Any person may request the company to provide him with a copy of –
  (*a*) any instrument creating or evidencing a charge over the company's property, or
  (*b*) any entry in the register of charges kept by the company, on payment of such fee as may be prescribed.
This subsection applies to any charge, whether or not particulars are required to be delivered to the registrar for registration.

(3) The company shall send the copy to him not later than ten days after the day on which the request is received or, if later, on which payment is received.

(4) If inspection of the copies or register is refused, or a copy requested is not sent within the time specified above –
  (*a*) the company and every officer of it who is in default is liable to a fine, and
  (*b*) the court may by order compel an immediate inspection of the copies or register or, as the case may be, direct that the copy be sent immediately.".

Supplementary provisions

102   Power to make further provision by regulations

The following section is inserted in Part XII of the Companies Act 1985 –

"Supplementary provisions

413   Power to make further provision by regulations

(1) The Secretary of State may by regulations make further provision as to the application of the provisions of this Part in relation to charges of any description specified in the regulations.

Nothing in the following provisions shall be construed as restricting the generality of that power.

(2) The regulations may require that where the charge is contained in or evidenced or varied by a written instrument there shall be delivered to the registrar for registration, instead of particulars or further particulars of the charge, the instrument itself or a certified copy of it together with such particulars as may be prescribed.

(3) The regulations may provide that a memorandum of a charge ceasing to affect property of the company shall not be accepted by the registrar unless supported by such evidence as may be prescribed, and that a memorandum not so supported shall be treated as not having been delivered.

(4) The regulations may also provide that where the instrument creating the charge is delivered to the registrar in support of such a memorandum, the registrar may mark the instrument as cancelled before returning it and shall send copies of the instrument cancelled to such persons as may be prescribed.

(5) The regulations may exclude or modify, in such circumstances and to such extent as may be prescribed, the operation of the provisions of this Part relating to the voidness of a charge.

(6) The regulations may require, in connection with the delivery of particulars, further particulars or a memorandum of the charge's ceasing to affect property of the company, the delivery of such supplementary information as may be prescribed, and may –

> (*a*) apply in relation to such supplementary information any provisions of this Part relating to particulars, further particulars or such a memorandum, and
>
> (*b*) provide that the particulars, further particulars or memorandum shall be treated as not having been delivered until the required supplementary information is delivered.

(7) Regulations under this section shall be made by statutory instrument which shall be subject to annulment in pursuance of a resolution of either House of Parliament.".

103 Other supplementary provisions

The following sections are inserted in Part XII of the Companies Act 1985 –

"414 Date of creation of charge

(1) References in this Part to the date of creation of a charge by a company shall be construed as follows.

(2) A charge created under the law of England and Wales shall be taken to be created –

> (*a*) in the case of a charge created by an instrument in writing, when the instrument is executed by the company or, if its execution by the company is conditional, upon the conditions being fulfilled, and
>
> (*b*) in any other case, when an enforceable agreement is entered into by the company conferring a security interest intended to take effect forthwith or upon the company acquiring an interest in property subject to the charge.

(3) A charge created under the law of Scotland shall be taken to be created –

> (*a*) in the case of a floating charge, when the instrument creating the floating charge is executed by the company, and
>
> (*b*) in any other case, when the right of the person entitled to the benefit of the charge is constituted as a real right.

(4) Where a charge is created in the United Kingdom but comprises property outside the United Kingdom, any further proceedings necessary to make the charge valid or effectual under the law of the country where the property is situated shall be disregarded in ascertaining the date on which the charge is to be taken to be created.

415 Prescribed particulars and related expressions

(1) References in this Part to the prescribed particulars of a charge are to such particulars of, or relating to, the charge as may be prescribed.

(2) The prescribed particulars may, without prejudice to the generality of subsection (1), include –

 (a) whether the company has undertaken not to create other charges ranking in priority to or *pari passu* with the charge, and

 (b) whether the charge is a market charge within the meaning of Part VII of the Companies Act 1989 or a charge to which the provisions of that Part apply as they apply to a market charge.

(3) References in this Part to the registered particulars of a charge at any time are to such particulars and further particulars of the charge as have at that time been duly delivered for registration.

(4) References in this Part to the registered particulars of a charge being complete and accurate at any time are to their including all the prescribed particulars which would be required to be delivered if the charge were then newly created.

416   Notice of matters disclosed on register

(1) A person taking a charge over a company's property shall be taken to have notice of any matter requiring registration and disclosed on the register at the time the charge is created.

(2) Otherwise, a person shall not be taken to have notice of any matter by reason of its being disclosed on the register or by reason of his having failed to search the register in the course of making such inquiries as ought reasonably to be made.

(3) The above provisions have effect subject to any other statutory provision as to whether a person is to be taken to have notice of any matter disclosed on the register.

417   Power of court to dispense with signature

(1) Where it is proposed to deliver further particulars of a chargee, or to deliver a memorandum of a charge ceasing to affect the company's property, and –

 (a) the chargee refuses to sign or authorise a person to sign on his behalf, or cannot be found, or

 (b) the company refuses to authorise a person to sign on its behalf,

the court may on the application of the company or the chargee, or of any other person having a sufficient interest in the matter, authorise the delivery of the particulars or memorandum without that signature.

(2) The order may be made on such terms as appear to the court to be appropriate.

(3) Where particulars or a memorandum are delivered to the registrar for registration in reliance on an order under this section, they must be accompanied by an office copy of the order.

In such a case the references in sections 401 and 403 to the particulars or memorandum being duly signed are to their being otherwise duly signed.

(4) The registrar shall file the office copy of the court order along with the particulars or memorandum.".

104   Interpretation, &c

The following sections are inserted in Part XII of the Companies Act 1985 –

"418   Regulations

Regulations under any provision of this Part, or prescribing anything for the purposes of any such provision –

(*a*) may make different provision for different cases, and

(*b*) may contain such supplementary, incidental and transitional provisions as appear to the Secretary of State to be appropriate.

419   Minor definitions

(1) In this Part –

"chargee" means the person for the time being entitled to exercise the security rights conferred by the charge;

"issue of debentures" means a group of debentures, or an amount of debenture stock, secured by the same charge, and

"series of debentures" means a group of debentures each containing or giving by reference to another instrument a charge to the benefit of which the holders of debentures of the series are entitled *pari passu*.

(2) References in this Part to the creation of a charge include the variation of a charge which is not registrable so as to include property by virtue of which it becomes registrable.

The provisions of section 414 (construction of references to date of creation of charge) apply in such a case with any necessary modifications.

(3) References in this Part to the date of acquisition of property by a company are –

(*a*) in England and Wales, to the date on which the acquisition is completed, and

(*b*) in Scotland, to the date or which the transaction is settled.

(4) In the application of this Part to a floating charge created under the law of Scotland, references to crystallisation shall be construed as references to the attachment of the charge.

(5) References in this Part to the beginning of insolvency proceedings are to –

(*a*) the presentation of a petition on which an administration order or winding-up order is made, or

(*b*) the passing of a resolution for voluntary winding up.

420   Index of defined expressions

The following Table shows the provisions of this Part defining or otherwise explaining expressions used in this Part (other than expressions used only in the same section) –

charge	sections 395(2) and 396(6)
charge requiring registration	section 396
chargee	section 419(1)
complete and accurate (in relation to registered particulars)	section 415(4)
creation of charge	section 419(2)
crystallisation (in relation to Scottish floating charge)	section 419(4)
date of acquisition (of property by a company)	section 419(3)
date of creation of charge	section 414
further particulars	section 401
insolvency proceedings, beginning of	section 419(5)
issue of debentures	section 419(1)
memorandum of charge ceasing to affect company's property	section 403
prescribed particulars	section 415(1) and (2)
property	section 395(2)
registered particulars	section 415(3)
registrar and registration in relation to a charge	section 395(4)
relevant event	section 399(2)
series of debentures	section 419(1).".

105   Charges on property of oversea company

The provisions set out in Schedule 15 are inserted in Part XXIII of the Companies Act 1985 (oversea companies), as a Chapter III (registration of charges).

106   Application of provisions to unregistered companies

In Schedule 22 to the Companies Act 1985 (provisions applying to unregistered companies), at the appropriate place insert –

"Part XII	Registration of company charges; copies of instruments and register to be kept by company.	Subject to section 718(3).".

107 Consequential amendments

The enactments specified in Schedule 16 have effect with the amendments specified there, which are consequential on the amendments made by the preceding provisions of this Part.

PART V
OTHER AMENDMENTS OF COMPANY LAW

A company's capacity and related matters

108 A company's capacity and the power of the directors to bind it

(1) In Chapter III of Part I of the Companies Act 1985 (a company's capacity; formalities of carrying on business), for section 35 substitute –

"35 A company's capacity not limited by its memorandum

(1) The validity of an act done by a company shall not be called into question on the ground of lack of capacity by reason of anything in the company's memorandum.

(2) A member of a company may bring proceedings to restrain the doing of an act which but for subsection (1) would be beyond the company's capacity; but no such proceedings shall lie in respect of an act to be done in fulfilment of a legal obligation arising from a previous act of the company.

(3) It remains the duty of the directors to observe any limitations on their powers flowing from the company's memorandum; and action by the directors which but for subsection (1) would be beyond the company's capacity may only be ratified by the company by special resolution.
A resolution ratifying such action shall not affect any liability incurred by the directors or any other person; relief from any such liability must be agreed to separately by special resolution.

(4) The operation of this section is restricted by section 30B(1) of the Charities Act 1960 and section 112(3) of the Companies Act 1989 in relation to companies which are charities; and section 322A below (invalidity of certain transactions to which directors or their associates are parties) has effect notwithstanding this section.

35A Power of directors to bind the company

(1) In favour of a person dealing with a company in good faith, the power of the board of directors to bind the company, or authorise others to do so, shall be deemed to be free of any limitation under the company's constitution.

(2) For this purpose –
    (*a*) a person "deals with" a company if he is a party to any transaction or other act to which the company is a party;
    (*b*) a person shall not be regarded as acting in bad faith by reason only of his knowing that an act is beyond the powers of the directors under the company's constitution;
    (*c*) a person shall be presumed to have acted in good faith unless the contrary is proved.

(3) The references above to limitations on the directors' powers under the company's constitution include limitations deriving –

> (*a*) from a resolution of the company in general meeting or a meeting of any class of shareholders, or
>
> (*b*) from any agreement between the members of the company or of any class of shareholders.

(4) Subsection (1) does not affect any right of a member of that company to bring proceedings to restrain the doing of an act which is beyond the powers of the directors; but no such proceedings shall lie in respect of an act to be done in fulfilment of a legal obligation arising from a previous act of the company.

(5) Nor does that subsection affect any liability incurred by the directors, or any other person, by reason of the directors' exceeding their powers.

(6) The operation of this section is restricted by section 30B(1) of the Charities Act 1960 and section 112(3) of the Companies Act 1989 in relation to companies which are charities; and section 322A below (invalidity of certain transactions to which directors or their associates are parties) has effect notwithstanding this section.

35B No duty to enquire as to capacity of company or authority of directors

A party to a transaction with a company is not bound to enquire as to whether it is permitted by the company's memorandum or as to any limitation on the powers of the board of directors to bind the company or authorise others to do so.".

(2) In Schedule 21 to the Companies Act 1985 (effect of registration of companies not formed under that Act), in paragraph 6 (general application of provisions of Act), after sub-paragraph (5) insert –

> "(6) Where by virtue of sub-paragraph (4) or (5) a company does not have power to alter a provision, it does not have power to ratify acts of the directors in contravention of the provision."

(3) In Schedule 22 to the Companies Act 1985 (provisions applying to unregistered companies), in the entries relating to Part I, in the first column for "section 35" substitute "sections 35 to 35B".

109 Invalidity of certain transactions involving directors

(1) In Part X of the Companies Act 1985 (enforcement of fair dealing by directors), after section 322 insert –

322A Invalidity of certain transactions involving directors, etc

(1) This section applies where a company enters into a transaction to which the parties include –

> (*a*) a director of the company or of its holding company, or
>
> (*b*) a person connected with such a director or a company with whom such a director is associated,

and the board of directors, in connection with the transaction, exceed any limitation on their powers under the company's constitution.

(2) The transaction is voidable at the instance of the company.

(3) Whether or not it is avoided, any such party to the transaction as is mentioned in subsection (1)(*a*) or (*b*), and any director of the company who authorised the transaction, is liable –

    (*a*) to account to the company for any gain which he has made directly or indirectly by the transaction, and

    (*b*) to indemnify the company for any loss or damage resulting from the transaction.

(4) Nothing in the above provisions shall be construed as excluding the operation of any other enactment or rule of law by virtue of which the transaction may be called in question or any liability to the company may arise.

(5) The transaction ceases to be voidable if –

    (*a*) restitution of any money or other asset which was the subject-matter of the transaction is no longer possible, or

    (*b*) the company is indemnified for any loss or damage resulting from the transaction, or

    (*c*) rights acquired bona fide for value and without actual notice of the directors' exceeding their powers by a person who is not party to the transaction would be affected by the avoidance, or

    (*d*) the transaction is ratified by the company in general meeting, by ordinary or special resolution or otherwise as the case may require.

(6) A person other than a director of the company is not liable under subsection (3) if he shows that at the time the transaction was entered into he did not know that the directors were exceeding their powers.

(7) This section does not affect the operation of section 35A in relation to any party to the transaction not within subsection (1)(*a*) or (*b*).

But where a transaction is voidable by virtue of this section and valid by virtue of that section in favour of such a person, the court may, on the application of that person or of the company, make such order affirming, severing or setting aside the transaction, on such terms, as appear to the court to be just.

(8) In this section "transaction" includes any act; and the reference in subsection (1) to limitations under the company's constitution includes limitations deriving –

    (*a*) from a resolution of the company in general meeting or a meeting of any class of shareholders, or

    (*b*) from any agreement between the members of the company or of any class of shareholders.".

(2) In Schedule 22 to the Companies Act 1985 (provisions applying to unregistered companies), in the entries relating to Part X, insert –

"section 322A	Invalidity of certain transactions involving directors, etc.	Subject to section 718(3)."

110   Statement of company's objects

In Chapter I of Part I of the Companies Act 1985 (company formation), after section 3 (forms of memorandum) insert –

"3A   Statement of company's objects: general commercial company

Where the company's memorandum states that the object of the company is to carry on business as a general commercial company –

> (*a*) the object of the company is to carry on any trade or business whatsoever, and
>
> (*b*) the company has power to do all such things as are incidental or conducive to the carrying on of any trade or business by it.".

(2) In the same Chapter, for section 4 (resolution to alter objects) substitute –

"4   Resolution to alter objects

(1) A company may by special resolution alter its memorandum with respect to the statement of the company's objects.

(2) If an application is made under the following section, an alteration does not have effect except in so far as it is confirmed by the court.".

111   Charitable companies

(1) In the Charities Act 1960, for section 30 (charitable companies) substitute –

"30   Charitable companies: winding up

Where a charity may be wound up by the High Court under the Insolvency Act 1986, a petition for it to be wound up under that Act by any court in England or Wales having jurisdiction may be presented by the Attorney General, as well as by any person authorised by that Act.

30A   Charitable companies: alteration of objects clause

(1) Where a charity is a company or other body corporate having power to alter the instruments establishing or regulating it as a body corporate, no exercise of that power which has the effect of the body ceasing to be a charity shall be valid so as to affect the application of –

> (*a*) any property acquired under any disposition or agreement previously made otherwise than for full consideration in money or money's worth, or any property representing property so acquired,
>
> (*b*) any property representing income which has accrued before the alteration is made, or
>
> (*c*) the income from any such property as aforesaid.

(2) Where a charity is a company, any alteration by it of the objects clause in its memorandum of association is ineffective without the prior written consent of the Commissioners; and it shall deliver a copy of that consent to the registrar of companies under section 6(1)(*a*) or (*b*) of the Companies Act 1985 along with the printed copy of the memorandum as altered.

(3) Section 6(3) of that Act (offences) applies in relation to a default in complying with subsection (2) as regards the delivery of a copy of the Commissioners' consent.

30B   Charitable companies: invalidity of certain transactions

(1) Sections 35 and 35A of the Companies Act 1985 (capacity of company not limited by its memorandum; power of directors to bind company) do not apply to

the acts of a company which is a charity except in favour of a person who –

(a) gives full consideration in money or money's worth in relation to the act in question, and

(b) does not know that the act is not permitted by the company's memorandum or, as the case may be, is beyond the powers of the directors,

or who does not know at the time the act is done that the company is a charity.

(2) However, where such a company purports to transfer or grant an interest in property, the fact that the act was not permitted by the company's memorandum or, as the case may be, that the directors in connection with the act exceeded any limitation on their powers under the company's constitution, does not affect the title of a person who subsequently acquires the property or any interest in it for full consideration without actual notice of any such circumstances affecting the validity of the company's act.

(3) In any proceedings arising out of subsection (1) the burden of proving –

(a) that a person knew that an act was not permitted by the company's memorandum or was beyond the powers of the directors, or

(b) that a person knew that the company was a charity,

lies on the person making that allegation.

(4) Where a company is a charity, the ratification of an act under section 35(3) of the Companies Act 1985, or the ratification of a transaction to which section 322A of that Act applies (invalidity of certain transactions to which directors or their associates are parties), is ineffective without the prior written consent of the Commissioners.

30C Charitable companies: status to appear on correspondence, etc

(1) Where a company is a charity and its name does not include the word "charity" or the word "charitable", the fact that the company is a charity shall be stated in English in legible characters –

(a) in all business letters of the company,

(b) in all its notices and other official publications,

(c) in all bills of exchange, promissory notes, endorsements, cheques and orders for money or goods purporting to be signed by or on behalf of the company,

(d) in all conveyances purporting to be executed by the company, and

(e) in all its bills of parcels, invoices, receipts and letters of credit.

(2) In subsection (1)(d) "conveyance" means any instrument creating, transferring, varying or extinguishing an interest in land.

(3) Section 349(2) to (4) of the Companies Act 1985 (offences in connection with failure to include required particulars in business letters, &c.) apply in relation to a contravention of subsection (1) above.".

(2) In section 46 of the Charities Act 1960 (definitions), at the appropriate place insert –
    "'company' means a company formed and registered under the Companies Act 1985, or to which the provisions of that Act apply as they apply to such a company;".

112 Charitable companies (Scotland)

(1) In the following provisions (which extend to Scotland only) –

(*a*) "company" means a company formed and registered under the Companies Act 1985, or to which the provisions of that Act apply as they apply to such a company; and

(*b*) "charity" means a body established for charitable purposes only (that expression having the same meaning as in the Income Tax Acts).

(2) Where a charity is a company or other body corporate having power to alter the instruments establishing or regulating it as a body corporate, no exercise of that power which has the effect of the body ceasing to be a charity shall be valid so as to affect the application of –

(*a*) any property acquired by virtue of any transfer, contract or obligation previously effected otherwise than for full consideration in money or money's worth, or any property representing property so acquired,

(*b*) any property representing income which has accrued before the alteration is made, or

(*c*) the income from any such property as aforesaid.

(3) Sections 35 and 35A of the Companies Act 1985 (capacity of company not limited by its memorandum; power of directors to bind company) , do not apply to the acts of a company which is a charity except in favour of a person who –

(*a*) gives full consideration in money or money's worth in relation to the act in question, and

(*b*) does not know that the act is not permitted by the company's memorandum or, as the case may be, is beyond the powers of the directors,

or who does not know at the time the act is done that the company is a charity.

(4) However, where such a company purports to transfer or grant an interest in property, the fact that the act was not permitted by the company's memorandum or, as the case may be, that the directors in connection with the act exceeded any limitation on their powers under the company's constitution, does not affect the title of a person who subsequently acquires the property or any interest in it for full consideration without actual notice of any such circumstances affecting the validity of the company's act.

(5) In any proceedings arising out of subsection (3) the burden of proving –

(*a*) that a person knew that an act was not permitted by the company's memorandum or was beyond the powers of the directors, or

(*b*) that a person knew that the company was a charity,

lies on the person making that allegation.

(6) Where a company is a charity and its name does not include the word "charity" or the word "charitable", the fact that the company is a charity shall be stated in English in legible characters –

(*a*) in all business letters of the company,

(*b*) in all its notices and other official publications,

(*c*) in all bills of exchange, promissory notes, endorsements, cheques and orders for money or goods purporting to be signed by or on behalf of the company,

(*d*) in all conveyances purporting to be executed by the company, and

(*e*) in all its bills of parcels, invoices, receipts and letters of credit.

(7) In subsection (6)(*d*) "conveyance" means any document for the creation, transfer, variation or extinction of an interest in land.

(8) Section 349(2) to (4) of the Companies Act 1985 (offences in connection with failure to include required particulars in business letters, &c.) apply in relation to a contravention of subsection (6) above.

De-regulation of private companies

113 Written resolutions of private companies

(1) Chapter IV of Part XI of the Companies Act 1985 (meetings and resolutions) is amended as follows.

(2) After section 381 insert –

"Written resolutions of private companies

381A Written resolutions of private companies

(1) Anything which in the case of a private company may be done –

(*a*) by resolution of the company in general meeting, or

(*b*) by resolution of a meeting of any class of members of the company,

may be done, without a meeting and without any previous notice being required, by resolution in writing signed by or on behalf of all the members of the company who at the date of the resolution would be entitled to attend and vote at such meeting.

(2) The signatures need not be on a single document provided each is on a document which accurately states the terms of the resolution.

(3) The date of the resolution means when the resolution is signed by or on behalf of the last member to sign.

(4) A resolution agreed to in accordance with this section has effect as if passed –

(*a*) by the company in general meeting, or

(*b*) by a meeting of the relevant class of members of the company,

as the case may be; and any reference in any enactment to a meeting at which a resolution is passed or to members voting in favour of a resolution shall be construed accordingly.

(5) Any reference in any enactment to the date of passing of a resolution is, in relation to a resolution agreed to in accordance with this section, a reference to the date of the resolution, unless section 381B(4) applies in which case it shall be construed as a reference to the date from which the resolution has effect.

(6) A resolution may be agreed to in accordance with this section which would otherwise be required to be passed as a special, extraordinary or elective resolution; and any reference in any enactment to a special, extraordinary or elective resolution includes such a resolution.

(7) This section has effect subject to the exceptions specified in Part I of Schedule 15A; and in relation to certain descriptions of resolution under this section the procedural requirements of this Act have effect with the adaptations specified in Part II of that Schedule.

381B Rights of auditors in relation to written resolution

(1) A copy of any written resolution proposed to be agreed to in accordance with section 381A shall be sent to the company's auditors.

(2) If the resolution concerns the auditors as auditors, they may within seven days from the day on which they receive the copy give notice to the company stating their opinion that the resolution should be considered by the company in general meeting or, as the case may be, by a meeting of the relevant class of members of the company.

(3) A written resolution shall not have effect unless –

    (*a*) the auditors notify the company that in their opinion the resolution –
        (i) does not concern them as auditors, or
        (ii) does so concern them but need not be considered by the company in general meeting, or as the case may be, by a meeting of the relevant class of members of the company, or

    (*b*) the period for giving a notice under subsection (2) expires without any notice having been given in accordance with that subsection.

(4) A written resolution previously agreed to in accordance with section 381A shall not have effect until that notification is given or, as the case may be, that period expires.

381C   Written resolutions: supplementary provisions

(1) Sections 381A and 381B have effect notwithstanding any provision of the company's memorandum or articles.

(2) Nothing in those sections affects any enactment or rule of law as to –

    (*a*) things done otherwise than by passing a resolution, or
    (*b*) cases in which a resolution is treated as having been passed, or a person is precluded from alleging that a resolution has not been duly passed.".

(3) After section 382 insert –

"382A   Recording of written resolutions

(1) Where a written resolution is agreed to in accordance with section 381A which has effect as if agreed by the company in general meeting, the company shall cause a record of the resolution (and of the signatures) to be entered in a book in the same way as minutes of proceedings of a general meeting of the company.

(2) Any such record, if purporting to be signed by a director of the company or by the company secretary, is evidence of the proceedings in agreeing to the resolution; and where a record is made in accordance with this section, then, until the contrary is proved, the requirements of this Act with respect to those proceedings shall be deemed to be complied with.

(3) Section 382(5) (penalties) applies in relation to a failure to comply with subsection (1) above as it applies in relation to a failure to comply with subsection (1) of that section; and section 383 (inspection of minute books) applies in relation to a record made in accordance with this section as it applies in relation to the minutes of a general meeting.".

114   Written resolutions: supplementary provisions

(1) In the Companies Act 1985 the following Schedule is inserted after Schedule 15 –

"SCHEDULE 15A
WRITTEN RESOLUTIONS OF PRIVATE COMPANIES

PART I
EXCEPTIONS

1. Section 381A does not apply to –
   (*a*) a resolution under section 303 removing a director before the expiration of his period of office, or
   (*b*) a resolution under section 391 removing an auditor before the expiration of his term of office.

PART II
ADAPTATION OF PROCEDURAL REQUIREMENTS

Introductory

2. – (1) In this Part of this Schedule (which adapts certain requirements of this Act in relation to proceedings under section 381A) –
   (*a*) a "written resolution" means a resolution agreed to, or proposed to be agreed to, in accordance with that section, and
   (*b*) a "relevant member" means a member by whom, or on whose behalf, the resolution is required to be signed in accordance with that section.

(2) A written resolution is not effective if any of the requirements of this Part of this Schedule is not complied with.

Section 95 (disapplication of pre-emption rights)

3. – (1) The following adaptations have effect in relation to a written resolution under section 95(2) (disapplication of pre-emption rights), or renewing a resolution under that provision.

(2) So much of section 95(5) as requires the circulation of a written statement by the directors with a notice of meeting does not apply, but such a statement must be supplied to each relevant member at or before the time at which the resolution is supplied to him for signature.

(3) Section 95(6) (offences) applies in relation to the inclusion in any such statement of matter which is misleading, false or deceptive in a material particular.

Section 155 (financial assistance for purchase of company's own shares or those of holding company)

4. In relation to a written resolution giving approval under section 155(4) or (5) (financial assistance for purchase of company's own shares or those of holding company), section 157(4)(*a*) (documents to be available at meeting) does not apply, but the documents referred to in that provision must be supplied to each relevant member at or before the time at which the resolution is supplied to him for signature.

Sections 164, 165 and 167 (authority for off-market purchase or contingent purchase contract of company's own shares)

5. – (1) The following adaptations have effect in relation to a written resolution –

 (*a*) conferring authority to make an off-market purchase of the company's own shares under section 164(2),

 (*b*) conferring authority to vary a contract for an off-market purchase of the company's own shares under section 164(7), or

 (*c*) varying, revoking or renewing any such authority under section 164(3).

(2) Section 164(5) (resolution ineffective if passed by exercise of voting rights by member holding shares to which the resolution relates) does not apply; but for the purposes of section 381A(1) a member holding shares to which the resolution relates shall not be regarded as a member who would be entitled to attend and vote.

(3) Section 164(6) (documents to be available at company's registered office and at meeting) does not apply, but the documents referred to in that provision and, where that provision applies by virtue of section 164(7), the further documents referred to in that provision must be supplied to each relevant member at or before the time at which the resolution is supplied to him for signature.

(4) The above adaptations also have effect in relation to a written resolution in relation to which the provisions of section 164(3) to (7) apply by virtue of –

 (*a*) section 165(2) (authority for contingent purchase contract), or

 (*b*) section 167(2) (approval of release of rights under contract approved under section 164 or 165).

Section 173 (approval for payment out of capital)

6. – (1) The following adaptations have effect in relation to a written resolution giving approval under section 173(2) (redemption or purchase of company's own shares out of capital).

(2) Section 174(2) (resolution ineffective if passed by exercise of voting rights by member holding shares to which the resolution relates) does not apply; but for the purposes of section 381A(1) a member holding shares to which the resolution relates shall not be regarded as a member who would be entitled to attend and vote.

(3) Section 174(4) (documents to be available at meeting) does not apply, but the documents referred to in that provision must be supplied to each relevant member at or before the time at which the resolution is supplied to him for signature.

Section 319 (approval of director's service contract)

7. In relation to a written resolution approving any such term as is mentioned in section 319(1) (director's contract of employment for more than five years), section 319(5) (documents to be available at company's registered office and at

meeting) does not apply, but the documents referred to in that provision must be supplied to each relevant member at or before the time at which the resolution is supplied to him for signature.

Section 337 (funding of director's expenditure in performing his duties)

8. In relation to a written resolution giving approval under section 337(3)(*a*) (funding a director's expenditure in performing his duties), the requirement of that provision that certain matters be disclosed at the meeting at which the resolution is passed does not apply, but those matters must be disclosed to each relevant member at or before the time at which the resolution is supplied to him for signature.".

(2) The Schedule inserted after Schedule 15 to the Companies Act 1985 by the Companies (Mergers and Divisions) Regulations 1987 is renumbered "15B"; and accordingly, in section 427A of that Act (also inserted by those regulations), in subsections (1) and (8) for "15A" substitute "15B".

115 Election by private company to dispense with certain requirements

(1) In Part IV of the Companies Act 1985 (allotment of shares and debentures), in section 80(1) (authority of company required for certain allotments) after "this section" insert "or section 80A"; and after that section insert –

"80A Election by private company as to duration of authority

(1) A private company may elect (by elective resolution in accordance with section 379A) that the provisions of this section shall apply, instead of the provisions of section 80(4) and (5), in relation to the giving or renewal, after the election, of an authority under that section.

(2) The authority must state the maximum amount of relevant securities that may be allotted under it and may be given –

    (*a*) for an indefinite period, or

    (*b*) for a fixed period, in which case it must state the date on which it will expire.

(3) In either case an authority (including an authority contained in the articles) may be revoked or varied by the company in general meeting.

(4) An authority given for a fixed period may be renewed or further renewed by the company in general meeting.

(5) A resolution renewing an authority –

    (*a*) must state, or re-state, the amount of relevant securities which may be allotted under the authority or, as the case may be, the amount remaining to be allotted under it, and

    (*b*) must state whether the authority is renewed for an indefinite period or for a fixed period, in which case it must state the date on which the renewed authority will expire.

(6) The references in this section to the maximum amount of relevant securities that may be allotted shall be construed in accordance with section 80(6).

(7) If an election under this section ceases to have effect, an authority then in force which was given for an indefinite period or for a fixed period of more than five years –

(*a*) if given five years or more before the election ceases to have effect, shall expire forthwith, and

(*b*) otherwise, shall have effect as if it had been given for a fixed period of five years.".

(2) In Chapter IV of Part XI of the Companies Act 1985 (meetings and resolutions), after section 366 (annual general meeting) insert –

"366A Election by private company to dispense with annual general meetings

(1) A private company may elect (by elective resolution in accordance with section 379A) to dispense with the holding of annual general meetings.

(2) An election has effect for the year in which it is made and subsequent years, but does not affect any liability already incurred by reason of default in holding an annual general meeting.

(3) In any year in which an annual general meeting would be required to be held but for the election, and in which no such meeting has been held, any member of the company may, by notice to the company not later than three months before the end of the year, require the holding of an annual general meeting in that year.

(4) If such a notice is given, the provisions of section 366(1) and (4) apply with respect to the calling of the meeting and the consequences of default.

(5) If the election ceases to have effect, the company is not obliged under section 366 to hold an annual general meeting in that year if, when the election ceases to have effect, less than three months of the year remains.

This does not affect any obligation of the company to hold an annual general meeting in that year in pursuance of a notice given under subsection (3).".

(3) In the same Chapter, in sections 369(4) and 378(3) (majority required to sanction short notice of meeting) insert –

"A private company may elect (by elective resolution in accordance with section 379A) that the above provisions shall have effect in relation to the company as if for the references to 95 per cent. there were substituted references to such lesser percentage, but not less than 90 per cent., as may be specified in the resolution or subsequently determined by the company in general meeting.".

116 Elective resolution of private company

(1) Chapter IV of Part XI of the Companies Act 1985 (meetings and resolutions) is amended as follows.

(2) After section 379 insert –

"379A Elective resolution of private company

(1) An election by a private company for the purposes of –

(*a*) section 80A (election as to duration of authority to allot shares),

(*b*) section 252 (election to dispense with laying of accounts and reports before general meeting), (*c*) section 366A (election to dispense with holding of annual general meeting),

(*d*) section 369(4) or 378(3) (election as to majority required to authorise short notice of meeting), or

(*e*) section 386 (election to dispense with appointment of auditors annually),

shall be made by resolution of the company in general meeting in accordance with this section.

Such a resolution is referred to in this Act as an "elective resolution".

(2) An elective resolution is not effective unless –

(*a*) at least 21 days' notice in writing is given of the meeting, stating that an elective resolution is to be proposed and stating the terms of the resolution, and

(*b*) the resolution is agreed to at the meeting, in person or by proxy, by all the members entitled to attend and vote at the meeting.

(3) The company may revoke an elective resolution by passing an ordinary resolution to that effect.

(4) An elective resolution shall cease to have effect if the company is re-registered as a public company.

(5) An elective resolution may be passed or revoked in accordance with this section, and the provisions referred to in subsection (1) have effect, notwithstanding any contrary provision in the company's articles of association.".

(3) In section 380 (registration of resolutions), in subsection (4) (resolutions to which the section applies), after paragraph (*b*) insert –

"(*bb*) an elective resolution or a resolution revoking such a resolution;".

117 Power to make further provision by regulations

(1) The Secretary of State may by regulations make provision enabling private companies to elect, by elective resolution in accordance with section 379A of the Companies Act 1985, to dispense with compliance with such requirements of that Act as may be specified in the regulations, being requirements which appear to the Secretary of State to relate primarily to the internal administration and procedure of companies.

(2) The regulations may add to, amend or repeal provisions of that Act; and may provide for any such provision to have effect, where an election is made, subject to such adaptations and modifications as appear to the Secretary of State to be appropriate.

(3) The regulations may make different provision for different cases and may contain such supplementary, incidental and transitional provisions as appear to the Secretary of State to be appropriate.

(4) Regulations under this section shall be made by statutory instrument.

(5) No regulations under this section shall be made unless a draft of the instrument containing the regulations has been laid before Parliament and approved by a resolution of each House.

Appointment and removal of auditors and related matters

118   Introduction

(1) The following sections amend the provisions of the Companies Act 1985 relating to auditors by inserting new provisions in Chapter V of Part XI of that Act.

(2) The new provisions, together with the amendment made by section 124, replace the present provisions of that Chapter except section 389 (qualification for appointment as auditor) which is replaced by provisions in Part II of this Act.

119   Appointment of auditors

(1) The following sections are inserted in Chapter V of Part XI of the Companies Act 1985 (auditors)–

"Appointment of auditors

384   Duty to appoint auditors

(1) Every company shall appoint an auditor or auditors in accordance with this Chapter.
This is subject to section 388A (dormant company exempt from obligation to appoint auditors).

(2) Auditors shall be appointed in accordance with section 385 (appointment at general meeting at which accounts are laid), except in the case of a private company which has elected to dispense with the laying of accounts in which case the appointment shall be made in accordance with section 385A.

(3) Reverences in this Chapter to the end of the time for appointing auditors are to the end of the time within which an appointment must be made under section 385(2) or 385A(2), according to whichever of those sections applies.

(4) Sections 385 and 385A have effect subject to section 386 under which a private company may elect to dispense with the obligation to appoint auditors annually.

385   Appointment at general meeting at which accounts laid

(1) This section applies to every public company and to a private company which has not elected to dispense with the laying of accounts.

(2) The company shall, at each general meeting at which accounts are laid, appoint an auditor or auditors to hold office from the conclusion of that meeting until the conclusion of the next general meeting at which accounts are laid.

(3) The first auditors of the company may be appointed by the directors at any time before the first general meeting of the company at which accounts are laid; and auditors so appointed shall hold office until the conclusion of that meeting.

(4) If the directors fail to exercise their powers under subsection (3), the powers may be exercised by the company in general meeting.

385A Appointment by private company which is not obliged to lay accounts

(1) This section applies to a private company which has elected in accordance with section 252 to dispense with the laying of accounts before the company in general meeting.

(2) Auditors shall be appointed by the company in general meeting before the end of the period of 28 days beginning with the day on which copies of the company's annual accounts for the previous financial year are sent to members under section 238 or, if notice is given under section 253(2) requiring the laying of the accounts before the company in general meeting, the conclusion of that meeting.

Auditors so appointed shall hold office from the end of that period or, as the case may be, the conclusion of that meeting until the end of the time for appointing auditors for the next financial year.

(3) The first auditors of the company may be appointed by the directors at any time before–

> (*a*) the end of the period of 28 days beginning with the day on which copies of the company's first annual accounts are sent to members under section 238, or
>
> (*b*) if notice is given under section 253(2) requiring the laying of the accounts before the company in general meeting, the beginning of that meeting;

and auditors so appointed shall hold office until the end of that period, or, as the case may be, the conclusion of that meeting.

(4) If the directors fail to exercise their powers under subsection (3), the powers may be exercised by the company in general meeting.

(5) Auditors holding office when the election is made shall, unless the company in general meeting determines otherwise, continue to hold office until the end of the time for appointing auditors for the next financial year; and auditors holding office when an election ceases to have effect shall continue to hold office until the conclusion of the next general meeting of the company at which accounts are laid.

386 Election by private company to dispense with annual appointment

(1) A private company may elect (by elective resolution in accordance with section 379A) to dispense with the obligation to appoint auditors annually.

(2) When such an election is in force the company's auditors shall be deemed to be re-appointed for each succeeding financial year on the expiry of the time for appointing auditors for that year, unless–

> (*a*) a resolution has been passed under section 250 by virtue of which the company is exempt from the obligation to appoint auditors, or
>
> (*b*) a resolution has been passed under section 393 to the effect that their appointment should be brought to an end.

(3) If the election ceases to be in force, the auditors then holding office shall continue to hold office–

> (*a*) where section 385 then applies, until the conclusion of the next general meeting of the company at which accounts are laid;

(*b*) where section 385A then applies, until the end of the time for appointing auditors for the next financial year under that section.

(4) No account shall be taken of any loss of the opportunity of further deemed re-appointment under this section in ascertaining the amount of any compensation or damages payable to an auditor on his ceasing to hold office for any reason.

387 Appointment by Secretary of State in default of appointment by company

(1) If in any case no auditors are appointed, re-appointed or deemed to be re-appointed before the end of the time for appointing auditors, the Secretary of State may appoint a person to fill the vacancy.

(2) In such a case the company shall within one week of the end of the time for appointing auditors give notice to the Secretary of State of his power having become exercisable.

If a company fails to give the notice required by this subsection, the company and every officer of it who is in default is guilty of an offence and liable to a fine and, for continued contravention, to a daily default fine.

388 Filling of casual vacancies

(1) The directors, or the company in general meeting, may fill a casual vacancy in the office of auditor.

(2) While such a vacancy continues, any surviving or continuing auditor or auditors may continue to act.

(3) Special notice is required for a resolution at a general meeting of a company–
    (*a*) filling a casual vacancy in the office of auditor, or
    (*b*) re-appointing as auditor a retiring auditor who was appointed by the directors to fill a casual vacancy.

(4) On receipt of notice of such an intended resolution the company shall forthwith send a copy of it–
    (*a*) to the person proposed to be appointed, and
    (*b*) if the casual vacancy was caused by the resignation of an auditor, to the auditor who resigned

388A Dormant company exempt from obligation to appoint auditors

(1) A company which by virtue of section 250 (dormant companies: exemption from provisions as to audit of accounts) is exempt from the provisions of Part VII relating to the audit of accounts is also exempt from the obligation to appoint auditors.

(2) The following provisions apply if the exemption ceases.

(3) Where section 385 applies (appointment at general meeting at which accounts are laid), the directors may appoint auditors at any time before the next meeting of the company at which accounts are to be laid; and auditors so appointed shall hold office until the conclusion of that meeting.

(4) Where section 385A applies (appointment by private company not obliged to lay accounts), the directors may appoint auditors at any time before–

    (*a*) the end of the period of 28 days beginning with the day on which copies of the company's annual accounts are next sent to members under section 238, or

    (*b*) if notice is given under section 253(2) requiring the laying of the accounts before the company in general meeting, the beginning of that meeting;

and auditors so appointed shall hold office until the end of that period or, as the case may be, the conclusion of that meeting.

(5) If the directors fail to exercise their powers under subsection (3) or (4), the powers may be exercised by the company in general meeting.".

(2) In Schedule 24 to the Companies Act 1985 (punishment of offences), at the appropriate place insert–

"387(2)	Company failing to give Secretary of State notice of non-appointment of auditors.	Summary.	One-fifth of the statutory maximum.	One-fiftieth of the statutory maximum."

(3) In section 46(2) of the Banking Act 1987 (duty of auditor of authorised institution to give notice to Bank of England of certain matters) for "appointed under section 384" substitute "appointed under Chapter V of Part XI"; and in section 46(4) (adaptation of references in relation to Northern Ireland) for "sections 384," substitute "Chapter V of Part XI and sections".

120 Rights of auditors

(1) The following sections are inserted in Chapter V of Part XI of the Companies Act 1985 (auditors)–

Rights of auditors

389A Rights to information

(1) The auditors of a company have a right of access at all times to the company's books, accounts and vouchers, and are entitled to require from the company's officers such information and explanations as they think necessary for the performance of their duties as auditors.

(2) An officer of a company commits an offence if he knowingly or recklessly makes to the company's auditors a statement (whether written or oral) which–

    (*a*) conveys or purports to convey any information or explanations which the auditors require, or are entitled to require, as auditors of the company, and

    (*b*) is misleading, false or deceptive in a material particular.

A person guilty of an offence under this subsection is liable to imprisonment or a fine, or both.

(3) A subsidiary undertaking which is a body corporate incorporated in Great Britain, and the auditors of such an undertaking, shall give to the auditors of any

parent company of the undertaking such information and explanations as they may reasonably require for the purposes of their duties as auditors of that company.

If a subsidiary undertaking fails to comply with this subsection, the undertaking and every officer of it who is in default is guilty of an offence and liable to a fine; and if an auditor fails without reasonable excuse to comply with this subsection he is guilty of an offence and liable to a fine.

(4) A parent company having a subsidiary undertaking which is not a body corporate incorporated in Great Britain shall, if required by its auditors to do so, take all such steps as are reasonably open to it to obtain from the subsidiary undertaking such information and explanations as they may reasonably require for the purposes of their duties as auditors of that company.

If a parent company fails to comply with this subsection, the company and every officer of it who is in default is guilty of an offence and liable to a fine.

(5) Section 734 (criminal proceedings against unincorporated bodies) applies to an offence under subsection (3).

390   Right to attend company meetings, &c

(1) A company's auditors are entitled–
- (a) to receive all notices of, and other communications relating to, any general meeting which a member of the company is entitled to receive;
- (b) to attend any general meeting of the company; and
- (c) to be heard at any general meeting which they attend on any part of the business of the meeting which concerns them as auditors.

(2) In relation to a written resolution proposed to be agreed to by a private company in accordance with section 381A, the company's auditors are entitled–
- (a) to receive all such communications relating to the resolution as, by virtue of any provision of Schedule 15A, are required to be supplied to a member of the company,
- (b) to give notice in accordance with section 381B of their opinion that the resolution concerns them as auditors and should be considered by the company in general meeting or, as the case may be, by a meeting of the relevant class of members of the company.
- (c) to attend any such meeting, and
- (d) to be heard at any such meeting which they attend on any part of the business of the meeting which concerns them as auditors.

(3) The right to attend or be heard at a meeting is exercisable in the case of a body corporate or partnership by an individual authorised by it in writing to act as its representative at the meeting.".

(2) In section 734 of the Companies Act 1985 (criminal proceedings against unincorporated bodies), in subsection (1) (offences in relation to which the provisions apply), after "under" insert "section 389A(3) or".

(3) In Schedule 24 to the Companies Act 1985 (punishment of offences) at the appropriate place insert–

"389A(2)	Officer of company making false, misleading or deceptive statement to auditors.	1. On indictment.	2 years or a fine; or both.
		2. Summary.	6 months or the statutory maximum; or both.
389A(3)	Subsidiary undertaking or its auditor failing to give information to auditors of parent company.	Summary.	One-fifth of the statutory maximum.
389A(4)	Parent company failing to obtain from subsidiary undertaking information for purposes of audit.	Summary.	One-fifth of the statutory maximum.".

(4) In Schedule 4 to the Iron and Steel Act 1982 (constitution and proceedings of publicly-owned companies that are private companies), in paragraph 3(6) (entitlement of auditors to attend and be heard at general meetings, &c.) for "387(1)" substitute "390(1)".

121 Remuneration of auditors

The following sections are inserted in Chapter V of Part XI of the Companies Act 1985 (auditors)–

"Remuneration of auditors

390A Remuneration of auditors

(1) The remuneration of auditors appointed by the company in general meeting shall be fixed by the company in general meeting or in such manner as the company in general meeting may determine.

(2) The remuneration of auditors appointed by the directors or the Secretary of State shall be fixed by the directors or the Secretary of State, as the case may be.

(3) There shall be stated in a note to the company's annual accounts the amount of the remuneration of the company's auditors in their capacity as such.

(4) For the purposes of this section "remuneration" includes sums paid in respect of expenses.

(5) This section applies in relation to benefits in kind as to payments in cash, and in relation to any such benefit references to its amount are to its estimated money value.
The nature of any such benefit shall also be disclosed.

390B Remuneration of auditors or their associates for non-audit work

(1) The Secretary of State may make provision by regulations for securing the disclosure of the amount of any remuneration received or receivable by a company's auditors or their associates in respect of services other than those of auditors in their capacity as such.

(2) The regulations may–
    (*a*) provide that "remuneration" includes sums paid in respect of expenses,

    (*b*) apply in relation to benefits in kind as to payments in cash, and in relation to any such benefit require disclosure of its nature and its estimated money value,

    (*c*) define "associate" in relation to an auditor,

    (*d*) require the disclosure of remuneration in respect of services rendered to associated undertakings of the company, and

    (*e*) define "associated undertaking" for that purpose.

(3) The regulations may require the auditors to disclose the relevant information in their report or require the relevant information to be disclosed in a note to the company's accounts and require the auditors to supply the directors of the company with such information as is necessary to enable that disclosure to be made.

(4) The regulations may make different provision for different cases.

(5) Regulations under this section shall be made by statutory instrument which shall be subject to annulment in pursuance of a resolution of either House of Parliament.".

122 Removal, resignation, &c of auditors

(1) The following sections are inserted in Chapter V of Part XI of the Companies Act 1985 (auditors)–

"Removal, resignation, &c of auditors

391 Removal of auditors

(1) A company may by ordinary resolution at any time remove an auditor from office, notwithstanding anything in any agreement between it and him.

(2) Where a resolution removing an auditor is passed at a general meeting of a company, the company shall within 14 days give notice of that fact in the prescribed form to the registrar.

If a company fails to give the notice required by this subsection, the company and every officer of it who is in default is guilty of an offence and liable to a fine and, for continued contravention, to a daily default fine.

(3) Nothing in this section shall be taken as depriving a person removed under it of compensation or damages payable to him in respect of the termination of his appointment as auditor or of any appointment terminating with that as auditor.

(4) An auditor of a company who has been removed has, notwithstanding his removal, the rights conferred by section 390 in relation to any general meeting of the company–

    (*a*) at which his term of office would otherwise have expired, or

    (*b*) at which it is proposed to fill the vacancy caused by his removal.

In such a case the references in that section to matters concerning the auditors as auditors shall be construed as references to matters concerning him as a former auditor.

391A Rights of auditors who are removed or not re-appointed

(1) Special notice is required for a resolution at a general meeting of a company–

> (*a*) removing an auditor before the expiration of his term of office, or
>
> (*b*) appointing as auditor a person other than a retiring auditor.

(2) On receipt of notice of such an intended resolution the company shall forthwith send a copy of it to the person proposed to be removed or, as the case may be, to the person proposed to be appointed and to the retiring auditor.

(3) The auditor proposed to be removed or (as the case may be) the retiring auditor may make with respect to the intended resolution representations in writing to the company (not exceeding a reasonable length) and request their notification to members of the company.

(4) The company shall (unless the representations are received by it too late for it to do so)–

> (*a*) in any notice of the resolution given to members of the company, state the fact of the representations having been made, and
>
> (*b*) send a copy of the representations to every member of the company to whom notice of the meeting is or has been sent.

(5) If a copy of any such representations is not sent out as required because received too late or because of the company's default, the auditor may (without prejudice to his right to be heard orally) require that the representations be read out at the meeting.

(6) Copies of the representations need not be sent out and the representations need not be read at the meeting if, on the application either of the company or of any other person claiming to be aggrieved, the court is satisfied that the rights conferred by this section are being abused to secure needless publicity for defamatory matter; and the court may order the company's costs on the application to be paid in whole or in part by the auditor, notwithstanding that he is not a party to the application.

392 Resignation of auditors

(1) An auditor of a company may resign his office by depositing a notice in writing to that effect at the company's registered office.

The notice is not effective unless it is accompanied by the statement required by section 394.

(2) An effective notice of resignation operates to bring the auditor's term of office to an end as of the date on which the notice is deposited or on such later date as may be specified in it.

(3) The company shall within 14 days of the deposit of a notice of resignation send a copy of the notice to the registrar of companies.

If default is made in complying with this subsection, the company and every officer of it who is in default is guilty of an offence and liable to a fine and, for continued contravention, a daily default fine.

392A Rights of resigning auditors

(1) This section applies where an auditor's notice of resignation is accompanied by a statement of circumstances which he considers should be brought to the

attention of members or creditors of the company.

(2) He may deposit with the notice a signed requisition calling on the directors of the company forthwith duly to convene an extraordinary general meeting of the company for the purpose of receiving and considering such explanation of the circumstances connected with his resignation as he may wish to place before the meeting.

(3) He may request the company to circulate to its members–

> (*a*) before the meeting convened on his requisition, or
>
> (*b*) before any general meeting at which his term of office would otherwise have expired or at which it is proposed to fill the vacancy caused by his resignation,

a statement in writing (not exceeding a reasonable length) of the circumstances connected with his resignation.

(4) The company shall (unless the statement is received too late for it to comply)–

> (*a*) in any notice of the meeting given to members of the company, state the fact of the statement having been made, and
>
> (*b*) send a copy of the statement to every member of the company to whom notice of the meeting is or has been sent.

(5) If the directors do not within 21 days from the date of the deposit of a requisition under this section proceed duly to convene a meeting for a day not more than 28 days after the date on which the notice convening the meeting is given, every director who failed to take all reasonable steps to secure that a meeting was convened as mentioned above is guilty of an offence and liable to a fine.

(6) If a copy of the statement mentioned above is not sent out as required because received too late or because of the company's default, the auditor may (without prejudice to his right to be heard orally) require that the statement be read out at the meeting.

(7) Copies of a statement need not be sent out and the statement need not be read out at the meeting if, on the application either of the company or of any other person who claims to be aggrieved, the court is satisfied that the rights conferred by this section are being abused to secure needless publicity for defamatory matter; and the court may order the company's costs on such an application to be paid in whole or in part by the auditor, notwithstanding that he is not a party to the application.

(8) An auditor who has resigned has, notwithstanding his resignation, the rights conferred by section 390 in relation to any such general meeting of the company as is mentioned in subsection (3)(*a*) or (*b*).

In such a case the references in that section to matters concerning the auditors as auditors shall be construed as references to matters concerning him as a former auditor.

393   Termination of appointment of auditors not appointed annually

(1) When an election is in force under section 386 (election by private company to dispense with annual appointment), any member of the company may deposit notice in writing at the company's registered office proposing that the appointment of the company's auditors be brought to an end.

No member may deposit more than one such notice in any financial year of the company.

(2) If such a notice is deposited it is the duty of the directors–

> (*a*) to convene a general meeting of the company for a date not more than 28 days after the date on which the notice was given, and
>
> (*b*) to propose at the meeting a resolution in a form enabling the company to decide whether the appointment of the company's auditors should be brought to an end.

(3) If the decision of the company at the meeting is that the appointment of the auditors should be brought to an end, the auditors shall not be deemed to be re-appointed when next they would be and, if the notice was deposited within the period immediately following the distribution of accounts, any deemed re-appointment for the financial year following that to which those accounts relate which has already occurred shall cease to have effect.

The period immediately following the distribution of accounts means the period beginning with the day on which copies of the company's annual accounts are sent to members of the company under section 238 and ending 14 days after that day.

(4) If the directors do not within 14 days from the date of the deposit of the notice proceed duly to convene a meeting, the member who deposited the notice (or, if there was more than one, any of them) may himself convene the meeting; but any meeting so convened shall not be held after the expiration of three months from that date.

(5) A meeting convened under this section by a member shall be convened in the same manner, as nearly as possible, as that in which meetings are to be convened by directors.

(6) Any reasonable expenses incurred by a member by reason of the failure of the directors duly to convene a meeting shall be made good to him by the company; and any such sums shall be recouped by the company from such of the directors as were in default of any sums payable, or to become payable, by the company by way of fees or other remuneration in respect of their services.

(7) This section has effect notwithstanding anything in any argeement between the company and its auditors; and no compensation or damages shall be payable by reason of the auditors' appointment being terminated under this section.".

(2) In Schedule 24 to the Companies Act 1985 (punishment of offences), at the appropriate place insert–

"391(2)	Failing to give notice to registrar of removal of auditor.	Summary.	One-fifth of the statutory maximum.	One-fiftieth of the statutory maximum.
392(3)	Company failing to forward notice of auditor's resignation to registrar.	1. On indictment. 2. Summary.	A fine The statutory maximum.	One-tenth of the statutory maximum.
392A(5)	Directors failing to convene meeting requisitioned by resigning auditor.	1. On indictment. 2. Summary.	A fine. The statutory maximum.".	

123   Statement by person ceasing to hold office as auditor

(1) The following section is inserted in Chapter V of Part XI of the Companies Act 1985 (auditors)–

"394   Statement by person ceasing to hold office as auditor

(1) Where an auditor ceases for any reason to hold office, he shall deposit at the company's registered office a statement of any circumstances connected with his ceasing to hold office which he considers should be brought to the attention of the members or creditors of the company or, if he considers that there are no such circumstances, a statement that there are none.

(2) In the case of resignation, the statement shall be deposited along with the notice of resignation; in the case of failure to seek re-appointment, the statement shall be deposited not less than 14 days before the end of the time allowed for next appointing auditors; in any other case, the statement shall be deposited not later than the end of the period of 14 days beginning with the date on which he ceases to hold office.

(3) If the statement is of circumstances which the auditor considers should be brought to the attention of the members or creditors of the company, the company shall within 14 days of the deposit of the statement either–

    (*a*) send a copy of it to every person who under section 238 is entitled to be sent copies of the accounts, or

    (*b*) apply to the court.

(4) The company shall if it applies to the court notify the auditor of the application.

(5) Unless the auditor receives notice of such an application before the end of the period of 21 days beginning with the day on which he deposited the statement, he shall within a further seven days send a copy of the statement to the registrar.

(6) If the court is satisfied that the auditor is using the statement to secure needless publicity for defamatory matter–

    (*a*) it shall direct that copies of the statement need not be sent out, and

    (*b*) it may further order the company's costs on the application to be paid in whole or in part by the auditor, notwithstanding that he is not a party to the application;

and the company shall within 14 days of the court's decision send to the persons mentioned in subsection (3)(*a*) a statement setting out the effect of the order.

(7) If the court is not so satisfied, the company shall within 14 days of the court's decision–

    (*a*) send copies of the statement to the persons mentioned in subsection (3)(*a*), and

    (*b*) notify the auditor of the court's decision;

and the auditor shall within seven days of receiving such notice send a copy of the statement to the registrar.

394A   Offences of failing to comply with s 394

(1) If a person ceasing to hold office as auditor fails to comply with section 394 he is guilty of an offence and liable to a fine.

(2) In proceedings for an offence under subsection (1) it is a defence for the person charged to show that he took all reasonable steps and exercised all due diligence to avoid the commission of the offence.

(3) Sections 733 (liability of individuals for corporate default) and 734 (criminal proceedings against unincorporated bodies) apply to an offence under subsection (1).

(4) If a company makes default in complying with section 394, the company and every officer of it who is in default is guilty of an offence and liable to a fine and, for continued contravention, to a daily default fine.".

(2) In Schedule 24 to the Companies Act 1985 (punishment of offences), at the appropriate place insert–

"394A(1)　Person ceasing to hold office as auditor failing to deposit statement as to circumstances.

"394A(1)	Person ceasing to hold office as auditor failing to deposit statement as to circumstances.	1. On indictment. 2. Summary.	A fine. The statutory maximum.	
394A(4)	Company failing to comply with requirements as to statement of person ceasing to hold office as auditor.	1. On indictment. 2. Summary.	A fine. The statutory maximum.	One-tenth of the statutory maximum.".

(3) In section 733 of the Companies Act 1985 (liability of individuals for corporate default), in subsection (1) (offences in relation to which provisions apply) after "216(3)" insert ",394A(1)".

(4) In section 734 of the Companies Act 1985 (criminal proceedings against unincorporated bodies), in subsection (1) (offences in relation to which the provisions apply), after "under" insert "section 394(1) or".

(5) In Schedule 22 to the Companies Act 1985 (unregistered companies), in the entry for sections 384 to 393, for "393" substitute "394A".

124　Auditors of trade unions and employers' associations

In section 11 of the Trade Union and Labour Relations Act 1974 (duties of trade unions and employers' associations as to auditors, &c.), after subsection (8) insert –

"(9) Where a trade union or employers' association to which this section applies is a company within the meaning of the Companies Act 1985 –

    (*a*) subsection (3) above, and the provisions of paragraphs 6 to 15 of Schedule 2 to this Act, do not apply, and

    (*b*) the rights and powers conferred, and duties imposed, by paragraphs 16 to 21 of that Schedule belong to the auditors of the company appointed under Chapter V of Part XI of that Act.".

Company records and related matters

125   Delivery of documents to the registrar

(1) For section 706 of the Companies Act 1985 (size, durability, &c. of documents delivered to the registrar) substitute –

"706   Delivery to the registrar of documents in legible form

(1) This section applies to the delivery to the registrar under any provision of the Companies Acts of documents in legible form.

(2) The document must –
- (*a*) state in a prominent position the registered number of the company to which it relates,
- (*b*) satisfy any requirements prescribed by regulations for the purposes of this section, and
- (*c*) conform to such requirements as the registrar may specify for the purpose of enabling him to copy the document.

(3) If a document is delivered to the registrar which does not comply with the requirements of this section, he may serve on the person by whom the document was delivered (or, if there are two or more such persons, on any of them) a notice indicating the respect in which the document does not comply.

(4) Where the registrar serves such a notice, then, unless a replacement document –
- (*a*) is delivered to him within 14 days after the service of the notice, and
- (*b*) complies with the requirements of this section (or section 707) or is not rejected by him for failure to comply with those requirements,

the original document shall be deemed not to have been delivered to him.

But for the purposes of any enactment imposing a penalty for failure to deliver, so far as it imposes a penalty for continued contravention, no account shall be taken of the period between the delivery of the original document and the end of the period of 14 days after service of the registrar's notice.

(5) Regulations made for the purposes of this section may make different provision with respect to different descriptions of document.".

(2) For section 707 of the Companies Act 1985 (power of registrar to accept information on microfilm, &c.) substitute –

"707   Delivery to the registrar of documents otherwise than in legible form

(1) This section applies to the delivery to the registrar under any provision of the Companies Acts of documents otherwise than in legible form.

(2) Any requirement to deliver a document to the registrar, or to deliver a document in the prescribed form, is satisfied by the communication to the registrar of the requisite information in any non-legible form prescribed for the purposes of this section by regulations or approved by the registrar.

(3) Where the document is required to be signed or sealed, it shall instead be authenticated in such manner as may be prescribed by regulations or approved by the registrar.

(4) The document must –

(a) contain in a prominent position the registered number of the company to which it relates,

(b) satisfy any requirements prescribed by regulations for the purposes of this section, and

(c) be furnished in such manner, and conform to such requirements, as the registrar may specify for the purpose of enabling him to read and copy the document.

(5) If a document is delivered to the registrar which does not comply with the requirements of this section, he may serve on the person by whom the document was delivered (or, if there are two or more such persons, on any of them) a notice indicating the respect in which the document does not comply.

(6) Where the registrar serves such a notice, then, unless a replacement document –

(a) is delivered to him within 14 days after the service of the notice, and

(b) complies with the requirements of this section (or section 706) or is not rejected by him for failure to comply with those requirements,

the original document shall be deemed not to have been delivered to him.

But for the purposes of any enactment imposing a penalty for failure to deliver, so far as it imposes a penalty for continued contravention, no account shall be taken of the period between the delivery of the original document and the end of the period of 14 days after service of the registrar's notice.

(7) The Secretary of State may by regulations make further provision with respect to the application of this section in relation to instantaneous forms of communication.

(8) Regulations made for the purposes of this section may make different provision with respect to different descriptions of document and different forms of communication, and as respects delivery to the registrar for England and Wales and delivery to the registrar for Scotland.".

126 Keeping and inspection of company records

(1) In Part XXIV of the Companies Act 1985 (the registrar of companies, his functions and offices), after the sections inserted by section 125 above, insert –

"707A The keeping of company records by the registrar

(1) The information contained in a document delivered to the registrar under the Companies Acts may be recorded and kept by him in any form he thinks fit, provided it is possible to inspect the information and to produce a copy of it in legible form.

This is sufficient compliance with any duty of his to keep, file or register the document.

(2) The originals of documents delivered to the registrar in legible form shall be kept by him for ten years, after which they may be destroyed.

(3) Where a company has been dissolved, the registrar may, at any time after the expiration of two years from the date of the dissolution, direct that any records in his custody relating to the company may be removed to the Public Record Office; and records in respect of which such a direction is given shall be

disposed of in accordance with the enactments relating to that Office and the rules made under them.

This subsection does not extend to Scotland.

(4) In subsection (3) "company" includes a company provisionally or completely registered under the Joint Stock Companies Act 1844.".

(2) For sections 709 and 710 of the Companies Act 1985 (inspection of documents kept by the registrar) substitute –

"709   Inspection, &c of records kept by the registrar

(1) Any person may inspect any records kept by the registrar for the purposes of the Companies Acts and may require –

  (*a*) a copy, in such form as the registrar considers appropriate, of any information contained in those records, or

  (*b*) a certified copy of, or extract from, any such record.

(2) The right of inspection extends to the originals of documents delivered to the registrar in legible form only where the record kept by the registrar of the contents of the document is illegible or unavailable.

(3) A copy of or extract from a record kept at any of the offices for the registration of companies in England and Wales or Scotland, certified in writing by the registrar (whose official position it is unnecessary to prove) to be an accurate record of the contents of any document delivered to him under the Companies Acts, is in all legal proceedings admissible in evidence as of equal validity with the original document and as evidence of any fact stated therein of which direct oral evidence would be admissible.

In England and Wales this is subject to compliance with any applicable rules of court under section 5 of the Civil Evidence Act 1968 or section 69(2) of the Police and Criminal Evidence Act 1984 (which relate to evidence from computer records).

(4) Copies of or extracts from records furnished by the registrar may, instead of being certified by him in writing to be an accurate record, be sealed with his official seal.

(5) No process for compelling the production of a record kept by the registrar shall issue from any court except with the leave of the court; and any such process shall bear on it a statement that it is issued with the leave of the court.

710   Certificate of incorporation

Any person may require a certificate of the incorporation of a company, signed by the registrar or authenticated by his official seal.

710A   Provision and authentication by registrar of documents in non-legible form

(1) Any requirement of the Companies Acts as to the supply by the registrar of a document may, if the registrar thinks fit, be satisfied by the communication by the registrar of the requisite information in any non-legible form prescribed for the purposes of this section by regulations or approved by him.

(2) Where the document is required to be signed by him or sealed with his

official seal, it shall instead be authenticated in such manner as may be prescribed by regulations or approved by the registrar.".

127 Supplementary provisions as to company records and related matters

(1) In Part XXIV of the Companies Act 1985 (the registrar of companies, his functions and offices), after section 715 insert –

"715A Interpretation

(1) In this Part –
"document" includes information recorded in any form; and
"legible", in the context of documents in legible or non-legible form, means capable of being read with the naked eye.

(2) References in this Part to delivering a document include sending, forwarding, producing or (in the case of a notice) giving it.".

(2) In section 708(1) of the Companies Act 1985 (fees) –
(*a*) in paragraph (*a*) for the words from "any notice or other document" to the end substitute "any document which under those Acts is required to be delivered to him", and
(*b*) in paragraph (*b*) omit "or other material".

(3) Omit sections 712 and 715 of the Companies Act 1985 (removal and destruction of old records).

(4) In section 713(1) (enforcement of duty to make returns, &c.), for the words from "file with" to "or other document" substitute "deliver a document to the registrar of companies".

(5) In section 735A(2) of the Companies Act 1985 (provisions applying to Insolvency Act 1986 and Company Directors Disqualification Act 1986 as to the Companies Acts) –
(*a*) after "707(1)," insert "707A(1),",
(*b*) after "708(1)(*a*) and (4)," insert "709(1) and (3),", and
(*c*) for "710(5)" substitute "710A".

(6) After section 735A of the Companies Act 1985 insert –

"735B Relationship of this Act to Parts IV and V of the Financial Services Act 1986

In sections 704(5), 706(1), 707(1), 707A(1), 708(1)(a) and (4), 709(1) and (3), 710A and 713(1) references to the Companies Acts include Parts IV and V of the Financial Services Act 1986.".

(7) In Schedule 22 to the Companies Act 1985 (unregistered companies), in the entry for Part XXIV for "sections 706, 708 to 710, 712 and 713" substitute "sections 706 to 710A, 713 and 715A".

Miscellaneous

128 Form of articles for partnership company

In Chapter I of Part I of the Companies Act 1985 (company formation), after section 8 (Tables A, C, D and E) insert –

"8A   Table G

(1) The Secretary of State may by regulations prescribe a Table G containing articles of association appropriate for a partnership company, that is, a company limited by shares whose shares are intended to be held to a substantial extent by or on behalf of its employees.

(2) A company limited by shares may for its articles adopt the whole or any part of that Table.

(3) If in consequence of regulations under this section Table G is altered, the alteration does not affect a company registered before the alteration takes effect, or repeal as respects that company any portion of the Table.

(4) Regulations under this section shall be made by statutory instrument which shall be subject to annulment in pursuance of a resolution of either House of Parliament.".

129   Membership of holding company

(1) In Chapter I of Part I of the Companies Act 1985 (company formation), for section 23 (membership of holding company) substitute –

"23   Membership of holding company

(1) Except as mentioned in this section, a body corporate cannot be a member of a company which is its holding company and any allotment or transfer of shares in a company to its subsidiary is void.

(2) The prohibition does not apply where the subsidiary is concerned only as personal representative or trustee unless, in the latter case, the holding company or a subsidiary of it is beneficially interested under the trust.

For the purpose of ascertaining whether the holding company or a subsidiary is so interested, there shall be disregarded –

   (a) any interest held only by way of security for the purposes of a transaction entered into by the holding company or subsidiary in the ordinary course of a business which includes the lending of money;

   (b) any such interest as is mentioned in Part I of Schedule 2.

(3) The prohibition does not apply where the subsidiary is concerned only as a market maker.

For this purpose a person is a market maker if –

   (a) he holds himself out at all normal times in compliance with the rules of a recognised investment exchange other than an overseas investment exchange (within the meaning of the Financial Services Act 1986) as willing to buy and sell securities at prices specified by him, and

   (b) he is recognised as so doing by that investment exchange.

(4) Where a body corporate became a holder of shares in a company –

   (a) before 1st July 1948, or

   (b) on or after that date and before the commencement of section 122 of the Companies Act 1989, in circumstances in which this section as it then had effect did not apply,

but at any time after the commencement of that section falls within the prohibition in subsection (1) above in respect of those shares, it may continue to be a member of that company; but for so long as that prohibition would apply, apart from this subsection, it has no right to vote in respect of those shares at meetings of the company or of any class of its members.

(5) Where a body corporate becomes a holder of shares in a company after the commencement of that section in circumstances in which the prohibition in subsection (1) does not apply, but subsequently falls within that prohibition in respect of those shares, it may continue to be a member of that company; but for so long as that prohibition would apply, apart from this subsection, it has no right to vote in respect of those shares at meetings of the company or of any class of its members.

(6) Where a body corporate is permitted to continue as a member of a company by virtue of subsection (4) or (5), an allotment to it of fully paid shares in the company may be validly made by way of capitalisation of reserves of the company; but for so long as the prohibition in subsection (1) would apply, apart from subsection (4) or (5), it has no right to vote in respect of those shares at meetings of the company or of any class of its members.

(7) The provisions of this section apply to a nominee acting on behalf of a subsidiary as to the subsidiary itself.

(8) In relation to a company other than a company limited by shares, the references in this section to shares shall be construed as references to the interest of its members as such, whatever the form of that interest.".

(2) In Schedule 2 to the Companies Act 1985 (interpretation of references to "beneficial interest"), in paragraphs 1(1), 3(1) and 4(2) for "as respects section 23(4)" substitute "as this paragraph applies for the purposes of section 23(2)".

130   Company contracts and execution of documents by companies

(1) In Chapter III of Part I of the Companies Act 1985 (a company's capacity; the formalities of carrying on business), for section 36 (form of company contracts) substitute –

"36   Company contracts: England and Wales

Under the law of England and Wales a contract may be made –
  (*a*)   by a company, by writing under its common seal, or
  (*b*)   on behalf of a company, by any person acting under its authority, express or implied;
and any formalities required by law in the case of a contract made by an individual also apply, unless a contrary intention appears, to a contract made by or on behalf of a company.".

(2) After that section insert –

"36A   Execution of documents: England and Wales

(1) Under the law of England and Wales the following provisions have effect with respect to the execution of documents by a company.

(2) A document is executed by a company by the affixing of its common seal.

(3) A company need not have a common seal, however, and the following subsections apply whether it does or not.

(4) A document signed by a director and the secretary of a company, or by two directors of a company, and expressed (in whatever form of words) to be executed by the company has the same effect as if executed under the common seal of the company.

(5) A document executed by a company which makes it clear on its face that it is intended by the person or persons making it to be a deed has effect, upon delivery, as a deed; and it shall be presumed, unless a contrary intention is proved, to be delivered upon its being so executed.

(6) In favour of a purchaser a document shall be deemed to have been duly executed by a company if it purports to be signed by a director and the secretary of the company, or by two directors of the company, and, where it makes it clear on its face that it is intended by the person or persons making it to be a deed, to have been delivered upon its being executed.

A "purchaser" means a purchaser in good faith for valuable consideration and includes a lessee, mortgagee or other person who for valuable consideration acquires an interest in property.".

(3) After the section inserted by subsection (2) insert –

"36B Execution of documents: Scotland

(1) Under the law of Scotland the following provisions have effect with respect to the execution of documents by a company.

(2) A document –
- (*a*) is signed by a company if it is signed on its behalf by a director, or by the secretary, of the company or by a person authorised to sign the document on its behalf, and
- (*b*) is subscribed by a company if it is subscribed on its behalf by being signed in accordance with the provisions of paragraph (*a*) at the end of the last page.

(3) A document shall be presumed, unless the contrary is shown, to have been subscribed by a company in accordance with subsection (2) if –
- (*a*) it bears to have been subscribed on behalf of the company by a director, or by the secretary, of the company or by a person bearing to have been authorised to subscribe the document on its behalf; and
- (*b*) it bears –
  - (i)   to have been signed by a person as a witness of the subscription of the director, secretary or other person subscribing on behalf of the company; or
  - (ii) (if the subscription is not so witnessed) to have been sealed with the common seal of the company.

(4) A presumption under subsection (3) as to subscription of a document does not include a presumption –
- (*a*) that a person bearing to subscribe the document as a director or the secretary of the company was such director or secretary; or
- (*b*) that a person subscribing the document on behalf of the company bearing to have been authorised to do so was authorised to do so.

(5) Notwithstanding subsection (3)(*b*)(ii), a company need not have a common seal.

(6) Any reference in any enactment (including an enactment contained in a subordinate instrument) to a probative document shall, in relation to a document executed by a company after the commencement of section 130 of the Companies Act 1989, be construed as a reference to a document which is presumed under subsection (3) above to be subscribed by the company.

(7) Subsections (1) to (4) above do not apply where an enactment (including an enactment contained in a subordinate instrument) provides otherwise.".

(4) After the section inserted by subsection (3) insert –

"36C   Pre-incorporation contracts, deeds and obligations

(1) A contract which purports to be made by or on behalf of a company at a time when the company has not been formed has effect, subject to any agreement to the contrary, as one made with the person purporting to act for the company or as agent for it, and he is personally liable on the contract accordingly.

(2) Subsection (1) applies –
    (*a*) to the making of a deed under the law of England and Wales, and
    (*b*) to the undertaking of an obligation under the law of Scotland,
as it applies to the making of a contract.".

(5) In Schedule 22 of the Companies Act 1985 (provisions applying to unregistered companies), at the appropriate place insert –

"Section 36	Company contracts.	Subject to section 718(3).
Sections 36A and 36B	Execution of documents.	Subject to section 718(3).
Section 36C	Pre-incorporation contracts, deeds and obligations.	Subject to section 718(3).".

(6) The Secretary of State may make provision by regulations applying sections 36 to 36C of the Companies Act 1985 (company contracts; execution of documents; pre-incorporation contracts, deeds and obligations) to companies incorporated outside Great Britain, subject to such exceptions, adaptations or modifications as may be specified in the regulations.

Regulations under this subsection shall be made by statutory instrument which shall be subject to annulment in pursuance of a resolution of either House of Parliament.

(7) Schedule 17 contains further minor and consequential amendments relating to company contracts, the execution of documents by companies and related matters.

131   Members' rights to damages, &c

(1) In Part IV of the Companies Act 1985 (allotment of shares and debentures), before section 112 and after the heading *"Other matters arising out of allotment &c"*, insert –

"111A   Right to damages, &c not affected

A person is not debarred from obtaining damages or other compensation from a company by reason only of his holding or having held shares in the company or any right to apply or subscribe for shares or to be included in the company's register in respect of shares.".

(2) In section 116 of the Companies Act 1985 (extended operation of certain provisions applying to public companies) for "and 110 to 115" substitute ", 110, 111 and 112 to 115".

132   Financial assistance for purposes of employees' share scheme

In Chapter VI of Part V of the Companies Act 1985 (financial assistance by company for purchase of its own shares), in section 153 (transactions not prohibited), for subsection (4)(*b*) (provision of money in accordance with employees' share scheme) substitute –
> "(*b*) the provision by a company, in good faith in the interests of the company, of financial assistance for the purposes of an employees' share scheme,".

133   Issue of redeemable shares

(1) In Part V of the Companies Act 1985 (share capital, its increase, maintenance and reduction), Chapter III (redeemable shares, purchase by a company of its own shares) is amended as follows.

(2) After section 159 (power to issue redeemable shares) insert –

"159A   Terms and manner of redemption

(1) Redeemable shares may not be issued unless the following conditions are satisfied as regards the terms and manner of redemption.

(2) The date on or by which, or dates between which, the shares are to be or may be redeemed must be specified in the company's articles or, if the articles so provide, fixed by the directors, and in the latter case the date or dates must be fixed before the shares are issued.

(3) Any other circumstances in which the shares are to be or may be redeemed must be specified in the company's articles.

(4) The amount payable on redemption must be specified in, or determined in accordance with, the company's articles, and in the latter case the articles must not provide for the amount to be determined by reference to any person's discretion or opinion.

(5) Any other terms and conditions of redemption shall be specified in the company's articles.

(6) Nothing in this section shall be construed as requiring a company to provide in its articles for any matter for which provision is made by this Act.".

(3) In section 160 (financing, &c. of redemption) –
   (*a*) omit subsection (3) (which is superseded by the new section 159A), and
   (*b*) in subsection (4) (cancellation of shares on redemption) for "redeemed under this section" substitute "redeemed under this Chapter".

(4) In section 162 (power of company to purchase own shares), for subsection (2) (application of provisions relating to redeemable shares) substitute –
> "(2) Sections 159, 160 and 161 apply to the purchase by a company under this section of its own shares as they apply to the redemption of redeemable shares.".

134   Disclosure of interests in shares

(1) Part VI of the Companies Act 1985 (disclosure of interests in shares) is amended as follows.

(2) In section 199(2) (notifiable interests), for the words from "the percentage" to the end substitute "3 per cent. of the nominal value of that share capital".

The order bringing the above amendment into force may make such provision as appears to the Secretary of State appropriate as to the obligations of a person whose interest in a company's shares becomes notifiable by virtue of the amendment coming into force.

(3) In sections 202(1) and (4) and 206(8) (which require notification of certain matters within a specified period) for "5 days" substitute "2 days".

(4) In section 202 (particulars to be contained in notification), for subsection (3) substitute –

> "(3) A notification (other than one stating that a person no longer has a notifiable interest) shall include the following particulars, so far as known to the person making the notification at the date when it is made –
> (a) the identity of each registered holder of shares to which the notification relates and the number of such shares held by each of them, and
> (b) the number of such shares in which the interest of the person giving the notification is such an interest as is mentioned in section 208(5).".

(5) After section 210 insert –

"210A Power to make further provision by regulations

(1) The Secretary of State may by regulations amend –
> (a) the definition of "relevant share capital" (section 198(2)),
> (b) the percentage giving rise to a "notifiable interest" (section 199(2)),
> (c) the periods within which an obligation of disclosure must be fulfilled or a notice must be given (sections 202(1) and (4) and 206(8)),
> (d) the provisions as to what is taken to be an interest in shares (section 208) and what interests are to be disregarded (section 209), and
> (e) the provisions as to company investigations (section 212);

and the regulations may amend, replace or repeal the provisions referred to above and make such other consequential amendments or repeals of provisions of this Part as appear to the Secretary of State to be appropriate.

(2) The regulations may in any case make different provision for different descriptions of company; and regulations under subsection (1)(b), (c) or (d) may make different provision for different descriptions of person, interest or share capital.

(3) The regulations may contain such transitional and other supplementary and incidental provisions as appear to the Secretary of State to be appropriate, and may in particular make provision as to the obligations of a person whose interest in a company's shares becomes or ceases to be notifiable by virtue of the regulations.

(4) Regulations under this section shall be made by statutory instrument.

(5) No regulations shall be made under this section unless a draft of the regulations has been laid before and approved by a resolution of each House of Parliament.".

(6) Any regulations made under section 209(1)(j) which are in force immediately before the repeal of that paragraph by this Act shall have effect as if made under section 210A(1)(d) as inserted by subsection (5) above.

135   Orders imposing restrictions on shares

(1) The Secretary of State may by regulations made by statutory instrument make such amendments of the provisions of the Companies Act 1985 relating to orders imposing restrictions on shares as appear to him necessary or expedient –

    (*a*) for enabling orders to be made in a form protecting the rights of third parties;

    (*b*) with respect to the circumstances in which restrictions may be relaxed or removed;

    (*c*) with respect to the making of interim orders by a court.

(2) The provisions referred to in subsection (1) are section 210(5), section 216(1) and (2), section 445 and Part XV of the Companies Act 1985.

(3) The regulations may make different provision for different cases and may contain such transitional and other supplementary and incidental provisions as appear to the Secretary of State to be appropriate.

(4) Regulations under this section shall not be made unless a draft of the regulations has been laid before Parliament and approved by resolution of each House of Parliament.

136   A company's registered office

For section 287 of the Companies Act 1985 (registered office) substitute –

"287   Registered office

    (1) A company shall at all times have a registered office to which all communications and notices may be addressed.

    (2) On incorporation the situation of the company's registered office is that specified in the statement sent to the registrar under section 10.

    (3) The company may change the situation of its registered office from time to time by giving notice in the prescribed form to the registrar.

    (4) The change takes effect upon the notice being registered by the registrar, but until the end of the period of 14 days beginning with the date on which it is registered a person may validly serve any document on the company at its previous registered office.

    (5) For the purposes of any duty of a company –

        (*a*) to keep at its registered office, or make available for public inspection there, any register, index or other document, or

        (*b*) to mention the address of its registered office in any document,

a company which has given notice to the registrar of a change in the situation of its registered office may act on the change as from such date, not more than 14 days after the notice is given, as it may determine.

    (6) Where a company unavoidably ceases to perform at its registered office any such duty as is mentioned in subsection (5)(*a*) in circumstances in which it was not practicable to give prior notice to the registrar of a change in the situation of its registered office, but –

        (*a*) resumes performance of that duty at other premises as soon as practicable, and

        (*b*) gives notice accordingly to the registrar of a change in the situation of its registered office within 14 days of doing so,

it shall not be treated as having failed to comply with that duty.

(7) In proceedings for an offence of failing to comply with any such duty as is mentioned in subsection (5), it is for the person charged to show that by reason of the matters referred to in that subsection or subsection (6) no offence was committed.".

137 Effecting of insurance for officers and auditors of company

(1) In section 310 of the Companies Act 1985 (provisions exempting officers and auditors from liability), for subsection (3) (permitted provisions) substitute –

"(3) This section does not prevent a company –
    (*a*) from purchasing and maintaining for any such officer or auditor insurance against any such liability, or
    (*b*) from indemnifying any such officer or auditor against any liability incurred by him –
        (i)   in defending any proceedings (whether civil or criminal) in which judgment is given in his favour or he is acquitted, or
        (ii) in connection with any application under section 144(3) or (4) (acquisition of shares by innocent nominee) or section 727 (general power to grant relief in case of honest and reasonable conduct) in which relief is granted to him by the court.".

(2) In Part I of Schedule 7 to the Companies Act 1985 (general matters to be dealt with in directors' report), after paragraph 5 insert –

"Insurance effected for officers or auditors

5A. Where in the financial year the company has purchased or maintained any such insurance as is mentioned in section 310(3)(*a*) (insurance of officers or auditors against liabilities in relation to the company), that fact shall be stated in the report.".

138 Increase of limits on certain exemptions

Part X of the Companies Act 1985 (enforcement of fair dealing by directors) is amended as follows –
    (*a*) in section 332(1)(*b*) (short-term quasi-loans) for "£1,000" substitute "£5,000";
    (*b*) in section 334 (loans of small amounts) for "£2,500" substitute "£5,000";
    (*c*) in section 338(4) and (6) (loans or quasi-loans by money–lending company) for "£50,000" substitute "£100,000".

139 Annual returns

(1) In Part XI of the Companies Act 1985 (company administration and procedure), for Chapter III (annual return) substitute –

"CHAPTER III
ANNUAL RETURN

363 Duty to deliver annual returns

(1) Every company shall deliver to the registrar successive annual returns each

of which is made up to a date not later than the date which is from time to time the company's "return date", that is –

(a) the anniversary of the company's incorporation, or

(b) if the company's last return delivered in accordance with this Chapter was made up to a different date, the anniversary of that date.

(2) Each return shall –

(a) be in the prescribed form,

(b) contain the information required by or under the following provisions of this Chapter, and

(c) be signed by a director or the secretary of the company;

and it shall be delivered to the registrar within 28 days after the date to which it is made up.

(3) If a company fails to deliver an annual return in accordance with this Chapter before the end of the period of 28 days after a return date, the company is guilty of an offence and liable to a fine and, in the case of continued contravention, to a daily default fine.

The contravention continues until such time as an annual return made up to that return date and complying with the requirements of subsection (2) (except as to date of delivery) is delivered by the company to the registrar.

(4) Where a company is guilty of an offence under subsection (3), every director or secretary of the company is similarly liable unless he shows that he took all reasonable steps to avoid the commission or continuation of the offence.

(5) The references in this section to a return being delivered "in accordance with this Chapter" are –

(a) in relation to a return made after the commencement of section 139 of the Companies Act 1989, to a return with respect to which all the requirements of subsection (2) are complied with;

(b) in relation to a return made before that commencement, to a return with respect to which the formal and substantive requirements of this Chapter as it then had effect were complied with, whether or not the return was delivered in time.

364   Contents of annual return: general

(1) Every annual return shall state the date to which it is made up and shall contain the following information –

(a) the address of the company's registered office;

(b) the type of company it is and its principal business activities;

(c) the name and address of the company secretary;

(d) the name and address of every director of the company;

(e) in the case of each individual director –

(i) his nationality, date of birth and business occupation, and

(ii) such particulars of other directorships and former names as are required to be contained in the company's register of directors;

(f) in the case of any corporate director, such particulars of other directorships as would be required to be contained in that register in the case of an individual;

(g) if the register of members is not kept at the company's registered office, the address of the place where it is kept;

(*h*) if any register of debenture holders (or a duplicate of any such register or a part of it) is not kept at the company's registered office, the address of the place where it is kept;

(*i*) if the company has elected –

    (i) to dispense under section 252 with the laying of accounts and reports before the company in general meeting, or

    (ii) to dispense under section 366A with the holding of annual general meetings,

a statement to that effect.

(2) The information as to the company's type shall be given by reference to the classification scheme prescribed for the purposes of this section.

(3) The information as to the company's principal business activities may be given by reference to one or more categories of any prescribed system of classifying business activities.

(4) A person's "name" and "address" mean, respectively –

(*a*) in the case of an individual, his Christian name (or other forename) and surname and his usual residential address;

(*b*) in the case of a corporation or Scottish firm, its corporate or firm name and its registered or principal office.

(5) In the case of a peer, or an individual usually known by a title, the title may be stated instead of his Christian name (or other forename) and surname or in addition to either or both of them.

(6) Where all the partners in a firm are joint secretaries, the name and principal office of the firm may be stated instead of the names and addresses of the partners.

364A Contents of annual return: particulars of share capital and shareholders

(1) The annual return of a company having a share capital shall contain the following information with respect to its share capital and members.

(2) The return shall state the total number of issued shares of the company at the date to which the return is made up and the aggregate nominal value of those shares.

(3) The return shall state with respect to each class of shares in the company –

(*a*) the nature of the class, and

(*b*) the total number and aggregate nominal value of issued shares of that class at the date to which the return is made up.

(4) The return shall contain a list of the names and addresses of every person who –

(*a*) is a member of the company on the date to which the return is made up, or

(*b*) has ceased to be a member of the company since the date to which the last return was made up (or, in the case of the first return, since the incorporation of the company);

and if the names are not arranged in alphabetical order the return shall have annexed to it an index sufficient to enable the name of any person in the list to be easily found.

(5) The return shall also state –

    (*a*) the number of shares of each class held by each member of the company at the date to which the return is made up, and

    (*b*) the number of shares of each class transferred since the date to which the last return was made up (or, in the case of the first return, since the incorporation of the company) by each member or person who has ceased to be a member, and the dates of registration of the transfers.

(6) The return may, if either of the two immediately preceding returns has given the full particulars required by subsections (4) and (5), give only such particulars as relate to persons ceasing to be or becoming members since the date of the last return and to shares transferred since that date.

(7) Subsections (4) and (5) do not require the inclusion of particulars entered in an overseas branch register if copies of those entries have not been received at the company's registered office by the date to which the return is made up.

Those particulars shall be included in the company's next annual return after they are received.

(8) Where the company has converted any of its shares into stock, the return shall give the corresponding information in relation to that stock, stating the amount of stock instead of the number or nominal value of shares.

365 Supplementary provisions: regulations and interpretation

(1) The Secretary of State may by regulations make further provision as to the information to be given in a company's annual return, which may amend or repeal the provisions of sections 364 and 364A.

(2) Regulations under this section shall be made by statutory instrument which shall be subject to annulment in pursuance of a resolution of either House of Parliament.

(3) For the purposes of this Chapter, except section 363(2)(*c*) (signature of annual return), a shadow director shall be deemed to be a director.".

(2) Where a company was, immediately before the commencement of this section, in default with respect to the delivery of one or more annual returns, this section does not affect its obligation to make such a return (in accordance with Chapter III of Part XI of the Companies Act 1985 as it then had effect) or any liability arising from failure to do so.

(3) In Schedule 24 to the Companies Act 1985 (punishment of offences) in the entry relating to section 363(7), in the first column for "363(7)" substitute "363(3)".

(4) In Schedule 1 to the Company Directors Disqualification Act 1986 (matters relevant to determining unfitness of directors), in paragraph 4 (failure of company to comply with certain provisions), for sub-paragraphs (*f*) and (*g*) substitute –

"(*f*) section 363 (duty of company to make annual returns);".

(5) In section 565(6) of the Income and Corporation Taxes Act 1988 (conditions for exemption from provisions relating to sub-contractors in construction industry: compliance with requirements of Companies Act 1985), in paragraph (*d*) for "sections 363, 364 and 365" substitute "sections 363 to 365".

140 Floating charges (Scotland)

(1) In section 463 of the Companies Act 1985 (effect of floating charge on winding up),

in subsection (1) for the words "On the commencement of the winding up of a company," there shall be substituted the words "Where a company goes into liquidation within the meaning of section 247(2) of the Insolvency Act 1986,".

(2) Section 464 of the Companies Act 1985 (ranking of floating charges) is amended as follows.

(3) In subsection (1)(*b*) at the beginning there shall be inserted the words "with the consent of the holder of any subsisting floating charge or fixed security which would be adversely affected,".

(4) After subsection (1) there shall be inserted the following subsection –

"(1A) Where an instrument creating a floating charge contains any such provision as is mentioned in subsection (1)(*a*), that provision shall be effective to confer priority on the floating charge over any fixed security or floating charge created after the date of the instrument.".

(5) For subsection (3) there shall be substituted –

"(3) The order of ranking of the floating charge with any other subsisting or future floating charges or fixed securities over all or any part of the company's property is determined in accordance with the provisions of subsections (4) and (5) except where it is determined in accordance with any provision such as is mentioned in paragraph (*a*) or (*b*) of subsection (1).".

(6) In subsection (5) at the end there shall be added the following paragraph –
"; and
   (*e*) (in the case of a floating charge to secure a contingent liability other than a liability arising under any further advances made from time to time) the maximum sum to which that contingent liability is capable of amounting whether or not it is contractually limited.".

(7) In subsection (6) after the words "subject to" there shall be inserted the words "Part XII and to".

(8) In section 466 of the Companies Act 1985 (alteration of floating charges), subsections (4) and (5) and in subsection (6) the words "falling under subsection (4) of this section" shall cease to have effect.

141 Application to declare dissolution of company void

(1) Section 651 of the Companies Act 1985 (power of court to declare dissolution of company void) is amended as follows.

(2) In subsection (1) omit the words "at any time within 2 years of the date of the dissolution".

(3) After subsection (3) add –

"(4) Subject to the following provisions, an application under this section may not be made after the end of the period of two years from the date of the dissolution of the company.

(5) An application for the purpose of bringing proceedings against the company –
   (*a*) for damages in respect of personal injuries (including any sum claimed by virtue of section 1(2)(*c*) of the Law Reform (Miscellaneous Provisions) Act 1934 (funeral expenses)), or

(*b*) for damages under the Fatal Accidents Act 1976 or the Damages (Scotland) Act 1976,

may be made at any time; but no order shall be made on such an application if it appears to the court that the proceedings would fail by virtue of any enactment as to the time within which proceedings must be brought.

(6) Nothing in subsection (5) affects the power of the court on making an order under this section to direct that the period between the dissolution of the company and the making of the order shall not count for the purposes of any such enactment.

(7) In subsection (5)(*a*) "personal injuries" includes any disease and any impairment of a person's physical or mental condition.".

(4) An application may be made under section 651(5) of the Companies Act 1985 as inserted by subsection (3) above (proceedings for damages for personal injury, &c.) in relation to a company dissolved before the commencement of this section notwithstanding that the time within which the dissolution might formerly have been declared void under that section had expired before commencement.

But no such application shall be made in relation to a company dissolved more than twenty years before the commencement of this section.

(5) Except as provided by subsection (4), the amendments made by this section do not apply in relation to a company which was dissolved more than two years before the commencement of this section.

142   Abolition of doctrine of deemed notice

(1) In Part XXIV of the Companies Act 1985 (the registrar of companies, his functions and offices), after section 711 insert –

"711A   Exclusion of deemed notice

(1) A person shall not be taken to have notice of any matter merely because of its being disclosed in any document kept by the registrar of companies (and thus available for inspection) or made available by the company for inspection.

(2) This does not affect the question whether a person is affected by notice of any matter by reason of a failure to make such inquiries as ought reasonably to be made.

(3) In this section 'document' includes any material which contains information.

(4) Nothing in this section affects the operation of –
(*a*) section 416 of this Act (under which a person taking a charge over a company's property is deemed to have notice of matters disclosed on the companies charges register), or
(*b*) section 198 of the Law of Property Act 1925 as it applies by virtue of section 3(7) of the Land Charges Act 1972 (under which the registration of certain land charges under Part XII, or Chapter III of Part XXIII, of this Act is deemed to constitute actual notice for all purposes connected with the land affected).".

(2) In Schedule 22 to the Companies Act 1985 (unregistered companies), in the entry for Part XXIV at the appropriate place insert –

"Section 711A Abolition of doctrine of deemed   Subject to section 718(3).".
notice.

143 Rights of inspection and related matters

(1) In Part XXV of the Companies Act 1985 (miscellaneous and supplementary provisions), after section 723 insert –

"723A Obligations of company as to inspection of registers, &c

(1) The Secretary of State may make provision by regulations as to the obligations of a company which is required by any provision of this Act –

(*a*) to make available for inspection any register, index or document, or

(*b*) to provide copies of any such register, index or document, or part of it;
and a company which fails to comply with the regulations shall be deemed to have refused inspection or, as the case may be, to have failed to provide a copy.

(2) The regulations may make provision as to the time, duration and manner of inspection, including the circumstances in which and extent to which the copying of information is permitted in the course of inspection.

(3) The regulations may define what may be required of the company as regards the nature, extent and manner of extracting or presenting any information for the purposes of inspection or the provision of copies.

(4) Where there is power to charge a fee, the regulations may make provision as to the amount of the fee and the basis of its calculation.

(5) Regulations under this section may make different provision for different classes of case.

(6) Nothing in any provision of this Act or in the regulations shall be construed as preventing a company from affording more extensive facilities than are required by the regulations or, where a fee may be charged, from charging a lesser fee than that prescribed or no fee at all.

(7) Regulations under this section shall be made by statutory instrument which shall be subject to annulment in pursuance of a resolution of either House of Parliament.".

(2) In section 169(5) of the Companies Act 1985 (contract for purchase by company of its own shares), omit the words from ", during business hours" to "for inspection)".

(3) In section 175(6) of the Companies Act 1985 (statutory declaration and auditors' report relating to payment out of capital), in paragraph (*b*) omit the words from "during business hours" to "period".

(4) In section 191 of the Companies Act 1985 (register of debenture holders) –

(*a*) in subsection (1), omit the words from "(but" to "for inspection)" and for the words from "a fee of 5 pence" to the end substitute "such fee as may be prescribed";

(*b*) in subsection (2) for the words from "10 pence" to the end substitute "such fee as may be prescribed"; and

(*c*) in subsection (3), after "on payment" insert "of such fee as may be prescribed" and omit paragraphs (*a*) and (*b*).

(5) In section 219 of the Companies Act 1985 (register of interests in shares, &c.) –

(*a*) in subsection (1), omit the words from "during" to "for inspection)"; and (*b*) in subsection (2) for the words from "10 pence" to "required to be copied" substitute "such fee as may be prescribed".

(6) In section 288 of the Companies Act 1985 (register of directors and secretaries), in subsection (3), omit the words from "during" to "for inspection)" and for the words from "5 pence" to the end substitute "such fee as may be prescribed".

(7) In section 318 of the Companies Act 1985 (directors' service contracts), in subsection (7) omit the words from ", during business hours" to "for inspection)".

(8) In section 356 of the Companies Act 1985 (register and index of members' names) –
  (*a*) in subsection (1), omit "during business hours" and for "the appropriate charge" substitute "such fee as may be prescribed";
  (*b*) omit subsection (2);
  (*c*) in subsection (3) for "the appropriate charge" substitute "such fee as may be prescribed"; and
  (*d*) omit subsection (4).

(9) In section 383 of the Companies Act 1985 (minutes of proceedings of general meetings) –
  (*a*) in subsection (1), omit "during business hours";
  (*b*) omit subsection (2); and
  (*c*) in subsection (3), after "entitled" insert "on payment of such fee as may be prescribed" and omit the words from "at a charge" to the end.

(10) In Part IV of Schedule 13 to the Companies Act 1985 (register of directors' interests) –
  (*a*) in paragraph 25, omit the words from "during" to "for inspection)" and for the words from "5 pence" to the end substitute "such fee as may be prescribed"; and
  (*b*) in paragraph 26(1), for the words from "10 pence" to the end substitute "such fee as may be prescribed".

(11) In Schedule 22 to the Companies Act 1985 (provisions applying to unregistered companies), in the entry relating to Part XXV at the appropriate place insert –

| "Section 723A | Rights of inspection and related matters. | To apply only so far as this provision has effect in relation to provisions applying by virtue of the foregoing provisions of this Schedule.". |

144 "Subsidiary", "holding company" and "wholly-owned subsidiary"

(1) In Part XXVI of the Companies Act 1985 (general interpretation provisions), for section 736 substitute –

"736 "Subsidiary", "holding company" and "wholly-owned subsidiary"

(1) A company is a "subsidiary" of another company, its "holding company", if that other company –
  (*a*) holds a majority of the voting rights in it, or
  (*b*) is a member of it and has the right to appoint or remove a majority of its board of directors, or
  (*c*) is a member of it and controls alone, pursuant to an agreement with other shareholders or members, a majority of the voting rights in it,

or if it is a subsidiary of a company which is itself a subsidiary of that other company.

(2) A company is a "wholly-owned subsidiary" of another company if it has no members except that other and that other's wholly-owned subsidiaries or persons acting on behalf of that other or its wholly-owned subsidiaries.

(3) In this section "company" includes any body corporate.

736A   Provisions supplementing s 736

(1) The provisions of this section explain expressions used in section 736 and otherwise supplement that section.

(2) In section 736(1)(*a*) and (*c*) the references to the voting rights in a company are to the rights conferred on shareholders in respect of their shares or, in the case of a company not having a share capital, on members, to vote at general meetings of the company on all, or substantially all, matters.

(3) In section 736(1)(*b*) the reference to the right to appoint or remove a majority of the board of directors is to the right to appoint or remove directors holding a majority of the voting rights at meetings of the board on all, or substantially all, matters; and for the purposes of that provision –

    (*a*) a company shall be treated as having the right to appoint to a directorship if –

        (i) a person's appointment to it follows necessarily from his appointment as director of the company, or

        (ii) the directorship is held by the company itself; and

    (*b*) a right to appoint or remove which is exercisable only with the consent or concurrence of another person shall be left out of account unless no other person has a right to appoint or, as the case may be, remove in relation to that directorship.

(4) Rights which are exercisable only in certain circumstances shall be taken into account only –

    (*a*) when the circumstances have arisen, and for so long as they continue to obtain, or

    (*b*) when the circumstances are within the control of the person having the rights;

and rights which are normally exercisable but are temporarily incapable of exercise shall continue to be taken into account.

(5) Rights held by a person in a fiduciary capacity shall be treated as not held by him.

(6) Rights held by a person as nominee for another shall be treated as held by the other; and rights shall be regarded as held as nominee for another if they are exercisable only on his instructions or with his consent or concurrence.

(7) Rights attached to shares held by way of security shall be treated as held by the person providing the security –

    (*a*) where apart from the right to exercise them for the purpose of preserving the value of the security, or of realising it, the rights are exercisable only in accordance with his instructions;

    (*b*) where the shares are held in connection with the granting of loans as part of normal business activities and apart from the right to exercise them for the purpose of preserving the value of the security, or of realising it, the rights are exercisable only in his interests.

(8) Rights shall be treated as held by a company if they are held by any of its subsidiaries; and nothing in subsection (6) or (7) shall be construed as requiring rights held by a company to be treated as held by any of its subsidiaries.

(9) For the purposes of subsection (7) rights shall be treated as being exercisable in accordance with the instructions or in the interests of a company if they are exercisable in accordance with the instructions of or, as the case may be, in the interests of –

(*a*) any subsidiary or holding company of that company, or

(*b*) any subsidiary of a holding company of that company.

(10) The voting rights in a company shall be reduced by any rights held by the company itself.

(11) References in any provision of subsections (5) to (10) to rights held by a person include rights falling to be treated as held by him by virtue of any other provision of those subsections but not rights which by virtue of any such provision are to be treated as not held by him.

(12) In this section "company" includes any body corporate.".

(2) Any reference in any enactment (including any enactment contained in subordinate legislation within the meaning of the Interpretation Act 1978) to a "subsidiary" or "holding company" within the meaning of section 736 of the Companies Act 1985 shall, subject to any express amendment or saving made by or under this Act, be read as referring to a subsidiary or holding company as defined in section 736 as substituted by subsection (1) above.

This applies whether the reference is specific or general, or express or implied.

(3) In Part XXVI of the Companies Act 1985 (general interpretation provisions), after section 736A insert –

"736B   Power to amend ss 736 and 736A

(1) The Secretary of State may by regulations amend sections 736 and 736A so as to alter the meaning of the expressions "holding company", "subsidiary" or "wholly-owned subsidiary".

(2) The regulations may make different provision for different cases or classes of case and may contain such incidental and supplementary provisions as the Secretary of State thinks fit.

(3) Regulations under this section shall be made by statutory instrument which shall be subject to annulment in pursuance of a resolution of either House of Parliament.

(4) Any amendment made by regulations under this section does not apply for the purposes of enactments outside the Companies Acts unless the regulations so provide.

(5) So much of section 23(3) of the Interpretation Act 1978 as applies section 17(2)(*a*) of that Act (effect of repeal and re-enactment) to deeds, instruments and documents other than enactments shall not apply in relation to any repeal and re-enactment effected by regulations made under this section.".

(4) Schedule 18 contains amendments and savings consequential on the amendments made by this section; and the Secretary of State may by regulations make such further amendments or savings as appear to him to be necessary or expedient.

(5) Regulations under this section shall be made by statutory instrument which shall be subject to annulment in pursuance of a resolution of either House of Parliament.

(6) So much of section 23(3) of the Interpretation Act 1978 as applies section 17(2)(*a*) of that Act (presumption as to meaning of references to enactments repealed and re-enacted) to deeds or other instruments or documents does not apply in relation to the repeal and re-enactment by this section of section 736 of the Companies Act 1985.

145 Minor amendments

The Companies Act 1985 has effect with the further amendments specified in Schedule 19.

PART VI
MERGERS AND RELATED MATTERS

146 Restriction on references where prior notice given

After section 75 of the Fair Trading Act 1973 there is inserted –

"Restriction on power to make merger reference where prior notice has been given

75A General rule where notice given by acquirer and no reference made within period for considering notice

(1) Notice may be given to the Director by a person authorised by regulations to do so of proposed arrangements which might result in the creation of a merger situation qualifying for investigation.

(2) The notice must be in the prescribed form and state that the existence of the proposal has been made public.

(3) If the period for considering the notice expires without any reference being made to the Commission with respect to the notified arrangements, no reference may be made under this Part of this Act to the Commission with respect to those arrangements or to the creation or possible creation of any merger situation qualifying for investigation which is created in consequence of carrying those arrangements into effect.

(4) Subsection (3) of this section is subject to sections 75B(5) and 75C of this Act.

(5) A notice under subsection (1) of this section is referred to in sections 75B to 75F of this Act as a "merger notice".

75B The role of the Director

(1) The Director shall, when the period for considering any merger notice begins, take such action as he considers appropriate to bring the existence of the proposal, the fact that the merger notice has been given and the date on which the

period for considering the notice may expire to the attention of those who in his opinion would be affected if the arrangements were carried into effect.

(2) The period for considering a merger notice is the period of twenty days, determined in accordance with subsection (9) of this section, beginning with the first day after –

(*a*) the notice has been received by the Director, and

(*b*) any fee payable to the Director in respect of the notice has been paid.

(3) The Director may, and shall if required to do so by the Secretary of State, by notice to the person who gave the merger notice –

(*a*) extend the period mentioned in subsection (2) of this section by a further ten days, and

(*b*) extend that period as extended under paragraph (*a*) of this subsection by a further fifteen days.

(4) The Director may by notice to the person who gave the merger notice request him to provide the Director within such period as may be specified in the notice with such information as may be so specified.

(5) If the Director gives to the person who gave the merger notice (in this subsection referred to as "the relevant person") a notice stating that the Secretary of State is seeking undertakings under section 75G of this Act, section 75A(3) of this Act does not prevent a reference being made to the Commission unless –

(*a*) after the Director has given that notice, the relevant person has given a notice to the Director stating that he does not intend to give such undertakings, and

(*b*) the period of ten days beginning with the first day after the notice under paragraph (*a*) of this subsection was received by the Director has expired.

(6) A notice by the Director under subsection (3), (4) or (5) of this section must either be given to the person who gave the merger notice before the period for considering the merger notice expires or be sent in a properly addressed and pre-paid letter posted to him at such time that, in the ordinary course of post, it would be delivered to him before that period expires.

(7) The Director may, at any time before the period for considering any merger notice expires, reject the notice if –

(*a*) he suspects that any information given in respect of the notified arrangements, whether in the merger notice or otherwise, by the person who gave the notice or any connected person is in any material respect false or misleading,

(*b*) he suspects that it is not proposed to carry the notified arrangements into effect, or

(*c*) any prescribed information is not given in the merger notice or any information requested by notice under subsection (4) of this section is not provided within the period specified in the notice.

(8) If –

(*a*) under subsection (3)(*b*) of this section the period for considering a merger notice has been extended by a further fifteen days, but

(*b*) the Director has not made any recommendation to the Secretary of State under section 76(*b*) of this Act as to whether or not it would in the Director's opinion be expedient for the Secretary of State to make a reference to the Commission with respect to the notified arrangements,

then, during the last five of those fifteen days, the power of the Secretary of State to make a reference to the Commission with respect to the notified arrangements is not affected by the absence of any such recommendation.

(9) In determining any period for the purposes of subsections (2), (3) and (5) of this section no account shall be taken of –

    (*a*) Saturday, Sunday, Good Friday and Christmas Day, and

    (*b*) any day which is a bank holiday in England and Wales.

75C Cases where power to refer unaffected

(1) Section 75A(3) of this Act does not prevent any reference being made to the Commission if –

    (*a*) before the end of the period for considering the merger notice, it is rejected by the Director under section 75B(7) of this Act,

    (*b*) before the end of that period, any of the enterprises to which the notified arrangements relate cease to be distinct from each other,

    (*c*) any information (whether prescribed information or not) that –

        (i) is, or ought to be, known to the person who gave the merger notice or any connected person, and

        (ii) is material to the notified arrangements;

    is not disclosed to the Secretary of State or the Director by such time before the end of that period as may be specified in regulations,

    (*d*) at any time after the merger notice is given but before the enterprises to which the notified arrangements relate cease to be distinct from each other, any of those enterprises ceases to be distinct from any enterprise other than an enterprise to which those arrangements relate,

    (*e*) the six months beginning with the end of the period for considering the merger notice expires without the enterprises to which the notified arrangements relate ceasing to be distinct from each other,

    (*f*) the merger notice is withdrawn, or

    (*g*) any information given in respect of the notified arrangements, whether in the merger notice or otherwise, by the person who gave the notice or any connected person is in any material respect false or misleading.

(2) Where –

    (*a*) two or more transactions which have occurred or, if any arrangements are carried into effect, will occur may be treated for the purposes of a merger reference as having occurred simultaneously on a particular date, and

    (*b*) subsection (3) of section 75A of this Act does not prevent such a reference with respect to the last of those transactions,

that subsection does not prevent such a reference with respect to any of those transactions which actually occurred less than six months before –

    (i) that date, or

    (ii) the actual occurrence of another of those transactions with respect to which such a reference may be made (whether or not by virtue of this subsection).

(3) In determining for the purposes of subsection (2) of this section the time at which any transaction actually occurred, no account shall be taken of any option or other conditional right until the option is exercised or the condition is satisfied.

75D Regulations

(1) The Secretary of State may make regulations for the purposes of sections 75A to 75C of this Act.

(2) The regulations may, in particular –

    (*a*) provide for section 75B(2) or (3) or section 75C(1)(*e*) of this Act to apply as if any reference to a period of days or months were a reference to a period specified in the regulations for the purposes of the provision in question,

    (*b*) provide for the manner in which any merger notice is authorised or required to be given, rejected or withdrawn, and the time at which any merger notice is to be treated as received or rejected,

    (*c*) provide for the manner in which any information requested by the Director or any other material information is authorised or required to be provided or disclosed, and the time at which such information is to be treated as provided or disclosed,

    (*d*) provide for the manner in which any notice under section 75B of this Act is authorised or required to be given,

    (*e*) provide for the time at which any notice under section 75B(5)(*a*) of this Act is to be treated as received,

    (*f*) provide for the address which is to be treated for the purposes of section 75B(6) of this Act and of the regulations as a person's proper address,

    (*g*) provide for the time at which any fee is to be treated as paid, and

    (*h*) provide that a person is, or is not, to be treated, in such circumstances as may be specified in the regulations, as acting on behalf of a person authorised by regulations to give a merger notice or a person who has given such a notice.

(3) The regulations may make different provision for different cases.

(4) Regulations under this section shall be made by statutory instrument.

75E Interpretation of sections 75A to 75D

In this section and sections 75A to 75D of this Act –

    "connected person", in relation to the person who gave a merger notice, means –

        (*a*) any person who, for the purposes of section 77 of this Act, is associated with him, or

        (*b*) any subsidiary of the person who gave the merger notice or of any person so associated with him,

    "merger notice" is to be interpreted in accordance with section 75A(5) of this Act,

    "notified arrangements" means the arrangements mentioned in the merger notice or arrangements not differing from them in any material respect, "prescribed" means prescribed by the Director by notice having effect for the time being and published in the London, Edinburgh and Belfast Gazettes,

"regulations" means regulations under section 75D of this Act, and

"subsidiary" has the meaning given by section 75(4K) of this Act,

and references to the enterprises to which the notified arrangements relate are references to those enterprises that would have ceased to be distinct from one another if the arrangements mentioned in the merger notice in question had been carried into effect at the time when the notice was given.

75F Power to amend sections 75B to 75D

(1) The Secretary of State may, for the purpose of determining the effect of giving a merger notice and the steps which may be or are to be taken by any person in connection with such a notice, by regulations made by statutory instrument amend sections 75B to 75D of this Act.

(2) The regulations may make different provision for different cases and may contain such incidental and supplementary provisions as the Secretary of State thinks fit.

(3) No regulations shall be made under this section unless a draft of the regulations has been laid before and approved by resolution of each House of Parliament.".

147 Undertakings as alternative to merger reference

In Part V of the Fair Trading Act 1973 after the sections inserted by section 146 of this Act there is inserted –

"Undertakings as alternative to merger reference

75G Acceptance of undertakings

(1) Where –
- (a) the Secretary of State has power to make a merger reference to the Commission under section 64 or 75 of this Act,
- (b) the Director has made a recommendation to the Secretary of State under section 76 of this Act that such a reference should be made, and
- (c) the Director has (in making that recommendation or subsequently) given advice to the Secretary of State specifying particular effects adverse to the public interest which in his opinion the creation of the merger situation qualifying for investigation may have or might be expected to have,

the Secretary of State may, instead of making a merger reference to the Commission, accept from such of the parties concerned as he considers appropriate undertakings complying with subsections (2) and (3) of this section to take specified action which the Secretary of State considers appropriate to remedy or prevent the effects adverse to the public interest specified in the advice.

(2) The undertakings must provide for one or more of the following –

(*a*) the division of a business by the sale of any part of the undertaking or assets or otherwise (for which purpose all the activities carried on by way of business by any one person or by any two or more interconnected bodies corporate may be treated as a single business),

(*b*) the division of a group of interconnected bodies corporate, and

(*c*) the separation, by the sale of any part of the undertaking or assets concerned or other means, of enterprises which are under common control otherwise than by reason of their being enterprises of interconnected bodies corporate.

(3) The undertakings may also contain provision –

(*a*) preventing or restricting the doing of things which might prevent or impede the division or separation,

(*b*) as to the carrying on of any activities or the safeguarding of any assets until the division or separation is effected,

(*c*) for any matters necessary to effect or take account of the division or separation, and

(*d*) for enabling the Secretary of State to ascertain whether the undertakings are being fulfilled.

(4) If the Secretary of State has accepted one or more undertakings under this section, no reference may be made to the Commission with respect to the creation or possible creation of the merger situation qualifying for investigation by reference to which the undertakings were accepted, except in a case falling within subsection (5) of this section.

(5) Subsection (4) of this section does not prevent a reference being made to the Commission if material facts about the arrangements or transactions, or proposed arrangements or transactions, in consequence of which the enterprises concerned ceased or may cease to be distinct enterprises were not –

(*a*) notified to the Secretary of State or the Director, or

(*b*) made public,

before the undertakings were accepted.

(6) In subsection (5) of this section "made public" has the same meaning as in section 64 of this Act.

75H Publication of undertakings

(1) The Secretary of State shall arrange for –

(*a*) any undertaking accepted by him under section 75G of this Act,

(*b*) the advice given by the Director for the purposes of subsection (1)(*c*) of that section in any case where such an undertaking has been accepted, and

(*c*) any variation or release of such an undertaking,

to be published in such manner as he may consider appropriate.

(2) In giving advice for the purposes of section 75G(1)(*c*) of this Act the Director shall have regard to the need for excluding, so far as practicable, any matter to which subsection (4) of this section applies.

(3) The Secretary of State shall exclude from any such advice as published under this section –

(*a*) any matter to which subsection (4) of this section applies and in relation to which he is satisfied that its publication in the advice would not be in the public interest, and

(b) any other matter in relation to which he is satisfied that its publication in the advice would be against the public interest.

(4) This subsection applies to –

(a) any matter which relates to the private affairs of an individual, where publication of that matter would or might, in the opinion of the Director or the Secretary of State, as the case may be, seriously and prejudicially affect the interests of that individual, and

(b) any matter which relates specifically to the affairs of a particular body of persons, whether corporate or unincorporate, where publication of that matter would or might, in the opinion of the Director or the Secretary of State, as the case may be, seriously and prejudicially affect the interests of that body, unless in his opinion the inclusion of that matter relating specifically to that body is necessary for the purposes of the advice.

(5) For the purposes of the law relating to defamation, absolute privilege shall attach to any advice given by the Director for the purposes of section 75G(1)(c) of this Act.

75J Review of undertakings

Where an undertaking has been accepted by the Secretary of State under section 75G of this Act, it shall be the duty of the Director –

(a) to keep under review the carrying out of that undertaking, and from time to time consider whether, by reason of any change of circumstances, the undertaking is no longer appropriate and either –
  (i) one or more of the parties to it can be released from it, or
  (ii) it needs to be varied or to be superseded by a new undertaking, and

(b) if it appears to him that the undertaking has not been or is not being fulfilled, that any person can be so released or that the undertaking needs to be varied or superseded, to give such advice to the Secretary of State as he may think proper in the circumstances.

75K Order of Secretary of State where undertaking not fulfilled

(1) The provisions of this section shall have effect where it appears to the Secretary of State that an undertaking accepted by him under section 75G of this Act has not been, is not being or will not be fulfilled.

(2) The Secretary of State may by order made by statutory instrument exercise such one or more of the powers specified in paragraphs 9A and 12 to 12C and Part II of Schedule 8 to this Act as he may consider it requisite to exercise for the purpose of remedying or preventing the adverse effects specified in the advice given by the Director for the purposes of section 75(G)(1)(c) of this Act; and those powers may be so exercised to such extent and in such manner as the Secretary of State considers requisite for that purpose.

(3) In determining whether, or to what extent or in what manner, to exercise any of those powers, the Secretary of State shall take into account any advice given by the Director under section 75J(b) of this Act.

(4) The provision contained in an order under this section may be different from that contained in the undertaking.

(5) On the making of an order under this section, the undertaking and any other undertaking accepted under section 75G of this Act by reference to the same merger situation qualifying for investigation are released by virtue of this section.".

148   Enforcement of undertakings

After section 93 of the Fair Trading Act 1973 there is inserted –

"93A   Enforcement of undertakings

(1) This section applies where a person (in this section referred to as "the responsible person") has given an undertaking which –

(a) has been accepted by the Secretary of State under section 75G of this Act,

(b) has been accepted by the appropriate Minister or Ministers under section 88 of this Act after the commencement of this section, or

(c) has been accepted by the Director under section 4 or 9 of the Competition Act 1980 after that time.

(2) Any person may bring civil proceedings in respect of any failure, or apprehended failure, of the responsible person to fulfil the undertaking, as if the obligations imposed by the undertaking on the responsible person had been imposed by an order to which section 90 of this Act applies.".

149   Temporary restrictions on share dealings

(1) In section 75 of the Fair Trading Act 1973 (reference in anticipation of merger), after subsection (4) there is inserted –

"(4A) Where a merger reference is made under this section, it shall be unlawful, except with the consent of the Secretary of State under subsection (4C) of this section –

(a) for any person carrying on any enterprise to which the reference relates or having control of any such enterprise or for any subsidiary of his, or

(b) for any person associated with him or for any subsidiary of such a person,

directly or indirectly to acquire, at any time during the period mentioned in subsection (4B) of this section, an interest in shares in a company if any enterprise to which the reference relates is carried on by or under the control of that company.

(4B) The period referred to in subsection (4A) of this section is the period beginning with the announcement by the Secretary of State of the making of the merger reference concerned and ending –

(a) where the reference is laid aside at any time, at that time,

(b) where the time (including any further period) allowed to the Commission for making a report on the reference expires without their having made such a report, on the expiration of that time,

(c) where a report of the Commission on the reference not including such conclusions as are referred to in section 73(1)(b) of this Act is laid before Parliament, at the end of the day on which the report is so laid, (*d*) where a report of the Commission on the reference including such conclusions is laid before Parliament, at the end of the period of forty days beginning with the day on which the report is so laid,

and where such a report is laid before each House on different days, it is to be treated for the purposes of this subsection as laid on the earlier day.

(4C) The consent of the Secretary of State –

(*a*) may be either general or special,

(*b*) may be revoked by the Secretary of State, and

(*c*) shall be published in such way as, in the opinion of the Secretary of State, to give any person entitled to the benefit of it an adequate opportunity of getting to know of it, unless in the Secretary of State's opinion publication is not necessary for that purpose.

(4D) Section 93 of this Act applies to any contravention or apprehended contravention of subsection (4A) of this section as it applies to a contravention or apprehended contravention of an order to which section 90 of this Act applies.

(4E) Subsections (4F) to (4K) of this section apply for the interpretation of subsection (4A).

(4F) The circumstances in which a person acquires an interest in shares include those where –

(*a*) he enters into a contract to acquire the shares (whether or not for cash),

(*b*) not being the registered holder, he acquires a right to exercise, or to control the exercise of, any right conferred by the holding of the shares, or

(*c*) he acquires a right to call for delivery of the shares to himself or to his order or to acquire an interest in the shares or assumes an obligation to acquire such an interest,

but does not include those where he acquires an interest in pursuance of an obligation assumed before the announcement by the Secretary of State of the making of the merger reference concerned.

(4G) The circumstances in which a person acquires a right mentioned in subsection (4F) of this section –

(*a*) include those where he acquires a right or assumes an obligation the exercise or fulfilment of which would give him that right, but

(*b*) does not include those where he is appointed as proxy to vote at a specified meeting of a company or of any class of its members or at any adjournment of the meeting or he is appointed by a corporation to act as its representative at any meeting of the company or of any class of its members,

and references to rights and obligations in this subsection and subsection (4F) of this section include conditional rights and conditional obligations.

(4H) Any reference to a person carrying on or having control of any enterprise includes a group of persons carrying on or having control of an enterprise and any member of such a group.

(4J) Sections 65(2) to (4) and 77(1) and (4) to (6) of this Act apply to determine whether any person or group of persons has control of any enterprise and whether persons are associated as they apply for the purposes of section 65 of this Act to determine whether enterprises are brought under common control.

(4K) "Subsidiary" has the meaning given by section 736 of the Companies Act 1985, but that section and section 736A of that Act also apply to determine whether a company is a subsidiary of an individual or of a group of persons as they apply to determine whether it is a subsidiary of a company and references to a subsidiary in subsections (8) and (9) of section 736A as so applied are to be read accordingly.

(4L) In this section –
"company" includes any body corporate, and
"share" means share in the capital of a company, and includes stock.

(4M) Nothing in subsection (4A) of this section makes anything done by a person outside the United Kingdom unlawful unless he is –

(a) a British citizen, a British Dependent Territories citizen, a British Overseas citizen or a British National (Overseas),

(b) a body corporate incorporated under the law of the United Kingdom or of a part of the United Kingdom, or

(c) a person carrying on business in the United Kingdom, either alone or in partnership with one or more other persons.".

(2) This section does not apply in relation to any merger reference made before the passing of this Act.

150 Obtaining control by stages

(1) After section 66 of the Fair Trading Act 1973 there is inserted –

"66A Obtaining control by stages

(1) Where an enterprise is brought under the control of a person or group of persons in the course of two or more transactions (referred to in this section as a "series of transactions") falling within subsection (2) of this section, those transactions may, if the Secretary of State or, as the case may be, the Commission thinks fit, be treated for the purposes of a merger reference as having occurred simultaneously on the date on which the latest of them occurred.

(2) The transactions falling within this subsection are –

(a) any transaction which –

(i) enables that person or group of persons directly or indirectly to control or materially to influence the policy of any person carrying on the enterprise,

(ii) enables that person or group of persons to do so to a greater degree, or

(iii) is a step (whether direct or indirect) towards enabling that person or group of persons to do so, and

(b) any transaction whereby that person or group of person acquires a controlling interest in the enterprise or, where the enterprise is carried on by a body corporate, in that body corporate.

(3) Where a series of transactions includes a transaction falling within subsection (2)(b) of this section, any transaction occurring after the occurrence of that transaction is to be disregarded for the purposes of subsection (1) of this section.

(4) Where the period within which a series of transactions occurs exceeds two

years, the transactions that may be treated as mentioned in subsection (1) of this section are any of those transactions that occur within a period of two years.

(5) Sections 65(2) to (4) and 77(1) and (4) to (6) of this Act apply for the purposes of this section to determine whether an enterprise is brought under the control of a person or group of persons and whether a transaction falls within subsection (2) of this section as they apply for the purposes of section 65 of this Act to determine whether enterprises are brought under common control.

(6) In determining for the purposes of this section the time at which any transaction occurs, no account shall be taken of any option or other conditional right until the option is exercised or the condition is satisfied.".

(2) This section does not apply in relation to any merger reference made before the passing of this Act.

151 False or misleading information

At the end of Part VIII of the Fair Trading Act 1973 there is inserted –

"93B False or misleading information

(1) If a person furnishes any information –
- (a) to the Secretary of State, the Director or the Commission in connection with any of their functions under Parts IV, V, VI or this Part of this Act or under the Competition Act 1980, or
- (b) to the Commission in connection with the functions of the Commission under the Telecommunications Act 1984 or the Airports Act 1986,

and either he knows the information to be false or misleading in a material particular, or he furnishes the information recklessly and it is false or misleading in a material particular, he is guilty of an offence.

(2) A person who –
- (a) furnishes any information to another which he knows to be false or misleading in a material particular, or
- (b) recklessly furnishes any information to another which is false or misleading in a material particular,

knowing that the information is to be used for the purpose of furnishing information as mentioned in subsection (1)(a) or (b) of this section, is guilty of an offence.

(3) A person guilty of an offence under subsection (1) or (2) of this section is liable –
- (a) on summary conviction, to a fine not exceeding the statutory maximum, and
- (b) on conviction on indictment, to imprisonment for a term not exceeding two years or to a fine or to both.

(4) Section 129(1) of this Act does not apply to an offence under this section.".

152 Fees

(1) The Secretary of State may by regulations made by statutory instrument require the payment to him or to the Director of such fees as may be prescribed by the regulations in

connection with the exercise by the Secretary of State, the Director and the Commission of their functions under Part V of the Fair Trading Act 1973.

(2) The regulations may provide for fees to be payable –
    (*a*) in respect of –
        (i) an application for the consent of the Secretary of State under section 58(1) of the Fair Trading Act 1973 to the transfer of a newspaper or of newspaper assets, and
        (ii) a notice under section 75A(1) of that Act, and
    (*b*) on the occurrence of any event specified in the regulations.

(3) The events that may be specified in the regulations by virtue of subsection (2)(*b*) above include –
    (*a*) the making by the Secretary of State of a merger reference to the Commission under section 64 or 75 of the Fair Trading Act 1973,
    (*b*) the announcement by the Secretary of State of his decision not to make a merger reference in any case where, at the time the announcement is made, he would under one of those sections have power to make such a reference.

(4) The regulations may also contain provision –
    (*a*) for ascertaining the persons by whom fees are payable,
    (*b*) specifying whether any fee is payable to the Secretary of State or to the Director,
    (*c*) for the amount of any fee to be calculated by reference to matters which may include –
        (i) in a case involving functions of the Secretary of State under sections 57 to 61 of the Fair Trading Act 1973, the number of newspapers concerned, the number of separate editions (determined in accordance with the regulations) of each newspaper and the average circulation per day of publication (within the meaning of Part V of that Act) of each newspaper, and
        (ii) in any other case, the value (determined in accordance with the regulations) of any assets concerned,
    (*d*) as to the time when any fee is to be paid, and
    (*e*) for the repayment by the Secretary of State or the Director of the whole or part of any fee in specified circumstances.

(5) The regulations may make different provision for different cases.

(6) Subsections (2) to (5) above do not prejudice the generality of subsection (1) above.

(7) In determining the amount of any fees to be prescribed by the regulations, the Secretary of State may take into account all costs incurred by him and by the Director in respect of the exercise by him, by the Commission and by the Director of their respective functions –
    (*a*) under Part V of the Fair Trading Act 1973, and
    (*b*) under Parts I, VII and VIII of that Act in relation to merger references or other matters arising under Part V.

(8) A statutory instrument containing regulations under this section shall be subject to annulment in pursuance of a resolution of either House of Parliament.

(9) Fees paid to the Secretary of State or the Director under this section shall be paid into the Consolidated Fund.

(10) In this section –
"the Commission",
"the Director", and
"merger reference",

have the same meaning as in the Fair Trading Act 1973, and "newspaper" has the same meaning as in Part V of that Act.

(11) References in this section to Part V of the Fair Trading Act 1973 and to merger references under section 64 or 75 of that Act or under that Part include sections 29 and 30 of the Water Act 1989 and any reference under section 29 of that Act.

153 Other amendments about mergers and related matters

Schedule 20 to this Act has effect.

PART VII
FINANCIAL MARKETS AND INSOLVENCY

Introduction

154 Introduction

This Part has effect for the purposes of safeguarding the operation of certain financial markets by provisions with respect to –
  (a) the insolvency, winding up or default of a person party to transactions in the market (sections 155 to 172),
  (b) the effectiveness or enforcement of certain charges given to secure obligations in connection with such transactions (sections 173 to 176), and
  (c) rights and remedies in relation to certain property provided as cover for margin in relation to such transactions or subject to such a charge (sections 177 to 181).

Recognised investment exchanges and clearing houses

155 Market contracts

(1) This Part applies to the following descriptions of contract connected with a recognised investment exchange or recognised clearing house.
The contracts are referred to in this Part as "market contracts".

(2) In relation to a recognised investment exchange, this Part applies to –
  (a) contracts entered into by a member or designated non-member of the exchange which are made on or otherwise subject to the rules of the exchange; and
  (b) contracts subject to the rules of the exchange entered into by the exchange for the purposes of or in connection with the provision of clearing services.
A "designated non-member" means a person in respect of whom action may be taken under the default rules of the exchange but who is not a member of the exchange.

(3) In relation to a recognised clearing house, this Part applies to contracts subject to the rules of the clearing house entered into by the clearing house for the purposes of or in connection with the provision of clearing services for a recognised investment exchange.

(4) The Secretary of State may by regulations make further provision as to the contracts to be treated as "market contracts", for the purposes of this Part, in relation to a recognised investment exchange or recognised clearing house.

(5) The regulations may add to, amend or repeal the provisions of subsections (2) and (3) above.

156   Additional requirements for recognition: default rules, &c

(1) The Financial Services Act 1986 shall have effect as if the requirements set out in Schedule 21 to this Act (the "additional requirements") were among those specified in that Act for recognition of an investment exchange or clearing house.

(2) In particular, that Act shall have effect –
- (*a*) as if the requirements set out in Part I of that Schedule were among those specified in Schedule 4 to that Act (requirements for recognition of UK investment exchange),
- (*b*) as if the requirements set out in Part II of that Schedule were among those specified in section 39(4) of that Act (requirements for recognition of UK clearing house), and
- (*c*) as if the requirement set out in Part III of that Schedule was among those specified in section 40(2) of that Act (requirements for recognition of overseas investment exchange or clearing house).

(3) The additional requirements do not affect the status of an investment exchange or clearing house recognised before the commencement of this section, but if the Secretary of State is of the opinion that any of those requirements is not met in the case of such a body, he shall within one month of commencement give notice to the body stating his opinion.

(4) Where the Secretary of State gives such a notice, he shall not –
- (*a*) take action to revoke the recognition of such a body on the ground that any of the additional requirements is not met, unless he considers it essential to do so in the interests of investors, or
- (*b*) apply on any such ground for a compliance order under section 12 of the Financial Services Act 1986,

until after the end of the period of six months beginning with the date on which the notice was given.

(5) The Secretary of State may extend, or further extend, that period if he considers there is good reason to do so.

157   Change in default rules

(1) A recognised UK investment exchange or recognised UK clearing house shall give the Secretary of State at least 14 days' notice of any proposal to amend, revoke or add to its default rules; and the Secretary of State may within 14 days from receipt of the notice direct the exchange or clearing house not to proceed with the proposal, in whole or in part.

(2) A direction under this section may be varied or revoked.

(3) Any amendment or revocation of, or addition to, the default rules of an exchange or clearing house in breach of a direction under this section is ineffective.

158   Modifications of the law of insolvency

(1) The general law of insolvency has effect in relation to market contracts, and action

taken under the rules of a recognised investment exchange or recognised clearing house with respect to such contracts, subject to the provisions of sections 159 to 165.

(2) So far as those provisions relate to insolvency proceedings in respect of a person other than a defaulter, they apply in relation to –

(*a*) proceedings in respect of a member or designated non-member of a recognised investment exchange or a member of a recognised clearing house, and

(*b*) proceedings in respect of a party to a market contract begun after a recognised investment exchange or recognised clearing house has taken action under its default rules in relation to a person party to the contract as principal,

but not in relation to any other insolvency proceedings, notwithstanding that rights or liabilities arising from market contracts fall to be dealt with in the proceedings.

(3) The reference in subsection (2)(*b*) to the beginning of insolvency proceedings is to –

(*a*) the presentation of a bankruptcy petition or a petition for sequestration of a person's estate, or

(*b*) the presentation of a petition for an administration order or a winding-up petition or the passing of a resolution for voluntary winding up, or

(*c*) the appointment of an administrative receiver.

(4) The Secretary of State may make further provision by regulations modifying the law of insolvency in relation to the matters mentioned in subsection (1).

(5) The regulations may add to, amend or repeal the provisions mentioned in subsection (1), and any other provision of this Part as it applies for the purposes of those provisions, or provide that those provisions have effect subject to such additions, exceptions or adaptations as are specified in the regulations.

159 Proceedings of exchange or clearing house take precedence over insolvency procedures

(1) None of the following shall be regarded as to any extent invalid at law on the ground of inconsistency with the law relating to the distribution of the assets of a person on bankruptcy, winding up or sequestration, or in the administration of an insolvent estate –

(*a*) a market contract,

(*b*) the default rules of a recognised investment exchange or recognised clearing house,

(*c*) the rules of a recognised investment exchange or recognised clearing house as to the settlement of market contracts not dealt with under its default rules.

(2) The powers of a relevant office-holder in his capacity as such, and the powers of the court under the Insolvency Act 1986 or the Bankruptcy (Scotland) Act 1985 shall not be exercised in such a way as to prevent or interfere with –

(*a*) the settlement in accordance with the rules of a recognised investment exchange or recognised clearing house of a market contract not dealt with under its default rules, or

(*b*) any action taken under the default rules of such an exchange or clearing house.

This does not prevent a relevant office-holder from afterwards seeking to recover any amount under section 163(4) or 164(4) or prevent the court from afterwards making any such order or decree as is mentioned in section 165(1) or (2) (but subject to subsections (3) and (4) of that section).

(3) Nothing in the following provisions of this Part shall be construed as affecting the generality of the above provisions.

(4) A debt or other liability arising out of a market contract which is the subject of default proceedings may not be proved in a winding up or bankruptcy, or in Scotland claimed in a winding up or sequestration, until the completion of the default proceedings.

A debt or other liability which by virtue of this subsection may not be proved or claimed shall not be taken into account for the purposes of any set-off until the completion of the default proceedings.

(5) For the purposes of subsection (4) the default proceedings shall be taken to be completed in relation to a person when a report is made under section 162 stating the sum (if any) certified to be due to or from him.

160 Duty to give assistance for purposes of default proceedings

It is the duty of –

(*a*) any person who has or had control of any assets of a defaulter, and

(*b*) any person who has or had control of any documents of or relating to a defaulter,

to give a recognised investment exchange or recognised clearing house such assistance as it may reasonably require for the purposes of its default proceedings.

This applies notwithstanding any duty of that person under the enactments relating to insolvency.

(2) A person shall not under this section be required to provide any information or produce any document which he would be entitled to refuse to provide or produce on grounds of legal professional privilege in proceedings in the High Court or on grounds of confidentiality as between client and professional legal adviser in proceedings in the Court of Session.

(3) Where original documents are supplied in pursuance of this section, the exchange or clearing house shall return them forthwith after the completion of the relevant default proceedings, and shall in the meantime allow reasonable access to them to the person by whom they were supplied and to any person who would be entitled to have access to them if they were still in the control of the person by whom they were supplied.

(4) The expenses of a relevant office-holder in giving assistance under this section are recoverable as part of the expenses incurred by him in the discharge of his duties; and he shall not be required under this section to take any action which involves expenses which cannot be so recovered, unless the exchange or clearing house undertakes to meet them.

There shall be treated as expenses of his such reasonable sums as he may determine in respect of time spent in giving the assistance.

(5) The Secretary of State may by regulations make further provision as to the duties of persons to give assistance to a recognised investment exchange or recognised clearing house for the purposes of its default proceedings, and the duties of the exchange or clearing house with respect to information supplied to it.

The regulations may add to, amend or repeal the provisions of subsections (1) to (4) above.

(6) In this section "document" includes information recorded in any form.

161 Supplementary provisions as to default proceedings

(1) If the court is satisfied on an application by a relevant office-holder that a party to a market contract with a defaulter intends to dissipate or apply his assets so as to prevent the office-holder recovering such sums as may become due upon the completion of the default proceedings, the court may grant such interlocutory relief (in Scotland, such interim order) as it thinks fit.

(2) A liquidator or trustee of a defaulter or, in Scotland, a permanent trustee on the sequestrated estate of the defaulter shall not –

(*a*) declare or pay any dividend to the creditors, or

(*b*) return any capital to contributories, unless he has retained what he reasonably considers to be an adequate reserve in respect of any claims arising as a result of the default proceedings of the exchange or clearing house concerned.

(3) The court may on an application by a relevant office-holder make such order as it thinks fit altering or dispensing from compliance with such of the duties of his office as are affected by the fact that default proceedings are pending or could be taken, or have been or could have been taken.

(4) Nothing in section 10(1)(*c*), 11(3), 126, 128, 130, 185 or 285 of the Insolvency Act 1986 (which restrict the taking of certain legal proceedings and other steps), and nothing in any rule of law in Scotland to the like effect as the said section 285, in the Bankruptcy (Scotland) Act 1985 or in the Debtors (Scotland) Act 1987 as to the effect of sequestration, shall affect any action taken by an exchange or clearing house for the purpose of its default proceedings.

162 Duty to report on completion of default proceedings

(1) A recognised investment exchange or recognised clearing house shall, on the completion of proceedings under its default rules, report to the Secretary of State on its proceedings stating in respect of each creditor or debtor the sum certified by them to be payable from or to the defaulter or, as the case may be, the fact that no sum is payable.

(2) The exchange or clearing house may make a single report or may make reports from time to time as proceedings are completed with respect to the transactions affecting particular persons.

(3) The exchange or clearing house shall supply a copy of every report under this section to the defaulter and to any relevant office-holder acting in relation to him or his estate.

(4) When a report under this section is received by the Secretary of State, he shall publish notice of that fact in such manner as he thinks appropriate for bringing it to the attention of creditors and debtors of the defaulter.

(5) An exchange or clearing house shall make available for inspection by a creditor or debtor of the defaulter so much of any report by it under this section as relates to the sum (if any) certified to be due to or from him or to the method by which that sum was determined.

(6) Any such person may require the exchange or clearing house, on payment of such reasonable fee as the exchange or clearing house may determine, to provide him with a copy of any part of a report which he is entitled to inspect.

163 Net sum payable on completion of default proceedings

(1) The following provisions apply with respect to the net sum certified by a recognised investment exchange or recognised clearing house, upon proceedings under its default rules being duly completed in accordance with this Part, to be payable by or to a defaulter.

(2) If, in England and Wales, a bankruptcy or winding-up order has been made, or a resolution for voluntary winding-up has been passed, the debt –

(*a*) is provable in the bankruptcy or winding up or, as the case may be, is payable to the relevant office-holder, and (*b*) shall be taken into account, where appropriate, under section 323 of the Insolvency Act 1986 (mutual dealings and set-off) or the corresponding provision applicable in the case of winding up,

in the same way as a debt due before the commencement of the bankruptcy, the date on which the body corporate goes into liquidation (within the meaning of section 247 of the Insolvency Act 1986) or, in the case of a partnership, the date of the winding-up order.

(3) If, in Scotland, an award of sequestration or a winding-up order has been made, or a resolution for voluntary winding up has been passed, the debt –

(*a*) may be claimed in the sequestration or winding up or, as the case may be, is payable to the relevant office-holder, and

(*b*) shall be taken into account for the purposes of any rule of law relating to set-off applicable in sequestration or winding up,

in the same way as a debt due before the date of sequestration (within the meaning of section 73(1) of the Bankruptcy (Scotland) Act 1985) or the commencement of the winding up (within the meaning of section 129 of the Insolvency Act 1986).

(4) However, where (or to the extent that) a sum is taken into account by virtue of subsection (2)(*b*) or (3)(*b*) which arises from a contract entered into at a time when the creditor had notice –

(*a*) that a bankruptcy petition or, in Scotland, a petition for sequestration was pending, or

(*b*) that a meeting of creditors had been summoned under section 98 of the Insolvency Act 1986 or that a winding-up petition was pending,

the value of any profit to him arising from the sum being so taken into account (or being so taken into account to that extent) is recoverable from him by the relevant office-holder unless the court directs otherwise.

(5) Subsection (4) does not apply in relation to a sum arising from a contract effected under the default rules of a recognised investment exchange or recognised clearing house.

(6) Any sum recoverable by virtue of subsection (4) ranks for priority, in the event of the insolvency of the person from whom it is due, immediately before preferential or, in Scotland, preferred debts.

164 Disclaimer of property, rescission of contracts, &c

(1) Sections 178, 186, 315 and 345 of the Insolvency Act 1986 (power to disclaim onerous property and court's power to order rescission of contracts, &c.) do not apply in relation to –

(*a*) a market contract, or

(*b*) a contract effected by the exchange or clearing house for the purpose of realising property provided as margin in relation to market contracts.

In the application of this subsection in Scotland, the reference to sections 178, 315 and 345 shall be construed as a reference to any rule of law having the like effect as those sections.

(2) In Scotland, a permanent trustee on the sequestrated estate of a defaulter or a liquidator is bound by any market contract to which that defaulter is a party and by any contract as is mentioned in subsection (1)(*b*) above notwithstanding section 42 of the Bankruptcy (Scotland) Act 1985 or any rule of law to the like effect applying in liquidations.

(3) Sections 127 and 284 of the Insolvency Act 1986 (avoidance of property dispositions effected after commencement of winding up or presentation of bankruptcy petition), and

section 32(8) of the Bankruptcy (Scotland) Act 1985 (effect of dealing with debtor relating to estate vested in permanent trustee), do not apply to –

    (*a*) a market contract, or any disposition of property in pursuance of such a contract,

    (*b*) the provision of margin in relation to market contracts,

    (*c*) a contract effected by the exchange or clearing house for the purpose of realising property provided as margin in relation to a market contract, or any disposition of property in pursuance of such a contract, or

    (*d*) any disposition of property in accordance with the rules of the exchange or clearing house as to the application of property provided as margin.

(4) However, where –

    (*a*) a market contract is entered into by a person who has notice that a petition has been presented for the winding up or bankruptcy or sequestration of the estate of the other party to the contract, or

    (*b*) margin in relation to a market contract is accepted by a person who has notice that such a petition has been presented in relation to the person by whom or on whose behalf the margin is provided,

the value of any profit to him arising from the contract or, as the case may be, the amount or value of the margin is recoverable from him by the relevant office-holder unless the court directs otherwise.

(5) Subsection (4)(*a*) does not apply where the person entering into the contract is a recognised investment exchange or recognised clearing house acting in accordance with its rules, or where the contract is effected under the default rules of such an exchange or clearing house; but subsection (4)(*b*) applies in relation to the provision of margin in relation to such a contract.

(6) Any sum recoverable by virtue of subsection (4) ranks for priority, in the event of the insolvency of the person from whom it is due, immediately before preferential or, in Scotland, preferred debts.

165 Adjustment of prior transactions

(1) No order shall be made in relation to a transaction to which this section applies under –

    (*a*) section 238 or 339 of the Insolvency Act 1986 (transactions at an under-value),

    (*b*) section 239 or 340 of that Act (preferences), or

    (*c*) section 423 of that Act (transactions defrauding creditors).

(2) As respects Scotland, no decree shall be granted in relation to any such transaction –

    (*a*) under section 34 or 36 of the Bankruptcy (Scotland) Act 1985 or section 242 or 243 of the Insolvency Act 1986 (gratuitous alienations and unfair preferences), or

    (*b*) at common law on grounds of gratuitous alienations or fraudulent preferences.

(3) This section applies to –

    (*a*) a market contract to which a recognised investment exchange or recognised clearing house is a party or which is entered into under its default rules, and

    (*b*) a disposition of property in pursuance of such a market contract.

(4) Where margin is provided in relation to a market contract and (by virtue of subsection (3)(*a*) or otherwise) no such order or decree as is mentioned in subsection (1) or (2) has been, or could be, made in relation to that contract, this section applies to –

(*a*) the provision of the margin,

(*b*) any contract effected by the exchange or clearing house in question for the purpose of realising the property provided as margin, and

(*c*) any disposition of property in accordance with the rules of the exchange or clearing house as to the application of property provided as margin.

166   Powers of Secretary of State to give directions

(1) The powers conferred by this section are exercisable in relation to a recognised UK investment exchange or recognised UK clearing house.

(2) Where in any case an exchange or clearing house has not taken action under its default rules –

(*a*) if it appears to the Secretary of State that it could take action, he may direct it to do so, and

(*b*) if it appears to the Secretary of State that it is proposing to take or may take action, he may direct it not to do so.

(3) Before giving such a direction the Secretary of State shall consult the exchange or clearing house in question; and he shall not give a direction unless he is satisfied, in the light of that consultation –

(*a*) in the case of a direction to take action, that failure to take action would involve undue risk to investors or other participants in the market, or

(*b*) in the case of a direction not to take action, that the taking of action would be premature or otherwise undesirable in the interests of investors or other participants in the market.

(4) A direction shall specify the grounds on which it is given.

(5) A direction not to take action may be expressed to have effect until the giving of a further direction (which may be a direction to take action or simply revoking the earlier direction).

(6) No direction shall be given not to take action if, in relation to the person in question –

(*a*) a bankruptcy order or an award of sequestration of his estate has been made, or an interim receiver or interim trustee has been appointed, or

(*b*) a winding up order has been made, a resolution for voluntary winding up has been passed or an administrator, administrative receiver or provisional liquidator has been appointed;

and any previous direction not to take action shall cease to have effect on the making or passing of any such order, award or appointment.

(7) Where an exchange or clearing house has taken or been directed to take action under its default rules, the Secretary of State may direct it to do or not to do such things (being things which it has power to do under its default rules) as are specified in the direction.

The Secretary of State shall not give such a direction unless he is satisfied that it will not impede or frustrate the proper and efficient conduct of the default proceedings.

(8) A direction under this section is enforceable, on the application of the Secretary of State, by injunction or, in Scotland, by an order under section 45 of the Court of Session Act 1988; and where an exchange or clearing house has not complied with a direction, the court may make such order as it thinks fit for restoring the position to what it would have been if the direction had been complied with.

167 Application to determine whether default proceedings to be taken

(1) Where there has been made or passed in relation to a member or designated non-member of a recognised investment exchange or a member of a recognised clearing house –

    (*a*) a bankruptcy order or an award of sequestration of his estate, or an order appointing an interim receiver of his property, or

    (*b*) an administration or winding up order, a resolution for voluntary winding up or an order appointing a provisional liquidator,

and the exchange or clearing house has not taken action under its default rules in consequence of the order, award or resolution or the matters giving rise to it, a relevant office-holder appointed by, or in consequence of or in connection with, the order, award or resolution may apply to the Secretary of State.

(2) The application shall specify the exchange or clearing house concerned and the grounds on which it is made.

(3) On receipt of the application the Secretary of State shall notify the exchange or clearing house, and unless within three business days after the day on which the notice is received the exchange or clearing house –

    (*a*) takes action under its default rules, or

    (*b*) notifies the Secretary of State that it proposes to do so forthwith,

then, subject as follows, the provisions of sections 158 to 165 above do not apply in relation to market contracts to which the member or designated non-member in question is a party or to anything done by the exchange or clearing house for the purposes of, or in connection with, the settlement of any such contract.

For this purpose a "business day" means any day which is not a Saturday or Sunday, Christmas Day, Good Friday or a bank holiday in any part of the United Kingdom under the Banking and Financial Dealings Act 1971.

(4) The provisions of sections 158 to 165 are not disapplied if before the end of the period mentioned in subsection (3) the Secretary of State gives the exchange or clearing house a direction under section 166(2)(*a*) (direction to take action under default rules).

No such direction may be given after the end of that period.

(5) If the exchange or clearing house notifies the Secretary of State that it proposes to take action under its default rules forthwith, it shall do so; and that duty is enforceable, on the application of the Secretary of State, by injunction or, in Scotland, by an order under section 45 of the Court of Session Act 1988.

168 Delegation of functions to designated agency

(1) Section 114 of the Financial Services Act 1986 (power to transfer functions to designated agency) applies to the functions of the Secretary of State under this Part in relation to a UK investment exchange or clearing house, with the exception of his functions with respect to the making of orders and regulations.

(2) If immediately before the commencement of this section –

    (*a*) a designated agency is exercising all functions in relation to such bodies which are capable of being transferred under that section, and

    (*b*) no draft order is lying before Parliament resuming any of those functions,

the order bringing this section into force shall have effect as a delegation order made under that section transferring to that agency all the functions which may be transferred by virtue of this section.

(3) The Secretary of State may –

(*a*) in the circumstances mentioned in subsection (3), (4) or (5) of section 115 of the Financial Services Act 1986, or

(*b*) if it appears to him that a designated agency is unable or unwilling to discharge all or any of the functions under this Part which have been transferred to it,

make an order under that section resuming all functions under this Part which have been transferred to the agency.

This does not affect his power to make an order under subsection (1) or (2) of that section with respect to such functions.

169 Supplementary provisions

(1) Section 61 of the Financial Services Act 1986 (injunctions and restitution orders) applies in relation to a contravention of any provision of the rules of a recognised investment exchange or recognised clearing house relating to the matters mentioned in Schedule 21 to this Act as it applies in relation to a contravention of any provision of such rules relating to the carrying on of investment business.

(2) The following provisions of the Financial Services Act 1986 –

section 12 (compliance orders), as it applies by virtue of section 37(8) or 39(8),

section 37(7)(*b*) (revocation of recognition of UK investment exchange), and

section 39(7)(*b*) (revocation of recognition of UK clearing house),

apply in relation to a failure by a recognised investment exchange or recognised clearing house to comply with an obligation under this Part as to a failure to comply with an obligation under that Act.

(3) Where the recognition of an investment exchange or clearing house is revoked under the Financial Services Act 1986, the Secretary of State may, before or after the revocation order, give such directions as he thinks fit with respect to the continued application of the provisions of this Part, with such exceptions, additions and adaptations as may be specified in the direction, in relation to cases where a relevant event of any description specified in the directions occurred before the revocation order takes effect.

(4) The references in sections 119 and 121 of the Financial Services Act 1986 (competition) to what is necessary for the protection of investors shall be construed as including references to what is necessary for the purposes of this Part.

(5) Section 204 of the Financial Services Act 1986 (service of notices) applies in relation to a notice, direction or other document required or authorised by or under this Part to be given to or served on any person other than the Secretary of State.

Other exchanges and clearing houses

170 Certain overseas exchanges and clearing houses

(1) The Secretary of State may by regulations provide that this Part applies in relation to contracts connected with an overseas investment exchange or clearing house which is approved by him, in accordance with such procedures as may be specified in the regulations, as satisfying such requirements as may be so specified, as it applies in relation to contracts connected with a recognised investment exchange or clearing house.

(2) The Secretary of State shall not approve an overseas investment exchange or clearing house unless he is satisfied –

(*a*) that the rules and practices of the body, together with the law of the country in which the body's head office is situated, provide adequate procedures for dealing

with the default of persons party to contracts connected with the body, and
 (*b*) that it is otherwise appropriate to approve the body.

(3) The reference in subsection (2)(*a*) to default is to a person being unable to meet his obligations.

(4) The regulations may apply in relation to the approval of a body under this section such of the provisions of the Financial Services Act 1986 as the Secretary of State considers appropriate.

(5) The Secretary of State may make regulations which, in relation to a body which is so approved –
 (*a*) apply such of the provisions of the Financial Services Act 1986 as the Secretary of State considers appropriate, and
 (*b*) provide that the provisions of this Part apply with such exceptions, additions and adaptations as appear to the Secretary of State to be necessary or expedient;
 and different provision may be made with respect to different bodies or descriptions of body.

(6) Where the regulations apply any provisions of the Financial Services Act 1986, they may provide that those provisions apply with such exceptions, additions and adaptations as appear to the Secretary of State to be necessary or expedient.

171 Certain money market institutions

(1) The Secretary of State may by regulations provide that this Part applies to contracts of any specified description in relation to which settlement arrangements are provided by a person for the time being included in a list maintained by the Bank of England for the purposes of this section, as it applies to contracts connected with a recognised investment exchange or recognised clearing house.

(2) The Secretary of State shall not make any such regulations unless he is satisfied, having regard to the extent to which the contracts in question –
 (*a*) involve, or are likely to involve, investments falling within paragraph 2 of Schedule 5 to the Financial Services Act 1986 (money market investments), or
 (*b*) are otherwise of a kind dealt in by persons supervised by the Bank of England,
 that it is appropriate that the arrangements should be subject to the supervision of the Bank of England.

(3) The approval of the Treasury is required for –
 (*a*) the conditions imposed by the Bank of England for admission to the list maintained by it for the purposes of this section, and
 (*b*) the arrangements for a person's admission to and removal from the list;
 and any regulations made under this section shall cease to have effect if the approval of the Treasury is withdrawn, but without prejudice to their having effect again if approval is given for fresh conditions or arrangements.

(4) The Bank of England shall publish the list as for the time being in force and provide a certified copy of it at the request of any person wishing to refer to it in legal proceedings.
 A certified copy shall be evidence (in Scotland, sufficient evidence) of the contents of the list; and a copy purporting to be certified by or on behalf of the Bank shall be deemed to have been duly certified unless the contrary is shown.

(5) Regulations under this section may, in relation to a person included in the list –
 (*a*) apply, with such exceptions, additions and adaptations as appear to the

Secretary of State to be necessary or expedient, such of the provisions of the Financial Services Act 1986 as he considers appropriate, and

(*b*) provide that the provisions of this Part apply with such exceptions, additions and adaptations as appear to the Secretary of State to be necessary or expedient.

(6) Before making any regulations under this section, the Secretary of State shall consult the Treasury and the Bank of England.

(7) In section 84(1) of the Banking Act 1987 (disclosure of information obtained under that Act), in the Table showing the authorities to which, and functions for the purposes of which, disclosure may be made, at the end add –

"A person included in the list maintained by the Bank for the purposes of section 171 of the Companies Act 1989.	Functions under settlement arrangements to which regulations under that section relate.".

172   Settlement arrangements provided by the Bank of England

(1) The Secretary of State may by regulations provide that this Part applies to contracts of any specified description in relation to which settlement arrangements are provided by the Bank of England, as it applies to contracts connected with a recognised investment exchange or recognised clearing house.

(2) Regulations under this section may provide that the provisions of this Part apply with such exceptions, additions and adaptations as appear to the Secretary of State to be necessary or expedient.

(3) Before making any regulations under this section, the Secretary of State shall consult the Treasury and the Bank of England.

Market charges

173   Market charges

(1) In this Part "market charge" means a charge, whether fixed or floating, granted –

(*a*) in favour of a recognised investment exchange, for the purpose of securing debts or liabilities arising in connection with the settlement of market contracts,

(*b*) in favour of a recognised clearing house, for the purpose of securing debts or liabilities arising in connection with their ensuring the performance of market contracts, or

(*c*) in favour of a person who agrees to make payments as a result of the transfer of specified securities made through the medium of a computer-based system established by the Bank of England and The Stock Exchange, for the purpose of securing debts or liabilities of the transferee arising in connection therewith.

(2) Where a charge is granted partly for purposes specified in subsection (1)(*a*), (*b*) or (*c*) and partly for other purposes, it is a "market charge" so far as it has effect for the specified purposes.

(3) In subsection (1)(*c*) –

"specified securities" means securities for the time being specified in the list in Schedule 1 to the Stock Transfer Act 1982, and includes any right to such securities; and "transfer", in relation to any such securities or right, means a transfer of the beneficial interest.

(4) The Secretary of State may by regulations make further provision as to the charges granted in favour of any such person as is mentioned in subsection (1)(*a*), (*b*) or (*c*) which are to be treated as "market charges" for the purposes of this Part; and the regulations may add to, amend or repeal the provisions of subsections (1) to (3) above.

(5) The regulations may provide that a charge shall or shall not be treated as a market charge if or to the extent that it secures obligations of a specified description, is a charge over property of a specified description or contains provisions of a specified description.

(6) Before making regulations under this section in relation to charges granted in favour of a person within subsection (1)(*c*), the Secretary of State shall consult the Treasury and the Bank of England.

174 Modifications of the law of insolvency

(1) The general law of insolvency has effect in relation to market charges and action taken in enforcing them subject to the provisions of section 175.

(2) The Secretary of State may by regulations make further provision modifying the law of insolvency in relation to the matters mentioned in subsection (1).

(3) The regulations may add to, amend or repeal the provisions mentioned in subsection (1), and any other provision of this Part as it applies for the purposes of those provisions, or provide that those provisions have effect with such exceptions, additions or adaptations as are specified in the regulations.

(4) The regulations may make different provision for cases defined by reference to the nature of the charge, the nature of the property subject to it, the circumstances, nature or extent of the obligations secured by it or any other relevant factor.

(5) Before making regulations under this section in relation to charges granted in favour of a person within section 173(1)(*c*), the Secretary of State shall consult the Treasury and the Bank of England.

175 Administration orders, &c

(1) The following provisions of the Insolvency Act 1986 (which relate to administration orders and administrators) do not apply in relation to a market charge –
  (*a*) sections 10(1)(*b*) and 11(3)(*c*) (restriction on enforcement of security while petition for administration order pending or order in force), and
  (*b*) section 15(1) and (2) (power of administrator to deal with charged property);
and section 11(2) of that Act (receiver to vacate office when so required by administrator) does not apply to a receiver appointed under a market charge.

(2) However, where a market charge falls to be enforced after an administration order has been made or a petition for an administration order has been presented, and there exists another charge over some or all of the same property ranking in priority to or *pari passu* with the market charge, the court may order that there shall be taken after enforcement of the market charge such steps as the court may direct for the purpose of ensuring that the chargee under the other charge is not prejudiced by the enforcement of the market charge.

(3) The following provisions of the Insolvency Act 1986 (which relate to the powers of receivers) do not apply in relation to a market charge –
  (*a*) section 43 (power of administrative receiver to dispose of charged property), and

(*b*) section 61 (power of receiver in Scotland to dispose of an interest in property).

(4) Sections 127 and 284 of the Insolvency Act 1986 (avoidance of property dispositions effected after commencement of winding up or presentation of bankruptcy petition), and section 32(8) of the Bankruptcy (Scotland) Act 1985 (effect of dealing with debtor relating to estate vested in permanent trustee), do not apply to a disposition of property as a result of which the property becomes subject to a market charge or any transaction pursuant to which that disposition is made.

(5) However, if a person (other than the chargee under the market charge) who is party to a disposition mentioned in subsection (4) has notice at the time of the disposition that a petition has been presented for the winding up or bankruptcy or sequestration of the estate of the party making the disposition, the value of any profit to him arising from the disposition is recoverable from him by the relevant office-holder unless the court directs otherwise.

(6) Any sum recoverable by virtue of subsection (5) ranks for priority, in the event of the insolvency of the person from whom it is due, immediately before preferential or, in Scotland, preferred debts.

(7) In a case falling within both subsection (4) above (as a disposition of property as a result of which the property becomes subject to a market charge) and section 164(3) (as the provision of margin in relation to a market contract), section 164(4) applies with respect to the recovery of the amount or value of the margin and subsection (5) above does not apply.

176   Power to make provision about certain other charges

(1) The Secretary of State may by regulations provide that the general law of insolvency has effect in relation to charges of such descriptions as may be specified in the regulations, and action taken in enforcing them, subject to such provisions as may be specified in the regulations.

(2) The regulations may specify any description of charge granted in favour of –
   (*a*) a body approved under section 170 (certain overseas exchanges and clearing houses),
   (*b*) a person included in the list maintained by the Bank of England for the purposes of section 171 (certain money market institutions),
   (*c*) the Bank of England,
   (*d*) an authorised person within the meaning of the Financial Services Act 1986, or
   (*e*) an international securities self-regulating organisation within the meaning of that Act,
for the purpose of securing debts or liabilities arising in connection with or as a result of the settlement of contracts or the transfer of assets, rights or interests on a financial market.

(3) The regulations may specify any description of charge granted for that purpose in favour of any other person in connection with exchange facilities or clearing services provided by a recognised investment exchange or recognised clearing house or by any such body, person, authority or organisation as is mentioned in subsection (2).

(4) Where a charge is granted partly for the purpose specified in subsection (2) and partly for other purposes, the power conferred by this section is exercisable in relation to the charge so far as it has effect for that purpose.

(5) The regulations may –
   (*a*) make the same or similar provision in relation to the charges to which they apply as is made by or under sections 174 and 175 in relation to market charges, or

(*b*) apply any of those provisions with such exceptions, additions or adaptations as are specified in the regulations.

(6) Before making regulations under this section relating to a description of charges defined by reference to their being granted –

(*a*) in favour of a person included in the list maintained by the Bank of England for the purposes of section 171, or in connection with exchange facilities or clearing services provided by a person included in that list, or

(*b*) in favour of the Bank of England, or in connection with settlement arrangements provided by the Bank,

the Secretary of State shall consult the Treasury and the Bank of England.

(7) Regulations under this section may provide that they apply or do not apply to a charge if or to the extent that it secures obligations of a specified description, is a charge over property of a specified description or contains provisions of a specified description.

Market property

177 Application of margin not affected by certain other interests

(1) The following provisions have effect with respect to the application by a recognised investment exchange or recognised clearing house of property (other than land) held by the exchange or clearing house as margin in relation to a market contract.

(2) So far as necessary to enable the property to be applied in accordance with the rules of the exchange or clearing house, it may be so applied notwithstanding any prior equitable interest or right, or any right or remedy arising from a breach of fiduciary duty, unless the exchange or clearing house had notice of the interest, right or breach of duty at the time the property was provided as margin.

(3) No right or remedy arising subsequently to the property being provided as margin may be enforced so as to prevent or interfere with the application of the property by the exchange or clearing house in accordance with its rules.

(4) Where an exchange or clearing house has power by virtue of the above provisions to apply property notwithstanding an interest, right or remedy, a person to whom the exchange or clearing house disposes of the property in accordance with its rules takes free from that interest, right or remedy.

178 Priority of floating market charge over subsequent charges

(1) The Secretary of State may by regulations provide that a market charge which is a floating charge has priority over a charge subsequently created or arising, including a fixed charge.

(2) The regulations may make different provision for cases defined, as regards the market charge or the subsequent charge, by reference to the description of charge, its terms, the circumstances in which it is created or arises, the nature of the charge, the person in favour of whom it is granted or arises or any other relevant factor.

179 Priority of market charge over unpaid vendor's lien

Where property subject to an unpaid vendor's lien becomes subject to a market charge, the charge has priority over the lien unless the chargee had actual notice of the lien at the time the property became subject to the charge.

180   Proceedings against market property by unsecured creditors

(1) Where property (other than land) is held by a recognised investment exchange or recognised clearing house as margin in relation to market contracts or is subject to a market charge, no execution or other legal process for the enforcement of a judgment or order may be commenced or continued, and no distress may be levied, against the property by a person not seeking to enforce any interest in or security over the property, except with the consent of –

(*a*) in the case of property provided as cover for margin, the investment exchange or clearing house in question, or

(*b*) in the case of property subject to a market charge, the person in whose favour the charge was granted.

(2) Where consent is given the proceedings may be commenced or continued notwithstanding any provision of the Insolvency Act 1986 or the Bankruptcy (Scotland) Act 1985.

(3) Where by virtue of this section a person would not be entitled to enforce a judgment or order against any property, any injunction or other remedy granted with a view to facilitating the enforcement of any such judgment or order shall not extend to that property.

(4) In the application of this section to Scotland, the reference to execution being commenced or continued includes a reference to diligence being carried out or continued, and the reference to distress being levied shall be omitted.

181   Power to apply provisions to other cases

(1) The power of the Secretary of State to make provision by regulations under –

(*a*) section 170, 171 or 172 (power to extend provisions relating to market contracts), or

(*b*) section 176 (power to extend provisions relating to market charges),

includes power to apply sections 177 to 180 to any description of property provided as cover for margin in relation to contracts in relation to which the power is exercised or, as the case may be, property subject to charges in relation to which the power is exercised.

(2) The regulations may provide that those sections apply with such exceptions, additions and adaptations as may be specified in the regulations.

Supplementary provisions

182   Powers of court in relation to certain proceedings begun before commencement

(1) The powers conferred by this section are exercisable by the court where insolvency proceedings in respect of –

(*a*) a member of a recognised investment exchange or a recognised clearing house, or

(*b*) a person by whom a market charge has been granted,

are begun on or after 22nd December 1988 and before the commencement of this section. That person is referred to in this section as "the relevant person".

(2) For the purposes of this section "insolvency proceedings" means proceedings under Part II, IV, V or IX of the Insolvency Act 1986 (administration, winding up and bankruptcy)

or under the Bankruptcy (Scotland) Act 1985; and references in this section to the beginning of such proceedings are to –

    (*a*) the presentation of a petition on which an administration order, winding-up order, bankruptcy order or award of sequestration is made, or

    (*b*) the passing of a resolution for voluntary winding up.

(3) This section applies in relation to –

    (*a*) in England and Wales, the administration of the insolvent estate of a deceased person, and

    (*b*) in Scotland, the administration by a judicial factor appointed under secion 11A of the Judicial Factors (Scotland) Act 1889 of the insolvent estate of a deceased person,

as it applies in relation to insolvency proceedings.

In such a case references to the beginning of the proceedings shall be construed as references to the death of the relevant person.

(4) The court may on an application made, within three months after the commencement of this section, by –

    (*a*) a recognised investment exchange or recognised clearing house, or

    (*b*) a person in whose favour a market charge has been granted,

make such order as it thinks fit for achieving, except so far as assets of the relevant person have been distributed before the making of the application, the same result as if the provisions of Schedule 22 had come into force on 22nd December 1988.

(5) The provisions of that Schedule ("the relevant provisions") reproduce the effect of certain provisions of this Part as they appeared in the Bill for this Act as introduced into the House of Lords and published on that date.

(6) The court may in particular –

    (*a*) require the relevant person or a relevant office-holder –

        (i) to return property provided as cover for margin or which was subject to a market charge, or to pay to the applicant or any other person the proceeds of realisation of such property, or

        (ii) to pay to the applicant or any other person such amount as the court estimates would have been payable to that person if the relevant provisions had come into force on 22nd December 1988 and market contracts had been settled in accordance with the rules of the recognised investment exchange or recognised clearing house, or a proportion of that amount if the property of the relevant person or relevant office-holder is not sufficient to meet the amount in full;

    (*b*) provide that contracts, rules and dispositions shall be treated as not having been void;

    (*c*) modify the functions of a relevant office-holder, or the duties of the applicant or any other person, in relation to the insolvency proceedings, or indemnify any such person in respect of acts or omissions which would have been proper if the relevant provisions had been in force;

    (*d*) provide that conduct which constituted an offence be treated as not having done so;

    (*e*) dismiss proceedings which could not have been brought if the relevant provisions had come into force on 22nd December 1988, and reverse the effect of any order of a court which could not, or would not, have been made if those provisions had come into force on that date.

(7) An order under this section shall not be made against a relevant office-holder if the effect would be that his remuneration, costs and expenses could not be met.

183   Insolvency proceedings in other jurisdictions

(1) The references to insolvency law in section 426 of the Insolvency Act 1986 (co-operation with courts exercising insolvency jurisdiction in other jurisdictions) include, in relation to a part of the United Kingdom, the provisions made by or under this Part and, in relation to a relevant country or territory within the meaning of that section, so much of the law of that country or territory as corresponds to any provisions made by or under this Part.

(2) A court shall not, in pursuance of that section or any other enactment or rule of law, recognise or give effect to –
>   (*a*) any order of a court exercising jurisdiction in relation to insolvency law in a country or territory outside the United Kingdom, or
>   (*b*) any act of a person appointed in such a country or territory to discharge any functions under insolvency law,

in so far as the making of the order or the doing of the act would be prohibited in the case of a court in the United Kingdom or a relevant office-holder by provisions made by or under this Part.

(3) Subsection (2) does not affect the recognition or enforcement of a judgment required to be recognised or enforced under or by virtue of the Civil Jurisdiction and Judgments Act 1982.

184   Indemnity for certain acts, &c

(1) Where a relevant office-holder takes any acion in relation to property of a defaulter which is liable to be dealt with in accordance with the default rules of a recognised investment exchange or recognised clearing house, and believes and has reasonable grounds for believing that he is entitled to take that action, he is not liable to any person in respect of any loss or damage resulting from his action except in so far as the loss or damage is caused by the office-holder's own negligence.

(2) Any failure by a recognised investment exchange or recognised clearing house to comply with its own rules in respect of any matter shall not prevent that matter being treated for the purposes of this Part as done in accordance with those rules so long as the failure does not substantially affect the rights of any person entitled to require compliance with the rules.

(3) No recognised investment exchange or recognised clearing house, nor any officer or servant or member of the governing body of a recognised investment exchange or recognised clearing house, shall be liable in damages for anything done or omitted in the discharge or purported discharge of any functions to which this subsection applies unless the act or omission is shown to have been in bad faith.

(4) The functions to which subsection (3) applies are the functions of the exchange or clearing house so far as relating to, or to matters arising out of –
>   (*a*) its default rules, or
>   (*b*) any obligations to which it is subject by virtue of this Part.

(5) No person exercising any functions by virtue of arrangements made pursuant to paragraph 5 or 12 of Schedule 21 (delegation of functions in connection with default procedures), nor any officer or servant of such a person, shall be liable in damages for

anything done or omitted in the discharge or purported discharge of those functions unless the act or omission is shown to have been in bad faith.

185 Power to make further provision by regulations

(1) The Secretary of State may by regulations make such further provision as appears to him necessary or expedient for the purposes of this Part.

(2) Provision may, in particular, be made –
    (*a*) for integrating the provisions of this Part with the general law of insolvency, and
    (*b*) for adapting the provisions of this Part in their application to overseas investment exchanges and clearing houses.

(3) Regulations under this section may add to, amend or repeal any of the provisions of this Part or provide that those provisions have effect subject to such additions, exceptions or adaptations as are specified in the regulations.

186 Supplementary provisions as to regulations

(1) Regulations under this Part may make different provision for different cases and may contain such incidental, transitional and other supplementary provisions as appear to the Secretary of State to be necessary or expedient.

(2) Regulations under this Part shall be made by statutory instrument which shall be subject to annulment in pursuance of a resolution of either House of Parliament.

187 Construction of references to parties to market contracts

(1) Where a person enters into market contracts in more than one capacity, the provisions of this Part apply (subject as follows) as if the contracts entered into in each different capacity were entered into by different persons.

(2) References in this Part to a market contract to which a person is a party include (subject as follows, and unless the context otherwise requires) contracts to which he is party as agent.

(3) The Secretary of State may by regulations –
    (*a*) modify or exclude the operation of subsections (1) and (2), and
    (*b*) make provision as to the circumstances in which a person is to be regarded for the purposes of those provisions as acting in different capacities.

188 Meaning of "default rules" and related expressions

(1) In this Part "default rules" means rules of a recognised investment exchange or recognised clearing house which provide for the taking of action in the event of a person appearing to be unable, or likely to become unable, to meet his obligations in respect of one or more market contracts connected with the exchange or clearing house.

(2) References in this Part to a "defaulter" are to a person in respect of whom action has been taken by a recognised investment exchange or recognised clearing house under its default rules, whether by declaring him to be a defaulter or otherwise; and references in this Part to "default" shall be construed accordingly.

(3) In this Part "default proceedings" means proceedings taken by a recognised investment exchange or recognised clearing house under its default rules.

(4) If an exchange or clearing house takes action under its default rules in respect of a person, all subsequent proceedings under its rules for the purposes of or in connection with

the settlement of market contracts to which the defaulter is a party shall be treated as done under its default rules.

189 Meaning of "relevant office-holder"

(1) The following are relevant office-holders for the purposes of this Part –

  (*a*) the official receiver,

  (*b*) any person acting in relation to a company as its liquidator, provisional liquidator, administrator or administrative receiver,

  (*c*) any person acting in relation to an individual (or, in Scotland, any debtor within the meaning of the Bankruptcy (Scotland) Act 1985) as his trustee in bankruptcy or interim receiver of his property or as permanent or interim trustee in the sequestration of his estate,

  (*d*) any person acting as administrator of an insolvent estate of a deceased person.

(2) In subsection (1)(*b*) "company" means any company, society, association, partnership or other body which may be wound up under the Insolvency Act 1986.

190 Minor definitions

(1) In this Part –

"administrative receiver" has the meaning given by section 251 of the Insolvency Act 1986;

"charge" means any form of security, including a mortgage and, in Scotland, a heritable security;

"clearing house" has the same meaning as in the Financial Services Act 1986;

"interim trustee" and "permanent trustee" have the same meaning as in the Bankruptcy (Scotland) Act 1985;

"investment" and "investment exchange" have the same meaning as in the Financial Services Act 1986;

"overseas", in relation to an investment exchange or clearing house, means having its head office outside the United Kingdom;

"recognised" means recognised under the Financial Services Act 1986;

"set-off", in relation to Scotland, includes compensation;

"The Stock Exchange" means The International Stock Exchange of the United Kingdom and the Republic of Ireland Limited;

"UK", in relation to an investment exchange or clearing house, means having its head office in the United Kingdom.

(2) References in this Part to settlement in relation to a market contract are to the discharge of the rights and liabilities of the parties to the contract, whether by performance, compromise or otherwise.

(3) In this Part the expressions "margin" and "cover for margin" have the same meaning.

(4) References in this Part to ensuring the performance of a transaction have the same meaning as in the Financial Services Act 1986.

(5) For the purposes of this Part a person shall be taken to have notice of a matter if he

deliberately failed to make enquiries as to that matter in circumstances in which a reasonable and honest person would have done so.

This does not apply for the purposes of a provision requiring "actual notice".

(6) References in this Part to the law of insolvency include references to every provision made by or under the Insolvency Act 1986 or the Bankruptcy (Scotland) Act 1985; and in relation to a building society references to insolvency law or to any provision of the Insolvency Act 1986 are to that law or provision as modified by the Building Societies Act 1986.

(7) In relation to Scotland, references in this Part –

(*a*) to sequestration include references to the administration by a judicial factor of the insolvent estate of a deceased person, and

(*b*) to an interim or permanent trustee include references to a judicial factor on the insolvent estate of a deceased person,

unless the context otherwise requires.

191 Index of defined expressions

The following Table shows provisions defining or otherwise explaining expressions used in this Part (other than provisions defining or explaining an expression used only in the same section or paragraph) –

administrative receiver	section 190(1)
charge	section 190(1)
clearing house	section 190(1)
cover for margin	section 190(3)
default rules (and related expressions)	section 188
designated non-member	section 155(2)
ensuring the performance of a transaction	section 190(4)
insolvency law (and similar expressions)	section 190(6)
interim trustee	section 190(1) and (7)(*b*)
investment	section 190(1)
investment exchange	section 190(1)
margin	section 190(3)
market charge	section 173
market contract	section 155
notice	section 190(5)
overseas (in relation to an investment exchange or clearing house)	section 190(1)
party (in relation to a market contract)	section 187
permanent trustee	section 190(1) and (7)(*b*)
recognised	section 190(1)
relevant office-holder	section 189
sequestration	section 190(7)(*a*)
set off (in relation to Scotland)	section 190(1)
settlement and related expressions (in relation to a market contract)	section 190(2)
The Stock Exchange	section 190(1)
trustee, interim or permanent (in relation to Scotland)	section 190(7)(*b*)
UK (in relation to an investment exchange or clearing house)	section 190(1)

PART VIII
AMENDMENTS OF THE FINANCIAL SERVICES ACT 1986

192   Statements of principle

In Chapter V of Part I of the Financial Services Act 1986 (conduct of investment business), after section 47 insert –

"47A   Statements of principle

(1) The Secretary of State may issue statements of principle with respect to the conduct and financial standing expected of persons authorised to carry on investment business.

(2) The conduct expected may include compliance with a code or standard issued by another person, as for the time being in force, and may allow for the exercise of discretion by any person pursuant to any such code or standard.

(3) Failure to comply with a statement of principle under this section is a ground for the taking of disciplinary action or the exercise of powers of intervention, but it does not of itself give rise to any right of action by investors or other persons affected or affect the validity of any transaction.

(4) The disciplinary action which may be taken by virtue of subsection (3) is –
   (a) the withdrawal or suspension of authorisation under section 28 or the termination or suspension of authorisation under section 33,
   (b) the giving of a disqualification direction under section 59,
   (c) the making of a public statement under section 60, or
   (d) the application by the Secretary of State for an injunction, interdict or other order under section 61(1);
and the reference in that subsection to powers of intervention is to the powers conferred by Chapter VI of this Part.

(5) Where a statement of principle relates to compliance with a code or standard issued by another person, the statement of principle may provide –
   (a) that failure to comply with the code or standard shall be a ground for the taking of disciplinary action, or the exercise of powers of intervention, only in such cases and to such extent as may be specified, and
   (b) that no such action shall be taken, or any such power exercised, except at the request of the person by whom the code of standard in question was issued.

(6) The Secretary of State shall exercise his powers in such manner as appears to him appropriate to secure compliance with statements of principle under this section.

47B   Modification or waiver of statements of principle in particular cases

(1) The relevant regulatory authority may on the application of any person –
   (a) modify a statement of principle issued under section 47A so as to adapt it to his circumstances or to any particular kind of business carried on by him, or

(*b*) dispense him from compliance with any such statement of principle, generally or in relation to any particular kind of business carried on by him.

(2) The powers conferred by this section shall not be exercised unless it appears to the relevant regulatory authority –

(*a*) that compliance with the statement of principle in question would be unduly burdensome for the applicant having regard to the benefit which compliance would confer on investors, and

(*b*) that the exercise of those powers will not result in any undue risk to investors.

(3) The powers conferred by this section may be exercised unconditionally or subject to conditions; and section 47A(3) applies in the case of failure to comply with a condition as in the case of failure to comply with a statement of principle.

(4) The relevant regulatory authority for the purposes of this section is –

(*a*) in the case of a member of a recognised self-regulating organisation or professional body, in relation to investment business in the carrying on of which he is subject to the rules of the organisation or body, that organisation or body;

(*b*) in any other case, or in relation to other investment business, the Secretary of State.

(5) The references in paragraph 4(1) of Schedule 2 and paragraph 4(2) of Schedule 3 (requirements for recognition of self-regulating organisations and professional bodies) to monitoring and enforcement of compliance with statements of principle include monitoring and enforcement of compliance with conditions imposed by the organisation or body under this section.".

193 Restriction of right to bring action for contravention of rules, regulations, &c

(1) In Chapter V of Part I of the Financial Services Act 1986 (conduct of investment business), after section 62 (actions for damages) insert –

"62A Restriction of right of action

(1) No action in respect of a contravention to which section 62 above applies shall lie at the suit of a person other than a private investor, except in such circumstances as may be specified by regulations made by the Secretary of State.

(2) The meaning of the expression "private investor" for the purposes of subsection (1) shall be defined by regulations made by the Secretary of State.

(3) Regulations under subsection (1) may make different provision with respect to different cases.

(4) The Secretary of State shall, before making any regulations affecting the right to bring an action in respect of a contravention of any rules or regulations made by a person other than himself, consult that person.".

(2) In section 114(5) of the Financial Services Act 1986 (transfer of functions to designated agency: excluded functions), after paragraph (*d*) insert –
"(*dd*) section 62A;".

(3) In Schedule 11 to the Financial Services Act 1986 (friendly societies), after paragraph 22 insert –

> "22A.–(1) No action in respect of a contravention to which paragraph 22(4) above applies shall lie at the suit of a person other than a private investor, except in such circumstances as may be specified by regulations made by the Registrar.
>
> (2) The meaning of the expression "private investor" for the purposes of sub-paragraph (1) shall be defined by regulations made by the Registrar.
>
> (3) Regulations under sub-paragraph (1) may make different provision with respect to different cases.
>
> (4) The Registrar shall, before making any regulations affecting the right to bring an action in respect of a contravention of any rules or regulations made by a person other than himself, consult that person.".

(4) In paragraph 28(5) of Schedule 11 to the Financial Services Act 1986 (transfer of Registrar's functions to transferee body), after "paragraphs 2 to 25" insert "(except paragraph 22A)".

194   Application of designated rules and regulations to members of self-regulating organisations

In Chapter V of Part I of the Financial Services Act 1986 (conduct of investment business), after section 63 insert –

> **"63A   Application of designated rules and regulations to members of self-regulating organisations**
>
> (1) The Secretary of State may in rules and regulations under –
>> (*a*) section 48 (conduct of business rules),
>> (*b*) section 49 (financial resources rules),
>> (*c*) section 55 (clients' money regulations), or
>> (*d*) section 56 (regulations as to unsolicited calls),
>
> designate provisions which apply, to such extent as may be specified, to a member of a recognised self-regulating organisation in respect of investment business in the carrying of which he is subject to the rules of the organisation.
>
> (2) It may be provided that the designated rules or regulations have effect, generally or to such extent as may be specified, subject to the rules of the organisation.
>
> (3) A member of a recognised self-regulating organisation who contravenes a rule or regulation applying to him by virtue of this section shall be treated as having contravened the rules of the organisation.
>
> (4) It may be provided that, to such extent as may be specified, the designated rules or regulations may not be modified or waived (under section 63B below or section 50) in relation to a member of a recognised self-regulating organisation.
>
> Where such provision is made any modification or waiver previously granted shall cease to have effect, subject to any transitional provision or saving contained in the rules or regulations.
>
> (5) Except as mentioned in subsection (1), the rules and regulations referred to in that subsection do not apply to a member of a recognised self-regulating

organisation in respect of investment business in the carrying on of which he is subject to the rules of the organisation.

63B Modification or waiver of designated rules and regulations

(1) A recognised self-regulating organisation may on the application of a member of the organisation –

> (*a*) modify a rule or regulation designated under section 63A so as to adapt it to his circumstances or to any particular kind of business carried on by him, or
>
> (*b*) dispense him from compliance with any such rule or regulation, generally or in relation to any particular kind of business carried on by him.

(2) The powers conferred by this section shall not be exercised unless it appears to the organisation –

> (*a*) that compliance with the rule or regulation in question would be unduly burdensome for the applicant having regard to the benefit which compliance would confer on investors, and
>
> (*b*) that the exercise of those powers will not result in any undue risk to investors.

(3) The powers conferred by this section may be exercised unconditionally or subject to conditions; and section 63A(3) applies in the case of a contravention of a condition as in the case of contravention of a designated rule or regulation.

(4) The reference in paragraph 4(1) of Schedule 2 (requirements for recognition of self-regulating organisations) to monitoring and enforcement of compliance with rules and regulations includes monitoring and enforcement of compliance with conditions imposed by the organisation under this section.".

195 Codes of practice

In Chapter V of Part I of the Financial Services Act 1986 (conduct of investment business), after the sections inserted by section 194 above, insert –

"63C Codes of practice

(1) The Secretary of State may issue codes of practice with respect to any matters dealt with by statements of principle issued under section 47A or by rules or regulations made under any provision of this Chapter.

(2) In determining whether a person has failed to comply with a statement of principle –

> (*a*) a failure by him to comply with any relevant provision of a code of practice may be relied on as tending to establish failure to comply with the statement of principle, and
>
> (*b*) compliance by him with the relevant provisions of a code of practice may be relied on as tending to negative any such failure.

(3) A contravention of a code of practice with respect to a matter dealt with by rules or regulations shall not of itself give rise to any liability or invalidate any transaction; but in determining whether a person's conduct amounts to contravention of a rule or regulation –

> (*a*) contravention by him of any relevant provision of a code of practice may be relied on as tending to establish liability, and

(*b*) compliance by him with the relevant provisions of a code of practice may be relied on as tending to negative liability.

(4) Where by virtue of section 63A (application of designated rules and regulations to members of self-regulating organisations) rules or regulations –

(*a*) do not apply, to any extent, to a member of a recognised self-regulating organisation, or

(*b*) apply, to any extent, subject to the rules of the organisation,

a code of practice with respect to a matter dealt with by the rules or regulations may contain provision limiting its application to a corresponding extent.".

196   Relations with other regulatory authorities

In Part I of the Financial Services Act 1986 (regulation of investment business), after section 128 insert –

"CHAPTER XV

RELATIONS WITH OTHER REGULATORY AUTHORITIES

128A   Relevance of other controls

In determining –

(*a*) in relation to a self-regulating organisation, whether the requirements of Schedule 2 are met, or

(*b*) in relation to a professional body, whether the requirements of Schedule 3 are met,

the Secretary of State shall take into account the effect of any other controls to which members of the organisation or body are subject.

128B   Relevance of information given and action taken by other regulatory authorities

(1) The following provisions apply in the case of –

(*a*) a person whose principal place of business is in a country or territory outside the United Kingdom, or

(*b*) a person whose principal business is other than investment business;

and in relation to such a person "the relevant regulatory authority" means the appropriate regulatory authority in that country or territory or, as the case may be, in relation to his principal business.

(2) The Secretary of State may regard himself as satisfied with respect to any matter relevant for the purposes of this Part if –

(*a*) the relevant regulatory authority informs him that it is satisfied with respect to that matter, and

(*b*) he is satisfied as to the nature and scope of the supervision exercised by that authority.

(3) In making any decision with respect to the exercise of his powers under this Part in relation to any such person, the Secretary of State may take into account whether the relevant regulatory authority has exercised, or proposes to exercise, its powers in relation to that person.

(4) The Secretary of State may enter into such arrangements with other regulatory authorities as he thinks fit for the purposes of this section.

(5) Where any functions under this Part have been transferred to a designated agency, nothing in this section shall be construed as affecting the responsibility of the Secretary of State for the discharge of Community obligations or other international obligations of the United Kingdom.

128C Enforcement in support of overseas regulatory authority

(1) The Secretary of State may exercise his disciplinary powers or powers of intervention at the request of, or for the purpose of assisting, an overseas regulatory authority.

(2) The disciplinary powers of the Secretary of State means his powers –
- (*a*) to withdraw or suspend authorisation under section 28 or to terminate or suspend authorisation under section 33,
- (*b*) to give a disqualification direction under section 59,
- (*c*) to make a public statement under section 60, or
- (*d*) to apply for an injunction, interdict or other order under section 61(1);

and the reference to his powers of intervention is to the powers conferred by Chapter VI of this Part.

(3) An "overseas regulatory authority" means an authority in a country or territory outside the United Kingdom which exercises –
- (*a*) any function corresponding to –
  - (i) a function of the Secretary of State under this Act, the Insurance Companies Act 1982 or the Companies Act 1985,
  - (ii) a function under this Act of a designated agency, transferee body or competent authority, or
  - (iii) a function of the Bank of England under the Banking Act 1987, or
- (*b*) any functions in connection with the investigation of, or the enforcement of rules (whether or not having the force of law) relating to, conduct of the kind prohibited by the Company Securities (Insider Dealing) Act 1985, or
- (*c*) any function prescribed for the purposes of this subsection, being a function which in the opinion of the Secretary of State relates to companies or financial services.

(4) In deciding whether to exercise those powers the Secretary of State may take into account, in particular –
- (*a*) whether corresponding assistance would be given in that country or territory to an authority exercising regulatory functions in the United Kingdom;
- (*b*) whether the case concerns the breach of a law, or other requirement, which has no close parallel in the United Kingdom or involves the assertion of a jurisdiction not recognised by the United Kingdom;
- (*c*) the seriousness of the case and its importance to persons in the United Kingdom;
- (*d*) whether it is otherwise appropriate in the public interest to give the assistance sought.

(5) The Secretary of State may decline to exercise those powers unless the overseas regulatory authority undertakes to make such contribution towards the cost of their exercise as the Secretary of State considers appropriate.

(6) The reference in subsection (3)(*c*) to financial services includes, in particular, investment business, insurance and banking.".

197   Construction of references to incurring civil liability

(1) In section 150(6) of the Financial Services Act 1986 (exclusion of liability in respect of false or misleading listing particulars), at the end insert –

"The reference above to a person incurring liability includes a reference to any other person being entitled as against that person to be granted any civil remedy or to rescind or repudiate any agreement.".

(2) In section 154(5) of the Financial Services Act 1986 (exclusion of civil liability in respect of advertisements or other information in connection with listing application), at the end insert –

"The reference above to a person incurring civil liability includes a reference to any other person being entitled as against that person to be granted any civil remedy or to rescind or repudiate any agreement.".

198   Offers of unlisted securities

(1) In Part V of the Financial Services Act 1986 (offers of unlisted securities), after section 160 insert –

"160A   Exemptions

(1) The Secretary of State may by order exempt from sections 159 and 160 when issued in such circumstances as may be specified in the order –

(*a*) advertisements appearing to him to have a private character, whether by reason of a connection between the person issuing them and those to whom they are addressed or otherwise;

(*b*) advertisements appearing to him to deal with investments only incidentally;

(*c*) advertisements issued to persons appearing to him to be sufficiently expert to understand any risks involved;

(*d*) such other classes of advertisements as he thinks fit.

(2) The Secretary of State may by order exempt from sections 159 and 160 an advertisement issued in whatever circumstances which relates to securities appearing to him to be of a kind that can be expected normally to be bought or dealt in only by persons sufficiently expert to understand any risks involved.

(3) An order under subsection (1) or (2) may require a person who by virtue of the order is authorised to issue an advertisement to comply with such requirements as are specified in the order.

(4) An order made by virtue of subsection (1) (*a*), (*b*) or (*c*) or subsection (2) shall be subject to annulment in pursuance of a resolution of either House of Parliament; and no order shall be made by virtue of subsection (1)(*d*) unless a draft of it has been laid before and approved by a resolution of each House of Parliament.".

(2) The following amendments of the Financial Services Act 1986 are consequential on that above.

(3) In section 159, in subsection (1) omit the words from the beginning to "section 161 below," and after subsection (2) insert –

"(3) Subsection (1) above has effect subject to section 160A (exemptions) and section 161 (exceptions).".

(4) In section 160, in subsection (1) omit the words from the beginning to "section 161 below", and for subsections (6) to (9) substitute –

"(6) Subsection (1) above has effect subject to section 160A (exemptions) and section 161 (exceptions).".

(5) In section 171, in subsection (1)(*b*) and subsection (3) for "section 160(6) or (7)" substitute "section 160A".

199 Offers of securities by private companies and old public companies

In Part V of the Financial Services Act 1986 (offers of unlisted securities), in section 170 (advertisements by private companies and old public companies), for subsections (2) to (4) substitute –

"2) The Secretary of State may by order exempt from subsection (1) when issued in such circumstances as may be specified in the order —
    (*a*) advertisements appearing to him to have a private character, whether by reason of a connection between the person issuing them and those to whom they are addressed or otherwise;
    (*b*) advertisements appearing to him to deal with investments only incidentally;
    (*c*) advertisements issued to persons appearing to him to be sufficiently expert to understand any risks involved;
    (*d*) such other classes of advertisements as he thinks fit.

(3) The Secretary of State may by order exempt from subsection (1) an advertisement issued in whatever circumstances which relates to securities appearing to him to be of a kind that can be expected normally to be bought or dealt in only by persons sufficiently expert to understand any risks involved.

(4) An order under subsection (2) or (3) may require a person who by virtue of the order is authorised to issue an advertisement to comply with such requirements as are specified in the order.

(4A) An order made by virtue of subsection (2)(*a*), (*b*) or (*c*) or subsection (3) shall be subject to annulment in pursuance of a resolution of either House of Parliament; and no order shall be made by virtue of subsection (2)(*d*) unless a draft of it has been laid before and approved by a resolution of each House of Parliament.".

200 Jurisdiction of High Court and Court of Session

(1) In the Financial Services Act 1986, for section 188 (jurisdiction as respects actions concerning designated agency, &c.), substitute –

"188 Jurisdiction of High Court and Court of Session

(1) Proceedings arising out of any act or omission (or proposed act or omission) of –
    (*a*) a recognised self-regulating organisation,
    (*b*) a designated agency,
    (*c*) a transferee body, or
    (*d*) the competent authority,

in the discharge or purported discharge of any of its functions under this Act may be brought in the High Court or the Court of Session.

(2) The jurisdiction conferred by subsection (1) is in addition to any other jurisdiction exercisable by those courts.".

(2) In Schedule 5 to the Civil Jurisdiction and Judgments Act 1982 (proceedings excluded from general provisions as to allocation of jurisdiction within the United Kingdom), for paragraph 10 substitute –

"*Financial Services Act 1986*

10. Proceedings such as are mentioned in section 188 of the Financial Services Act 1986.".

201 Directions to secure compliance with international obligations

In the Financial Services Act 1986, for section 192 (international obligations) substitute –

"192 International obligations

(1) If it appears to the Secretary of State –
  (*a*) that any action proposed to be taken by an authority or body to which this section applies would be incompatible with Community obligations or any other international obligations of the United Kingdom, or
  (*b*) that any action which that authority or body has power to take is required for the purpose of implementing any such obligation,
he may direct the authority or body not to take or, as the case may be, to take the action in question.

(2) The authorities and bodies to which this section applies are the following –
  (*a*) a recognised self-regulating organisation,
  (*b*) a recognised investment exchange (other than an overseas investment exchange),
  (*c*) a recognised clearing house (other than an overseas clearing house),
  (*d*) a designated agency,
  (*e*) a transferee body,
  (*f*) a competent authority.

(3) This section also applies to an approved exchange within the meaning of Part V of this Act in respect of any action which it proposes to take or has power to take in respect of rules applying to a prospectus by virtue of a direction under section 162(3) above.

(4) A direction under this section may include such supplementary or incidental requirements as the Secretary of State thinks necessary or expedient.

(5) Where the function of making or revoking a recognition order in respect of an authority or body to which this section applies is exercisable by a designated agency, any direction in respect of that authority or body shall be a direction requiring the agency to give the authority or body such a direction as is specified in the direction given by the Secretary of State.

(6) A direction under this section is enforceable, on the application of the

person who gave it, by injunction or, in Scotland, by an order under section 45 of the Court of Session Act 1988.".

202 Offers of short-dated debentures

In section 195 of the Financial Services Act 1986 (circumstances in which certain offers of debentures not treated as offers to the public), for "repaid within less than one year of the date of issue" substitute "repaid within five years of the date of issue".

203 Standard of protection for investors

(1) In Schedule 2 to the Financial Services Act 1986 (requirements for recognition of self-regulating organisations), in paragraph 3 (safeguards for investors) for sub-paragraphs (1) and (2) substitute –

"(1) The organisation must have rules governing the carrying on of investment business by its members which, together with the statements of principle, rules, regulations and codes of practice to which its members are subject under Chapter V of Part I of this Act, are such as to afford an adequate level of protection for investors.

(2) In determining in any case whether an adequate level of protection is afforded for investors of any description, regard shall be had to the nature of the investment business carried on by members of the organisation, the kinds of investors involved and the effectiveness of the organisation's arrangements for enforcing compliance.".

(2) In Schedule 3 to the Financial Services Act 1986 (requirements for recognition of professional bodies), for paragraph 3 (safeguards for investors) substitute –

"3. – (1) The body must have rules regulating the carrying on of investment business by persons certified by it which, together with the statements of principle, rules, regulations and codes of practice to which those persons are subject under Chapter V of Part I of this Act, afford an adequate level of protection for investors.

(2) In determining in any case whether an adequate level of protection is afforded for investors of any description, regard shall be had to the nature of the investment business carried on by persons certified by the body, the kinds of investors involved and the effectiveness of the body's arrangements for enforcing compliance.".

(3) The order bringing this section into force may provide that, for a transitional period, a self-regulating organisation or professional body may elect whether to comply with the new requirement having effect by virtue of subsection (1) or (2) above or with the requirement which it replaces.

The Secretary of State may by order specify when the transitional period is to end.

204 Costs of compliance

(1) In Schedule 2 to the Financial Services Act 1986 (requirements for recognition of self-regulating organisations), after paragraph 3 insert –

"Taking account of costs of compliance

3A. The organisation must have satisfactory arrangements for taking account, in framing its rules, of the cost to those to whom the rules would apply of complying with those rules and any other controls to which they are subject.";

and in Schedule 3 to that Act (requirements for recognition of professional body), after paragraph 3 insert –

"Taking account of costs of compliance

3A. The body must have satisfactory arrangements for taking account, in framing its rules, of the cost to those to whom the rules would apply of complying with those rules and any other controls to which they are subject.".

(2) The additional requirements having effect by virtue of subsection (1) do not affect the status of a self-regulating organisation or professional body recognised before the commencement of that subsection; but if the Secretary of State is of the opinion that any of those requirements is not met in the case of such an organisation or body, he shall within one month of commencement give notice to the organisation or body stating his opinion.

(3) Where the Secretary of State gives such a notice, he shall not –
>   (*a*) take action to revoke the recognition of such an organisation or body on the ground that any of the additional requirements is not met, unless he considers it essential to do so in the interests of investors, or
>   (*b*) apply on any such ground for a compliance order under section 12 of the Financial Services Act 1986,

until after the end of the period of six months beginning with the date on which the notice was given.

(4) In Schedule 7 to the Financial Services Act 1986 (qualifications of designated agency), after paragraph 2 insert –

"Taking account of costs of compliance

2A. – (1) The agency must have satisfactory arrangements for taking account, in framing any provisions which it proposes to make in the exercise of its legislative functions, of the cost to those to whom the provisions would apply of complying with those provisions and any other controls to which they are subject.

(2) In this paragraph "legislative functions" means the functions of issuing or making statements of principle, rules, regulations or codes of practice.".

(5) The additional requirement having effect by virtue of subsection (4) above does not affect the status of a designated agency to which functions have been transferred before the commencement of that subsection; but if the Secretary of State is of the opinion the requirement is not met in the case of such an agency, he shall within one month of commencement give notice to the agency stating his opinion.

(6) Where the Secretary of State gives such a notice, he shall not take action under section 115(2) of the Financial Services Act 1986 to resume any functions exercisable by such an agency on the ground that the additional requirement is not met until after the end of the period of six months beginning with the date on which the notice was given.

(7) References in this section to a recognised self-regulating organisation include a recognised self-regulating organisation for friendly societies and references to a designated agency include a transferee body (within the meaning of that Act).

In relation to such an organisation or body –

(*a*) references to the Secretary of State shall be construed as references to the Registrar (within the meaning of Schedule 11 to the Financial Services Act 1986), and

(*b*) the reference to section 12 of that Act shall be contrued as a reference to paragraph 6 of that Schedule.

205 Requirements for recognition of investment exchange

(1) In Schedule 4 to the Financial Services Act 1986 (requirements for recognition of investment exchanges), after paragraph 5 insert –

"Supplementary

6. – (1) The provisions of this Schedule relate to an exchange only so far as it provides facilities for the carrying on of investment business; and nothing in this Schedule shall be construed as requiring an exchange to limit dealings on the exchange to dealings in investments.

(2) The references in this Schedule, and elsewhere in this Act, to ensuring the performance of transactions on an exchange are to providing satisfactory procedures (including default procedures) for the settlement of transactions on the exchange.".

(2) The above amendment shall be deemed always to have had effect.

(3) In section 207(1) of the Financial Services Act 1986 (interpretation), at the appropriate place insert –

""ensure" and "ensuring", in relation to the performance of transactions on an investment exchange, have the meaning given in paragraph 6 of Schedule 4 to this Act;".

206 Consequential amendments and delegation of functions on commencement

(1) The Financial Services Act 1986 has effect with the amendments specified in Schedule 23 which are consequential on the amendments made by sections 192, 194 and 195.

(2) If immediately before the commencement of any provision of this Part, which amends Part I of the Financial Services Act 1986 –

(*a*) a designated agency is exercising by virtue of a delegation order under section 114 of that Act any functions of the Secretary of State under that Part, and

(*b*) no draft order is lying before Parliament resuming any of those functions,

the order bringing that provision into force may make, in relation to any functions conferred on the Secretary of State by the amendment, any such provision as may be made by an order under that section.

(3) If immediately before the commencement of any provision of Schedule 23, which amends Part III of the Financial Services Act 1986 –

(*a*) a transferee body (within the meaning of that Act) is exercising by virtue of a transfer order under paragraph 28 of Schedule 11 to that Act any functions of the Registrar under that Part, and

(*b*) no draft order is lying before Parliament resuming any of those functions,
the order bringing that provision into force may make, in relation to any functions
conferred on the Registrar by the amendment, any such provision as may be made by an
order under that paragraph.

(4) References in the Financial Services Act 1986 to a delegation order made under
section 114 of that Act or to a transfer order made under paragraph 28 of Schedule 11 to
that Act include an order made containing any such provision as is authorised by subsection
(2) or (3).

PART IX
TRANSFER OF SECURITIES

207 Transfer of securities

(1) The Secretary of State may make provision by regulations for enabling title to
securities to be evidenced and transferred without a written instrument.
In this section –

- (*a*) "securities" means shares, stock, debentures, debenture stock, loan stock,
  bonds, units of a collective investment scheme within the meaning of the
  Financial Services Act 1986 and other securities of any description; and
- (*b*) references to title to securities include any legal or equitable interest in
  securities; and
- (*c*) references to a transfer of title include a transfer by way of security.

(2) The regulations may make provision –

- (*a*) for procedures for recording and transferring title to securities, and
- (*b*) for the regulation of those procedures and the persons responsible for or
  involved in their operation.

(3) The regulations shall contain such safeguards as appear to the Secretary of State
appropriate for the protection of investors and for ensuring that competition is not
restricted, distorted or prevented.

(4) The regulations may for the purpose of enabling or facilitating the operation of the
new procedures make provision with respect to the rights and obligations of persons in
relation to securities dealt with under the procedures.
But the regulations shall be framed so as to secure that the rights and obligations in
relation to securities dealt with under the new procedures correspond, so far as practicable,
with those which would arise apart from any regulations under this section.

(5) The regulations may include such supplementary, incidental and transitional
provisions as appear to the Secretary of State to be necessary or expedient.
In particular, provision may be made for the purpose of giving effect to –

- (*a*) the transmission of title to securities by operation of law;
- (*b*) any restriction on the transfer of title to securities arising by virtue of the
  provisions of any enactment or instrument, court order or agreement;
- (*c*) any power conferred by any such provision on a person to deal with securities on
  behalf of the person entitled.

(6) The regulations may make provision with respect to the persons responsible for the
operation of the new procedures –

- (*a*) as to the consequences of their insolvency or incapacity, or (*b*) as to the transfer from them to other persons of their functions in relation to the new procedures.

(7) The regulations may for the purposes mentioned above –

(*a*) modify or exclude any provision of any enactment or instrument, or any rule of law;

(*b*) apply, with such modifications as may be appropriate, the provisions of any enactment or instrument (including provisions creating criminal offences);

(*c*) require the payment of fees, or enable persons to require the payment of fees, of such amounts as may be specified in the regulations or determined in accordance with them;

(*d*) empower the Secretary of State to delegate to any person willing and able to discharge them any functions of his under the regulations.

(8) The regulations may make different provision for different cases.

(9) Regulations under this section shall be made by statutory instrument; and no such regulations shall be made unless a draft of the instrument has been laid before and approved by resolution of each House of Parliament.

PART X
MISCELLANEOUS AND GENERAL PROVISIONS

Miscellaneous

208 Summary proceedings in Scotland for offences in connection with disqualification of directors

In section 21 of the Company Directors Disqualification Act 1986 (application of provisions of the Insolvency Act 1986), after subsection (3) add –

"(4) For the purposes of summary proceedings in Scotland, section 431 of that Act applies to summary proceedings for an offence under section 11 or 13 of this Act as it applies to summary proceedings for an offence under Parts I to VII of that Act.".

209 Prosecutions in connection with insider dealing

In section 8 of the Company Securities (Insider Dealing) Act 1985 (punishment of contraventions), in subsection (2) (institution of proceedings in England and Wales), for "by the Secretary of State or by, or with the consent of, the Director of Public Prosecutions" substitute "by, or with the consent of, the Secretary of State or the Director of Public Prosecutions".

210 Restriction of duty to supply statements of premium income

(1) Schedule 3 to the Policyholders Protection Act 1975 (provisions with respect to levies on authorised insurance companies) is amended as follows.

(2) For paragraph 4 (statements of premium income to be sent to Secretary of State) substitute –

"4. – (1) The Secretary of State may by notice in writing require an authorised insurance company to send him a statement of –

   (*a*) any income of the company for the year preceding that in which the notice is received by the company which is income liable to the general business levy, and

   (*b*) any income of the company for that year which is income liable to the long term business levy.

(2) An authorised insurance company which receives a notice under this paragraph shall send that statement required by the notice to the Secretary of State within three months of receiving the notice.

(3) Where an authorised insurance company is required under this paragraph to send a statement to the Secretary of State in respect of income of both descriptions mentioned in sub-paragraph (1)(*a*) and (*b*) above it shall send a separate statement in respect of income of each description.".

(3) In paragraph 5(3) (application of provisions of the Insurance Companies Act 1982 to failure to meet obligation imposed by paragraph 4) for "the obligation imposed on an insurance company in paragraph 4" substitute "an obligation imposed on an insurance company under paragraph 4".

(4) In paragraph 6 (declaration and enforcement of levies) omit sub-paragraph (4) (provision about notices).

(5) After paragraph 7 insert –

"Notices under paragraphs 4 and 6

8. A notice under paragraph 4 or 6 above may be sent by post, and a letter containing such a notice shall be deemed to be properly addressed if it is addressed to the insurance company to which it is sent at its last known place of business in the United Kingdom.".

211 Building societies: miscellaneous amendments

(1) In section 104 of the Building Societies Act 1986 (power to assimilate law relating to building societies and law relating to companies), in subsection (2) (relevant provisions of that Act), omit the word "and" before paragraph (*d*) and after that paragraph add –
   "; and
   (*e*) section 110 (provisions exempting officers and auditors from liability).".

(2) In Schedule 15 to the Building Societies Act 1986 (application of companies winding-up legislation) –
   (*a*) in paragraph 1(*a*) (provisions of Insolvency Act 1986 applied) for "and XII" substitute ", XII and XIII";
   (*b*) in paragraph 3(2)(*b*) (adaptations: references to be omitted), omit ", a shadow director".

(3) In the Company Directors Disqualification Act 1986, after section 22 insert –

"22A Application of Act to building societies

(1) This Act applies to building societies as it applies to companies.

(2) References in this Act to a company, or to a director or an officer of a company include, respectively, references to a building society within the

meaning of the Building Societies Act 1986 or to a director or officer, within the meaning of that Act, of a building society.

(3) In relation to a building society the definition of "shadow director" in section 22(5) applies with the substitution of "building society" for "company".

(4) In the application of Schedule 1 to the directors of a building society, references to provisions of the Insolvency Act or the Companies Act include references to the corresponding provisions of the Building Societies Act 1986.".

General

212 Repeals

The enactments mentioned in Schedule 24 are repealed to the extent specified there.

213 Provisions extending to Northern Ireland

(1) The provisions of this Act extend to Northern Ireland so far as they amend, or provide for the amendment of, an enactment which so extends.

(2) So far as any provision of this Act amends the Companies Act 1985 or the Insolvency Act 1986, its application to companies registered or incorporated in Northern Ireland is subject to section 745(1) of the Companies Act 1985 or section 441(2) of the Insolvency Act 1986, as the case may be.

(3) In Part III (investigations and powers to obtain information), sections 82 to 91, (powers exercisable to assist overseas regulatory authorities) extend to Northern Ireland.

(4) Part VI (mergers and related matters) extends to Northern Ireland.

(5) In Part VII (financial markets and insolvency) the following provisions extend to Northern Ireland –
  - (*a*) sections 154 and 155 (introductory provisions and definition of "market contract"),
  - (*b*) section 156 and Schedule 21 (additional requirements for recognition of investment exchange or clearing house),
  - (*c*) sections 157, 160, 162, and 166 to 169 (provisions relating to recognised investment exchange and clearing houses),
  - (*d*) sections 170 to 172 (power to extend provisions to other financial markets),
  - (*e*) section 184 (indemnity for certain acts), and
  - (*f*) sections 185 to 191 (supplementary provisions).

(6) Part VIII (amendments of Financial Services Act 1986) extends to Northern Ireland.

(7) Part IX (transfer of securities) extends to Northern Ireland.

Subject to any Order made after the passing of this Act by virtue of section 3(1)(*a*) of the Northern Ireland Constitution Act 1973, the transfer of securities shall not be a transferred matter for the purposes of that Act but shall for the purposes of section 3(2) be treated as specified in Schedule 3 to that Act.

(8) In Part X (miscellaneous and general provisions), this section and sections 214 to 216 (general provisions) extend to Northern Ireland.

(9) Except as mentioned above, the provisions of this Act do not extend to Northern Ireland.

214 Making of corresponding provision for Northern Ireland

(1) An Order in Council under paragraph 1(1)(*b*) of Schedule 1 to the Northern Ireland Act 1974 (legislation for Northern Ireland in the interim period) which contains a statement that it is only made for purposes corresponding to the purposes of provisions of this Act to which this section applies –

    (*a*) shall not be subject to paragraph 1(4) and (5) of that Schedule (affirmative resolution of both Houses of Parliament), but

    (*b*) shall be subject to annulment in pursuance of a resolution of either House of Parliament.

(2) The provisions of this Act to which this section applies are –

    (*a*) Parts I to V, and

    (*b*) Part VII, except sections 156, 157 and 169 and Schedule 21.

215 Commencement and transitional provisions

(1) The following provisions of this Act come into force on Royal Assent –

    (*a*) in Part V (amendments of company law), section 141 (application to declare dissolution of company void);

    (*b*) in Part VI (mergers) –

        (i) sections 147 to 150, and

        (ii) paragraphs 2 to 12, 14 to 16, 18 to 20, 22 to 25 of Schedule 20, and section 153 so far as relating to those paragraphs;

    (*c*) in Part VIII (amendments of the Financial Services Act 1986), section 202 (offers of short-dated debentures);

    (*d*) in Part X (miscellaneous and general provisions), the repeals made by Schedule 24 in sections 71, 74, 88 and 89 of, and Schedule 9 to, the Fair Trading Act 1973, and section 212 so far as relating to those repeals.

(2) The other provisions of this Act come into force on such day as the Secretary of State may appoint by order made by statutory instrument; and different days may be appointed for different provisions and different purposes.

(3) An order bringing into force any provision may contain such transitional provisions and savings as appear to the Secretary of State to be necessary or expedient.

(4) The Secretary of State may also by order under this section amend any enactment which refers to the commencement of a provision brought into force by the order so as to substitute a reference to the actual date on which it comes into force.

216 Short title

This Act may be cited as the Companies Act 1989.

SCHEDULES

Section 4(2)

SCHEDULE 1

FORM AND CONTENT OF COMPANY ACCOUNTS

1. Schedule 4 to the Companies Act 1985 (form and content of company accounts) is amended as follows.

Group undertakings

2. – (1) For "group companies", wherever occurring, substitute "group undertakings".

(2) That expression occurs –
- (*a*) in Balance Sheet Format 1, in Items B.III.1 and 2, C.II.2, C.III.1, E.6 and H.6;
- (*b*) in Balance Sheet Format 2 –
  - (i) under the heading "ASSETS", in Items B.III.1 and 2, C.II.2 and C.III.1;
  - (ii) under the heading "LIABILITIES", in Item C.6;
- (*c*) in the Profit and Loss Accounts Formats –
  - (i) in Format 1, Item 7;
  - (ii) in Format 2, Item 9;
  - (iii) in Format 3, Item B.3;
  - (iv) in Format 4, Item B.5;
- (*d*) in Notes (15) and (16) to the profit and loss account formats; and
- (*e*) in the second sentence of paragraph 53(2) (exclusion from requirement to state separately certain loans).

Participating interests

3. – (1) For "shares in related companies", wherever occurring, substitute "participating interests".

(2) That expression occurs –
- (*a*) in Balance Sheet Format 1, Item B.III.3;
- (*b*) in Balance Sheet Format 2, under the heading "ASSETS", in Item B.III.3;
- (*c*) in the Profit and Loss Accounts Formats –
  - (i) in Format 1, Item 8;
  - (ii) in Format 2, Item 10;
  - (iii) in Format 3, Item B.4;
  - (iv) in Format 4, Item B.6.

4. – (1) For "related companies", wherever occurring in any other context, substitute "undertakings in which the company has a participating interest".

(2) Those contexts are –
- (*a*) in Balance Sheet Format 1, in Items B.III.4, C.II.3, E.7 and H.7;
- (*b*) in Balance Sheet Format 2 –
  - (i) under the heading "ASSETS", in Items B.III.4 and C.II.3;
  - (ii) under the heading "LIABILITIES", in Item C.7.

Consistency of accounting policies

5. For paragraph 11 (consistency of accounting policy from one year to the next) substitute –

"11. Accounting policies shall be applied consistently within the same accounts and from one financial year to the next.".

Revaluation reserve

6. In paragraph 34 (revaluation reserve), for sub-paragraph (3) (circumstances in which reduction of reserve required or permitted) substitute –

"(3) An amount may be transferred from the revaluation reserve –
> (*a*)   to the profit and loss account, if the amount was previously charged to that account or represents realised profit, or
> (*b*)   on capitalisation;

and the revaluation reserve shall be reduced to the extent that the amounts transferred to it are no longer necessary for the purposes of the valuation method used.

(3A) In sub-paragraph (3)(*b*) "capitalisation", in relation to an amount standing to the credit of the revaluation reserve, means applying it in wholly or partly paying up unissued shares in the company to be allotted to members of the company as fully or partly paid shares.

(3B) The revaluation reserve shall not be reduced except as mentioned in this paragraph.".

Compliance with accounting standards

7. After paragraph 36 (disclosure of accounting policies) insert –

"36A. It shall be stated whether the accounts have been prepared in accordance with applicable accounting standards and particulars of any material departure from those standards and the reasons for it shall be given.".

Provision for taxation

8. For paragraph 47 (provision for taxation) substitute –

"47. The amount of any provision for deferred taxation shall be stated separately from the amount of any provision for other taxation.".

Loans in connection with assistance for purchase of company's own shares

9. In paragraph 51(2) (disclosure of outstanding loans in connection with certain cases of financial assistance for purchase of company's own shares), after "153(4)(*b*)" insert ",(*bb*)".

Obligation to show corresponding amounts for previous financial year

10. In paragraph 58(3) (exceptions from obligation to show corresponding amount for previous financial year), for paragraphs (*a*) to (*c*) substitute –

"(*a*) paragraph 13 of Schedule 4A (details of accounting treatment of acquisitions),
(*b*) paragraphs 2, 8(3), 16, 21(1)(*d*), 22(4) and (5), 24(3) and (4) and 27(3) and (4) of Schedule 5 (shareholdings in other undertakings),
(*c*) Parts II and III of Schedule 6 (loans and other dealings in favour of directors and others), and
(*d*) paragraphs 42 and 46 above (fixed assets and reserves and provisions).".

Special provisions where company is parent company or subsidiary undertaking

11. – (1) For the heading to Part IV (special provisions where the company is a holding or subsidiary company) substitute –

"PART IV
SPECIAL PROVISIONS WHERE COMPANY IS A PARENT COMPANY OR
SUBSIDIARY UNDERTAKING".

(2) In that Part for paragraph 59 substitute –

"Dealings with or interests in group undertakings

59. Where a company is a parent company or a subsidiary undertaking and any item required by Part I of this Schedule to be shown in the company's balance sheet in relation to group undertakings includes –

    (*a*) amounts attributable to dealings with or interests in any parent undertaking or fellow subsidiary undertaking, or

    (*b*) amounts attributable to dealings with or interests in any subsidiary undertaking of the company,

the aggregate amounts within paragraphs (*a*) and (*b*) respectively shall be shown as separate items, either by way of subdivision of the relevant item in the balance sheet or in a note to the company's accounts.".

(3) After that paragraph insert –

"Guarantees and other financial commitments in favour of group undertakings

59A. Commitments within any of sub-paragraphs (1) to (5) of paragraph 50 (guarantees and other financial commitments) which are undertaken on behalf of or for the benefit of –

    (*a*) any parent undertaking or fellow subsidiary undertaking, or

    (*b*) any subsidiary undertaking of the company,

shall be stated separately from the other commitments within that sub-paragraph, and commitments within paragraph (*a*) shall also be stated separately from those within paragraph (*b*).".

Section 5(2) # SCHEDULE 2

[SCHEDULE 4A TO THE COMPANIES ACT 1985]
FORM AND CONTENT OF GROUP ACCOUNTS

General rules

1. – (1) Group accounts shall comply so far as practicable with the provisions of Schedule 4 as if the undertakings included in the consolidation ("the group") were a single company.

(2) In particular, for the purposes of paragraph 59 of that Schedule (dealings with or interests in group undertakings) as it applies to group accounts –

    (*a*) any subsidiary undertakings of the parent company not included in the consolidation shall be treated as subsidiary undertakings of the group, and

    (*b*) if the parent company is itself a subsidiary undertaking, the group shall be treated as a subsidiary undertaking of any parent undertaking of that company, and the reference to fellow-subsidiary undertakings shall be construed accordingly.

(3) Where the parent company is treated as an investment company for the purposes of Part V of that Schedule (special provisions for investment companies) the group shall be similarly treated.

2. – (1) The consolidated balance sheet and profit and loss account shall incorporate in full the information contained in the individual accounts of the undertakings included in the consolidation, subject to the adjustments authorised or required by the following provisions of this Schedule and to

such other adjustments (if any) as may be appropriate in accordance with generally accepted accounting principles or practice.

(2) If the financial year of a subsidiary undertaking included in the consolidation differs from that of the parent company, the group accounts shall be made up –

    (*a*)   from the accounts of the subsidiary undertaking for its financial year last ending before the end of the parent company's financial year, provided that year ended no more than three months before that of the parent company, or

    (*b*)   from interim accounts prepared by the subsidiary undertaking as at the end of the parent company's financial year.

3. – (1) Where assets and liabilities to be included in the group accounts have been valued or otherwise determined by undertakings according to accounting rules differing from those used for the group accounts, the values or amounts shall be adjusted so as to accord with the rules used for the group accounts.

(2) If it appears to the directors of the parent company that there are special reasons for departing from sub-paragraph (1) they may do so, but particulars of any such departure, the reasons for it and its effect shall be given in a note to the accounts.

(3) The adjustments referred to in this paragraph need not be made if they are not material for the purpose of giving a true and fair view.

4. Any differences of accounting rules as between a parent company's individual accounts for a financial year and its group accounts shall be disclosed in a note to the latter accounts and the reasons for the difference given.

5. Amounts which in the particular context of any provision of this Schedule are not material may be disregarded for the purposes of that provision.

Elimination of group transactions

6. – (1) Debts and claims between undertakings included in the consolidation, and income and expenditure relating to transactions between such undertakings, shall be eliminated in preparing the group accounts.

(2) Where profits and losses resulting from transactions between undertakings includedin the consolidation are included in the book value of assets, they shall be eliminated in preparing the group accounts.

(3) The elimination required by sub-paragraph (2) may be effected in proportion to the group's interest in the shares of the undertakings.

(4) Sub-paragraphs (1) and (2) need not be complied with if the amounts concerned are not material for the purpose of giving a true and fair view.

Acquisition and merger accounting

7. – (1) The following provisions apply where an undertaking becomes a subsidiary undertaking of the parent company.

(2) That event is referred to in those provisions as an "acquisition", and references to the "undertaking acquired" shall be construed accordingly.

8. An acquisition shall be accounted for by the acquisition method of accounting unless the conditions for accounting for it as a merger are met and the merger method of accounting is adopted.

9. – (1) The acquisition method of accounting is as follows.

(2) The identifiable assets and liabilities of the undertaking acquired shall be included in the consolidated balance sheet at their fair values as at the date of acquisition.

In this paragraph the "identifiable" assets or liabilities of the undertaking acquired means the assets or liabilities which are capable of being disposed of or discharged separately, without disposing of a business of the undertaking.

(3) The income and expenditure of the undertaking acquired shall be brought into the group accounts only as from the date of the acquisition.

(4) There shall be set off against the acquisition cost of the interest in the shares of the undertaking held by the parent company and its subsidiary undertakings the interest of the parent company and its subsidiary undertakings in the adjusted capital and reserves of the undertaking acquired.
For this purpose –

> "the acquisition cost" means the amount of any cash consideration and the fair value of any other consideration, together with such amount (if any) in respect of fees and other expenses of the acquisition as the company may determine, and

> "the adjusted capital and reserves" of the undertaking acquired means its capital and reserves at the date of the acquisition after adjusting the identifiable assets and liabilities of the undertaking to fair values as at that date.

(5) The resulting amount if positive shall be treated as goodwill, and if negative as a negative consolidation difference.

10. – (1) The conditions for accounting for an acquisition as a merger are –
>   (a)   that at least 90 per cent. of the nominal value of the relevant shares in the undertaking acquired is held by or on behalf of the parent company and its subsidiary undertakings,
>   (b)   that the proportion referred to in paragraph (a) was attained pursuant to an arrangement providing for the issue of equity shares by the parent company or one or more of its subsidiary undertakings,
>   (c)   that the fair value of any consideration other than the issue of equity shares given pursuant to the arrangement by the parent company and its subsidiary undertakings did not exceed 10 per cent. of the nominal value of the equity shares issued, and
>   (d)   that adoption of the merger method of accounting accords with generally accepted accounting principles of practice.

(2) The reference in sub-paragraph (1)(a) to the "relevant shares" in an undertaking acquired is to those carrying unrestricted rights to participate both in distributions and in the assets of the undertaking upon liquidation.

11. – (1) The merger method of accounting is as follows.

(2) The assets and liabilities of the undertaking acquired shall be brought into the group accounts at the figures at which they stand in the undertaking's accounts, subject to any adjustment authorised or required by this Schedule.

(3) The income and expenditure of the undertaking acquired shall be included in the group accounts for the entire financial year, including the period before the acquisition.

(4) The group accounts shall show corresponding amounts relating to the previous financial year as if the undertaking acquired had been included in the consolidation throughout that year.

(5) There shall be set off against the aggregate of –
>   (a)   the appropriate amount in respect of qualifying shares issued by the parent company or its subsidiary undertakings in consideration for the acquisition of shares in the undertaking acquired, and
>   (b)   the fair value of any other consideration for the acquisition of shares in the undertaking acquired, determined as at the date when those shares were acquired,
the nominal value of the issued share capital of the undertaking acquired held by the parent company and its subsidiary undertakings.

(6) The resulting amount shall be shown as an adjustment to the consolidated reserves.

(7) In sub-paragraph (5)(a) "qualifying shares" means –
>   (a)   shares in relation to which section 131 (merger relief) applies, in respect of which the appropriate amount is the nominal value; or

(*b*) shares in relation to which section 132 (relief in respect of group reconstructions) applies, in respect of which the appropriate amount is the nominal value together with any minimum premium value within the meaning of that section.

12. – (1) Where a group is acquired, paragraphs 9 to 11 apply with the following adaptations.

(2) References to shares of the undertaking acquired shall be construed as references to shares of the parent undertaking of the group.

(3) Other references to the undertaking acquired shall be construed as references to the group; and references to the assets and liabilities, income and expenditure and capital and reserves of the undertaking acquired shall be construed as references to the assets and liabilites, income and expenditure and capital and reserves of the group after making the set-offs and other adjustments required by this Schedule in the case of group accounts.

13. – (1) The following information with respect to acquisitions taking place in the financial year shall be given in a note to the accounts.

(2) There shall be stated –
(*a*) the name of the undertaking acquired or, where a group was acquired, the name of the parent undertaking of that group, and
(*b*) whether the acquisition has been accounted for by the acquisition or the merger method of accounting;
and in relation to an acquisition which significantly affects the figures shown in the group accounts, the following further information shall be given.

(3) The composition and fair value of the consideration for the acquisition given by the parent company and its subsidiary undertakings shall be stated.

(4) The profit or loss of the undertaking or group acquired shall be stated –
(*a*) for the period from the beginning of the financial year of the undertaking or, as the case may be, of the parent undertaking of the group, up to the date of the acquisition, and
(*b*) for the previous financial year of that undertaking or parent undertaking;
and there shall also be stated the date on which the financial year referred to in paragraph (*a*) began.

(5) Where the acquisition method of accounting has been adopted, the book values immediately prior to the acquisition, and the fair values at the date of acquisition, of each class of assets and liabilities of the undertaking or group acquired shall be stated in tabular form, including a statement of the amount of any goodwill or negative consolidation difference arising on the acquisition, together with an explanation of any significant adjustments made.

(6) Where the merger method of accounting has been adopted, an explanation shall be given of any significant adjustments made in relation to the amounts of the assets and liabilities of the undertaking or group acquired, together with a statement of any resulting adjustment to the consolidated reserves (including the re-statement of opening consolidated reserves).

(7) In ascertaining for the purposes of sub-paragraph (4), (5) or (6) the profit or loss of a group, the book values and fair values of assets and liabilities of a group or the amount of the assets and liabilities of a group, the set-offs and other adjustments required by this Schedule in the case of group accounts shall be made.

14. – (1) There shall also be stated in a note to the accounts the cumulative amount of goodwill resulting from acquisitions in that and earlier financial years which has been written off.

(2) That figure shall be shown net of any goodwill attributable to subsidiary undertakings or businesses disposed of prior to the balance sheet date.

15. Where during the financial year there has been a disposal of an undertaking or group which significantly affects the figures shown in the group accounts, there shall be stated in a note to the accounts –
(*a*) the name of that undertaking or, as the case may be, of the parent undertaking of that group, and
(*b*) the extent to which the profit or loss shown in the group accounts is attributable to profit or loss of that undertaking or group.

16. The information required by paragraph 13, 14 or 15 above need not be disclosed with respect to an undertaking which –
  (a)   is established under the law of a country outside the United Kingdom, or
  (b)   carries on business outside the United Kingdom,
if in the opinion of the directors of the parent company the disclosure would be seriously prejudicial to the business of that undertaking or to the business of the parent company or any of its subsidiary undertakings and the Secretary of State agrees that the information should not be disclosed.

Minority interests

17. – (1) The formats set out in Schedule 4 have effect in relation to group accounts with the following additions.

(2) In the Balance Sheet Formats a further item headed "Minority interests" shall be added –
  (a)   in Format 1, either after item J or at the end (after item K), and
  (b)   in Format 2, under the general heading "LIABILITIES", between items A and B;
and under that item shall be shown the amount of capital and reserves attributable to shares in subsidiary undertakings included in the consolidation held by or on behalf of persons other than the parent company and its subsidiary undertakings.

(3) In the Profit and Loss Account Formats a further item headed "Minority interests" shall be added –
  (a)   in Format 1, between items 14 and 15,
  (b)   in Format 2, between items 16 and 17,
  (c)   in Format 3, between items 7 and 8 in both sections A and B, and
  (d)   in Format 4, between items 9 and 10 in both sections A and B;
and under that item shall be shown the amount of any profit or loss on ordinary activities attributable to shares in subsidiary undertakings included in the consolidation held by or on behalf of persons other than the parent company and its subsidiary undertakings.

(4) In the Profit and Loss Account Formats a further item headed "Minority interests" shall be added –
  (a)   in Format 1, between items 18 and 19,
  (b)   in Format 2, between items 20 and 21,
  (c)   in Format 3, between items 9 and 10 in section A and between items 8 and 9 in section B, and
  (d)   in Format 4, between items 11 and 12 in section A and between items 10 and 11 in section B;
and under that item shall be shown the amount of any profit or loss on extraordinary activities attributable to shares in subsidiary undertakings included in the consolidation held by or on behalf of persons other than the parent company and its subsidiary undertakings.

(5) For the purposes of paragraph 3(3) and (4) of Schedule 4 (power to adapt or combine items) –
  (a)   the additional item required by sub-paragraph (2) above shall be treated as one to which a letter is assigned, and
  (b)   the additional items required by sub-paragraphs (3) and (4) above shall be treated as ones to which an Arabic number is assigned.

Interests in subsidiary undertakings excluded from consolidation

18. The interest of the group in subsidiary undertakings excluded from consolidation under section 229(4) (undertakings with activities different from those of undertakings included in the consolidation), and the amount of profit or loss attributable to such an interest, shall be shown in the consolidated balance sheet or, as the case may be, in the consolidated profit and loss account by the equity method of accounting (including dealing with any goodwill arising in accordance with paragraphs 17 to 19 and 21 of Schedule 4).

Joint ventures

19. – (1) Where an undertaking included in the consolidation manages another undertaking jointly with one or more undertakings not included in the consolidation, that other undertaking ("the joint venture") may, if it is not –

    (*a*) a body corporate, or

    (*b*) a subsidiary undertaking of the parent company,

be dealt with in the group accounts by the method of proportional consolidation.

(2) The provisions of this Part relating to the preparation of consolidated accounts apply, with any necessary modifications, to proportional consolidation under this paragraph.

Associated undertakings

20. – (1) An "associated undertaking" means an undertaking in which an undertaking included in the consolidation has a participating interest and over whose operating and financial policy it exercises a significant influence, and which is not –

    (*a*) a subsidiary undertaking of the parent company, or

    (*b*) a joint venture dealt with in accordance with paragraph 19.

(2) Where an undertaking holds 20 per cent. or more of the voting rights in another undertaking, it shall be presumed to exercise such an influence over it unless the contrary is shown.

(3) The voting rights in an undertaking means the rights conferred on shareholders in respect of their shares or, in the case of an undertaking not having a share capital, on members, to vote at general meetings of the undertaking on all, or substantially all, matters.

(4) The provisions of paragraphs 5 to 11 of Schedule 10A (rights to be taken into account and attribution of rights) apply in determining for the purposes of this paragraph whether an undertaking holds 20 per cent. or more of the voting rights in another undertaking.

21. – (1) The formats set out in Schedule 4 have effect in relation to group accounts with the following modifications.

(2) In the Balance Sheet Formats the items headed "Participating interests", that is –

    (*a*) in Format 1, item B.III.3, and

    (*b*) in Format 2, item B.III.3 under the heading "ASSETS",

shall be replaced by two items, "Interests in associated undertakings" and "Other participating interests".

(3) In the Profit and Loss Account Formats, the items headed "Income from participating interests", that is –

    (*a*) in Format 1, item 8,

    (*b*) in Format 2, item 10,

    (*c*) in Format 3, item B.4, and

    (*d*) in Format 4, item B.6,

shall be replaced by two items, "Income from interests in associated undertakings" and "Income from other participating interests".

22. – (1) The interest of an undertaking in an associated undertaking, and the amount of profit or loss attributable to such an interest, shall be shown by the equity method of accounting (including dealing with any goodwill arising in accordance with paragraphs 17 to 19 and 21 of Schedule 4).

(2) Where the associated undertaking is itself a parent undertaking, the net assets and profits or losses to be taken into account are those of the parent and its subsidiary undertakings (after making any consolidation adjustments).

(3) The equity method of accounting need not be applied if the amounts in question are not material for the purpose of giving a true and fair view.

SCHEDULE 3

[SCHEDULE 5 TO THE COMPANIES ACT 1985]
DISCLOSURE OF INFORMATION: RELATED UNDERTAKINGS

PART I
COMPANIES NOT REQUIRED TO PREPARE GROUP ACCOUNTS

Subsidiary undertakings

1. – (1) The following information shall be given where at the end of the financial year the company has subsidiary undertakings.

(2) The name of each subsidiary undertaking shall be stated.

(3) There shall be stated with respect to each subsidiary undertaking –
    (*a*) if it is incorporated outside Great Britain, the country in which it is incorporated;
    (*b*) if it is incorporated in Great Britain, whether it is registered in England and Wales or in Scotland;
    (*c*) if it is unincorporated, the address of its principal place of business.

(4) The reason why the company is not required to prepare group accounts shall be stated.

(5) If the reason is that all the subsidiary undertakings of the company fall within the exclusions provided for in section 229, it shall be stated with respect to each subsidiary undertaking which of those exclusions applies.

Holdings in subsidiary undertakings

2. – (1) There shall be stated in relation to shares of each class held by the company in a subsidiary undertaking –
    (*a*) the identity of the class, and
    (*b*) the proportion of the nominal value of the shares of that class represented by those shares.

(2) The shares held by or on behalf of the company itself shall be distinguished from those attributed to the company which are held by or on behalf of a subsidiary undertaking.

Financial information about subsidiary undertakings

3. – (1) There shall be disclosed with respect to each subsidiary undertaking –
    (*a*) the aggregate amount of its capital and reserves as at the end of its relevant financial year, and
    (*b*) its profit or loss for that year.

(2) That information need not be given if the company is exempt by virtue of section 228 from the requirement to prepare group accounts (parent company included in accounts of larger group).

(3) That information need not be given if –
    (*a*) the subsidiary undertaking is not required by any provision of this Act to deliver a copy of its balance sheet for its relevant financial year and does not otherwise publish that balance sheet in Great Britain or elsewhere, and
    (*b*) the company's holding is less than 50 per cent. of the nominal value of the shares in the undertaking.

(4) Information otherwise required by this paragraph need not be given if it is not material.

(5) For the purposes of this paragraph the "relevant financial year" of a subsidiary undertaking is –
    (*a*) if its financial year ends with that of the company, that year, and

(*b*)   if not, its financial year ending last before the end of the company's financial year.

Financial years of subsidiary undertakings

4. Where the financial year of one or more subsidiary undertakings did not end with that of the company, there shall be stated in relation to each such undertaking –

(*a*)   the reasons why the company's directors consider that its financial year should not end with that of the company, and

(*b*)   the date on which its last financial year ended (last before the end of the company's financial year).

Instead of the dates required by paragraph (*b*) being given for each subsidiary undertaking the earliest and latest of those dates may be given.

Further information about subsidiary undertakings

5. – (1) There shall be disclosed –

(*a*)   any qualifications contained in the auditors' reports on the accounts of subsidiary undertakings for financial years ending with or during the financial year of the company, and

(*b*)   any note or saving contained in such accounts to call attention to a matter which, apart from the note or saving, would properly have been referred to in such a qualification,

in so far as the matter which is the subject of the qualification or note is not covered by the company's own accounts and is material from the point of view of its members.

(2) The aggregate amount of the total investment of the company in the shares of subsidiary undertakings shall be stated by way of the equity method of valuation, unless –

(*a*)   the company is exempt from the requirement to prepare group accounts by virtue of section 228 (parent company included in accounts of larger group), and

(*b*)   the directors state their opinion that the aggregate value of the assets of the company consisting of shares in, or amounts owing (whether on account of a loan or otherwise) from, the company's subsidiary undertakings is not less than the aggregate of the amounts at which those assets are stated or included in the company's balance sheet.

(3) In so far as information required by this paragraph is not obtainable, a statement to that effect shall be given instead.

Shares and debentures of company held by subsidiary undertakings

6. – (1) The number, description and amount of the shares in and debentures of the company held by or on behalf of its subsidiary undertakings shall be disclosed.

(2) Sub-paragraph (1) does not apply in relation to shares or debentures in the case of which the subsidiary undertaking is concerned as personal representative or, subject as follows, as trustee.

(3) The exception for shares or debentures in relation to which the subsidiary undertaking is concerned as trustee does not apply if the company, or any subsidiary undertaking of the company, is beneficially interested under the trust, otherwise than by way of security only for the purposes of a transaction entered into by it in the ordinary course of a business which includes the lending of money.

(4) Schedule 2 to this Act has effect for the interpretation of the reference in sub-paragraph (3) to a beneficial interest under a trust.

Significant holdings in undertakings other than subsidiary undertakings

7. – (1) The information required by paragraphs 8 and 9 shall be given where at the end of the financial year the company has a significant holding in an undertaking which is not a subsidiary undertaking of the company.

(2) A holding is significant for this purpose if –
- (*a*) it amounts to 10 per cent. or more of the nominal value of any class of shares in the undertaking, or
- (*b*) the amount of the holding (as stated or included in the company's accounts) exceeds one-tenth of the amount (as so stated) of the company's assets.

8. – (1) The name of the undertaking shall be stated.

(2) There shall be stated –
- (*a*) if the undertaking is incorporated outside Great Britain, the country in which it is incorporated;
- (*b*) if it is incorporated in Great Britain, whether it is registered in England and Wales or in Scotland;
- (*c*) if it is unincorporated, the address of its principal place of business.

(3) There shall also be stated –
- (*a*) the identity of each class of shares in the undertaking held by the company, and
- (*b*) the proportion of the nominal value of the shares of that class represented by those shares.

9. – (1) Where the company has a significant holding in an undertaking amounting to 20 per cent. or more of the nominal value of the shares in the undertaking, there shall also be stated –
- (*a*) the aggregate amount of the capital and reserves of the undertaking as at the end of its relevant financial year, and
- (*b*) its profit or loss for that year.

(2) That information need not be given if –
- (*a*) the company is exempt by virtue of section 228 from the requirement to prepare group accounts (parent company included in accounts of larger group), and
- (*b*) the investment of the company in all undertakings in which it has such a holding as is mentioned in sub-paragraph (1) is shown, in aggregate, in the notes to the accounts by way of the equity method of valuation.

(3) That information need not be given in respect of an undertaking if –
- (*a*) the undertaking is not required by any provision of this Act to deliver a copy of its balance sheet for its relevant financial year and does not otherwise publish that balance sheet in Great Britain or elsewhere, and
- (*b*) the company's holding is less than 50 per cent. of the nominal value of the shares in the undertaking.

(4) Information otherwise required by this paragraph need not be given if it is not material.

(5) For the purposes of this paragraph the "relevant financial year" of an undertaking is –
- (*a*) if its financial year ends with that of the company, that year, and
- (*b*) if not, its financial year ending last before the end of the company's financial year.

Arrangements attracting merger relief

10. – (1) This paragraph applies to arrangements attracting merger relief, that is, where a company allots shares in consideration for the issue, transfer or cancellation of shares in another body corporate ("the other company") in circumstances such that section 130 of this Act (share premium account) does not, by virtue of section 131(2) (merger relief), apply to the premiums on the shares.

(2) If the company makes such an arrangement during the financial year, the following information shall be given –
- (*a*) the name of the other company,
- (*b*) the number, nominal value and class of shares allotted,
- (*c*) the number, nominal value and class of shares in the other company issued, transferred or cancelled, and
- (*d*) particulars of the accounting treatment adopted in the company's accounts in respect of the issue, transfer or cancellation.

(3) Where the company made such an arrangement during the financial year, or during either of the two preceding financial years, and there is included in the company's profit and loss account –

    (*a*)   any profit or loss realised during the financial year by the company on the disposal of –
        (i)   any shares in the other company, or
        (ii) any assets which were fixed assets of the other company or any of its subsidiary undertakings at the time of the arrangement, or
    (*b*)   any part of any profit or loss realised during the financial year by the company on the disposal of any shares (other than shares in the other company) which was attributable to the fact that there were at the time of the disposal amongst the assets of the company which issued the shares, or any of its subsidiary undertakings, such shares or assets as are described in paragraph (*a*) above,

then, the net amount of that profit or loss or, as the case may be, the part so attributable shall be shown, together with an explanation of the transactions to which the information relates.

(4) For the purposes of this paragraph the time of the arrangement shall be taken to be –

    (*a*)   where as a result of the arrangement the other company becomes a subsidiary undertaking of the company, the date on which it does so or, if the arrangement in question becomes binding only on the fulfilment of a condition, the date on which that condition is fulfilled;
    (*b*)   if the other company is already a subsidiary undertaking of the company, the date on which the shares are allotted or, if they are allotted on different days, the first day.

Parent undertaking drawing up accounts for larger group

11. – (1) Where the company is a subsidiary undertaking, the following information shall be given with respect to the parent undertaking of –

    (*a*)   the largest group of undertakings for which group accounts are drawn up and of which the company is a member, and
    (*b*)   the smallest such group of undertakings.

(2) The name of the parent undertaking shall be stated.

(3) There shall be stated –

    (*a*)   if the undertaking is incorporated outside Great Britain, the country in which it is incorporated;
    (*b*)   if it is incorporated in Great Britain, whether it is registered in England and Wales or in Scotland;
    (*c*)   if it is unincorporated, the address of its principal place of business.

(4) If copies of the group accounts referred to in sub-paragraph (1) are available to the public, there shall also be stated the addresses from which copies of the accounts can be obtained.

Identification of ultimate parent company

12. – (1) Where the company is a subsidiary undertaking, the following information shall be given with respect to the company (if any) regarded by the directors as being the company's ultimate parent company.

(2) The name of that company shall be stated.

(3) If known to the directors, there shall be stated –

    (*a*)   if that company is incorporated outside Great Britain, the country in which it is incorporated;
    (*b*)   if it is incorporated in Great Britain, whether it is registered in England and Wales or in Scotland.

(4) In this paragraph "company" includes any body corporate.

Constructions of references to shares held by company

13. – (1) References in this Part of this Schedule to shares held by a company shall be construed as follows.

(2) For the purposes of paragraphs 2 to 5 (information about subsidiary undertakings) –

    (*a*)   there shall be attributed to the company any shares held by a subsidiary undertaking, or by a person acting on behalf of the company or a subsidiary undertaking; but

    (*b*)   there shall be treated as not held by the company any shares held on behalf of a person other than the company or a subsidiary undertaking.

(3) For the purposes of paragraphs 7 to 9 (information about undertakings other than subsidiary undertakings) –

    (*a*)   there shall be attributed to the company shares held on its behalf by any person; but

    (*b*)   there shall be treated as not held by a company shares held on behalf of a person other than the company.

(4) For the purposes of any of those provisions, shares held by way of security shall be treated as held by the person providing the security –

    (*a*)   where apart from the right to exercise them for the purpose of preserving the value of the security, or of realising it, the rights attached to the shares are exercisable only in accordance with his instructions, and

    (*b*)   where the shares are held in connection with the granting of loans as part of normal business activities and apart from the right to exercise them for the purposes of preserving the value of the security, or of realising it, the rights attached to the shares are exercisable only in his interests.

PART II
COMPANIES REQUIRED TO PREPARE GROUP ACCOUNTS

Introductory

14. In this Part of this Schedule "the group" means the group consisting of the parent company and its subsidiary undertakings.

Subsidiary undertakings

15. – (1) The following information shall be given with respect to the undertakings which are subsidiary undertakings of the parent company at the end of the financial year.

(2) The name of each undertaking shall be stated.

(3) There shall be stated –

    (*a*)   if the undertaking is incorporated outside Great Britain, the country in which it is incorporated;

    (*b*)   if it is incorporated in Great Britain, whether it is registered in England and Wales or in Scotland;

    (*c*)   if it is unincorporated, the address of its principal place of business.

(4) It shall also be stated whether the subsidiary undertaking is included in the consolidation and, if it is not, the reasons for excluding it from consolidation shall be given.

(5) It shall be stated with respect to each subsidiary undertaking by virtue of which of the conditions specified in section 258(2) or (4) it is a subsidiary undertaking of its immediate parent undertaking.

That information need not be given if the relevant condition is that specified in subsection (2)(*a*) of that section (holding of a majority of the voting rights) and the immediate parent undertaking holds the same proportion of the shares in the undertaking as it holds voting rights.

Holdings in subsidiary undertakings

16. – (1) The following information shall be given with respect to the shares of a subsidiary undertaking held –

    (*a*) by the parent company, and

    (*b*) by the group;

and the information under paragraphs (*a*) and (*b*) shall (if different) be shown separately.

(2) There shall be stated –

    (*a*) the identity of each class of shares held, and

    (*b*) the proportion of the nominal value of the shares of that class represented by those shares.

Financial information about subsidiary undertakings not included in the consolidation

17. – (1) There shall be shown with respect to each subsidiary undertaking not included in the consolidation –

    (*a*) the aggregate amount of its capital and reserves as at the end of its relevant financial year, and

    (*b*) its profit or loss for that year.

(2) That information need not be given if the group's investment in the undertaking is included in the accounts by way of the equity method of valuation or if –

    (*a*) the undertaking is not required by any provision of this Act to deliver a copy of its balance sheet for its relevant financial year and does not otherwise publish that balance sheet in Great Britain or elsewhere, and

    (*b*) the holding of the group is less than 50 per cent. of the nominal value of the shares in the undertaking.

(3) Information otherwise required by this paragraph need not be given if it is not material.

(4) For the purposes of this paragraph the "relevant financial year" of a subsidiary undertaking is –

    (*a*) if its financial year ends with that of the company, that year, and

    (*b*) if not, its financial year ending last before the end of the company's financial year.

Further information about subsidiary undertakings excluded from consolidation

18. – (1) The following information shall be given with respect to subsidiary undertakings excluded from consolidation.

(2) There shall be disclosed –

    (*a*) any qualifications contained in the auditors' reports on the accounts of the undertaking for financial years ending with or during the financial year of the company, and

    (*b*) any note or saving contained in such accounts to call attention to a matter which, apart from the note or saving, would properly have been referred to in such a qualification,

in so far as the matter which is the subject of the qualification or note is not covered by the consolidated accounts and is material from the point of view of the members of the parent company.

(3) In so far as information required by this paragraph is not obtainable, a statement to that effect shall be given instead.

Financial years of subsidiary undertakings

19. Where the financial year of one or more subsidiary undertakings did not end with that of the company, there shall be stated in relation to each such undertaking –

    (*a*) the reasons why the company's directors consider that its financial year should not end with that of the company, and

    (*b*) the date on which its last financial year ended (last before the end of the company's financial year).

Instead of the dates required by paragraph (*b*) being given for each subsidiary undertaking the earliest and latest of those dates may be given.

Shares and debentures of company held by subsidiary undertakings

20. – (1) The number, description and amount of the shares in and debentures of the company held by or on behalf of its subsidiary undertakings shall be disclosed.

(2) Sub-paragraph (1) does not apply in relation to shares or debentures in the case of which the subsidiary undertaking is concerned as personal representative or, subject as follows, as trustee.

(3) The exception for shares or debentures in relation to which the subsidiary undertaking is concerned as trustee does not apply if the company or any of its subsidiary undertakings is beneficially interested under the trust, otherwise than by way of security only for the purposes of a transaction entered into by it in the ordinary course of a business which includes the lending of money.

(4) Schedule 2 to this Act has effect for the interpretation of the reference in sub-paragraph (3) to a beneficial interest under a trust.

Joint ventures

21. – (1) The following information shall be given where an undertaking is dealt with in the consolidated accounts by the method of proportional consolidation in accordance with paragraph 19 of Schedule 4A (joint ventures) –
- (*a*) the name of the undertaking;
- (*b*) the address of the principal place of business of the undertaking;
- (*c*) the factors on which joint management of the undertaking is based; and
- (*d*) the proportion of the capital of the undertaking held by undertakings included in the consolidation.

(2) Where the financial year of the undertaking did not end with that of the company, there shall be stated the date on which a financial year of the undertaking last ended before that date.

Associated undertakings

22. – (1) The following information shall be given where an undertaking included in the consolidation has an interest in an associated undertaking.

(2) The name of the associated undertaking shall be stated.

(3) There shall be stated –
- (*a*) if the undertaking is incorporated outside Great Britain, the country in which it is incorporated;
- (*b*) if it is incorporated in Great Britain, whether it is registered in England and Wales or in Scotland;
- (*c*) if it is unincorporated, the address of its principal place of business.

(4) The following information shall be given with respect to the shares of the undertaking held –
- (*a*) by the parent company, and
- (*b*) by the group;

and the information under paragraphs (*a*) and (*b*) shall be shown separately.

(5) There shall be stated –
- (*a*) the identity of each class of shares held, and
- (*b*) the proportion of the nominal value of the shares of that class represented by those shares.

(6) In this paragraph "associated undertaking" has the meaning given by paragraph 20 of Schedule 4A; and the information required by this paragraph shall be given notwithstanding that paragraph 22(3) of that Schedule (materiality) applies in relation to the accounts themselves.

Other significant holdings of parent company or group

23. – (1) The information required by paragraphs 24 and 25 shall be given where at the end of the financial year the parent company has a significant holding in an undertaking which is not one of its subsidiary undertakings and does not fall within paragraph 21 (joint ventures) or paragraph 22 (associated undertakings).

(2) A holding is significant for this purpose if –
   (*a*) it amounts to 10 per cent. or more of the nominal value of any class of shares in the undertaking, or
   (*b*) the amount of the holding (as stated or included in the company's individual accounts) exceeds one-tenth of the amount of its assets (as so stated).

24. – (1) The name of the undertaking shall be stated.

(2) There shall be stated –
   (*a*) if the undertaking is incorporated outside Great Britain, the country in which it is incorporated;
   (*b*) if it is incorporated in Great Britain, whether it is registered in England and Wales or in Scotland;
   (*c*) if it is unincorporated, the address of its principal place of business.

(3) The following information shall be given with respect to the shares of the undertaking held by the parent company.

(4) There shall be stated –
   (*a*) the identity of each class of shares held, and
   (*b*) the proportion of the nominal value of the shares of that class represented by those shares.

25. – (1) Where the company has a significant holding in an undertaking amounting to 20 per cent. or more of the nominal value of the shares in the undertaking, there shall also be stated –
   (*a*) the aggregate amount of the capital and reserves of the undertaking as at the end of its relevant financial year, and
   (*b*) its profit or loss for that year.

(2) That information need not be given in respect of an undertaking if –
   (*a*) the undertaking is not required by any provision of this Act to deliver a copy of its balance sheet for its relevant financial year and does not otherwise publish that balance sheet in Great Britain or elsewhere, and
   (*b*) the company's holding is less than 50 per cent. of the nominal value of the shares in the undertaking.

(3) Information otherwise required by this paragraph need not be given if it is not material.

(4) For the purposes of this paragraph the "relevant financial year" of an undertaking is –
   (*a*) if its financial year ends with that of the company, that year, and
   (*b*) if not, its financial year ending last before the end of the company's financial year.

26. – (1) The information required by paragraphs 27 and 28 shall be given where at the end of the financial year the group has a significant holding in an undertaking which is not a subsidiary undertaking of the parent company and does not fall within paragraph 21 (joint ventures) or paragraph 22 (associated undertakings).

(2) A holding is significant for this purpose if –
   (*a*) it amounts to 10 per cent. or more of the nominal value of any class of shares in the undertaking, or
   (*b*) the amount of the holding (as stated or included in the group accounts) exceeds one-tenth of the amount of the group's assets (as so stated).

27. – (1) The name of the undertaking shall be stated.

(2) There shall be stated –

(*a*) if the undertaking is incorporated outside Great Britain, the country in which it is incorporated;

(*b*) if it is incorporated in Great Britain, whether it is registered in England and Wales or in Scotland;

(*c*) if it is unincorporated, the address of its principal place of business.

(3) The following information shall be given with respect to the shares of the undertaking held by the group.

(4) There shall be stated –

(*a*) the identity of each class of shares held, and

(*b*) the proportion of the nominal value of the shares of that class represented by those shares.

28. – (1) Where the holding of the group amounts to 20 per cent. or more of the nominal value of the shares in the undertaking, there shall also be stated –

(*a*) the aggregate amount of the capital and reserves of the undertaking as at the end of its relevant financial year, and

(*b*) its profit or loss for that year.

(2) That information need not be given if –

(*a*) the undertaking is not required by any provision of this Act to deliver a copy of its balance sheet for its relevant financial year and does not otherwise publish that balance sheet in Great Britain or elsewhere, and

(*b*) the holding of the group is less than 50 per cent. of the nominal value of the shares in the undertaking.

(3) Information otherwise required by this paragraph need not be given if it is not material.

(4) For the purposes of this paragraph the "relevant financial year" of an outside undertaking is –

(*a*) if its financial year ends with that of the parent company, that year, and

(*b*) if not, its financial year ending last before the end of the parent company's financial year.

Arrangements attracting merger relief

29. – (1) This paragraph applies to arrangements attracting merger relief, that is, where a company allots shares in consideration for the issue, transfer or cancellation of shares in another body corporate ("the other company") in circumstances such that section 130 of this Act (share premium account) does not, by virtue of section 131(2) (merger relief), apply to the premiums on the shares.

(2) If the parent company made such an arrangement during the financial year, the following information shall be given –

(*a*) the name of the other company,

(*b*) the number, nominal value and class of shares allotted,

(*c*) the number, nominal value and class of shares in the other company issued, transferred or cancelled, and

(*d*) particulars of the accounting treatment adopted in the parent company's individual and group accounts in respect of the issue, transfer or cancellation, and

(*e*) particulars of the extent to which and manner in which the profit or loss for the financial year shown in the group accounts is affected by any profit or loss of the other company, or any of its subsidiary undertakings, which arose before the time of the arrangement.

(3) Where the parent company made such an arrangement during the financial year, or during either of the two preceding financial years, and there is included in the consolidated profit and loss account –

(*a*) any profit or loss realised during the financial year on the disposal of –

(i) any shares in the other company, or

(ii) any assets which were fixed assets of the other company or any of its subsidiary undertakings at the time of the arrangement, or

(*b*) any part of any profit or loss realised during the financial year on the disposal of any shares (other than shares in the other company) which was attributable to the fact that there were at the time of the disposal amongst the assets of the company which issued the shares, or any of its subsidiary undertakings, such shares or assets as are described in paragraph (*a*) above,

then, the net amount of that profit or loss or, as the case may be, the part so attributable shall be shown, together with an explanation of the transactions to which the information relates.

(4) For the purposes of this paragraph the time of the arrangement shall be taken to be –

    (*a*) where as a result of the arrangement the other company becomes a subsidiary undertaking of the company in question, the date on which it does so or, if the arrangement in question becomes binding only on the fulfilment of a condition, the date on which that condition is fulfilled;

    (*b*) if the other company is already a subsidiary undertaking of that company, the date on which the shares are allotted or, if they are allotted on different days, the first day.

Parent undertaking drawing up accounts for larger group

30. – (1) Where the parent company is itself a subsidiary undertaking, the following information shall be given with respect to that parent undertaking of the company which heads –

    (*a*) the largest group of undertakings for which group accounts are drawn up and of which that company is a member, and

    (*b*) the smallest such group of undertakings.

(2) The name of the parent undertaking shall be stated.

(3) There shall be stated –

    (*a*) if the undertaking is incorporated outside Great Britain, the country in which it is incorporated;

    (*b*) if it is incorporated in Great Britain, whether it is registered in England and Wales or in Scotland;

    (*c*) if it is unincorporated, the address of its principal place of business.

(4) If copies of the group accounts referred to in sub-paragraph (1) are available to the public, there shall also be stated the addresses from which copies of the accounts can be obtained.

Identification of ultimate parent company

31. – (1) Where the parent company is itself a subsidiary undertaking, the following information shall be given with respect to the company (if any) regarded by the directors as being that company's ultimate parent company.

(2) The name of that company shall be stated.

(3) If known to the directors, there shall be stated –

    (*a*) if that company is incorporated outside Great Britain, the country in which it is incorporated;

    (*b*) if it is incorporated in Great Britain, whether it is registered in England and Wales or in Scotland.

(4) In this paragraph "company" includes any body corporate.

Construction of references to shares held by parent company or group

32. – (1) References in this Part of this Schedule to shares held by the parent company or the group shall be construed as follows.

(2) For the purposes of paragraphs 16, 22(4) and (5) and 23 to 25 (information about holdings in subsidiary and other undertakings) –

(*a*) there shall be attributed to the parent company shares held on its behalf by any person; but

(*b*) there shall be treated as not held by the parent company shares held on behalf of a person other than the company.

(3) References to shares held by the group are to any shares held by or on behalf of the parent company or any of its subsidiary undertakings; but there shall be treated as not held by the group any shares held on behalf of a person other than the parent company or any of its subsidiary undertakings.

(4) Shares held by way of security shall be treated as held by the person providing the security –

(*a*) where apart from the right to exercise them for the purpose of preserving the value of the security, or of realising it, the rights attached to the shares are exercisable only in accordance with his instructions, and

(*b*) where the shares are held in connection with the granting of loans as part of normal business activities and apart from the right to exercise them for the purpose of preserving the value of the security, or of realising it, the rights attached to the shares are exercisable only in his interests.

Section 6(4)

SCHEDULE 4

DISCLOSURE OF INFORMATION: EMOLUMENTS AND OTHER BENEFITS OF DIRECTORS AND OTHERS

1. Schedule 6 to the Companies Act 1985 is amended as follows.

2. For the heading substitute –

"DISCLOSURE OF INFORMATION: EMOLUMENTS AND OTHER BENEFITS OF DIRECTORS AND OTHERS".

3. Insert the following provisions (which reproduce, with amendments, the former Part V of Schedule 5 to that Act) as Part I –

"PART I
CHAIRMAN'S AND DIRECTORS' EMOLUMENTS, PENSIONS AND COMPENSATION FOR LOSS OF OFFICE

Aggregate amount of directors' emoluments

1. – (1) The aggregate amount of directors' emoluments shall be shown.

(2) This means the emoluments paid to or receivable by any person in respect of –
   (*a*) his services as a director of the company, or
   (*b*) his services while director of the company –
      (i) as director of any of its subsidiary undertakings, or
      (ii) otherwise in connection with the management of the affairs of the company or any of its subsidiary undertakings.

(3) There shall also be shown, separately, the aggregate amount within sub-paragraph (2)(*a*) and (*b*)(i) and the aggregate amount within sub-paragraph (2)(*b*)(ii).

(4) For the purposes of this paragraph the "emoluments" of a person include –
   (*a*) fees and percentages,
   (*b*) sums paid by way of expenses allowance (so far as those sums are chargeable to United Kingdom income tax),
   (*c*) contributions paid in respect of him under any pension scheme, and

    (*d*) the estimated money value of any other benefits received by him otherwise than in cash,

and emoluments in respect of a person's accepting office as director shall be treated as emoluments in respect of his services as director.

Details of chairman's and directors' emoluments

2. Where the company is a parent company or a subsidiary undertaking, or where the amount shown in compliance with paragraph 1(1) is £60,000 or more, the information required by paragraphs 3 to 6 shall be given with respect to the emoluments of the chairman and directors, and emoluments waived.

3. – (1) The emoluments of the chairman shall be shown.

(2) The "chairman" means the person elected by the directors to be chairman of their meetings, and includes a person who, though not so elected, holds an office (however designated) which in accordance with the company's constitution carries with it functions substantially similar to those discharged by a person so elected.

(3) Where there has been more than one chairman during the year, the emoluments of each shall be stated so far as attributable to the period during which he was chairman.

(4) The emoluments of a person need not be shown if his duties as chairman were wholly or mainly discharged outside the United Kingdom.

4. – (1) The following information shall be given with respect to the emoluments of directors.

(2) There shall be shown the number of directors whose emoluments fell within each of the following bands –

        not more than £5,000,
        more than £5,000 but not more than £10,000,
        more than £10,000 but not more than £15,000,
        and so on.

(3) If the emoluments of any of the directors exceeded that of the chairman, there shall be shown the greatest amount of emoluments of any director.

(4) Where more than one person has been chairman during the year, the reference in sub-paragraph (3) to the emoluments of the chairman is to the aggregate of the emoluments of each person who has been chairman, so far as attributable to the period during which he was chairman.

(5) The information required by sub-paragraph (2) need not be given in respect of a director who discharged his duties as such wholly or mainly outside the United Kingdom; and any such director shall be left out of account for the purposes of sub-paragraph (3).

5. In paragraphs 3 and 4 "emoluments" has the same meaning as in paragraph 1, except that it does not include contributions paid in respect of a person under a pension scheme.

Emoluments waived

6. – (1) There shall be shown –
    (*a*) the number of directors who have waived rights to receive emoluments which, but for the waiver, would have fallen to be included in the amount shown under paragraph 1(1), and
    (*b*) the aggregate amount of those emoluments.

(2) For the purposes of this paragraph it shall be assumed that a sum not receivable in respect of a period would have been paid at the time at which it was due, and if such a sum was payable only on demand, it shall be deemed to have been due at the time of the waiver.

Pensions of directors and past directors

7. – (1) There shall be shown the aggregate amount of directors' or past directors' pensions.

(2) This amount does not include any pension paid or receivable under a pension scheme if the scheme is such that the contributions under it are substantially adequate for the maintenance of the scheme; but, subject to this, it includes any pension paid or receivable in respect of any such services of a director or past director as are mentioned in paragraph 1(2), whether to or by him or, on his nomination or by virtue of dependence on or other connection with him, to or by any other person.

(3) The amount shown shall distinguish between pensions in respect of services as director, whether of the company or any of its subsidiary undertakings, and other pensions.

(4) References to pensions include benefits otherwise than in cash and in relation to so much of a pension as consists of such a benefit references to its amount are to the estimated money value of the benefit.
The nature of any such benefit shall also be disclosed.

Compensation to directors for loss of office

8. – (1) There shall be shown the aggregate amount of any compensation to directors or past directors in respect of loss of office.

(2) This amount includes compensation received or receivable by a director or past director for –
   (a) loss of office as director of the company, or
   (b) loss, while director of the company or on or in connection with his ceasing to be a director of it, of –
      (i) any other office in connection with the management of the company's affairs, or
      (ii) any office as director or otherwise in connection with the management of the affairs of any subsidiary undertaking of the company;
and shall distinguish between compensation in respect of the office of director, whether of the company or any of its subsidiary undertakings, and compensation in respect of other offices.

(3) References to compensation include benefits otherwise than in cash; and in relation to such compensation references to its amount are to the estimated money value of the benefit.
The nature of any such compensation shall be disclosed.

(4) References to compensation for loss of office include compensation in consideration for, or in connection with, a person's retirement from office.

Sums paid to third parties in respect of directors' services

9. – (1) There shall be shown the aggregate amount of any consideration paid to or receivable by third parties for making available the services of any person –
   (a) as a director of the company, or
   (b) while director of the company –
      (i) as director of any of its subsidiary undertakings, or
      (ii) otherwise in connection with the management of the affairs of the company or any of its subsidiary undertakings.

(2) The reference to consideration includes benefits otherwise than in cash; and in relation to such consideration the reference to its amount is to the estimated money value of the benefit.
The nature of any such consideration shall be disclosed.

(3) The reference to third parties is to persons other than –
   (a) the director himself or a person connected with him or body corporate controlled by him, and

(*b*)   the company or any of its subsidiary undertakings.

Supplementary

10. – (1) The following applies with respect to the amounts to be shown under paragraphs 1, 7, 8 and 9.

(2) The amount in each case includes all relevant sums paid by or receivable from –
   (*a*)   the company; and
   (*b*)   the company's subsidiary undertakings; and
   (*c*)   any other person,

except sums to be accounted for to the company or any of its subsidiary undertakings or, by virtue of sections 314 and 315 of this Act (duty of directors to make disclosure on company takeover; consequence of non-compliance), to past or present members of the company or any of its subsidiaries or any class of those members.

(3) The amount to be shown under paragraph 8 shall distinguish between the sums respectively paid by or receivable from the company, the company's subsidiary undertakings and persons other than the company and its subsidiary undertakings.

(4) References to amounts paid to or receivable by a person include amounts paid to or receivable by a person connected with him or a body corporate controlled by him (but not so as to require an amount to be counted twice).

11. – (1) The amounts to be shown for any financial year under paragraphs 1, 7, 8 and 9 are the sums receivable in respect of that year (whenever paid) or, in the case of sums not receivable in respect of a period, the sums paid during that year.

(2) But where –
   (*a*)   any sums are not shown in a note to the accounts for the relevant financial year on the ground that the person receiving them is liable to account for them as mentioned in paragraph 10(2), but the liability is thereafter wholly or partly released or is not enforced within a period of 2 years; or
   (*b*)   any sums paid by way of expenses allowance are charged to United Kingdom income tax after the end of the relevant financial year,

those sums shall, to the extent to which the liability is released or not enforced or they are charged as mentioned above (as the case may be), be shown in a note to the first accounts in which it is practicable to show them and shall be distinguished from the amounts to be shown apart from this provision.

12. Where it is necessary to do so for the purpose of making any distinction required by the preceding paragraphs in an amount to be shown in compliance with this Part of this Schedule, the directors may apportion any payments between the matters in respect of which these have been paid or are receivable in such manner as they think appropriate.

Interpretation

13. – (1) The following applies for the interpretation of this Part of this Schedule.

(2) A reference to a subsidiary undertaking of the company –
   (*a*)   in relation to a person who is or was, while a director of the company, a director also, by virtue of the company's nomination (direct or indirect) of any other undertaking, includes (subject to the following sub-paragraph) that undertaking, whether or not it is or was in fact a subsidiary undertaking of the company, and
   (*b*)   for the purposes of paragraphs 1 to 7 (including any provision of this Part of this Schedule referring to paragraph 1) is to an undertaking which is a subsidiary undertaking at the time the services were rendered, and for the purposes of paragraph 8 to a subsidiary undertaking immediately before the loss of office as director.

(3) The following definitions apply –
   (*a*)   "pension" includes any superannuation allowance, superannuation gratuity or similar payment,

(*b*) "pension scheme" means a scheme for the provision of pensions in respect of services as director or otherwise which is maintained in whole or in part by means of contributions, and

(*c*) "contribution", in relation to a pension scheme, means any payment (including an insurance premium) paid for the purposes of the scheme by or in respect of persons rendering services in respect of which pensions will or may become payable under the scheme except that it does not include any payment in respect of two or more persons if the amount paid in respect of each of them is not ascertainable.

(4) References in this Part of this Schedule to a person being "connected" with a director, and to a director "controlling" a body corporate, shall be construed in accordance with section 346.

Supplementary

14. This Part of this Schedule requires information to be given only so far as it is contained in the company's books and papers or the company has the right to obtain it from the persons concerned.".

4. – (1) For the heading to the present Part I substitute –

"PART II
LOANS, QUASI-LOANS AND OTHER DEALINGS IN
FAVOUR OF DIRECTORS"

(2) Paragraphs 1 to 3 and 5 to 14 of that Part shall be renumbered 15 to 27, and internal cross-references in that Part shall be renumbered accordingly.

(3) Paragraph 4 is omitted.

(4) In paragraph 1 (renumbered 15) for "group accounts" substitute "The group accounts of a holding company, or if it is not required to prepare group accounts its individual accounts,".

(5) For the heading before paragraph 11 (renumbered 24) substitute –

"Excluded transactions"

5. In paragraph 14 (renumbered 27), make the existing provision sub-paragraph (1) and after it insert –

"(2) In this Part of this Schedule "director" includes a shadow director.".

6. – (1) For the heading to the present Part II substitute –

"PART III
OTHER TRANSACTIONS, ARRANGEMENTS AND AGREEMENTS"

(2) Paragraphs 15 to 17 of that Part shall be renumbered 28 to 30, and internal cross-references in that Part shall be renumbered accordingly.

(3) In paragraph 16 (renumbered 29), for "made as mentioned in section 233(1)" substitute "made by the company or a subsidiary of it for persons who at any time during the financial year were officers of the company (but not directors or shadow directors)".

7. Omit the present Part III (disclosure required in case of banking companies), the substance of which is reproduced in Part IV of Schedule 7 to this Act.

Section 8(2)   SCHEDULE 5

MATTERS TO BE INCLUDED IN DIRECTORS' REPORT

1. Schedule 7 to the Companies Act 1985 (matters to be included in directors' report) is amended as follows.

Subsidiary undertakings

2. – (1) In paragraph 1(1) (significant changes in fixed assets) for "subsidiaries" substitute "subsidiary undertakings".

(2) In paragraph 6 (general information), for "subsidiaries" in each place where it occurs (three times) substitute "subsidiary undertakings".

Directors' interests

3. For paragraph 2 (directors' interests) substitute –

"2. – (1) The information required by paragraphs 2A and 2B shall be given in the directors' report, or by way of notes to the company's annual accounts, with respect to each person who at the end of the financial year was a director of the company.

(2) In those paragraphs –
- (a) 'the register' means the register of directors' interests kept by the company under section 325; and
- (b) references to a body corporate being in the same group as the company are to its being a subsidiary or holding company, or another subsidiary of a holding company, of the company.

2A. – (1) It shall be stated with respect to each director whether, according to the register, he was at the end of the financial year interested in shares in or debentures of the company or any other body corporate in the same group.

(2) If he was so interested, there shall be stated the number of shares in and amount of debentures of each body (specifying it) in which, according to the register, he was then interested.

(3) If a director was interested at the end of the financial year in shares in or debentures of the company or any other body corporate in the same group –
- (a) it shall also be stated whether, according to the register, he was at the beginning of the financial year (or, if he was not then a director, when he became one) interested in shares in or debentures of the company or any other body corporate in the same group, and
- (b) if he was so interested, there shall be stated the number of shares in and amount of debentures of each body (specifying it) in which, according to the register, he was then interested.

(4) In this paragraph references to an interest in shares or debentures have the same meaning as in section 324; and references to the interest of a director include any interest falling to be treated as his for the purposes of that section.

(5) The reference above to the time when a person became a director is, in the case of a person who became a director on more than one occasion, to the time when he first became a director.

2B. – (1) It shall be stated with respect to each director whether, according to the register, any right to subscribe for shares in or debentures of the company or another body corporate in the same group was during the financial year granted to, or exercised by, the director or a member of his immediate family.

(2) If any such right was granted to, or exercised by, any such person during the financial year, there shall be stated the number of shares in and amount of debentures of each body (specifying it) in respect of which, according to the register, the right was granted or exercised.

(3) A director's 'immediate family' means his or her spouse and infant children; and for this purpose "children" includes step-children, and "infant", in relation to Scotland, means pupil or minor.

(4) The reference above to a member of the director's immediate family does not include a person who is himself or herself a director of the company.".

Section 13(2)   SCHEDULE 6

[SCHEDULE 8 TO THE COMPANIES ACT 1985]
EXEMPTIONS FOR SMALL AND MEDIUM-SIZED COMPANIES

PART I
SMALL COMPANIES

Balance sheet

1. – (1) The company may deliver a copy of an abbreviated version of the full balance sheet, showing only those items to which a letter or Roman number is assigned in the balance sheet format adopted under Part I of Schedule 4, but in other respects corresponding to the full balance sheet.

(2) If a copy of an abbreviated balance sheet is delivered, there shall be disclosed in it or in a note to the company's accounts delivered –
  (a) the aggregate of the amounts required by note (5) of the notes on the balance sheet formats set out in Part I of Schedule 4 to be shown separately for each item included under debtors (amounts falling due after one year), and
  (b) the aggregate of the amounts required by note (13) of those notes to be shown separately for each item included under creditors in Format 2 (amounts falling due within one year or after more than one year).
(3) The provisions of section 233 as to the signing of the copy of the balance sheet delivered to the registrar apply to a copy of an abbreviated balance sheet delivered in accordance with this paragraph.

Profit and loss account

2. A copy of the company's profit and loss account need not be delivered.

Disclosure of information in notes to accounts

3. – (1) Of the information required by Part III of Schedule 4 (information to be given in notes to accounts if not given in the accounts themselves) only the information required by the following provisions need be given –
  paragraph 36 (accounting policies),
  paragraph 38 (share capital),
  paragraph 39 (particulars of allotments),
  paragraph 42 (fixed assets), so far as it relates to those items to which a letter or Roman number is assigned in the balance sheet format adopted,
  paragraph 48(1) and (4) (particulars of debts),
  paragraph 58(1) (basis of conversion of foreign currency amounts into sterling),
  paragraph 58(2) (corresponding amounts for previous financial year), so far as it relates to

amounts stated in a note to the company's accounts by virtue of a requirement of Schedule 4 or under any other provision of this Act.

(2) Of the information required by Schedule 5 to be given in notes to the accounts, the information required by the following provisions need not be given –

paragraph 4 (financial years of subsidiary undertakings),
paragraph 5 (additional information about subsidiary undertakings),
paragraph 6 (shares and debentures of company held by subsidiary undertakings),
paragraph 10 (arrangements attracting merger relief).

(3) Of the information required by Schedule 6 to be given in notes to the accounts, the information required by Part I (directors' and chairman's emoluments, pensions and compensation for loss of office) need not be given.

Directors' report

4. A copy of the directors' report need not be delivered.

PART II
MEDIUM-SIZED COMPANIES

Profit and loss account

5. The company may deliver a profit and loss account in which the following items listed in the profit and loss account formats set out in Part I of Schedule 4 are combined as one item under the heading "gross profit or loss" –

Items 1, 2, 3 and 6 in Format 1;
Items 1 to 5 in Format 2;
Items A.1, B.1 and B.2 in Format 3;
Items A.1, A.2 and B.1 to B.4 in Format 4.

Disclosure of information in notes to accounts

6. The information required by paragraph 55 of Schedule 4 (particulars of turnover) need not be given.

PART III
SUPPLEMENTARY PROVISIONS

Statement that advantage taken of exemptions

7. – (1) Where the directors of a company take advantage of the exemptions conferred by Part I or Part II of this Schedule, the company's balance sheet shall contain –

(a) a statement that advantage is taken of the exemptions conferred by Part I or, as the case may be, Part II of this Schedule, and

(b) a statement of the grounds on which, in the directors' opinion, the company is entitled to those exemptions.

(2) The statements shall appear in the balance sheet immediately above the signature required by section 233.

Special auditors' report

8. – (1) If the directors of a company propose to take advantage of the exemptions conferred by Part I or II of this Schedule, it is the auditors' duty to provide them with a report stating whether in their opinion the company is entitled to those exemptions and whether the documents to be proposed to be delivered in accordance with this Schedule are properly prepared.

(2) The accounts delivered shall be accompanied by a special report of the auditors stating that in their opinion –
   (a)   the company is entitled to the exemptions claimed in the directors' statement, and
   (b)   the accounts to be delivered are properly prepared in accordance with this Schedule.

(3) In such a case a copy of the auditors' report under section 235 need not be delivered separately, but the full text of it shall be reproduced in the special report; and if the report under section 235 is qualified there shall be included in the special report any further material necessary to understand the qualification.

(4) Section 236 (signature of auditors' report) applies to a special report under this paragraph as it applies to a report under section 235.

Dormant companies

9. Paragraphs 7 and 8 above do not apply where the company is exempt by virtue of section 250 (dormant companies) from the obligation to appoint auditors.

Requirements in connection with publication of accounts

10. – (1) Where advantage is taken of the exemptions conferred by Part I or II of this Schedule, section 240 (requirements in connection with publication of accounts) has effect with the following adaptations.

(2) Accounts delivered in accordance with this Schedule and accounts in the form in which they would be required to be delivered apart from this Schedule are both "statutory accounts" for the purposes of that section.

(3) References in that section to the auditors' report under section 235 shall be read, in relation to accounts delivered in accordance with this Schedule, as references to the special report under paragraph 8 above.

Section 18(3) and (4)   # SCHEDULE 7

SPECIAL PROVISIONS FOR
BANKING AND INSURANCE COMPANIES AND GROUPS

Preliminary

Schedule 9 to the Companies Act 1985 is amended in accordance with this Schedule, as follows –
   (a)   for the heading of the Schedule substitute "SPECIAL PROVISIONS FOR BANKING AND INSURANCE COMPANIES AND GROUPS";
   (b)   omit the introductory paragraph preceding Part I, together with its heading;
   (c)   make the present provisions of Parts I to V of the Schedule (as amended by Part I of this Schedule) Part I of the Schedule, and accordingly –
      (i)   for the descriptive Part heading before paragraph 2 substitute "FORM AND CONTENT OF ACCOUNTS", and
      (ii)   omit the Part headings before paragraphs 19, 27, 31 and 32;

(*d*) the provisions of Parts II, III and IV of this Schedule have effect as Parts II, III and IV of Schedule 9 to the Companies Act 1985.

PART I
FORM AND CONTENT OF ACCOUNTS

1. In paragraph 10(1)(*c*) of Schedule 9 to the Companies Act 1985 (disclosure of outstanding loans in connection with certain cases of financial assistance for purchase of company's own shares), after "153(4)(*b*)" insert ",(*bb*)".

2. In paragraph 13 of that Schedule (information supplementing balance sheet, omit sub-paragraph (3) (information as to acquisition of, or creation of lien or charge over, company's own shares).

3. In paragraph 17(5) of that Schedule (statement of turnover: companies exempt from requirement) for "neither a holding company nor a subsidiary of another body corporate" substitute "neither a parent company nor a subsidiary undertaking".

4. After paragrah 18 of that Schedule insert –

"Supplementary provisions

18A. – (1) Accounting policies shall be applied consistently within the same accounts and from one financial year to the next.

(2) If it appears to the directors of a company that there are special reasons for departing from the principle stated in sub-paragraph (1) in preparing the company's accounts in respect of any financial year, they may do so; but particulars of the departure, the reasons for it and its effect shall be given in a note to the accounts.

18B. It shall be stated whether the accounts have been prepared in accordance with applicable accounting standards, and particulars shall be given of any material departure from those standards.

18C. – (1) In respect of every item shown in the balance sheet or profit and loss account, or stated in a note to the accounts, there shall be shown or stated the corresponding amount for the financial year immediately preceding that to which the accounts relate, subject to sub-paragraph (3).

(2) Where the corresponding amount is not comparable, it shall be adjusted and particulars of the adjustment and the reasons for it shall be given in a note to the accounts.

(3) Sub-paragraph (1) does not apply in relation to an amount shown –
  (*a*) as an amount the source or application of which is required by paragraph 8 above (reserves and provisions),
  (*b*) in pursuance of paragraph 13(10) above (acquisitions and disposals of fixed assets),
  (*c*) by virtue of paragraph 13 of Schedule 4A (details of accounting treatment of acquisitions),
  (*d*) by virtue of paragraph 2, 8(3), 16, 21(1)(*d*), 22(4) or (5), 24(3) or (4) or 27(3) or (4) of Schedule 5 (shareholdings in other undertakings), or
  (*e*) by virtue of Part II or III of Schedule 6 (loans and other dealings in favour of directors and others).".

5. – (1) Before paragraph 19 of that Schedule insert the heading "*Provisions where company is parent company or subsidiary undertaking*"; and that paragraph is amended as follows.

(2) In sub-paragraph (1) for the words from "is a holding company" onwards substitute "is a parent company".

(3) In sub-paragraph (2) –
> (*a*) for "subsidiaries" (four times) substitute "subsidiary undertakings", and
> (*b*) in paragraph (*a*), for "Part I" substitute "paragraphs 5, 6, 10, 13 and 14".

(4) Omit sub-paragraphs (3) to (7).

6. For paragraph 20 of that Schedule substitute –

> "20. – (1) This paragraph applies where the company is a subsidiary undertaking.
>
> (2) The balance sheet of the company shall show –
>> (*a*) the aggregate amount of its indebtedness to undertakings of which it is a subsidiary undertaking or which are fellow subsidiary undertakings, and
>> (*b*) the aggregate amount of the indebtedness of all such undertakings to it,
>
> distinguishing in each case between indebtedness in respect of debentures and otherwise.
>
> (3) The balance sheet shall also show the aggregate amount of assets consisting of shares in fellow subsidiary undertakings.".

7. Omit paragraphs 21 to 26 of that Schedule.

8. – (1) Before paragraph 27 of that Schedule insert the heading "*Exceptions for certain companies*"; and that paragraph is amended as follows.

(2) In sub-paragraph (2) –
> (*a*) for "Part I of this Schedule" substitute "paragraphs 2 to 18 of this Schedule", and
> (*b*) in paragraph (*b*) for the words from "paragraphs 15" to the end substitute "and paragraph 15".

(3) In sub-paragraph (4), omit "of the said Part I".

9. In paragraph 28 of that Schedule, in sub-paragraph (1) (twice) and in sub-paragraph (2) for "Part I" substitute "paragraphs 2 to 18".

10. After that paragraph insert –

> "28A. Where a company is entitled to, and has availed itself of, any of the provisions of paragraph 27 or 28 of this Schedule, section 235(2) only requires the auditors to state whether in their opinion the accounts have been properly prepared in accordance with this Act.".

11. Omit paragraphs 29 to 31 of that Schedule.

12. Before paragraph 32 of that Schedule insert the heading "*Interpretation*"; and in sub-paragraphs (1) and (2) of that paragraph for "this Schedule" substitute "this Part of this Schedule".

13. In paragraph 36 of that Schedule for "this Schedule" substitute "this Part of this Schedule".

PART II
[PART II OF SCHEDULE 9 TO THE COMPANIES ACT 1985]
ACCOUNTS OF BANKING OR INSURANCE GROUP

Undertakings to be included in consolidation

1. The following descriptions of undertaking shall not be excluded from consolidation under section 229(4) (exclusion of undertakings whose activities are different from those of the undertakings consolidated) –
> (*a*) in the case of a banking group, an undertaking (other than a credit institution) whose activities are a direct extension of or ancillary to banking business;
> (*b*) in the case of an insurance group, an undertaking (other than one carrying on insurance business) whose activities are a direct extension of or ancillary to insurance business.

For the purposes of paragraph (*a*) "banking" means the carrying on of a deposit-taking business within the meaning of the Banking Act 1987.

General application of provisions applicable to individual accounts

2. – (1) In paragraph 1 of Schedule 4A (application to group accounts of provisions applicable to individual accounts), the reference in sub-paragraph (1) to the provisions of Schedule 4 shall be construed as a reference to the provisions of Part I of this Schedule; and accordingly –
    (*a*) the reference in sub-paragraph (2) to paragraph 59 of Schedule 4 shall be construed as a reference to paragraphs 19(2) and 20 of Part I of this Schedule; and
    (*b*) sub-paragraph (3) shall be omitted.

(2) The general application of the provisions of Part I of this Schedule in place of those of Schedule 4 is subject to the following provisions.

Treatment of goodwill

3. – (1) The rules in paragraph 21 of Schedule 4 relating to the treatment of goodwill, and the rules in paragraphs 17 to 19 of that Schedule (valuation of fixed assets) so far as they relate to goodwill, apply for the purpose of dealing with any goodwill arising on consolidation.

(2) Goodwill shall be shown as a separate item in the balance sheet under an appropriate heading; and this applies notwithstanding anything in paragraph 10(1)(*b*) or (2) of Part I of this Schedule (under which goodwill, patents and trade marks may be stated in the company's individual accounts as a single item).

Minority interests and associated undertakings

4. The information required by paragraphs 17 and 20 to 22 of Schedule 4A (minority interests and associated undertakings) to be shown under separate items in the formats set out in Part I of Schedule 4 shall be shown separately in the balance sheet and profit and loss account under appropriate headings.

Companies entitled to benefit of exemptions

5. – (1) Where a banking or insurance company is entitled to the exemptions conferred by paragraph 27 or 28 of Part I of this Schedule, a group headed by that company is similarly entitled.

(2) Paragraphs 27(4), 28(2) and 28A (accounts not to be taken to be other than true and fair; duty of auditors) apply accordingly where advantage is taken of those exemptions in relation to group accounts.

Information as to undertaking in which shares held as result of financial assistance operation

6. – (1) The following provisions apply where the parent company of a banking group has a subsidiary undertaking which –
    (*a*) is a credit institution of which shares are held as a result of a financial assistance operation with a view to its reorganisation or rescue, and
    (*b*) is excluded from consolidation under section 229(3)(*c*) (interest held with a view to resale).

(2) Information as to the nature and terms of the operation shall be given in a note to the group accounts and there shall be appended to the copy of the group accounts delivered to the registrar in accordance with section 242 a copy of the undertaking's latest individual accounts and, if it is a parent undertaking, its latest group accounts.

If the accounts appended are required by law to be audited, a copy of the auditors' report shall also be appended.

(3) If any document required to be appended is in a language other than English, the directors shall annex to the copy of that document delivered a translation of it into English, certified in the prescribed manner to be a correct translation.

(4) The above requirements are subject to the following qualifications –

    (*a*) an undertaking is not required to prepare for the purposes of this paragraph accounts which would not otherwise be prepared, and if no accounts satisfying the above requirements are prepared none need be appended;

    (*b*) the accounts of an undertaking need not be appended if they would not otherwise be required to be published, or made available for public inspection, anywhere in the world, but in that case the reason for not appending the accounts shall be stated in a note to the consolidated accounts.

(5) Where a copy of an undertaking's accounts is required to be appended to the copy of the group accounts delivered to the registrar, that fact shall be stated in a note to the group accounts.

(6) Subsections (2) to (4) of section 242 (penalties, &c. in case of default) apply in relation to the requirements of this paragraph as regards the delivery of documents to the registrar as they apply in relation to the requirements of subsection (1) of that section.

PART III
[PART III OF SCHEDULE 9 TO THE COMPANIES ACT 1985]
ADDITIONAL DISCLOSURE: RELATED UNDERTAKINGS

1. Where accounts are prepared in accordance with the special provisions of this Part relating to banking companies or groups, there shall be disregarded for the purposes of –

    (*a*) paragraphs 7(2)(*a*), 23(2)(*a*) and 26(2)(*a*) of Schedule 5 (information about significant holdings in undertakings other than subsidiary undertakings: definition of 10 per cent. holding) and

    (*b*) paragraphs 9(1), 25(1) and 28(1) of that Schedule (additional information in case of 20 per cent. holding),

any holding of shares not comprised in the equity share capital of the undertaking in question.

PART IV
[PART IV OF SCHEDULE 9 TO THE COMPANIES ACT 1985]
ADDITIONAL DISCLOSURE: EMOLUMENTS AND OTHER BENEFITS OF
DIRECTORS AND OTHERS

1. The provisions of this Part of this Schedule have effect with respect to the application of Schedule 6 (additional disclosure: emoluments and other benefits of directors and others) to a banking company or the holding company of such a company.

Loans, quasi-loans and other dealings

2. Part II of Schedule 6 (loans, quasi-loans and other dealings) does not apply for the purposes of accounts prepared by a banking company, or a company which is the holding company of a banking company, in relation to a transaction or arrangement of a kind mentioned in section 330, or an agreement to enter into such a transaction or arrangement, to which that banking company is a party.

Other transactions, arrangements and agreements

3. – (1) Part III of Schedule 6 (other transactions, arrangements and agreements) applies for the purposes of accounts prepared by a banking company, or a company which is the holding company of a banking company, only in relation to a transaction, arrangement or agreement made by that banking company for –

    (*a*) a person who was a director of the company preparing the accounts, or who was connected with such a director, or

    (*b*) a person who was a chief executive or manager (within the meaning of the Banking Act 1987) of that company or its holding company.

(2) References in that Part to officers of the company shall be construed accordingly as including references to such persons.

(3) In this paragraph "director" includes a shadow director.

(4) For the purposes of that Part as it applies by virtue of this paragraph, a company which a person does not control shall not be treated as connected with him.

(5) Section 346 of this Act applies for the purposes of this paragraph as regards the interpretation of references to a person being connected with a director or controlling a company.

Section 18(5)   # SCHEDULE 8

[SCHEDULE 10 TO THE COMPANIES ACT 1985]
DIRECTORS' REPORT WHERE ACCOUNTS PREPARED IN ACCORDANCE WITH SPECIAL PROVISIONS FOR BANKING OR INSURANCE COMPANIES OR GROUPS

Recent issues

1. – (1) This paragraph applies where a company prepares individual accounts in accordance with the special provisions of this Part relating to banking or insurance companies.

(2) If in the financial year to which the accounts relate the company has issued any shares or debentures, the directors' report shall state the reason for making the issue, the classes of shares or debentures issued and, as respects each class, the number of shares or amount of debentures issued and the consideration received by the company for the issue.

Turnover and profitability

2. – (1) This paragraph applies where a company prepares group accounts in accordance with the special provisions of this Part relating to banking or insurance groups.

(2) If in the course of the financial year to which the accounts relate the group carried on business of two or more classes (other than banking or discounting or a class prescribed for the purposes of paragraph 17(2) of Part I of Schedule 9) that in the opinion of the directors differ substantially from each other, there shall be contained in the directors' report a statement of –

    (*a*) the proportions in which the turnover for the financial year (so far as stated in the consolidated accounts) is divided amongst those classes (describing them), and

    (*b*) as regards business of each class, the extent or approximate extent (expressed in money terms) to which, in the opinion of the directors, the carrying on of business of that class contributed to or restricted the profit or loss of the group for that year (before taxation).

(3) In sub-paragraph (2) "the group" means the undertakings included in the consolidation.

(4) For the purposes of this paragraph classes of business which in the opinion of the directors do not differ substantially from each other shall be treated as one class.

Labour force and wages paid

3. – (1) This paragraph applies where a company prepares individual or group accounts in accordance with the special provisions of this Part relating to banking or insurance companies or groups.

(2) There shall be stated in the directors' report –

(*a*)   the average number of persons employed by the company or, if the company prepares group accounts, by the company and its subsidiary undertakings, and

(*b*)   the aggregate amount of the remuneration paid or payable to persons so employed.

(3) The average number of persons employed shall be determined by adding together the number of persons employed (whether throughout the week or not) in each week of the financial year and dividing that total by the number of weeks in the financial year.

(4) The aggregate amount of the remuneration paid or payable means the total amount of remuneration paid or payable in respect of the financial year; and for this purpose remuneration means gross remuneration and includes bonuses, whether payable under contract or not.

(5) The information required by this paragraph need not be given if the average number of persons employed is less than 100.

(6) No account shall be taken for the purposes of this paragraph of persons who worked wholly or mainly outside the United Kingdom.

(7) This paragraph does not apply to a company which is a wholly-owned subsidiary of a company incorporated in Great Britain.

Section 21(2)   # SCHEDULE 9

[SCHEDULE 10A TO THE COMPANIES ACT 1985]
PARENT AND SUBSIDIARY UNDERTAKINGS: SUPPLEMENTARY PROVISIONS

Introduction

1. The provisions of this Schedule explain expressions used in section 258 (parent and subsidiary undertakings) and otherwise supplement that section.

Voting rights in an undertaking

2. – (1) In section 258(2)(*a*) and (*d*) the references to the voting rights in an undertaking are to the rights conferred on shareholders in respect of their shares or, in the case of an undertaking not having a share capital, on members, to vote at general meetings of the undertaking on all, or substantially all, matters.

(2) In relation to an undertaking which does not have general meetings at which matters are decided by the exercise of voting rights, the references to holding a majority of the voting rights in the undertaking shall be construed as references to having the right under the constitution of the undertaking to direct the overall policy of the undertaking or to alter the terms of its constitution.

Right to appoint or remove a majority of the directors

3. – (1) In section 258(2)(*b*) the reference to the right to appoint or remove a majority of the board of directors is to the right to appoint or remove directors holding a majority of the voting rights at meetings of the board on all, or substantially all, matters.

(2) An undertaking shall be treated as having the right to appoint to a directorship if –

(*a*) a person's appointment to it follows necessarily from his appointment as director of the undertaking, or

(*b*) the directorship is held by the undertaking itself.

(3) A right to appoint or remove which is exercisable only with the consent or concurrence of another person shall be left out of account unless no other person has a right to appoint or, as the case may be, remove in relation to that directorship.

Right to exercise dominant influence

4. – (1) For the purposes of section 258(2)(*c*) an undertaking shall not be regarded as having the right to exercise a dominant influence over another undertaking unless it has a right to give directions with respect to the operating and financial policies of that other undertaking which its directors are obliged to comply with whether or not they are for the benefit of that other undertaking.

(2) A "control contract" means a contract in writing conferring such a right which –

(*a*) is of a kind authorised by the memorandum or articles of the undertaking in relation to which the right is exercisable, and

(*b*) is permitted by the law under which that undertaking is established.

(3) This paragraph shall not be read as affecting the construction of the expression "actually exercises a dominant influence" in section 258(4)(*a*).

Rights exercisable only in certain circumstances or temporarily incapable of exercise

5. – (1) Rights which are exercisable only in certain circumstances shall be taken into account only –

(*a*) when the circumstances have arisen, and for so long as they continue to obtain, or

(*b*) when the circumstances are within the control of the person having the rights.

(2) Rights which are normally exercisable but are temporarily incapable of exercise shall continue to be taken into account.

Rights held by one person on behalf of another

6. Rights held by a person in a fiduciary capacity shall be treated as not held by him.

7. – (1) Rights held by a person as nominee for another shall be treated as held by the other.

(2) Rights shall be regarded as held as nominee for another if they are exercisable only on his instructions or with his consent or concurrence.

Rights attached to shares held by way of security

8. Rights attached to shares held by way of security shall be treated as held by the person providing the security –

(*a*) where apart from the right to exercise them for the purpose of preserving the value of the security, or of realising it, the rights are exercisable only in accordance with his instructions, and

(*b*) where the shares are held in connection with the granting of loans as part of normal business activities and apart from the right to exercise them for the purpose of preserving the value of the security, or of realising it, the rights are exercisable only in his interests.

Rights attributed to parent undertaking

9. – (1) Rights shall be treated as held by a parent undertaking if they are held by any of its subsidiary undertakings.

(2) Nothing in paragraph 7 or 8 shall be construed as requiring rights held by a parent undertaking to be treated as held by any of its subsidiary undertakings.

(3) For the purposes of paragraph 8 rights shall be treated as being exercisable in accordance with the instructions or in the interests of an undertaking if they are exercisable in accordance with the instructions of or, as the case may be, in the interests of any group undertaking.

Disregard of certain rights

10. The voting rights in an undertaking shall be reduced by any rights held by the undertaking itself.

Supplementary

11. References in any provision of paragraphs 6 to 10 to rights held by a person include rights falling to be treated as held by him by virtue of any other provision of those paragraphs but not rights which by virtue of any such provision are to be treated as not held by him.

Section 23

SCHEDULE 10

AMENDMENTS CONSEQUENTIAL ON PART I

PART I
AMENDMENTS OF THE COMPANIES ACT 1985

1. In section 46 (meaning of "unqualified" auditors' report in section 43(3)), for subsections (2) to (6) substitute –

"(2) If the balance sheet was prepared for a financial year of the company, the reference is to an auditors' report stating without material qualification the auditors' opinion that the balance sheet has been properly prepared in accordance with this Act.

(3) If the balance sheet was not prepared for a financial year of the company, the reference is to an auditors' report stating without material qualification the auditors' opinion that the balance sheet has been properly prepared in accordance with the provisions of this Act which would have applied if it had been so prepared.

For the purposes of an auditors' report under this subsection the provisions of this Act shall be deemed to apply with such modifications as are necessary by reason of the fact that the balance sheet is not prepared for a financial year of the company.

(4) A qualification shall be regarded as material unless the auditors state in their report that the matter giving rise to the qualification is not material for the purpose of determining (by reference to the company's balance sheet) whether at the balance sheet date the amount of the company's net assets was not less than the aggregate of its called up share capital and undistributable reserves.

In this subsection 'net assets' and 'undistributable reserves' have the meaning given by section 264(2) and (3).".

2. In section 209(5)(*a*)(i) for "an authorised institution" substitute "a banking company".

3. In sections 211(9) and 215(4) for "paragraph 3 or 10 of Schedule 5" substitute "section 231(3)".

4. In section 271(3), for "section 236" substitute "section 235".

5. In section 272(3) –
    (*a*) for "section 228" substitute "section 226", and
    (*b*) for "section 238" substitute "section 233".

6. In sections 272(5) and 273(7) for "section 241(3)(*b*)" substitute "the second sentence of section 242(1)".

7. In section 276(*b*) for "34(4)(*b*)" substitute "34(3)(*a*)".

8. For section 279 substitute –

"279   Distributions by banking or insurance companies

Where a company's accounts relevant for the purposes of this Part are prepared in accordance with the special provisions of Part VII relating to banking or insurance companies, sections 264 to 275 apply with the modifications shown in Schedule 11.".

9. In section 289(4) for "section 252(5)" substitute "section 250(3)".

10. In sections 338(4), 339(4), 343(1)(*a*) and 344(2) for "an authorised institution", wherever occurring, substitute "a banking company".

11. In section 343(2) and 4 for "paragraph 4 of Schedule 6, be required by section 232" substitute "paragraph 2 of Part IV of Schedule 9, be required".

12. In section 699(3) for "section 241(3)" substitute "section 242(1)".

13. In Part XXIII (oversea companies), for Chapter II (delivery of accounts) substitute –

"CHAPTER II
DELIVERY OF ACCOUNTS AND REPORTS

700   Preparation of accounts and reports by oversea companies

(1) Every oversea company shall in respect of each financial year of the company prepare the like accounts and directors' report, and cause to be prepared such an auditors' report, as would be required if the company were formed and registered under this Act.

(2) The Secretary of State may by order –
- (*a*) modify the requirements referred to in subsection (1) for the purpose of their application to oversea companies;
- (*b*) exempt an oversea company from those requirements or from such of them as may be specified in the order.

(3) An order may make different provision for different cases or classes of case and may contain such incidental and supplementary provisions as the Secretary of State thinks fit.

(4) An order under this section shall be made by statutory instrument which shall be subject to annulment in pursuance of a resolution of either House of Parliament.

701   Oversea company's financial year and accounting reference periods

(1) Sections 223 to 225 (financial year and accounting reference periods) apply to an oversea company, subject to the following modifications.

(2) For the references to the incorporation of the company substitute references to the company establishing a place of business in Great Britain.

(3) Omit section 225(4) (restriction on frequency with which current accounting reference period may be extended).

702   Delivery to registrar of accounts and reports of oversea company

(1) An oversea company shall in respect of each financial year of the company deliver to the registrar copies of the accounts and reports prepared in accordance with section 700.

If any document comprised in those accounts or reports is in a language other than English, the directors shall annex to the copy delivered a translation of it into English, certified in the prescribed manner to be a correct translation.

(2) In relation to an oversea company the period allowed for delivering accounts and reports is 13 months after the end of the relevant accounting reference period.

This is subject to the following provisions of this section.

(3) If the relevant accounting reference period is the company's first and is a period of more than 12 months, the period allowed is 13 months from the first anniversary of the company's establishing a place of business in Great Britain.

(4) If the relevant accounting period is treated as shortened by virtue of a notice given by the company under section 225 (alteration of accounting reference date), the period allowed is that applicable in accordance with the above provisions or three months from the date of the notice under that section, whichever last expires.

(5) If for any special reason the Secretary of State thinks fit he may, on an application made before the expiry of the period otherwise allowed, by notice in writing to an oversea company extend that period by such further period as may be specified in the notice.

(6) In this section "the relevant accounting reference period" means the accounting reference period by reference to which the financial year for the accounts in question was determined.

703 Penalty for non-compliance

(1) If the requirements of section 702(1) are not complied with before the end of the period allowed for delivering accounts and reports, or if the accounts and reports delivered do not comply wth the requirements of this Act, the company and every person who immediately before the end of that period was a director of the company is guilty of an offence and liable to a fine and, for continued contravention, to a daily default fine.

(2) It is a defence for a person charged with such an offence to prove that he took all reasonable steps for securing that the requirements in question would be complied with.

(3) It is not a defence in relation to a failure to deliver copies to the registrar to prove that the documents in question were not in fact prepared as required by this Act.".

14. In section 711(1)(*k*) for "section 241 (annual accounts)" substitute "section 242(1) (accounts and reports)".

15. For section 742 (expressions used in connection with accounts) substitute –

"742 Expressions used in connection with accounts

(1) In this Act, unless a contrary intention appears, the following expressions have the same meaning as in Part VII (accounts) –

"annual accounts",
"accounting reference date" and "accounting reference period",
"balance sheet" and "balance sheet" date,
"current assets",
"financial year", in relation to a company,
"fixed assets",
"parent company" and "parent undertaking",
"profit and loss account", and
"subsidiary undertaking".

(2) References in this Act to "realised profits" and "realised losses", in relation to a company's accounts, shall be construed in accordance with section 262(3).".

16. In section 744 (interpretation), omit the definition of "authorised institution" and at the appropriate place insert –

"'banking company' means a company which is authorised under the Banking Act 1987;".

17. In Schedule 1, in paragraph 2(2)(*a*) for "section 252(5)" substitute "section 250(3)".

18. – (1) Schedule 2 (interpretation of references to "beneficial interest") is amended as follows.

(2) After the heading at the beginning of the Schedule, and before the cross-heading preceding paragraph 1, insert the following heading –

"PART I
REFERENCES IN SECTIONS 23, 145, 146 AND 148".

(3) In paragraph 1 –
    (*a*) in sub-paragraph (1) omit "paragraph 60(2) of Schedule 4, or paragraph 19(3) of Schedule 9"; and
    (*b*) omit sub-paragraph (5).

(4) In paragraph 3 –
    (*a*) in sub-paragraph (1) omit ", paragraph 60(2) of Schedule 4 or paragraph 19(3) of Schedule 9"; and
    (*b*) omit sub-paragraph (3).

(5) In paragraph 4 –
    (*a*) in sub-paragraph (1) omit "(whether as personal representative or otherwise)", and
    (*b*) in sub-paragraph (2) omit ",paragraph 60(2) of Schedule 4 and paragraph 19(3) of Schedule 9";
and at the end add –

"(3) As respects sections 145, 146 and 148, sub-paragraph (1) above applies where a company is a personal representative as it applies where a company is a trustee.".

(6) In paragraph 5(1) for "this Schedule" substitute "this Part of this Schedule".

(7) After paragraph 5 insert the following –

"PART II
REFERENCES IN SCHEDULE 5

Residual interests under pension and employees' share schemes

6. – (1) Where shares in an undertaking are held on trust for the purposes of a pension scheme or an employees' share scheme, there shall be disregarded any residual interest which has not vested in possession, being an interest of the undertaking or any of its subsidiary undertakings.

(2) In this paragraph a "residual interest" means a right of the undertaking in question (the "residual beneficiary") to receive any of the trust property in the event of –
    (*a*) all the liabilities arising under the scheme having been satisfied or provided for, or
    (*b*) the residual beneficiary ceasing to participate in the scheme, or
    (*c*) the trust property at any time exceeding what is necessary for satisfying the liabilities arising or expected to arise under the scheme.

(3) In sub-paragraph (2) references to a right include a right dependent on the exercise of a discretion vested by the scheme in the trustee or any other person; and references to liabilities arising under a scheme include liabilities that have resulted or may result from the exercise of any such discretion.

(4) For the purposes of this paragraph a residual interest vests in possession –
    (*a*) in a case within sub-paragraph (2)(*a*), on the occurrence of the event there mentioned, whether or not the amount of the property receivable pursuant to the right mentioned in that sub-paragraph is then ascertained;

(*b*)   in a case within sub-paragraph (2)(*b*) or (*c*), when the residual beneficiary becomes entitled to require the trustee to transfer to that beneficiary any of the property receivable pursuant to that right.

Employer's charges and other rights of recovery

7. – (1) Where shares in an undertaking are held on trust, there shall be disregarded –

    (*a*)   if the trust is for the purposes of a pension scheme, any such rights as are mentioned in sub-paragraph (2) below;

    (*b*)   if the trust is for the purposes of an employees' share scheme, any such rights as are mentioned in paragraph (*a*) of that sub-paragraph,

being rights of the undertaking or any of its subsidiary undertakings.

(2) The rights referred to are –

    (*a*)   any charge or lien on, or set-off against, any benefit or other right or interest under the scheme for the purpose of enabling the employer or former employer of a member of the scheme to obtain the discharge of a monetary obligation due to him from the member, and

    (*b*)   any right to receive from the trustee of the scheme, or as trustee of the scheme to retain, an amount that can be recovered or retained under section 47 of the Social Security Pensions Act 1975 (deduction of premium from refund of pension contributions) or otherwise as reimbursement or partial reimbursement for any state scheme premium paid in connection with the scheme under Part III of that Act.

Trustee's right to expenses, remuneration, indemnity, &c.

8. Where an undertaking is a trustee, there shall be disregarded any rights which the undertaking has in its capacity as trustee including, in particular, any right to recover its expenses or be remunerated out of the trust property and any right to be indemnified out of the property for any liability incurred by reason of any act or omission of the undertaking in the performance of its duties as trustee.

Supplementary

9. – (1) The following applies for the interpretation of this Part of this Schedule.

(2) "Undertaking" and "shares", in relation to an undertaking, have the same meaning as in Part VII.

(3) This Part of this Schedule applies in relation to debentures as it applies in relation to shares.

(4) "Pension scheme" means any scheme for the provision of benefits consisting of or including relevant benefits for or in respect of employees or former employees; and "relevant benefits" means any pension, lump sum, gratuity or other like benefit given or to be given on retirement or on death or in anticipation of retirement or, in connection with past service, after retirement or death.

(5) In sub-paragraph (4) of this paragraph and in paragraph 7(2) "employee" and "employer" shall be read as if a director of an undertaking were employed by it.".

19. – (1) Part II of Schedule 3 (prospectuses: auditors' and accountants' reports to be set out) is amended as follows.

(2) In paragraph 16 (auditors' reports), in sub-paragraph (2) for "subsidiaries" substitute "subsidiary undertakings" and for sub-paragraph (3) substitute –

"(3) If the company has subsidiary undertakings, the report shall –

    (*a*) deal separately with the company's profits or losses as provided by sub-paragraph (2), and in addition deal either –

        (i) as a whole with the combined profits or losses of its subsidiary undertakings, so far as they concern members of the company, or

        (ii) individually with the profits or losses of each of its subsidiary undertakings, so far as they concern members of the company,

or, instead of dealing separately with the company's profits or losses, deal as a whole with the profits or losses of the company and (so far as they concern members of the company) with the combined profits and losses of its subsidiary undertakings; and

    (*b*) deal separately with the company's assets and liabilities as provided by sub-paragraph (2), and in addition deal either –

        (i) as a whole with the combined assets and liabilities of its subsidiary undertakings, with or without the company's assets and liabilities, or

        (ii) individually with the assets and liabilities of each of its subsidiary undertakings,

indicating, as respects the assets and liabilities of its subsidiary undertakings, the allowance to be made for persons other than members of the company.".

(3) For paragraph 18 (accountants' reports) substitute –

"18. – (1) The following provisions apply if –

    (*a*) the proceeds of the issue are to be applied directly or indirectly in any manner resulting in the acquisition by the company of shares in any other undertaking, or any part of the proceeds is to be so applied, and

    (*b*) by reason of that acquisition or anything to be done in consequence of or in connection with it, that undertaking will become a subsidiary undertaking of the company.

(2) There shall be set out in the prospectus a report made by accountants upon –

    (*a*) the profits or losses of the other undertaking in respect of each of the five financial years immediately preceding the issue of the prospectus, and

    (*b*) the assets and liabilities of the other undertaking at the last date to which its accounts were made up.

(3) The report shall –

    (*a*) indicate how the profits or losses of the other undertaking would in respect of the shares to be acquired have concerned members of the company and what allowance would have fallen to be made, in relation to assets and liabilities so dealt with, for holders of other shares, if the company had at all material times held the shares to be acquired, and

    (*b*) where the other undertaking is a parent undertaking, deal with the profits or losses and the assets and liabilities of the undertaking and its subsidiary undertakings in the manner provided by paragraph 16(3) above in relation to the company and its subsidiary undertakings.

(4) In this paragraph "undertaking" and "shares", in relation to an undertaking, have the same meaning as in Part VII.".

(4) In paragraph 22 (eligibility of accountants to make reports), for sub-paragraph (2) substitute –

"(2) Such a report shall not be made by an accountant who is an officer or servant, or a partner of or in the employment of an officer or servant, of –

    (*a*) the company or any of its subsidiary undertakings,

    (*b*) a parent undertaking of the company or any subsidiary undertaking of such an undertaking.".

20. In paragraph 12(*b*) of Schedule 4, for "section 238" substitute "section 233".

21. – (1) Schedule 11 is amended as follows.

(2) For the heading substitute "MODIFICATIONS OF PART VIII WHERE COMPANY'S ACCOUNTS PREPARED IN ACCORDANCE WITH SPECIAL PROVISIONS FOR BANKING OR INSURANCE COMPANIES".

(3) In paragraphs 1 and 2(*a*) for "Schedule 9" substitute "Part I of Schedule 9".

(4) In paragraph 4 –
- (*a*) in sub-paragraph (*a*) for "Schedule 9" substitute "Part I of Schedule 9", and
- (*b*) omit sub-paragraphs (*b*) and (*c*).

(5) In paragraph 5 –
- (*a*) in sub-paragraph (*a*) for "Part III of Schedule 9" substitute "paragraph 27 or 28 of Schedule 9", and
- (*b*) omit sub-paragraph (*b*).

(6) In paragraph 6 –
- (*a*) in sub-paragraph (*a*), for "section 228" substitute "section 226" and for "section 258 and Schedule 9" substitute "section 255 and Part I of Schedule 9", and
- (*b*) in sub-paragraph (*b*), for "Part III of Schedule 9" substitute "paragraph 27 or 28 of Schedule 9".

(7) In paragraph 7(*a*) for "Schedule 9" substitute "Part I of Schedule 9".

22 – (1) In Schedule 15A (renumbered 15B) (provisions applicable to mergers and divisions of public companies), paragraph 6 (documents to be made available for inspection) is amended as follows.

(2) In sub-paragraph (1)(*b*) (directors' report on merger or division), after "directors' report" insert "referred to in paragraph 4 above".

(3) For sub-paragraph (1)(*d*) and (*e*) substitute –
> "(*d*) the company's annual accounts, together with the relevant directors' report and auditors' report, for the last three financial years ending on or before the relevant date; and
> (*e*) if the last of those financial years ended more than six months before the relevant date, an accounting statement in the form described in the following provisions.".

(4) In sub-paragraph (1), after the paragraphs add –
> "In paragraphs (*d*) and (*e*) "the relevant date" means one month before the first meeting of the company summoned under section 425(1) or for the purposes of paragraph 1.".

(5) For sub-paragraphs (2) to (5) substitute –

> "(2) The accounting statement shall consist of –
> - (*a*) a balance sheet dealing with the state of the affairs of the company as at a date not more than three months before the draft terms were adopted by the directors, and
> - (*b*) where the company would be required to prepare group accounts if that date were the last day of a financial year, a consolidated balance sheet dealing with the state of affairs of the company and its subsidiary undertakings as at that date.

> (3) The requirements of this Act as to balance sheets forming part of a company's annual accounts, and the matters to be included in notes thereto, apply to any balance sheet required for the accounting statement, with such modifications as are necessary by reason of its being prepared otherwise than as at the last day of a financial year.

> (4) Any balance sheet required for the accounting statement shall be approved by the board of directors and signed on behalf of the board by a director of the company.

> (5) In relation to a company within the meaning of Article 3 of the Companies (Northern Ireland) Order 1986, the references in this paragraph to the requirements of this Act shall be construed as reference to the corresponding requirements of that Order.".

23. In Schedule 22 (provisions applying to unregistered companies), in the entry relating to Part VII, in column 1, for "Schedule 10" substitute "Schedules 10 and 10A".

24. – (1) Schedule 24 (punishment of offences) is amended as follows.

(2) The existing entries for provisions in Part VII are amended as follows, and shall be re-ordered according to the new order of the sections in that Part:

Provision of Part VII	Amendment
223(1)	In column 1, for "223(1)" substitute "221(5) or 222(4)".
223(2)	In column 1, for "223(2)" substitute "222(6)". In column 2, for "222(4)" substitute "222(5)".
231(3)	In column 1, for "231(3)" substitute "231(6)".
231(4)	In column 1, for "231(4)" substitute "232(4)". In column 2, for "Schedule 5, Part V" substitute "Schedule 6, Part I".
235(7)	In column 1, for "235(7)" substitute "234(5)". In column 2, for "the section" substitute "Part VII".
238(2)	In column 1, for "238(2)" substitute "233(6)".
240(5)	In column 1, for "240(5)" substitute "238(5)". In column 2, for "company balance sheet" substitute "company's annual accounts".
243(1)	In column 1, for "243(1)" substitute "241(2) or 242(2)". In column 2, for "company accounts" substitute "company's annual accounts, directors' report and auditors' report".
245(1)	Omit the entry.
245(2)	Omit the entry.
246(2)	In column 1, for "246(2)" substitute "239(3)". In column (2) after "accounts" insert "and reports".
254(6)	In column 1, for "254(6)" substitute "240(6)". In column 2 for the present words substitute "Failure to comply with requirements in connection with publication of accounts".
255(5)	Omit the entry.
260(3)	Omit the entry.

(3) At the appropriate places insert the following new entries –

"233(5) Approving defective accounts.	1. On indictment 2. Summary.	A fine. The statutory maximum.
234A(4) Laying, circulating or delivering directors' report without required signature.	Summary.	One-fifth of the statutory maximum.
236(4) Laying, circulating or delivering auditors' report without required signature.	Summary.	One-fifth of the statutory maximum.

| 251(6) | Failure to comply with requirements in relation to summary financial statements. | Summary. | One-fifth of the statutory maximum.". |

(4) In the entry for section 703(1) (failure by oversea company to comply with requirements as to accounts and reports), in column 2 for the words from "s.700" to the end substitute "requirements as to accounts and reports".

PART II
AMENDMENTS OF OTHER ENACTMENTS

Betting, Gaming and Lotteries Act 1963 (c.2)

25. In Schedule 2 to the Betting, Gaming and Lotteries Act 1963 (registered pool promoters),in paragraph 24(2) (duties with respect to delivery of accounts and audit) for the words from "and the following provisions" to "their report)" substitute "and sections 235(2) and 237(1) and (3) of the Companies Act 1985 (matters to be stated in auditors' report and responsibility of auditors in preparing their report)".

Harbours Act 1964 (c.40)

26. – (1) Section 42 of the Harbours Act 1964 (accounts and reports of statutory harbour undertakers) is amended as follows.

(2) For subsection (2) substitute –

> "(2) Where a statutory harbour undertaker is a parent undertaking with subsidiary undertakings which carry on harbour activities or any associated activities, then, it shall be the duty of the company also to prepare group accounts relating to the harbour activities and associated activities carried on by it and its subsidiary undertakings."

(3) In subsection (6) (application of provisions of the Companies Act 1985) –
>   (a) in paragraph (a) for "company accounts" substitute "individual company accounts";
>   (b) in paragraph (c) omit the words "required to be attached to a company's balance sheet".

(4) In subsection (9), for the definition of "holding company" and "subsidiary" substitute –
> "'parent undertaking' and 'subsidiary undertaking' have the same meaning as in Part VII of the Companies Act 1985;".

Coal Industry Act 1971 (c.16)

27. – (1) Section 8 of the Coal Industry Act 1971 (further provisions as to accounts of British Coal Corporation) is amended as follows.

(2) In subsections (1) and (2) for "subsidiaries" (three times) substitute "subsidiary undertakings".

(3) After subsection (2) insert –

> "(3) In this section 'subsidiary undertaking' has the same meaning as in Part VII of the Companies Act 1985.".

Aircraft and Shipbuilding Industries Act 1977 (c.3)

28. – (1) Section 17 of the Aircraft and Shipbuilding Industries Act 1977 (British Shipbuilders: accounts and audit) is amended as follows.

(2) In subsection (1)(*c*) (duty to prepare consolidated accounts) for "subsidiaries" substitute "subsidiary undertakings".

(3) In subsection (9) (copies of accounts to be sent to the Secretary of State) for "subsidiaries" substitute "subsidiary undertakings" and for "subsidiary" substitute "subsidiary undertaking".

(4) After subsection (9) add –

> "(10) In this section 'subsidiary undertaking' has the same meaning as in Part VII of the Companies Act 1985.".

Crown Agents Act 1979 (c.43)

29. In section 22 of the Crown Agents Act 1979 (accounts and audit), in subsection (2) (duty to prepare consolidated accounts) for "subsidiaries" (three times) substitute "subsidiary undertakings", and at the end of that subsection add –
> "In this subsection 'subsidiary undertaking' has the same meaning as in Part VII of the Companies Act 1985.".

British Telecommunications Act 1981 (c.38)

30. In section 75 of the British Telecommunications Act 1981 (accounts of the Post Office), in subsection (1)(*c*)(i) for "subsidiaries" substitute "subsidiary undertakings within the meaning of Part VII of the Companies Act 1985".

Transport Act 1981 (c.56)

31. In section 11(4) of the Transport Act 1981, for "section 235" substitute "section 234".

Iron and Steel Act 1982 (c.25)

32. In section 24(5) of the Iron and Steel Act 1982 (meaning of "directors' report") for the words from "which, under section 235" to the end substitute "which is required to be prepared under section 234 of the Companies Act 1985".

Oil and Pipelines Act 1985 (c.62)

33. In Schedule 3 to the Oil and Pipelines Act 1985 (Oil and Pipelines Agency: financial and other provisions), in paragraph 9(2) (duty to prepare consolidated accounts) for "subsidiaries" (three times) substitute "subsidiary undertakings", and at the end of that sub-paragraph add –
> "In this sub-paragraph "subsidiary undertaking" has the same meaning as in Part VII of the Companies Act 1985.".

Patents, Designs and Marks Act 1986 (c.39)

34. In Schedule 2 to the Patents, Designs and Marks Act 1986 (service marks), in paragraph 1(2) (provisions in which reference to trade mark includes service mark) for sub-paragraph (ii) substitute –
> "(ii) Part I of Schedule 4 and paragraphs 5(2)(*d*) and 10(1)(*b*) and (2) of Schedule 9 (form of company balance sheets); and".

Company Directors Disqualification Act 1986 (c.46)

35. – (1) The Company Directors Disqualification Act 1986 is amended as follows.

(2) In section 3(3)(*b*) (default orders) –

    (*a*) in sub-paragraph (i) for "section 244" substitute "section 242(4)", and

    (*b*) after that sub-paragraph insert –

            "(*ia*)section 245B of that Act (order requiring preparation of revised accounts),".

(3) In Schedule 1, for paragraph 5 substitute –

    "5. The extent of the director's responsibility for any failure by the directors of the company to comply with –

        (*a*) section 226 or 227 of the Companies Act (duty to prepare annual accounts), or

        (*b*) section 233 of that Act (approval and signature of accounts).".

Financial Services Act 1986 (c.60)

36. – (1) The Financial Services Act 1986 is amended as follows.

(2) In section 117(4) and (5), for "section 227" substitute "section 226".

(3) In Schedule 1, for paragraph 30 substitute –

    "30. – (1) For the purposes of this Schedule a group shall be treated as including any body corporate in which a member of the group holds a qualifying capital interest.

    (2) A qualifying capital interest means an interest in relevant shares of the body corporate which the member holds on a long-term basis for the purpose of securing a contribution to its own activities by the exercise of control or influence arising from that interest.

    (3) Relevant shares means shares comprised in the equity share capital of the body corporate of a class carrying rights to vote in all circumstances at general meetings of the body.

    (4) A holding of 20 per cent. or more of the nominal value of the relevant shares of a body corporate shall be presumed to be a qualifying capital interest unless the contrary is shown.

    (5) In this paragraph "equity share capital" has the same meaning as in the Companies Act 1985 and the Companies (Northern Ireland) Order 1986.".

Banking Act 1987 (c.22)

37. – (1) The Banking Act 1987 is amended as follows.

(2) In section 46(2) (duties of auditor of authorised institution), in paragraph (*c*) for "section 236" substitute "section 235(2)" and for "section 237" substitute "section 235(3) or section 237"; and in section 46(4) (adaptation of references for Northern Ireland) for "236 and 237" substitute "235(2) and 235(3) and 237".

(3) After section 105 insert –

"105A Meaning of 'related company'

    (1) In this Act a 'related company', in relation to an institution or the holding company of an institution, means a body corporate (other than a subsidiary) in which the institution or holding company holds a qualifying capital interest.

    (2) A qualifying capital interest means an interest in relevant shares of the body corporate which the institution or holding company holds on a long-term basis for the purpose of securing a contribution to its own activities by the exercise of control or influence arising from that interest.

(3) Relevant shares means shares comprised in the equity share capital of the body corporate of a class carrying rights to vote in all circumstances at general meetings of the body.

(4) A holding of 20 per cent. or more of the nominal value of the relevant shares of a body corporate shall be presumed to be a qualifying capital interest unless the contrary is shown.

(5) In this paragraph 'equity share capital' has the same meaning as in the Companies Act 1985 and the Companies (Northern Ireland) Order 1986.".

(4) In section 106(1) (interpretation), for the definition of "related company" substitute –
"'related company' has the meaning given by section 105A above;".

Income and Corporation Taxes Act 1988 (c.1)

38. – (1) The Income and Corporation Taxes Act 1988 is amended as follows.

(2) In section 180 (annual return of registered profit-related pay scheme), in subsection (3) for "section 242(3)" substitute "section 244(3)".

(3) In section 565(6) (conditions for exemption from provisions relating to sub-contractors in construction industry: compliance with requirements of Companies Act 1985), in paragraph (a) for "section 227 and 241" substitute "sections 226, 241 and 242".

Dartford – Thurrock Crossing Act 1988 (c.20)

39. In section 33 of the Dartford-Thurrock Crossing Act 1988 (duty to lay before Parliament copies of accounts of persons appointed to levy tolls), for subsection (2) substitute –

"(2) In relation to a company 'accounts' in subsection (1) means the company's annual accounts for a financial year, together with the relevant directors' report and the auditors' report on those accounts.
Expressions used in this subsection have the same meaning as in Part VII of the Companies Act 1985.".

Section 30(5)   # SCHEDULE 11
RECOGNITION OF SUPERVISORY BODY

PART I
GRANT AND REVOCATION OF RECOGNITION

Application for recognition of supervisory body

1. – (1) A supervisory body may apply to the Secretary of State for an order declaring it to be a recognised supervisory body for the purposes of this Part of this Act.

(2) Any such application –
    (a)   shall be made in such manner as the Secretary of State may direct, and
    (b)   shall be accompanied by such information as the Secretary of State may reasonably require for the purpose of determining the application.

(3) At any time after receiving an application and before determining it the Secretary of State may require the applicant to furnish additional information.

(4) The directions and requirements given or imposed under sub-paragraphs (2) and (3) may differ as between different applications.

(5) Any information to be furnished to the Secretary of State under this paragraph shall, if he so requires, be in such form or verified in such manner as he may specify.

(6) Every application shall be accompanied by a copy of the applicant's rules and of any guidance issued by the applicant which is intended to have continuing effect and is issued in writing or other legible form.

Grant and refusal of recognition

2. – (1) The Secretary of State may, on an application duly made in accordance with paragraph 1 and after being furnished with all such information as he may require under that paragraph, make or refuse to make an order (a "recognition order") declaring the applicant to be a recognised supervisory body for the purposes of this Part of this Act.

(2) The Secretary of State shall not make a recognition order unless it appears to him, from the information furnished by the body and having regard to any other information in his possession, that the requirements of Part II of this Schedule are satisfied as respects that body.

(3) The Secretary of State may refuse to make a recognition order in respect of a body if he considers that its recognition is unnecessary having regard to the existence of one or more other bodies which maintain and enforce rules as to the appointment and conduct of company auditors and which have been or are likely to be recognised.

(4) Where the Secretary of State refuses an application for a recognition order he shall give the applicant a written notice to that effect specifying which requirements in the opinion of the Secretary of State are not satisfied or stating that the application is refused on the ground mentioned in sub-paragraph (3).

(5) A recognition order shall state the date on which it takes effect.

Revocation of recognition

3. – (1) A recognition order may be revoked by a further order made by the Secretary of State if at any time it appears to him –
   (a)   that any requirement of Part II of this Schedule is not satisfied in the case of the body to which the recognition order relates ("the recognised body"),
   (b)   that the recognised body has failed to comply with any obligation to which it is subject by virtue of this Part of this Act, or
   (c)   that the continued recognition of the body is undesirable having regard to the existence of one or more other bodies which have been or are to be recognised.

(2) An order revoking a recognition order shall state the date on which it takes effect and that date shall not be earlier than three months after the day on which the revocation order is made.

(3) Before revoking a recognition order the Secretary of State shall give written notice of his intention to do so to the recognised body, take such steps as he considers reasonably practicable for bringing the notice to the attention of members of the body and publish it in such manner as he thinks appropriate for bringing it to the attention of any other persons who are in his opinion likely to be affected.

(4) A notice under sub-paragraph (3) shall state the reasons for which the Secretary of State proposes to act and give particulars of the rights conferred by sub-paragraph (5).

(5) A body on which a notice is served under sub-paragraph (3), any member of the body and any other person who appears to the Secretary of State to be affected may within three months after the date of service or publication, or within such longer time as the Secretary of State may allow, make written representations to the Secretary of State and, if desired, oral representations to a person

appointed for that purpose by the Secretary of State; and the Secretary of State shall have regard to any representations made in accordance with this sub-paragraph in determining whether to revoke the recognition order.

(6) If in any case the Secretary of State considers it essential to do so in the public interest he may revoke a recognition order without regard to the restriction imposed by sub-paragraph (2) and notwithstanding that no notice has been given or published under sub-paragraph (3) or that the time for making representations in pursuance of such a notice has not expired.

(7) An order revoking a recognition order may contain such transitional provisions as the Secretary of State thinks necessary or expedient.

(8) A recognition order may be revoked at the request or with the consent of the recognised body and any such revocation shall not be subject to the restrictions imposed by sub-paragraphs (1) and (2) or the requirements of sub-paragraphs (3) to (5).

(9) On making an order revoking a recognition order the Secretary of State shall give the body written notice of the making of the order, take such steps as he considers reasonably practicable for bringing the making of the order to the attention of members of the body and publish a notice of the making of the order in such manner as he thinks appropriate for bringing it to the attention of any other persons who are in his opinion likely to be affected.

PART II
REQUIREMENTS FOR RECOGNITION

Holding of appropriate qualification

4. – (1) The body must have rules to the effect that a person is not eligible for appointment as a company auditor unless –
> (*a*) in the case of an individual, he holds an appropriate qualification;
> (*b*) in the case of a firm –
>> (i) the individuals responsible for company audit work on behalf of the firm hold an appropriate qualification, and
>> (ii) the firm is controlled by qualified persons (see paragraph 5 below).

(2) This does not prevent the body from imposing more stringent requirements.

(3) A firm which has ceased to comply with the conditions mentioned in sub-paragraph (1)(*b*) may be permitted to remain eligible for appointment as a company auditor for a period of not more than three months.

5. – (1) The following provisions explain what is meant in paragraph 4(1)(*b*)(ii) by a firm being "controlled by qualified persons".

(2) For this purpose references to a person being qualified are, in relation to an individual, to his holding an appropriate qualification, and in relation to a firm, to its being eligible for appointment as a company auditor.

(3) A firm shall be treated as controlled by qualified persons if, and only if –
> (*a*) a majority of the members of the firm are qualified persons, and
> (*b*) where the firm's affairs are managed by a board of directors, committee or other management body, a majority of the members of that body are qualified persons or, if the body consists of two persons only, that at least one of them is a qualified person.

(4) A majority of the members of a firm means –
> (*a*) where under the firm's constitution matters are decided upon by the exercise of voting rights, members holding a majority of the rights to vote on all, or substantially all, matters;
> (*b*) in any other case, members having such rights under the constitution of the firm as enable them to direct its overall policy or alter its constitution.

(5) A majority of the members of the management body of a firm means –
- (*a*) where matters are decided at meetings of the management body by the exercise of voting rights, members holding a majority of the rights to vote on all, or substantially all, matters at such meetings;
- (*b*) in any other case, members having such rights under the constitution of the firm as enable them to direct its overall policy or alter its constitution.

(6) The provisions of paragraphs 5 to 11 of Schedule 10A to the Companies Act 1985 (rights to be taken into account and attribution of rights) apply for the purposes of this paragraph.

Auditors to be fit and proper persons

6. – (1) The body must have adequate rules and practices designed to ensure that the persons eligible under its rules for appointment as a company auditor are fit and proper persons to be so appointed.

(2) The matters which the body may take into account for this purpose in relation to a person must include –
- (*a*) any matter relating to any person who is or will be employed by or associated with him for the purposes of or in connection with company audit work; and
- (*b*) in the case of a body corporate, any matter relating to any director or controller of the body, to any other body corporate in the same group or to any director or controller of any such other body; and
- (*c*) in the case of a partnership, any matter relating to any of the partners, any director or controller of any of the partners, any body corporate in the same group as any of the partners and any director or controller of any such other body.

(3) In sub-paragraph (2)(*b*) and (*c*) "controller", in relation to a body corporate, means a person who either alone or with any associate or associates is entitled to exercise or control the exercise of 15 per cent. or more of the rights to vote on all, or substantially all, matters at general meetings of the body or another body corporate of which it is a subsidiary.

Professional integrity and independence

7. – (1) The body must have adequate rules and practices designed to ensure –
- (*a*) that company audit work is conducted properly and with integrity, and
- (*b*) that persons are not appointed company auditor in circumstances in which they have any interest likely to conflict with the proper conduct of the audit.

(2) The body must also have adequate rules and practices designed to ensure that no firm is eligible under its rules for appointment as a company auditor unless the firm has arrangements to prevent –
- (*a*) individuals who do not hold an appropriate qualification, and
- (*b*) persons who are not members of the firm,

from being able to exert any influence over the way in which an audit is conducted in circumstances in which that influence would be likley to affect the independence or integrity of the audit.

Technical standards

8. The body must have rules and practices as to the technical standards to be applied in company audit work and as to the manner in which those standards are to be applied in practice.

Procedures for maintaining competence

9. The body must have rules and practices designed to ensure that persons eligible under its rules for appointment as a company auditor continue to maintain an appropriate level of competence in the conduct of company audits.

Monitoring and enforcement

10. – (1) The body must have adequate arrangements and resources for the effective monitoring and enforcement of compliance with its rules.

(2) The arrangements for monitoring may make provision for that function to be performed on behalf of the body (and without affecting its responsibility) by any other body or person who is able and willing to perform it.

Membership, eligibility and discipline

11. The rules and practices of the body relating to –
    (*a*)   the admission and expulsion of members,
    (*b*)   the grant and withdrawal of eligibility for appointment as a company auditor, and
    (*c*)   the discipline it exercises over its members,
must be fair and reasonable and include adequate provision for appeals.

Investigation of complaints

12. – (1) The body must have effective arrangements for the investigation of complaints –
    (*a*)   against persons who are eligible under its rules to be appointed company auditor, or
    (*b*)   against the body in respect of matters arising out of its functions as a supervisory body.

(2) The arrangements may make provision for the whole or part of that function to be performed by and to be the responsibility of a body or person independent of the body itself.

Meeting of claims arising out of audit work

13. – (1) The body must have adequate rules or arrangements designed to ensure that persons eligible under its rules for appointment as a company auditor take such steps as may reasonably be expected of them to secure that they are able to meet claims against them arising out of company audit work.

(2) This may be achieved by professional indemnity insurance or other appropriate arrangements.

Register of auditors and other information to be made available

14. The body must have rules requiring persons eligible under its rules for appointment as a company auditor to comply with any obligations imposed on them by regulations under section 35 or 36.

Taking account of costs of compliance

15. The body must have satisfactory arrangements for taking account, in framing its rules, of the cost to those to whom the rules would apply of complying with those rules and any other controls to which they are subject.

Promotion and maintenance of standards

16. The body must be able and willing to promote and maintain high standards of integrity in the conduct of company audit work and to co-operate, by the sharing of information and otherwise, with the Secretary of State and any other authority, body or person having responsibility in the United Kingdom for the qualification, supervision or regulation of auditors.

SCHEDULE 12

RECOGNITION OF PROFESSIONAL QUALIFICATION

PART I
GRANT AND REVOCATION OF RECOGNITION

Application for recognition of professional qualification

1. – (1) A qualifying body may apply to the Secretary of State for an order declaring a qualification offered by it to be a recognised professional qualification for the purposes of this Part of this Act.

(2) Any such application –
 (a) shall be made in such manner as the Secretary of State may direct, and
 (b) shall be accompanied by such information as the Secretary of State may reasonably require for the purpose of determining the application.

(3) At any time after receiving an application and before determining it the Secretary of State may require the applicant to furnish additional information.

(4) The directions and requirements given or imposed under sub-paragraphs (2) and (3) may differ as between different applications.

(5) Any information to be furnished to the Secretary of State under this section shall, if he so requires, be in such form or verified in such manner as he may specify.
 In the case of examination standards, the verification required may include independent moderation of the examinations over such period as the Secretary of State considers necessary.

(6) Every application shall be accompanied by a copy of the applicant's rules and of any guidance issued by it which is intended to have continuing effect and is issued in writing or other legible form.

Grant and refusal of recognition

2. – (1) The Secretary of State may, on an application duly made in accordance with paragraph 1 and after being furnished with all such information as he may require under that paragraph, make or refuse to make an order (a "recognition order") declaring the qualification in respect of which the application was made to be a recognised professional qualification for the purposes of this Part of this Act.
 In this Part of this Act a "recognised qualifying body" means a qualifying body offering a recognised professional qualification.

(2) The Secretary of State shall not make a recognition order unless it appears to him, from the information furnished by the applicant and having regard to any other information in his possession, that the requirements of Part II of this Schedule are satisfied as respects the qualification.

(3) Where the Secretary of State refuses an application for a recognition order he shall give the applicant a written notice to that effect specifying which requriements, in his opinion, are not satisfied.

(4) A recognition order shall state the date on which it takes effect.

Revocation of recognition

3. – (1) A recognition order may be revoked by a further order made by the Secretary of State if at any time it appears to him –
 (a) that any requirement of Part II of this Schedule is not satisfied in relation to the qualification to which the recognition order relates, or

(*b*) that the qualifying body has failed to comply with any obligation to which it is subject by virtue of this Part of this Act.

(2) An order revoking a recognition order shall state the date on which it takes effect and the date shall not be earlier than three months after the day on which the revocation order is made.

(3) Before revoking a recognition order the Secretary of State shall give written notice of his intention to do so to the qualifying body, take such steps as he considers reasonably practicable for bringing the notice to the attention of persons holding the qualification or in the course of studying for it and publish it in such manner as he thinks appropriate for bringing it to the attention of any other persons who are in his opinion likely to be affected.

(4) A notice under sub-paragraph (3) shall state the reasons for which the Secretary of State proposes to act and give particulars of the rights conferred by sub-paragraph (5).

(5) A body on which a notice is served under sub-paragraph (3), any person holding the qualification or in the course of studying for it and any other person who appears to the Secretary of State to be affected may within three months after the date of service or publication, or within such longer time as the Secretary of State may allow, make written representations to the Secretary of State and, if desired, oral representations to a person appointed for that purpose by the Secretary of State; and the Secretary of State shall have regard to any representations made in accordance with this subsection in determining whether to revoke the recognition order.

(6) If in any case the Secretary of State considers it essential to do so in the public interest he may revoke a recognition order without regard to the restriction imposed by sub-paragraph (2) and notwithstanding that no notice has been given or published under sub-paragraph (3) or that the time for making representations in pursuance of such a notice has not expired.

(7) An order revoking a recognition order may contain such transitional provisions as the Secretary of State thinks necessary or expedient.

(8) A recognition order may be revoked at the request or with the consent of the qualifying body and any such revocation shall not be subject to the restrictions imposed by sub-paragraphs (1) and (2) or the requirements of sub-paragraphs (3) to (5).

(9) On making an order revoking a recognition order the Secretary of State shall give the qualifying body written notice of the making of the order, take such steps as he considers reasonably practicable for bringing the making of the order to the attention of persons holding the qualification or in the course of studying for it and publish a notice of the making of the order in such manner as he thinks appropriate for bringing it to the attention of any other persons who are in his opinion likely to be affected.

PART II
REQUIREMENTS FOR RECOGNITION

Entry requirements

4. – (1) The qualification must only be open to persons who have attained university entrance level or have a sufficient period of professional experience.

(2) In relation to a person who has not been admitted to a university or other similar establishment in the United Kingdom, attaining university entrance level means –
    (*a*) being educated to such a standard as would entitle him to be considered for such admission on the basis of –
        (i) academic or professional qualifications obtained in the United Kingdom and recognised by the Secretary of State to be of an appropriate standard, or
        (ii) academic or professional qualifications obtained outside the United Kingdom which the Secretary of State considers to be of an equivalent standard; or

(*b*)   being assessed on the basis of written tests of a kind appearing to the Secretary of State to be adequate for the purpose, with or without oral examination, as of such a standard of ability as would entitle him to be considered for such admission.

(3) The assessment, tests and oral examination referred to in sub-paragraph (2)(*b*) may be conducted by the qualifying body or by some other body approved by the Secretary of State.

Course of theoretical instruction

5. The qualification must be restricted to persons who have completed a course of theoretical instruction in the subjects prescribed for the purposes of paragraph 7 or have a sufficient period of professional experience.

Sufficient period of professional experience

6. – (1) The references in paragraphs 4 and 5 to a sufficient period of professional experience are to not less than seven years' experience in a professional capacity in the fields of finance, law and accountancy.

(2) Periods of theoretical instruction in the fields of finance, law and accountancy may be deducted from the required period of professional experience, provided the instruction –
(*a*)   lasted at least one year, and
(*b*)   is attested by an examination recognised by the Secretary of State for the purposes of this paragraph;
but the period of professional experience may not be so reduced by more than four years.

(3) The period of professional experience together with the practical training required in the case of persons satisfying the requirement in paragraph 5 by virtue of having a sufficient period of professional experience must not be shorter than the course of theoretical instruction referred to in that paragraph and the practical training required in the case of persons satisfying the requirement of that paragraph by virtue of having completed such a course.

Examination

7. – (1) The qualification must be restricted to persons who have passed an examination (at least part of which is in writing) testing –
(*a*)   theoretical knowledge of the subjects prescribed for the purposes of this paragraph by regulations made by the Secretary of State, and
(*b*)   ability to apply that knowledge in practice,
and requiring a standard of attainment at least equivalent to that required to obtain a degree from a university or similar establishment in the United Kingdom.

(2) The qualification may be awarded to a person without his theoretical knowledge of a subject being tested by examination if he has passed a university or other examination of equivalent standard in that subject or holds a university degree or equivalent qualification in it.

(3) The qualification may be awarded to a person without his ability to apply his theoretical knowledge of a subject in practice being tested by examination if he has received practical training in that subject which is attested by an examination or diploma recognised by the Secretary of State for the purposes of this paragraph.

(4) Regulations under this paragraph shall be made by statutory instrument which shall be subject to annulment in pursuance of a resolution of either House of Parliament.

Practical training

8. – (1) The qualification must be restricted to persons who have completed at least three years' practical training of which –

    (*a*) part was spent being trained in company audit work, and

    (*b*) a substantial part was spent being trained in company audit work or other audit work of a description approved by the Secretary of State as being similar to company audit work.

For this purpose "company audit work" includes the work of a person appointed as auditor under the Companies (Northern Ireland) Order 1986 or under the law of a country or territory outside the United Kingdom where it appears to the Secretary of State that the law and practice with respect to the audit of company accounts is similar to that in the United Kindom.

(2) The training must be given by persons approved by the body offering the qualification as persons as to whom the body is satisfied, in the light of undertakings given by them and the supervision to which they are subject (whether by the body itself or some other body or organisation), that they will provide adequate training.

(3) At least two-thirds of the training must be given by a fully-qualified auditor, that is, a person –

    (*a*) eligible in accordance with this Part of this Act to be appointed as a company auditor, or

    (*b*) satisfying the corresponding requirements of the law of Northern Ireland or another member State of the European Economic Community.

The body offering the qualification

9. – (1) The body offering the qualification must have –

    (*a*) rules and arrangements adequate to ensure compliance with the requirements of paragraphs 4 to 8, and

    (*b*) adequate arrangements for the effective monitoring of its continued compliance with those requirements.

(2) The arrangements must include arrangements for monitoring the standard of its examinations and the adequacy of the practical training given by the persons approved by it for that purpose.

Section 46(6)   # SCHEDULE 13

SUPPLEMENTARY PROVISIONS WITH RESPECT TO DELEGATION ORDER

Introductory

1. The following provisions have effect in relation to a body established by a delegation order under section 46; and any power to make provision by order is to make provison by order under that section.

Status

2. The body shall not be regarded as acting on behalf of the Crown and its members, officers and employees shall not be regarded as Crown servants.

Name, members and chairman

3. – (1) The body shall be known by such name as may be specified in the delegation order.

(2) The body shall consist of such persons (not being less than eight) as the Secretary of State may appoint after such consultation as he thinks appropriate; and the chairman of the body shall be such person as the Secretary of State may appoint from amongst its members.

(3) The Secretary of State may make provision by order as to the terms on which the members of the body are to hold and vacate office and as to the terms on which a person appointed as chairman is to hold and vacate the office of chairman.

Financial provisions

4. – (1) The body shall pay to its chairman and members such remuneration, and such allowances in respect of expenses properly incurred by them in the performance of their duties, as the Secretary of State may determine.

(2) As regards any chairman or member in whose case the Secretary of State so determines, the body shall pay or make provision for the payment of–

    (*a*)   such pension, allowance or gratuity to or in respect of that person on his retirement or death, or

    (*b*)   such contributions or other payment towards the provision of such a pension, allowance or gratuity,

as the Secretary of State may determine.

(3) Where a person ceases to be a member of the body otherwise than on the expiry of his term of office and it appears to the Secretary of State that there are special circumstances which make it right for him to receive compensation, the body shall make a payment to him by way of compensation of such amount as the Secretary of State may determine.

Proceedings

5. – (1) The delegation order may contain such provision as the Secretary of State considers appropriate with respect to the proceedings of the body.

(2) The order may, in particular –

    (*a*)   authorise the body to discharge any functions by means of committees consisting wholly or partly of members of the body;

    (*b*)   provide that the validity of proceedings of the body, or of any such committee, is not affected by any vacancy among the members or any defect in the appointment of any member.

Fees

6. – (1) The body may retain fees payable to it.

(2) The fees shall be applied for meeting the expenses of the body in discharging its functions and for any purposes incidental to those functions.

(3) Those expenses include any expenses incurred by the body on such staff, accommodation, services and other facilities as appear to it to be necessary or expedient for the proper performance of its functions.

(4) In prescribing the amount of fees in the exercise of the functions transferred to it the body shall prescribe such fees as appear to it sufficient to defray those expenses, taking one year with another.

(5) Any exercise by the body of the power to prescribe fees requires the approval of the Secretary of State; and the Secretary of State may, after consultation with the body, by order vary or revoke any regulations made by it prescribing fees.

Legislative functions

7. – (1) Regulations made by the body in the exercise of the functions transferred to it shall be made by instrument in writing, but not by statutory instrument.

(2) The instrument shall specify the provision of this Part of this Act under which it is made.

(3) The Secretary of State may by order impose such requirements as he thinks necessary or expedient as to the circumstances and manner in which the body must consult on any regulations it proposes to make.

8. – (1) Immediately after an instrument is made it shall be printed and made available to the public with or without payment.

(2) A person shall not be taken to have contravened any regulation if he shows that at the time of the alleged contravention the instrument containing the regulation had not been made available as required by this paragraph.

9. – (1) The production of a printed copy of an instrument purporting to be made by the body on which is endorsed a certificate signed by an officer of the body authorised by it for the purpose and stating –

    (*a*)   that the instrument was made by the body,

    (*b*)   that the copy is a true copy of the instrument, and

    (*c*)   that on a specified date the instrument was made available to the public as required by paragraph 8,

is prima facie evidence or, in Scotland, sufficient evidence of the facts stated in the certificate.

(2) A certificate purporting to be signed as mentioned in sub-paragraph (1) shall be deemed to have been duly signed unless the contrary is shown.

(3) Any person wishing in any legal proceedings to cite an instrument made by the body may require the body to cause a copy of it to be endorsed with such a certificate as is mentioned in this paragraph.

Report and accounts

10. – (1) The body shall at least once in each year for which the delegation order is in force make a report to the Secretary of State on the discharge of the functions transferred to it and on such other matters as the Secretary of State may by order require.

(2) The Secretary of State shall lay before Parliament copies of each report received by him under this paragraph.

(3) The Secretary of State may, with the consent of the Treasury, give directions to the body with respect to its accounts and the audit of its accounts and it is the duty of the body to comply with the directions.

(4) A person shall not be appointed auditor of the body unless he is eligible for appointment as a company auditor under section 25.

Other supplementary provisions

11. – (1) The transfer of a function to a body established by a delegation order does not affect anything previously done in the exercise of the function transferred; and the resumption of a function so transferred does not affect anything previously done in exercise of the function resumed.

(2) The Secretary of State may by order make such transitional and other supplementary provision as he thinks necessary or expedient in relation to the transfer or resumption of a function.

(3) The provision that may be made in connection with the transfer of a function includes, in particular, provision –

    (*a*)   for modifying or excluding any provision of this Part of this Act in its application to the function transferred;

    (*b*)   for applying to the body established by the delegation order, in connection with the function transferred, any provision applying to the Secretary of State which is contained in or made under any other enactment;

    (*c*)   for the transfer of any property, rights or liabilities from the Secretary of State to that body;

    (*d*)   for the carrying on and completion by that body of anything in process of being done by the Secretary of State when the order takes effect;

    (*e*)   for the substitution of that body for the Secretary of State in any instrument, contract or legal proceedings.

(4) The provision that may be made in connection with the resumption of a function includes, in particular, provision –

    (*a*) for the transfer of any property, rights or liabilities from that body to the Secretary of State;

    (*b*) for the carrying on and completion by the Secretary of State of anything in process of being done by that body when the order takes effect;

    (*c*) for the substitution of the Secretary of State for that body in any instrument, contract or legal proceedings.

12. Where a delegation order is revoked, the Secretary of State may by order make provision –

    (*a*) for the payment of compensation to persons ceasing to be employed by the body established by the delegation order; and

    (*b*) as to the winding up and dissolution of the body.

Section 47(1)

SCHEDULE 14

SUPERVISORY AND QUALIFYING BODIES: RESTRICTIVE PRACTICES

PART I
PREVENTION OF RESTRICTIVE PRACTICES

Refusal of recognition on grounds related to competition

1. – (1) The Secretary of State shall before deciding whether to make a recognition order in respect of a supervisory body or professional qualification send to the Director General of Fair Trading (in this Schedule referred to as "the Director") a copy of the rules and of any guidance which the Secretary of State is required to consider in making that decision together with such other information as the Secretary of State considers will assist the Director.

(2) The Director shall consider whether the rules or guidance have, or are intended or likely to have, to any significant extent the effect of restricting, distorting or preventing competition, and shall report to the Secretary of State; and the Secretary of State shall have regard to his report in deciding whether to make a recognition order.

(3) The Secretary of State shall not make a recognition order if it appears to him that the rules and any guidance of which copies are furnished with the application have, or are intended or likely to have, to any significant extent the effect of restricting, distorting or preventing competition, unless it appears to him that the effect is reasonably justifiable having regard to the purposes of this Part of this Act.

Notification of changes to rules or guidance

2. – (1) Where a recognised supervisory or qualifying body amends, revokes or adds to its rules or guidance in a manner which may reasonably be regarded as likely –

    (*a*) to restrict, distort or prevent competition to any significant extent, or

    (*b*) otherwise to affect the question whether the recognition order granted to the body should continue in force,

it shall within seven days give the Secretary of State written notice of the amendment, revocation or addition.

(2) Notice need not be given under sub-paragraph (1) of the revocation of guidance not intended to have continuing effect or issued otherwise than in writing or other legible form, or of any amendment or addition to guidance which does not result in or consist of guidance which is intended to have continuing effect and is issued in writing or other legible form.

Continuing scrutiny by the Director General of Fair Trading

3. – (1) The Director shall keep under review the rules made or guidance issued by a recognised supervisory or qualifying body, and if he is of the opinion that any rules or guidance of such a body have, or are intended or likely to have, to any significant extent the effect of restricting, distorting or preventing competition, he shall report his opinion to the Secretary of State, stating what in his opinion the effect is or is likely to be.

(2) The Secretary of State shall send to the Director copies of any notice received by him under paragraph 2, together with such other information as he considers will assist the Director.

(3) The Director may report to the Secretary of State his opinion that any matter mentioned in such a notice does not have, and is not intended or likely to have, to any significant extent the effect of restricting, distorting or preventing competition.

(4) The Director may from time to time consider whether –
  (a) any practices of a recognised supervisory or qualifying body in its capacity as such, or
  (b) any relevant practices required or contemplated by the rules or guidance of such a body or otherwise attributable to its conduct in its capacity as such,
have, or are intended or likely to have, to any significant extent the effect of restricting, distorting or preventing competition and, if so, what that effect is or is likely to be; and if he is of that opinion he shall make a report to the Secretary of State stating his opinion and what the effect is or is likely to be.

(5) The practices relevant for the purposes of sub-paragraph (4)(b) in the case of a recognised supervisory body are practices engaged in for the purposes of, or in connection with, appointment as a company auditor or the conduct of company audit work by persons who –
  (a) are eligible under its rules for appointment as a company auditor, or
  (b) hold an appropriate qualification and are directors or other officers of bodies corporate which are so eligible or partners in, or employees of, partnerships which are so eligible.

(6) The practices relevant for the purposes of sub-paragraph (4)(b) in the case of a recognised qualifying body are –
  (a) practices engaged in by persons in the course of seeking to obtain a recognised professional qualification from that body, and
  (b) practices engaged in by persons approved by the body for the purposes of giving practical training to persons seeking such a qualification and which relate to such training.

Investigatory powers of the Director

4. – (1) The following powers are exercisable by the Director for the purpose of investigating any matter in connection with his functions under paragraph 1 or 3.

(2) The Director may by a notice in writing require any person to produce, at a time and place specified in the notice, to the Director or to any person appointed by him for the purpose, any documents which are specified or described in the notice and which are documents in his custody or under his control and relating to any matter relevant to the investigation.

(3) The Director may by a notice in writing require any person to furnish to the Director such information as may be specified or described in the notice, and specify the time within which and the manner and form in which any such information is to be furnished.

(4) A person shall not under this paragraph be required to produce any document or disclose any information which he would be entitled to refuse to produce or disclose on grounds of legal professional privilege in proceedings in the High Court or on the ground of confidentiality as between client and professional legal adviser in proceedings in the Court of Session.

(5) Subsections (6) to (8) of section 85 of the Fair Trading Act 1973 (enforcement provisions) apply in relation to a notice under this paragraph as they apply in relation to a notice under subsection (1) of that section but as if, in subsection (7) of that section, for the words from "any one" to "the Commission" there were substituted "the Director".

Publication of Director's reports

5. – (1) The Director may, if he thinks fit, publish any report made by him under paragraph 1 or 3.

(2) He shall exclude from a published report, so far as practicable, any matter which relates to the affairs of a particular person (other than the supervisory or qualifying body concerned) the publication of which would or might in his opinion seriously and prejudicially affect the interests of that person.

Powers exercisable by the Secretary of State in consequence of report

6. – (1) The powers conferred by this section are exercisable by the Secretary of State if, having received and considered a report from the Director under paragraph 3(1) or (4), it appears to him that –
   (a)   any rules made or guidance issued by a recognised supervisory or qualifying body, or
   (b)   any such practices as are mentioned in paragraph 3(4),

have, or are intended or likely to have, to any significant extent the effect of restricting, distorting or preventing competition and that that effect is greater than is reasonably justifiable having regard to the purposes of this Part of this Act.

(2) The powers are –
   (a)   to revoke the recognition order granted to the body concerned,
   (b)   to direct it to take specified steps for the purpose of securing that the rules, guidance or practices in question do not have the effect mentioned in sub-paragraph (1), and
   (c)   to make alterations in the rules of the body for that purpose.

(3) The provisions of paragraph 3(2) to (5), (7) and (9) of Schedule 11 or, as the case may be, Schedule 12 have effect in relation to the revocation of a recognition order under sub-paragraph (2)(a) above as they have effect in relation to the revocation of such an order under that Schedule.

(4) Before the Secretary of State exercises the power conferred by sub-paragraph (2)(b) or (c) above he shall –
   (a)   give written notice of his intention to do so to the body concerned and take such steps (whether by publication or otherwise) as he thinks appropriate for bringing the notice to the attention of any other person who in his opinion is likely to be affected by the exercise of the power, and
   (b)   have regard to any representations made within such time as he considers reasonable by the body or any such other person.

(5) A notice under sub-paragraph (4) shall give particulars of the manner in which the Secretary of State proposes to exercise the power in question and state the reasons for which he proposes to act; and the statement of reasons may include matters contained in any report received by him under paragraph 4.

Supplementary provisions

7. – (1) A direction under paragraph 6 is, on the application of the Secretary of State, enforceable by injunction or, in Scotland, by an order under section 45 of the Court of Session Act 1988.

(2) The fact that any rules made by a recognised supervisory or qualifying body have been altered by the Secretary of State, or pursuant to a direction of the Secretary of State, under paragraph 6 does not preclude their subsequent alteration or revocation by that body.

(3) In determining for the purposes of this Part of this Schedule whether any guidance has, or is likely to have, any particular effect the Secretary of State and the Director may assume that the persons to whom it is addressed will act in conformity with it.

PART II
CONSEQUENTIAL EXEMPTIONS FROM COMPETITION LAW

Fair Trading Act 1973 (c. 41)

8. – (1) For the purpose of determining whether a monopoly situation within the meaning of the Fair Trading Act 1973 exists by reason of the circumstances mentioned in section 7(1)(*c*) of that Act (supply of services by or for group of two or more persons), no account shall be taken of –
    (*a*) the rules of or guidance issued by a recognised supervisory or qualifying body, or
    (*b*) conduct constituting such a practice as is mentioned in paragraph 3(4) above.

(2) Where a recognition order is revoked there shall be disregarded for the purpose mentioned in sub-paragraph (1) any such conduct as is mentioned in that sub-paragraph which occurred while the order was in force.

(3) Where on a monopoly reference under section 50 or 51 of the Fair Trading Act 1973 falling within section 49 of that Act (monopoly reference not limited to the facts) the Monopolies and Mergers Commission find that a monopoly situation within the meaning of that Act exists and –
    (*a*) that the person (or, if more than one, any of the persons) in whose favour it exists is –
        (i) a recognised supervisory or qualifying body, or
        (ii) a person of a description mentioned in paragraph 3(5) or (6) above, or
    (*b*) that any such person's conduct in doing anything to which the rules of such a body relate is subject to guidance issued by the body,
the Commission in making their report on that reference shall exclude from their consideration the question whether the rules or guidance of the body concerned, or the acts or omissions of that body in its capacity as such, operate or may be expected to operate against the public interest.

Restrictive Trade Practices Act 1976 (c. 34)

9. – (1) The Restrictive Trade Practices Act 1976 does not apply to an agreement for the constitution of a recognised supervisory or qualifying body in so far as it relates to rules of or guidance issued by the body, and incidental matters connected therewith, including any term deemed to be contained in it by virtue of section 8(2) or 16(3) of that Act.

(2) Nor does that Act apply to an agreement the parties to which consist of or include –
    (*a*) a recognised supervisory or qualifying body, or
    (*b*) any such person as is mentioned in paragraph 3(5) or (6) above,
by reason that it includes any terms the inclusion of which is required or contemplated by the rules or guidance of that body.

(3) Where an agreement ceases by virtue of this paragraph to be subject to registration –
    (*a*) the Director shall remove from the register maintained by him under the Act of 1976 any particulars which are entered or filed in that register in respect of the agreement, and
    (*b*) any proceedings in respect of the agreement which are pending before the Restrictive Practices Court shall be discontinued.

(4) Where a recognition order is revoked, sub-paragraphs (1) and (2) above shall continue to apply for a period of six months beginning with the day on which the revocation takes effect, as if the order were still in force.

(5) Where an agreement which has been exempt from registration by virtue of this paragraph ceases to be exempt in consequence of the revocation of a recognition order, the time within which particulars of the agreement are to be furnished in accordance with section 24 of and Schedule 2 to the Act of 1976 shall be the period of one month beginning with the day on which the agreement ceased to be exempt from registration.

(6) Where in the case of an agreement registered under the 1976 Act a term ceases to fall within sub-paragraph (2) above in consequence of the revocation of a recognition order and particulars of that term have not previously been furnished to the Director under section 24 of that Act, those

particulars shall be furnished to him within the period of one month beginning with the day on which the term ceased to fall within that sub-paragraph.

Competition Act 1980 (c. 21)

10. – (1) No course of conduct constituting any such practice as is mentioned in paragraph 3(4) above shall constitute an anti-competitive practice for the purposes of the Competition Act 1980.

(2) Where a recognition order is revoked there shall not be treated as an anti-competitive practice for the purposes of that Act any such course of conduct as is mentioned in sub-paragraph(1) which occurred while the order was in force.

Section 50 # SCHEDULE 15

CHARGES ON PROPERTY OF OVERSEA COMPANIES

The following provisions are inserted in Part XXIII of the Companies Act 1985 –

"CHAPTER III
REGISTRATION OF CHARGES

703A Introductory provisions

(1) The provisions of this Chapter have effect for securing the registration in Great Britain of charges on the property of a registered oversea company.

(2) Section 395(2) and (3) (meaning of "charge" and "property") have effect for the purposes of this Chapter.

(3) A "registered oversea company", in relation to England and Wales or Scotland, means an oversea company which has duly delivered documents to the registrar for that part of Great Britain under section 691 and has not subsequently given notice to him under section 696(4) that it has ceased to have an established place of business in that part.

(4) References in this Chapter to the registrar shall be construed in accordance with section 703E below and references to registration, in relation to a charge, are to registration in the register kept by him under this Chapter.

703B Charges requiring registration

(1) The charges requiring registration under this Chapter are those which if created by a company registered in Great Britain would require registration under Part XII of this Act.

(2) Whether a charge is one requiring registration under this Chapter shall be determined –
> (*a*) in the case of a charge over property of a company at the date it delivers documents for registration under section 691, as at that date,
> (*b*) in the case of a charge created by a registered oversea company, as at the date the charge is created, and
> (*c*) in the case of a charge over property acquired by a registered oversea company, as at the date of the acquisition.

(3) In the following provisions of this chapter references to a charge are, unless the context otherwise requires, to a charge requiring registration under this Chapter.

Where a charge not otherwise requiring registration relates to property by virtue of which it requires to be registered and to other property, the references are to the charge so far as it relates to property of the former description.

703C   The register

(1) The registrar shall keep for each registered oversea company a register, in such form as he thinks fit, of charges on property of the company.

(2) The register shall consist of a file containing with respect to each such charge the particulars and other information delivered to the registrar under or by virtue of the following provisions of this Chapter.

(3) Section 397(3) to (5) (registrar's certificate as to date of delivery of particulars) applies in relation to the delivery of any particulars or other information under this Chapter.

703D   Company's duty to deliver particulars of charges for registration

(1) If when an oversea company delivers documents for registration under section 691 any of its property is situated in Great Britain and subject to a charge, it is the company's duty at the same time to deliver the prescribed particulars of the charge, in the prescribed form, to the registrar for registration.

(2) Where a registered oversea company –
> (*a*)   creates a charge on property situated in Great Britain, or
> (*b*)   acquires property which is situated in Great Britain and subject to a charge,

it is the company's duty to deliver the prescribed particulars of the charge, in the prescribed form, to the registrar for registration within 21 days after the date of the charge's creation or, as the case may be, the date of the acquisition.

This subsection does not apply if the property subject to the charge is at the end of that period no longer situated in Great Britain.

(3) Where the preceding subsections do not apply and property of a registered oversea company is for a continuous period of four months situated in Great Britain and subject to a charge, it is the company's duty before the end of that period to deliver the prescribed particulars of the charge, in the prescribed form, to the registrar for registration.

(4) Particulars of a charge required to be delivered under subsections (1), (2) or (3) may be delivered for registration by any person interested in the charge.

(5) If a company fails to comply with subsection (1), (2) or (3), then, unless particulars of the charge have been delivered for registration by another person, the company and every officer of it who is in default is liable to a fine.

(6) Section 398(2), (4) and (5) (recovery of fees paid in connection with registration, filing of particulars in register and sending of copy of particulars filed and note as to date) apply in relation to particulars delivered under this Chapter.

703E   Registrar to whom particulars, &c to be delivered

(1) The particulars required to be delivered by section 703D(1) (charges over property of oversea company becoming registered in a part of Great Britain) shall be delivered to the registrar to whom the documents are delivered under section 691.

(2) The particulars required to be delivered by section 703D(2) or (3) (charges over property of registered oversea company) shall be delivered –
> (*a*)   if the company is registered in one part of Great Britain and not in the other, to the registrar for the part in which it is registered, and

(b) if the company is registered in both parts of Great Britain but the property subject to the charge is situated in one part of Great Britain only, to the registrar for that part;

and in any other case the particulars shall be delivered to the registrars for both parts of Great Britain.

(3) Other documents required or authorised by virtue of this Chapter to be delivered to the registrar shall be delivered to the registrar or registrars to whom particulars of the charge to which they relate have been, or ought to have been, delivered.

(4) If a company gives notice under section 696(4) that it has ceased to have an established place of business in either part of Great Britain, charges over property of the company shall cease to be subject to the provisions of this Chapter, as regards registration in that part of Great Britain, as from the date on which notice is so given.

This is without prejudice to rights arising by reason of events occurring before that date.

703F Effect of failure to deliver particulars, late delivery and effect of errors and omissions

(1) The following provisions of Part XII –
- (a) section 399 (effect of failure to deliver particulars),
- (b) section 400 (late delivery of particulars), and
- (c) section 402 (effect of errors and omissions in particulars delivered),

apply, with the following modifications, in relation to a charge created by a registered oversea company of which particulars are required to be delivered under this Chapter.

(2) Those provisions do not apply to a charge of which particulars are required to be delivered under section 703D(1) (charges existing when company delivers documents under section 691).

(3) In relation to a charge of which particulars are required to be delivered under section 703D(3) (charges registrable by virtue of property being within Great Britain for requisite period), the references to the period of 21 days after the charge's creation shall be construed as references to the period of four months referred to in that subsection.

703G Delivery of further particulars or memorandum

Sections 401 and 403 (delivery of further particulars and memorandum of charge ceasing to affect company's property) apply in relation to a charge of which particulars have been delivered under this Chapter.

703H Further provisions with respect to voidness of charges

(1) The following provisions of Part XII apply in relation to the voidness of a charge by virtue of this Chapter –
- (a) section 404 (exclusion of voidness as against unregistered charges),
- (b) section 405 (restrictions on cases in which charge is void),
- (c) section 406 (effect of exercise of power of sale), and
- (d) section 407 (effect of voidness on obligation secured).

(2) In relation to a charge of which particulars are required to be delivered under section 703D(3) (charges registrable by virtue of property being within Great Britain for requisite period), the reference in section 404 to the period of 21 days after the charge's creation shall be construed as a reference to the period of four months referred to in that subsection.

703I Additional information to be registered

(1) Section 408 (particulars of taking up of issue of debentures) applies in relation to a charge of which particulars have been delivered under this Chapter.

(2) Section 409 (notice of appointment of receiver or manager) applies in relation to the appointment of a receiver or manager of property of a registered oversea company.

(3) Regulations under section 410 (notice of crystallisation of floating charge, &c.) may apply in relation to a charge of which particulars have been delivered under this Chapter; but subject to such exceptions, adaptations and modifications as may be specified in the regulations.

703J   Copies of instruments and register to be kept by company

(1) Sections 411 and 412 (copies of instruments and register to be kept by company) apply in relation to a registered oversea company and any charge over property of the company situated in Great Britain.

(2) They apply to any charge, whether or not particulars are required to be delivered to the registrar.

(3) In relation to such a company the references to the company's registered office shall be construed as references to its principal place of business in Great Britain.

703K   Power to make further provision by regulations

(1) The Secretary of State may by regulations make further provision as to the application of the provisions of this Chapter, or the provisions of Part XII applied by this Chapter, in relation to charges of any description specified in the regulations.

(2) The regulations may apply any provisions of regulations made under section 413 (power to make further provision with respect to application of Part XII) or make any provision which may be made under that section with respect to the application of provisions of Part XII.

703L   Provisions as to situation of property

(1) The following provisions apply for determining for the purposes of this Chapter whether a vehicle which is the property of an oversea company is situated in Great Britain –
- (*a*) a ship, aircraft or hovercraft shall be regarded as situated in Great Britain if, and only if, it is registered in Great Britain;
- (*b*) any other description of vehicle shall be regarded as situated in Great Britain on a day if, and only if, at any time on that day the management of the vehicle is directed from a place of business of the company in Great Britain;

and for the purposes of this Chapter a vehicle shall not be regarded as situated in one part of Great Britain only.

(2) For the purposes of this Chapter as it applies to a charge on future property, the subject-matter of the charge shall be treated as situated in Great Britain unless it relates exclusively to property of a kind which cannot, after being acquired or coming into existence, be situated in Great Britain; and references to property situated in a part of Great Britain shall be similarly construed.

703M   Other supplementary provisions

The following provisions of Part XII apply for the purposes of this Chapter –
- (*a*) section 414 (construction of references to date of creation of charge),
- (*b*) section 415 (prescribed particulars and related expressions),
- (*c*) section 416 (notice of matters disclosed on the register),
- (*d*) section 417 (power of court to dispense with signature),
- (*e*) section 418 (regulations) and
- (*f*) section 419 (minor definitions).

703N   Index of defined expressions

The following Table shows the provisions of this Chapter and Part XII defining or otherwise explaining expressions used in this Chapter (other than expressions used only in the same section) –

charge	sections 703A(2), 703B(3) and 395(2)
charge requiring registration	sections 703B(1) and 396
creation of charge	sections 703M(*f*) and 419(2)
date of acquisition (of property by a company)	sections 703M(*f*) and 419(3)
date of creation of charge	sections 703M(*a*) and 414
property	sections 703A(2) and 395(2)
registered oversea company	section 703A(3)
registrar and registration in relation to a charge	sections 703A(4) and 703E
situated in Great Britain	
in relation to vehicles	section 703L(1)
in relation to future property	section 703L(2)".

Section 107

SCHEDULE 16

AMENDMENTS CONSEQUENTIAL ON PART IV

Land Charges Act 1972 (c. 61)

1. – (1) Section 3 of the Land Charges Act 1972 (registration of land charges) is amended as follows.

(2) In subsection (7) (registration in companies charges register to have same effect as registration under that Act), for "any of the enactments mentioned in subsection (8) below" substitute "Part XII, or Chapter III of Part XXIII, of the Companies Act 1985 (or corresponding earlier enactments)".

(3) In subsection (8) for "The enactments" substitute "The corresponding earlier enactments" and at the end insert "as originally enacted".

Companies Act 1985 (c.6)

2. – (1) Schedule 24 to the Companies Act 1985 (punishment of offences) is amended as follows.

(2) For the entries relating to sections 399(3) to 423(3) (offences under Part XII: registration of charges) substitute –

"398(3)	Company failing to deliver particulars of charge to registrar.	1. On indictment. 2. Summary.	A fine. The statutory maximum.
408(3)	Company failing to deliver particulars of taking up of issue of debentures.	Summary.	One-fifth of the statutory maximum.
409(4)	Failure to give notice to registrar of appointment of receiver or manager, or of his ceasing to act.	Summary.	.One-fifth of the statutory maximum.
410(4)	Failure to comply with requirements of regulations under s.410.	Summary.	One-fifth of the statutory maximum.
411(4)	Failure to keep copies of charging instruments or register at registered office.	1. On indictment. 2. Summary.	A fine. The statutory maximum.

| 412(4) | Refusing inspection of charging instrument or register or failing to supply copies. | Summary. | One-fifth of the statutory maximum.". |

(3) After the entry relating to section 703(1) insert –

| "703D(5) | Oversea company failing to deliver particulars of charge to registrar. | 1. On indictment. 2. Summary. | A fine. The statutory maximum.". |

Insolvency Act 1986 (c. 45)

3. – (1) The Insolvency Act 1986 is amended as follows.

(2) In section 9(3) (restrictions on making administration order where administrative receiver has been appointed), in paragraph (*b*) (exceptions) insert –

      "(i) be void against the administrator to any extent by virtue of the provisions of Part XII of the Companies Act 1985 (registration of company charges),";

and renumber the existing sub-paragraphs as (ii) to (iv).

(3) In sections 45(5), 53(2), 54(3) and 62(5) (offences of failing to deliver documents relating to appointment or cessation of appointment of receiver) omit the words "and, for continued contravention, to a daily default fine".

Company Directors Disqualification Act 1986 (c. 46)

4. In Schedule 1 to the Company Directors Disqualification Act 1986 (matters relevant to determining unfitness of directors), in paragraph 4 (failure of company to comply with certain provisions), for sub-paragraph (*h*) substitute –

      "(*h*) sections 398 and 703D (duty of company to deliver particulars of charges on its property).".

Section 130(7)   # SCHEDULE 17

COMPANY CONTRACTS, SEALS, &C.: FURTHER PROVISIONS

Execution of deeds abroad

1. – (1) Section 38 of the Companies Act 1985 (execution of deeds abroad) is amended as follows.

(2) In subsection (1) (appointment of attorney to execute deeds), after "A company may" insert "under the law of England and Wales".

(3) For subsection (2) (effect of deed executed by attorney) substitute –

      "(2) A deed executed by such an attorney on behalf of the company has the same effect as if executed under the company's common seal.".

Official seal for use abroad

2. – (1) Section 39 of the Companies Act 1985 (power to have official seal for use abroad) is amended as follows.

(2) In subsection (1), after "A company" insert "which has a common seal" and for "the common seal of the company" substitute "its common seal".

(3) For subsection (2) (effect of sealing with official seal) substitute –

"(2) The official seal when duly affixed to a document has the same effect as the company's common seal.".

(4) In subsection (3) (instrument authorising person to affix official seal), after "by writing under its common seal" insert "or, in the case of a company registered in Scotland, subscribed in accordance with section 36B,".

Official seal for share certificates, &c.

3. – (1) Section 40 of the Companies Act 1985 (official seal for share certificates, &c.) is amended as follows.

(2) After "A company" insert "which has a common seal" and for "the company's common seal" substitute "its common seal".

(3) At the end add –
"The official seal when duly affixed to a document has the same effect as the company's common seal.".

Authentication of documents

4. In section 41 of the Companies Act 1985 (authentication of documents), for the words from "may be signed" to the end substitute "is sufficiently authenticated for the purposes of the law of England and Wales by the signature of a director, secretary or other authorised officer of the company.".

Share certificate as evidence of title

5. For section 186 of the Companies Act 1985 (certificate to be evidence of title) substitute –

"186 Certificate to be evidence of title

(1) A certificate under the common seal of the company (or, in the case of a company registered in Scotland, subscribed in accordance with section 36B) specifying any shares held by a member is –
   (*a*) in England and Wales, prima facie evidence, and
   (*b*) in Scotland, sufficient evidence unless the contrary is shown,
of his title to the shares.".

Share warrants to bearer

6. For section 188 of the Companies Act 1985 (issue and effect of share warrant to bearer) substitute –

"188 Issue and effect of share warrant to bearer

(1) A company limited by shares may, if so authorised by its articles, issue with respect to any fully paid shares a warrant (a "share warrant") stating that the bearer of the warrant is entitled to the shares specified in it.

(2) A share warrant issued under the company's common seal (or, in the case of a company registered in Scotland, subscribed in accordance with section 36B) entitles the bearer to the shares specified in it; and the shares may be transferred by delivery of the warrant.

(3) A company which issues a share warrant may, if so authorised by its articles, provide (by coupons or otherwise) for the payment of the future dividends on the shares included in the warrant.".

Identification of company on common seal

7. In section 350 of the Companies Act 1985 (identification of company on company seal), for subsection (1) substitute –

"(1) A company which has a common seal shall have its name engraved in legible characters on the seal; and if it fails to comply with this subsection it is liable to a fine.".

Floating charges under Scots law

8. In section 462 of the Companies Act 1985 (power of company to create floating charge), for subsections (2) and (3) substitute –

"(2) In the case of a company which the Court of Session has jurisdiction to wind up, a floating charge may be created only by a written instrument which is presumed under section 36B to be subscribed by the company.".

9. In section 466(2) of the Companies Act 1985 (execution of instrument altering floating charge) –
   (*a*) at the beginning of the subsection insert "Without prejudice to any enactment or rule of law regarding the execution of documents,";
   (*b*) omit paragraph (*a*);
   (*c*) at the end of paragraph (*b*) insert ";or", and
   (*d*) omit paragraph (*d*) and the word "or" preceding it.

10. In section 53(3) of the Insolvency Act 1986 (execution of instrument appointing receiver), in paragraph (*a*) for "in accordance with the provisions of section 36 of the Companies Act as if it were a contract" substitute "in accordance with section 36B of the Companies Act 1985".

Section 144(4)   SCHEDULE 18

"SUBSIDIARY" AND RELATED EXPRESSIONS: CONSEQUENTIAL
AMENDMENTS AND SAVINGS

Coal Industry Nationalisation Act 1946 (c. 59)

1. In Schedule 2A to the Coal Industry Nationalisation Act 1946 (eligbility for superannuation benefits), in the definition of "subsidiary" in paragraph 5 of the Table, for "section 154 of the Companies Act 1948" substitute "section 736 of the Companies Act 1985".

Electricity Act 1947 (c.54)

2. In section 67 of the Electricity Act 1947 (interpretation) –
   (*a*) in the definition of "holding company" for "the definition contained in the Companies Act 1947" substitute "section 736 of the Companies Act 1985", and
   (*b*) in the definition of "subsidiary company" for "the Companies Act 1947" substitute "section 736 of the Companies Act 1985".

Landlord and Tenant Act 1954 (c. 56)

3. In section 42 of the Landlord and Tenant Act 1954 (groups of companies), in subsection (1) for

"the same meaning as is assigned to it for the purposes of the Companies Act 1985 by section 736 of that Act" substitute "the meaning given by section 736 of the Companies Act 1985".

Transport Act 1962 (c. 46)

4. In the Transport Act 1946, in the definition of "subsidiary" in section 92(1) (interpretation) omit the words "(taking references in that section to a company as being references to a body corporate)".

Harbours Act 1964 (c. 40)

5. In section 57(1) of the Harbours Act 1964 (interpretation), in the definition of "marine work" for "section 154 of the Companies Act 1948" substitute "section 736 of the Companies Act 1985".

General Rate Act 1967 (c. 9)

6. In section 32A of the General Rate Act 1967 (rateable premises of Transport Boards), in the definition of "subsidiary" in subsection (6) omit the words "(taking references in that section to a company as being references to a body corporate)".

Transport Act 1968 (c. 73)

7. For the purposes of Part V of the Transport Act 1968 (licensing of road haulage operators) as it applies in relation to licences granted before the commencement of section 144(1), the expression "subsidiary" has the meaning given by section 736 of the Companies Act 1985 as originally enacted.

Post Office Act 1969 (c. 48)

8. In section 86 of the Post Office Act 1969 (interpretation), in subsection (2) for "736(5)(*b*)" substitute "736".

Industry Act 1972 (c. 63)

9. In section 10 of the Industry Act 1972 (construction credits), in subsection (9) for "for the purposes of the Companies Act 1985 by section 736 of that Act" substitute "by section 736 of the Companies Act 1985".

Coal Industry Act 1973 (c. 8)

10. In section 12(1) of the Coal Industry Act 1973 (interpretation) for the definition of "subsidiary" and "wholly-owned subsidiary" substitute –
     "'subsidiary' and 'wholly-owned subsidiary' have the meanings given by section 736 of the Companies Act 1985;".

Industry Act 1975 (c. 68)

11. In section 37(1) of the Industry Act 1975 (interpretation), in the definition of "wholly-owned subsidiary" for "section 736(5)(*b*)" substitute "section 736".

Scottish Development Agency Act 1975 (c.69)

12. In section 25(1) of the Scottish Development Agency Act 1975 (interpretation), in the definition of "wholly-owned subsidiary" for "section 736(5)(*b*)" substitute "section 736".

Welsh Development Agency Act 1975 (c. 70)

13. In section 27(1) of the Welsh Development Agency Act 1975 (interpretation), in the definition of "wholly-owned subsidiary" for "section736(5)(*b*)" substitute "section 736".

Restrictive Trade Practices Act 1976 (c. 41)

14. – (1) This paragraph applies to agreements (within the meaning of the Restrictive Trade Practices Act 1976) made before the commencement of section 144(1); and "registrable" means subject to registration under that Act.

(2) An agreement which was not registrable before the commencement of section 144(1) shall not be treated as registrable afterwards by reason only of that provision having come into force; and an agreement which was registrable before the commencement of that provision shall not cease to be registrable by reason of that provision coming into force.

Industrial Common Ownership Act 1976 (c. 78)

15. In section 2(5) of the Industrial Common Ownership Act 1976 (common ownership and co-operative enterprises) for "for the purposes of the Companies Act 1985" substitute "as defined by section 736 of the Companies Act 1985 or for the purposes of".

Aircraft and Shipbuilding Industries Act 1977 (c. 3)

16. In section 56(1) of the Aircraft and Shipbuilding Industries Act 1977 (interpretation), in the definition of "subsidiary" for "the same meaning as in" substitute "the meaning given by section 736 of".

Nuclear Industry (Finance) Act 1977 (c. 7)

17. In section 3 of the Nuclear Industry (Finance) Act 1977 (expenditure on acquisition of shares in National Nuclear Corporation Ltd and subsidiaries), after "within the meaning of" insert "section 736 of". .

Coal Industry Act 1977 (c. 39)

18. In section 14(1) of the Coal Industry Act 1977 (interpretation), in the definition of "wholly-owned subsidiary" for "section 736(5)(*b*)" substitute "section 736".

Shipbuilding (Redundancy Payments) Act 1978 (c.11)

19. In section 1(4) of the Shipbuilding (Redundancy Payments) Act 1978 (schemes for payments to redundant workers), for the definitions of "subsidiary" and "wholly-owned subsidiary" substitute –
> "'subsidiary' and 'wholly-owned subsidiary' have the meanings given by section 736 of the Companies Act 1985;".

Capital Gains Tax Act 1979 (c. 14)

20. In section 149 of the Capital Gains Tax Act 1979 (employee trusts), in subsection (7) for "the same meaning as in" substitute "the meaning given by section 736 of".

Crown Agents Act 1979 (c. 43)

21. In section 31(1) of the Crown Agents Act 1979 (interpretation), in the definition of "wholly-owned subsidiary" for "section 736(5)(b)" substitute "section 736(2)".

Competition Act 1980 (c. 21)

22. In sections 11(3)(*f*) and 12 of the Competition Act 1980 (references relating to public bodies, &c.), after "within the meaning of" insert "section 736 of".

British Aerospace Act 1980 (c. 26)

23. In section 14(1) of the British Aerospace Act 1980 (interpretation) –
   (*a*) in the definition of "subsidiary" for "the same meaning as in", and
   (*b*) in the definition of "wholly-owned subsidiary" for "the same meaning as it has for the purposes of section 150 of the Companies Act 1948",
substitute "the meaning given by section 736 of the Companies Act 1985".

Local Government, Planning and Land Act 1980 (c. 65)

24. In sections 100(1), 141(7) and 170(1)(*d*) and (2) of the Local Government, Planning and Land Act 1980 (which refer to wholly-owned subsidiaries) for "within the meaning of section 736(5)(b)" substitute "as defined by section 736".

British Telecommunications Act 1981 (c. 38)

25. In section 85 of the British Telecommunications Act 1981 (interpretation), for subsection (2) substitute –

> "(2) Any reference in this Act to a subsidiary or wholly-owned subsidiary shall be construed in accordance wth section 736 of the Companies Act 1985.".

Transport Act 1981 (c.56)

26. In section 4(2) of the Transport Act 1981 (interpretation of provisions relating to activities of British Railways Board), for "section 154 of the Companies Act 1985" substitute "section 736 of the Companies Act 1985".

Value Added Tax Act 1983 (c. 55)

27. In section 29 of the Value Added Tax Act 1983 (groups of companies), in subsection (8) after "within the meaning of" insert "section 736 of".

Telecommunications Act 1984 (c. 12)

28. In section 73(1) of the Telecommunications Act 1984 (interpretation of Part V), for "the same meaning as in" substitute "the meaning given by section 736 of".

London Regional Transport Act 1984 (c. 32)

29. In section 68 of the London Regional Transport Act 1984 (interpretation), for the definition of "subsidiary" substitute –
"" subsidiary" (subject to section 62 of this Act) has the meaning given by section 736 of the Companies Act 1985;".

Inheritance Tax Act 1984 (c. 51)

30. – (1) The Inheritance Tax Act 1984 is amended as follows.

(2) In section 13 (dispositions by close companies for benefit of employees), in the definition of "subsidiary" in subsection (5) for "the same meaning as in" substitute "the meaning given by section 736 of".

(3) In section 103 (introductory provisions relating to relief for business property), in subsection (2) for "the same meanings as in" substitute "the meanings given by section 736 of".

(4) In section 234 (interest on instalments) in subsection (3) for "within the meaning of" substitute "as defined in section 736 of".

Ordnance Factories and Military Services Act 1984 (c. 59)

31. In section 14 of the Ordnance Factories and Military Services Act 1984 (interpretation), for the definitions of "subsidiary" and "wholly-owned subsidiary" substitute –
"" subsidiary" and "wholly-owned subsidiary" have the meanings given by section 736 of the Companies Act 1985.".

Companies Act 1985 (c. 6)

32. – (1) The following provisions have effect with respect to the operation of section 23 of the Companies Act 1985 (prohibition on subsidiary being a member of its holding company).

(2) In relation to times, circumstances and purposes before the commencement of section 144(1) of this Act, the references in section 23 to a subsidiary or holding company shall be construed in accordance with section 736 of the Companies Act 1985 as originally enacted.

(3) Where a body corporate becomes or ceases to be a subsidiary of a holding company by reason of section 144(1) coming into force, the prohibition in section 23 of the Companies Act 1985 shall apply (in the absence of exempting circumstances), or cease to apply, accordingly.

33. – (1) Section 153 of the Companies Act 1985 (transactions excepted from prohibition on company giving financial assistance for acquisition of its own shares) is amended as follows.

(2) In subsection (4)(*bb*) (employees' share schemes) for "a company connected with it" substitute "a company in the same group".

(3) For subsection (5) substitute –

> "(5) For the purposes of subsection (4)(*bb*) a company is in the same group as another company if it is a holding company or subsidiary of that company, or a subsidiary of a holding company of that company.".

34. Section 293 of the Companies Act 1985 (age limit for directors) does not apply in relation to a director of a company if –
> (*a*) he had attained the age of 70 before the commencement of section 144(1) of this Act, and
> (*b*) the company became a subsidiary of a public company by reason only of the commencement of that subsection.

35. Nothing in section 144(1) affects the operation of Part XIIIA of the Companies Act 1985 (takeover offers) in relation to a takeover offer made before the commencement of that subsection.

36. For the purposes of section 719 of the Companies Act 1985 (power to provide for employees on transfer or cessation of business), a company which immediately before the commencement of section 144(1) was a subsidiary of another company shall not be treated as ceasing to be such a subsidiary by reason of that subsection coming into force.

37. For the purposes of section 743 of the Companies Act 1985 (meaning of "employees' share scheme"), a company which immediately before the commencement of section 144(1) was a subsidiary of another company shall not be treated as ceasing to be such a subsidiary by reason of that subsection coming into force.

38. In Schedule 25 to the Companies Act 1985 "subsidiary" has the meaning given by section 736 of that Act as originally enacted.

Transport Act 1985 (c. 67)

39. In section 137(1) of the Transport Act 1985 (interpretation), in the definition of "subsidiary" for the words from "as defined" to the end substitute "within the meaning of section 736 of the Companies Act 1985 as originally enacted (and not as substituted by section 144(1) of the Companies Act 1989);".

Housing Act 1985 (c. 68)

40. In section 622 of the Housing Act 1985 (minor definitions: general), in the definition of "subsidiary" for "the same meaning as in" substitute "the meaning given by section 736 of".

Housing Associations Act 1985 (c. 69)

41. In section 101 of the Housing Associations Act 1985 (minor definitions: Part II), in the definition of "subsidiary" for "the same meaning as in" substitute "the meaning given by section 736 of".

Atomic Energy Authority Act 1986 (c. 3)

42. In section 9 of the Atomic Energy Authority Act 1986 (interpretation), in the definition of "subsidiary" and "wholly-owned subsidiary" for "have the same meaning as in" substitute "have the meaning given by section 736 of".

Airports Act 1986 (c. 31)

43. In section 82 of the Airports Act 1986 (general interpretation), in the definition of "subsidiary" for "has the same meaning as in" substitute "has the meaning given by section 736 of".

Gas Act 1986 (c. 44)

44. In the Gas Act 1986 –
    (*a*) in section 48(1) (interpretation of Part I), in the definitions of "holding company" and "subsidiary", and
    (*b*) in section 61(1) (interpretation of Part II), in the definition of "subsidiary",
for "has the same meaning as in" substitute "has the meaning given by section 736 of".

Building Societies Act 1986 (c. 53)

45. In section 119 of the Building Societies Act 1986 (interpretation), in the definition of "subsidiary" for "has the same meaning as in" substitute "has the meaning given by section 736 of".

Income and Corporation Taxes Act 1988 (c. 1)

46. In section 141 of the Income and Corporation Taxes Act 1988 (benefits in kind: non-cash vouchers), in the definition of "subsidiary" in subsection (7) for "section 736(5)(*b*)" substitute "section 736".

British Steel Act 1988 (c. 35)

47. In section 15(1) of the British Steel Act 1988 (interpretation) in the definition of "subsidiary" for "has the same meaning as in" substitute "has the meaning given by section 736 of".

Section 145　　　　　　　# SCHEDULE 19

MINOR AMENDMENTS OF THE COMPANIES ACT 1985

Correction of cross-reference

1. In section 131(1) of the Companies Act 1985 (merger relief) for "section 132(4)" substitute "section 132(8)".
This amendment shall be deemed always to have had effect.

Particulars to be given of directors and secretaries

2. – (1) Section 289 of the Companies Act 1985 (particulars of directors required to be entered in register) is amended as follows.

    (2) In subsection (1)(*a*) (particulars of individual directors)
        (*a*) in sub-paragraph (i) for "Christian name and surname" and in sub-paragraph (ii) for "Christian name or surname" substitute "name", and
        (*b*) for sub-paragraph (vii) substitute –
        "(vii) the date of his birth;".

    (3) In subsection (1)(*b*) (particulars of other directors) after "corporation" insert "or Scottish firm" and after "corporate" insert "or firm".

    (4) For subsection (2) substitute –

        "(2) In subsection (1)(*a*) –
            (*a*) "name" means a person's Christian name (or other forename) and surname, except that in the case of a peer, or an individual usually known by a title, the

title may be stated instead of his Christian name (or other forename) and surname, or in addition to either or both of them; and

(*b*) the reference to a former name does not include –
- (i)   in the case of a peer, or an individual normally known by a British title, the name by which he was known previous to the adoption of or succession to the title, or
- (ii) in the case of any person, a former name which was changed or disused before he attained the age of 18 years or which has been changed or disused for 20 years or more, or
- (iii) in the case of a married woman, the name by which she was known previous to the marriage.".

3. – (1) Section 290 of the Companies Act 1985 (particulars of secretaries to be entered in register) is amended as follows.

(2) In subsection (1)(*a*) (particulars of individuals) for "Christian name and surname" and "Christian name or surname" substitute "name".

(3) For subsection (3) substitute –

"(3) Section 289(2)(*a*) and (*b*) apply for the purposes of the obligation under subsection (1)(*a*) of this section to state the name or former name of an individual.".

4. – (1) Section 305 of the Companies Act 1985 (directors' names on company correspondence, &c.) is amended as follows.

(2) In subsection (1) for the words from "the Christian name" onwards substitute "the name of every director of the company".

(3) For subsection (4) substitute –

"(4) For the purposes of the obligation under subsection (1) to state the name of every director of the company, a person's "name" means –
- (*a*) in the case of an individual, his Christian name (or other forename) and surname; and
- (*b*) in the case of a corporation or Scottish firm, its corporate or firm name.

(5) The initial or a recognised abbreviation of a person's Christian name or other forename may be stated instead of the full Christian name or other forename.

(6) In the case of a peer, or an individual usually known by a title, the title may be stated instead of his Christian name (or other forename) and surname or in addition to either or both of them.

(7) In this section "director" includes a shadow director and the reference in subsection (3) to an "officer" shall be construed accordingly.".

5. – (1) Section 686 of the Companies Act 1985 (documents to be delivered to registrar on registration of company not formed under companies legislaton) is amended as follows.

(2) In subsection (1) (particulars to be delivered to registrar), for paragraph (*b*) (particulars of directors and managers) substitute –

"(*b*) a list showing with respect to each director or manager of the company –
- (i)   in the case of an individual, his name, address, occupation and date of birth,
- (ii) in the case of a corporation or Scottish firm, its corporate or firm name and registered or principal office,".

(3) After that subsection insert –

"(1A) For the purposes of subsection (1)(*b*)(i) a person's 'name' means his Christian name (or other forename) and surname, except that in the case of a peer, or an individual usually known by a title, the title may be stated instead of his Christian name (or other forename) and surname or in addition to either or both of them.".

6. In section 691 of the Companies Act 1985 (documents to be delivered to registrar on registration of oversea company), for subsection (2) (particulars of directors and secretary) substitute –

"(2) The list referred to in subsection (1)(*b*)(i) shall contain the following particulars with respect to each director –

    (*a*) in the case of an individual –
        (i)   his name,
        (ii) any former name,
        (iii) his usual residential address,
        (iv) his nationality,
        (v) his business occupation (if any),
        (vi) if he has no business occupation but holds other directorships, particulars of them, and
        (vii) his date of birth;
    (*b*) in the case of a corporation or Scottish firm, its corporate or firm name and registered or principal office.

(3) The list referred to in subsection (1)(*b*)(i) shall contain the following particulars with respect to the secretary (or, where there are joint secretaries, with respect to each of them) –

    (*a*) in the case of an individual, his name, any former name and his usual residential address;
    (*b*) in the case of a corporation or Scottish firm, its corporate or firm name and registered or principal office.

Where all the partners in a firm are joint secretaries of the company, the name and principal office of the firm may be stated instead of the particulars required by paragraph (*a*).

(4) In subsections (2)(*a*) and (3)(*a*) above –

    (*a*) "name" means a person's Christian name (or other forename) and surname, except that in the case of a peer, or an individual usually known by a title, the title may be stated instead of his Christian name (or other forename) and surname, or in addition to either or both of them; and
    (*b*) the reference to a former name does not include –
        (i)   in the case of a peer, or an individual normally known by a British title, the name by which he was known previous to the adoption of or succession to the title, or
        (ii) in the case of any person, a former name which was changed or disused before he attained the age of 18 years or which has been changed or disused for 20 years or more, or
        (iii) in the case of a married woman, the name by which she was known previous to the marriage.".

7. – (1) Schedule 1 to the Companies Act 1985 (particulars of directors and secretaries to be sent to registrar) is amended as follows.

(2) In paragraph 1(*a*) (particulars of individual directors) –

    (*a*) for "Christian name and surname" and "Christian name or surname" substitute "name"; and
    (*b*) for the words from "and, in the case" to the end substitute "and his date of birth".

(3) In paragraph 1(*b*) (particulars of other directors) after "corporation" insert "or Scottish firm" and after "corporate" insert "or firm".

(4) In paragraph 3(1)(*a*) (particulars of individual secretaries) for "Christian name and surname" (twice) substitute "name".

(5) For paragraph 4 substitute –

"4. In paragraphs 1(*a*) and 3(1)(*a*) above –

    (*a*) "name" means a person's Christian name (or other forename) and surname, except that in the case of a peer, or an individual usually known by a title, the title may be stated instead of his Christian name (or other forename) and surname or in addition to either or both of them; and

(b) the reference to a former name does not include –

(i) in the case of a peer, or an individual normally known by a British title, the name by which he was known previous to the adoption of or succession to the title, or

(ii) in the case of any person, a former name which was changed or disused before he attained the age of 18 years or which has been changed or disused for 20 years or more, or

(iii) in the case of a married woman, the name by which she was known previous to the marriage.".

Transactions with directors not requiring authorisation

8. In section 321 of the Companies Act 1985 (exceptions from provisions requiring authorisation for substantial property transactions with diretors, &c.), after subsection (3) insert –

"(4) Section 320(1) does not apply to a transaction on a recognised investment exchange which is effected by a director, or a person connected with him, through the agency of a person who in relation to the transaction acts as an independent broker.

For this purpose an "independent broker" means –

(a) in relation to a transaction on behalf of a director, a person who independently of the director selects the person with whom the transaction is to be effected, and

(b) in relation to a transaction on behalf of a person connected with a director, a person who independently of that person or the director selects the person with whom the transaction is to be effected;

and "recognised", in relation to an investment exchange, means recognised under the Financial Services Act 1986.".

Time limit for holding extraordinary general meeting convened on members' requisition

9. In section 368 of the Companies Act 1985 (extraordinary general meeting on members' requisition), after subsection (7) add –

"(8) the directors are deemed not to have duly convened a meeting if they convene a meeting for a date more than 28 days after the date of the notice convening the meeting.".

Removal of restriction on transfer of shares

10. – (1) In section 456(3) of the Companies Act 1985 (removal of restrictions by order of court), in paragraph (b) (order where shares to be sold) –

(a) for "sold" substitute "transferred for valuable consideration", and

(b) for "sale" substitute "transfer".

(2) In section 454(2) and (3) (which refer to section 456(3)(b) for "sell" and "sale" substitute "transfer".

Protection of company's members against unfair prejudice

11. In Part XVII of the Companies Act 1985 (protection of company's members against unfair prejudice) –

(a) in section 459(1) (application by company member), and

(b) in section 460(1)(b) (application by Secretary of State),

for "unfairly prejudicial to the interests of some part of the members" substitute "unfairly prejudicial to the interests of its members generally or of some part of its members".

Requirements for registration by joint stock companies

12. In section 684(1) of the Companies Act 1985 (requirements for registration by joint stock companies: documents to be delivered to registrar), in paragraph (*b*) (list of members on specified day) for "(not more than 6 clear days before the day of registration)" substitute "(not more than 28 clear days before the day of registration)".

Delivery of documents by oversea companies

13. In Chapter I of Part XXIII of the Companies Act 1985 (oversea companies: registration, &c.), for section 696 (office where documents to be filed) substitute –

"696   Registrar to whom documents to be delivered

(1) References to the registrar in relation to an oversea company (except references in Chapter III of this Part (registration of charges): see section 703E), shall be construed in accordance with the following provisions.

(2) The documents which an oversea company is required to deliver to the registrar shall be delivered –
(*a*) to the registrar for England and Wales if the company has established a place of business in England and Wales, and
(*b*) to the registrar for Scotland if the company has established a place of business in Scotland;
and if the company has an established place of business in both parts of Great Britain, the documents shall be delivered to both registrars.

(3) If a company ceases to have a place of business in either part of Great Britain, it shall forthwith give notice of that fact to the registrar for that part; and from the date on which notice is so given it is no longer obliged to deliver documents to that registrar.".

Companies' registered numbers

14. For section 705 of the Companies Act 1985 (companies' registered numbers) substitute –

"705   Companies' registered numbers

(1) The registrar shall allocate to every company a number, which shall be known as the company's registered number.

(2) Companies' registered numbers shall be in such form, consisting of one or more sequences of figures or letters, as the registrar may from time to time determine.

(3) The registrar may upon adopting a new form of registered number make such changes of existing registered numbers as appear to him necessary.

(4) A change of a company's registered number has effect from the date on which the company is notified by the registrar of the change; but for a period of three years beginning with the date on which that notification is sent by the registrar the requirement of section 351(1)(*a*) as to the use of the company's registered number on business letters and order forms is satisfied by the use of either the old number or the new.

(5) In this section "company" includes –
(*a*) any oversea company which has complied with section 691 (delivery of statutes to registrar, &c.), other than a company which appears to the registrar not to have a place of business in Great Britain; and
(*b*) any body to which any provision of this Act applies by virtue of section 718 (unregistered companies).".

Exemptions from limit of 20 on members of partnership

15. – (1) Section 716 of the Companies Act 1985 (prohibition of formation of company, association or partnership with more than 20 members unless registered as company, &c.) is amended as follows.

(2) In subsection (2) (exemptions), after paragraph (*c*) insert –

> "(*d*) for any purpose prescribed by regulations (which may include a purpose mentioned above), of a partnership of a description so prescribed.";

and omit the words inserted by paragraph 22 of Schedule 16 to the Financial Services Act 1986.

(3) For subsections (3) and (4) substitute –

> "(3) In subsection (2)(*a*) "solicitor" –
>> (*a*) in relation to England and Wales, means solicitor of the Supreme Court, and
>> (*b*) in relation to Scotland, means a person enrolled or deemed enrolled as a solicitor in pursuance of the Solicitors (Scotland) Act 1980.

> (4) In subsection (2)(*c*) "recognised stock exchange" means –
>> (*a*) the International Stock Exchange of the United Kingdom and the Republic of Ireland Limited, and
>> (*b*) any other stock exchange for the time being recognised for the purposes of this section by the Secretary of State by order made by statutory instrument.".

16. – (1) Section 717 of the Companies Act 1985 (limited partnerships: limit on numbers of members) is amended as follows.

(2) In subsection (1) (exemptions from limit of 20 members under section 4(2) of Limited Partnerships Act 1907), after paragraph (*c*) insert –

> "(*d*) to a partnership carrying on business of any description prescribed by regulations (which may include a business of any description mentioned above), of a partnership of a description so prescribed.";

and omit the words inserted by paragraph 22 of Schedule 16 to the Financial Services Act 1986.

(3) For subsections (2) and (3) substitute –

> "(2) In subsection (1)(*a*) "solicitor" –
>> (*a*) in relation to England and Wales, means solicitor of the Supreme Court, and
>> (*b*) in relation to Scotland, means a person enrolled or deemed enrolled as a solicitor in pursuance of the Solicitors (Scotland) Act 1980.

> (3) In subsection (1)(*c*) "recognised stock exchange" means –
>> (*a*) The International Stock Exchange of the United Kingdom and the Republic of Ireland Limited, and
>> (*b*) any other stock exchange for the time being recognised for the purposes of this section by the Secretary of State by order made by statutory instrument.".

Meaning of "officer who is in default"

17. In section 730 of the Companies Act 1985 (punishment of offences), in subsection (5) (meaning of "officer who is in default"), after "company" (twice) insert "or other body".

Offences committed by partnerships and other unincorporated bodies

18. In section 734 of the Companies Act 1985 (criminal proceedings against unincorporated bodies) at the end add –

> "(5) Where such an offence committed by a partnership is proved to have been committed with the consent or connivance of, or to be attributable to any neglect on the part of, a partner, he as well as the partnership is guilty of the offence and liable to be proceeded against and punished accordingly.

(6) Where such an offence committed by an unincorporated body (other than a partnership) is proved to have been committed with the consent or connivance of, or to be attributable to any neglect on the part of, any officer of the body or any member of its governing body, he as well as the body is guilty of the offence and liable to be proceeded against and punished accordingly.".

Meaning of "office copy" in Scotland

19. In Part XXVI of the Companies Act 1985 (interpretation), after section 743 insert –

"743A   Meaning of "office copy" in Scotland

References in this Act to an office copy of a court order shall be construed, as respects Scotland, as references to a certified copy interlocutor.".

Index of defined expressions

20. In Part XXVI of the Companies Act 1985 (interpretation), after section 744 insert –

"744A   Index of defined expressions

The following Table shows provisions defining or otherwise explaining expressions for the purposes of this Act generally –

accounting reference date, accounting reference period	sections 224 and 742(1)
acquisition (in relation to a non-cash asset)	section 739(2)
agent	section 744
allotment (and related expressions)	section 738
annual accounts	sections 261(2), 262(1) and 742(1)
annual general meeting	section 366
annual return	section 363
articles	section 744
authorised minimum	section 118
balance sheet and balance sheet date	sections 261(2), 262(1) and 742(1)
bank holiday	section 744
banking company	section 744
body corporate	section 740
books and papers, books or papers	section 744
called-up share capital	section 737(1)
capital redemption reserve	section 170(1)
the Companies Acts	section 744
companies charges register	section 397
company	section 735(1)
the Consequential Provisions Act	section 744
corporation	section 740
the court (in relation to a company)	section 744
current assets	sections 262(1) and 742(1)
debenture	section 744
director	section 741(1)
document	section 744
elective resolution	section 379A

employees' share scheme	section 743
equity share capital	section 744
existing company	section 735(1)
extraordinary general meeting	section 368
extraordinary resolution	section 378(1)
financial year (of a company)	sections 223 and 742(1)
fixed assets	sections 262(1) and 742(1)
floating charge (in Scotland)	section 462
the former Companies Acts	section 735(1)
the Gazette	section 744
hire-purchase agreement	section 744
holding company	section 736
the Insider Dealing Act	section 744
the Insolvency Act	section 735A(1)
insurance company	section 744
the Joint Stock Companies Acts	section 735(3)
limited company	section 1(2)
member (of a company)	section 22
memorandum (in relation to a company)	section 744
non-cash asset	section 739(1)
number (in relation to shares)	section 744
office copy (in relation to a court order in Scotland)	section 743A
officer (in relation to a body corporate)	section 744
official seal (in relation to the registrar of companies)	section 744
oversea company	section 744
overseas branch register	section 362
paid up (and related expressions)	section 738
parent company and parent undertaking	sections 258 and 742(1)
place of business	section 744
prescribed	section 744
private company	section 1(3)
profit and loss account	sections 261(2), 262(1) and 742(1)
prospectus	section 744
public company	section 1(3)
realised profits or losses	sections 262(3) and 742(2)
registered number (of a company)	section 705(1)
registered office (of a company)	section 287
registrar and registrar of companies	section 744
resolution for reducing share capital	section 135(3)
shadow director	sections 741(2) and (3)
share	section 744
share premium account	section 130(1)
share warrant	section 188
special notice (in relation to a resolution)	section 379
special resolution	section 378(2)
subsidiary	section 736
subsidiary undertaking	sections 258 and 742(1)
transfer (in relation to a non-cash asset)	section 739(2)
uncalled share capital	section 737(2)
undistributable reserves	section 264(3)
unlimited company	section 1(2)
unregistered company	section 718
wholly-owned subsidiary	section 736(2).".

Fraudulent trading by unregistered companies

21. In Schedule 22 to the Companies Act 1985 (provisions applying to unregistered companies), at the appropriate place insert –
"Part XVI Fraudulent trading by a company -".

Section 153

SCHEDULE 20

AMENDMENTS ABOUT MERGERS AND RELATED MATTERS

Fair Trading Act 1973 (c. 41)

1. In section 46 of the Fair Trading Act 1973, subsection (3) is omitted.

2. – (1) In section 60 of that Act –
    (*a*) in subsection (1) for "the period of three months beginning with the date of the" there is substituted "such period (not being longer than three months beginning with the date of the reference) as may be specified in the",
    (*b*) in subsection (2) for "original period of three months" there is substituted "period specified in the newspaper merger reference", and
    (*c*) in subsection (3) for "subsection (1)" there is substituted "the newspaper merger reference".

(2) This paragraph does not apply in relation to any newspaper merger reference made before the passing of this Act.

3. In section 63(1) of that Act, for "to 75 of this Act shall have effect in relation to merger references other than" there is substituted "to 75K of this Act shall not have effect in relation to".

4. In section 66 of that Act –
    (*a*) in subsections (1) and (3), after "the Secretary of State" there is inserted "or the Commission", and
    (*b*) in subsection (4), after "this section" there is inserted "and to section 66A of this Act".

5. – (1) In section 67 of that Act, in subsection (2)(*a*), for the words from "any enterprise" to the end there is substituted –
        "(i) any enterprise which remains under the same ownership and control, or
        (ii) if none of the enterprises remains under the same ownership and control, the enterprise having the assets with the highest value, and".

(2) In subsection (4) of that section –
    (*a*) after "section 66" there is inserted "or subsection (1) of section 66A", and
    (*b*) for "that subsection" there is substituted "either of those subsections".

6. In section 68(4) of that Act, after "the Secretary of State" there is inserted "or, as the case may be, the Commission".

7. In section 71 of that Act –
    (*a*) in subsection (1) the words "made under section 69(4) of this Act", and
    (*b*) subsection (2),
are omitted.

8. In section 74(1) of that Act –
    (*a*) the words "and does not impose on the Commission a limitation under section 69(4) of this Act" are omitted, and
    (*b*) in paragraph (*d*), for "paragraph 12" there is substituted "paragraphs 12 and 12A".

9. In section 75(4) of that Act –
    (*a*) after "sections 66" there is inserted "66A", and
    (*b*) for paragraphs (*a*) and (*b*) there is substituted –

"(*a*) section 66 shall apply, where an event by which any enterprises cease as between themselves to be distinct enterprises will occur if the arrangements are carried into effect, as if the event had occurred immediately before the date of the reference;

(*aa*) section 66A shall apply, where a transaction falling within subsection (2) of that section will occur if the arrangements are carried into effect, as if the transaction had occurred immediately before the date of the reference;

(*b*) in section 67(4) the references to subsection (1) of section 66 and subsection (1) of section 66A shall be construed as references to those subsections as modified in accordance with paragraph (*a*) or (*aa*) of this subsection;".

10. Paragraphs 4 to 9 (and the repeals in Schedule 24 corresponding to paragraphs 7 and 8(a)) do not apply in relation to any merger reference made before the passing of this Act.

11. At the end of section 76 of that Act there is added –

"(2) In exercising his duty under this section the Director shall take into consideration any representations made to him by persons appearing to him to have a substantial interest in any such arrangements or transactions or by bodies appearing to him to represent substantial numbers of persons who have such an interest.".

12. – (1) In section 83 of that Act, after subsection (3) there is inserted –

"(3A) Without prejudice to subsection (3) above, if the Minister or Ministers to whom any such report is made consider that it would not be in the public interest to disclose –

(*a*) any matter contained in the report relating to the private affairs of an individual whose interests would, in the opinion of the Minister or Ministers, be seriously and prejudicially affected by the publication of that matter, or

(*b*) any matter contained in the report relating specifically to the affairs of a particular person whose interests would, in the opinion of the Minster or Ministers, be seriously and prejudicially affected by the publication of that matter,

the Minister or Ministers shall exclude that matter from the copies of the report as laid before Parliament and from the report as published under this section.".

(2) This paragraph does not apply in relation to any report made before the passing of this Act.

13. – (1) In section 85 of that Act, for subsection (7) there is substituted –

"(7) If any person (referred to in subsection (7A) of this section as 'the defaulter') refuses or otherwise fails to comply with any notice under subsection (1) of this section, any one of those who, in relation to the investigation in question, are performing the functions of the Commission may certify that fact in writing to the court and the court may enquire into the case.

(7A) If, after hearing any witness who may be produced against or on behalf of the defaulter and any statement which may be offered in defence, the court is satisfied that the defaulter did without reasonable excuse refuse or otherwise fail to comply with the notice, the court may punish the defaulter (and, in the case of a body corporate, any director or officer) in like manner as if the defaulter had been guilty of contempt of court.".

(2) Subsections (5) and (6)(*b*) of that section are omitted.

14. – (1) In section 88 of that Act, in subsection (1) for the words from "if requested" to "the relevant parties" there is substituted "to comply with any request of the appropriate Minister or Ministers to consult with any persons mentioned in the request (referred to below in this section as 'the relevant parties')".

(2) After subsection (2) of that section there is inserted –

"(2A) where –
    (*a*) an undertaking is given under this section after the commencement of this subsection, or
    (*b*) an undertaking given under this section is varied or released after that time,
the Minister to whom the undertaking is or was given shall cause the undertaking or, as the case may be, the variation or release to be published in such manner as the Minister may consider appropriate.".

(3) In subsection (4) of that section –
    (*a*) in paragraph (*a*) for "it" there is substituted "the undertaking is no longer appropriate and either the relevant parties (or any of them) can be released from the undertaking or the undertaking", and
    (*b*) in paragraph (*b*) for "that it" there is substituted "that any person can be so released or that an undertaking",
and in subsection (5), after "varied" (in both places) there is inserted "or revoked".

(4) In subsection (6) of that section the words from "'the relevant parties'" to the "and" immediately following paragraph (*c*) are omitted.

(5) Sub-paragraphs (1) and (4) (and the repeal in Schedule 24 corresponding to sub-paragraph (4)) do not apply in relation to any report made before the passing of this Act.

15. – (1) In section 89 of that Act, in subsection (1), for paragraphs (*a*) and (*b*) there is substituted –
    "(*a*) in the circumstances specified in subsection (1) of any of the following sections –
        (i)   sections 56, 73 and 75K of this Act, and
        (ii) section 10 of the Competition Act 1980,
      the Secretary of State makes, has made, or has under consideration the making of, an order under the section in question exercising any of the powers specified in Schedule 8 to this Act, or
    (*b*) in the circumstances specified in subsection (1) of section 12 of the Competition Act 1980 the Secretary of State makes, has made, or has under consideration the making of, an order under subsection (5) of that section exercising any of those powers.".

(2) In subsection (2) of that section, "Part II of" is omitted.

(3) In subsection (3) of that section, after paragraph (*b*) there is inserted –
    "(*bb*) require any person to furnish any such information to the Director as may be specified or described in the order;".

(4) The amendments made by sub-paragraphs (1) to (3) have effect in relation to the making of any order under section 89 of the Fair Trading Act 1973 after the passing of this Act, whether the principal order (within the meaning of that section) was made before or after that time.

16. – (1) Section 90 of that Act is amended as follows.

(2) In subsection (1) after "section 74" there is inserted ", section 75K".

(3) For subsection (5) there is substituted –

    "(5) Nothing in any order to which this section applies shall have effect so as to –
    (*a*) cancel or modify conditions in licences granted –
        (i)   under a patent granted under the Patents Act 1949 or the Patents Act 1977 or a European patent (UK) (within the meaning of the Patents Act 1977), or
        (ii) in respect of a design registered under the Registered Designs Act 1949,
      by the proprietor of the patent or design, or
    (*b*) require an entry to be made in the register of patents or the register of designs to the effect that licences under such a patent or such a design are to be available as of right.".

17. In section 132(1) of that Act, after "85(6)" there is inserted "section 93B".

18. – (1) In Schedule 3 to that Act, in paragraph 16(2) for "75" there is substituted "73".

(2) This paragraph does not apply in relation to any report made before the passing of this Act.

19. – (1) Schedule 8 to that Act is amended as follows.

(2) After paragraph 9 there is inserted –

> "9A – (1) An order may require a person supplying goods or services to publish –
>> (*a*) any such accounting information in relation to the supply of the goods or services, and
>> (*b*) any such information in relation to –
>>> (i) the quantities of goods or services supplied, or
>>> (ii) the geographical areas in which they are supplied,
>> as may be specified or described in the order.
>
> (2) In this paragraph "accounting information", in relation to a supply of goods or services, means information as to –
>> (*a*) the costs of the supply, including fixed costs and overheads,
>> (*b*) the manner in which fixed costs and overheads are calculated and apportioned for accounting purposes of the supplier, and
>> (*c*) the income attributable to the supply.".

(3) After paragraph 12 there is inserted –

> "12A. An order may require any person to furnish any such information to the Director as may be specified or described in the order.
>
> 12B. An order may require any activities to be carried on separately from any other activities.
>
> 12C. An order may prohibit or restrict the exercise of any right to vote exercisable by virtue of the holding of any shares, stock or securities.".

20. – (1) In Schedule 9 to that Act, in paragraph 4 the words from "either" to the end are omitted.

(2) This paragraph has effect in relation to the laying of any draft order under paragraph 4 of Schedule 9 to the Fair Trading Act 1973 after the passing of this Act, whether the notice under that Schedule was published before or after that time.

Competition Act 1980 (c. 21)

21. In section 3(8) of the Competition Act 1980 –
  (*a*) for "(5)" there is substituted "(6)", and
  (*b*) at the end there is inserted "but as if, in subsection (7) of that section, for the words from 'any one' to 'the Commission' there were substituted 'the Director'".

22. In section 4(4) of that Act for paragraph (*a*) there is substituted –
> "(*a*) to arrange for –
>> (i) any undertaking accepted by him under this section, and
>> (ii) any variation or release of such an undertaking after the passing of the Companies Act 1989,
>> to be published in such manner as appears to him to be appropriate,".

23. In section 9(4) of that Act –
  (*a*) in paragraph (*a*), after "undertaking" there is inserted "and of any variation of it after the passing of the Companies Act 1989", and
  (*b*) in paragraph (*b*), after "undertaking" there is inserted "and any variation or release of it after that time".

24. In section 29(1)(*a*) of that Act after "section" there is inserted "75G or".

Telecommunications Act 1984 (c. 12)

25. – (1) In section 13(9) of the Telecommunications Act 1984, after "Commission)" there is inserted "together with section 24 of the Competition Act 1980 (modification of provisions about performance of Commission's functions)".

(2) The Monopolies and Mergers Commission (Performance of Functions) Order 1989 shall have effect as if sub-paragraph (1) above had come into force immediately before the making of the Order.

Financial Services Act 1986 (c. 60)

26. In section 123(3) of the Financial Services Act 1986 –
    (*a*) for "(5)" there is substituted "(6)", and
    (*b*) at the end there is inserted "but as if, in subsection (7) of that section, for the words from 'any one" to 'the Commission" there were substituted 'the Director'".

Section 156(1)
SCHEDULE 21
ADDITIONAL REQUIREMENTS FOR RECOGNITION

PART I
U.K. INVESTMENT EXCHANGES

Default rules

1. – (1) The exchange must have default rules which, in the event of a member of the exchange appearing to be unable to meet his obligations in respect of one or more market contracts, enable action to be taken in respect of unsettled market contracts to which he is party.

(2) The rules may authorise the taking of the same or similar action in relation to a member who appears to be likely to become unable to meet his obligations in respect of one or more market contracts.

(3) The rules must enable action to be taken in respect of all unsettled market contracts, other than those entered into by a recognised clearing house for the purposes of or in connection with the provision of clearing services for the exchange.

(4) As regards contracts entered into by the exchange for the purposes of or in connection with the provision of its own clearing services, the rules must contain provision corresponding to that required by paragraphs 9 to 11 below in the case of a UK clearing house.

(5) As regards other contracts the rules must contain provision complying with paragraphs 2 and 3 below.

Content of rules

2. – (1) The rules must provide for all rights and liabilities between those party as principal to unsettled market contracts to which the defaulter is party as principal to be discharged and for there to be paid by one party to the other such sum of money (if any) as may be determined in accordance with the rules.

(2) The rules must further provide –
    (*a*) for the sums so payable in respect of different contracts between the same parties to be aggregated or set off so as to produce a net sum, and

(*b*) for the certification by or on behalf of the exchange of the net sum payable or, as the case may be, of the fact that no sum is payable.

(3) The rules may make special provision with respect to, or exclude from the provisions required by sub-paragraphs (1) and (2), contracts of any description prescribed for the purposes of this sub-paragraph by regulations made by the Secretary of State.

Notification to other parties affected

3. The exchange must have adequate arrangements for securing that –
   (*a*) parties to unsettled market contracts with a defaulter acting as principal are notified as soon as reasonably practicable of the default and of any decision taken under the rules in relation to contracts to which they are a party; and
   (*b*) parties to unsettled market contracts with a defaulter acting as agent and the defaulter's principals are notified as soon as reasonably practicable of the default and of the identity of the other party to the contract.

Application of default rules to designated non-members

4. – (1) The rules may make the same or similar provision in relation to designated non-members as in relation to members of the exchange.

(2) If such provision is made, the exchange must have adequate procedures –
   (*a*) for designating the persons, or descriptions of person, in respect of whom action may be taken,
   (*b*) for keeping under review the question which persons or descriptions of person should be or remain so designated, and
   (*c*) for withdrawing such designation.

(3) The procedures shall be designed to secure that a person is not or does not remain designated if failure by him to meet his obligations in respect of one or more market contracts would be unlikely adversely to affect the operation of the market, and that a description of persons is not or does not remain designated if failure by a person of that description to meet his obligations in respect of one or more market contracts would be unlikely adversely to affect the operation of the market.

(4) The exchange must have adequate arrangements –
   (*a*) for bringing a designation or withdrawal of designation to the attention of the person or description of persons concerned, and
   (*b*) where a description of persons is designated, or the designation of a description of persons is withdrawn, for ascertaining which persons fall within that description.

Delegation of functions in connection with default procedures

5. The rules may make provision for the whole or part of the functions mentioned in paragraphs 1 to 4 to be performed by another body or person on behalf of the exchange.

Co-operation with other authorities

6. The exchange must be able and willing to co-operate, by the sharing of information and otherwise, with the Secretary of State, any relevant office-holder and any other authority or body having responsibility for any matter arising out of, or connected with, the default of a member of the exchange or any designated non-member.

Margin

7. Where the exchange provides its own clearing arrangements and margined transactions are effected, paragraph 14 below applies as it applies in relation to a clearing house.

PART II
U.K. CLEARING HOUSES

Default rules

8. – (1) The clearing house must have default rules which, in the event of a member of the clearing house appearing to be unable to meet his obligations in respect of one or more market contracts, enable action to be taken to close out his position in relation to all unsettled market contracts to which he is a party.

(2) The rules may authorise the taking of the same or similar action where a member appears to be likely to become unable to meet his obligations in respect of one or more market contracts.

Content of rules

9. – (1) The rules must provide for all rights and liabilities of the defaulter under or in respect of unsettled market contracts to be discharged and for there to be paid by or to the defaulter such sum of money (if any) as may be determined in accordance with the rules.

(2) The rules must further provide –
- (*a*) for the sums so payable by or to the defaulter in respect of different contracts to be aggregated or set off so as to produce a net sum;
- (*b*) for that sum –
  - (i) if payable by the defaulter to the clearing house, to be set off against any property provided by or on behalf of the defaulter as cover for margin (or the proceeds of realisation of such property) so as to produce a further net sum, and
  - (ii) if payable by the clearing house to the defaulter to be aggregated with any property provided by or on behalf of the defaulter as cover for margin (or the proceeds of realisation of such property); and
- (*c*) for the certification by or on behalf of the clearing house of the sum finally payable or, as the case may be, of the fact that no sum is payable.

10. – (1) The reference in paragraph 9 to the rights and liabilities of a defaulter under or in respect of an unsettled market contract includes (without prejudice to the generality of that provision) rights and liabilities arising in consequence of action taken under provisions of the rules authorising –
- (*a*) the effecting by the clearing house of corresponding contracts in relation to unsettled market contracts to which the defaulter is a party;
- (*b*) the transfer of the defaulter's position under an unsettled market contract to another member of the clearing house;
- (*c*) the exercise by the clearing house of any option granted by an unsettled market contract.

(2) A "corresponding contract" means a contract on the same terms (except as to price or premium) as the market contract, but under which the person who is the buyer under the market contract agrees to sell and the person who is the seller under the market contract agrees to buy.

This sub-paragraph applies with any necessary modifications in relation to a market contract which is not an agreement to sell.

(3) The reference in paragraph 9 to the rights and liabilities of a defaulter under or in respect of an unsettled market contract does not include, where he acts as agent, rights or liabilities of his arising out of the relationship of principal and agent.

Notification to other parties affected

11. The clearing house must have adequate arrangements for securing that parties to unsettled market contracts with a defaulter are notified as soon as reasonably practicable of the default and of any decision taken under the rules in relation to contracts to which they are a party.

Delegation of functions in connection with default procedures

12. The rules may make provision for the whole or part of the functions mentioned in paragraphs 8 to 11 to be performed by another body or person on behalf of the clearing house.

Co-operation with other authorities

13. The clearing house must be able and willing to co-operate, by the sharing of information and otherwise, with the Secretary of State, any relevant office-holder and any other authority or body having responsibility for any matter arising out of, or connected with, the default of a member of the clearing house.

Margin

14. – (1) The rules of the clearing house must provide that, in the event of a default, margin provided by the defaulter for his own account is not to be applied to meet a shortfall on a client account.

(2) This is without prejudice to the requirements of any relevant regulations under section 55 of the Financial Services Act 1986 (clients' money).

PART III
OVERSEAS INVESTMENT EXCHANGES AND CLEARING HOUSES

15. – (1) The rules and practices of the body, together with the law of the country in which the body's head office is situated, must be such as to provide adequate procedures for dealing with the default of persons party to market contracts connected with the body.

(2) The reference in sub-paragraph (1) to default is to a person being unable to meet his obligations.

Section 182(4)   SCHEDULE 22

FINANCIAL MARKETS AND INSOLVENCY: PROVISIONS APPLYING TO PRE-COMMENCEMENT CASES

Introductory

1. The provisions of this Schedule have effect for the purpose of safeguarding the operation of certain financial markets –
   (a) in the event of the insolvency, winding up or default of a person party to transactions in the market (paragraphs 2 to 8), and
   (b) as regards the effectiveness or enforcement of certain charges given to secure obligations in connection with such transactions (paragraphs 9 to 12).

Recognised investment exchanges and clearing houses

2. – (1) This Schedule applies to the following descriptions of contract connected with a recognised investment exchange or recognised clearing house.

The contracts are referred to in this Schedule as "market contracts".

(2) In relation to a recognised investment exchange, this Schedule applies to –

(*a*) contracts entered into by a member or designated non-member of the exchange which are –

    (i)   made on or otherwise subject to the rules of the exchange,

    (ii) on terms expressed to be as traded on the exchange, or

    (iii) on the same terms as those on which an equivalent contract would be made on the exchange; and

(*b*) contracts subject to the rules of the exchange entered into by the exchange for the purposes of or in connection with the provision of clearing services.

A "designated non-member" means a person in respect of whom action may be taken under the default rules of the exchange but who is not a member of the exchange.

(3) In relation to a recognised clearing house, this Schedule applies to contracts subject to the rules of the clearing house entered into by the clearing house for the purposes of or in connection with the provision of clearing services for a recognised investment exchange.

This includes contracts effected under or in consequence of action taken by the clearing house under its default rules.

3. The general law of insolvency has effect in relation to market contracts, and action taken under the rules of a recognised investment exchange or recognised clearing house with respect to such contracts, subject to the following provisions of this Schedule.

4. – (1) None of the following shall be regarded as to any extent invalid at law on the ground of inconsistency with the law relating to the distribution of the assets of a person on bankruptcy, winding up or sequestration, or in the administration of an insolvent estate –

(*a*) a market contract,

(*b*) the rules of a recognised investment exchange or recognised clearing house as to the settlement of market contracts,

(*c*) the default rules of a recognised investment exchange or recognised clearing house.

(2) The powers of a relevant office-holder in his capacity as such, and the powers of the court under the Insolvency Act 1986 or the Bankruptcy (Scotland) Act 1985, shall not be exercised in such a way as to prevent or interfere with –

(*a*) the settlement of a market contract in accordance with the rules of a recognised investment exchange or recognised clearing house,

(*b*) any action taken under the default rules of such an exchange or clearing house.

(3) Nothing in the following provisions of this Schedule shall be construed as affecting the generality of sub-paragraph (2).

(4) A debt or other liability arising out of a market contract which is the subject of default proceedings may not be proved in a winding up or bankruptcy, or in Scotland claimed in a winding up or sequestration, until the completion of the default proceedings.

A debt or other liability which by virtue of this sub-paragraph may not be proved or claimed shall not be taken into account for the purposes of any set-off until the completion of the default proceedings.

5. – (1) A liquidator or trustee of a defaulter shall not –

(*a*) declare or pay any dividend to the creditors, or

(*b*) return any capital to contributories,

unless he has retained what he reasonably considers to be an adequate reserve in respect of any claims arising as a result of the default proceedings of the exchange or clearing house concerned.

(2) Nothing in section 11(3), 130 or 285 of the Insolvency Act 1986 (which restrict the taking of certain legal proceedings and other steps), and nothing in the Bankruptcy (Scotland) Act 1985, shall affect any action taken by an exchange or clearing house for the purpose of its default proceedings.

6. – (1) The following provisions apply with respect to the net sum certified by a recognised investment exchange or recognised clearing house, upon the completion of proceedings under its default rules, to be payable by or to a defaulter.

(2) If, in England and Wales, a bankruptcy or winding up order has been made, or a resolution for voluntary winding up has been passed, the debt –

(a)   is provable in the bankruptcy or winding up or, as the case may be, is payable to the relevant office-holder, and

(b)   shall be taken into account, where appropriate, under section 323 of the Insolvency Act 1986 (mutual dealings and set-off) or the corresponding provision applicable in the case of a winding up,

in the same way as a debt due before the commencement of the bankruptcy or winding up.

(3) If, in Scotland, an award of sequestration or a winding up order has been made, or a resolution for voluntary winding up has been passed, the debt –

(a)   may be claimed in the sequestration or winding up or, as the case may be, is payable to the relevant office-holder, and

(b)   shall be taken into account for the purposes of any rule of law relating to compensation or set-off applicable in sequestration or winding up,

in the same way as a debt due before the date of sequestration (within the meaning of section 73(1) of the Bankruptcy (Scotland) Act 1985) or the commencement of the winding up.

7. – (1) Sections 178, 186, 315 and 345 of the Insolvency Act 1986 (power to disclaim onerous property and court's power to order rescission of contracts, &c.) do not apply in relation to –

(a)   a market contract, or

(b)   a contract effected by the exchange or clearing house for the purpose of realising property provided as margin in relation to market contracts.

In the application of this sub-paragraph in Scotland, the reference to sections 178 and 315 shall be construed as a reference to any rule of law having the like effect as those sections.

(2) Sections 127 and 284 of the Insolvency Act 1986 (avoidance of property dispositions effected after commencement of winding up or presentation of bankruptcy petition) do not apply to –

(a)   a market contract, or any disposition of property in pursuance of such a contract,

(b)   the provision of margin in relation to market contracts,

(c)   a contract effected by the exchange or clearing house for the purpose of realising property provided as margin in relation to a market contract, or any disposition of property in pursuance of such a contract, or

(d)   any disposition of property in accordance with the rules of the exchange or clearing house as to the application of property provided as margin.

(3) However, if a person enters into a market contract knowing that a petition has been presented for the winding up or bankruptcy of the other party to the contract, the value of any profit or benefit to him arising from the contract is recoverable from him by the relevant office-holder unless the court directs otherwise.

(4) Any sum recoverable by virtue of sub-paragraph (3) has the same priority, in the event of the insolvency of the person from whom it is due, as if it were secured by a fixed charge.

8. – (1) No order shall be made in relation to a market contract under –

(a)   section 238 or 339 of the Insolvency Act 1986 (transactions at an under-value),

(b)   section 239 or 340 of that Act (preferences), or

(c)   section 423 of that Act (transactions defrauding creditors),

unless the court is satisfied that the person in favour of whom the contract was made knew at the time he entered into it that it was at an under-value (within the meaning of the relevant provision) or, as the case may be, that a preference was being given.

(2) As respects Scotland, no decree shall be granted in relation to a market contract –
>   (*a*)   under section 34 or 36 of the Bankruptcy (Scotland) Act 1985 or section 242 or 243 of the Insolvency Act 1986 (gratuitous alienations and unfair preferences), or
>   (*b*)   at common law,

unless the court is satisfied that the person with whom the contract was made knew at the time he entered into it that it was challengeable under any of the provisions mentioned in paragraph (*a*) or at common law.

(3) Sub-paragraphs (1) and (2) apply in relation to –
>   (*a*)   a disposition of property in pursuance of a market contract,
>   (*b*)   the provision of margin in relation to market contracts,
>   (*c*)   a contract effected by a recognised investment exchange or recognised clearing house for the purpose of realising property provided as margin, or
>   (*d*)   a disposition of property in accordance with the rules of the exchange or clearing house as to the application of property provided as margin,

as they apply in relation to the making of a market contract.

Market charges

9. – (1) The charges to which paragraphs 10 to 12 apply are charges, whether fixed or floating, granted –
>   (*a*)   in favour of a recognised investment exchange, for the purpose of securing debts or liabilities arising in connection with the settlement of market contracts,
>   (*b*)   in favour of a recognised clearing house, for the purpose of securing debts or liabilities arising in connection with their ensuring the performance of market contracts, or
>   (*c*)   in favour of a person who agrees to make payments as a result of the transfer of specified securities made through the medium of a computer-based system established by the Bank of England and The Stock Exchange, for the purpose of securing debts or liabilities of the transferee arising in connection with the payments.

Those charges are referred to in this Schedule as "market charges".

(2) Where a charge is granted partly for purposes specified in sub-paragraph (1)(*a*), (*b*) or (*c*) and partly for other purposes, paragraphs 10 to 12 apply to it so far as it has effect for the specified purposes; and the expression "market charge" shall be construed accordingly.

(3) In this paragraph and paragraphs 10 to 12 –
>   "charge" means any form of security, including a mortgage and, in Scotland, a heritable security; and
>   "specified securities" means securities for the time being specified in the list in Schedule 1 to the Stock Transfer Act 1982, and includes any right to such securities.

10. The general law of insolvency has effect in relation to market charges and action taken in enforcing them subject to the following provisions of this Schedule.

11. – (1) Sections 10(1)(*b*) and 11(3)(*c*) of the Insolvency Act 1986 (no enforcement of security while petition for administration order pending or order in force) do not apply to a market charge.

(2) Section 11(2) of that Act (receiver to vacate office when so required by administrator) does not apply to a receiver appointed under a market charge.

(3) Section 15(1) and (2) of that Act (administrator's power to deal with charged property) do not apply to a market charge.

(4) Sections 127 and 284 of that Act (avoidance of property dispositions effected after commencement of winding up or presentation of bankruptcy petition) do not apply to –
>   (*a*)   a disposition of property as a result of which the property becomes subject to a market charge, or any transaction pursuant to which that disposition is made, or
>   (*b*)   any disposition of property made in enforcing a market charge.

(5) However, if a person (other than the chargee under the market charge) who is a party to a disposition mentioned in sub-paragraph (4)(*a*) knows at the time of the disposition that a petition has been presented for the winding up or bankruptcy of the party making the disposition, the value of any profit or benefit to him arising from the disposition is recoverable from him by the relevant office-holder unless the court directs otherwise.

(6) Any sum recoverable by virtue of sub-paragraph (5) has the same priority, in the event of the insolvency of the person from whom it is due, as if it were secured by a fixed charge.

12. – (1) No legal proceedings, execution or other legal process may be commenced or continued, and no distress may be levied against property which is, or becomes, subject to a market charge except with the consent of the person in whose favour the charge was granted or the leave of the court.

(2) The court may give leave subject to such terms as it thinks fit.

(3) Sub-paragraph (1) does not apply to proceedings to enforce any security over, or any equitable interest in, the property.

(4) Sections 10(1)(*c*), 11(3)(*d*), 130(3) and 285(3) of the Insolvency Act 1986 (which restrict the taking of certain legal proceedings and other steps) have effect accordingly.

(5) In the application of this paragraph to Scotland, the reference to execution being commenced or continued includes a reference to diligence being carried out or continued, and the reference to distress being levied shall be omitted.

Supplementary provisions

13. – (1) In this Schedule "default rules" means –
   (*a*) in relation to a recognised investment exchange, rules which provide in the event of a member or designated non-member of the exchange appearing to be unable, or likely to become unable, to meet his obligations in respect of one or more market contracts, for the settlement forthwith of all unsettled market contracts to which he is a party as principal, other than those whose performance is ensured by a recognised clearing house;
   (*b*) in relation to a recognised clearing house, rules which provide in the event of a member of the clearing house appearing to be unable, or likely to become unable, to meet his obligations in respect of any market contract, for the closing out of his position in relation to all market contracts to which he is a party.

(2) References in this Schedule to a "defaulter" are to a person in respect of whom action has been taken by a recognised investment exchange or recognised clearing house under its default rules, whether by declaring him to be a defaulter or otherwise; and references in this Schedule to "default" shall be construed accordingly.

(3) In this Schedule "default proceedings" means proceedings taken by a recognised investment exchange or recognised clearing house under its default rules.

14. – (1) The following are relevant office-holders for the purposes of this Schedule –
   (*a*) the official receiver,
   (*b*) any person acting in relation to a company as its liquidator, provisional liquidator, administrator or administrative receiver,
   (*c*) any person acting in relation to an individual (or, in Scotland, a deceased debtor) as his trustee in bankruptcy or interim receiver of his property or as permanent or interim trustee in the sequestration of his estate.
   (*d*) any person acting as administrator (or, in Scotland, as judicial factor) of an insolvent estate of a deceased person.

(2) Sub-paragraph (1)(*c*) applies in relation to a partnership, and any debtor within the meaning of the Bankruptcy (Scotland) Act 1985, as it applies in relation to an individual.

(3) In this paragraph –
   "administrative receiver" has the meaning given by section 251 of the Insolvency Act 1986;

"company" means a company within the meaning of section 735(1) of the Companies Act 1985 or a company which may be wound up under Part V of the Insolvency Act 1986 (unregistered companies); and

"interim trustee" and "permanent trustee" have the same meaning as in the Bankruptcy (Scotland) Act 1985.

15. – (1) In this Schedule –

"clearing house" has the same meaning as in the Financial Services Act 1986;

"investment" and "investment exchange" have the same meaning as in the Financial Services Act 1986;

"recognised" means recognised under the Financial Services Act 1986;

"The Stock Exchange" means The International Stock Exchange of the United Kingdom and the Republic of Ireland Limited.

(2) References in this Schedule to ensuring the performance of a transaction have the same meaning as in the Financial Services Act 1986.

(3) References in this Schedule to a market contract to which a person is a party include, unless the contrary intention appears, contracts to which he is party as agent.

Section 206(1)   SCHEDULE 23

CONSEQUENTIAL AMENDMENTS OF THE FINANCIAL SERVICES ACT 1986

PART I
GENERAL AMENDMENTS

1. – (1) Section 13 of the Financial Services Act 1986 (power to direct alteration of rules of recognised self-regulating organisation) is amended as follows.

(2) Omit subsection (1).

(3) For subsection (2) substitute –

"(2) If at any time it appears to the Secretary of State that –
(a) a recognised self-regulating organisation is concerned with two or more kinds of investment business, and
(b) the requirement in paragraph 3(1) of Schedule 2 to this Act is not satisfied in respect of investment business of one or more but not all of those kinds,
he may, instead of revoking the recognition order or making an application under section 12 above, direct the organisation to alter, or himself alter, its rules so that they preclude a member from carrying on investment business of a kind in respect of which that requirement is not satisfied, unless he is an authorised person otherwise than by virtue of membership of the organisation or is an exempted person in respect of that business.".

(4) For subsection (3) substitute –

"(3) A direction under this section is enforceable on the application of the Secretary of State by injunction or, in Scotland, by an order under section 45 of the Court of Session Act 1988.".

(5) Omit subsections (4) to (6).

2. – (1) Section 48 of the Financial Services Act 1986 (conduct of business rules) is amended as follows.

(2) In subsection (1) omit the words "members of a recognised self-regulating organisation or" and "organisation or".

(3) After subsection (10) insert –

"(11) Section 63A below (application of designated rules) has effect as regards the application of rules under this section to members of recognised self-regulating organisations in respect of investment business in the carrying on of which they are subject to the rules of the organisation.".

3. – (1) Section 49 of the Financial Services Act 1986 (financial resources rules) is amended as follows.

(2) For subsection (1) substitute –

"(1) The Secretary of State may make rules requiring –
    (*a*) a person authorised to carry on investment business by virtue of section 25 or 31 above, or
    (*b*) a member of a recognised self-regulating organisation carrying on investment business in the carrying on of which he is subject to the rules of the organisation,
to have and maintain in respect of that business such financial resources as are required by the rules.".

(3) After subsection (2) insert –

"(3) Section 63A below (application of designated rules) has effect as regards the application of rules under this section to members of recognised self-regulating organisations in respect of investment business in the carrying on of which they are subject to the rules of the organisation.".

4. In section 50 of the Financial Services Act 1986 (power of Secretary of State to modify conduct of business and financial resources rules for particular cases), after subsection (3) insert –

"(4) The powers conferred by subsection (1) above shall not be exercised in a case where the powers conferred by section 63B below are exercisable (powers of recognised self-regulating organisation in relation to designated rules).".

5. In section 52 of the Financial Services Act 1986 (notification regulations), in subsection (3) (application to member of recognised self-regulating organisation or professional body), for "subject to any of the rules made under section 48 above" substitute "not subject to the rules of that organisation or body".

6. – (1) Section 55 of the Financial Services Act 1986 (clients' money) is amended as follows.

(2) In subsection (2)(*b*) and (*e*) omit the words "a member of a recognised self-regulating organisation or" and "organisation or".

(3) In subsection (3) omit the words "organisation or".

(4) After subsection (5) insert –

"(6) Section 63A below (application of designated regulations) has effect as regards the application of regulations under this section to members of recognised self-regulating organisations in respect of investment business in the carrying on of which they are subject to the rules of the organisation.".

7. In section 56 of the Financial Services Act 1986 (unsolicited calls), for subsection (7) substitute –

"(7) Section 63A below (application of designated regulations) has effect as regards the application of regulations under this section to members of recognised self-regulating organisations in respect of investment business in the carrying on of which they are subject to the rules of the organisation.
As it applies to such persons in respect of such business the reference in subsection (1) above to conduct permitted by regulations made by the Secretary of State shall be construed –
    (*a*) where or to the extent that the regulations do not apply, as a reference to conduct permitted by the rules of the organisation; and
    (*b*) where or to the extent that the regulations do apply but are expressed to have effect subject to the rules of the organisation, as a reference to conduct permitted by the regulations together with the rules of the organisation.

(7A) In the application of this section to anything done by a person certified by a recognised professional body in carrying on investment business in the carrying on of which he is subject to the rules of the body, the reference in subsection (1) above to conduct permitted by regulations made by the Secretary of State shall be construed as a reference to conduct permitted by the rules of the body.".

8. In section 86 of the Financial Services Act 1986 (collective investment schemes constituted in other member States), in subsection (7) (restriction on application of conduct of business rules), at the end add –

"This subsection also applies to statements of principle under section 47A and codes of practice under section 63A so far as they relate to matters falling within the rule-making power in section 48.".

9. In section 95 of the Financial Services Act 1986 (collective investment schemes: contraventions), after subsection (2) add –

"(3) The disciplinary action which may be taken by virtue of section 47A(3) (failure to comply with statement of principle) includes –

(*a*) the giving of a direction under section 91(2), and

(*b*) the application by the Secretary of State for an order under section 93;

and subsection (6) of section 47A (duty of the Secretary of State as to exercise of powers) has effect accordingly.".

10. – (1) Section 107 of the Financial Services Act 1986 (appointment of auditors) is amended as follows.

(2) For subsection (1) (power to make rules) substitute –

"(1) The Secretary of State may make rules requiring –

(*a*) a person authorised to carry on investment business by virtue of section 25 or 31 above, or

(*b*) a member of a recognised self-regulating organisation carrying on investment business in the carrying on of which he is subject to the rules of the organisation,

and who, apart from the rules, is not required by or under any enactment to appoint an auditor, to appoint as an auditor a person satisfying such conditions as to qualifications and otherwise as may be specified in or imposed under the rules.".

(3) After subsection (3) add –

"(4) In its application to members of recognised self-regulating organisations, this section has effect subject to section 107A below.".

11. After section 107 of the Financial Services Act 1986 insert –

"107A   Application of audit rules to members of self-regulating organisations

(1) The Secretary of State may in rules under section 107 designate provisions which apply, to such extent as may be specified, to a member of a recognised self-regulating organisation in respect of investment business in the carrying on of which he is subject to the rules of the organisation.

(2) It may be provided that the designated rules have effect, generally or to such extent as may be specified, subject to the rules of the organisation.

(3) A member of a recognised self-regulating organisation who contravenes a rule applying to him by virtue of that section shall be treated as having contravened the rules of the organisation.

(4) Except as mentioned above, rules made under section 107 do not apply to members of recognised self-regulating organisations in respect of investment business in the carrying on of which they are subject to the rules of the organisation.

(5) A recognised self-regulating organisation may on the application of a member of the organisation –

    (*a*)   modify a rule designated under this section so as to adapt it to his circumstances or to any particular kind of business carried on by him, or

    (*b*)   dispense him from compliance with any such rule, generally or in relation to any particular kind of business carried on by him.

(6) The powers conferred by subsection (5) shall not be exercised unless it appears to the organisation –

    (*a*)   that compliance with the rule in question would be unduly burdensome for the applicant having regard to the benefit which compliance would confer on investors, and

    (*b*)   that the exercise of those powers will not result in any undue risk to investors.

(7) The powers conferred by subsection (5) may be exercised unconditionally or subject to conditions; and subsection (3) applies in the case of a contravention of a condition as in the case of contravention of a designated rule.

(8) The reference in paragraph 4(1) of Schedule 2 (requirements for recognition of self-regulating organisations) to monitoring and enforcement of compliance with rules includes monitoring and enforcement of compliance with conditions imposed by the organisation under subsection (7).".

12. – (1) Section 114 of the Financial Services Act 1986 (power to transfer functions to designated agency) is amended as follows.

(2) For subsection (9) substitute –

"(9) The Secretary of State shall not make a delegation order transferring any legislative functions unless –

    (*a*)   the agency has furnished him with a copy of the instruments it proposes to issue or make in the exercise of those functions, and

    (*b*)   he is satisfied that those instruments will afford investors an adequate level of protection and, in the case of such provisions as are mentioned in Schedule 8 to this Act, comply with the principles set out in that Schedule.

In this subsection "legislative functions" means the functions of issuing or making statements of principle, rules, regulations or codes of practice.".

(3) In subsection (12) for "rules or regulations made" substitute "statements of principle, rules, regulations or codes of practice issued or made".

13. – (1) Section 115 of the Financial Services Act 1986 (resumption of transferred functions) is amended as follows.

(2) For subsection (5) substitute –

"(5) Where the transferred functions consist of or include any legislative functions, an order may be made under subsection (2) above if at any time it appears to the Secretary of State that the instruments issued or made by the agency do not satisfy the requirements of section 114(9)(*b*) above.".

(3) In subsection (7) –

    (*a*)   in the opening words, for "subsection (2)(*b*) above" substitute "this section", and

    (*b*)   in paragraph (*a*) for "functions of making rules or regulations" substitute "functions of issuing or making statements of principle, rules, regulations or codes of practice.".

14. – (1) Section 119 of the Financial Services Act 1986 (competition scrutiny: recognition orders) is amended as follows.

(2) In subsection (1) (considerations relevant to making of recognition order), for paragraphs (*a*) and (*b*) substitute –

    "(*a*)   in the case of a self-regulating organisation, the rules and any guidance of which copies are furnished with the application for the order, together with any statements of principle, rules, regulations or codes of practice to which members of the organisation would be subject by virtue of Chapter V of this Part,

(*b*) in the case of an investment exchange, the rules and any guidance of which copies are furnished with the application for the order, together with any arrangements of which particulars are furnished with the application,

(*c*) in the case of a clearing house, the rules and any guidance of which copies are furnished with the application for the order,".

(3) In subsection (2) (circumstances in which powers are exercisable in relation to recognised body), for paragraphs (*a*) to (*c*) substitute –

"(*a*) in the case of a self-regulating organisation,

(i)   any rules made or guidance issued by the organisation,

(ii)   any practices of the organisation, or

(iii) any practices of persons who are members of, or otherwise subject to the rules made by, the organisation,

together with any statements of principle, rules, regulations or codes of practice to which members of the organisation are subject by virtue of Chapter V of this Part,

(*b*) in the case of a recognised investment exchange –

(i)   any rules made or guidance issued by the exchange,

(ii)   any practices of the exchange, or

(iii) any practices of persons who are members of, or otherwise subject to the rules made by, the exchange,

(*c*) in the case of a recognised clearing house –

(i)   any rules made or guidance issued by the clearing house,

(ii)   any practices of the clearing house, or

(iii) any practices of persons who are members of, or otherwise subject to the rules made by, the clearing house,

or any clearing arrangements made by the clearing house,".

(4) In subsection (3) (powers exercisable in relation to recognised body) –

(*a*) in paragraph (*b*) for "the rules" substitute "its rules, or the", and

(*b*) in paragraph (*c*) for "the rules" substitute "its rules".

(5) In subsection (5) (construction of references to practices) –

(*a*) for "paragraph (*b*)" substitute "paragraph (*a*)(ii), (*b*)(iii) and (*c*)(ii)", and

(*b*) omit the words from "and the practices referred to in paragraph (*c*)" to the end.

(6) After that subsection insert –

"(6) The practices referred to in paragraph (*a*)(iii), (*b*)(iii) and (*c*)(iii) of subsection (2) above are –

(*a*) in relation to a recognised self-regulating organisation, practices in relation to business in respect of which the persons in question are subject to –

(i)   the rules of the organisation, or

(ii)   statements of principle, rules, regulations or codes of practice to which its members are subject by virtue of Chapter V of this Part,

and which are required or contemplated by the rules of the organisation or by those statements, rules, regulations or codes, or by guidance issued by the organisation,

(*b*) in relation to a recognised investment exchange or clearing house, practices in relation to business in respect of which the persons in question are subject to the rules of the exchange or clearing house, and which are required or contemplated by its rules or guidance,

or which are otherwise attributable to the conduct or the organisation, exchange or clearing house as such.".

15. – (1) Section 121 of the Financial Services Act 1986 (competition scrutiny: designated agencies) is amended as follows.

(2) In subsection (1) for "rules, regulations" substitute "statements of principle, rules, regulations, codes of practice".

(3) In subsection (2)(*a*) and (*c*) for "rules or regulations made" substitute "statements of principle, rules, regulations or codes of practice issued or made".

(4) In subsection (3)(*b*) for "rules, regulations" substitute "statements of principle, rules, regulations, codes of practice".

(5) In subsection (4) for "rules or regulations" (twice) substitute "statements of principle, rules, regulations or codes of practice".

16. – (1) Section 122 of the Financial Services Act 1986 (reports by Director General of Fair Trading) is amended as follows.

(2) In subsection (1) for "and regulations" substitute, ", statements of principle, regulations and codes of practice".

(3) In subsection (2) for "regulations," substitute "statements of principle, regulations, codes of practice,".

(4) In subsection (4) –
> (*a*) in paragraph (*a*) for "rules, guidance, arrangements and regulations" substitute "rules, statements of principle, regulations, codes of practice, guidance and arrangements", and
> (*b*) in the words following the paragraphs, for "rules, guidance, arrangements, regulations" substitute "rules, statements of principle, regulations, codes of practice, guidance, arrangements", and for "rules, guidance, arrangements or regulations" substitute "rules, statements of principle, regulations, codes of practice, guidance or arrangements".

17. – (1) Section 124 of the Financial Services Act 1986 (matters to be left out of account for certain purposes in connection with competition scrutiny) is amended as follows.

(2) In subsection (1) (matters to be left out of account in determining whether monopoly situation exists), in paragraph (*c*) for "rules or regulations made or guidance issued" substitute "statements of principle, rules, regulations, codes of practice or guidance issued or made".

(3) In subsection (3) (matters to be excluded from consideration where monopoly situation exists) –
> (*a*) in paragraph (*a*), for "rules or regulations made" substitute "statements of principle, rules, regulations or codes of practice issued or made",
> (*b*) in paragraph (*b*), for "rules or regulations" substitute "statements of principle, rules, regulations or codes of practice", and
> (*c*) in the closing words, for "rules, regulations" substitute "statements of principle, rules, regulations, codes of practice".

18. For section 205 of the Financial Services Act 1986 (regulations, rules and orders) substitute –

"205 General power to make regulations

The Secretary of State may make regulations prescribing anything which by this Act is authorised or required to be prescribed.

205A Supplementary provisions with respect to subordinate legislation

(1) The following provisions apply to any power of the Secretary of State under this Act –
> (*a*) to issue statements of principle,
> (*b*) to make rules or regulations,
> (*c*) to make orders (other than such orders as are excepted by subsection (4) below), or
> (*d*) to issue codes of practice.

(2) any such power is exercisable by statutory instrument and includes power to make different provision for different cases.

(3) Except as otherwise provided, a statutory instrument containing statements of principle, rules or regulations shall be subject to annulment in pursuance of a resolution of either House of Parliament.

(4) The above provisions do not apply to a recognition order, an order declaring a collective investment scheme to be an authorised unit trust scheme or a recognised scheme or to an order revoking any such order.".

19. In section 206(1) of the Financial Services Act 1986 (publication of information and advice) –
 (*a*) in paragraph (*a*), for "rules and regulations made" substitute "statements of principle, rules, regulations and codes of practice issued or made", and
 (*b*) in paragraph (*b*) for "rules or regulations" substitute "statements of principle, rules, regulations or codes of practice".

20. In Schedule 2 to the Financial Services Act 1986 (requirements for recognition of self-regulating organisations), in paragraph 4(1) (monitoring and enforcement) for "rules or regulations" substitute "statements of principle, rules, regulations or codes of pratice".

21. In Schedule 3 to the Financial Services Act 1986 (requirements for recognition of professional bodies), in paragraph 4(2) (monitoring and enforcement) for "rules or regulations" substitute "statements of principle, rules, regulations or codes of practice".

22. In Schedule 7 to the Financial Services Act 1986 (qualifications of designated agency), in paragraph 2(2) (arrangements for discharge of functions: matters to be decided upon by the governing body) for "rules or regulations must be made" substitute "statements of principle, rules, regulations and codes of practice must be issued or made".

23. – (1) Schedule 8 to the Financial Services Act 1986 (principles applicable to designated agency's rules and regulations) is amended as follows.

(2) In the heading for "RULES AND REGULATIONS" substitute "LEGISLATIVE PROVISIONS".

(3) For paragraph 1, and the cross-heading preceding it, substitute –

"Introduction

1. – (1) In this Schedule "legislative provisions" means the provisions of statements of principle, rules, regulations and codes of practice issued or made under Part I of this Act.

(2) References in this Schedule to "conduct of business provisions" are to rules made under section 48 of this Act and statements of principle and codes of practice so far as they relate to matters falling within that rule-making power.

(3) References in this Schedule to provisions made for the purposes of a specified section or Chapter are to rules or regulations made under that section or Chapter and statements of principle and codes of practice so far as they relate to matters falling within that power to make rules or regulations.

Standards

1A. The conduct of business provisions and the other legislative provisions must promote high standards of integrity and fair dealing in the conduct of investment business.".

(4) In paragraphs 2 to 7, 9, 11 and 12 for "conduct of business rules" substitute "conduct of business provisions".

(5) In paragraph 7 for "those rules and rules under" substitute "those provisions and provisions made for the purposes of".

(6) In paragraph 8 for "Rules made under" substitute "Provisions made for the purposes of".

(7) In paragraph 9 for "regulations made under" substitute "provisions made for the purposes of".

(8) In paragraph 10 for "Rules made under" substitute "Provisions made for the purposes of" and for "under those sections" substitute "for the purposes of those sections".

(9) In paragraph 12 for "rules and regulations made under" substitute "provisions made for the purposes of".

24. – (1) Schedule 9 to the Financial Services Act 1986 (designated agency: exercise of transferred functions) is amended as follows.

(2) In paragraph 4(1) (copies of instruments to be sent to Secretary of State), for "any rules or regulations made" substitute "any statements of principle, rules, regulations or codes of practice issued or made".

(3) For paragraphs 5 and 6 substitute –

"5. Paragraphs 6 to 9 below have effect instead of section 205A of this Act in relation to statements of principle, rules, regulations and codes of practice issued or made by a designated agency in the exercise of powers transferred to it by a delegation order.

6. Any such power is exercisable by instrument in writing and includes power to make different provision for different cases.".

(4) In paragraph 8 (instruments to be printed and made available to public) –
   (a) in sub-paragraph (1) for "is made" substitute "is issued or made", and
   (b) in sub-paragraph (2) for "rule or regulation" (twice) substitute "statement of principle, rule, regulation or code of practice".

(5) In paragraph 9 (proof of instruments), for "made by the agency" (twice) substitute "made or issued by the agency".

(6) For paragraph 12 (consultation) substitute –

"12. – (1) Where a designated agency proposes, in the exercise of powers transferred to it by a delegation order, to issue or make any statements of principle, rules, regulations or codes of practice, it shall publish the proposed instrument in such manner as appears to it best calculated to bring the proposals to the attention of the public, together with a statement that representations about the proposals (and, in particular, representations as to the cost of complying with the proposed provision) can be made to the agency within a specified time.

(2) Before issuing or making the instrument the agency shall have regard to any representations duly made in accordance with the statement.

(3) The above requirements do not apply –
   (a) where the agency considers that the delay involved in complying with them would be prejudicial to the interests of investors;
   (b) to the issuing or making of an instrument in the same, or substantially the same, terms as a proposed instrument which was furnished by the agency to the Secretary of State for the purposes of section 114(9) of this Act.".

25. – (1) Schedule 10 to the Financial Services Act 1986 (application of investment business provisions to regulated insurance companies) is amended as follows.

(2) In paragraph 4 (modification of conduct of business rules), after sub-paragraph (2) insert –

"(2A) Sub-paragraphs (1) and (2) also apply to statements of principle under section 47A and codes of practice under section 63A so far as they relate to matters falling within the rule-making power in section 48.".

(3) In paragraph 7 (withdrawal of authorisation) after sub-paragraph (2) insert –

"(3) The disciplinary action which may be taken by virtue of section 47A(3) of this Act (failure to comply with statement of principle) includes –
>   (*a*)   the withdrawal of authorisation under section 11(2)(*a*) of the Insurance Companies Act 1982, and
>   (*b*)   the giving of a direction under section 13(2A) of that Act;

and subsection (6) of section 47A (duty of the Secretary of State as to exercise of powers) has effect accordingly.".

PART II
AMENDMENTS RELATING TO FRIENDLY SOCIETIES

26. Schedule 11 to the Financial Services Act 1986 (friendly societies) is amended as follows.

27. In paragraph 3(2) (competition scrutiny: recognition of self-regulating organisation for friendly societies), after "sent to him under this sub-paragraph" insert ",together with any statements of principle, rules, regulations or codes of practice to which members of the organisation would be subject by virtue of this Schedule,".

28. – (1) Paragraph 4 (requirements for recognition of self-regulating organisation for friendly societies) is amended as follows.
(2) In sub-paragraph (4) –
>   (*a*)   in paragraph (*a*) for "22" substitute "22D", and
>   (*b*)   omit paragraph (*b*).

(3) In sub-paragraph (5) for "22" substitute "22D".

29. Omit paragraph 7.

30. – (1) Paragraph 10 (competition scrutiny: circumstances in which powers are exercisable in relation to recognised self-regulating organisation for friendly societies) is amended as follows.

(2) In sub-paragraph (1), after paragraph (*c*) insert "together with any statements of principle, rules, regulations or codes of practice to which members of the organisation are subject by virtue of this Schedule,".

(3) In sub-paragraph (2) –
>   (*a*)   in paragraph (*b*), for "the rules" substitute "its rules, or the", and
>   (*b*)   in paragraph (*c*), for "the rules" substitute "its rules".

(4) In sub-paragraph (3) (construction of references to practices), omit the words from "and the practices referred to in paragraph (*c*)" to the end; and after that sub-paragraph insert –

"(3A) The practices referred to in paragraph (*c*) of sub-paragraph (1) above are practices in relation to business in respect of which the persons in question are subject to –
>   (*a*)   the rules of the organisation, or
>   (*b*)   statements of principle, rules, regulations or codes of practice to which its members are subject by virtue of this Schedule,

and which are required or contemplated by the rules of the organisation or by those statements, rules, regulations or codes, or by guidance issued by the organisation, or which are otherwise attributable to the conduct of the organisation as such.".

31. In paragraph 13, for "Paragraphs 14 to 25" substitute "Paragraphs 13A to 25".

32. Before paragraph 14 and after the heading "*Conduct of investment business*", insert –

"13A. – (1) The Registrar may issue statements of principle with respect to the conduct expected of regulated friendly societies.

(2) The conduct expected may include compliance with a code or standard issued by another person, as for the time being in force, and may allow for the exercise of discretion by any person pursuant to any such code or standard.

(3) Failure to comply with a statement of principle under this paragraph is a ground for the taking of disciplinary action or the exercise of powers of intervention, but it does not give rise to any right of action by investors or other persons affected or affect the validity of any transaction.

(4) The disciplinary action which may be taken by virtue of sub-paragraph (3) is –
>   (*a*)   the making of a public statement under paragraph 21, or
>   (*b*)   the application by the Registrar for an injunction, interdict or other order under paragraph 22(1), or
>   (*c*)   any action under paragraph 26 or 27 of this Schedule;

and the reference in that sub-paragraph to powers of intervention is to the powers conferred by Chapter VI of Part I of this Act.

(5) Where a statement of principle relates to compliance with a code or standard issued by another person, the statement of principle may provide –
>   (*a*)   that failure to comply with the code or standard shall be a ground for the taking of disciplinary action, or the exercise of powers of intervention, only in such cases and to such extent as may be specified; and
>   (*b*)   that no such action shall be taken, or any such power exercised, except at the request of the person by whom the code or standard in question was issued.

(6) The Registrar shall exercise his powers in such manner as appears to him appropriate to secure compliance with statements of principle under this paragraph.

13B. – (1) The relevant regulatory authority may on the application of a regulated friendly society –
>   (*a*)   modify a statement of principle issued under paragraph 13A so as to adapt it to the circumstances of the society or to any particular kind of business carried on by it, or
>   (*b*)   dispense the society from compliance with any such statement of principle, generally or in relation to any particular kind of business carried on by it.

(2) The powers conferred by this paragraph shall not be exercised unless it appears to the relevant regulatory authority –
>   (*a*)   that compliance with the statement of principle in question would be unduly burdensome for the applicant having regard to the benefit which compliance would confer on investors, and
>   (*b*)   that the exercise of those powers will not result in any undue risk to investors.

(3) The powers conferred by this paragraph may be exercised unconditionally or subject to conditions; and paragraph 13A(3) applies in the case of failure to comply with a condition as in the case of failure to comply with a statement of principle.

(4) The relevant regulatory authority for the purposes of this paragraph is –
>   (*a*)   in the case of a member society of a recognised self-regulating organisation for friendly societies, in relation to investment business in the carrying on of which it is subject to the rules of the organisation, that organisation;
>   (*b*)   in any other case, or in relation to other investment business, the Registrar.

(5) The reference in paragraph 4(1) of Schedule 2 as applied by paragraph 4 above (requirements of recognition of self-regulating organisation for friendly societies) to monitoring and enforcement of compliance with statements of principle includes monitoring and enforcement of compliance with conditions imposed by the organisation under this paragraph.".

33. – (1) Paragraph 14 (conduct of business rules) is amended as follows.

(2) In sub-paragraph (1), omit the words "other than a member society".

(3) After sub-paragraph (2) insert –

> "(2A) Paragraph 22B below has effect as regards the application of rules under this paragraph to member societies in respect of investment business in the carrying on of which they are subject to the rules of a recognised self-regulating organisation for friendly societies.".

(4) In sub-paragraph (3), omit the word "and" after paragraph (*a*); and after paragraph (*b*) insert –

> "; and
>> (*c*) for the references in subsection (4) to section 63B and a recognised self-regulating organisation there shall be substituted references to paragraph 13B and a recognised self-regulating organisation for friendly societies.".

34. – (1) Paragraph 19 (clients' money regulations) is amended as follows.

(2) In sub-paragraph (2) for the words from "(but with the substitution" to the end substitute "(but with the substitution for the reference in paragraph (*e*) of subsection (2) to the Secretary of State of a reference to the Registrar)".

(3) After that sub-paragraph insert –

> "(3) Paragraph 22B below has effect as regards the application of regulations under this paragraph to member societies in respect of investment business in the carrying on of which they are subject to the rules of a recognised self-regulating organisation for friendly societies.".

35. For paragraph 20 (unsolicited calls) substitute –

> "20. – (1) Regulations under section 56(1) of this Act shall not permit anything to be done by a regulated friendly society but that section shall not apply to anything done by such a society in the course of or in consequence of an unsolicited call which, as respects the society, constitutes the carrying on of regulated business, if it is permitted to be done by the society by regulations made by the Registrar with the consent of the Secretary of State.

> (2) Paragraph 22B below has effect as regards the application of regulations under this paragraph to member societies in respect of investment business in the carrying on of which they are subject to the rules of a recognised self-regulating organisation for friendly societies.

> (3) As it applies to such persons in respect of such business, the reference in sub-paragraph (1) above to conduct permitted by regulations made by the Registrar with the consent of the Secretary of State shall be construed –
>> (*a*) where or to the extent that the regulations do not apply, as a reference to conduct permitted by the rules of the organisation; and
>> (*b*) where or to the extent that the regulations do apply but are expressed to have effect subject to the rules of the organisation, as a reference to conduct permitted by the regulations together with the rules of the organisation.".

36. After paragraph 22 (and after the paragraph inserted by section 193(3)) insert –

"22B. – (1) The Registrar may in rules and regulations under –
>> (*a*) paragraph 14 (conduct of business rules),
>> (*b*) paragraph 19 (client's money regulations), or
>> (*c*) paragraph 20 (regulations as to unsolicited calls),

designate provisions which apply, to such extent as may be specified, to a member society in respect of investment business in the carrying on of which it is subject to the rules of a recognised self-regulating organisation for friendly societies.

(2) It may be provided that the designated rules or regulations have effect, generally or to such extent as may be specified, subject to the rules of the organisation.

(3) A member society which contravenes a rule or regulation applying to it by virtue of this

paragraph shall be treated as having contravened the rules of the relevant recognised self-regulating organisation for friendly societies.

(4) It may be provided that, to such extent as may be specified, the designated rules or regulations may not be modified or waived (under paragraph 22C below or section 50) in relation to a member society.

Where such provision is made any modification or waiver previously granted shall cease to have effect, subject to any transitional provision or saving contained in the rules or regulations.

(5) Except as mentioned in sub-paragraph (1), the rules and regulations referred to in that sub-paragraph do not apply to a member society in respect of investment business in the carrying on of which it is subject to the rules of a recognised self-regulating organisation for friendly societies.

22C. – (1) A recognised self-regulating organisation for friendly societies may on the application of a society which is a member of the organisation–

  (*a*) modify a rule or regulation designated under paragraph 22B so as to adapt it to the circumstances of the society or to any particular kind of business carried on by it, or
  (*b*) dispense the society from compliance with any such rule or regulation, generally or in relation to any particular kind of business carried on by it.

(2) The powers conferred by this paragraph shall not be exercised unless it appears to the organisation –

  (*a*) that compliance with the rule or regulation in question would be unduly burdensome for the applicant having regard to the benefit which compliance would confer on investors, and
  (*b*) that the exercise of those powers will not result in any undue risk to investors.

(3) The powers conferred by this paragraph may be exercised unconditionally or subject to conditions; and paragraph 22B(3) applies in the case of a contravention of a condition as in the case of contravention of a designated rule or regulation.

(4) The reference in paragraph 4(1) of Schedule 2 as applied by paragraph 4 above (requirements for recognition of self-regulating organisation for friendly societies) to monitoring and enforcement of compliance with rules and regulations includes monitoring and enforcement of compliance with conditions imposed by the organisation under this paragraph.

22D. – (1) The Registrar may issue codes of practice with respect to any matters dealt with by statements of principle issued under paragraph 13A or by rules or regulations made under any provision of this Schedule.

(2) In determining whether a society has failed to comply with a statement of principle –

  (*a*) a failure by it to comply with any relevant provision of a code of practice may be relied on as tending to establish failure to comply with the statement of principle, and
  (*b*) compliance by it with the relevant provisions of a code of practice may be relied on as tending to negative any such failure.

(3) A contravention of a code of practice with respect to a matter dealt with by rules or regulations shall not of itself give rise to any liability or invalidate any transaction; but in determining whether a society's conduct amounts to contravention of a rule or regulation –

  (*a*) contravention by it of any relevant provision of a code of practice may be relied on as tending to establish liability, and
  (*b*) compliance by it with the relevant provision of a code of practice may be relied on as tending to negative liability.

(4) Where by virtue of paragraph 22B (application of designated rules and regulations to member societies) rules or regulations –

  (*a*) do not apply, to any extent, to a member society of a recognised self-regulating organisation for friendly societies, or
  (*b*) apply, to any extent, subject to the rules of the organisation,

a code of practice with respect to a matter dealt with by the rules or regulations may contain provision limiting its application to a corresponding extent.".

37. For paragraph 29 (transfer of functions of making rules or regulations) substitute –

"29. – (1) The Registrar shall not make a transfer order transferring any legislative functions to a transferee body unless –

(*a*) the body has furnished him and the Secretary of State with a copy of the instruments it proposes to issue or make in the exercise of those functions, and

(*b*) they are both satisfied that those instruments will –
   (i) afford investors an adequate level of protection,
   (ii) in the case of provisions corresponding to those mentioned in Schedule 8 to this Act, comply with the principles set out in that Schedule, and
   (iii) take proper account of the supervision of friendly societies by the Registrar under the enactments relating to friendly societies.

(2) In this paragraph "legislative functions" means the functions of issuing or making statements of principle, rules, regulations or codes of practice.".

38. In paragraph 30(2), for "rules or regulations made" substitute "statements of principle, rules, regulations or codes of practice issued or made".

39. In paragraph 31(6)(*c*), for "as if the reference to section 205(2) were a reference to paragraph 45(1) below" substitute "as if the reference to section 205A were a reference to paragraph 45(1) and (3) below".

40. For paragraph 34 substitute –

"34. – (1) A transferee body to which the Registrar has transferred any legislative functions may exercise those functions without the consent of the Secretary of State.

(2) In this paragraph "legislative functions" means the functions of issuing or making statements of principle, rules, regulations or codes of practice.".

41. In paragraph 36 (competition scrutiny: transferee bodies) in sub-paragraphs (1) and (3)(*b*) for "rules, regulations" substitute "statements of principle, rules, regulations, codes of practice".

42. In paragraph 38(1) (publication of information and advice) –
(*a*) in paragraph (*a*), for "rules and regulations made" substitute "statements of principle, rules, regulations and codes of practice issued or made", and
(*b*) in paragraph (*b*) for "rules or regulations" substitute "statements of principle, rules, regulations or codes of practice".

43. In paragraph 45 –
(*a*) in sub-paragraph (1) for "make regulations, rules or orders" substitute "issue or make statements of principle, rules, regulations, orders or codes of practice", and
(*b*) in sub-paragraph (3) for "regulations, rules or orders" substitute "statements of principle, rules, regulations, orders or codes of practice.".

Section 212   **SCHEDULE 24**

REPEALS

Chapter	Short title	Extent of repeal
1964 c. 40.	Harbours Act 1964.	In section 42(6), the words "required to be attached to a company's balance sheet".
1973 c. 41.	Fair Trading Act 1973.	Section 46(3). In section 71, in subsection (1) the words "made under section 69(4) of this Act" and subsection (2). In section 74(1), the words from "and does not" to "section 69(4) of this Act". In section 85, subsection (5) and, in subsection (6), paragraph (*b*) and the word "or" preceding it.

<table>
<tr><td>73 c. 41.
continued</td><td>Fair Trading
Act 1973
continued</td><td>In section 88(6), the words from "the relevant parties" to the "and" immediately following paragraph (c).
In section 89(2), the words "Part II of".
In Schedule 9, in paragraph 4 the words from "either" to the end.</td></tr>
<tr><td>1985 c. 6.</td><td>Companies Act 1985.</td><td>Section 160(3)</td></tr>
</table>

In section 169(5), the words from ", during business hours" to "for inspection)".

In section 175(6)(b), the words from "during business hours" to "period".

In section 191 –

(a) in subsection (1), the words from "(but" to "for inspection)";

(b) in subsection (3), paragraphs (a) and (b).

Section 201

In section 202(1), the words "(except where section 201(3) applies)".

Section 209(1)(j).

In section 219(1), the words from "during" to "for inspection)".

In section 288(3), the words from "during" to "for inspection)".

In section 318(7), the words from "during" to "for inspection)".

In section 356 –

(a) in subsection (1), the words "during business hours";

(b) subsections (2) and (4).

In section 383 –

(a) in subsection (1), the words "during business hours";

(b) subsection (2);

(c) in subsection (3), the words from "at a charge" to the end.

Section 389.

Section 435.

Section 440.

Section 443(4).

In section 446 –

(a) in subsection (3), paragraph (b) and the word "and" preceding it;

(b) subsection (7).

Section 447(1).

In section 449(1) –

(a) the words "or 448";

(b) paragraph (e).

Section 452(1)(b).

In section 460(1), the words "(inspection of company's books and papers)" and "under section 440".

In section 464(5), at the end of paragraph (c), the word "and".

In section 466 –

(a) in subsection (2), paragraph (a) and (d) and the word "or" preceding the latter;

(b) subsections (4) and (5);

(*c*) in subsection (6), the words "falling under subsection (4) of this section".

In section 651(1), the words "at any time within 2 years of the date of the dissolution".

In section 708(1)(*b*), the words "or other material".

Sections 712 and 715.

In section 716(2), the words following paragraph (*c*).

In section 717(1), the words following paragraph (*c*).

In section 733(3), the words from "then" to "216(3)".

In section 735A(1), the words "440, 449(1)(*a*) and (*d*)".

In section 744, the definitions of "annual return", "authorised institution", "authorised minimum", "expert", "floating charge", "joint stock company" and "undistributable reserves".

In section 746, the words "Except as provided by section 243(6),".

In Schedule 2 –

(*a*) in paragraph 1(1), the words "paragraph 60(2) of Schedule 4 or paragraph 19(3) of Schedule 9";

(*b*) paragraph 1(5);

(*c*) in paragraph 2(1), the word "23,";

(*d*) paragraph 2(2);

(*e*) in paragraph 3(1), the words "paragraph 60(2) of Schedule 4 or paragraph 19(3) of Schedule 9";

(*f*) paragraph 3(3);

(*g*) in paragraph 4(1), the words "(whether as personal representative or otherwise)";

(*h*) in paragraph 4(2), the words "paragraph 60(2) of Schedule 4 or paragraph 19(3) of Schedule 9".

In Schedule 4, paragraphs 50(6), 53(7), 60 to 70, 74, 75, 77 to 81, 87, 90 to 92 and 95.

In Schedule 9 –

(*a*) paragraphs 1, 13(3) and (18), 16, 18(5), 19(3) to (7) and 21 to 26;

(*b*) in paragraph 27(4), the words "of the said Part I";

(*c*) in paragraph 28, in sub-paragraph (1) the words "to which Part II of the Insurance Companies Act 1982 applies" and in sub-paragraph (2) the words "of Part I of this Schedule";

(*d*) paragraphs 29 to 31.

In Schedule 11 –

(*a*) paragraph 4(*b*) and (*c*); (*b*) paragraph 4(*b*) and (*c*);

(*b*) paragraph 5(*b*).

In Schedule 13, in paragraph 25, the words from "during" to "for inspection)".

Schedule 15.

In Schedule 22 –

(*a*) the entry relating to section 36(4);

(*b*) in the entry relating to sections 363 to 365, the words "(with Schedule 15)";

(*c*) in the entry relating to sections 384 to 393, in column 2, the word "qualifications".

In Schedule 24, the entries relating to sections 245(1), 245(2), 255(5), 260(3), 287(3), 365(3),

384(5), 386(2), 389(10), 390(7), 391(4), 392(2) and 393.

1985 c.65	Insolvency Act 1985.	In Schedule 6, paragraphs 7(3), 23 and 45.
1986 c.45	Insolvency Act 1986.	In sections 45(5), 53(2), 54(3) and 62(5), the words "and, for continued contravention, to a daily default fine".

In sections 45(5), 53(2), 54(3) and 62(5), the words "and, for continued contravention, to a daily default fine".

In Schedule 10, the entries in column 5 relating to sections 45(5), 53(2), 54(3) and 62(5).

In Part I of Schedule 13, the entries relating to sections 222(4), 225 and 733(3).

1986 c.46. Company Directors Disqualification Act 1986.

In section 21(2), the words "and section 431 (summary proceedings)".

1986 c. 53. Building Societies Act 1986.

In Schedule 15, in paragraph 3(2)(*b*), the words ", a shadow director".

In Schedule 18, paragraphs 16 and 17.

1986 c.60. Financial Services Act 1986.

In section 13 –
(*a*) subsection (1);
(*b*) subsections (4) to (6).
In section 48(1), the words "members of a recognised self-regulating organisation or" and "organisation or".
In section 55 –
(*a*) in subsection (2)(*b*) and (*e*), the words "a member of a recognised self-regulating organisation or" and "organisation or";
(*b*) in subsection (3), the words "organisation or".
In section 94 –
(*a*) in subsection (3), the words "except section 435(1)(*a*) and (*b*) and (2)";
(*b*) in subsection (4), the words "or its affairs", "and the affairs mentioned in subsection (1) or (2) above" and "or director".
Section 105(7).
In section 119(5), the words from "and the practices referred to in paragraph (*c*)" to the end.
In sections 159(1) and 160(1), the words from the beginning to "section 161 below".
In section 179(3), the word "and" preceding paragraph (i).
Section 180(6).
Section 196(3).
Section 198(1).
In section 199(9), the words from "and, in relation" to the end.
In Schedule 11 –
(*a*) paragraph 4(4)(*b*);
(*b*) paragraph 7;
(*c*) in paragraph 10(3), the words from "and the pratices referred to in paragraph (*c*)" to the end;
(*d*) in paragraph 14(1), the words "other than a member society";
(*e*) in paragraph 14(3), the word "and" after paragraph (*a*).
In Schedule 16, paragraph 22.

1987 c. 22.	Banking Act 1987.	In the Table in section 84(1), the entry relating to persons appointed under section 94, 106 or 177 of the Financial Services Act 1986. Section 90(1). In Schedule 6 – (*a*) paragraph 18(1) to (6); (*b*) in paragraph 18(7), the words "and (1A)"; (*c*) paragraph 18(8) and (9); (*d*) in paragraph 27(3) the words "and (6)".
1987 c. 41.	Criminal Justice (Scotland) Act 1987.	Section 55(*a*)
1988 c. 1.	Income and Corporation Taxes Act 1988.	Section 565(6)(*b*).
1988 c. 33.	Criminal Justice Act 1988.	Section 145(*a*).
1988 c. 48.	Copyright, Designs and Patents Act 1988.	In Schedule 7, paragraph 31.

INDEX